WORLD TRADE ORGANIZATION

Dispute Settlement Reports

2000
Volume X

Pages 4591-5118

AF777209

CAMBRIDGE
UNIVERSITY PRESS

PUBLISHED BY THE PRESS SYNDICATE OF THE UNIVERSITY OF CAMBRIDGE
The Pitt Building, Trumpington Street, Cambridge, United Kingdom

CAMBRIDGE UNIVERSITY PRESS
The Edinburgh Building, Cambridge CB2 2RU, UK
40 West 20th Street, New York, NY 10011–4211, USA
477 Williamstown Road, Port Melbourne, VIC 3207, Australia
Ruiz de Alarcón 13, 28014 Madrid, Spain
Dock House, The Waterfront, Cape Town 8001, South Africa

http://www.cambridge.org

Printed in the United Kingdom at the University Press, Cambridge

French edition and Spanish edition paperbacks of this title are both available directly from WTO Publications, World Trade Organization, Centre William Rappard, 154 rue de Lausanne, CH-1211 Geneva 21, Switzerland http://www.wto.org

ISBN 0 521 82856 2 hardback

THE WTO DISPUTE SETTLEMENT REPORTS

The *Dispute Settlement Reports* of the World Trade Organization (the "WTO") include panel and Appellate Body reports, as well as arbitration awards, in disputes concerning the rights and obligations of WTO Members under the provisions of the *Marrakesh Agreement Establishing the World Trade Organization.* The *Dispute Settlement Reports* are available in English, French and Spanish. Starting with 1999, the first volume of each year contains a cumulative index of published disputes.

This volume may be cited as DSR 2000:X

TABLE OF CONTENTS

UNITED STATES - ANTI-DUMPING ACT OF 1916

Complaint by the European Communities

Report of the Panel

WT/DS136/R

Adopted by the Dispute Settlement Body
on 26 September 2000
as Upheld by the Appellate Body Report

TABLE OF CONTENTS

I. INTRODUCTION

1.1 On 4 June 1998, the European Communities requested consultations with the United States pursuant to Article 4 of the Understanding on Rules and Procedures Governing the Settlement of Disputes (hereinafter the "DSU"), Article XXIII of the General Agreement on Tariffs and Trade 1994 (hereinafter the "GATT 1994") and Article 17.3 of the Agreement on Implementation of Article VI of the General Agreement on Tariffs and Trade 1994 (hereinafter the "Anti-Dumping Agreement") regarding failure on the part of the United States to repeal Title VIII of the US Revenue Act of 1916, also known as the US Antidumping Act of 1916 (hereinafter the "1916 Act").[1]

1.2 Consultations were held in Geneva on 29 July 1998, but did not lead to a mutually satisfactory resolution of the matter.

1.3 On 11 November 1998, the European Communities requested the Dispute Settlement Body (hereinafter the "DSB") to establish a panel pursuant to Article XXIII of the GATT 1994, Articles 4 and 6 of the DSU and Article 17 of the Anti-Dumping Agreement.[2] The European Communities claimed that the 1916 Act was inconsistent with Article XVI:4 of the Marrakesh Agreement Establishing the World Trade Organization (hereinafter the "Agreement Establishing the WTO" - the Marrakesh Agreement Establishing the World Trade Organization including its annexes being referred to as the "WTO Agreement"); Articles VI:1 and VI:2 of the GATT 1994; and Articles 1, 2.1, 2.2, 3, 4 and 5 of the Anti-Dumping Agreement.[3] In the alternative, the European Communities claimed that the 1916 Act was in breach of Article III:4 of the GATT 1994.

1.4 On 1 February 1999, the DSB established a panel pursuant to the request made by the European Communities, in accordance with Article 6 of the DSU. In document WT/DS136/3, the Secretariat reported that the parties had agreed that the panel would have the standard terms of reference. The terms of reference are the following:

> "To examine, in the light of the relevant provisions of the covered agreements cited by the European Communities in document WT/DS136/2, the matter referred to the DSB by the European Communities in that document and to make such findings as will assist the DSB in making the recommendations or in giving the rulings provided for in those agreements."

1.5 Document WT/DS136/3 also reported that, on 1 April 1999, the Panel was constituted as follows:

Chairman:	Mr. Johann Human
Members:	Mr. Dimitrij Grčar
	Professor Eugeniusz Piontek

1.6 India, Japan and Mexico reserved their rights to participate in the Panel proceedings as third parties. All of them presented arguments to the Panel.

1.7 The Panel met with the parties on 13 - 14 July 1999 as well as 14 - 15 September 1999. It met with third parties on 14 July 1999. The Panel issued its interim report to the parties on 20 December 1999. The Panel issued its final report to the parties on 14 February 2000.

---

1 See WT/DS136/1.

2 See WT/DS/136/2.

3 The provisions listed by the European Communities in WT/DS/136/2 as being infringed by the 1916 Act are, in the view of the European Communities, not necessarily the only violations of the mentioned Agreements. See WT/DS/136/2.

II. FACTUAL ASPECTS

A. *Description of the US 1916 Act*

2.1 The 1916 Act at issue in the present dispute was enacted by the US Congress under the heading of "Unfair Competition" in Title VIII of the Revenue Act of 1916.[4] It provides as follows:

> "It shall be unlawful for any person importing or assisting in importing any articles from any foreign country into the United States, commonly and systematically to import, sell or cause to be imported or sold such articles within the United States at a price substantially less than the actual market value or wholesale price of such articles, at the time of exportation to the United States, in the principal markets of the country of their production, or of other foreign countries to which they are commonly exported after adding to such market value or wholesale price, freight, duty, and other charges and expenses necessarily incident to the importation and sale thereof in the United States: *Provided*, That such act or acts be done with the intent of destroying or injuring an industry in the United States, or of preventing the establishment of an industry in the United States, or of restraining or monopolizing any part of trade and commerce in such articles in the United States.
>
> Any person who violates or combines or conspires with any other person to violate this section is guilty of a misdemeanour, and, on conviction thereof, shall be punished by a fine not exceeding $5,000, or imprisonment not exceeding one year, or both, in the discretion of the court.
>
> Any person injured in his business or property by reason of any violation of, or combination or conspiracy to violate, this section, may sue therefor in the district court of the United States for the district in which the defendant resides or is found or has an agent, without respect to the amount in controversy, and shall recover threefold the damages sustained, and the cost of the suit, including a reasonable attorney's fee.
>
> The foregoing provisions shall not be construed to deprive the proper State courts of jurisdiction in actions for damages thereunder."[5]

2.2 Thus, the business activity which the 1916 Act prohibits is a form of international price discrimination, which has two basic components:

(a) An importer must have sold a foreign-produced product within the United States at a price which is "substantially less" than the price at which the same product is sold in the country of the foreign producer.

(b) The importer must have undertaken this price discrimination "commonly and systematically."

---

4 Act of 8 September 1916. The Revenue Act of 1916 can be found at 39 Stat. 756 (1916).

5 15 U.S.C. § 72.

2.3 It is a condition for criminal or civil liability under the 1916 Act that the importer must have undertaken this price discrimination with "an intent of destroying or injuring an industry in the United States, or of preventing the establishment of an industry in the United States, or of restraining or monopolizing any part of trade and commerce in such articles in the United States."

2.4 Another characteristic of the 1916 Act is that it provides for a private right of action in federal district court and the remedy of treble damages for a private complainant, based on the injury sustained by that complainant in its business or property, as well as for criminal penalties in an action brought by the US government.

2.5 The 1916 Act is codified in Title 15 of the United States Code, entitled "Commerce and Trade".[6]

B. Description of Other Relevant US Acts

1. Antidumping Act of 1921 and Tariff Act of 1930

2.6 In 1921, the United States enacted the "Antidumping Act of 1921."[7] It empowered the Secretary of the Treasury to impose duties on dumped goods without regard to the dumper's intent. Whereas the Antidumping Act of 1921 was later repealed, it is on this Act that the United States' Tariff Act of 1930, as amended (hereinafter the "Tariff Act of 1930"),[8] is built. The Tariff Act of 1930 is implemented through proceedings governed by regulations promulgated by the US Department of Commerce[9] and the US International Trade Commission[10].

2.7 The 1921 Antidumping Act was, and the 1930 Tariff Act, as amended, is, codified in Title 19 of the United States Code, entitled "Customs Duties".

2.8 The United States has notified Title VII of the Tariff Act of 1930, as amended, and its implementing regulations to the WTO's Committee on Anti-Dumping Practices in accordance with Articles 18.4 and 18.5 of the Anti-Dumping Agreement.

2. Robinson-Patman Act

2.9 Section 2 of the Clayton Act, as amended by the Robinson-Patman Act in 1936, provides in pertinent part:

> "It shall be unlawful for any person engaged in commerce, in the course of such commerce, either directly or indirectly, to discriminate in price between different purchasers of commodities of like grade and quality, where either or any of the purchases involved in such discrimination are in commerce, where such commodities are sold for use, consumption, or resale within the United States [...] and where the effect of such discrimination may be substantially to lessen competition or tend to create a monopoly in any line of commerce, or to

---

6 See 15 U.S.C. §§ 71-74.

7 The Antidumping Act of 1921 was codified at 19 U.S.C. §§ 160-71 (repealed).

8 The Tariff Act of 1930 is codified at 19 U.S.C. §§ 1671 et seq.

9 See 19 C.F.R. Part 351.

10 See 19 C.F.R. Part 200.

> injure, destroy, or prevent competition with any person who either grants or knowingly receives the benefit of such discrimination or with customers of either of them."[11]

2.10 Section 2(f) of the Clayton Act, as amended by the Robinson-Patman Act, applies the same principles to the conduct of a buyer, by making it unlawful for a buyer "knowingly to induce or receive discrimination in price" prohibited by other parts of the Act.[12] A violation of this provision is subject to criminal penalties and also is actionable in a private right of action, where treble damages and injunctive relief are available.

2.11 To establish price discrimination in an action under the Robinson-Patman Act, there first must be evidence of two actual sales at different prices, with both sales occurring in US commerce.[13] Thus, the Robinson-Patman Act does not apply to cross-border price discrimination.[14] In addition, a successful price discrimination claim requires a showing of an anti-competitive effect. Case law has established that, if the claim is directed at so-called "primary line injury," meaning injury to the price discriminator's rivals, which corresponds to the situation addressed by the 1916 Act, the requisite anti-competitive effect can be demonstrated through a showing of (i) pricing below an appropriate measure of cost and (ii) the likelihood that the predator will recoup its losses in the future.[15]

2.12 The Robinson-Patman Act is codified in Title 15 of the United States Code, entitled "Commerce and Trade."[16]

C. *Instances of Application of the US 1916 Act*

2.13 The 1916 Act has been invoked infrequently. Before the 1970s, there was only one reported 1916 Act court case, *H. Wagner and Adler Co. v. Mali*[17].[18]

2.14 In line with the infrequent invocation of the 1916 Act, there is a limited number of judicial interpretations of its specific provisions.[19] In this regard, it should be

---

[11] 15 U.S.C. 13(a).

[12] See 15 U.S.C. 13(f).

[13] See *International Telephone & Telegraph Corp. et al.*, 104 F.T.C. 280, 417, citing E. Kinter, *A Robinson-Patman Primer*, 3rd ed. (1979), p. 35.

[14] In answering a question of the Panel regarding, *inter alia*, whether the Robinson-Patman Act applies to imported products, the United States notes, however, that imported goods that have become a part of domestic commerce may be subject to the Robinson-Patman Act.

[15] See *Brooke Group Ltd. v. Brown & Williamson Tobacco Corp.*, 509 U.S. 209, 222-23 (1993) (hereinafter "*Brooke Group*").

[16] Also located in Title 15 are the Sherman Act (15 U.S.C. §§ 1-7, to be found at 26 Stat. 209 (1890)), the Clayton Act (15 U.S.C. §§ 12-27, to be found at 38 Stat. 730 (1914)) and the Federal Trade Commission Act (15 U.S.C. §§ 41-58, to be found at 38 Stat. 717 (1914)).

[17] F.2d 666 (2d Cir. 1935).

[18] In response to a question of the Panel regarding whether the 1916 Act was applied before the 1970s, the United States confirmed its understanding that there was only one reported 1916 Act case before the 1970s. The United States also notes, however, that not all filed cases lead to reported decisions.

[19] Those interpretations can be found in the following - final or interlocutory - court decisions: *H. Wagner and Adler Co. v. Mali, Op. Cit.*; *In re Japanese Electronic Products Antitrust Litigation*, 388 F.Supp. 565 (Judicial Panel on Multidistrict Litigation, 1975) (hereinafter "*In re Japanese*

noted that, under the US legal system, the judicial branch of the government is the final authority regarding the meaning of federal laws, such as statutes passed by the legislative branch, i.e. the US Congress. It should also be noted, however, that no claims under the 1916 Act have ever been reviewed by the US Supreme Court, which is the highest federal court in the United States.[20] All court decisions so far have been rendered by US circuit courts of appeals or US district courts.[21]

2.15 All of the court decisions addressing the meaning of the 1916 Act and its various provisions to date also have involved private civil complaints rather than criminal prosecutions. Yet no complainant in a civil suit has so far recovered treble damages and the cost of the suit. However, in one recent civil case involving a 1916 Act claim, *Wheeling-Pittsburgh*[22], some defendants have elected to settle rather than proceed to trial.

2.16 The US Department of Justice, the agency responsible for prosecuting criminal violations of the 1916 Act, has never successfully prosecuted a criminal case under the 1916 Act.[23] Accordingly, no criminal sanctions have ever been imposed pursuant to the 1916 Act.

Electronic Products I"); *Zenith Radio Corp. v. Matsushita Electric Industrial Co., Ltd.*, 402 F.Supp. 244 (E.D. Pa. 1975) (hereinafter "*Zenith I*"); *Zenith Radio Corp. v. Matsushita Electric Industrial Co., Ltd.*, 402 F.Supp. 251 (E.D. Pa. 1975) (hereinafter "*Zenith II*"); *Outboard Marine Corp. v. Pezetel*, 461 F. Supp. 384 (D. Del. 1978); *Schwimmer v. Sony Corp. of America*, 471 F. Supp. 793 (E.D.N.Y. 1979); *Schwimmer v. Sony Corp. of America*, 637 F.2d 41 (2nd Cir. 1980); *Jewel Foliage Co. v. Uniflora Overseas Florida*, 497 F. Supp. 513 (M.D. Fla. 1980); *Zenith Radio Corp. v. Matsushita Electric Industrial Co., Ltd.*, 494 F.Supp. 1190 (E.D. Pa. 1980) (hereinafter "*Zenith III*"); *In re Japanese Electronic Products Antitrust Litigation (Zenith Radio Corp. v. Matsushita Electric Industrial Co., Ltd.)*, 723 F.2d 319 (3d Cir. 1983) (hereinafter "*In re Japanese Electronic Products II*"); *Western Concrete Structures Co. v. Mitsui & Co.*, 760 F.2d 1013 (9th Cir. 1985); *Isra Fruit Ltd. v. Agrexco Agr. Export Co.*, 631 F. Supp. 984 (S.D.N.Y. 1986); *In re Japanese Electronic Products Antitrust Litigation (Zenith Radio Corp. v. Matsushita Electric Industrial Co., Ltd.)*, 807 F.2d 44 (3d Cir. 1986) (hereinafter "*In re Japanese Electronic Products III*") *Helmac Products Corp. v. Roth (Plastics) Corp.*, 814 F. Supp. 560 (E.D. Mich. 1992) (hereinafter "*Helmac I*"); *Helmac Products Corp. v. Roth (Plastics) Corp.*, 814 F.Supp. 581 (E.D. Mich. 1993) (hereinafter "*Helmac II*"); *Geneva Steel Company v. Ranger Steel Supply Corp.*, 980 F.Supp. 1209 (D. Utah 1997) (hereinafter "*Geneva Steel*"); *Wheeling-Pittsburgh Steel Corporation v. Mitsui Co.*, 35 F.Supp.2d. 597 (S.D. Ohio 1999) (hereinafter "*Wheeling-Pittsburgh*").

[20] The only reported case in which the US Supreme Court has considered the 1916 Act was *United States v. Cooper Corp.*, 312 U.S. 600 (1941), although the issue in that case was whether the United States is a "person" within the meaning of Section 7 of the US Sherman Act entitled to sue for treble damages thereunder.

[21] In the United States, the federal judicial branch is established on three levels. Generally, the lowest level is the trial court level, consisting of the various US district courts. At least one district court can be found in each of the 50 States. The next level consists of the US circuit courts of appeals, which are intermediate appellate courts responsible for reviewing district court decisions. There are 12 federal court circuits. At the highest level of the federal court system is the US Supreme Court, which, at its discretion, hears appeals from decisions of the circuit courts.

[22] The case is still pending while the remaining litigants conduct discovery.

[23] In response to a question of the Panel regarding the number of cases considered for prosecution by the US Department of Justice, the United States notes that, so far as it can determine, the US Department of Justice has never prosecuted nor seriously considered prosecuting a criminal case under the 1916 Act. In *Zenith III*, *Op. Cit.*, p. 1212, the following is stated regarding enforcement of the 1916 Act's criminal provisions until the early 1970s:

III. CLAIMS AND MAIN ARGUMENTS

A. *Requests Dealt with by the Panel in the Course of the Proceedings*

1. *Preliminary Objection by the United States and Request for a Ruling by the Panel*

3.1 As a preliminary matter, the **United States** considers[24] that the European Communities claims for the first time in its first written submission that the 1916 Act also violates Articles 1 and 18.1 of the Anti-Dumping Agreement because these provisions make anti-dumping duties the exclusive remedy for dumping. The relevant WTO dispute settlement provisions - Articles 6.2 and 7 of the DSU and Articles 17.4 and 17.5 of the Anti-Dumping Agreement - preclude the Panel from considering these two claims because they were not included in the European Communities' request for the establishment of a panel.[25]

3.2 The United States notes that Article 7 of the DSU provides that the Panel's mandate is to examine the "matter" described in the panel request.[26] The Appellate Body has definitively described the "matter" which is properly before a panel to examine. In *Guatemala - Cement*, it explained that the complaining Member must, in its panel request,

> "identify the *specific measures at issue* and provide a brief summary of the *legal basis of the complaint* sufficient to present the problem clearly. [...] The "matter referred to the DSB", therefore, consists of two elements: the specific *measures* at issue and the *legal basis of the complaint* (or the *claims*)."[27]

"Apparently there have been four attempts to enforce the criminal provisions of the Act, but none of them has been successful and none has given rise to a reported judicial decision. Marks, *United States Antidumping Laws - A* Government *Overview* 43 Antitrust L.J. 580, 581 (1974)."

24 See the US First Written Submission, dated 3 June 1999, p.2.

25 The United States refers to WT/DS136/3.

26 The United States notes that Article 1.2 of the DSU explains that its rules and procedures govern a dispute subject to any special or additional rules and procedures contained in the covered agreements. The same Article provides that, to the extent that there is a "difference" between the rules and procedures of the DSU and the special or additional rules and procedures set forth in a covered agreement, the special or additional rules and procedures in the covered agreement "shall prevail." However, as established in the Appellate Body Report on *Guatemala - Anti-Dumping Investigation Regarding Portland Cement from Mexico,* WT/DS60/AB/R, adopted 25 November 1998, DSR 1998:IX, 3767, paras. 65-66 (hereinafter "Appellate Body Report on *Guatemala - Cement*"), if there is no "difference," the rules and procedures of the DSU *apply together with* the special or additional rules and procedures of the covered agreement. The Appellate Body expressly held that there is no "difference" between Articles 6.2 and 7 of the DSU, and Articles 17.4 and 17.5 of the Antidumping Agreement. *Ibid.*, paras. 67-68. Accordingly, Articles 6.2 and 7 of the DSU apply together with Articles 17.4 and 17.5 of the Antidumping Agreement when the claims at issue are being made under the Antidumping Agreement. When applied together, these Articles permit a panel to consider only the "matter" set forth in the complaining Member's panel request where, as here, the terms of reference are exclusively defined by reference to the panel request. *Ibid.*, paras. 70-72.

27 Appellate Body Report, *Guatemala - Cement, supra*, footnote 26, para. 72 (emphasis in original).

3.3 According to the United States, the Appellate Body has also settled that the complaining Member may set out the "legal basis for the complaint" - its "claims" - in a summary fashion and that the minimum requirement is simply for the complaining Member to list provisions of a WTO agreement[28].[29] Vague references to unidentified "other" provisions, however, do not satisfy the standards of Article 6.2 of the DSU.[30] If a particular "legal basis of the complaint" - a "claim" - is not set forth in the panel request, it is not properly before the panel. Likewise, Article 6.2 is not satisfied by only identifying the claims in the complaining Member's first written submission. In *European Communities - Bananas*, the Appellate Body explained that a deficiency in a panel request cannot be cured by the complaining Member's first submission:

> "Article 6.2 of the DSU requires that the *claims*, but not the *arguments*, must all be specified sufficiently in the request for the establishment of a panel in order to allow the defending party [...] to know the legal basis of the complaint. If a *claim* is not specified in the request for the establishment of a panel, then a faulty request cannot be subsequently 'cured' by a complaining party's argumentation in its first written submission to the panel or in any other submission or statement made later in the panel proceeding."[31]

3.4 The United States contends that, under these standards, the European Communities' panel request in the present dispute is insufficient to place claims that the 1916 Act violated Articles 1 and 18.1 of the Anti-Dumping Agreement before the Panel. The European Communities, in its panel request, characterised the 1916 Act as an anti-dumping statute and claimed that the 1916 Act was inconsistent with Article VI:2 of the GATT 1994, which, according to the European Communities, "specif[ies] that anti-dumping duties are the only possible remedy to dumping whereas the 1916 Act is having recourse to treble damages and fines and/or imprisonment."[32] The European Communities at no point claimed - in its panel request or even in its request for consultations - that the 1916 Act was similarly inconsistent with any provision of the Anti-Dumping Agreement or, in particular, with Article 1 or Article 18.1 of the Anti-Dumping Agreement.[33]

---

[28] The term "WTO agreement(s)" is used hereinafter to refer to the various agreements contained in Annex 1 and 2 of the WTO Agreement.

[29] The United States refers to the Appellate Body Report on *India - Patent Protection for Pharmaceutical and Agricultural Chemical Products,* WT/DS50/AB/R, adopted 16 January 1998, DSR 1998:I, 9, paras. 88-91 (hereinafter "Appellate Body Report on *India - Patents*"); Report of the Appellate Body on *European Communities - Regime for the Importation, Sale and Distribution of Bananas*, WT/DS27/AB/R, adopted 25 September 1997, DSR 1997:II, 591, para. 141 (hereinafter "Appellate Body Report on *European Communities - Bananas*").

[30] The United States refers to the Panel Report on *European Communities - Regime for the Importation, Sale and Distribution of Bananas*, WT/DS27/R/USA, adopted 25 September 1997, DSR 1997:II, 943, paras. 7.29-7.30 (hereinafter "Panel Report on *European Communities - Bananas*").

[31] Appellate Body Report, *European Communities - Bananas, supra*, footnote 29, para. 143 (emphasis in original).

[32] WT/DS136/1.

[33] The United States notes that the European Communities did reference Article 1 of the Anti-dumping Agreement but only with regard to a separate claim that Article 1 requires "the carrying out

3.5 The United States submits that until receipt of the European Communities' first written submission, the United States had no notice that the European Communities was asserting claims under Articles 1 and 18.1 of the Anti-Dumping Agreement. The Appellate Body has explained that a defective panel request cannot be cured by a later submission or statement. Accordingly, the European Communities' claims under Articles 1 and 18.1 of the Anti-Dumping Agreement are not properly before the Panel.

3.6 The United States therefore requests that the Panel rule that the claims are not before it and are eliminated from the instant proceeding. The United States requests that the Panel rule expeditiously and, if possible, by the time of its first meeting.

3.7 In response to a question of the Panel regarding its position *vis-à-vis* the US request, the **European Communities** states[34] that the United States requests the Panel to exclude claims that the European Communities has not made. The relevant EC claims are that by providing for a remedy other than duties against dumping the 1916 Act violates Article XVI:4 of the Agreement Establishing the WTO and Article VI:2 of the GATT 1994. The European Communities makes no separate claims that this feature of the 1916 Act violates Article 1 and 18.1 of the Anti-Dumping Agreement. These provisions were merely mentioned as arguments in support of the European Communities' claims. Accordingly, the US request for a preliminary ruling can be dismissed as being without object.

3.8 The position taken by the Panel in the course of the proceedings *vis-à-vis* the US request is reflected in section VI.B.1 of this report.

2. *Request by Japan for Enhanced Third Party Rights*

3.9 **Japan**, which is a third party in the present case and has requested the establishment of another panel in respect of the 1916 Act,[35] requests to be granted enhanced third party rights.[36] In particular, Japan requests to receive all the necessary documents, including submissions and written versions of statements by the parties, and that it be granted permission to attend all the meetings of the second substantive meeting of the Panel.[37]

3.10 In reply to a request by the Panel for the views of the parties, the **European Communities** states that it is happy to support the request of Japan, provided that the

of an investigation (which has to respect a set of procedural rules) prior to the imposition of any duty." Never did the European Communities identify Article 1 of the Antidumping Agreement as the basis for a claim that antidumping duties are the sole remedy for dumping. The United States also refers to the Panel Report on *European Communities - Imposition of Anti-Dumping Duties on Imports of Cotton Yarn from Brazil*, adopted on 5 July 1995, ADP/137, paras. 442-447 for the proposition that if there is more than one legal basis for alleging a breach of the same provision of an agreement, a separate and distinct claim is required.

[34] See the European Communities' letter to the Chairman of the Panel, dated 6 July 1999.

[35] See WT/DS162/3. That panel was established on 26 July 1999 and composed on 11 August 1999 (WT/DS162/4).

[36] As stated in Japan's letter to the Chairman of the Panel, dated 2 September 1999.

[37] Japan made its request for enhanced third party rights after the first substantive meeting of the Panel.

European Communities' similar request in the case initiated by Japan in respect of the 1916 Act (WT/DS162) is also accepted by the Panel.

3.11 The **United States,** in reply to the same request by the Panel, notes that it strongly objects expanded third party rights for Japan in the present case, since the circumstances of the case do not warrant it.

3.12 For the United States, expanded third party rights are not needed in order to obtain access to the parties' submissions. The United States supports full transparency in the WTO and will be making its submissions and oral statements available to the public. Furthermore, the United States recalls that it has requested in both panel proceedings dealing with the 1916 Act (WT/DS136 and WT/DS162) that each party provide a non-confidential summary of the information contained in each submission that could be disclosed to the public unless the party has made the submission public. The United States further recalls that the DSU provides that parties shall make such non-confidential versions available upon request. Accordingly, both the European Communities and Japan will have access to each others' submissions as soon as they comply with the requirements of the DSU in this regard.

3.13 The United States argues, moreover, that, as individual complaining parties, Japan and the European Communities have more than adequate opportunity to present their views and respond to the arguments of the United States. In *EC Measures Concerning Meat and Meat Products (Hormones)*[38], the panel allowed expanded third party rights because the panel had stated that it intended to conduct concurrent deliberations in those cases meaning that its deliberations were going to be based upon the arguments and presentations in both cases, including presentations by experts made jointly to both panels. The panel proceeded with this approach despite the fact that the United States had expressed its unequivocal concern with the panel's "concurrent deliberations" approach. Thus, because the panel was going to consider arguments made in one case in the course of deciding another case, the United States requested and was allowed enhanced third party rights. Otherwise, without an opportunity for the United States to respond, the panel would have been considering what would have been, in effect, *ex parte* submissions.

3.14 The United States notes that, in the present case, the Panel has not stated that it intends to conduct concurrent deliberations, and for the reasons expressed in the *European Communities - Hormones* proceeding, the United States would not support concurrent deliberations. Accordingly, the European Communities will not be denied an opportunity to respond to arguments of the United States that will be considered by the Panel in making its decision in the case initiated by the European Communities. The same holds true for Japan in its case. The apparent purpose for the request for expanded third party rights is to provide the third parties with an opportunity to make an additional submission in their own panel process. There is no provision in the DSU for such additional submissions.

3.15 The position taken by the Panel in the course of the proceedings *vis-à-vis* Japan's request is reflected in section VI.B.2 of this report.

---

[38] Panel Report on *EC Measures Concerning Meat and Meat Products (Hormones)*, WT/DS26/R/USA, WT/DS48/R/CAN, adopted 13 February 1998, DSR 1998:III, 699 (hereinafter Panel Report on "*European Communities - Hormones*").

B. Overview of the Claims of the Parties and Findings Requested

3.16 The **European Communities** requests the Panel to find that by maintaining the 1916 Act the United States has violated:

(a) Article VI:1 and VI:2 of the GATT 1994 and Articles 1, 2.1, 2.2, 3, 4 and 5.5 of the Anti-Dumping Agreement;

(b) Article III:4 of the GATT 1994[39];

(c) Article XVI:4 of the Agreement Establishing the WTO;

and that by doing so it has nullified and impaired benefits accruing to the European Communities under those Agreements.

3.17 The European Communities requests the Panel to hold that the 1916 Act is an anti-dumping measure since it is targeted at imports and at price discrimination between the exporters' market or third country market and the importing country's market in terms which are in substance identical to those laid down in Article VI:1 of the GATT 1994. Since the conditions under which action may be taken under the 1916 Act allow action to be taken which would not be allowed under Article VI of the GATT 1994 or the Anti-Dumping Agreement and in particular because the remedies provided in the 1916 Act are not those allowed under Article VI:2 of the GATT 1994, the Panel should hold that the 1916 Act as such violates Article VI:1 and VI:2 of the GATT 1994 and the cited provisions of the Anti-Dumping Agreement.

3.18 In the alternative, the European Communities asks the Panel to find that the 1916 Act violates the national treatment requirement of Article III:4 of the GATT 1994 because the 1916 Act leads to the application of stricter disciplines on imported goods than domestic goods.

3.19 Finally, the European Communities considers that the Panel should also find that the 1916 Act is in violation of Article XVI:4 of the Agreement Establishing the WTO because the United States has failed to ensure, in respect of the 1916 Act, that its laws are in conformity with its WTO obligations.

3.20 The **United States** requests the Panel to find that nothing in Article VI:2 of the GATT 1994 provides that anti-dumping duties are the exclusive remedy for dumping. If the Panel therefore rejects the European Communities' Article VI:2 claim, it need not reach the question of whether the 1916 Act is governed by Article VI and the Anti-Dumping Agreement. The United States also requests the Panel to reject the European Communities' other claims under Article VI:1 and the Anti-Dumping Agreement, because the European Communities has failed to demonstrate that the procedures in Article VI:1 and the various other provisions asserted under the Anti-Dumping Agreement are required to be followed in response to injurious dumping.

3.21 The United States moreover requests the Panel to hold that the 1916 Act is in any event not inconsistent with either Article VI of the GATT 1994 or the Anti-Dumping Agreement because the 1916 Act is not an anti-dumping statute under US law and therefore is not governed by Article VI of the GATT 1994 or the Anti-Dumping Agreement. The United States submits that the 1916 Act is specifically

[39] This claim is made in the alternative. See section III.G.1 below.

targeted at a very narrow type of objectionable business activity involving antitrust-like predatory intent.

3.22 The United States further requests the Panel to dismiss the European Communities' claim that the 1916 Act accords less favorable treatment to imported goods than the Robinson-Patman Act accords to like domestic goods. The Panel's decision in this regard should be informed by the fact that the 1916 Act establishes a standard for relief which has never been met in the case of importers and imported goods.

3.23 The United States also asks the Panel to conclude that the 1916 Act as such is in any event WTO-consistent because it is susceptible to an interpretation that permits action consistent with the United States' WTO obligations.

3.24 Finally, the United States requests the Panel to find no violation of Article XVI:4 of the Agreement Establishing the WTO. Article XVI:4 of the Agreement Establishing the WTO is not relevant, unless the 1916 Act is shown to be inconsistent with a separate WTO obligation of the United States. The United States submits that this is not the case.

C. The Distinction between Discretionary and Mandatory Legislation and its Relevance to the Present Case

3.25 In response to a question of the Panel to both parties regarding whether the 1916 Act should be viewed as mandatory or non-mandatory legislation within the meaning given to those terms by GATT 1947/WTO practice, the **United States** notes that both the civil and the criminal provisions constitute non-mandatory legislation in the context of the European Communities' claims under Articles III:4 and VI:2 of the GATT 1994.

3.26 The United States recalls that GATT 1947 and WTO panels have uniformly drawn a distinction between mandatory and discretionary legislation. Only legislation which mandates WTO-inconsistent action can itself be WTO-inconsistent. In this regard, the panel in *Canada - Measures Affecting the Export of Civilian Aircraft* recently stated:

> "We recall the distinction that GATT/WTO panels have consistently drawn between discretionary legislation and mandatory legislation. For example, in *United States - Tobacco*, the panel "recalled that panels had consistently ruled that legislation which mandated action inconsistent with the General Agreement could be challenged as such, whereas legislation which merely gave the discretion to the executive authority [...] to act inconsistently with the General Agreement could not be challenged as such; only the actual application of such legislation inconsistent with the General Agreement could be subject to challenge" [citation omitted]."[40]

[40] Panel Report on *Canada - Measures Affecting the Export of Civilian Aircraft*, WT/DS70/R, adopted 20 August 1999, as upheld by the Appellate Body Report, DSR 1999:IV, 1443, para. 9.124 (hereinafter "Panel Report on *Canada - Aircraft*"), citing the Panel Report on *United States - Measures Affecting the Importation, Internal Sale and Use of Tobacco*, adopted on 4 October 1994, BISD 41S/131, para 118 (hereinafter "*United States - Tobacco*").

3.27 The United States further notes that in *EEC - Regulation on Imports of Parts and Components*[41], the panel found that "the mere existence" of the anti-circumvention provision of the European Communities' anti-dumping legislation was not inconsistent with the European Communities' GATT 1947 obligations, even though the European Communities had taken GATT-inconsistent measures under that provision.[42] The panel based its finding on its conclusion that the anti-circumvention provision "does not mandate the imposition of duties or other measures by the EEC Commission and Council; it merely authorizes the Commission and the Council to take certain actions"[43]. In the present dispute, the European Communities is challenging no specific measures taken under the 1916 Act. Rather, it is challenging the mere existence of the 1916 Act. Thus, for that challenge to succeed, the European Communities must demonstrate not only that the 1916 Act authorizes WTO-inconsistent action, but that it mandates such action. In other words, it must show that this legislation is not susceptible to an interpretation that would permit the US government to comply with its WTO obligations.

3.28 The United States further recalls that, in applying the discretionary/mandatory distinction, panels have found that legislation explicitly directing action inconsistent with GATT 1947 principles does not mandate inconsistent action so long as it provides the possibility for authorities to avoid such action. For example, in *United States - Taxes on Petroleum and Certain Imported Substances*,[44] the Superfund Act required importers to supply sufficient information regarding the chemical inputs of taxable substances to enable the tax authorities to determine the amount of tax to be imposed; otherwise, a penalty tax would be imposed in the amount of five percent *ad valorem* or a different rate to be prescribed in regulations by the Secretary of the Treasury by a different methodology. The regulations in question had not yet been issued. Nevertheless, the panel concluded:

> "[W]hether [the regulations] will eliminate the need to impose the penalty tax and whether they will establish complete equivalence between domestic and imported products, as required by Article III:2, first sentence, remain open questions. From the perspective of the overall objectives of the General Agreement it is regrettable that the Superfund Act explicitly directs the United States tax authorities to impose a tax inconsistent with the national treatment principle but, since the Superfund Act also gives them the possibility to avoid the need to impose that tax by issuing regulations, the existence of the penalty rate provisions as such does not constitute a violation of the United States obligations under the General Agreement."[45]

---

41 Panel Report on *EEC - Regulation on Imports of Parts and Components*, adopted on 16 May 1990, BISD 37S/132 (hereinafter "*EEC - Parts and Components*").

42 The United States refers to *EEC - Parts and Components*, *Op. Cit.*, paras. 5.9, 5.21, 5.25-5.26.

43 *Ibid.*, para. 5.25.

44 Panel Report on *United States - Taxes on Petroleum and Certain Imported Substances*, adopted on 17 June 1987, BISD 34S/136 (hereinafter "*US - Superfund*").

45 *Ibid.*, para. 5.2.9.

3.29 The United States also notes that, in *Thailand - Restrictions on Importation of and Internal Taxes on Cigarettes*[46] the panel examined Thailand's Tobacco Act, which established a higher ceiling tax rate for imported cigarettes than for domestic cigarettes. While the Act explicitly gave Thai officials the authority to implement discriminatory tax rates, this did not render the statute mandatory. The panel concluded that "the possibility that the Tobacco Act might be applied contrary to Article III:2 was, by itself, not sufficient to make it inconsistent with the General Agreement."[47]

3.30 The United States recalls, finally, the findings of the panel in the *United States - Tobacco* case. That case is factually analogous to the instant case and therefore offers guidance to the Panel. The panel in the *United States - Tobacco* case found that a law did not mandate GATT-inconsistent action where the language of that law was susceptible of a range of meanings, including meanings permitting GATT-consistent action. Specifically, the panel examined the question whether a statute requiring that "comparable" inspection fees be assessed for imported and domestic tobacco mandated that these fees had to be identical for each, without respect to differences in inspection costs. If so, the statute was inconsistent with Article VIII:1(a) of the GATT 1947, which prohibited the imposition of fees in excess of services rendered.[48] The United States argued that the term "comparable" need not be interpreted to mean "identical," and that the law did not preclude a fee structure commensurate with the cost of services rendered.[49] The panel agreed with the United States:

> "[T]he Panel noted that there was no clear interpretation on the meaning of the term "comparable" as used in the 1993 legislative amendment. It appeared to the Panel that the term "comparable", including the ordinary meaning thereof, was susceptible of a range of meanings. The Panel considered that this range of meanings could encompass the interpretation advanced by the United States in this proceeding, an interpretation which could potentially enable USDA to comply with the obligation of Article VIII:1(a) not to impose fees in excess of the cost of services rendered, while at the same time meeting the comparability requirement of [the US law]."[50]

The United States adds that the panel therefore found that the complaining party had "not demonstrated that [the US law] *could not* be applied in a manner ensuring that fees charged for inspecting tobacco were not in excess of the cost of services rendered."[51]

---

[46] Panel Report on *Thailand - Restrictions on Importation of and Internal Taxes on Cigarettes*, adopted on 7 November 1990, BISD 37S/200 (hereinafter "*Thailand - Cigarettes*").

[47] *Ibid.*, para. 86. The United States further notes that the panel, at para. 88, found that the actual implementation of the tax rates through regulations was also consistent with Thai obligations, since these rates were non-discriminatory.

[48] The United States refers to *United States - Tobacco, Op. Cit.*, para. 118.

[49] The United States refers to *United States - Tobacco, Op. Cit.*, para. 122.

[50] *Ibid.*, para. 123.

[51] *Ibid.* (emphasis added by the United States).

3.31 In the view of the United States, there is thus a strict burden on a complaining party seeking to establish that a Member's legislation *as such* mandates a violation of WTO obligations: the complaining party must demonstrate that the legislation, as interpreted in accordance with the domestic law of the Member, precludes any possibility of action consistent with the Member's WTO obligations. Moreover, where legislation is susceptible of multiple interpretations, the complaining party must demonstrate that none of these interpretations permits WTO-consistent action.

3.32 The United States contends that, in the present case, the European Communities has failed to meet that burden. The 1916 Act is susceptible to an interpretation that is WTO-consistent. In fact, all final judicial decisions that have considered the 1916 Act have interpreted it as such. Indeed, US courts have repeatedly admonished that the 1916 Act should be interpreted whenever possible to parallel the unfair competition law applicable to domestic commerce.[52] Interpreting the 1916 Act to parallel domestic unfair competition law is clearly consistent with WTO obligations because the WTO does not govern competition laws. Moreover, any susceptibility that particular elements of a 1916 Act claim may have to a range of possible meanings is ultimately of no consequence because the 1916 Act remains different from an anti-dumping statute under the entire range of conceivable interpretations.

3.33 Turning to the basis for the distinction, the United States notes that the distinction in GATT 1947/WTO jurisprudence between discretionary and mandatory legislation is not based upon a particular provision of the WTO Agreement, nor is it limited in its application to a particular WTO provision. In the cases discussed above, for example, this distinction was applied in the context of both Article III and Article VIII of the GATT 1947. The distinction is a general principle developed by panels that most likely has its origin in the presumption against conflicts between national and international laws. It is both general international practice and that of the United States that statutory language is to be interpreted so as to avoid conflicts with international obligations. There is thus a presumption against a conflict between international and national law. In general,

> "[a]lthough national courts must apply national laws even if they conflict with international law, there is a presumption against the existence of such a conflict. As international law is based upon the common consent of the different states, it is improbable that a state would intentionally enact a rule conflicting with international law. A rule of national law which ostensibly seems to conflict with international law must, therefore, if possible always be so interpreted as to avoid such conflict."[53]

3.34 The United States recalls that, under US law, it is an elementary principle of statutory construction that "an act of Congress ought never to be construed to violate the law of nations if any other possible construction remains"[54]. While international obligations cannot override inconsistent requirements of domestic law, "ambiguous

---

[52] The United States refers to *Zenith III*, *Op. Cit.*, p. 1223.

[53] *Oppenheim's International Law*, 9th ed., pp. 81-82 (footnote omitted).

[54] *Murray v. Schooner Charming Betsy*, 6 U.S. (2 Cranch) 64, 118 (1804).

statutory provisions [...] [should] be construed, where possible, to be consistent with international obligations of the United States"[55].

3.35 According to the United States, GATT 1947 jurisprudence distinguishing between mandatory and discretionary legislation does no more than apply the general principle that there is a presumption against conflicts between national and international law. If a law is susceptible to an interpretation that is WTO-consistent, there is a presumption that domestic authorities will interpret that law so as to avoid a conflict with WTO obligations. This presumption may be seen as underlying the *United States - Tobacco* panel's finding that a domestic law susceptible of multiple interpretations would not violate a state's international obligations so long as one possible interpretation permits action consistent with those obligations.[56] This principle applies with equal force in the present case. The 1916 Act is a discretionary statute susceptible of an interpretation that permits action consistent with the United States' WTO obligations under both Article III:4 and Article VI:2, as all judicial decisions to date establish as a matter of fact. Accordingly, the Panel should rule that the 1916 Act, as such, is fully consistent with the United States' WTO obligations.

3.36 In response to the Panel's question and the US arguments, the **European Communities** notes that the provisions of the 1916 Act are "mandatory" legislation as this term is used in GATT 1947/WTO practice. According to that practice, mandatory measures are those which, under national law, require the executive authority to impose a measure. For example, in *Denial of Most-Favoured-Nation Treatment As To Non-Rubber Footwear From Brazil*, the following definition can be found:

> "[...] the Panel examined whether this legislation as such is consistent with Article I:1. The Panel noted that the CONTRACTING PARTIES had decided in previous cases that legislation mandatorily *requiring the executive authority to impose a measure* inconsistent with the General Agreement was inconsistent with that Agreement *as such*, whether or not an occasion for the actual application of the legislation had arisen. The Panel recalled that the backdating provisions of the two Acts *are mandatory legislation*, that is *they impose on the executive authority requirements which cannot be modified by executive action*, and it therefore found that these provisions *as such, not merely their application in concrete cases*, have to be consistent with Article I:1."[57]

3.37 The European Communities recalls that the United States relies in particular on the *EEC - Parts and Components* case. However, that case concerned authorising provisions in respect of which there was discretion for the administration. Whether

---

[55] *Footwear Distributors and Retailers of America v. United States*, 852 F. Supp. 1078, 1088 (CIT), appeal dismissed, 43 F.3d 1486 (Table) (Fed. Cir. 1994), citing *DeBartolo Corp. v. Florida Gulf Coast Building and Trades Council*, 485 U.S. 568 (1988). The United States also refers to the Restatement (Third) of the Foreign Relations of the United States, s. 114 (1987).

[56] The United States refers to *United States - Tobacco*, *Op. Cit.*, para. 123.

[57] Panel Report on *Denial of Most-Favoured-Nation Treatment as to Non-Rubber Footwear from Brazil*, adopted on 19 June 1992, BISD 39S/128, para. 6.13 (footnote omitted; emphasis added by the European Communities).

these provisions produced any effects in practice depended on the discretion of an administration. There is no such discretion in the case of the 1916 Act.

3.38 In light of the foregoing, the European Communities considers that there are two main reasons why the 1916 Act is mandatory legislation. First, when a private party brings an action under the 1916 Act there is no room at all for government discretion.[58] Second, once a court has found that the 1916 Act standard is met, it is required to grant relief to the complainant. The wording of paragraph 2 of the 1916 Act is unequivocal:

> "Any person who violates or combines or conspires with any other person to violate this section is guilty of a misdemeanour, and, *on conviction thereof, shall* be punished by a fine not exceeding $5,000, or imprisonment not exceeding one year, or both, in the discretion of the court."[59]

3.39 The European Communities notes that the only margin of discretion left to a court is concerned with the type and level of the sanction that will be applied. And even that discretion can be exercised only within statutory limits. Moreover, if it is true, as the United States submits, that the actual meaning of the 1916 Act depends on courts' interpretation of its provisions, it is even clearer that the government has no discretion at all to influence courts' decisions. Nor can the government modify the 1916 Act's legal requirements. This further confirms that the 1916 Act is "mandatory".

3.40 The European Communities further recalls that, in response to a question of the Panel regarding what discretion a US court has in dismissing a 1916 Act case or in deciding not to impose treble damages, for example, because doing so would be contrary to international law obligations of the United States, the United States replies that

> "[a] court would not have discretion to dismiss a well-founded case under the 1916 Act [...] nor would a court have discretion not to impose treble damages that had been properly established."

The European Communities thus considers that neither the administration nor the courts have discretion over civil claims.

3.41 The European Communities points out, moreover, that the situation concerning the criminal liability provisions is somewhat different but that the legislation is still not discretionary within the meaning of GATT 1947/WTO jurisprudence. In this connection, it is important to note that the 1916 Act makes "unlawful" and "misdemeanours" the offences that it describes. The most pertinent analogy under GATT 1947 case law is the report of the panel on *United States - Measures Affecting Alcoholic and Malt Beverages.*[60] One of the many measures examined in that case concerned the maximum price laws in Massachusetts and Rhode Island. The panel held

---

[58] The European Communities notes that criminal prosecution under the 1916 Act is the only case within the discretion of the US government.

[59] Emphasis added by the European Communities.

[60] Panel Report on *United States - Measures Affecting Alcoholic and Malt Beverages*, adopted on 19 June 1992, BISD 39S/206 (hereinafter "*United States - Malt Beverages*").

those laws to violate the GATT 1947 even though they were not being enforced, saying:

> "Even if Massachusetts may not currently be using its police powers to enforce this mandatory legislation, the measure continues to be mandatory legislation which may influence the decisions of economic operators."[61]

3.42 The European Communities argues that the reason why the panel in *United States - Malt Beverages* considered the legislation in issue in that case to have legal effects is that good corporate citizens, like all good citizens, avoid acting unlawfully and indeed committing misdemeanours, whether or not the law is being actively enforced and they risk actual punishment. The same reasoning is applicable to the present case.

3.43 The European Communities notes, in addition, that the US Department of Justice may only decline to bring a criminal case under certain defined conditions, none of which include a consideration of whether or not the action would be WTO-compatible. Also, once the decision to bring a case has been taken by the US Department of Justice, the courts are obliged to try it and impose a penalty if the conditions and criteria of the 1916 Act are met. That is, courts are obliged to do in criminal cases what the United States said that they are obliged to do in civil cases. In other words, it is mandatory for them to take action against dumping which is inconsistent with WTO rules. Thus, both the civil and criminal provisions of the 1916 Act create legal effects and in neither case does this depend on the administration taking some discretionary action.

3.44 The European Communities submits, finally, that the unadopted report of the panel on *EC - Anti-Dumping Duties on Audio Tapes in Cassettes Originating in Japan*[62] as well as the adopted report of the panel on *United States - Definition of Industry concerning Wine and Grape Products*[63] support its view that the 1916 Act is not discretionary legislation as this term is used in GATT 1947/WTO jurisprudence.[64]

3.45 In response, the **United States** reiterates its view that the 1916 Act should be viewed as discretionary legislation. In reply to a question of the Panel regarding the discretion enjoyed by the US Department of Justice as to whether to bring a criminal case or not, the United States states that the Department of Justice, an executive branch agency, has the discretion to decide whether or not to bring a criminal prosecution under the 1916 Act. In other words, while the 1916 Act authorises the Department of Justice to bring a criminal prosecution, it does not mandate it.

3.46 The United States notes, in this regard, that the standards used by the Department of Justice in deciding whether to conduct criminal proceedings, including investigative measures, are set out in a public document known as the "United States

---

[61] *Ibid.*, para. 5.60.

[62] Panel Report on *EC - Anti-Dumping Duties on Audio Tapes in Cassettes Originating in Japan*, ADP/136 (unadopted), dated 28 April 1995 (hereinafter "*EC - Audio Cassettes*").

[63] Panel Report on *United States - Definition of Industry concerning Wine and Grape Products*, adopted by the Committee on Subsidies and Countervailing Measures on 28 April 1992, BISD 39S/436 (hereinafter "*United States - Definition of Wine Industry*").

[64] See section III.H.2 below.

Attorneys' Manual", specifically, Ch. 9-27 of that Manual entitled "Principles of Federal Prosecution." This document explains that the Department enjoys wide discretion regarding whether, when and how it will bring criminal charges. For example, section 9-27.220 states that, where there is sufficient admissible evidence of a federal offence, the government may nonetheless decline to prosecute because (1) no substantial federal interest would be served by prosecution; (2) the person is subject to effective prosecution in another jurisdiction; or (3) there exists an adequate non-criminal alternative to prosecution. In section 9-27.230, "Substantial Federal Interest" is defined to include, *inter alia*, "federal law enforcement priorities" and "the nature and seriousness of the offense."[65]

3.47 The United States further notes that in cases where the United States, acting through the Department of Justice, is itself a party to litigation, it has direct responsibility for ensuring that its own claims and actions comport with US laws and obligations, and for informing the court of such considerations. Also, where appropriate, the Department can seek to intervene in a private civil litigation in order to protect a federal government interest. The Department does not routinely intervene in private litigation, however, and it remains a matter of judgment when and before what courts it should be done.

3.48 As concerns civil cases, the United States contends that the European Communities misses the point with its argument that when a private party brings an action under the 1916 Act there is no room for government discretion. The question in these circumstances is not whether the executive authority has discretion, but whether the law mandates a violation of a WTO obligation. In the instant case, to answer that question the Panel must determine whether the law is susceptible to an interpretation that is WTO-consistent. Although prior cases applying the mandatory/discretionary distinction have involved executive enforcement of a measure, there is no reason that the principle cannot apply to a measure that is enforced through the judicial branch.

3.49 The United States argues, finally, that the European Communities' reliance on the *United States - Malt Beverages* case is misplaced. The issue in that case was whether the non-enforcement of mandatory legislation rendered the legislation non-actionable. Indeed, this is plainly reflected in the section quoted by the European Communities. Yet, that is not the question in the instant case. The question in the instant case is whether the law is mandatory, not whether the law is being enforced.

3.50 In response to a question of the Panel regarding whether the mandatory/discretionary distinction applies also to cases of judicial enforcement of a measure, the **European Communities** states that, contrary to the view expressed by the United States, the mandatory/discretionary distinction does not apply to such cases. Courts only declare what the law is. Or, as Montesquieu noted, the judiciary is "la bouche de la loi". Accordingly, a court does not make law, it only applies it.

3.51 The European Communities further notes that the US constitution is founded on the principle of the separation of powers. The United States cannot argue that its courts regard themselves in general as having discretion as to whether or not to apply

---

[65] The United States notes in this connection that Sections One and Two of the Sherman Antitrust Act of 1890 can be and often are enforced through criminal as well as civil proceedings, while the Clayton Antitrust Act is enforceable only through civil actions.

the law, similar to that possessed by the executive arm of government when powers are delegated. Even if this were to be the case in some special areas, such as awarding specific remedies, it does not apply to the adjudication of a dispute under the 1916 Act.

3.52 The European Communities does acknowledge that it may sometimes appear that courts have a number of options in interpreting the law. However, that is simply a reflection of the difficulty of predicting the outcome of a complex debate. No court would admit to being free to choose between a number of options for interpreting the law. All courts endeavour in good faith to establish the true meaning of the law on the basis of the text and established principles of interpretation.

3.53 The European Communities considers that the most pertinent WTO decision for the present case is *India - Patent Protection*. In that case, the Appellate Body concluded that the Indian courts would apply the (mandatory) law even in the face of directly contradictory administrative practice. This conclusion reflects the principle that courts do not have discretion in the same way as administrations do.

3.54 The European Communities argues, moreover, that the cases that have been invoked by the United States all concern cases where the administration was taking action and also had the power to complete, amend or add to the legislation so as to avoid a violation. Clearly, courts are not in the same position and do not have the power to adopt additional or amending rules. In any event, even if one could imagine situations where courts are given discretionary powers to amend or add to legislation in the same way as an administration typically might, that certainly is not the case with the 1916 Act.

3.55 The European Communities also points out that the provisions of the 1947 Protocol of Provisional Application demonstrate that, historically, it was administrative discretion that was considered relevant. That is also one reason why Article XVI:4 of the Agreement Establishing the WTO speaks of "domestic laws, regulations and *administrative* procedures".[66]

3.56 The European Communities notes, finally, that the United States apparently attempts to confuse the issue before the Panel by assimilating discretion in the application of legislation with ambiguity in the interpretation of legislation, which allegedly exists in the instant case. However, there is no basis even under the GATT 1947 to defend legislation which is on its face GATT-inconsistent on the ground that courts might one day interpret it in a GATT-consistent manner.

3.57 The European Communities recalls that the only GATT 1947 case in which there is any reference to interpretation is *United States - Tobacco*, which the United States claims is particularly pertinent to the present dispute. The *United States - Tobacco* case involved a situation in which domestic legislation was incomplete.[67] There was a requirement on the administration to promulgate fees for the inspection of imported tobacco at a level "comparable" to that for domestic tobacco but at the same time the administration had the power to adjust the level of fees for the inspec-

66 Article XVI:4 of the Agreement Establishing the WTO reads as follows: "Each Member shall ensure the conformity of its laws, regulations and administrative procedures with its obligations as provided in the annexed Agreements." (no emphasis in the original)

67 The European Communities refers to *United States - Tobacco*, *Op. Cit.*, paras. 114-118.

tion of domestic tobacco. The panel therefore understandably held that there was no basis to hold that the administration, in fixing the level of fees for imported tobacco, would do so at a level inconsistent with Article VIII:1(a) of the GATT 1947. In other words, the panel held that at such stage there was no mandatory legislation inconsistent with the GATT 1947. In the instant case, there is of course no power for the US administration to complete or amend the 1916 Act which would allow it to make it compatible with WTO rules. All the requirements are already laid down in the 1916 Act.

3.58 The **United States** takes issue with the European Communities' description of the *United States - Tobacco* case as involving domestic legislation that was "incomplete," meaning according to the European Communities that the agency had not yet promulgated its regulations. The United States does not agree that that somehow distinguishes the panel's application of the mandatory/discretionary distinction from the present case. In the *United States - Tobacco* case, the panel considered whether a term in a statute could be interpreted by the relevant government authorities - which happened to be executive branch authorities - in a WTO-consistent manner. Thus, the only difference is that executive branch authorities were involved instead of judicial branch authorities. There is no reason why the same principle should not apply in the present case. The focus in a mandatory/discretionary analysis is not on which branch of government is applying the law, but whether there is room in the application of the law for the relevant government authorities to act in a WTO-consistent manner. In the present case, not only is there room for such an interpretation, but the law has already been so interpreted. Accordingly, the Panel should find that the 1916 Act as such is WTO-consistent.

3.59 The **European Communities** considers that, even if there were any basis for arguing on the basis of the GATT 1947 that any aspect of the 1916 Act is discretionary and not a *per se* violation of the US obligations, the situation is in any event different under the WTO Agreement, since Article XVI:4 of the Agreement Establishing the WTO expressly requires Members to "ensure the conformity of its laws, regulations and administrative procedures with its obligations" under the WTO agreements.[68]

3.60 The **United States** replies that the mandatory/discretionary distinction is still being applied in cases brought under the WTO, as is evidenced by the report of the panel on *Canada - Aircraft*.

D. Applicability of Article VI of the GATT 1994 and the Anti-Dumping Agreement

1. The Meaning and Scope of Article VI of the GATT 1994 and The Anti-Dumping Agreement

3.61 The **European Communities** submits that Article VI of the GATT 1994[69] acknowledges the existence of a particular problem in international trade and then

---

[68] See also part III. H. below.

[69] Article VI:1 of the GATT 1994 provides as follows:

proceeds to provide a solution. Three steps are envisaged in this respect: First, Article VI defines the practice of dumping. Second, it sets out certain other conditions that need to be fulfilled for the application of remedial measures, such as the existence of injury. And third, it authorises the remedial measures which can be taken to deal with dumping.

3.62 Regarding the first step, i.e. the definition of the practice of dumping, the European Communities recalls that Article VI:1 of the GATT 1994 defines dumping as follows:

> "[…] For the purposes of this Article, a product is considered as being introduced into the commerce of an importing country at less than its normal value, if the price of the product exported from one country to another
>
> (a) is less than the comparable price, in the ordinary course of trade, for the like product when destined for consumption in the exporting country, or,
>
> (b) in the absence of such domestic price, is less than either
>
> (i) the highest comparable price for the like product for export to any third country in the ordinary course of trade, or
>
> (ii) the cost of production of the product in the country of origin plus a reasonable addition for selling cost and profit.
>
> Due allowance shall be made in each case for differences in conditions and terms of sale, for differences in taxation, and for other differences affecting price comparability."

3.63 The European Communities considers that a first essential feature of the above-noted definition is that it refers to rules targeting imports. The definition is based on the concept of price discrimination between the price of these imports and the normal value, which is the domestic price - "the comparable price, in the ordinary course of trade" - in the exporting country or, in the absence of such a price, the

---

"The contracting parties recognize that dumping, by which products of one country are introduced into the commerce of another country at less than the normal value of the products, is to be condemned if it causes or threatens material injury to an established industry in the territory of a contracting party or materially retards the establishment of a domestic industry. For the purposes of this Article, a product is considered as being introduced into the commerce of an importing country at less than its normal value, if the price of the product exported from one country to another

(a) is less than the comparable price, in the ordinary course of trade, for the like product when destined for consumption in the exporting country, or,

(b) in the absence of such domestic price, is less than either

i) the highest comparable price for the like product for export to any third country in the ordinary course of trade, or

ii) the cost of production of the product in the country of origin plus a reasonable addition for selling cost and profit.

Due allowance shall be made in each case for differences in conditions and terms of sale, for differences in taxation, and for other differences affecting price comparability."

highest comparable price for export to any third country in the ordinary course of trade, or the cost of production plus a reasonable addition for selling cost and profit. This analysis yields the definition of the kinds of rules which are anti-dumping rules subject to the discipline of Article VI of the GATT 1994:

(i) The rules are targeted at imports and by the fact of their importation.

(ii) The practice is defined by reference to discrimination between the prices of the imported products and domestic prices in the country of export or, in the absence of such prices, export prices to a third country or cost of production.

3.64 As concerns the pre-conditions for taking action against dumping, the European Communities notes that the most important pre-condition is stated to be injury. Article VI:1 provides that dumping as defined is "to be condemned" *if* it "causes or threatens material injury to an established industry in the territory of a contracting party or materially retards the establishment of a domestic industry."

3.65 Finally, with respect to the remedial measures which can be taken, the European Communities refers to Article VI:2, which reads as follows:

> "In order to offset or prevent dumping, a contracting party may levy on any dumped product an anti-dumping duty not greater in amount than the margin of dumping in respect of such product. For the purposes of this Article, the margin of dumping is the price difference determined in accordance with the provisions of paragraph 1."

According to the European Communities, this language establishes the application of anti-dumping duties as the sole means authorized by the GATT 1994 by which a contracting party can seek to deal with the problem of dumped imports.

3.66 The European Communities maintains that it is only dumping meeting the definition that is to be condemned, and then only in the stated circumstances of injury, threat of injury or material retardation. Anti-dumping duties may be applied "in order to offset or prevent dumping", but only in an amount no greater than the margin of dumping as defined. The reference to "offsetting" as well as "preventing" also makes clear that anti-dumping duties are the exclusive remedy established by the GATT 1994 for dealing with the problem of dumping, whether past, present or future.

3.67 The European Communities further submits that the Anti-Dumping Agreement is fully consistent with Article VI and defines in greater detail the conditions and in particular the requirements for an investigation that need to be fulfilled to allow anti-dumping action to be taken. Article 1 of the Anti-Dumping Agreement confirms that an anti-dumping measure can be applied only under the circumstances provided for in Article VI of the GATT 1994 and pursuant to investigations conducted in accordance with the Agreement, while Article 18.1 of the Anti-Dumping Agreement stipulates that action can be taken against the import of dumped products from another WTO Member *only if* the dumping causes or threatens material injury, and that no other measures can be taken than those provided for by Article VI of the GATT 1994 and the Anti-Dumping Agreement.

3.68 According to the **United States**, the cornerstone of the European Communities' claim that the 1916 Act violates Article VI and the Anti-Dumping Agreement is its argument that the WTO anti-dumping rules capture any measure which targets imports and is based upon the concept of price discrimination. The text of Article VI or the Anti-Dumping Agreement does not, however, support the European Communities' position. Nowhere does Article VI or the Anti-Dumping Agreement state that its disciplines govern *any* law based upon the concept of price discrimination *regardless* of any other elements required to be proven under the law. In fact, the European Communities' argument is inconsistent with the text of Article VI. In this regard, paragraph 1 of Article VI begins by explaining that "dumping [...] is to be condemned if it causes or threatens material injury to an established industry in the territory of a Member or materially retards the establishment of a domestic industry." Paragraph 2 then provides that, "[i]n order to offset or prevent" this injurious dumping, "a Member may levy on any dumped product an anti-dumping duty not greater in amount than the margin of dumping in respect of such product." Article VI thus only addresses actions taken for the purpose of offsetting or preventing injurious dumping. It does not purport to address actions taken that are not designed to offset or prevent injurious dumping, as is the case with the 1916 Act.

3.69 The United States argues, moreover, that to read into the text of Article VI the limitation that all laws with any kind of international price discrimination component must conform to the anti-dumping rules, as the European Communities advocates, would extend the anti-dumping rules far into a realm which pre-dated them and whose objectives, underlying principles and targeted conduct are quite different - namely, the realm of antitrust or competition laws. If the Panel were to rule that Article VI applies to all forms of international price discrimination, and regardless of the nature of the injury sustained, the 1916 Act would not be the only casualty. Such a ruling would seem to mean that other Members' antitrust legislation prohibiting various forms of discriminatory or low pricing, including Articles 81 and 82 of the EC Treaty, Canada's Competition Act, Japan's Antimonopoly Act, Mexico's Federal Competition Law, India's Monopolies and Restrictive Trade Practices Act, as well as the US Sherman Act, would be WTO-inconsistent to the extent that those laws address attempted monopolization or an abuse of dominance undertaken through predatory, cross-border pricing practices. That result could not have been intended by Article VI and the Anti-Dumping Agreement.

3.70 According to the United States, the negotiating history of the GATT 1947 supports the contention that Article VI of the GATT 1994 is not intended as a remedy for predatory pricing. The GATT 1947 was agreed to during negotiations which paralleled the negotiations for a proposed larger agreement, the Havana Charter for an International Trade Organization. The Havana Charter contained one article addressing anti-dumping and several separate articles addressing private anti-competitive practices, among other matters. The GATT 1947 was agreed to first and was intended to be an interim agreement until the Havana Charter could be finalized, although, as is well known, it never was. In any event, the GATT 1947 incorporated *verbatim*, in Article VI, the article on anti-dumping that had been negotiated as part of the Havana Charter. The GATT 1947, however, did not incorporate any of the Havana Charter articles addressing private anti-competitive practices.

3.71 The United States contends that the subsequent history of the GATT 1947 further supports this point. In particular, in 1958, the contracting parties decided to appoint a group of experts to "study and make recommendations with regard to whether, and to what extent if at all, and how the Contracting Parties should undertake to deal with restrictive business practices in international trade."[70] In 1960, the Group of Experts issued a report in which it recommended that the contracting parties engage in consultations if there was an alleged restrictive business practice, but that it was unrealistic to recommend a multilateral agreement on the control of international restrictive business practices.[71]

3.72 The United States submits, finally, that a 1989 OECD Report also illustrated that predatory pricing is not considered the target of anti-dumping rules. The Report states that "predatory pricing is subject to the competition laws and policies of most OECD countries, but there has been a lively controversy over what standards should be applied."[72]

3.73 The **European Communities** considers that the United States is using the term "predatory" in a misleading manner by confusing the US antitrust notion of predation with its more ordinary meaning. According to the European Communities, it is often said that one of the clearest targets of Article VI of the GATT 1994 is precisely "predatory" dumping. Indeed, that is one of the forms of dumping that has always been considered covered by Article VI. When the first Anti-Dumping Code was negotiated, the issue of whether dumping measures authorized under multilateral rules should be limited to predatory conduct was discussed. A Note submitted by the US delegation for consideration by the Group on Anti-Dumping Policies in 1966 made the following observations:

> "An historical purpose of anti-dumping measures has been to regulate so-called predatory price discrimination whose objective is to use monopoly power in one's home market to maintain high prices and to reduce prices in an export market in order to destroy competitors and establish an additional market monopoly. [...] The Draft Code is not, however, restricted to such conduct, *as indeed Article VI is not thus restricted*."[73]

3.74 The European Communities also notes that it is a misrepresentation of the EC position for the United States to claim that the European Communities is saying that Article VI and the Antidumping Agreement govern *any* international price discrimination law *regardless* of the other substantive elements of that law. The discriminatory pricing required for action to be taken under anti-dumping laws is qualitatively different from discriminatory pricing addressed by competition laws. The criteria for determining whether a law is subject to the disciplines of Article VI and the Anti-Dumping Agreement are (i) whether the law is targeted at imports, and (ii) whether it defines the regulated conduct as price discrimination in the form of lower prices in the market of the importing country than those practised on the market of the country of export. This approach is confirmed by the basic theory of anti-dumping which recognizes a particular problem posed by price discrimination of this kind, requiring

---

70 Resolution of 5 November 1958 on "Restrictive Business Practices - Appointment of Group of Experts", BISD 7S/29.

71 The United States refers to document L/1015, adopted on 2 June 1960, BISD 9S/170, para. 5,7.

72 OECD, *Predatory Pricing* (1989), p. 3.

73 TN.64/NTB/W/3 (emphasis added by the European Communities).

an analysis distinct from that applying to price discrimination within the same market.

3.75 The European Communities points out, finally, that the 1916 Act is directed against price discrimination in the form of lower prices in the market of the importing country than on the market of the country of export. This is exactly what Article VI:1 of the GATT 1994 defines as dumping and does not correspond at all to any known "antitrust" definition of discriminatory pricing.

3.76 The **United States** submits that the distinction between antitrust and anti-dumping is not based upon whether price discrimination occurs within a single market or across markets. That is not the factor that distinguishes anti-dumping analysis from antitrust analysis. At least in the United States, it is not correct to say that antitrust price discrimination is solely a problem within one and the same market. In primary line cases under the Robinson-Patman Act, for example, price differences have been found within the same market or between two markets.

3.77 The United States recalls, moreover, that it has asked the European Communities whether it would consider the 1916 Act WTO-consistent if it were amended to apply to both domestic and imported goods. The European Communities, in its response to the US question, rewords the 1916 Act so that it applies to discriminatory sales between US customers and sales between US customers and foreign customers.[74] The European Communities then reasons that the hypothetical law is not governed by Article VI and the Anti-Dumping Agreement because it does not target imports and does not define the comparison for price discrimination by using the words "lower prices in the market of the importing country than practised in the market of the exporting country."

3.78 According to the United States, there is, however, no substantive difference between the actual 1916 Act and the hypothetical law drafted by the European Communities which it considers to be outside the reach of the anti-dumping disciplines. The same cross-border transaction would be captured by both forms of the law. In each instance of a cross-border transaction, the price comparison would be between the price in the United States and the price in a foreign market. To say that one law is WTO-consistent because it also applies to domestic goods is to elevate form over substance and demonstrates that the European Communities' legal approach to the proper scope of Article VI and the Anti-Dumping Agreement in the present case is results-driven and without merit. For example, under the European Communities' theory, if the Sherman Act and Article 82 of the EC Treaty had been drafted in separate pieces of legislation, the measure applicable to imports would be

---

74 The hypothetical law drafted by the European Communities reads as follows:

> "It shall be unlawful for any person engaged in commerce, in the course of such commerce, either directly or indirectly, to sell commodities of like grade and quality in the United States at prices which are lower than those applied to other purchasers in the United States or in foreign markets [subject to applicable adjustments for differences in transport and other costs];Provided, That such act or acts be done with the intent of destroying or injuring an industry in the United States, or of preventing the establishment of an industry in the United States, or of restraining or monopolizing any part of the trade and commerce in such articles in the United States."

WTO-inconsistent; but because those laws apply to imports and domestic goods, the portion that applies to imports would be consistent with WTO obligations.

3.79 The **European Communities** disputes that it is elevating form over substance. A split Sherman Act applying only to imports would not look at all like the 1916 Act. It would not have a prohibition of price discrimination looking like the definition of dumping in Article VI:1 of the GATT 1994. Also, it is not possible to make the 1916 Act apply to domestic goods without completely changing its nature. The 1916 Act is based on price discrimination between the domestic market of an exporter and the import market. Such distinctions make no sense when applied to a single domestic market.

3.80 In response, the **United States** maintains its view that Article VI and the Anti-Dumping Agreement do not govern competition laws simply because those laws incorporate the element of price discrimination. The existence of an antitrust objective in a law regulating cross-border price discrimination should remove it from the scope of Article VI of the GATT 1994. The issue of cross-border predation is an entirely legitimate and traditional subject of antitrust concern, whether under United States, European or other antitrust laws. Predatory behaviour may constitute monopolisation, abuse of dominance or anti-competitive price discrimination whether the markets concerned are local, regional, national or even international. It would be most unfortunate if the Panel were to rule that antitrust enforcement bodies are powerless to deal with harmful conduct because some of that conduct occurs beyond national borders, and that only domestic conduct, domestic parties or even domestic products are legitimate subjects of competition policy concern, whatever their economic impacts.

3.81 The United States adds that the Panel is in any event not called upon to define the exact parameters of Article VI and the Anti-Dumping Agreement for all possible purposes. Rather, the Panel must only decide whether the 1916 Act, a law with substantively different requirements from the anti-dumping rules and which targets a different practice than the anti-dumping rules, is nonetheless governed by Article VI and the Anti-Dumping Agreement. There is simply nothing in the text, or the objectives, of those agreements that would justify such a far-reaching extension of their disciplines.

2. *The Nature of the 1916 Act: Anti-Dumping or Antitrust Law?*

(a) The Text and Distinctive Features of the 1916 Act

3.82 The **European Communities** notes that the question to be answered by the Panel is whether the 1916 Act is of such a nature as to be subject to the rules of Article VI of the GATT 1994. The European Communities recalls that the objective criteria for determining whether a law is subject to the disciplines of Article VI and the Anti-Dumping Agreement are (i) whether the law is targeted at imports, and (ii) whether it defines the regulated conduct as price discrimination in the form of lower prices in the market of the importing country than those practised on the market of the country of export. On that basis, the 1916 Act is a law which is subject to Article VI of the GATT 1994 because

(i) it is targeted at imports. Its prohibition is directed at "any person importing or assisting in importing any articles in the United States". Such persons who breach the prohibition are guilty of a misdemeanour, and are liable for treble damages to persons who are injured by the prohibited conduct; and

(ii) the regulated conduct is defined by reference to discrimination between the price of the imported products and "the actual market value or wholesale price of such articles [...] in the principal markets of the country of their production, or of other foreign countries to which they are commonly exported".

3.83 The 1916 Act does not, in the view of the European Communities, escape the discipline of Article VI because it requires the prohibited conduct to be "common and systematic", or because the price differential must be "substantial". Article VI applies whether the dumping is limited in occurrence and sporadic, or frequent and systematic. It applies whether the dumping margin is large or small. It takes into account the magnitude and frequency of the dumping only through the rule that the level of anti-dumping duty imposed may not exceed the level of dumping found.

3.84 The European Communities further argues that the 1916 Act does not escape the discipline of Article VI because sanctions can only be imposed under the 1916 Act if one or more of the enumerated specific intents are found. The discipline of Article VI applies to any rule directed at dumping. Once it is established that the rule or law is subject to Article VI, then the sole remedies permitted by Article VI are conditional on a finding of (i) dumping in accordance with the definition of Article VI and (ii) material injury, threat of material injury, or material retardation. Substituting the specific intent tests incorporated in the 1916 Act for the injury tests required by Article VI in no way serves to take the 1916 Act out of the discipline of Article VI. Quite the contrary, it is one of the grounds which cause the 1916 Act to infringe Article VI, since the 1916 Act permits the application of sanctions in circumstances other than the only ones envisaged by Article VI - namely where there is material injury, threat of material injury or material retardation.

3.85 The European Communities notes that, likewise, a law which applies tests other than those provided for in Article VI cannot be saved by an argument that the quantum of difficulty, from the point of view of the party seeking relief, is greater in the case of that law than would be the case if it merely followed the injury test of Article VI. Applying different conditions does not take the measure outside the scope of Article VI of the GATT 1994, it simply violates the requirements of Article VI. In any event, it is far from clear that the specific intent tests of the 1916 Act are necessarily more difficult to meet than the injury tests of Article VI. For example, as regards the test relating to "the intent of destroying or injuring an industry in the United States", it is presumably difficult to show an intent to *destroy* an industry in the United States. But showing an intent to injure an industry may be much easier: an internal memorandum or exchange of correspondence between an importer and an exporter, estimating that, with a price reduction of, say, 10%, the imported product would increase its market share by 15%, and that some or all of this would be taken from domestic producers, would presumably be sufficient to establish an "intent of [...] injuring" a US industry. It is not at all difficult to imagine the existence of such evidence. Given the pre-trial discovery rules applicable in litigation in the United States, it is quite possible that such evidence could be obtained by a plaintiff.

3.86 The **United States** argues that a review of the text of the 1916 Act establishes that the 1916 Act is a predatory pricing statute with antitrust objectives, not an anti-dumping measure within the purview of Article VI and the Anti-Dumping Agreement. The 1916 Act is not a statute that addresses the "dumping" and "injury" that would make it an anti-dumping statute within the meaning of Article VI of the GATT 1994. The 1916 Act is designed to combat a specific form of international price discrimination. This price discrimination not only must involve substantial price differences but also must be undertaken commonly and systematically and with a specified intent. The 1916 Act is not directed at the simple price differences that cause material injury captured by the Anti-Dumping Agreement, nor is it based on the Anti-Dumping Agreement's notion of material injury to a domestic industry. The 1916 Act is directed at a very different type of harmful business activity than that addressed by Article VI and the Anti-Dumping Agreement.

3.87 The United States further argues that a review of the various substantive and procedural requirements of the 1916 Act confirms that they are the same as, or similar to, the requirements applicable under US antitrust statutes. For example:

(a) The 1916 Act requires a finding of price differences, like the Robinson-Patman Act.[75] The price differences under the 1916 Act must be "substantial" in amount and undertaken "commonly and systematically," while the Robinson-Patman Act only requires two consummated sales to different buyers at different prices.[76]

(b) The 1916 Act requires a finding that the pricing at issue be undertaken with a predatory intent. This predatory pricing requirement is similar to that found in Section 2 of the Sherman Act and in so-called primary line cases under the Robinson-Patman Act, although neither of those Acts normally requires proof of any intent, at least in civil cases. There is an intent requirement in criminal antitrust cases, such as a criminal offense under the Sherman Act.[77]

(c) The 1916 Act applies to articles of "like grade and quality," just as that term is used in the Robinson-Patman Act.[78]

(d) The statute of limitations for bringing a lawsuit under the 1916 Act is the same as that under the Clayton Act and the Robinson-Patman Act, i.e. four years.[79]

---

[75] The United States refers to 15 U.S.C. 13(a).

[76] The United States refers to *International Telephone & Telegraph Corp. et al.*, 104 F.T.C. 280, 417, citing E. Kinter, *A Robinson-Patman Primer*, 3rd ed. (1979), p. 35.

[77] The United States refers to *U.S. v. Brown*, 936 F.2d 1042, 1046 (9th Cir. 1991).

[78] The United States refers to *Zenith III, Op. Cit.*, p. 1197. The United States notes that the *Zenith* court, at pp. 1226-1227 explained that "we find that the same standard of 'like grade and quality' limited product comparisons under section 2 of the Clayton Act prior to the Robinson-Patman amendments. Since the Clayton Act was passed in 1914, the same standard is applicable under the Antidumping Act of 1916."

[79] The United States refers to *Helmac I, Op. Cit.*, pp. 566-67, noting that where the 1916 Act did not set forth applicable statute of limitations, the Court relied on the purpose of the US Congress in

(e) The 1916 Act provides for enforcement through either a civil lawsuit brought by a private party before a US court or a criminal prosecution brought by the US Department of Justice. These remedies mirror those available under the antitrust laws, including the Sherman Act, the Clayton Act and the Robinson-Patman Act.[80]

(f) The issue of whether a private party has the requisite standing to bring a 1916 Act lawsuit is determined by reference to antitrust standing principles.[81]

(g) The 1916 Act authorizes the award of treble damages to a successful private litigant. This remedy is somewhat unusual under US civil law, but it is a common remedy for violations of US antitrust statutes. Indeed, in the third paragraph of the 1916 Act, the US Congress basically replicated the then-existing language of Section 4 of the Clayton Act[82] and Section 7 of the Sherman Act,[83] which authorized treble damages for "any person who shall be injured in his business or property" by reason of any conduct proscribed by US antitrust laws.

(h) With regard to its criminal provisions, the 1916 Act is virtually identical to, and specifies the same penalties as, the criminal provisions of the Sherman Act in force in 1916.

3.88 The **European Communities** considers that these differences derive from the time at which the 1916 Act was adopted and the peculiarly US form of remedies chosen. For example, the availability of treble damages is by no means an indication that the measure is an antitrust measure, but rather relates to the fact that the US Congress disapproves of certain conduct or activities. Treble damages have been provided for in US legislation in a number of cases which have nothing to do with antitrust.[84] Moreover, the European Communities is not aware of any other jurisdic-

enacting the 1916 Act to interpret the 1916 Act as having same statute of limitations as other antitrust statutes.

[80] In response to a question asked by the Panel in a different context, the United States notes, however, that the Clayton Act is enforceable only through civil actions.

[81] The United States refers to, e.g., *Isra Fruit Ltd. v. Agrexco Agr. Export Co., Op. Cit.*, pp. 988-89; *Jewel Foliage Co. v. Uniflora Overseas Florida, Op. Cit.*, p. 516; *Schwimmer v. Sony Corp., Op. Cit.*, pp. 796-97.

[82] The United States notes that the relevant Clayton Act language can be found at 38 Stat. 731 (1914).

[83] The United States notes that the relevant Sherman Act language can be found at 26 Stat. 210 (1890). The United States further notes that the US Congress later amended this part of the Sherman Act.

[84] The European Communities lists the following cases: 35 U.S.C. Sec. 296 (Title 35 - Patents / Part III Patents and protection of patent rights / Chapter 29 - Remedies for infringement of patent, and other actions); 7 U.S.C. Sec. 2570 (Title 7 - Agriculture / Chapter 57 - Plant Variety Protection / Subchapter III - Plant Variety Protection and Rights); 12 U.S.C Sec. 2607 (Title 12 - Banks and Banking / Chapter 27 - Real Estate Settlement Procedures); 25 U.S.C.S. § 305e (United States Code Service; Title 25 - Indians / Chapter 7A - Promotion of Social and Economic Welfare); 15 U.S.C. Sec. 1117 (Title 15 - Commerce and Trade / Chapter 22 - Trade-marks / Subchapter III - General Provisions); 15 U.S.C. Sec. 1693f (Title 15 - Commerce and Trade / Chapter 41 - Consumer Credit Protection / Subchapter VI - Electronic Fund Transfers); 18 U.S.C. Sec. 1964 (Title 18 - Crimes and

tion which provides for treble damages in this way. Treble damages is not a feature of an antitrust measure, it is an indication of a US measure.

3.89 The **United States** further argues that there are significant differences between the 1916 Act and the anti-dumping rules. As a trade remedy, the anti-dumping rules are triggered only in response to the practice of "dumping," i.e. a situation where an exporter sells its product abroad at lower prices than it does at home or at prices that are below cost, which causes "material injury" to producers of the product in the importing country. Once these facts are established, the investigating authorities may impose duties to offset prospectively the injurious dumping. In contrast, the 1916 Act takes action against a different type of harmful business activity. Under the 1916 Act, mere dumping is not enough. The complainant must show price discrimination which is common and systematic as well as substantial, and the complainant must demonstrate a predatory intent. There is also no requirement that actual or threatened "material injury" to a domestic industry be shown. The complainant instead is required to show damages to its business or property. Thus, while an importer may violate the 1916 Act, it cannot be said that the same facts would satisfy the requirements for the imposition of anti-dumping duties.

3.90 The United States contends that the differences between anti-dumping rules and the 1916 Act are readily seen when the requirements of the Anti-Dumping Agreement are contrasted with those of the 1916 Act:

(a) The price differences required under the two sets of rules are quite different. Under the 1916 Act, the price in the United States must be "substantially less" than the price abroad. Under the Anti-Dumping Agreement, normally a mere price difference above a *de minimis* level is all that is required, i.e. the price in the United States only has to be lower than the price abroad.

(b) The 1916 Act requires that the substantial price differences be undertaken "commonly and systematically." There is no similar requirement under the Anti-Dumping Agreement.

(c) The 1916 Act requires the complainant to establish "the intent of destroying or injuring an industry in the United States, or of preventing the establishment of an industry in the United States, or of restraining or monopolizing any part of trade and commerce in such articles in the United States." Under US law, this intent must be "predatory" in nature. The Anti-Dumping Agreement, in contrast, imposes no intent requirement of any kind.

(d) In a private action, the 1916 Act requires a showing of damages suffered by the individual complaining party. The Anti-Dumping Agreement, in contrast, requires that material injury to a domestic industry be found to exist.

Criminal Procedure / Chapter 96 - Racketeer Influenced and Corrupt Organizations); 22 U.S.C. Sec. 6082 (Title 22 - Foreign Relations and Intercourse / Chapter 69A - Cuban Liberty and Democratic Solidarity (Libertad) / Subchapter III - Protection of Property Rights of United States Nationals).

3.91 The **European Communities** concedes that there are differences between the requirements of the 1916 Act and those of Article VI of the GATT 1994, but these differences do not avoid a violation. They are in large part the reasons why there is a violation. Accordingly, the differences identified by the United States raise the following questions:

(a) As for the requisite price differences, the European Communities inquires whether the United States means to say that WTO dumping provisions do not reach "substantial" price discrimination, but only price discrimination which is between "*de minimis*" and "substantial".

(b) With respect to the second distinguishing feature identified by the United States, i.e. the requisite frequency of price discrimination, the European Communities inquires whether the US position is that WTO dumping provisions do not cover "common and systematic" dumping.

(c) Regarding the intent requirement, the European Communities inquires whether the United States means to say that price discrimination causing "material injury" is outside the scope of WTO dumping provisions if it is also deliberate. The European Communities recalls, in this regard, that the 1916 Act requires a number of alternative "intents", only some of which refer to competition. The intent to injure the US industry is sufficient to found liability and requires no effect on competition.

(d) Finally, in relation to the last distinguishing feature, i.e. the showing of damages suffered by individual companies, the European Communities inquires whether the US position is that where there is material injury to the domestic industry within the meaning of WTO dumping provisions there would not be damage to one or other individual company.

3.92 The European Communities argues, in addition, that the fact that the 1916 Act only prohibits price discrimination where the price is lower in the United States than elsewhere and thus is limited to protecting the US market against low prices also suggests that the 1916 Act is an anti-dumping measure rather than an antitrust measure.

3.93 In response to the last EC argument, the **United States** notes that the 1916 Act and its interpretation necessarily focus on anti-competitive effects in the United States. In the words of the US Supreme Court:

> "Respondents cannot recover antitrust damages based solely on an alleged cartelization of the Japanese market, because American antitrust laws do not regulate the competitive conditions in other nations' economies."[85]

3.94 The United States also reiterates its view that, however the 1916 Act is characterized, the fact remains that to succeed under it, a plaintiff must plead and prove

[85] *Matsushita Electrical Industrial Co., Ltd. v. Zenith Radio Corp.*, 475 U.S. 574, 582 (1986) (hereinafter "*Matsushita Electrical*"), quoting *United States v. Aluminum Co. of America*, 148 F.2d. 416, 433 (2d Cir. 1945) (L. Hand, J.).

many elements that make it qualitatively different from a measure intended to remedy dumping. Foremost among these elements is the specific predatory intent requirement.

3.95 The **European Communities** rejects the US argument that the 1916 Act is qualitatively different from a measure intended to remedy dumping. The European Communities recalls that the primary requirement of the 1916 Act corresponds to dumping within the meaning of Article VI of the GATT 1994. Certain of the additional requirements such as "common and systematic" dumping and "substantial" dumping margin may require dumping to be more severe than under Article VI of the GATT 1994, but this does not make the description of Article VI inapplicable. Article VI covers all dumping practices, including those which are "common and systematic". Article VI covers all forms of "price dumping", as defined therein. The only form of dumping whose exclusion from the scope of the GATT 1947 was ever discussed is "non-price" dumping.[86]

3.96 The **United States** considers that the European Communities attempts to minimise the qualitative differences between the 1916 Act and an anti-dumping measure by arguing that the "primary requirement" of the 1916 Act corresponds to "dumping" and that the other elements required to be proved under the 1916 Act are simply a "few additional conditions" that do not suffice to remove it from the anti-dumping rules. This mischaracterization is an attempt by the European Communities to justify labelling the 1916 Act as an "anti-dumping" measure.

3.97 The **European Communities** replies that the purpose of Article VI and the Anti-Dumping Agreement would be undermined if WTO Members could justify the application of measures other than anti-dumping duties - for example, civil liability for damages or criminal penalties - on the basis that the conduct to which they are applied is defined in a manner which, while incorporating the essential elements of the definition of dumping, differs by the addition of one or another additional condition like, for example, providing that the additional remedy is available in case of aggravated dumping, or if the objective definition of dumping is accompanied by certain specific intents. This is exactly what the 1916 Act does, it being understood that the 1916 Act was not enacted in order to circumvent the discipline of Article VI of the GATT 1994, which was only adopted three decades later. But to accept that the 1916 Act is compatible with Article VI of the GATT 1994 would entail accepting that Article VI can be circumvented by national legislation simply by resorting to the expedient of "bolting on" a few additional definitional elements and providing a remedy other than anti-dumping duties.

3.98 For the **United States**, it remains clear from the text of the statute, its legislative history and the relevant case law that it is the additional elements and their purpose which make the 1916 Act qualitatively different from a mere anti-dumping measure. These elements are not "conditions" any more than the requirement that the plaintiff must establish the requisite price difference. All of the elements of the 1916 Act must be demonstrated to establish liability. There is no basis for assuming that one element is more important or takes precedence over another.

---

[86] The European Communities refers to GATT, *Analytical Index: Guide to GATT Law and Practice* (1994), p. 204.

(b) The Theoretical Distinction between Anti-Dumping and Antitrust

3.99 According to the **European Communities**, nothing in the GATT 1994, the Anti-Dumping Agreement or any other WTO text supports the proposition that, from a WTO perspective, there is a clear dichotomy between two mutually exclusive categories of national legislation: anti-dumping legislation which is subject to Article VI of the GATT 1994 and the Anti-Dumping Agreement, on the one hand, and antitrust rules which are not subject to those rules, on the other. Indeed, there is nothing in the GATT 1994 and the Anti-Dumping Agreement which deals with or touches on antitrust at all. Accordingly, there is nothing in these texts to prevent laws and rules considered by national courts or legislatures to be "antitrust" in nature from being subject to Article VI and the Anti-Dumping Agreement. The dichotomy on which the United States bases its argument is a false one.[87]

3.100 In reply to a question of the Panel regarding how the basic features, principles and underlying economic assumptions of anti-dumping and antitrust rules differ, the European Communities notes, first of all, that the anti-dumping and antitrust rules in many cases had common origins and rely on common notions.[88] Anti-dumping legislation began to appear in various countries at the beginning of the twentieth century, at about the same time as antitrust legislation appeared in the United States. While the two types of legislation appear to have sprung from the same matrix of ideas prevailing at that time, anti-dumping legislation has from the start been posited on the notion that international trade poses a particular set of problems which require specific legislative solutions and remedies. This notion has increased in importance as tariff and other barriers to international trade have been reduced. In the negotiation of the WTO Anti-Dumping Agreement "the European Communities and the United States [...] took the view that effective and workable anti-dumping rules are essential to maintaining an open and liberal trading system".[89]

3.101 The European Communities further points out that the core element in most accounts of the rationale of dumping is that where national markets are economically separate, economic operators in one market may exploit the different economic conditions prevailing in the two markets to apply different prices. In particular, when there are entry barriers in one market, producers in that market may exploit those barriers to apply high prices in their domestic market, and use the resulting profits to subsidise exports to another market. Such practices may cause injury to actual or

---

87 The European Communities notes that, in any event, even in the United States it was recognized that the 1916 Act addresses the same practices as addressed by anti-dumping legislation in other countries, namely practices described as "the sale of imported merchandise at less than its prevailing market or wholesale price in the country of production". The European Communities refers to the United States Tariff Commission, *Information Concerning Dumping and Other Foreign Competition in the United States and Canada's Anti-Dumping Law*, Printed for the use of the Committeee on Ways and Means, House of Representatives (1919), p. 9.

88 The European Communities notes that this is why the 1916 Act is inspired by points addressed in the Sherman Act.

89 M. Koulen, "The New Anti-Dumping Code Through its Negotiating History", in *The Uruguay Round Results*, J. Bourgeois, ed. (1995), p. 160.

potential producers in the export market concerned. To the European Communities, the following description of the economic concept of dumping is a typical one:

> "To the economist, dumping is traditionally defined only as price discrimination between national markets, a definition first proposed by Viner. There was need of a restricted definition for the purposes of economic theory and that advanced by Viner enabled the topic to be subsumed within the overall theory of monopoly and imperfect competition.
>
> A necessary condition for price discrimination is that the total market for a product can be broken down into two or more sub-markets and that at least one of the sub-markets is isolated from the others. In addition, the seller has to have a certain degree of monopoly power in one or more of the isolated sub-markets. In these circumstances, price discrimination is profitable if there is a difference in the elasticities of demand in the separate sub-markets, thus enabling a higher price to be charged for the product in the sub-market in which demand is less elastic.
>
> The factors which cause isolation in international trade are high tariffs, import restrictions and other non-tariff barriers, such as statutorily imposed technical standards. These factors are usually found in the domestic market of the supplier and strengthen his power on that market. They create a less elastic demand for this product and enable him to charge higher prices. The price discrimination need not be between the domestic and export market, however, and may be practised instead between different export markets."[90]

3.102 The European Communities points out that a similar line of argument is found in the following passage taken from a US law review note:

> "[T]he recoupment requirement - at least as defined in *Brooke Group* - is too narrow in the international context because it fails to consider the ability of firms with a monopoly or oligopoly in their home markets simultaneously to recoup losses from dumping by increasing monopoly returns at home. Dumping in the US allows foreign producers to reap the economies of scale of producing at optimal capacity while restricting sales at home to protect their home market monopoly prices."[91]

3.103 The European Communities further argues that the GATT 1947 reflects the fact that, by 1947, the idea had coalesced that, in deciding whether to apply anti-dumping measures, the investigating authority should look to a set of defined possible injurious effects to be determined with respect to an "industry" in the country of importation. "Industry" means producers. "Injury" is therefore to be determined by reference to the situation of producers. While there may be an underlying assumption

---

[90] H.-F. Beseler and N. Williams, *Anti-dumping and Anti-subsidy Law, The European Communities*, (1986), p.41 (citations omitted).

[91] Note, *Rethinking the 1916 Antidumping Act*, 110 Harv. L. Rev. 1555, 1566 (1997).

that injury to producers will ultimately lead to injury to consumers, this is not explicit in the rules, and there is no requirement that the injury investigation examine effects of dumping practices on consumers.

3.104 The European Communities notes that, by contrast, it is often said that antitrust law protects competition, not competitors.[92] Modern antitrust theory increasingly tends to explicitly equate competition and consumer welfare.[93] This is reflected in the reasoning and language used by the US Supreme Court in *Brooke Group* which held that in order to prove a "primary line" violation of the Robinson-Patman Act, a plaintiff must plead and prove predation, consisting of (i) prices below "an appropriate measure" of the defendant's costs, and (ii) a demonstration that the competitor has a reasonable prospect of recouping its investment in below-cost pricing. The Court held that the essential requirements for primary line violations of the Robinson-Patman Act are the same as for claims of monopolisation by predatory pricing under Section 2 of the Sherman Act. Noting criticism of earlier case law made in light of "the antitrust laws' traditional concern for consumer welfare and price competition", the Court said that "the essence of the claim under either statute is the same: A business rival has priced its products in an unfair manner with the object to eliminate or retard competition and thereby gain and exercise control over prices in the relevant market."[94]

3.105 For the European Communities, it follows from these theoretical considerations that the essential characteristic of an anti-dumping law covered by the discipline of Article VI and the Anti-Dumping Agreement is that it is aimed at providing a remedy against imports where there is price discrimination consisting of the imports being sold at a lower price than that applied to sales of the same products in the market from which they are exported. Anti-dumping theory and legislation is based on the idea that the kind of price discrimination between different markets described in Article VI of the GATT 1994 poses a problem which is different from, and requires a different set of remedies from, the problem of price discrimination within one and the same market.

3.106 The **United States** disagrees with the European Communities' suggestion that there is a complete dichotomy between antitrust laws and their pursuit of consumer welfare, and trade laws and their focus on producer welfare. This purported dichotomy exaggerates reality. While it is certainly true that the purpose of some very well known antitrust laws is to preserve the competitive process in order to enhance economic efficiency and increase consumer welfare, it is also true that quite a number of

---

92 The European Communities points out that antitrust statutes, at least as regards the United States, use general language referring to competition as such: "restraint of trade or commerce among the several States, or with foreign nations" (Section 1 of the Sherman Act); "monopoliz[ing] or attempt[ing] to monopolize [...] any part of the trade or commerce among the several States, or with foreign nations" (Section 2 of the Sherman Act); price discrimination whose effect may be "substantially to lessen competition or tend to create a monopoly in any line of commerce, or to injure, destroy, or prevent competition with any person who either grants or knowingly received the benefit of such discrimination, or with customers of either of them" (Section 2 of the Clayton Act, as amended by the Robinson-Patman Act).

93 The European Communities also notes, however, that there is no commonly accepted standard for what constitutes a "competition" law.

94 *Brooke Group*, *Op. Cit.*, p. 222.

antitrust laws have other purposes, including the protection of small enterprises or other individual competitors.

3.107 The United States points out that one example of other antitrust purposes can be found in the Robinson-Patman Act, where, in the "secondary line" context[95], the statutory concern is for adverse effects on individual competitors, as well as on competition itself. Furthermore, even the European Communities' main antitrust instruments, Articles 81 and 82 of the EC Treaty, retain elements of concern for competitors as well as competition:

> "In the E.C., however, there is concern also that large firms may make it hard for smaller firms to compete, even if the latter are less efficient. The preamble to the [Rome] treaty refers to many factors other than efficiency, such as social policy, fair competition, small and medium-sized undertakings, peace and liberty. To protect small firms that are less efficient, it may be necessary to control the conduct of firms that have no power over price."[96]

3.108 The United States also recalls that, unlike US antitrust law, the parallel provisions of EC law condemning abuses of dominant position do not require presentation of "recoupment" evidence to show "predatory pricing."[97] Moreover, EC Member States' own antitrust laws may take similar positions. For example, France noted in its 1996 Annual Report to the OECD Competition Law and Policy Committee that "the aim of the provisions contained in the Law of 1 July 1996 is to fight the practice of artificially low retail prices without the need to prove the existence of an anticompetitive agreement or dominant position."[98] Likewise, the UK's Office of Fair Trading recently released a "Consultation Draft" discussing the "abuse of dominance" provision in Britain's 1998 Competition Act:

> "In *Akzo* and *Tetra-Pak II* the European Court of Justice found the undertakings' conduct to be an abuse without explicitly considering whether recouping losses would be feasible. The Director General [of the OFT] therefore does not consider that he would necessarily be required to establish that predation was feasible."[99]

3.109 According to the United States, it can be seen from these examples that the fact that a measure may include protection for competitors does not remove the measure from the category of antitrust laws. It thus remains a challenge for antitrust laws to protect competition without unduly protecting competitors, or to protect competitors without unduly prejudicing competition. This "antitrust paradox" reflects the historic reality that antitrust laws have social and political as well as economic goals.

---

[95] The United States recalls that in a "secondary line" context certain buyers of a good receive less advantageous sales terms from a given seller than other competing buyers.

[96] Korah, *An Introductory Guide to EC Competition Law and Practice*, 6th ed., Oxford (1997), p. 76; and see also Amato, *Antitrust and the Boundaries of Power* (1997), chs. 3 and 5.

[97] The United States refers to Korah, *Op. Cit.*, pp. 97-107; *Tetra Pak II* (C333/94P)[1997] C.E.C., 4 MLR 662.

[98] DAFFE/CLP(97)11/08, October 1997, at para. 68.

[99] Office of Fair Trading, *Formal Consultation Draft - Competition Act 1998 - the Chapter II Prohibition* (OFT 402 1998), Part 4, especially para. 4.31.

3.110 The **European Communities** objects to the claim of the United States that the European Communities is relying on a "complete dichotomy between antitrust and anti-dumping laws". The European Communities' position is the opposite. Antitrust and anti-dumping rules have in many cases common origins and rely on common notions. The point is that there is a definition of, and disciplines for, anti-dumping measures and so the only question for the Panel is whether the 1916 Act comes within and violates the anti-dumping disciplines, not whether there is a "dichotomy".

3.111 The **United States** further contends, in response to the same question asked by the Panel to the European Communities, that anti-dumping rules and antitrust laws have different objectives, are founded on different principles, and seek to remedy different problems. The anti-dumping rules are not intended as a remedy for the predatory pricing practices of firms or for any other private anti-competitive practices typically condemned by antitrust laws. Rather, the anti-dumping rules are a trade remedy which WTO Members have agreed is necessary to the maintenance of the multilateral trading system. Without this and other trade remedies, there could have been no agreement on broader GATT 1947 and later WTO packages of market-opening agreements, especially given the imperfections which remain in the multilateral trading system. In contrast, antitrust laws remedy, among other things, private pricing practices which are objectionable because they are instruments of cartelization, monopolisation or abuse of dominant position. While it is true that the anti-dumping rules address certain private pricing practices, it is not because these pricing practices - that is, injurious dumping practices - are anti-competitive in an antitrust sense. Injurious dumping practices will not normally qualify as anti-competitive when analysed under the distinct rules of most national antitrust laws.

3.112 The United States further points out that, as a trade remedy, the anti-dumping rules are triggered only in response to the practice of "dumping," i.e. a situation where an exporter sells its product abroad at lower prices than it does at home or at prices that are below cost, which causes "material injury" to producers of the product in the importing country. Once these facts are established, the investigating authorities may impose duties to offset prospectively the injurious dumping. While this simple definition of injurious dumping may suggest certain comparisons with competition laws addressing price discrimination, any careful analysis shows major differences between the principles upon which anti-dumping rules and the competition laws are founded.

3.113 The United States recalls, in this regard, that, although some dumping may be due to business advantages and market segmentation which have arisen in response to commercial forces, more typically it is a government's industrial policies or key aspects of the national economic system which a government has created, promoted, or tolerated that enable injurious dumping to take place. Principally of concern are certain government industrial policies or practices which in most instances are not directly or fully subject to any type of WTO prohibitions or disciplines. In other instances, these policies or practices may not fully conform to WTO disciplines or, even if they do, may not leave all Members on an equal footing because of differences in starting levels of openness and transparency among Members. These policies still are objectionable because they distort market structures or processes and, as a result, provide artificial advantages to home market producers and often do so at the expense of home market consumers. These artificial advantages generally translate into increased profits for these producers in their home market, which make possible and, for various reasons, may encourage these producers to engage in injurious dumping abroad.

3.114 The United States states that one broad category of objectionable policies can be found in government industrial policies which combine limits on domestic competition with market access barriers that keep out foreign competitors. Here, the possible combinations are quite extensive. On the one hand, the existence of only limited domestic competition may be due to many different types of industrial policies falling under the umbrella of government actions intended to influence the structure of the home market with the aim of affecting the number or type of producers, including (1) government policies limiting the number of producers in a particular industry, such as through the restrictive award of licenses, (2) State monopolies, (3) government policies favoring a "national champion" firm within an industry, (4) government policies which divide up and stabilize market shares and (5) any of a variety of other government policies which regulate commerce by creating, promoting or tolerating monopolies or oligopolies or by favoring some domestic competitors over other domestic and foreign competitors. Other general categories of objectionable policies include domestic price controls, government subsidisation and state trading arrangements.

3.115 The United States argues that anti-dumping rules are a practical, albeit indirect, response to these trade-distorting policies. The anti-dumping rules allow Members to respond through the imposition of offsetting duties when confronted with one harmful result of these policies, namely, injurious dumping in export markets by the producers that benefit from these policies. From this perspective, the anti-dumping rules represent an effort to maintain a "level playing field" among producers in different countries. Anti-dumping duties are designed to offset, quantitatively, the artificial advantages realized by the exporting country's producers so that producers in the importing country may compete, at least in the importing country's market, on an equal footing with the exporting country's producers.

3.116 The United States points out that anti-dumping rules also help to neutralise inequities that may arise from differences in national economic systems, even as international trade liberalises. For example, differing social and legal arrangements for employment and under-employment, or differing debt-equity structures and debt burdens, often made possible by indirect government intervention in the banking system, can favor the exporting country's producers over the importing country's producers and lead to injurious dumping. Other circumstances that can lead to injurious dumping can include certain competition-inhibiting private conduct, cross-subsidisation that can result from the legal organisation and operation of foreign business groupings and, in the case of non-market economies or some economies in transition, export directives and prices and costs not entirely based on market principles.

3.117 The United States considers that the anti-dumping rules thus implicitly recognize that there is an accepted norm for the behavior of governments in the broad multilateral trade context, i.e. a government should not pursue industrial policies which distort market structures or processes and thereby provide artificial advantages to domestic producers to the detriment of producers in other countries. The anti-dumping rules also recognize that there should be a remedy for certain harms caused when different economic systems interact.

3.118 Turning to competition laws, the United States notes that they appropriately do not take these matters into consideration, and they do not address the underlying problems at which the anti-dumping rules are directed. Instead, competition laws remedy private business practices which, in themselves, are objectionable because they are anti-competitive in an antitrust sense. The primary objectives of competition policy, as expressed in competition laws, are to promote economic efficiency and to maximize consumer welfare through innovation and the optimal allocation of resources in competitive markets. The competition laws therefore are largely directed at the competitive practices of private firms and market structures, with the objective of assuring a competitive market. In some countries, the competition laws have additional, less central objectives, such as the preservation of a decentralised economy, support of small businesses or maintenance of economic and social stability.

3.119 The United States acknowledges that the anti-dumping rules address certain private pricing practices as do the competition laws. However, dumping practices are not anti-competitive in an antitrust sense. The anti-dumping rules provide a remedy against injurious dumping as an indirect response to a foreign government's market-distortive industrial policies or differences in national economic systems. As a result, although dumping by foreign producers can, for example, send false signals to the importing country's market that distort investment patterns, dumping practices will not normally qualify as anti-competitive when analysed under the distinct rules of most national competition laws.

3.120 The United States recalls that, in the Working Group on the Interaction between Trade and Competition Policy in 1998, the European Communities recognized the distinction between anti-dumping law and competition law:

> "Antidumping law and competition law apply in different economic, legal and institutional contexts. Competition law prohibits and subjects to strict penalties certain forms of pricing behaviour by firms. While competition law applies in principle within the context of an integrated market, antidumping law applies in an economic setting which is still characterized by border measures and other regulatory obstacles and distortions of trade."[100]

3.121 The United States notes that, in addition, during the meeting at which the Working Group considered the above-mentioned document, a representative of the European Communities "reiterated that the submission by his delegation argued that anti-dumping rules and competition rules applied in different economic, legal and institutional contexts and that therefore there could be no question of the replacement of one set of rules for the other, and no question of simply making a mechanical transposition from competition law into anti-dumping law of concepts which were intended to deal with a totally different kind of problem and underlay a totally different type of instrument."[101]

[100] WT/WGTCP/W/78.

[101] WT/WGTCP/M/5, para. 71.

3.122 In response, the **European Communities** asserts that the United States seeks to develop a new theory of dumping which cannot be reconciled with the wording of Article VI of the GATT 1994 and the Anti-Dumping Agreement as well as decades of US enforcement. The European Communities inquires whether the United States is henceforth going to refrain from applying anti-dumping duties where there is no underlying government trade-distorting policy or practice. Likewise, the European Communities wonders whether the United States is in future going to accept as defences from exporters in dumping cases the argument that "I have no protected domestic market" or "I am not dumping, I am engaging in predatory pricing".

3.123 The European Communities adds that, to state that anti-dumping rules respond to government trade-distorting policies may have far-reaching implications which had certainly never been intended by GATT 1947 contracting parties. This argument implies that anti-dumping rules exercise some sort of indirect constraint on the domestic policies of a dumper's home country - even in areas outside trade policy like industrial policy or social relations, to which the United States refers. There is no underpinning for this in the wording of WTO dumping provisions or in the negotiating history. The only policy limitation underlying WTO dumping rules is the obligation to conform Members' anti-dumping policy to WTO rules and to take WTO-consistent anti-dumping measures.

3.124 The **United States** denies that it is developing a new theory of dumping. The United States refers to the fact that its notion of dumping is discussed in detail in the US paper submitted to the Working Group on the Interaction between Trade and Competition Policy. Moreover, in the same Working Group, the European Communities itself recognized basically the same concepts. Furthermore, it is worth noting that the District Court in *Wheeling-Pittsburgh* even recognized this distinction. In this regard, that court stated that "dumping itself has long been noted to constitute a harmful international trade practice which may, through *government, as opposed to market-driven action*, cause sharp increases in imported goods, to the detriment of domestic producers."[102]

(c) Statements by US Executive Branch Officials

3.125 The **European Communities** argues that the US government's denial that the 1916 Act is an instrument to counter dumping is also in contradiction with a number of official statements made by US Government officials in 1985 and 1986 at the occasion of the discussions on the adoption of section 236 and section 1655, two bills to amend the 1916 Act.[103]

3.126 The European Communities notes that the Chairman of the US Federal Trade Commission, on 17 June 1985, wrote in a letter to the US Senate Committee of the Judiciary that the provisions of the 1916 Act "establish liability, provided that the *dumping* is done" under the conditions described in the statute. In a footnote he further clarifies that "[u]nder the Anti-Dumping 1916 Act dumping is the difference

[102] *Wheeling-Pittsburgh, Op. Cit.*, p. 604 (emphasis added by the United States).

[103] The European Communities notes that the amendments, aimed, *inter alia,* at making the criteria for applying the 1916 Act less stringent, were never adopted.

between the price in the US and the price in foreign countries".[104] Moreover, according to the European Communities, the testimony of 18 July 1986 of USTR General Counsel Alan Holmer to the US Senate Finance Committee states, *inter alia*, that the 1916 Act is legal under the GATT 1947 and the Anti-Dumping Code only because it is grandfathered pursuant to the 1947 Protocol of Provisional Application.[105] Similar statements were also made by former US Trade Representative Clayton Yeutter and by the Department of Justice.[106]

3.127 In the view of the European Communities, this shows that, in the past, US Government bodies not only held the view that the 1916 Act concerns dumping practices, but also that, without grandfathering, it would have been GATT-illegal. The United States failed to seek a grandfather exception under the GATT 1994.[107] The logical conclusion, according to the European Communities, is that, since US authorities admitted that the 1916 Act benefited from grandfathering under the GATT 1947 and since the 1916 Act does not benefit from any grandfather clause under the GATT 1994, it is in breach of the WTO Agreement and the GATT 1994.

3.128 In addition, the European Communities refers to the 1995 Antitrust Enforcement Guidelines for International Operations of the US Department of Justice and the US Federal Trade Commission. Those guidelines expressly mention that "the 1916 Act is not an antitrust statute [...]. It is a trade statute that creates a private claim against importers [...]"[108].

---

[104] Emphasis added by the European Communities.

[105] The European Communities refers to pages 4 and 5 of the testimony where it is stated, *inter alia*, that "[t]he Antidumping Code [...] expressly limits the remedy for dumping to the prospective collection of antidumping duties to offset the margin of dumping. [...] Article 16 [of the Tokyo Round Anti-Dumping Code, now Article 18.1 of the WTO AD Agreement] must stand for the proposition that a government can provide its citizens one, and only one, remedy for dumping. That remedy is the collection of duties in a manner consistent with the Antidumping Code. We believe that our reading flows logically from the letter and spirit of the GATT and the Antidumping Code. It also follows that S. 1655 would violate the Code by imposing additional sanctions on top of normal antidumping duties. [...] While the same criticism can be levelled at the Antidumping Act of 1916, that Act was "grandfathered" by the Protocol of Provisional application when the U.S. joined the GATT in 1947. Because of this legal technicality, the 1916 Act in its present form is legal under the GATT."

[106] The European Communities refers to a letter, dated 18 February 1986, from US Trade Representative C. Yeutter to Sen. S. Thurmond, 18 February 1986, where it is stated, as criticism in connection with proposed amendments to the 1916 Act, that "[w]hile many of the above objections can be levelled at the Antidumping Act of 1916, that Act was grandfathered by the Protocol of Provisional Application upon U.S. accession to the GATT and is therefore GATT-legal." The European Communities also refers to another letter, dated 4 February 1986, from Assistant Attorney General J. Bolton to Sen. S. Thurmond, where it is stated that "[t]o the extent that any provisions of the current 1916 Act are inconsistent with the GATT, they are protected by the "grandfather clause", para. 1(b) of the 1947 Protocol of Provisional Application of the GATT".

[107] The European Communities notes the existence of para. 3(a) of the introductory language to the GATT 1994 which only mentions "measures taken by a Member under specific mandatory legislation, enacted by that Member before it became a contracting party to the GATT 1947, that prohibits the use, sale or lease of foreign-built or foreign-reconstructed vessels in commercial applications between points in national waters or the waters of an exclusive economic zone".

[108] Section 2.82 of the Guidelines. The European Communities notes that the full text is available on the Internet at http://www.usdoj.gov/atr/public/guidelines/internat.txt.

3.129 In response, the **United States** states that, assuming *arguendo* that the European Communities' characterisation of the statements at issue is accurate, the simple answer to the EC argument is that the two government agencies commenting on the proposed 1986 legislation, i.e. the US Department of Justice and USTR, were mistaken as a matter of fact.

3.130 The United States considers that the GATT 1947 document L/2375/Add. 1 of 19 March 1965 shows that the US government did not include the 1916 Act anywhere in the survey of existing mandatory legislation not in conformity with Part II of the GATT 1947. Indeed, at one point, the US government specifically notified statutes that were not in conformity with Articles III and VI of the GATT 1947, which are the two Articles which the European Communities claims the 1916 Act violates. The 1916 Act was not among them. The plain import of document L/2375/Add.1 is that, in the United States' view, the 1916 Act was GATT-legal and therefore did not require "grandfathering".

3.131 The United States confirms that its notification in document L/2375/Add.1 was not binding, but maintains that it was nevertheless an official statement of the US government's position regarding the GATT-legality of the 1916 Act in a GATT 1947 forum. The United States did not have the occasion to address the GATT-legality of the 1916 Act in the only other possible GATT 1947 forum, i.e. a dispute resolution proceeding, because no contracting party challenged the 1916 Act under the GATT 1947, and this despite the fact that the United States had never invoked the "grandfathering" protection made available by the Protocol of Provisional Application.

3.132 The United States further points out that the notification by the United States contained in document L/2375/Add.1, which is an official statement of the US government, contradicts, as a factual matter, the statements cited by the European Communities. Therefore, the Panel should attach no weight to those statements when deciding whether the 1916 Act violates Articles III:4 and VI:2 of the GATT 1994.

3.133 The United States considers it more significant, however, that the inference which the European Communities draws from the statements made by the two agencies is not accurate. In each of the statements, the agency official first discusses why the proposed legislation, which would have amended the 1916 Act, was GATT-illegal. Then, the agency official explains that while the 1916 Act pre-dates the GATT 1947 and is therefore eligible for "grandfathering" if ever challenged as GATT-illegal, the 1916 Act would no longer be eligible for "grandfathering", under GATT 1947 jurisprudence, if it were amended. For example, Assistant Attorney General John Bolton of the US Department of Justice states:

> "*To the extent that any provisions of the current 1916 Act are inconsistent with the GATT*, they are protected by the "grandfather clause," paragraph 1(b) of the 1947 Protocol of Provisional Application of the GATT. Any amendment to the 1916 Act that is inconsistent with the GATT or the [Antidumping] Code would not benefit from that pro-

tection, however, and accordingly, would contravene our international obligations."[109]

3.134 For the United States it is clear from this statement that the official is not admitting or even suggesting that the 1916 Act, without the proposed amendments, was GATT-illegal. Rather, the official is merely saying that the 1916 Act is eligible for "grandfathering" only if it is not amended and that it would be GATT-illegal if amended as proposed, given that the proposed amendments are GATT-illegal.

3.135 The United States submits that the statements of the two officials from USTR are very similar and attempt to convey the same message, although they are perhaps not as clearly made. For example, former US Trade Representative Clayton Yeutter, after detailing various reasons why the proposed amendments to the 1916 Act were GATT-illegal, states:

> "While many of the above objections *can be leveled at* the Anti-dumping Act of 1916, that act was "grandfathered" upon U.S. accession to the GATT and is therefore GATT-legal. By significantly amending the 1916 Act, S. 1655 would remove the protection of the GATT "grandfather clause" [...]."[110]

3.136 In the view of the United States, it emerges from this statement that, like the US Department of Justice official, former US Trade Representative Yeutter is simply attempting to make the point that the "grandfathering" available to protect the 1916 Act from objections like those applicable to the proposed amendments in question would be lost if the 1916 Act were amended. He is not attempting to opine that those objections actually would be valid if levelled against the 1916 Act.

3.137 The United States also points out that the European Communities provided an incomplete quotation from the 1995 Antitrust Enforcement Guidelines for International Operations of the US Department of Justice and the US Federal Trade Commission.[111]

3.138 The United States considers that, for all these reasons, the statements cited by the European Communities deserve to be given no weight by the Panel in determining whether the 1916 Act violates Articles III:4 and VI:2 of the GATT 1994.

---

[109] Letter of 4 February 1986 from Assistant Attorney General J. Bolton to Sen. S. Thurmond, p. 5 (emphasis added by the United States).

[110] Letter of 18 February 1986 from US Trade Representative C. Yeutter to Sen. S. Thurmond (emphasis added by the United States). The United States also refers to the Letter of 4 February 1986 from Assistant Attorney General J. Bolton to Sen. S. Thurmond, p. 5.

[111] Section 2.82 of the 1995 Antitrust Enforcement Guidelines provides as follows:

> "The Revenue Act of 1916, better known as the Antidumping Act, 15 U.S.C. 71, 74, is not an antitrust statute, but its subject-matter is closely related to the antitrust rules regarding predation. It is a trade statute that creates a private claim against importers who sell goods into the United States at prices substantially below the prices charged for the same goods in their home markets. In order to state a claim, a plaintiff must show both that such lower prices were commonly and systematically charged, and that the importer had the specific intent to injure or destroy an industry in the United States, or to prevent the establishment of an industry."

(d) The Classification of the 1916 Act in the US Legal System

3.139 The **United States** notes that the 1916 Act's placement in the United States Code constitutes further evidence of its antitrust nature. When the 1916 Act was codified in the United States Code, it was placed under Title 15, entitled "Commerce and Trade." Also located in Title 15 are the Sherman Act, the Clayton Act and the Federal Trade Commission Act, which are all antitrust laws. In contrast, the US anti-dumping laws are codified in Title 19, entitled "Customs Duties". Moreover, it should be noted that the 1916 Act was enacted under the heading of "Unfair Competition" in Title VIII of the Revenue Act of 1916. For the United States, in US terminology, dumping is not unfair competition.

3.140 The **European Communities** responds that, so long as the 1916 Act has the objective criteria which bring it under Article VI of the GATT 1994, it does not matter whether it is classified in the US legal system as antitrust or anti-dumping. In fact, the 1916 Act is not considered an antitrust measure in the United States, as is evidenced by the Antitrust Enforcement Guidelines for International Operations of the US Justice Department.

3.141 For the European Communities, it is plain, moreover, that dumping is a form of unfair competition whereas antitrust measures are distinguishable notably because they are designed to protect competition, not competitors. The United States itself has regularly recognized that dumping is unfair competition. For example, in the report of the panel on *United States - Imposition of Anti-Dumping Duties on Imports of Fresh and Chilled Atlantic Salmon from Norway*[112] the US position on the nature of Article VI of the GATT 1947 is reported in the following terms:

> "The drafters of the General Agreement had recognized in 1947 that distortions to international *competition* caused by unfair trade practices could be so severe that effective remedies to curb such distortions were essential: indeed, as essential to an overall programme of liberalization of international trade as, for example, the m.f.n. principle and the national treatment principle."[113]

3.142 The **United States** rejects the EC assertion that the 1916 Act is not considered an antitrust measure in the United States. Until at least as recently as 1994, the US Congress considered the 1916 Act to be an antitrust statute because it is included in a compilation of selected antitrust statutes under the heading "Principal Antitrust Laws" that was prepared by the US Congress.[114]

3.143 The **European Communities** notes that it does not know the US Congress document of 1994 and maintains its view that it is a recent invention to consider the 1916 Act as an antitrust statute.

---

[112] Panel Report on *United States - Imposition of Anti-Dumping Duties on Imports of Fresh and Chilled Atlantic Salmon from Norway*, adopted by the Committee on Anti-Dumping Practices on 27 April 1994, BISD 41S/229 (hereinafter "*United States - Anti-Dumping Duties on Salmon from Norway*").

[113] *Ibid.*, para. 74 (emphasis added by the European Communities).

[114] The document referred to by the United States was not submitted to the Panel.

(e) Simultaneous or Consecutive Filings of 1916 Act Claims and 1930 Tariff Act Petitions in Cases Involving the Same Matter

3.144 In response to a question of the Panel to the United States regarding whether there have ever been situations where complaints in respect of the same matter were simultaneously filed under the 1916 Act and the relevant provisions of the 1930 Tariff Act dealing with anti-dumping, the **United States** replies that the situation that most closely approximates the situation described can be found with regard to the matter underlying the *Geneva Steel* case. In *Geneva Steel*, the plaintiff filed a 1916 Act complaint in federal court in September of 1996 addressing the allegedly predatory pricing practices of certain importers of steel plate, and two months later it filed anti-dumping petitions on steel plate with the US Department of Commerce. Thus, although these filings were not simultaneous, they were close in time. Of course, even if these filings had been made simultaneously, it would not be accurate to describe them as addressing the "same matter," as the Panel's question suggests. In this regard, the 1916 Act provides retroactive relief, i.e. treble damages for past conduct. The US anti-dumping law, in contrast, provides prospective relief. It remedies, through the imposition of duties, transactions occurring after the initiation of the anti-dumping investigation. As a result, the same transactions would not be remedied by the simultaneous filings of a 1916 Act complaint and an anti-dumping petition.

3.145 The United States notes that a similar but more complicated situation arose with regard to the matter underlying the *Wheeling-Pittsburgh* case. There, the plaintiff filed a lawsuit against Japanese and Russian importers of hot-rolled steel in state court asserting novel claims under state law but no claim under the 1916 Act, a federal law. For various reasons, that lawsuit was subsequently transferred to federal court and all of the state claims were dismissed. The plaintiff nevertheless was allowed to amend its complaint to state a claim under the 1916 Act. It is the recollection of the United States that, by the time the 1916 Act claim was brought, anti-dumping investigations of hot-rolled steel were already underway.

3.146 The United States notes, finally, that the matter underlying the *Zenith III* case, Japanese television sets, involved both the filing of 1916 Act claims and an anti-dumping petition. The anti-dumping petitions were filed with the then-responsible agency, the US Department of Treasury, in March 1968. In December 1970, the plaintiff NUE (National Union Electric Corporation) filed suit under the 1916 Act among other statutes. In September 1974, the plaintiff Zenith filed a claim under the 1916 Act.

3.147 With regard to another question of the Panel to the United States regarding whether there has ever been any situation where a complaint under the 1916 Act was initiated after an anti-dumping investigation in respect of the same matter was unsuccessful, the United States notes that it is not aware of any situation where a 1916 Act complaint was filed in the wake of an unsuccessful anti-dumping investigation.

(f) The Relevant US Case Law

(i) The Distinction between Issues of Fact and Issues of Law

3.148 The **European Communities** notes that the question whether a given national law is subject to and compatible with the disciplines of the WTO Agreement and the GATT 1994 is a matter of WTO law, which it is for the Panel to decide under the DSU, and subject to appeal to the Appellate Body. The Panel cannot be bound by the views of national courts of WTO Members on this question. Words like "antitrust", "unfair competition", and "predatory" may have different meanings in different Member states. They may be used in different ways at different times. Allowing their use to determine the scope of application of the discipline of Article VI would effectively invite Members themselves to choose to withdraw their legislation from WTO disciplines simply by choosing the right label. On the other hand, judgments of national courts are relevant insofar as they offer guidance on the meaning or interpretation of national laws, and it is appropriate for the Panel to take them into account for that purpose.

3.149 The European Communities claims that it is clear on the face of the 1916 Act that it targets imported products through sanctions applied to importers and that the regulated conduct is defined by reference to discrimination between the import price and prices on the domestic market or export prices to a third country. The debate down the years among lower courts in the United States as to whether the 1916 Anti-Dumping Act is a trade law or an antitrust law[115] is therefore not relevant for WTO purposes.

3.150 The European Communities considers that, while the Panel must consider US case law and other official pronouncements in order to establish the meaning and substantive content of the 1916 Act, it need not attach importance to the characterisation of the 1916 Act by US courts as being or not being an anti-dumping measure since this is a matter of WTO law, which US courts do not address but which the Panel must. In performing this task, the Panel should not have regard to, and should in any event not be bound by, labels such as "antitrust" or "protectionist" which domestic courts apply for one or another domestic purpose.

3.151 According to the European Communities, the Panel should have regard to the elements which are relevant for the purposes of Article VI of the GATT 1994, i.e. whether the practice which is targeted by the 1916 Act is covered by Article VI. Article VI does not only regulate dumping. It also defines what is meant by dumping. Therefore, the Panel should examine whether the 1916 Act, as interpreted by US Courts, is directed at this kind of practice, irrespective of any categorisation of the 1916 Act as "antitrust" legislation and of the legislative purpose of the statute by US courts for their domestic purposes.

3.152 The European Communities finds support for its position in the report of the panel on *EEC - Parts and Components*. The panel in that case examined whether the description or categorisation of a charge under the domestic law of a contracting

---

[115] The European Communities refers to *Zenith III, Op. Cit.*; *Wheeling-Pittsburgh, Op. Cit.*; *Geneva Steel, Op. Cit.*.

party is relevant in determining whether it is subject to the requirements of Article II or those of Article III:2 of the GATT 1994. The panel found that "if the description or categorization under the domestic law of a contracting party were to provide the required 'connection with importation', contracting parties could determine themselves which of these provisions would apply to their charges"[116]. Likewise, if categorisation of the 1916 Act as a dumping statute by US courts and authorities were necessary or relevant to establish whether dumping takes place within the meaning of Article VI of the GATT 1994, the United States could determine itself whether Article VI would apply to its statute. Clearly, the purpose of this provision could then be easily circumvented.

3.153 According to the **United States**, in all cases, the role of a panel is fundamentally the same: the panel must first assess the facts presented and then determine their conformity with the relevant agreement, which generally entails interpreting the scope and applicability of those agreements to the facts. In the present case, the assessment of the facts could be easily blurred or confused with interpreting the scope of the relevant agreements. It is important that the Panel not lose sight of the distinction between its role as a fact finder in the present case and its role in determining questions of law. The proper interpretation of the 1916 Act is a question of fact to be established, as it is an accepted principle of international law that municipal law is a fact to be proven before an international tribunal.[117] Because it is expedient to its positions in the present case, the European Communities would have the Panel ignore the US case law interpreting the 1916 Act. However, the Panel is not called upon to interpret the 1916 Act as such. Rather, the Panel must assess the current state of jurisprudence in the United States regarding the 1916 Act in order to determine the fact of the 1916 Act. It is not the role of the Panel to agree or disagree with judicial decisions interpreting and applying the 1916 Act. The danger in the Panel interpreting the 1916 Act as such is that the Panel might adopt an interpretation of the law that does not match the true application of the law in the United States. To do so would result in a Panel report based upon hypothetical facts. In order to avoid such an outcome, the Panel should deem the case law interpreting the 1916 Act as dispositive for purposes of determining the fact of US law.[118]

3.154 In support of its position, the United States refers to the *Brazilian Loans* case in which the Permanent Court of International Justice (hereinafter the "PCIJ") deemed controlling the manner in which French courts had interpreted French legis-

---

[116] *EC - Parts and Components, Op. Cit.*, para 5.7.

[117] The United States refers to the decision of the Permanent Court of International Justice (hereinafter the "PCIJ") in *Case Concerning Certain German Interests in Polish Upper Silesia*, PCIJ Rep. 1926, Series A, No. 7, p. 19; *Case Concerning the Payment in Gold of Brazilian Federal Loans Contracted in France*, PCIJ Rep. 1929, Series A, No. 21, pp. 124-25 (hereinafter "*Brazilian Loans*").

[118] The United States refers to the Separate Opinion of Judge Lauterpacht in the PCIJ decision in *Case Concerning the Guardianship of an Infant*, ICJ Rep. 1958, Sep. Op., p. 91. According to the United States, it is settled practice among States that international judicial bodies should accept, and treat as binding, questions of municipal law and practice decided by competent municipal courts. The United States refers to the PCIJ decision in *Case Concerning the Payment of Various Serbian Loans Issued in France*, PCIJ Rep. 1929, Series A, No. 20, p. 46; *Brazilian Loans, Op. Cit.*, pp. 124-25.

lation. The PCIJ admonished in that case that a tribunal of international law should "pay the utmost regard to the decisions of the municipal courts of a country, for it is with the aid of their jurisprudence that it will be enabled to decide what are the rules which in actual fact, are applied in the country the law of which is recognized as applicable in a given case."[119] This principle "rests in part on the concept of the reserved domain of domestic jurisdiction, and in part on the practical need of avoiding contradictory versions of the law of a state from different sources."[120]

3.155 In the view of the United States, it therefore follows that the interpretation of the 1916 Act by US courts offers more than just guidance to the Panel. It is their interpretation that is dispositive for purposes of determining the nature of the 1916 Act. The Panel is not called upon to opine upon or interpret the statute itself by agreeing or disagreeing with any particular court's interpretation. In *India - Patents*, the Appellate Body noted approvingly that the panel had not interpreted Indian law as such, but, rather, had reviewed the law to determine whether it was WTO-consistent. Accordingly, it is the responsibility of the Panel to ascertain the interpretation afforded to the 1916 Act by the weight of judicial authority in the United States. This is not to say that that the Panel has no interpretative role in the instant case. As confirmed by the Appellate Body in *India - Patents*, once the Panel has determined the interpretation of the municipal law as a matter of fact, it is the Panel's function to determine the applicability of the relevant WTO agreements to those facts.[121] These are questions of law to be determined by the Panel in the first instance. In the present case, the Panel is called upon to determine the scope of Article VI and Article III of the GATT 1994.

3.156 The **European Communities** rejects the US contention that it does not consider US judicial decisions relevant for WTO purposes. The interpretation of the 1916 Act, i.e. determining what it means, including, notably, what must be pleaded and proved in order to establish a claim under it, is a matter of US law and therefore of fact before the present Panel. The Panel should of course look to the text of the statute and the pronouncements of US courts and other authorities to determine this question. By contrast, the question of what is the meaning and the extent of the disciplines laid down in Article VI of the GATT 1994, and the question of whether a Member's legislation with certain features is covered by and is in conformity with Article VI, are matters of WTO law to be determined by the Panel.

3.157 In reply to a question of the Panel regarding the relevance to the present case of the Appellate Body's report in the *India - Patents* case, the European Communities points out that that report is particularly relevant to the present case because it states in very clear terms the task to which the Panel is called. In that report, the Appellate Body distinguished between the possible objectives pursued when interpreting domestic law in international tribunals and other dispute settlement fora, including in WTO dispute settlement, and upheld the panel's review of India's legislation. The considerations developed in the *India - Patents* Appellate Body report also apply to

---

[119] *Brazilian Loans*, *Op. Cit.*, pp. 124-25.

[120] I. Brownlie, *Principles of Public International Law*, 4th ed., Clarendon Press (1990), p.41.

[121] The United States refers to the Appellate Body Report on *India - Patents*, *supra*, footnote 29, paras. 65-66.

the present dispute. As the Appellate Body found in that case, it is essential that the Panel carry out "an examination of the relevant aspects of [US] municipal law" in order to determine whether the US provisions are in conformity with the obligations laid down in the GATT 1994, the Agreement Establishing the WTO and the Anti-Dumping Agreement. As the Appellate Body pointed out, "[t]here [is] simply *no way for the Panel to make this determination without engaging in an examination of [domestic] law*."[122] In the same vein as the European Communities has argued before the present Panel, the Appellate Body concluded that "[t]o say that the Panel should have done otherwise would be to say that only India can assess whether Indian law is consistent with India's obligations under the *WTO Agreement*. This, clearly, cannot be so." [123]

3.158 In response, the **United States** notes that the European Communities agrees that the nature of the 1916 Act is a question of fact for the Panel and that US judicial decisions interpreting the 1916 Act are dispositive for this purpose.

(ii) Comments on the Case Law in General

3.159 The **European Communities** asserts that US courts' views on whether the 1916 Act is a trade law or an antitrust law are far from consonant. It is sufficient to note that while some judgments, notably those of the District Court and the Circuit Court of Appeals in the *Zenith III* case, suggest that the 1916 Act is solely an antitrust law and not a trade law, this view has been strongly contested. For example, the District Court in *Geneva Steel* held:

> "The 1916 Act means what its plain language says. In addition to its antitrust prohibitions, the Act has a protectionist component that prohibits conduct designed to injure the domestic steel industry."[124]

3.160 The European Communities points out that even those Courts that claim that the 1916 Act is solely an antitrust statute acknowledge that establishing that dumping took place remains the first prerequisite to apply the 1916 Act. For instance, in *In re Japanese Electronic Products II*, which described the 1916 Act as "complex antitrust litigation", the Court of Appeals for the Third Circuit held that:

> "The 1916 Act makes it illegal to *dump* imported goods on the US market with the purpose of destroying or injuring US industry. [...] The first element necessary to a finding of *dumping* under the 1916 Act is proof that a price differential exists between two comparable products, one of which is imported or sold in the US and the other of which is sold in the exporting country."[125]

3.161 The European Communities reiterates in this connection that the fact that the conduct targeted by a statute is defined by reference to discrimination between the price of the imported products and a benchmark which is generally the price of the product in the exporting country, is sufficient to determine that the statute is directed

---

[122] Appellate Body Report, *India - Patents, supra,* footnote 29, para 66 (emphasis added).

[123] *Ibid.*, para 66.

[124] *Geneva Steel, Op. Cit.*, p. 1214.

[125] *In re Japanese Products II*, Op. Cit, pp. 322 and 324 (emphasis added by the European Communities).

at dumping and is subject to the disciplines of Article VI of the GATT 1994. There is, therefore, no need to discuss the case law any further.

3.162 Nor does the European Communities accept that for the purposes of establishing the applicability of Article VI of the GATT 1994 it is necessary to examine the question whether the law protects competitors as distinct from competition, or whether the specific intent requirement relates to an intent to injure industry as opposed to an intent to injure competition. The language quoted above makes clear that US courts themselves have taken sharply different positions on these questions, and there is nothing to suggest that there will be greater clarity in the foreseeable future.

3.163 The **United States** contends that the prevailing view among US courts that have addressed the issue supports interpreting the 1916 Act as an antitrust-like statute. Contrary to the European Communities' suggestion that US courts have taken different positions, the prevailing view among US courts that have addressed the issue, which include the US Supreme Court in the *Cooper* case, is that the 1916 Act is an antitrust-like statute. It is their interpretation of the 1916 Act that, as a factual matter, must control in the present dispute. More fundamentally, the prevailing interpretation of the 1916 Act shows that the 1916 Act is not a statute that addresses the "dumping" and "injury" that would make it an anti-dumping statute within the meaning of Article VI of the GATT 1994. As the courts have recognized, the 1916 Act is designed to combat a specific form of international price discrimination. This price discrimination not only must involve substantial price differences but also must be undertaken commonly and systematically and with a specified intent. The 1916 Act is not directed at the simple price differences that cause material injury captured by the Anti-Dumping Agreement, nor is it based on the Anti-Dumping Agreement's notion of material injury to a domestic industry.

3.164 The United States notes that, in *Zenith III*, the US court decision on the interpretation of the specific provisions of the 1916 Act, the Court explained that the 1916 Act was part of the corpus of US antitrust law of the era and, therefore, any given provision generally should be interpreted in a manner consistent with antitrust principles.[126] Every other final and conclusive US court decision in this area, moreover, has supported the *Zenith III* analysis.[127] More specifically, these court decisions confirm that the 1916 Act is directed at a very different type of harmful business activity from that addressed by Article VI and the Anti-Dumping Agreement. While the Court of Appeals for the Third Circuit used the term "dumping" in connection with the 1916 Act, it apparently did so in a non-technical sense. Moreover, contrary to the European Communities' assertion, the Court did not state that a finding of "dumping" is itself a necessary precondition to apply the 1916 Act.

3.165 The **European Communities** adds that the domestic case law so heavily relied on by the United States is much less supportive of the US position than the United States would have the Panel believe. In most of the cases cited by the United

---

[126] The United States refers to *Zenith III*, *Op. Cit.*, p. 1212, 1223.

[127] The United States refers to *Schwimmer v. Sony Corp.*, *Op. Cit.*; *Outboard Marine Corp. v. Pezetel*, *Op. Cit.*; *Jewel Foliage Co. v. Uniflora Overseas Florida*, *Op. Cit.*; *Western Concrete Structures Co. v. Mitsui & Co.*, *Op. Cit.*; *Isra Fruit Ltd. v. Agrexco Agr. Export Co.*, *Op. Cit.*; *Helmac I*, *Op. Cit.*; *Helmac II*, *Op. Cit.*.

States as identifying the 1916 Act as "antitrust-like", a careful reading reveals that the problem of categorization was raised as a step in resolving other issues very far removed from those now before the Panel. Among those other issues are: Is the "comparability" test under the 1916 Act the same or different from that under the Robinson-Patman Act?[128] What is the applicable prescription period for claims under the 1916 Act?[129] May an importer of competing products sue under the 1916 Act, or is standing to sue limited to domestic producers?[130]

3.166 The **United States** maintains its position that the prevailing view among US courts is that the 1916 Act is an antitrust-like statute, and it is their interpretation which must control in the present dispute.

(iii) United States v. Cooper Corp.

3.167 The **United States** asserts that the US Supreme Court, which is the highest court in the United States and the final arbiter of a statute's meaning, recognized the 1916 Act as an antitrust statute in *United States v. Cooper Corp.*[131] In that case, the Supreme Court expressly described the 1916 Act as "supplemental" to the Sherman Act, the United States' first and most basic antitrust law.[132]

3.168 The **European Communities** contests this US assertion. According to the European Communities, the issue in *Cooper* was whether the United States is a "person" within the meaning of Section 7 of the Sherman Act, entitled to sue for treble damages thereunder. What the Court did in examining the Sherman Act was to list what it described as "supplemental legislation". That list included "the antidumping provisions of the Revenue Act of 1916".[133] This statement from the Supreme Court should rather be interpreted as a confirmation that the 1916 Act is an anti-dumping act.

3.169 The **United States** disagrees with the European Communities that by calling the 1916 Act "supplemental" to the Sherman Antitrust Act, the foremost antitrust law in the United States, the Court thereby "confirmed" that it is an anti-dumping measure. In any event, it should be noted that the leading lower court case addressing how specific provisions of the 1916 Act should be interpreted is *Zenith III.* It "conclude[d] [...], on the basis of the statutory text, that the 1916 Act *is an antitrust, not a protectionist statute.*"[134]

---

[128] The European Communities refers to *Zenith III, Op. Cit.*.

[129] The European Communities refers to *Helmac I, Op. Cit.*.

[130] The European Communities refers to *Isra Fruit Ltd. V. Agrexco Agr. Export Co., Op. Cit.*; *Western Concrete Structures Co., Inc. v. Mitsui & Company (USA) Inc., Op. Cit.*; *Jewel Foliage Company v. Uniflora Overseas Florida, Inc., Op. Cit.*; *Schwimmer v. Sony Corp., Op. Cit.*; *Outboard Marine Corporation v. Pezetel, Op. Cit.*.

[131] 312 U.S. 600 (1941) (hereinafter "*Cooper*").

[132] The United States refers to *Cooper, Op. Cit.*, pp. 608 -610.

[133] The European Communities refers to *Cooper, Op. Cit.*, pp. 608-610.

[134] *Zenith III, Op. Cit.*, p. 1214 (emphasis added by the United States).

(iv) Zenith Radio Corp. v. Matsushita Electric Industrial Co. and In re Japanese Electronic Products Antitrust Litigation

3.170 The **European Communities** asserts that in fact none of the cases referred to by the United States clearly establish, even for purely domestic purposes, let alone in a manner that would be relevant for the WTO, that the 1916 Act is an antitrust statute. The closest there is to such a case is the District Court's judgment in the *Zenith III* case. The issue in that case was whether products sold by the defendants in the United States and Japan were sufficiently comparable to give rise to a claim under the 1916 Act. The Court held that they were not, a judgment partially reversed by the Circuit Court of Appeals. The District Court's judgment is based on an analysis of the 1916 Act as having two features:

(i) The 1916 Act is "intended to complement the antitrust laws by imposing on importers substantially the same legal strictures relating to price discrimination as those which had already been imposed on domestic businesses by the Clayton Antitrust Act of 1914", with the result that the "like grade and quality" test of the Robinson-Patman Act should also be used for the 1916 Act.[135] The Court found that this test was narrower than the standard under the 1921 Antidumping Act, which permits a degree of discretion to the administering authority on this issue.

(ii) The value of imported merchandise is determined by reference to the sales of "similar" merchandise, because the 1916 Act borrows the language from the 1913 Tariff Act.

3.171 The European Communities points out that the question whether the standards under the 1916 Act were more rigorous than those under the 1921 Antidumping Act arose because anti-dumping duties had been assessed against some of the products involved in the litigation under the 1916 Act, and the plaintiffs sought to rely on this to establish comparability.

3.172 The European Communities further recalls that the Court of Appeals agreed that the 1916 Act should be interpreted consistently with its purpose, which was "to prohibit anticompetitive pricing".[136] But it held that products could be comparable under the Act even though "products sold in Japan have technical components that make them work in Japan, and those sold in the United States have technical components that make them work in the United States. Considered in terms of consumer utility, i.e. consumer use and preference, marketability, and commercial interchangeability, the purchaser of a CEP [consumer electronic product] in Japan buys the same thing as the purchaser of a CEP in the United States: an operable CEP. Because the two consumers purchase the same thing, we would, absent other factors, expect them to pay the same price."[137]

[135] The European Communities refers to *Zenith III*, *Op. Cit.*, p. 1197.
[136] *In re Japanese Electronic Products II*, *Op. Cit.*, p. 324.
[137] *Ibid.*, p. 325.

3.173 The European Communities asserts that the analysis of the District Court concerning the relationship between the 1916 Act and the antitrust laws is not, however, convincing for WTO purposes or even, as the later US cases show, for purposes of US law. The following arguments support this contention:

(a) The legislative history materials invoked, dating from the period of 1916 to 1921, date from a period when there was no clearly accepted theoretical distinction between antitrust and protectionist legislation.

(b) The "intent" of a law cannot determine whether it is subject to the discipline of Article VI of the GATT 1994. Otherwise, the discipline could be avoided simply by changing the label and explanation given to a law.

(c) Nothing in the opinions of either the District Court or the Circuit Court of Appeals holds or suggests that the predation standards which are applicable under the antitrust laws, but which had not been fully developed at the time of the *Zenith* judgments, should also be read into the 1916 Act.

3.174 In the view of the **United States**, the nature of the 1916 Act was squarely addressed in the *Zenith III* case. In that case, the District Court specifically considered the character of the 1916 Act because, according to the Court, "the character of the statute is of salient concern in its construction."[138] To that end, the Court stated that its task "was to ascertain whether the Act was intended to be part of the corpus of antitrust law, or whether the Act was intended to be 'protectionist' legislation, as that term is used in discussion of tariff barriers to free trade."[139] After examining the similarities between the 1916 Act and other antitrust statutes, the Court concluded that the 1916 Act "*is an antitrust, not a protectionist statute*."[140] The Court also explained that "[t]hat conclusion is strongly corroborated by the political and legal history of the relevant era, and the legislative history of the 1916 Act."[141]

3.175 The United States notes that the *Zenith III* Court also quoted the relevant congressional report, which states that the purpose of the 1916 Act was to adopt a provision "[i]n order that persons, partnerships, corporations, and associations in foreign countries, whose goods are sold in this country, may be placed in the same position as our manufacturers with reference to unfair competition [...] ."[142] The Court also recounted how Representative Kitchin, the chairman of the House Committee on Ways and Means and the House sponsor of the 1916 Act, stated "in unambiguous terms" that the 1916 Act was "intended to do no more than to impose on importers the same pricing restrictions which had already been imposed on domestic businesses by the Clayton Antitrust Act of 1914."[143] The Court stated that

> "Representative Kitchin, explaining his bill at the outset of its consideration by the full House of Representatives, explained:

---

[138] *Zenith III*, *Op. Cit.*, p. 1212.

[139] *Ibid.*, p. 1212.

[140] *Ibid.*, p. 1214 (emphasis added by the United States).

[141] *Ibid.*, p. 1214.

[142] *Ibid.*, p. 1221, quoting H.R. Rep. No. 922, 64th Cong., 1st Sess. 9-10 (1916).

[143] *Ibid.*, p. 1222.

> We believe that the *same* unfair competition law which now applies to the domestic trader should apply to the foreign import trader."[144]

3.176 The United States also points out that the *Zenith III* Court further explained that, at the time of the enactment of the 1916 Act, "unfair competition" referred to the activities addressed by the antitrust laws of the era. The Court quoted the following explanations by the US Secretary of Commerce, William Redfield, in 1915:

> "'Unfair competition' is forbidden by law in domestic trade, and the Federal Trade Commission exists to determine the facts and takes steps to abate the evil wherever found. The door, however, is still open to "unfair competition" from abroad which may seriously affect American industries for the worse. It is not normal competition of which I speak, but abnormal. [...] If it shall pass beyond fair competition and exert or seek to exert a monopolistic power over any part of our commerce, we ought to prevent it."[145]

3.177 The United States further recalls that the *Zenith* Court ultimately concluded that it would be guided by the following principles when interpreting the 1916 Act:

> "The principal lesson which we draw from the legislative history of the 1916 Act, viewed against the historical background of the first [Woodrow] Wilson Administration, is that the statute should be interpreted whenever possible to parallel the "unfair competition" law applicable to domestic commerce. Since the 1916 Antidumping Act is a price discrimination law, it should be read in tandem with the domestic price discrimination law, section 2 of the Clayton Act, which was amended by the Robinson-Patman Act in 1936. And, in order to be faithful to the intention of Congress to subject importers to the "same unfair competition law," *we should not interpret the 1916 Act to impose on importers legal strictures which are more rigorous than those applied to domestic enterprises.*"[146]

3.178 The United States notes, finally, that, on appeal, the Third Circuit Court of Appeals found that the 1916 Act was enacted "to do with unfair competition" and concluded that the "primary aim of the 1916 Act is to prohibit *anti-competitive pricing"*.[147] It also held that the plaintiff must show a specific, not just general, predatory intent to injure or destroy an industry.[148]

3.179 In response, the **European Communities** maintains its view that there is no case law stating that plaintiffs in a 1916 action should provide evidence of predatory intent within the meaning of the Robinson-Patman Act and as defined by the *Brooke Group* ruling. The Third Circuit's 1983 opinion in the *Zenith* case, uses the 1916 Act's phrase "intent of destroying or injuring an industry in the United States" inter-

---

144 *Ibid.*, p. 1222, quoting 53 Cong. Rec. App. 1938 (1916) (footnote omitted; emphasis added by the United States).

145 *Ibid.*, p. 1219, quoting Annual Report of the Secretary of Commerce 43 (1915).

146 *Ibid.*, p. 1223 (footnote omitted; emphasis added by the United States).

147 *In re Japanese Electronic Products II, Op. Cit.*, p. 324 (emphasis added by the United States).

148 The United States refers to *In re Japanese Electronic Products II, Op. Cit.*, pp. 327-328.

changeably with the phrase "specific predatory intent".[149] However, the word "predatory" is not used as a term of art incorporating the concepts of sales "below an appropriate measure of cost" and reasonable prospect of recoupment of losses. It is necessary to quote extensively from the opinion to show exactly what the Court means. The following passage of the opinion summarises the evidence which the Court considered sufficient to create a genuine issue of fact[150] on the issue of specific intent under the 1916 Act:

> "To make out a claim that defendants conspired under the antitrust laws, plaintiffs need only show that defendants conspired with general intent to restrain trade [citations]. However, a showing of general intent does not necessarily constitute a prima facie showing of the specific intent required by the 1916 Act [...]. After reviewing the record in this case, we hold that evidence supporting plaintiffs' theory that defendants entered into the alleged conspiracy also creates a genuine issue of fact as to whether defendants agreed to dump CEPs on the United States market with the specific intent to destroy or injure an industry in the United States.
>
> Evidence supporting plaintiff's conspiracy theory would support an inference of predation in the United States market. This evidence is offered to show that the Japanese defendants agreed to stabilise prices at artificially high levels in Japan, insulating themselves by agreement from price-cutting competition at home. There is also evidence that defendants at the same time entered into an agreement to sell the fruits of the excess capacity of the Japanese CEP industry in the United States at low prices. We assume that the minimum price agreement, of which all the Japanese defendants were members, was mandated by the Ministry of International Trade and Industry [MITI]. Plaintiffs offer this evidence to show that defendants used the prices in that agreement as reference prices. Finally, plaintiffs point to evidence that defendants sought to conceal sales below MITI prices by a system of rebating.
>
> The Japanese defendants also allegedly eliminated the possibility of price-cutting competition amongst themselves in the United States by agreeing to [certain customer allocation rules] [...]. By thus allocating the market, defendants allegedly brought to bear the full force of their low-price conspiracy on their United States competitors in an effort to drive them out of the market.
>
> Furthermore, plaintiffs' experts [...] concluded that during the time of the alleged conspiracy, defendants operated an export cartel directed towards the United States with the specific intent to undersell their

[149] The European Communities refers to *In re Japanese Electronic Products II*, *Op. Cit.*, pp. 327-28.

[150] The European Communities notes that a "genuine issue of facts" is created where the court concludes that, based on the facts pleaded and the evidence presented before trial, the trier of fact could reach a conclusion favourable to the plaintiff.

> United States competitors and eventually to drive them out of business. [...]
>
> We believe that the evidence in this summary judgment record creates a genuine issue of fact as to whether defendants conspired to dump CEPs in the United States with the specific intent to injure or destroy an industry in the United States [...]."[151]

3.180 In the view of the European Communities, there is clearly no reference to sales below costs or to recoupment of losses in the quoted passage. The evidence cited is presented as circumstantial evidence of intent to injure and destroy an industry, "injure and destroy" and "predation" being used in an every-day, non-technical sense.

3.181 The European Communities also notes in this connection that in the *Wheeling Pittsburgh* case, it is held that under the 1916 Act "predatory pricing" means something different than under antitrust law and that this distinction renders the predatory pricing element as defined by *Brooke Group* inapplicable to "*dumping* cases", basically because in the context of international trade the whole premise of *Brooke Group* is lacking. This is echoed in the following passage taken from a US law review note:

> "[T]he recoupment requirement - at least as defined in *Brooke Group* - is too narrow in the international context because it fails to consider the ability of firms with a monopoly or oligopoly in their home markets simultaneously to recoup losses from dumping by increasing monopoly returns at home. Dumping in the US allows foreign producers to reap the economies of scale of producing at optimal capacity while restricting sales at home to protect their home market monopoly prices."[152]

3.182 The European Communities points out that, in this view, dumping can allow recoupment through high prices in the domestic market, simultaneous to selling at low prices in an export market, which was exactly what the plaintiffs alleged in *Zenith III*. In this theory of dumping, there could not be any need to show a prospect of recoupment later in time as referred to in *Brooke Group*, since recoupment is already occurring at the same time in another market.

3.183 The **United States** concedes that the Third Circuit Court of Appeals did not further elaborate on the element of "specific predatory intent" in its 1982 opinion, but points out that the meaning of this element was in any event clarified in a subsequent decision. In 1986, the *Zenith* case was remanded from the US Supreme Court and the Third Circuit Court of Appeals again had an opportunity to consider the plaintiffs' 1916 Act claims. The United States considers that some background information is helpful to fully understanding the Third Circuit's 1986 decision.

3.184 The United States thus recalls that Zenith and another US company named NEU commenced litigation against Japanese television set manufacturers in the early 1970s, complaining of Sherman Act, Robinson-Patman Act, 1916 Act and other

[151] *In re Japanese Electronic Products II, Op. Cit.*, pp. 328-29.

[152] Note, *Rethinking the 1916 Anti-Dumping Act, Op. Cit.*, pp. 1555-1572.

violations of federal law. During a series of decisions by the District Court and the Court of Appeals in the years 1980-83, the Sherman Act and 1916 Act claims were first dismissed by the District Court for lack of evidentiary support and then reinstated by the Third Circuit. The US Supreme Court then accepted the Sherman Act antitrust claims for review. Those claims were based on the theory that defendants had conspired to monopolise the US market by using excess profits in the Japanese home market to launch a predatory pricing attack on the United States. The Supreme Court reversed the Court of Appeals and remanded, stating that the plaintiff had not developed any credible proof of an illegal conspiracy to monopolise. The Supreme Court held that claims under the Sherman Act for conspiracies or attempts to monopolise through predatory low pricing could only be established by proof that such prices were below some appropriate measure of costs as well as evidence of a realistic expectation of recouping prior losses through future monopoly rents.[153] The Court of Appeals was ordered to consider its prior orders in the *Zenith* case in light of the Supreme Court's decision. On remand, the Third Circuit dismissed the plaintiffs' 1916 Act claims, like the Sherman Act claims, upon the basis that there was no evidence of the possibility of recoupment. The Court reasoned that "[s]ince the Sherman Act conspiracy charge failed in the Supreme Court, our holding on the Antidumping [1916] Act conspiracy claim must fail with it."[154]

3.185 According to the United States, the Supreme Court's decision in *Matsushita Electrical* actually laid the groundwork for the Supreme Court's decision in *Brooke Group* some 7 years later. In *Brooke Group*, the Supreme Court re-examined the so-called "primary line"[155] provisions of the Robinson-Patman Act and held that proof of recoupment was required in order to establish a predatory pricing claim. In doing so, the Supreme Court relied heavily upon its decision in *Matsushita Electrical.*

3.186 The United States therefore argues that, contrary to the European Communities' assertion that antitrust predation standards have never been read into the 1916 Act, in *In re Japanese Electronic Products III*, the 1916 Act claims were dismissed by the Court of Appeals based upon the same predatory pricing/recoupment standards that were established for the Robinson Patman Act by *Brooke Group* some years later. The Supreme Court's 1986 *Matsushita Electronical* decision was and remains a foundation of US antitrust jurisprudence on predatory pricing issues.

3.187 According to the **European Communities**, it is incorrect to deduce from the 1986 *In re Japanese Electronic Products III* decision that the legal standard applied there for the 1916 Act claims was the same as that applied by the Supreme Court to the Sherman Act claims. To understand the correct meaning of many of the pronouncements made by the various courts concerned, it is necessary to consider the detailed context in which they were made. The original complaint in the *Zenith III*

153 The United States refers to *Matsushita Electrical, Op. Cit.*. The United States notes that the Supreme Court reiterated this standard in the same year in another antitrust case, *Cargill, Inc. v. Monfort of Colorado, Inc.*, 479 U.S. 104 (1986), deciding what constitutes proof of injury to competition in the Clayton Act context of mergers and acquisitions.

154 *In re Japanese Electronic Products III*, *Op. Cit.*, pp. 48-49.

155 The United States recalls that "primary line" stands for adverse effects upon direct competitors of the defendant, as opposed to "secondary line," which refers to adverse effects on competitors of the defendant's favoured downstream customers.

case was based on both Sections 1 and 2 of the Sherman Act and the 1916 Act. The District Court granted summary judgment on both sets of claims.[156] The Court of Appeals reversed the judgments of the District Court on both sets of claims so that, if there had been no appeal to the Supreme Court, they would have been tried by the District Court. The Supreme Court, however, granted *certiorari* as regards the Sherman Act claims, but not the 1916 Act claims. It reversed the judgment of the Third Circuit Court of Appeals, with instructions that the case should be remanded to the Court of Appeals "for further proceedings in conformity with the opinion of this Court". The Court of Appeals, in its subsequent 1986 judgment, expressed some perplexity as to what this signified in relation to the 1916 Act claims. It first considered the consequences of the Supreme Court's judgment with respect to the Sherman Act claims which were the only ones that the latter had considered. It concluded that the District Court's summary judgment on the Sherman Act claims must be reinstated, using reasoning to which it is difficult to do justice without quoting it *verbatim*:

> "The conspiracy on which the plaintiffs rely in support of their Sherman Act claims is a horizontal conspiracy among Japanese manufacturers of consumer electronic products to maintain artificially high prices in the Japanese home market to help support sales at low prices in the American export market, thereby injuring American manufacturers competing with them in the latter market. When this court first reviewed the summary judgment record, we concluded it permitted findings that there are high entry barriers in the Japanese home market; that the Japanese manufacturers have higher fixed costs and higher debt-equity ratios than their American counterparts; that the Japanese manufacturers, individually and in the aggregate, created higher plant capacities than could reasonably be absorbed by the Japanese home market, thereby creating an incentive to dispose of the excess capacity in a market outside Japan [citation]. We also concluded that there is direct and circumstantial evidence of an agreement to stabilize Japanese home market prices to realize the profits needed to support sales at low prices in the United States [citation]. Despite these conclusions, the Supreme Court conclusively held that the defendants 'had no motive to enter into the alleged conspiracy'. [citation] [...]. The Supreme Court [...] conclusively held that 'in light of the absence of any rational motive to conspire, neither [defendants'] pricing practices, nor their conduct in the Japanese market, nor their agreements respecting prices and distribution in the American market, suffice to create a "genuine issue for trial".' citation] These holdings are the law of the case and are binding on this court. Consequently the plaintiffs are now foreclosed from arguing that there was a motive to

[156] The European Communities recalls that summary judgment is granted where the court concludes that, based on the facts pleaded and the evidence presented before trial, the trier of fact could not reach a conclusion favourable to the plaintiff (there is no "genuine issue of fact"), so the case should be dismissed without a trial.

> enter into the alleged conspiracy. They are also foreclosed from arguing that the direct and circumstantial evidence to which this court referred in its prior opinion is sufficient to overcome a motion for summary judgment."[157]

3.188 The European Communities concedes that, in concluding that there was no motive to enter into the alleged conspiracy, the Supreme Court had invoked the antitrust theory of predation, including the theory which holds that true predation can only occur where sales are made below "an appropriate measure of costs" and there is a reasonable prospect of recoupment of the losses so incurred. But the European Communities notes that the Supreme Court had done this in the context of its plenary review of the evidentiary record to determine whether there was a genuine issue of fact which required rejection of the motion for summary judgment. The Supreme Court observed that the Japanese companies "have no motive to sustain [the losses resulting from selling in the US market at low prices] absent some strong likelihood that the alleged conspiracy in this country will eventually pay off" and added that "courts should not permit fact-finders to infer conspiracies when such inferences are implausible".[158] This holding was, and was treated by the Court of Appeals as, a holding regarding the facts presented in the case rather than one regarding the interpretation of the language of the Sherman Act.

3.189 The European Communities notes that it was in this context that the Third Circuit Court of Appeals' 1986 opinion came to reconsider the 1916 Act claims which the Supreme Court had not treated. The Court of Appeals said:

> "Since it is now the law of the case that there is insufficient evidence of a conspiracy to price predatorily in the American market, it is necessary to reconsider our disposition of the Antidumping Act claim. As we explained in our earlier opinion, the Antidumping Act of 1916 includes as a substantive element in the cause of action a proviso that the acts complained of 'be done with the intent of destroying or injuring an industry in the United States' [citation]. The plaintiffs assert that the Japanese manufacturers individually and collectively have engaged in illegal dumping. *With respect to the conspiracy claims, we earlier held 'that the evidence supporting plaintiffs' theory that defendants entered into the alleged conspiracy also creates a genuine issue of fact as to whether defendants agreed to dump* [*consumer electronic products*] *on the United States market with the specific intent to destroy or injure an industry in the United States'.* [citation] *Since the Sherman Act conspiracy charge failed in the Supreme Court, our holding on the Antidumping Act conspiracy claim must fail with it. The Antidumping Act claims against individual Japanese manufacturers are equally vulnerable because we relied, in reversing summary judgment on those claims, on the evidence tending to show that the*

---

[157] *In re Japanese Electronic Products III*, *Op. Cit.*, p. 46.
[158] *Matsushita Electrical*, *Op. Cit.*, at 593.

individual manufacturers joined in a conspiracy to sell in the American market at predatory prices [...]."[159]

3.190 The European Communities contends that it is evident from the foregoing that the reasoning of the Court of Appeals is narrowly logical:

(a) Based on a plenary review of the factual record, the Supreme Court has held that there is no triable issue of fact as regards the Sherman Act claims;

(b) the Third Circuit Court of Appeals held in an earlier opinion that the evidence in the factual record in the case supporting the finding of a violation of the Sherman Act is the same evidence which could support findings of an agreement by the Japanese exporters to engage in conduct infringing the 1916 Act, and of individual infringements of the 1916 Act by them;

(c) therefore, following the Supreme Court's ruling, and in light of its earlier insistence that the factual basis for the Sherman Act claims and the 1916 Act claims was identical, the Court of Appeals considered to be compelled to dismiss the 1916 Act claims.

3.191 For the European Communities, it is clear that the Third Circuit Court of Appeals in no way held that there is a general requirement, as a matter of statutory interpretation, to prove pricing below cost and a reasonable prospect of recoupment in relation to claims made under the 1916 Act where the claim is based on specific intent to destroy or injure a US industry. Further confirmation is given by the fact that no subsequent court has ever sought to give to the 1986 opinion of the Third Circuit in *In re Japanese Electronic Products III* case the meaning which the United States tries to give it.

3.192 In the view of the European Communities, the decisive feature of the *Zenith III* litigation is that in that specific case the 1916 Act claim had been discussed on the basis of the same evidence which was dismissed for the antitrust claim. The Third Circuit Court of Appeals concluded as follows:

> "There is no *other* evidence tending to show that any of the defendants still in the case *dumped* consumer electronic products with the required intent to injure or destroy a United States industry."[160]

The European Communities considers that this statement contains the legal standard which is relevant for the 1916 Act: whether imports are dumped or not. Furthermore, the statement of the Court does not prove that a 1916 Act claim would not have been upheld if based on *other* evidence or arguments, and this irrespective of the fate of possible claims of antitrust nature. In other words, if there had been other evidence, the Third Circuit Court of Appeals could have found a violation of the 1916 Act even though there was no violation of antitrust law.

3.193 The **United States** submits that the European Communities' analysis of the 1986 *In re Japanese Electronic Products III* decision is untenable. In finding that the

---

159 *In re Japanese Electronic Products III, Op. Cit.*, pp. 47-48 (emphasis added by the European Communities).

160 *Ibid.*, p. 48 (emphasis added by the European Communities).

evidence in the record did not support a claim under the 1916 Act because it was the same evidence the Supreme Court had held to be legally insufficient under the Sherman Act, the Third Circuit Court of Appeals necessarily applied the same legal standard. The reason why the evidence was insufficient under the 1916 Act was because there were no facts in the record that could satisfy the legal standard applied by the Court. And the legal standard that was applied by the Third Circuit in that case was the same as the one applied by the Supreme Court to the Sherman Act claims - namely, that there must be evidence of below cost pricing and possibility of recoupment.

3.194 The United States further points out that even the author of the law review note which the European Communities attached to its second submission agrees with its reasoning. The author states:

> "On remand, the Third Circuit failed to acknowledge any significant differences between a 1916 Act claim and a Sherman Act predatory pricing claim, holding that '[s]ince the Sherman Act conspiracy charged failed in the Supreme Court, our holding on the Antidumping Act conspiracy claim must fail with it.' *This decision implies that a 1916 Act defendant must have a reasonable prospect of recouping its lost profits before "predatory" intent can rationally be attributed to it.*"[161]

(v) Helmac Products Corp. v. Roth (Plastics) Corp.

3.195 The **European Communities** contends that the *Helmac I* case is far from categorical on whether the "nature" of the 1916 Act is that of a classical antitrust law such as the Sherman Act or the Robinson-Patman Act.[162] The fact that the 1916 Act has objectives other than protecting competition is confirmed by the statement in *Helmac I* that "[b]esides injury to competition the Antidumping Act also provides a cause of action when defendants attempt to, among other things, injure an industry in the United States".[163]

3.196 The European Communities also notes that the Court in *Helmac I* said that :

> "This does not mean that the Antidumping Act of 1916 must be interpreted consistently with the antitrust statutes in all situations. The language differences may have serious implications in other contexts. Such a possibility is recognised in Zenith Radio. 'The principal lesson which we draw from the legislative history of the 1916 Act [...] is that the statute should be interpreted *whenever possible* to parallel the unfair competition law applicable to domestic commerce'. [citation] Despite its characterisation of the Antidumping Act of 1916 as an anti-

---

[161] Note, *Op. Cit.*, p. 1559 (footnote omitted and emphasis added by the United States).

[162] The European Communities recalls that the main point in *Helmac I* was for the Court to decide which statute of limitations is applicable to the 1916 Act, i.e. the 4 year statute of limitations of the Clayton Act or the 5 year statute of limitation of the Tariff Act.

[163] *Helmac I, Op. Cit.*, p. 575-576.

> trust statute, the Zenith Radio concluded that Congress intended to incorporate certain principles provided in the *Tariff Act* of 1913."[164]

3.197 Beyond the issue of the mere label of the 1916 Act, *Helmac I* confirms, in the view of the European Communities, such as was the case with *Zenith III*[165] that the existence of dumping, in the classical sense of the word, is a prerequisite for action under the 1916 Act :

> "While Zenith is helpful for analysis of the applicability of anti-trust law to an *anti-dumping* case under the Antidumping Act of 1916 [...]."[166]
>
> [...]
>
> "In an *anti-dumping* claim, there are two competitors, one foreign and one domestic, operating on the same level of the marketing chain. [...] Under the Robinson-Patman Act there are two levels of activity at issue."[167]

3.198 The European Communities further notes that the Court in *Helmac I* takes the view that, unlike in Robinson-Patman Act cases, the requirement that sales must take place before action is taken should not stand in 1916 Act cases:

> "There is no similar requirement in an *antidumping* claim. When one competitor unilaterally decides to lower his price with the requisite intent, that creates the violation. Thus I conclude that the actual sales requirement of a Robinson-Patman claim cannot be transferred to an *antidumping* claim."[168]

3.199 The European Communities infers from these quotations that

(a) *Helmac I* and also *Zenith III* consider that the existence of dumping, i.e. price discrimination between two different national markets, is essential to undertake action under the 1916 Act;

(b) *Helmac I* rather considers that the underlying objective of the 1916 Act is to counter dumping;

(c) therefore *Helmac I* considers that there are differences of interpretation and application between the 1916 Act and classical antitrust rules such as the Robinson-Patman Act, i.e. in the *Helmac I* case regarding whether an offer for sale is sufficient to trigger action.

3.200 The **United States** considers unsustainable the European Communities' claim that the *Helmac I* Court found that the "underlying objective of the 1916 Act is to counter dumping." The decision merely reflects that the District Court found multiple

---

164 *Helmac I, Op. Cit.*, p. 566 (emphasis added by the European Communities).

165 The European Communities recalls that the court in *In re Japanese Electronic Products II*, stated at pp. 321 and 324, that "the 1916 Act makes it illegal to dump imported goods on the US market with the purpose of destroying or injuring US industry. [...] The first element necessary to a finding of dumping under the 1916 Act is proof that a price differential exists between two comparable products, one of which is imported or sold in the US and the other of which is sold in the exporting country."

166 *Helmac I, Op. Cit.*, p. 573 (emphasis added by the European Communities).

167 *Ibid.*, p. 574 (emphasis added by the European Communities).

168 *Helmac I, Op. Cit.*, p. 574 (emphasis added by the European Communities).

statutory objectives, all of which, broadly speaking, can be considered to come within "competition policy". Moreover, a review of the decision shows that the European Communities' assertion is contradicted by the facts. As the European Communities has noted, the *Helmac I* Court, citing the *Zenith III* decision, exhorted that the 1916 Act, "should be interpreted whenever possible to parallel the 'unfair competition' law applicable to domestic commerce."[169] In any event, the *Helmac I* Court's statement that the 1916 Act is not required to be interpreted consistent with other antitrust laws is not relevant to the Panel's analysis. The relevant point is that the 1916 Act is susceptible to a WTO-consistent interpretation and, in fact, has been so interpreted to date.

(vi) Geneva Steel Corp. v. Ranger Steel Supply Corp. and Wheeling-Pittsburgh v. Mitsui & Co.

3.201 The **European Communities** argues that the *Geneva Steel* and *Wheeling-Pittsburgh* cases have confirmed the close link between the 1916 Act and the Trade Act of 1930 as amended, which provides for application of anti-dumping duties. For example, in the most recent case, the *Wheeling-Pittsburgh* case, the Court held:

> "Under the United States Constitution, only Congress and the President may regulate international trade. Congress has enacted both [the 1916 Act] as well as the Trade Act of 1930, as amended, [citation]. [The 1916 Act] permits any party injured by international dumping to bring a lawsuit in federal court and recover triple the amount of damages suffered, together with attorney's fees. [...] The Trade Act permits the United States International Trade Commission, upon a finding of dumping, to file a complaint on behalf of an entire industry. Based upon a finding of dumping, the United States Commerce Department is authorized to increase the tariff charged on any unlawfully dumped foreign goods in an amount which would raise the cost of the imported product to the fair market price."[170]

3.202 The European Communities further argues that, unlike the other cases quoted by the United States, the *Geneva Steel* and *Wheeling-Pittsburgh* cases squarely address the nature of the 1916 Act, and do so from the point of view of whether antitrust predation standards should be read into the specific requirements of the 1916 Act. They hold that such standards need not be met as regards the specific intent to destroy or injure a US industry. The *Zenith III* case did not hold to the contrary. The earlier case law does discuss the legislative intent of Congress, but not, as the United States claims, "the interpretation of the intent element of the 1916 Act". Consequently, the 1916 Act has a protectionist component that prohibits dumping designed to injure the domestic industry. The following passage of the *Geneva Steel* decision confirms this:

---

[169] *Ibid.*, p. 566.

[170] *Wheeling-Pittsburgh Steel Corp. v. Mitsui & Co.*, 1999 WL 38856, (S.D. Ohio), 22 January 1999.

> "[T]he language of the Act itself, in addition to prohibiting antitrust violations, clearly and literally prohibits non-antitrust and no-predatory pricing conduct. By the words it chose, Congress protected United States industries from unfair dumping, whether the dumper possessed predatory intent or not."[171]

3.203 The European Communities does acknowledge, however, that both District Court rulings establish a distinction between "dumping undertaken with the intent to injure industry", i.e. the first three intents, and "dumping undertaken with anti-competitive predatory intent", i.e. the last two intents. Both Courts admit that the last two types of intent under the 1916 Act, i.e. intent to restrain or monopolise commerce, have similarities to domestic antitrust law and do not exclude that the *Brooke Group* requirements may well apply here. They do not further examine this issue, however, as these grounds were not invoked by the respective plaintiffs. Both Courts also point out that their reasoning is supported by the majority of case law, particularly *Helmac I*, though with the exception of the *Zenith III* case.

3.204 The European Communities argues, however, that this distinction made by both District Courts between two kinds of dumping is based exclusively upon concepts and principles of US antitrust law, namely the "intent" that the defendants must be shown to have. Under Article VI of the GATT 1994, dumping is not a matter of intent. It is a matter of selling at a price lower than the one in the country of exportation, and that is precisely the conduct that needs to be shown in the first place under the 1916 Act. The showing of intent under the 1916 Act only comes after "dumping" has been established.

3.205 In response, the **United States** first of all notes that it is the view of the *Geneva Steel* preliminary decision that the 1916 Act has five alternative intents. This does not represent the view of the highest court in the United States to have considered this issue.

3.206 The United States further notes, as a threshold matter, that the *Geneva Steel* and *Wheeling-Pittsburgh* decisions - district court rulings on motions to dismiss - are interlocutory decisions and thus neither final nor conclusive under US law. Therefore they cannot, at the present time, be considered by the Panel as authoritative interpretations of US law. Both cases are currently in the discovery stage, which means that no trial has taken place. A federal district court decision on a motion to dismiss is considered as "final" only once all of the claims in the case have been tried or otherwise adjudicated and the district court has entered judgment.[172] At that point, the district court decision becomes "appealable," meaning that a party to the case may take an appeal to a circuit court of appeals. If no party appeals the case, the district court's decision becomes "conclusive" and therefore binding on the parties. However, even a final district court decision is not binding on other district courts or appellate

---

[171] *Geneva Steel, Op. Cit.*, p. 1217.

[172] The United States refers to *Cohen v. Beneficial Industrial Loan Corp.*, 337 U.S. 541, 545-47 (1949); *International Society for Krishna Consciousness, Inc. v. Air Canada*, 727 F.2d 253, 254-55 (2d Cir. 1984).

courts and it does not have persuasive value unless it has been soundly reasoned.[173] If a party does appeal the case, the appellate court, in turn, will conduct a review and either affirm, modify or reverse the district court's decision. The appellate court's decision then is the "conclusive" decision in the case, assuming that it is not subsequently reviewed by the US Supreme Court.[174] A "conclusive" appellate court decision is binding precedent on all of the district courts in the appellate court's circuit, and on other panels of judges sitting in the same court of appeals, but offers only persuasive precedent to courts in other circuits.[175]

3.207 The United States considers, moreover, that, under WTO jurisprudence, it is premature for the European Communities to base any aspect of its challenge to the 1916 Act under Article VI:2 of the GATT 1994 on the *Geneva Steel* or *Wheeling-Pittsburgh* decisions. Just as with discretionary authority which the executive may or may not exercise,[176] the mere possibility that the District Courts' decisions in those cases will become final and conclusive under US law is not enough to allow either decision to form any basis of a Panel finding that the 1916 Act is inconsistent with Article VI:2 of the GATT 1994. As long as it remains possible that either the District Court or the Circuit Court, on appeal, will interpret the 1916 Act in a manner that is entirely consistent with Article VI:2 of the GATT 1994, neither decision should be considered.

3.208 The United States also is of the view that, even if the Panel were to consider them, it may only consider how these preliminary decisions affect the prevailing interpretation in the United States. It cannot consider whether these decisions constitute violations themselves because the Panel's terms of reference do not include decisions as measures being challenged. The European Communities has challenged the 1916 Act as such, and not any specific application of the 1916 Act.

3.209 The United States also argues that, in any event, the *Geneva Steel* and *Wheeling-Pittsburgh* decisions do not treat the 1916 Act as an anti-dumping statute. More specifically, these decisions do not interpret the 1916 Act in a way that renders it a statute addressing the "dumping" and "injury" condemned by Article VI. These decisions differ from the other court decisions only in their more expansive reading of one element of a 1916 Act claim, i.e. the element setting forth the requisite intent. In fact, in *Wheeling-Pittsburgh*, the Court ruled that a showing of "predatory" intent is required although it is not necessary to show the possibility of recoupment. Under the *Geneva Steel* decision, a complainant could show either the traditional antitrust predatory intent or an intent to injure a US industry. Just like all of the other court decisions, however, both Courts require the complainant to show intent as well as

---

[173] The United States refers to *Threadgill v. Armstrong World Industries Inc.*, 928 F.2d 1366, 1371 (3d Cir. 1991).

[174] The United States refers to *Metropolitan Water Co. v. Kaw Valley Drainage District*, 223 U.S. 519, 524 (1912).

[175] The United States notes that there are twelve federal court circuits in the United States. Each district court is assigned to a circuit for purposes of appeal.

[176] The United States refers to, e.g., *United States - Tobacco, Op. Cit.*, paras. 118 and 121; *United States - Restrictions on Imports of Tuna*, unadopted, dated 3 September 1991, DS21/R, paras. 5.20-5.21; *United States - Superfund, Op. Cit.*, para. 5.2.9.

each of the other elements of a 1916 Act claim. Thus, even under these decisions, the basic differences between the 1916 Act and the Anti-Dumping Agreement remain.

3.210 The United States contends, finally, that the conclusion that the 1916 Act is not an anti-dumping statute remains sound even if the 1916 Act could be considered to have a "protectionist" component. To begin with, the concept of "protectionism" here means a focus on the protection of industry. This component of the 1916 Act still can be said to reflect antitrust standards of earlier eras, such as those found in the 1936 Robinson-Patman Act. Indeed, many governments, including the United States, continue to maintain statutes today that in some ways protect competitors. The fact that a measure may include protection for competitors does not remove the measure from the category of antitrust laws.

3.211 The **European Communities** notes that, according to the United States, the *Geneva Steel* and *Wheeling-Pittsburgh* rulings are not "authoritative". However, the United States cannot dispute, and does not deny, the fact that they are not merely hypothetical and that they are there. H For the European Communities, that is sufficient to make them relevant. Also, the mere fact that these cases depart from what the United States appears to describe as being the most authoritative ruling as yet, i.e. *Zenith III*, rather reveals the unauthoritative nature of this case.

3.212 The **United States** replies that, even if the two preliminary decisions in *Geneva Steel* and *Wheeling-Pittsburgh* are considered by the Panel in the context of analysing possible interpretations of the 1916 Act, they do not change the fact that the 1916 Act is susceptible to an interpretation that is WTO-consistent. This is demonstrated through the *Zenith III* line of cases as well as the other decisions applying antitrust principles to decide the issue at hand. In any event, the *Geneva Steel* and *Wheeling-Pittsburgh* decisions differed from the *Zenith III* line of cases only in their characterization of the intent requirement. This interpretation, however, does not transform the 1916 Act into an anti-dumping statute. Both Courts still required that the requisite specific intent to injure or destroy be pleaded as well as the other elements of the 1916 Act. In *Wheeling-Pittsburgh*, the Court expressly described the intent required as "predatory intent".[177] Furthermore, neither Court required that the plaintiff plead and prove material injury to the domestic industry as required in dumping.

E. Violation of Article VI:2 of the GATT 1994

1. General Arguments

3.213 The **European Communities** submits that the WTO anti-dumping rules, laid down in Article VI of the GATT 1994 and in the Anti-Dumping Agreement, establish a comprehensive and complete multilateral regime to define and address the issue of dumping in international trade. This comprehensive nature also pertains to the regulation of the measures that can be taken once injurious dumping within the meaning of Article VI of the GATT 1994 is found. In that case, as is made clear by Article VI:2 of the GATT 1994, "[i]n order to offset or prevent dumping, a contracting party may levy on any dumped product an anti-dumping duty not greater in

[177] The United States refers to *Wheeling-Pittsburgh, Op. Cit.*, p. 604.

amount than the margin of dumping in respect of such product". This exclusive character cannot but be clearer if the several provisions included in Article VI are examined together. That Article, *inter alia,* assigns a specific function to anti-dumping measures and repeatedly sets precise maximum quantitative limits to their permissible level. The function of anti-dumping measures is to "offset" dumping or "prevent" dumping in the case of threat of material injury. This is then further emphasized in Article 9.1 of the Anti-Dumping Agreement, where it is suggested to limit the duty to the amount necessary to offset the *injury* suffered by the domestic industry, which may be less than the full dumping margin. The imposition of duties is additionally limited in those paragraphs of Article VI of the GATT 1994 which prohibit parties from cumulating anti-dumping and countervailing duties to counter the same practice. It cannot go unnoticed that all those limitations and qualifications applying to the imposition of anti-dumping duties would have absolutely no purpose and absolutely no result if WTO Members were free to choose any other type of measure and then with no maximum limits as to amount and impact.

3.214 The European Communities recalls that the remedial measures provided for by the 1916 Anti-Dumping Act are treble damages and/or criminal penalties. These remedies are not duties. They do not fall into the only type of measures allowed under multilateral anti-dumping rules to counter dumping practices, nor are they authorised by other WTO provisions.

3.215 The European Communities contends that recognition of the fact that duties are the sole allowed remedies was again made by the US authorities. The testimony of USTR General Counsel Alan Holmer to the US Senate Finance Committee on 18 July 1986 contains the following portions:

> "The Antidumping Code, however, expressly *limits the* remedy for dumping to the prospective collection of antidumping duties *to offset the margin* of dumping. Article 16 of the Code states: 'No specific action against dumping of exports from another Party can be taken except in accordance with the provisions of the General Agreement, as interpreted by this Agreement.' *This language prohibits the use of additional sanctions, such as fines, embargoes, imprisonment or other draconian measures.*
>
> [...]
>
> It has also been argued that "the Code also does not affect other actions that are not in the nature of 'duties' that may affect goods that are 'dumped.'" The thrust of this argument is that if a government chooses to address dumping through the imposition of duties, it must do so under the procedures set out in the Antidumping Code, but at the same time, a government is free to use any other means that it chooses to punish dumping. This interpretation of Article 16, however, appears rather implausible if one considers its consequences. Under this view, *a foreign government would be perfectly within its rights to convict an American businessman of dumping and imprison him for a period of 10 years, since the government would have a right to use whatever alternative sanctions for dumping it pleased.*
>
> *It follows that Article 16 must stand for the proposition that a government can provide its citizens one, and only one, remedy for dump-*

> *ing. That remedy is the collection of duties in a manner consistent with the Antidumping Code.* We believe that our reading flows logically from the letter and spirit of the GATT and the Antidumping Code. It also follows that S. 1655 would violate the Code by imposing additional sanctions on top of normal antidumping duties.
>
> *While the same criticism can be leveled at the Antidumping Act of 1916, that Act was 'grandfathered' by the Protocol of Provisional Application when the U.S. joined the GATT in 1947.*"[178]

The European Communities adds that Article 16 of the 1979 Anti-Dumping Code is identical to Article 18 of the WTO Anti-Dumping Agreement.

3.216 The European Communities maintains that the compensatory, remedial objective of the measure authorized in Article VI of the GATT 1994 assumes that only a quantifiable price measure may offset a precisely quantified dumping margin or, possibly, a lower injury level. In other words, only a measure increasing the costs of the exporters up to the point of somehow forcing them to raise prices on their export markets where they have been found to dump is really fit to "offset" dumping. The remedial objective cannot be served by criminal liability and sanctions when their result is to "deprive of liberty" one of the economic actors involved in trade in foreign goods, such as importers in the case of the 1916 Act. As to pecuniary criminal sanctions, even if they were to be within the maximum level imposed by Article VI of the GATT 1994, the additional criminal liability element involved is already beyond the remedial objective described in Article VI and in the Anti-Dumping Agreement. It will obviously also be beyond that objective whenever the level of the penalty exceeds the dumping margin.

3.217 The **United States** argues that, for the European Communities' claim under Article VI:2 to succeed, it must establish two points: first, it must establish that Article VI:2 provides that anti-dumping duties are the sole remedy for dumping; and, second, it must establish that the 1916 Act is the type of measure governed by Article VI and the Anti-Dumping Agreement. The European Communities' claim under Article VI:2 is defective from the outset because nothing in Article VI:2 addresses whether anti-dumping duties are the sole remedy for dumping. Even assuming *arguendo* that Article VI:2 provides the sole remedy for dumping, the European Communities' claim still fails because the 1916 Act, as a statute directed at anti-competitive conduct, is not governed by Article VI of the GATT 1994 or the Anti-Dumping Agreement.

2. *The Text and Relevant Context of Article VI:2 of the GATT 1994*

3.218 The **United States** is of the view that the European Communities' claim fails at the outset because nothing in Article VI:2 of the GATT 1994[179] addresses whether anti-dumping duties are the exclusive remedy for dumping.

---

[178] Testimony of 18 July 1986 of USTR General Counsel Alan Holmer to the US Senate Finance Committee, pp. 4-5 (emphasis added by the European Communities).

[179] Para. 2 of Article VI provides as follows:

3.219 The United States notes that paragraph 2 simply states that a Member "may" levy an anti-dumping duty to offset or prevent dumping. It does not in any way suggest that remedies for dumping other than anti-dumping duties are prohibited. For example, it does not state that a Member "may only" levy anti-dumping duties. If the word "only" had been intended, the text could and would have said so. The European Communities, while focusing on the phrase "in order to offset or prevent dumping," ignores the fact that the directive in the paragraph is permissive and unqualified.

3.220 In the view of the **European Communities**, the United States is reading Article VI:2 of the GATT 1994 out of context and contrary to its clear object and purpose. A provision in an Agreement such as the GATT 1994 stating that something "may" be done does not necessarily mean that any alternative action, which could be more or less restrictive of trade, is in no way restricted. Whether it has this meaning or whether it implies on the contrary that no other action may be taken depends on the context in which the word "may" is being used.

3.221 The European Communities points out that the context of Article VI comprises Articles III to XIX of the GATT 1994, all of which regulate problems in international trade. Thus, Article VI regulates the action that members may take against dumping and the conditions under which they may take this action. Article VI:2 expressly states that the action which may be taken is to levy an anti-dumping duty. It is contrary to the object and purpose of Article VI to argue, as the United States appears to, that nothing in Article VI restricts the ability of members to take other action to prevent dumping, for example imprisoning the importers.

3.222 The **United States** considers that the European Communities' argument relating to the meaning of the term "may" is defective because the European Communities disregards the immediate context provided by paragraphs 3 to 6 of Article VI and instead argues that the context of Article VI comprises Articles III to XIX of the GATT 1994, without, however, explaining why this turns "may" in Article VI:2 into "shall" or "may only."

3.223 In the opinion of the United States, it is significant that the use in Article VI:2 of the permissive term "may" contrasts with the four immediately following paragraphs of Article VI, where express prohibitions on the imposition of duties are stated. In each of these paragraphs, Article VI uses the mandatory term "shall" and clearly conveys what is not permitted. For example, paragraph 5 provides as follows:

> "*No* product of the territory of any Member imported into the territory of any other Member *shall* be subject to both anti-dumping and countervailing duties to compensate for the same situation of dumping or export subsidization."[180]

3.224 The United States notes that paragraph 6(a) of Article VI uses a similar formulation:

> "In order to offset or prevent dumping, a contracting party may levy on any dumped product an anti-dumping duty not greater in amount than the margin of dumping in respect of such product. For purposes of this Article, the margin of dumping is the price difference determined in accordance with the provisions of para. 1."

[180] Emphasis added by the United States.

> "*No* contracting party *shall* levy any anti-dumping [...] duty on the importation of any product of the territory of another Member unless it determines that the effect of the dumping [...] is such as to cause or threaten material injury to an established domestic industry, or is such as to retard materially the establishment of a domestic industry."[181]

3.225 The United States asserts, moreover, that the only WTO provisions that arguably address the issue of any possible limitations on the remedies available for dumping are found not in the GATT 1994, but rather in the Anti-Dumping Agreement. The United States does not, however, examine the possible relevance of any provisions of the Anti-Dumping Agreement because the European Communities has not brought any claims under those provisions before the Panel.

3.226 The **European Communities** responds that words must always be interpreted in context. The relevant context in the present case is Article VI of the GATT 1994, which seeks to regulate the problem of dumping, just as other GATT 1994 provisions regulate other problems. The US approach to context is simplistic. It merely points out that paragraphs 3 to 6 of Article VI contain the word "shall" and Article VI:2 does not. It pays no attention to the structure of Article VI. Article VI of the GATT 1994 starts off in paragraph 1 with a definition of a problem, then specifies the action that may be taken to combat it and then imposes certain restrictions on the imposition of those duties.

3.227 The European Communities further contends that the only reason why paragraph 2 of Article VI uses the word "may" is because it was not intended that WTO Members should be obliged to impose anti-dumping duties, i.e. to take action against dumping at all. The ordinary meaning of Article VI:2 when read in context and having regard to the structure of Article VI is that other remedies than duties, such as fines and treble damages, cannot be imposed.

3. *The Negotiating History*

3.228 The **European Communities** asserts that its view that duties are the sole allowed remedies is borne out by the negotiating history of Article VI of the GATT 1994. According to the European Communities, despite attempts by some contracting parties to the GATT 1947 to provide for other types of offsetting measures, both during the preparatory work and the Review Session of 1955, Article VI was intentionally limited to anti-dumping duties.

3.229 The European Communities points out that the original text of Article VI of the GATT 1947 - that is, the text actually adopted in 1947 - did contain an explicit prohibition of anti-dumping measures other than duties. The structure of the original Article VI was different from what it is now. If the original text is examined, it is seen that it started with a prohibition of duties above a certain level of remedy authorized[182] and ended with the explicit statement that duties were the sole allowed remedy.

---

[181] Emphasis added by the United States.

[182] The European Communities refers to the language of the original text of Article VI:1 which reads:

3.230 The European Communities recalls that the revised text, which originated in Article 34 of the Havana Charter, followed a different drafting technique. Under the revised approach, an explicit rule making duties the exclusive remedy was no longer considered necessary. It is instructive, in this regard, to recall the explanation given by the 1948 Working Party on "Modifications to the General Agreement" for changing the text of Article VI of the GATT 1947. The Report of the Working Party notes in this regard:

> "While agreeing that there is no substantive difference between Article VI of the General Agreement and Article 34 of the Charter, the working party recommends the replacement of that article, as the text adopted at Havana contains a useful indication of the principle governing the operation of that article and constitutes a clearer formulation of the rules laid down in that article. The working party, endorsing the views expressed by [the Subcommittee on Article 34 at the Havana Conference] agreed that measures other than compensatory anti-dumping and countervailing duties may not be applied to counteract dumping or subsidization except in so far as such other measures are permitted under other provisions of the General Agreement."[183]

3.231 The European Communities takes the view that, by expressly stating that there was no substantive change, the Working Party has made it quite clear that there was no intention, in changing the text of Article VI of the GATT 1947, to allow other remedies than duties against dumping.

3.232 The European Communities also recalls another relevant statement of the same Working Party. The Report of the Working Party notes that it "[...] agreed that measures other than compensatory anti-dumping and countervailing duties may not be applied to counteract dumping or subsidization except insofar as such other measures are permitted under other provisions of the General Agreement."[184] In doing so, it confirmed, in the view of the European Communities, the "definite understanding" of the relevant Subcommittee of the Havana Conference, from which the text of Article VI was taken. Therefore, it results not only from the negotiating history of the GATT 1947, but also from subsequent interpretation that duties are the only authorized remedy to counter dumping practices under Article VI of the GATT 1994.

The European Communities further points out that the United States itself acknowledged that the negotiating history of Article VI confirms the exclusivity of the duty remedy. As can be seen from the report of the panel on *United States - Anti-Dumping Duties on Salmon from Norway,* the United States argued before that panel as follows:

> "No anti-dumping duty shall be levied on any product of the territory of any contracting party imported into the territory of any other contracting party in excess of an amount equal to the margin of dumping under which such product is being imported [...]."

[183] BISD II/41, 42, para. 12.

[184] Reprinted in GATT, *Analytical Index: Guide to GATT Law and Practice* (1994), pp. 216-217.

> "Regarding the negotiating history of the General Agreement, the United States also observed that injurious dumping had been viewed with such concern during the original GATT negotiations that proposals had been considered to permit imposition of tougher countermeasures than merely offsetting duties. However, in the end the Article VI remedy *had been limited to such duties*."[185]

3.233 The **United States** disputes that the negotiating history confirms the European Communities' view. The negotiating history of Article VI shows that GATT 1947 originally included a paragraph in Article VI - paragraph 7 - which provided in pertinent part:

> "No measures other than anti-dumping [...] duties shall be applied by any contracting party [...] for the purpose of offsetting dumping [...]."[186]

3.234 The United States recalls, however, that paragraph 7 existed for only about one year. Article VI was modified soon after GATT 1947 came into force, with the initial relevant discussions on this matter taking place in early 1948 during the so-called "Havana Conference," which addressed the draft charter of the International Trade Organization (hereinafter the "ITO"), a document which was similar in many respects to the GATT 1947. At that time, members of the Subcommittee on Article 34 considered a provision in the draft ITO charter, identical to the original paragraph 7 of Article VI of the GATT 1947, and decided to remove it. The record of these discussions explains:

> "The Subcommittee agreed to the deletion of paragraph 6 of the Geneva draft which expressly prohibited the use of measures other than anti-dumping or countervailing duties against dumping or subsidization. It did so with the definite understanding that measures other than compensatory anti-dumping [...] duties may not be applied to counteract dumping [...] except insofar as such other measures are permitted under other provisions of the Charter."[187]

3.235 The United States further notes that, later that year, during the Second Session of the GATT 1947, the Working Party on Modifications to the General Agreement referenced the work of the ITO Subcommittee on Article 34 and agreed, *inter alia*, to replace the entire then-existing Article VI with its counterpart under the draft ITO charter, which in final form contained no provision like paragraph 7 of Article VI of the GATT 1947. In a report, the Working Party explained:

> "The working party, endorsing the views expressed by [the ITO Subcommittee on Article 34], agreed that measures other than compensatory anti-dumping [...] duties may not be applied to counteract

---

185 *United States - Anti-Dumping Duties on Salmon from Norway*, *Op. Cit.*, para. 75 (footnote omitted; emphasis added by the European Communities).

186 Reproduced in GATT, *Analytical Index: Guide to GATT Law and Practice*, 6th ed. (1995), p. 238.

187 Reports of Committees and Principal Sub-Committees, ICITO I/8, p. 74, para. 25 (Geneva, September 1948), quoted in GATT, *Analytical Index: Guide to GATT Law and Practice*, *Op. Cit.*, p. 238.

dumping [...] except insofar as such other measures are permitted under other provisions of the General Agreement."[188]

3.236 The United States points out that, many years later, a paragraph similar in many respects to the original paragraph 7 of Article VI of the GATT 1947 appeared in Article 16.1 of the Tokyo Round Anti-Dumping Code. It provided:

"No specific action against dumping of exports from another Party can be taken except in accordance with the provisions of the General Agreement, as interpreted by this Agreement."

3.237 The United States also recalls that in a footnote to Article 16.1 it was stated that Article 16.1 "is not intended to preclude action under other relevant provisions of the General Agreement, as appropriate." A provision virtually identical to Article 16.1 of the Tokyo Round Anti-Dumping Code now appears in the Anti-Dumping Agreement, in Article 18.1, except that now it refers to the GATT 1994 instead of the GATT 1947.

3.238 In the **European Communities'** view, the introduction of an explicit prohibition of measures other than duties in Article 16.1 of the Tokyo Round Anti-Dumping Code cannot be argued to have changed the meaning of Article VI of the GATT 1947.[189] On the contrary, it confirmed that meaning. Thus, there does not appear to be a rule in Article VI that is not either referred to or repeated in the Code. The reason for this was that the Code and the GATT 1947 were distinct legal sets of rules, with different membership and separate means of enforcement. A claimant under the Code needed to be able to invoke any rule in Article VI. If repetition was necessary for the express provisions of Article VI, it was *a fortiori* necessary for those which had been recognized to be implied in such article. In the light of the foregoing it is therefore not surprising that the Code repeated explicitly the implicit Article VI rule that duties are the exclusive remedy for dumping.

3.239 The European Communities further submits that when the Tokyo Round Code was modified and transposed into the WTO Agreement's text, what happened was a conversion of an earlier treaty, and the non-removal rather than insertion of a clause. It would have been a rather unusual step to remove an explicit clause from an agreement on the basis that the point was implicit. It would have looked rather like a deliberate repeal of the rule.

3.240 The **United States** replies that, in any event, the negotiating history of Article VI does not indicate which of the provisions in Article VI of the GATT 1947 is the one that made the original paragraph 7 unnecessary by implicitly establishing that anti-dumping duties are the exclusive remedy for dumping. There is no indication that the provision in question is paragraph 2.

---

188 BISD II/41, 42, para. 12.

189 The European Communities refers to J. H. Jackson, *World Trade and the Law of GATT*, The Bobbs-Merrill Co. (1969), pp. 405-408, 420.

4. *The Relevance of Article 18.1 of the Anti-Dumping Agreement*

3.241 The **European Communities** contends that the adoption of the WTO Anti-Dumping Agreement has not changed the content of Article VI in respect of the limitation to duties because it includes no derogation or conflicting rule on this point. To the contrary, the WTO Anti-Dumping Agreement, and specifically Article 18.1 thereof, does nothing but confirm Article VI in this respect.

3.242 The European Communities therefore considers that it is sufficient to rely on Article VI to claim that the 1916 Act violates WTO rules by providing for remedies other than duties in order to counter dumping practices.

3.243 The **United States** rejects the European Communities' argument that Article VI:2 of the GATT 1994 makes anti-dumping duties the exclusive remedy for dumping and that it is therefore sufficient for the Panel to rely solely on that provision for this proposition. Moreover, the European Communities' view that Article 18.1 of the WTO Anti-Dumping Agreement "does nothing but confirm Article VI in this respect" is also wrong.

3.244 The United States argues, first, that the negotiating history of Article VI does not indicate which of the provisions in Article VI of the GATT 1947 is the one that made the original paragraph 7 unnecessary by implicitly establishing that anti-dumping duties are the exclusive remedy for dumping. There is no indication that the provision in question is paragraph 2.

3.245 The United States notes, second, that during the Tokyo Round, a provision wholly separate from Article VI:2 of the GATT 1947 - Article 16.1 of the Tokyo Round Anti-Dumping Code - was adopted to deal directly with the issue of whether, and to what extent, anti-dumping duties are the exclusive remedy for dumping. This provision, like its successor, Article 18.1 of the WTO Anti-Dumping Agreement, uses carefully crafted language to express the intended limitation regarding remedies other than anti-dumping duties, and it is much more precise than any rule that could be derived from the negotiating history of Article VI. The inclusion of these later provisions would seem to suggest the opposite of the European Communities' argument. That is, the fact that Article 16.1 of the Tokyo Round Anti-Dumping Code and its successor, Article 18.1 of the Anti-Dumping Agreement, needed to be added is evidence that Article VI:2 does not mean what the European Communities claims. Otherwise, these later provisions would be redundant and unnecessary. Interpretations which render parts of a treaty superfluous should be avoided.

3.246 The United States recalls, finally, that with the Uruguay Round and the coming into force of the GATT 1994 and the WTO Anti-Dumping Agreement, yet another fundamental change took place that further renders the European Communities' reliance on the negotiating history of Article VI inapposite. Specifically, the relationship between Article VI and the Anti-Dumping Agreement is different from the relationship that had existed between Article VI and the Tokyo Round Anti-Dumping Code. While it previously was possible for a panel to find a violation based independently on a paragraph in Article VI of the GATT 1947, it is now no longer possible for a panel to do so. Any violation must now include an invocation of a particular provision of the Anti-Dumping Agreement. In *Brazil - Measures Affecting Desiccated Coconut*[190], the Appellate Body explained this fundamental change in the context of considering whether Article VI of the GATT 1994 may be applied independently of the Agreement on Subsidies and Countervailing Measures (hereinafter the "SCM Agreement"). In support of its finding that Article VI may *not* be independently applied, the Appellate Body reasoned that Article VI of the GATT 1994 and the SCM Agreement now constitute a "package of rights and obligations," given the structure of the WTO Agreement, to which the GATT 1994 and the SCM Agreement are annexed.[191] The Appellate Body, quoting from the panel report, stated that the SCM Agreement and Article VI "together define, clarify and in some cases modify the whole package of rights and obligations of a potential user of countervailing measures."[192] Like Article VI of the GATT 1994 and the SCM Agreement, Article VI of the GATT 1994 and the Anti-Dumping Agreement constitute a package of rights and obligations regarding the use of anti-dumping measures. The plain language of Articles 1 and 18.1 shows that these provisions do not merely interpret Article VI, but, rather, go beyond by imposing a limitation on anti-dumping measures where Article VI:2 has none. It is therefore not proper for a panel to apply Article VI independently.

3.247 The United States notes that, in the present case, inexplicably, the European Communities has excluded from its panel request what may be the only relevant part of the package of rights and obligations regarding the use of anti-dumping measures, i.e. Article 18.1 of the Anti-Dumping Agreement. Indeed, regardless of whether it is the only relevant part of this package, it certainly is an essential part of it. In addition, if the Panel were to entertain a claim solely based upon Article VI:2 of the GATT 1994, it would run the very real risk of inconsistent decisions when one panel reviews a claim solely based on Article VI:2 and another panel reviews a claim under Article 18.1 of the Anti-Dumping Agreement.

3.248 The United States submits that, for all these reasons, the Panel should reject the European Communities' argument that Article VI:2, *standing alone*, mandates that anti-dumping duties are the only remedy for dumping.

3.249 In response, the **European Communities** notes that the United States seems to accept that Article VI does not allow remedies against dumping other than duties when it insists "that the negotiating history of Article VI does not indicate which of the provisions in Article VI of the GATT 1947 is the one that made the original paragraph 7 unnecessary by implicitly establishing that anti-dumping duties are the exclusive remedy for dumping". Moreover, in relation to the US argument that "there is no indication that the provision in question is paragraph 2", the European Communities inquires which provision it could be other than paragraph 2 read in the context of the other provisions of Article VI.

---

190 Appellate Body Report, *Brazil - Measures Affecting Desiccated Coconut* ("*Brazil - Desiccated Coconut*"), WT/DS22/AB/R, adopted 20 March 1997, DSR 1997:I, 167.

191 The United States refers to *Brazil - Desiccated Coconut, supra,* footnote 190, at 182

192 *Brazil - Desiccated Coconut, supra,* footnote 190, at 182, quoting from para. 246 of the panel report.

3.250 Regarding Article 16.1 of the Tokyo Round Anti-Dumping Code, the European Communities reiterates its view that the introduction of an explicit prohibition of measures other than duties in Article 16.1 of the Tokyo Round Anti-Dumping Code cannot be argued to have changed the meaning of Article VI of the GATT 1947.[193] On the contrary, it confirmed that meaning. Thus, there does not appear to be a rule in Article VI that is not either referred to or repeated in the Code. The reason for this was that the Code and the GATT 1947 were distinct legal sets of rules, with different membership and separate means of enforcement. A claimant under the Code needed to be able to invoke any rule in Article VI. If repetition was necessary for the express provisions of Article VI, it was *a fortiori* necessary for those which had been recognized to be implied in such article. In the light of the foregoing it is therefore not surprising that the Code repeated explicitly the implicit Article VI rule that duties are the exclusive remedy for dumping.

3.251 The European Communities further submits that when the Tokyo Round Code was modified and transposed into the WTO Agreement's text, what happened was a conversion of an earlier treaty, and the non-removal rather than insertion of a clause. It would have been a rather unusual step to remove an explicit clause from an agreement on the basis that the point was implicit. It would have looked rather like a deliberate repeal of the rule.

3.252 As concerns the United States' reliance on *Brazil - Desiccated Coconut*, the European Communities notes that the reference made by the Appellate Body to an indivisible relationship between Article VI of the GATT 1994 and the SCM Agreement rather supports the view that a separate citation of the Anti-Dumping Agreement in the present case is not necessary. The Appellate Body in *Brazil - Desiccated Coconut* held that Article VI cannot be read independently of the SCM Agreement and that they "together define, clarify and in some cases modify the whole package of rights and obligations [...]"[194]. The European Communities agrees that the same applies to the Anti-Dumping Agreement. Yet the United States in fact asks the Panel to do the opposite of what the Appellate Body found to be necessary. The United States seems to admit that there is within the "package" an obligation not to apply remedies other than duties against dumping but asks the Panel to only look at Article VI:2 and exclude any argument under Article 1 and 18 of the Anti-Dumping Agreement.

3.253 The European Communities argues that, at any rate, its request for a panel clearly identified a violation of the obligation not to use measures other than duties to combat dumping and considered that this obligation was implicit in Article VI:2 of the GATT 1994. If other parts of the "package" are considered relevant to this obligation they can and must be applied by the Panel, just as the panel and the Appellate Body in *Brazil - Desiccated Coconut* applied provisions of the SCM Agreement that had not been referred to in the request for establishment of that panel.

3.254 In conclusion, the European Communities reiterates its view that the provision violated is Article VI:2 of the GATT 1994. If the Panel should disagree that this is the provision which contains the clearly described violation, it should apply Article

[193] The European Communities refers to J. H. Jackson, *Op. Cit.*, pp. 405-408, 420.

[194] Appellate Body Report, *Brazil - Desiccated Coconut*, *supra*, footnote 190, at 182, quoting from para. 246 of the panel report.

18.1 of the Anti-Dumping Agreement to be faithful to the conclusions of the Appellate Body in *Brazil - Desiccated Coconut.* Article 18.1 of the Anti-Dumping Agreement is not in conflict with Article VI, as the United States has also agreed. Therefore, Article 18.1 cannot modify the meaning of Article VI.

3.255 The **United States** notes that the European Communities attempts to cure its defective panel request by suggesting that, while it is not asserting claims under Articles 1 and 18.1 of the Anti-Dumping Agreement, the Panel should consider them as merely "arguments." The Panel should reject such an attempt. The European Communities chose to rely upon Article VI:2 of the GATT 1994 for its position that Article VI and the Anti-Dumping Agreement provide the sole remedy for dumping. It could have included Articles 1 and 18.1 of the Anti-Dumping Agreement in its panel request, but, inexplicably, it chose not to. The European Communities should not be allowed to bootstrap what are in reality new claims into the present case by suggesting that they are only "arguments." For the Panel to analyse whether these newly invoked articles support the European Communities' other claims would be the same as considering them as claims themselves. In both instances, the Panel would be required to determine whether those provisions provide an exclusive remedy for dumping. The European Communities should not be allowed to so easily circumvent the requirements of the DSU.

3.256 The United States in fact takes the view that the Panel does not even have the authority to consider whether Articles 1 and 18.1 of the Anti-Dumping Agreement support the proposition that Article VI of the GATT 1994 provides the sole remedy for dumping. To do so would exceed the jurisdiction of the Panel. In *India - Patents*, the Appellate Body made clear that a panel has authority to consider only those claims which are included in the complaining party's panel request.[195] The Appellate Body stated definitively in that case that "[a] panel cannot assume jurisdiction that it does not have." Because Articles 1 and 18.1 of the Anti-Dumping Agreement were not included in the European Communities' panel request, the Panel does not have the authority to consider them.

3.257 In response to the US argument that the Panel cannot analyse whether Articles 1 and 18.1 of the Anti-Dumping Agreement support the EC position, the **European Communities** recalls that the Appellate Body in *European Communities - Bananas* stated that

> "Article 6.2 of the DSU requires that the *claims*, but not the *arguments*, must all be specified sufficiently in the request for the establishment of a panel in order to allow the defending party and any third parties to know the legal basis of the complaint."[196]

3.258 The European Communities further notes that there is nothing in the DSU that requires the *numbers* of the provisions of the covered agreements to be cited in a request for the establishment of a panel. The obligation in Article 6.2 of the DSU is to provide a brief summary of the legal basis of the complaint sufficient to state the problem clearly. The Appellate Body has merely said in *European Communities -*

[195] The United States refers to Appellate Body Report, *India - Patents, supra*, footnote 29, paras. 92-93.

[196] Appellate Body Report, *European Communities - Bananas, supra*, footnote 29, para. 143.

Bananas that citing the numbers of the provisions suffices, it has not said it is the only way to set out the legal basis.[197] There can be no doubt that the European Communities has clearly described the obligation concerned and the United States has neither contested this nor misunderstood the obligation described, it is merely disagreeing about the number to be given to it.

3.259 The **United States** rejects the EC argument that "[t]here is nothing in the DSU that requires the *numbers* of the provisions of the covered agreements to be cited in a request for the establishment of a panel." The United States wonders how a Member identifies a provision of a covered agreement other than by listing its number. The Appellate Body certainly anticipates that the complaining Member will list the number of the relevant provision when setting forth a claim. In *India - Patents*, the Appellate Body explained:

> "In *European Communities - Bananas*, we accepted the view of the panel in that case that it was "sufficient for the Complaining Parties to list the provisions of the specific agreements alleged to have been violated without setting out detailed arguments as to which specific aspects of the measures at issue relate to which specific provisions of those agreements", and we also agreed with the panel that the request in that case was sufficiently specific to comply with the "minimum standards" established by Article 6.2 of the DSU. In this case, in contrast, there is a failure to identify a specific provision of an agreement that is alleged to have been violated. This falls below the "minimum standards" that we were willing to accept in *European Communities - Bananas*."[198]

3.260 The United States recalls that, in the present case, it is not simply a matter of the European Communities' failure to identify the *number* of the provision on which it was basing its claim. The European Communities did not even identify the *covered agreement*. The European Communities recognizes that it should have identified Article 18.1 of the Anti-Dumping Agreement. Where the European Communities set forth its claim in its panel request, however, the European Communities did not merely fail to reference Article 18.1. It also failed even to identify the Anti-Dumping Agreement as the relevant covered agreement. Thus, the European Communities is left with no basis for arguing that anti-dumping duties are the exclusive remedy for dumping. It cannot rely on Article VI:2 of the GATT 1994, and it did not list Article 18.1 of the Anti-Dumping Agreement in its panel request.

5. *The Interpretation of the Footnote to Article 18.1 of the Anti-Dumping Agreement*

3.261 In reply to a question of the Panel to both parties regarding the correct interpretation of the footnote to Article 18.1[199] of the Anti-Dumping Agreement, the

---

[197] The European Communities refers to the Appellate Body Report on *European Communities - Bananas, supra*, footnote 29, para. 141.

[198] Appellate Body Report, *India - Patents, supra*, footnote 29, para. 91 (footnote omitted).

[199] Article 18.1 and its footnote provide as follows:

European Communities points out that the ordinary meaning of the footnote in this provision and of its predecessor in Article 16.1 of the Tokyo Round Anti-Dumping Code is that the Anti-Dumping Agreement does not prevent Members from taking appropriate action under other trade defence instruments provided within the GATT 1994, such as countervailing duty action and safeguard action.

3.262 The European Communities asserts that this interpretation is confirmed by the negotiating history. The factors taken into account by the negotiators in deciding to delete a corresponding provision when drafting the Havana Charter, and when amending the GATT 1947, were exactly the same. It is true that in the first case the negotiators used the phrase "other provisions of the Charter" whereas those in the second spoke of "other provisions of the General Agreement". However, it is clear that the Charter negotiators had in mind the Charter provisions that were incorporated in the General Agreement.

3.263 In support of its position, the European Communities references the Report of the Working Party established by Sub-Committee C of the Third Committee of the Havana Conference where, according to the European Communities, it appears clearly from paragraphs 3(iv) and 6 that the express prohibition of other measures against dumping was agreed to be unnecessary, removed and replaced by a statement to the minutes that other measures were not allowed because of concerns that some parties had about the implications for enforcing their rights under Articles 13 and 14 which correspond to what is now Article XVIII of the GATT 1994.[200]

3.264 The European Communities argues that, even if it could be argued that the Charter negotiators intended to preserve a wider range of possible measures, those who negotiated the 1948 amendments to the GATT 1947 clearly did not, since they explicitly refer to "other provisions of the General Agreement". The GATT 1947 negotiators were prepared to refer to the Havana Charter where that was their intention, as is apparent, for instance, from the Note *ad* Article II:4 of the GATT 1947.

3.265 The European Communities considers, finally, that the fact that this footnote was considered necessary merely confirms the EC view that alternative action against dumping such as treble damages, fines and imprisonment are not compatible with WTO rules.

3.266 The **United States**, in reply to the same question of the Panel, reiterates at the outset its view that the Panel should not reach the issue of the correct interpretation of Article 18.1 of the Anti-Dumping Agreement or its footnote. As a legal matter, Article 18.1 is not within the Panel's terms of reference.

3.267 Nevertheless, in response to the Panel's question, the United States notes that the footnote to Article 18.1 should be interpreted as meaning that a Member can take measures which deal with injurious dumping even when such measures are not ex-

---

> "18.1 No specific action against dumping of exports from another Member can be taken except in accordance with the provisions of GATT 1994, as interpreted by this Agreement.[24]
>
> [...]
>
> [24] This is not intended to preclude action under other relevant provisions of GATT 1994, as appropriate."

[200] The European Communities refers to document E.CONF.2/C.3/C/18, paras. 3(iv) and 6.

plicitly set forth in Article VI of the GATT 1994 or the Anti-Dumping Agreement, as long as the measure is not inconsistent with other GATT 1994 provisions.

3.268 The United States recalls that language nearly identical to that used in Article 18.1 and its footnote can be found in Article 16.1 of the Tokyo Round Anti-Dumping Code and its footnote. The meaning of the footnote to Article 16.1 was clear. No action against dumping could be taken except consistently with the GATT 1947. This merely restates the basic principle of *pacta sunt servanda*: every treaty in force is binding on the parties to it and must be performed by them in good faith. However, it is also clear that there was never any intention to eliminate the other GATT-consistent options available to address a factual situation that constituted a case of injurious dumping. A contracting party that was a party to the Code retained the option to address such dumping by eliminating the injury, for instance by raising the duty on the product concerned on an MFN basis to a level not in excess of the relevant tariff binding. Or it could renegotiate the duty on the product consistent with Article XXVIII of the GATT 1947. Or it could provide adjustment assistance for the industry or workers injured by the dumping. Or, if the factual situation also supported the taking of a safeguard action under Article XIX of the GATT 1947 or a countervailing duty under Article VI of the GATT 1947, the contracting party concerned could pursue those avenues.

3.269 The United States further points out that, read literally, Article 16.1 alone might have been misinterpreted to lock any government into levying anti-dumping duties whenever it was faced with a factual situation constituting injurious dumping. The footnote preserved flexibility to take any other measure that was otherwise GATT-consistent. The same conclusions hold today. If a WTO Member is faced with a factual situation constituting injurious dumping, it is not locked into levying anti-dumping duties, but has the option of taking other measures that are in accordance with the GATT 1994. If the measure is of a nature that is simply not regulated by the GATT 1994, as is the case for the 1916 Act, the measure is *a fortiori* consistent with the GATT 1994.

F. *Violations of Article VI:1 of the GATT 1994 and Articles 1, 2.1, 2.2, 3, 4 and 5.5 of the Anti-Dumping Agreement*

3.270 The **European Communities** notes that the 1916 Act prohibits dumping under different conditions than those laid down in Article VI of the GATT 1994 and the Anti-Dumping Agreement and applies different procedures and remedies than provided for therein. This gives rise to numerous violations of specific provisions of Article VI of the GATT 1994 and the Anti-Dumping Agreement.[201]

3.271 The European Communities submits that Article VI:1 of the GATT 1994 provides that dumping is to be condemned if it causes or threatens material injury and that Article 3 of the Anti-Dumping Agreement lays down a detailed definition of this notion and how injury may be established. The 1916 Act does not require actual

[201] The European Communities notes that, even if the Panel were to consider that the provisions of Article VI:2 did not contain mandatory language, all of the other provisions of Article VI:1 and the Anti-Dumping Agreement invoked by the European Communities contain clearly mandatory language.

injury at all, let alone material injury, but only one or more of the intents, including the intent to injure a domestic industry, no matter how threatening such intent may actually be. As a practical matter, evidence of actual injury will often be used to prove intent to injure under the 1916 Act. Where this occurs, there is nothing in the 1916 Act which ensures that the injury shown must correspond to the "material injury" standard of Article VI of the GATT 1994 and the Anti-Dumping Agreement. Furthermore, because other intents are relevant under the 1916 Act, in certain circumstances measures will be authorised under the 1916 Act without any inquiry into the effects on the US industry. Accordingly, the 1916 Act violates Article VI:1 of the GATT 1994 and Article 3 of the Anti-Dumping Agreement.

3.272 The European Communities further argues that remedies under the 1916 Act are available to private parties without the mediation of governmental authorities. The absence of an administrative procedure means that no investigation conforming to the requirements of the Anti-Dumping Agreement is conducted. Court proceedings are not a substitute for such administrative investigations. In the case of civil damages proceedings, the proceeding is conducted in the framework of the adversarial relationship between the parties. In both civil and criminal proceedings, the ultimate factual finding is made by the judge and/or a jury, who do not have the specialist knowledge of the subject of national authorities - a factor which is important in such a technical area. The conduct of the proceedings is determined by the parties to the proceedings, without the intervention and the responsibility of the importing country's administrative authorities. Accordingly, the 1916 Act fails to respect a number of procedural and due process requirements set forth in the Anti-Dumping Agreement, for example:

(a) the requirement that national authorities verify the information in a complaint before the investigation is opened;[202]

(b) the requirement that notice be given to the government of the exporting country before an anti-dumping investigation is launched;[203]

(c) the requirement that a complaint only be made on behalf of the domestic industry and be supported by a minimum proportion of the domestic industry. This representativity requirement serves an important function of avoiding frivolous complaints and the harassment of exporters and importers;[204]

(d) the possibility for governments of exporting countries to make comments on proposed findings;[205]

(e) the possibility for industrial users and representative consumer organisations to provide information on dumping, injury and causality,[206]

(f) the requirement that measures not be retroactive.[207]

---

[202] The European Communities refers to Article 5.3 of the Anti-Dumping Agreement.

[203] The European Communities refers to Article 5.5 of the Anti-Dumping Agreement.

[204] The European Communities refers to Articles 4 and 5.4 of the Anti-Dumping Agreement.

[205] The European Communities refers to Articles 6.9 and 6.11 of the Anti-Dumping Agreement.

[206] The European Communities refers to Article 6.12 of the Anti-Dumping Agreement.

[207] The European Communities refers to Article 10 of the Anti-Dumping Agreement.

3.273 The **United States** considers that the European Communities' claims under Article VI:1 of the GATT 1994 and the Anti-Dumping Agreement are adjuncts to its claim under Article VI:2 of the GATT 1994 and that each of these claims rests on the assumption that the Panel has already found the 1916 Act to be in violation of Article VI:2 of the GATT 1994. Thus, each of these claims has the same two premises of the alleged violation of Article VI:2 of the GATT 1994, namely, that Article VI:2 of the GATT 1994 makes anti-dumping duties the exclusive remedy for dumping and, further, that the 1916 Act is an anti-dumping statute that provides remedies for dumping other than anti-dumping duties. Because these two premises are erroneous, the European Communities' various claims under the GATT 1994 and the Anti-Dumping Agreement have no merit. Nothing in Article VI:2 of the GATT 1994 provides that anti-dumping duties are the exclusive remedy for dumping. Moreover, even assuming *arguendo* that Article VI:2 of the GATT 1994 makes anti-dumping duties the exclusive remedy for dumping, that provision nevertheless does not govern the 1916 Act because the 1916 Act is not an anti-dumping statute, and it does not provide remedies directed at the type of harmful conduct condemned by Article VI. Accordingly, like the European Communities' claim under Article VI:2, the Panel should reject the European Communities' various other claims under Article VI of the GATT 1994 and the Anti-Dumping Agreement.

3.274 The **European Communities** rejects the US argument that its claims based on Article VI:1 of the GATT 1994 and Articles 2.1, 2.2, 3, 4 and 5.5 of the Anti-Dumping Agreement depend on the claim that duties are the exclusive remedy and fall away if the European Communities' exclusive remedy claim fails.

3.275 The European Communities argues that Article VI:1 defines dumping and provides that it is to be condemned if it causes injury, threat of injury or material retardation. It follows clearly that measures taken against dumping are only consistent with Article VI:1 if there is a finding of both (i) dumping in accordance with the definition in that Article and (ii) injury, threat of injury or material retardation caused by such dumping. There is no mention of anti-dumping duties, so these principles would apply even if other measures could be taken consistently with Article VI:2.

3.276 According to the European Communities, the same argument applies to the cited Articles of the Anti-Dumping Agreement. Article 1 provides in relevant part that "[a]n anti-dumping measure shall be applied only under the circumstances provided for in Article VI of GATT 1994 and pursuant to investigations initiated and conducted in accordance with the provisions of this agreement". Articles 2.1 and 2.2 set forth amplified rules on the substantive definition of dumping. Article 3 does the same for injury. Article 4 defines "domestic industry", which is relevant for the injury definition. Article 5.5 provides that, "after receipt of a properly documented application and before proceeding to initiate an investigation, the authorities shall notify the government of the exporting Member concerned". It can easily be seen that all these provisions make no mention of the application of duties as a remedy, and would have to be applied even if it were to be decided that measures other than duties, such as civil damages or criminal penalties, could, consistently with Article VI of the GATT 1994, be applied to remedy dumping.

3.277 The **United States** considers that the European Communities has failed to demonstrate that the various procedural and substantive requirements found in Article VI:1 and the Anti-Dumping Agreement mandate compliance in and of themselves. The European Communities argues that the provisions setting forth these procedural and substantive requirements do not themselves indicate that they apply only when a Member is imposing a measure set forth in the Anti-Dumping Agreement, such as duties. From that assertion, the European Communities concludes that these procedural and substantive requirements apply even when a remedy not set forth in the Anti-Dumping Agreement is imposed. This argument lacks merit. For one thing, it wholly ignores the context provided by the remaining provisions of Article VI and the Anti-Dumping Agreement, all of which are geared toward a Member's imposition of a measure set forth in the Anti-Dumping Agreement, such as duties. If duties are not the exclusive remedy, then it makes no sense to interpret the other provisions of Article VI and the Anti-Dumping Agreement as mandating compliance with their procedures and investigation requirement.

3.278 According to the United States, the European Communities' argument also is defective on a more basic level. It looks at provisions which themselves are silent as to whether they apply only to measures set forth in the Anti-Dumping Agreement or, alternatively, apply to all measures counteracting dumping, even those not set forth in the Anti-Dumping Agreement. Then, without explaining why, the European Communities arbitrarily chooses to read this silence as nevertheless supporting the alternative that supports its claims in the present case. When a WTO agreement is truly silent on a particular matter, however, there is no basis for a panel to find a violation. A panel must terminate its analysis and find no violation.[208]

3.279 The **European Communities** replies that it finds this argument unconvincing since the provisions are also silent as to whether they apply to the steel industry or not but no-one would think - or at least the European Communities would not think of - arguing that there is therefore "no basis for a panel to find a violation" when they are so applied. An obligation which is not restricted in its scope applies generally. In this case the obligation to comply with the procedural requirements of Article VI of the GATT 1994 and the Anti-Dumping Agreement apply to all anti-dumping action and not just to duties.

3.280 The **United States** argues that, in any event, the Panel need not even reach these questions if it concludes, as it should, that the European Communities has failed to show that the 1916 Act is an anti-dumping statute governed by Article VI of the GATT 1994 and the Anti-Dumping Agreement.

G. Violation of Article III:4 of the GATT 1994

1. Introduction

3.281 The **European Communities** argues that if the Panel considers that the 1916 Act is fully within the scope of Article VI of the GATT 1994 and therefore subject to its disciplines, then there is no need to consider the EC claim under Article III:4 of the GATT 1994. If the Panel considers, however, that all or any portion of the 1916

[208] The United States refers to the Panel Report on *United States - Imposition of Countervailing Duties on Imports of Fresh and Chilled Atlantic Salmon from Norway*, unadopted, dated 4 December 1992, SCM/153, paras. 243-46 and 247-49; Panel Report on *New Zealand - Imports of Electrical Transformers from Finland*, adopted on 18 July 1985, BISD 32/S55, paras. 4.2-4.3.

Act is consistent with Article VI of the GATT 1994 and the Anti-Dumping Agreement, then it should consider the European Communities' claim under Article III:4 of the GATT 1994 with respect to that portion of the 1916 Act found to be consistent with Article VI of the GATT 1994 and the Anti-Dumping Agreement.

3.282 The European Communities is of the view that the 1916 Act infringes Article III:4 of the GATT 1994[209] since it accords to products of contracting parties imported into the United States treatment less favourable that that accorded to like products of US origin.

3.283 The **United States** considers that a review of the historical applications of the 1916 Act and the Robinson-Patman Act conclusively demonstrates that the 1916 Act raises no national treatment concerns under Article III:4 of the GATT 1994. In addition, even if the 1916 Act and the Robinson-Patman Act are compared using an element-by-element approach, no national treatment concerns arise.

2. *The 1916 Act as a Law Affecting the Internal Sale of Imported Products and the Robinson-Patman Act as Comparable Legislation*

3.284 For the **European Communities**, the 1916 Act is a law and it also affects the internal sale of products because it prohibits, *inter alia*, the sale or offering for sale of products below a certain price. The fact that a product cannot be sold at a freely established price affects, indeed may inhibit, its sale. The fact that the measure applies to importers does not prevent the applicability of Article III:4. The US measure before the panel on *United States - Section 337 Tariff Act 1930*[210] also applied to importers by imposing penalties on them but was still held to affect imported products.[211] Furthermore, the circumstances under which a product is imported cannot prevent a product from being "like" comparable domestic products. Indeed, the very fact that the 1916 Act applies exclusively to imported products already establishes a *prima facie* breach of Article III of the GATT 1994 since domestic products are not subject to the requirements of the 1916 Act.

3.285 The European Communities further notes that the 1916 Act is a price discrimination law addressed to the specific case of differences between the price on the US market of goods imported into the United States and the price of the same goods on the domestic market of the exporter or on third country markets. The comparable legislation applying to price discrimination on the US market in respect of US do-

---

[209] Article III:4 of the GATT 1994 provides as follows:

> "The products of the territory of any contracting party imported into the territory of any other contracting party shall be accorded treatment no less favourable than that accorded to like products of national origin in respect of all laws, regulations and requirements affecting their internal sale, offering for sale, purchase, transportation, distribution or use. The provisions of this para. shall not prevent the application of differential internal transportation charges which are based exclusively on the economic operation of the means of transport and not on the nationality of the product."

[210] Panel Report on *United States - Section 337 of the Tariff Act of 1930*, adopted on 7 November 1989, BISD 36S/345 (hereinafter "*United States - Section 337*").

[211] The European Communities refers to *United States - Section 337*, *Op. Cit.*, para. 5.10.

mestic products is the Robinson-Patman Act.[212] The Robinson-Patman Act provides as follows:

> "It shall be unlawful for any person engaged in commerce, in the course of such commerce, either directly or indirectly to discriminate in price between different purchasers of commodities of like grade and quality, [...] and where the effect of such discrimination may be to substantially lessen competition or tend to create a monopoly in any line of commerce, or to injure, destroy, or prevent competition with any person who either grants or knowingly receives the benefit of such discrimination or with customers of either of them."[213]

3.286 The **United States** takes issue with the European Communities' assertion that a *prima facie* breach is established by the fact that the 1916 Act applies exclusively to imported products. According to the United States, no such presumption arises. The panel on *United States - Section 337* recognized that the nature of the inquiry in an Article III:4 dispute is one of substance, not form. It explained that:

> "the mere fact that imported products are subject [...] to legal provisions that are different than those applying to products of national origin is in itself not conclusive in establishing inconsistency with Article III:4. In such cases, it has to be assessed whether or not such differences in the legal provisions applicable do or do not accord to imported products less favorable treatment."[214]

3.287 The United States does agree with the European Communities, however, that the comparable statute applicable to domestic goods is Section 2 of the Clayton Act, as amended by the Robinson-Patman Act.[215]

3. *The "No Less Favourable Treatment" Standard*

(a) General Arguments

3.288 According to the **European Communities**, if the text of the Robinson-Patman Act is compared with that of the 1916 Act, it can be seen that while the two texts have in common a requirement that price discrimination be found in respect of the relevant markets, they differ as regards the other elements which must be proved in order for an infringement of the law to be present. In the case of the 1916 Act, the additional requirements are the intent to (i) destroy a US industry, or (ii) injure a US industry, or (iii) prevent the establishment of a US industry, or (iv) restrain trade and commerce, or (v) monopolise trade and commerce. By contrast, in the Robinson-Patman Act, the additional requirements are:

---

[212] The European Communities refers to Section 2 of the Clayton Act, as amended by the Robinson-Patman Act in 1936 (15 U.S.C. § 13). According to the European Communities, it is established that this statute applies only to differences in price within the US market, not to differences between prices on the US market and prices on a foreign market. The European Communities refers to *Zenith I, Op. Cit.*, p. 248.

[213] 15 U.S.C. § 13(a).

[214] *United States - Section 337, Op. Cit.*, para.5.11.

[215] The United States refers to *Zenith III, Op. Cit.*, pp. 1213-1214.

> "the effect of such discrimination may be to substantially lessen competition or tend to create a monopoly in any line of commerce, or to injure, destroy, or prevent competition with any person who either grants or knowingly receives the benefit of such discrimination or with customers of either of them."

3.289 The European Communities further notes that among Robinson-Patman cases a distinction is made between the probable impact of price discrimination (i) on direct competitors of the discriminating seller (primary line injury), (ii) on the favoured and disfavoured buyers of the discriminating seller (second-line injury) and (iii) on the customers of either of them (third-line injury). Primary line discrimination is the only direct domestic analogue of international price discrimination as condemned in the 1916 Act. The US Supreme Court has held in the *Brooke Group* case that in order for the requisite effect on competition to be present, it must be shown that (i) the defendant charged prices below an appropriate measure of cost, and (ii) it had a reasonable prospect of recouping its investment in below cost prices.

3.290 In light of the foregoing, the European Communities contends that a careful comparison of the two laws, taking into account not only the respective texts but also the additional requirements read into the Robinson-Patman Act as a condition for finding primary line violations, demonstrates that it is substantially more difficult to prove a violation of the Robinson-Patman Act than it is to prove a violation of the 1916 Act. As a consequence, the 1916 Act allows the application of measures to imported products under less favourable conditions than those applicable to domestic products, thus resulting in less favourable treatment of imported products in violation of Article III:4 of the GATT 1994.

3.291 The European Communities points out, finally, that, in the *Zenith III* case, the District Court merely held that the 1916 Act should "whenever possible" be interpreted to parallel the Robinson-Patman Act [...]. The term "whenever possible" suggests that it should not necessarily always be the case, as was confirmed in the *Helmac I* case.

3.292 The **United States** is of the view that any analysis of the compatibility of the 1916 Act with the national treatment provisions of Article III:4 of the GATT 1994 should begin and end with one fundamental point. The 1916 Act has rarely been invoked. More importantly, the 1916 Act establishes a standard for relief which has never been met in the case of importers and imported goods. The Robinson-Patman Act, in contrast, has been successfully invoked in a vast number of civil cases.[216] From this perspective, the 1916 Act can be seen to treat importers and imported goods *more* favourably than the Robinson-Patman Act treats US sellers and their goods.

[216] The United States notes that only in a very small number of cases has the US Department of Justice invoked the criminal provisions of the Robinson-Patman Act over the years, or obtained convictions. The United States refers to ABA Antitrust Law Developments, 4th ed. (1997), a US antirust reference work, which notes, at page 490: "Section 3 [the criminal law provision of the Robinson-Patman Act] has rarely been enforced, and no prosecutions have been brought under that section since the 1960s."

3.293 In this connection, the United States recalls that, since the 1993 *Brooke Group* decision, there have been more than forty reported court of appeals and district court opinions in more than forty different cases that have addressed allegations that the price discrimination provisions of the Robinson-Patman Act have been violated, including cases leading to more than ten court of appeals and district court decisions in 1998 alone.[217] By comparison, only two district court determinations - at very early stages in their respective proceedings - have during that same period addressed allegations that the 1916 Act has been violated. This vast disparity alone establishes that the price discrimination proscriptions of the Robinson-Patman Act create far more danger of liability for domestic firms than the 1916 Act creates for importers, and therefore treat domestic firms far less favorably than the 1916 Act treats importers. Moreover, while liability for an importer under the 1916 Act can arise only from injury to the firms with which it competes, domestic firm liability under the Robinson-Patman Act can arise both from that type of injury and from injury to one or more downstream purchasers. As a consequence, cases involving secondary line liability, in addition to those involving primary line liability, are also relevant to any comparison to the 1916 Act.

3.294 The United States further notes that the conclusion that the Robinson-Patman Act treats domestic firms less favorably than the 1916 Act treats importers is strengthened by the number of primary line price discrimination cases since *Brooke Group*. In particular, since the *Brooke Group* decision, four court of appeals decisions, arising from three cases addressing allegations of primary line price discrimination, have been issued.[218] To the extent that the success of a particular case can be measured by the level of the federal court system to which it rises, all of these lawsuits alleging primary line discrimination were more successful than either of the two 1916 Act lawsuits. Moreover, fourteen district court decisions addressing primary line discrimination - in addition to those which led to some of the above court of appeals decisions - have been issued.[219] These figures suggest that allegations of

---

[217] The United States refers to, e.g., *Godfrey v. Pulitzer Publishing Co.*, 161 F.3d 1137 (8th Cir. 1998); *George Haug Co. v. Rolls Royce Motor Cars, Inc.*, 148 F.3d 136 (2d Cir. 1998); *Kentmaster Manufacturing Co. v. Jarvis Products Corp.*, 146 F.3d 691 (9th Cir. 1998), amended, No. 96-56341, 1999 WL 19636 (9th Cir. Jan. 20, 1999); *Metro Ford Truck Sales, Inc. v. Ford Motor Co.*, 145 F.3d 320 (5th Cir. 1998); *Sally Bridges v. MacLean-Stevens Studios, Inc.*, 35 F.Supp. 2d 20, 28 (D. Me. 1998); *Malek Wholesaler, Inc. v. First Film Extruding, Ltd.*, 1998 U.S.Dist. LEXIS 3674 (N.D. Ill. Mar. 20, 1998); *City of New York v. Coastal Oil New York, Inc.*, 1998-1 Trade Cas. (CCH) ¶ 72,087 (S.D.N.Y. 1998); *Liberty Lincoln-Mercury v. Ford Motor Co.*, 134 F.3d 557 (3d Cir. 1998); *Hoover Color Corp. v. Bayer Corp.*, 24 F. Supp. 2d 571 (W.D. Va. 1998); *Bell v. Fur Breeders Agricultural Cooperative*, 3 F. Supp. 2d 1241 (D. Utah 1998); *Precision Printing Co. v. Unisource Worldwide, Inc.*, 993 F. Supp. 338 (W.D. Pa. 1998); *Rebel Oil Co., Inc. v. Atlantic Richfield Co.*, 957 F.Supp. 1184, 1192 (D. Nev. 1997), affirmed, 146 F.3d 1088 (9th Cir.), cert. denied, 119 S. Ct. 541 (1998).

[218] The United States refers to *Kentmaster Manufacturing Co. v. Jarvis Products Corp.*, 146 F.3d 691, 694-95 (9th Cir. 1998), amended, No. 96-56341, 1999 WL 19636 (9th Cir. Jan. 20, 1999); *Coastal Fuels of Puerto Rico, Inc. v. Caribbean Petroleum Corp.*, 79 F.3d 182, 188 (1st Cir. 1996); *Rebel Oil Co. v. Atlantic Richfield Co.*, 146 F.3d 1088, 1091 (9th Cir. 1998), cert. denied, 119 S.Ct. 541 (1998), and 51 F.3d 1421, 1429 (9th Cir. 1995).

[219] The United States refers to *J&S Oil, Inc. v. Irving Oil Corp.*, 1999-2 Trade Cas. (CCH) ¶ 72,615 (D.Me. August 4, 1999), at 85551-54; *Wynn ex rel. Alabama v. Philip Morris Inc.*, 51 F.Supp. 2d 1232, 1247 (N.D. Ala. 1999); *Malek Wholesaler, Inc. v. First Film Extruding, Ltd.*, 1998 U.S. Dist.

primary line discrimination under the Robinson-Patman Act - even without considering allegations of secondary line discrimination - have continued to pose far more of a threat of liability to domestic firms than the 1916 Act poses to foreign firms.

3.295 The United States contends, moreover, that, even if provisions of the 1916 Act and the Robinson-Patman Act are compared in detail, no national treatment concerns arise. This is because the 1916 Act is intended to prevent unfair competition by extending the prohibitions of unfair competition in domestic commerce embodied in Section 2 of the Clayton Act of 1914 to importers.[220] Consistent with that construction, the prevailing interpretation among the courts that have considered the 1916 Act is either an explicit or implicit endorsement of the following principles enunciated by the District Court in *Zenith III*:

> "The principal lesson which we draw from the legislative history of the 1916 Act, viewed against the historical background of the first Wilson administration, is that the statute should be interpreted whenever possible to parallel the "unfair competition" law applicable to domestic commerce. Since the 1916 Antidumping Act is a price discrimination law, it should be read in tandem with the domestic price discrimination law, section 2 of the Clayton Act, which was amended by the Robinson-Patman Act in 1936."[221]

3.296 As regards the District Court's use of the term "whenever possible", the United States notes that it cannot speculate why the Court employed the term. A court decides one case at a time, and does not act as though it were a legislature. The important point is that the District Court recognized the similarity of the language with other antitrust statutes and held that the issue in question, the standard for comparability of products, should be based upon antitrust principles. It should be noted that the District Court in *Zenith III* also stated the following:

> "[The 1916 Act] was intended to complement the antitrust laws by imposing on importers substantially the same legal strictures relating

LEXIS 3674 (N.D. Ill. March 24, 1998); *Taylor Publishing Company v. Jostens, Inc.*, 36 F.Supp. 2d 360, 372-73 (E.D. Tex. 1999); *Sally Bridges v. MacLean-Stevens Studios, Inc.*, 35 F.Supp. 2d 20, 27-28 (D. Me. 1998); *City of New York v. Coastal Oil New York, Inc.*, 1998-1 Trade Cas. (CCH) ¶ 72,087 (S.D.N.Y. 1998); *Stearns Airport Equip. Co. v. FMC Corp.*, 977 F.Supp. 1269, 1273 (N.D. Tex. 1997); *Cardinal Indus. v. Pressman Toy Corp.*, 1997-1 Trade Cas. (CCH) ¶ 71,738 (S.D.N.Y. Dec. 17, 1996); *The Zeller Corp. v. Federal-Mogul Corp.*, 1997-1 Trade Cas. (CCH) ¶ 71,805 (N.D. Ohio June 25, 1996); *Anti-Monopoly, Inc. v. Hasbro, Inc.*, 958 F.Supp. 895, 906 (S.D.N.Y. 1997), and 1995-2 Trade Cas. ¶ 71,095 (S.D.N.Y. 1995), at 75,241; *Clark v. Flow Measurement, Inc.*, 948 F.Supp. 519, 522-29 (D. S.C. 1996); *C.B. Trucking, Inc. v. Waste Management, Inc. and WMX*, 944 F.Supp. 66, 68-69 (D. Mass. 1996); *En Vogue v. UK Optical, Ltd. and British Optical Import Company*, 843 F.Supp. 838, 845-47 (E.D.N.Y. 1994); *Lago & Sons Dairy, Inc. v. H.P. Hood, Inc.*, 1994 U.S. Dist. LEXIS 12909 (D. N.H. 1994).

[220] The United States notes that the US Department of Justice, in a letter from Samuel J. Graham, Assistant Attorney General, dated 30 June 1916, published in N.Y. Times on 4 July 1916 at page 10, stated that the "purpose" of the 1916 Act should be to prevent unfair competition. Just as we have said to our own people by the Clayton Act that they should not indulge in unfair competition, so we propose to say the same to the foreigner."

[221] *Zenith III*, *Op. Cit.*, p. 1223. The United States also refers to page 1214 of the same decision where it is stated that "[a]s a price discrimination statute, the Antidumping Act of 1916 is functionally similar to the price discrimination statutes which are applicable to domestic business."

to price discrimination as those which had already been imposed on domestic businesses by the Clayton Antitrust Act of 1914.[222]

[...]

[I]n order to be faithful to the intention of Congress to subject importers to "the same unfair competition law" [that is applicable to domestic commerce], we should not interpret the 1916 Act to impose on importers legal strictures which are more rigorous than those applied to domestic enterprises."[223]

3.297 According to the United States, consistent with these pronouncements, a comparison of the provisions of the 1916 Act with those of the Robinson-Patman Act makes it clear that the 1916 Act actually provides *more* favourable treatment than the Robinson-Patman Act in many ways and, in any event, does not in any instance provide less favourable treatment.

(b) The Relevance of Trade Effects

3.298 The **European Communities** asserts that the approach taken by the United States in respect of the European Communities' claim under Article III:4 of the GATT 1994 is fundamentally flawed. In effect, it seeks to apply a test which focuses on which law - the one applying to imports or the one applying to domestic products - is more often invoked successfully and what are the relative degrees of difficulty of successfully asserting a claim under the respective laws. However, as established in a long series of panel reports and confirmed by the Appellate Body, Article III of the GATT 1994 protects competitive opportunities and not trade flows.[224] Hence, in order to establish a violation of Article III:4 it is not necessary to show that the measure challenged has had any actual effects. The mere possibility that a measure may result in some circumstances in less favourable treatment being afforded to imported products is already sufficient to establish a violation of Article III:4. Thus, in the *EEC - Animal Feed Proteins* case.

"[...] the Panel examined whether a purchase regulation which does not necessarily discriminate against imported products but is capable of doing so is consistent with Article III:4. The Panel noted that the exposure of a particular imported product to a risk of discrimination constitutes, by itself, a form of discrimination. The Panel therefore concluded that purchase regulations creating such a risk must be considered to be according less favourable treatment within the meaning of Article III:4."[225]

---

[222] *Zenith III, Op. Cit.*, p. 1196-1197.

[223] *Ibid.*, p. 1223.

[224] The European Communities refers to, e.g., the Appellate Body Report on *Japan - Taxes on Alcoholic Beverages* ("*Japan - Alcoholic Beverages* "), WT/DS8/R, WT/DS10/R, WT/DS11/R, adopted 1 November 1996, DSR 1996:I, 97, at 109-110, and the panel reports cited therein.

[225] Panel Report on *EEC - Payments and Subsidies Paid to Processors and Producers of Oilseeds and Related Animal-Feed Proteins*, adopted on 25 January 1990, BISD 37S/86, para 141.

3.299 In the view of the European Communities, whether the conditions for applying the 1916 Act make it more or less difficult to apply is completely irrelevant for the purposes of establishing a claim under Article III:4.

3.300 The **United States** replies that it does not argue that the European Communities' claim under Article III:4 should be dismissed because the 1916 Act has not had any trade effects. Although there may be some merit to that argument, the United States has chosen not to make it.

(c) The Relevance of the Absence of Successful Invocations of the 1916 Act

3.301 The **European Communities** rejects the US contention that the 1916 Act treats importers of foreign goods more favourably than the Robinson-Patman Act treats sellers of US goods because the latter has been successfully invoked much more often than the former. The European Communities refers the Panel to the panel report on *United States - Standards for Reformulated and Conventional Gasoline*[226] where the panel rejected the argument that the US measures involved in that case could be justified because imported gasoline was treated "on the whole" no less favourably than domestic gasoline. The United States did not appeal this element of the panel report. The panel in the gasoline standards case rejected the "on the whole" reasoning because it would mean that less favourable treatment in one instance could be offset by more favourable treatment in another instance and noted that such an approach had also been rejected by the GATT 1947.[227] It is therefore clear that under Article III:4 an analysis has to be carried out at the level of an individual product, not at the level of the application of the law to all possible products. Any individual product must be treated no less favourably than a like domestic product, and this in all cases.

3.302 The **United States** responds that the European Communities fails to understand the US position. The United States does not argue that the 1916 Act on the whole treats imported goods more favourably than domestic goods and only in a few instances treats imported goods less favourably than domestic goods. The argument made by the United States is unqualified, just as is Article III:4. It is a fact that the 1916 Act establishes a standard for relief that is virtually impossible to satisfy and that has never been met in the case of importers and imported goods. The intent requirement of the 1916 Act is an overarching factor that is present in every instance, not just "on the whole" and exerts offsetting influence to any other perceived disadvantage. The Robinson-Patman Act, in contrast, has been successfully invoked on innumerable occasions to obtain relief involving US sellers and their goods.

3.303 The United States does not suggest that the Panel base its finding regarding the European Communities' Article III:4 claim entirely upon the fact that the 1916 Act has never been successfully invoked. But this fact is relevant to the Panel's de-

---

[226] Panel Report on *United States - Standards for Reformulated and Conventional Gasoline*, WT/DS2/R, adopted 20 May 1996, DSR 1996:I, 29 (hereinafter "Panel Report on *United States - Gasoline*").

[227] The European Communities refers to the Panel Report on *United States - Gasoline*, supra, footnote 226, para. 6.14, which refers to *United States - Section 337*, *Op. Cit.*, para. 5.14.

termination of whether the alleged differences between the 1916 Act and the Robinson-Patman Act afford less favourable treatment. The difference in terms of the successful invocation of the respective Acts shows that the 1916 Act requirements, taken together, are less rigorous for *every* importer, than the requirements under the Robinson-Patman Act. As a result, the 1916 Act treats importers and imported goods more favourably than the Robinson-Patman Act treats US sellers and their goods.

3.304 The **European Communities** considers that the fact that the 1916 Act has not often been invoked is due to a number of factors which do nothing to demonstrate that it provides more favourable treatment to imports than the Robinson-Patman Act does to domestic goods. The following factors explain why the 1916 Act has not been invoked so often:

(a) proceedings tend to be complex and time-consuming, and thus very expensive to the defendants;

(b) plaintiffs have an alternative remedy in normal (Article VI-compliant) anti-dumping action. This may often be more convenient and explains why there have not been many 1916 Act cases. The true comparison should therefore arguably be between all dumping price discrimination cases and domestic Robinson-Patman Act cases;

(c) in the *Wheeling-Pittsburgh* case a settlement was reached among the parties, which means that the complainant did find relief. The terms of the settlement were not made public, but it is known that the companies have agreed to certain import restrictions and pledged to purchase a certain amount of Wheeling-Pittsburgh steel.

3.305 The **United States** reiterates its view that the substantive reason for the complete absence of successful recoveries under the 1916 Act is found in the requirement that the complaining party show a specific, predatory intent on behalf of the defendant importer. This requirement has been described by the courts, in the particular context of the 1916 Act, as virtually impossible to satisfy. Even the interlocutory decision in *Geneva Steel*, which virtually forms the basis for the European Communities' whole position in the present case, acknowledged that

> "[...] the burden of proving such improper intent may not be easy. Absent some compelling evidence, it may be *nearly impossible*."[228]

3.306 Notwithstanding this US contention, the **European Communities** asserts, however, that the 1916 Act is still regarded as an efficient means of action. Recently, for example, a San Francisco law firm has been encouraging (potential) clients to resort to the 1916 Act against illegal exports, which shows that the 1916 Act is still regarded as an efficient means of action. The letter states in relevant part:

> "We believe that a legal action on behalf of the numerous steel companies who have been injured as a result of illegal steel dumping by companies from Japan, Brazil, South Korea, Russia and other countries is a viable and appropriate means to recover losses that have been incurred. The claims would be based on the 1916 Antidumping Act [...] which creates a private cause of action for dumping [...]. Our pro-

228 *Geneva Steel*, *Op. Cit.*, p. 1224 (emphasis added by the United States).

> posed action is similar to, but different in important respects, from actions already brought by Wheeling-Pittsburgh and Geneva Steel. These plaintiffs did not utilize the leverage that *multiple* plaintiffs can have in obtaining a significant recovery."

According to the European Communities, the letter also shows the growing effectiveness of the harassment value of the 1916 Act.

3.307 The **United States** maintains its view that one element of a 1916 Act claim - the requirement of a specific, predatory intent - renders the 1916 Act more favourable to importers and imported goods than is the Robinson-Patman Act to US sellers and their goods in every instance. The courts have interpreted this requirement as virtually impossible to satisfy, and the historical applications of the 1916 Act support this view, as there has never been a successful case brought under the 1916 Act. When this factor is taken into account to the extent that it might be capable of exerting an offsetting influence in each individual case, the only reasonable conclusion is that the 1916 Act treats importers and imported goods more favourably than the Robinson-Patman Act treats US sellers and their goods.

3.308 The United States submits, moreover, that this approach was followed by the panel in *United States - Section 337*. There, the panel explained that "an element of more favourable treatment would only be relevant if it would always accompany and offset an element of differential treatment causing less favourable treatment."[229] The panel found that some of the procedural advantages given to foreign respondents under Section 337 operate in all cases, and therefore it "took these factors into account to the extent that they might be capable of exerting an offsetting influence in each individual case of less favourable treatment resulting from an element cited by the Community."[230]

3.309 The United States thus concludes that it would be entirely appropriate for the Panel to begin and end its analysis of the European Communities' Article III:4 claim based upon the fact that the intent requirement is virtually impossible to satisfy.

(d) Element-by-Element Comparison of the 1916 Act and the the Robinson-Patman Act

3.310 The **European Communities** asserts that there are four principal differences between the 1916 Act and the Robinson-Patman Act that result in unfavourable treatment being afforded to imported products in violation of Article III:4 of the GATT 1994. These concern (i) the intent requirements under each Act, (ii) the measurement of price discrimination, (iii) the sufficiency of offers for sale for supporting claims under each Act, and (iv) the available defences under each Act.

3.311 The **United States** reiterates its view that the intent requirement of the 1916 Act is virtually impossible to satisfy. It is therefore unnecessary or at least inconsequential for the Panel to consider how one element of the 1916 Act might compare to a corresponding element of the Robinson-Patman Act. Even if the Panel were to find a particular element of the 1916 Act to be more rigorous than a corresponding ele-

229 *United States - Section 337, Op. Cit.*, para. 5.16.
230 *Ibid.*, para. 5.17.

ment of the Robinson-Patman Act, that finding could not transform the 1916 Act into a more rigorous statute than the Robinson-Patman Act, given that, when all of the requirements of the 1916 Act are viewed together, they are not more rigorous than the Robinson-Patman Act requirements in light of the 1916 Act's intent standard.

3.312 The United States further notes that, in any event, a careful comparison of each of these differences confirms what is manifest from a review of the actual application of the Acts. That is, the 1916 Act actually affords *more* favourable treatment to imported goods than the Robinson-Patman Act does regarding domestic goods.

(i) The Injury/Predation Standards

3.313 The **European Communities** notes that, under the Robinson-Patman Act, the pleading and proof requirements that a primary line complainant must meet in order to demonstrate that it is suffering from a predatory pricing policy are now well established since the US Supreme Court issued its decision in the *Brooke Group* case. Two conditions must be fulfilled in order to successfully demonstrate predatory pricing: (i) the defendant is charging prices below an appropriate measure of cost, namely, average variable costs[231] and (ii) that it has a reasonable prospect to recoup its investment in below cost prices. In its *Brooke Group* ruling, the Supreme Court defines in detail the conditions that must be met for such a recoupment to occur :

(i) Below cost pricing must be capable of driving the firm's rivals out of the market or causing them to raise their prices to supra-competitive levels within a disciplined oligopoly;

(ii) there must be a likelihood that the predatory scheme will cause a rise in prices above a competitive level that would be sufficient to compensate for the amounts expended on the predatory action.

3.314 The European Communities points out, in this regard, that determining whether recoupment of predatory losses is likely requires an estimate of the cost of the alleged predation and a close analysis of both the scheme alleged by the plaintiff and the structure and conditions of the relevant market. This represents a burden of proof which it is very difficult to sustain as the Supreme Court itself has recognised.[232] In its *Brooke Group* judgment, the Court held that "predatory pricing schemes are rarely tried and even more rarely successful" and "the costs of erroneous liability are high"[233].

---

[231] The European Communities refers to, e.g., *McGahee v. Northern Propane Gas Co.*, 858 F.2d 1487, 1504 (11th Cir. 1988); cert. denied, 490 U.S. 1084 (1989); *Northeastern Tel. Co. v. AT&T*, 651 F.2d 76, 87-88 (2d Cir. 1981), cert. denied, 455 U.S. 943 (1982); *Chillicothe Sand & Gravel Co. v. Martin Marietta Corp.*, 615 F.2d 427, 432 (7th Cir. 1980); *Janich Bros. v. American Distilling Co.*, 570 F.2d 848, 858 (9th Cir. 1977), cert. denied, 439 U.S. 829 (1978).

[232] The European Communities refers to *Matsushita Electric, Op. Cit.*

[233] The European Communities recalls that the primary line provisions of Section 2(a) of the Robinson-Patman Act which make price discrimination unlawful "where the effect of such discrimination may be to substantially less competition or tend to create a monopoly in any line of commerce or to injure, destroy or prevent competition with any" competing seller of the goods in question, has been interpreted as "really referring to the effect upon competition and not merely upon competitors".

3.315 The European Communities further recalls that the anti-competitive intents and effects which must be proved in order to establish a primary line Robinson-Patman Act infringement are not required by the 1916 Act. Under the 1916 Act, discriminatory pricing must rather be conducted with the intent of injuring, destroying or preventing the establishment of a US industry. In the *Wheeling-Pittsburgh* case, the Ohio District Court in its Opinion and Order of 22 January 1999[234] found that the complaining party had the duty to demonstrate that the defendants sold their products with the intent to injure or destroy the domestic hot-rolled steel industry but that the additional "predatory pricing" tests as set forth in *Brooke Group* were not applicable to the case before it, since such proof was not required in dumping cases.

3.316 The European Communities submits that the practical result of the difference between the "predatory pricing" test under the Robinson-Patman Act and the "intent to injure" test under the 1916 Act is that the same conduct by two firms, one selling imported products and the other selling domestic products, could be deemed to infringe the 1916 Act in the case of the imported products, and not to infringe the Robinson-Patman Act in the case of the domestic products. This was recognized by the US Court in the *Helmac I* case.[235]

3.317 The European Communities concedes that if it were to be definitively established by a judgment of the US Supreme Court that *Brooke Group* predation is required for a violation of the 1916 Act, all possibility of discrimination in the sense of Article III:4 of the GATT 1994 would be eliminated in respect of the injury/predation elements. But the European Communities denies that there is a reasonable prospect of this occurring. Such a holding would go against the clear language of the 1916 Act.

3.318 In this regard, the European Communities states that, while some courts have made general holdings that the 1916 Act is an antitrust, not a trade statute, others, in the more recent past, have held that it is both. On the assumption that a case raising the issue reached it, the US Supreme Court remains free to interpret the 1916 Act according to its own convictions. In its opinion of 22 January 1999, issued within the context of the *Wheeling-Pittsburgh* case, the Ohio District Court notes that there is no requirement in the US constitution that Congress should impose the same standards of conduct on the importers of goods as it does on domestic producers of goods. If the hypothetical approach of the United States to developments in its Supreme Court case law were followed, it could be said, inferring from actual 1916 Act case law, that there is at least a reasonable prospect that the Supreme Court will take the same view.

3.319 The European Communities concludes that, in these circumstances, the Panel can only take the 1916 Act to mean what its plain language says and what the courts which have considered it to date have taken it to mean. Since a number of them clearly consider that the 1916 Act is at least in part a trade law not incorporating antitrust predation requirements, and since plaintiffs are clearly continuing to pursue litigation on this assumption, discrimination under Article III:4 of the GATT 1994 is present.

---

234 The European Communities refers to *Wheeling-Pittsburgh*, *Op. Cit.*, p. 603.

235 The European Communities refers to *Helmac I*, *Op. Cit.*, p. 575 et seq..

3.320 The **United States** points out that the 1916 Act requires a complainant to show that the defendant possessed a specified intent, i.e. an intent to injure, destroy or prevent the establishment of a US industry or to restrain or monopolise trade. The prevailing judicial interpretation of the 1916 Act is that the intent requirement is a predatory intent requirement. Under the Robinson-Patman Act, the comparable element is the requirement that the complainant show "anti-competitive effect" which is commonly called "predatory pricing." This is demonstrated through proving an appropriate measure of below cost pricing and the possibility of recouping the predatory losses.[236]

3.321 The United States notes that the question thus becomes whether this supposed difference between the laws constitutes unfavourable treatment for imported goods. The European Communities concedes that a requirement of predatory intent under the 1916 Act like that required under the Robinson-Patman Act would eliminate all Article III:4 concerns with regard to the 1916 Act. In fact, the current state of US case law holds that evidence of the requisite intent under the 1916 Act is essentially the same predatory intent contemplated by the Robinson-Patman Act. As a factual matter, it is the US case law interpreting the 1916 Act that is dispositive in determining the nature of the 1916 Act. Thus, based upon the European Communities' statement and the prevailing judicial interpretation of the intent requirement, the Panel should find that the 1916 Act is fully consistent with Article III:4 as it accords the exact same treatment to foreign goods as the Robinson-Patman accords like domestic goods.

3.322 According to the **European Communities**, the United States has not demonstrated that the requisite intent under the 1916 Act is essentially the same predatory intent contemplated by the Robinson-Patman Act. It uses the terms "predation" and "predatory intent" very loosely, without recognizing the difference between (i) the narrow and antitrust specific meaning now applied also to primary line infringements of the Robinson-Patman Act as a result of the *Brooke Group* decision of the Supreme Court, which requires, as a condition to establishing predation, a showing of sales below an appropriate measure of cost and a reasonable prospect of recoupment of the losses from selling below cost and (ii) the broader every-day meaning of "predatory" which does indeed correspond to "intent to injure or destroy".

3.323 In response, the **United States** notes that it is not familiar with the "broader every-day meaning" of the term "predatory" and the European Communities has neglected to provide a source for this definition. In any event, whether the term is considered an "everyday" term or otherwise, the European Communities cannot dispute that the term "predatory" is an antitrust term.

3.324 The **European Communities**, however, maintains its view that when the 1916 Act refers to "intent to injure or destroy [...] US industry", it means "injure or destroy" in the broad every-day sense of these terms, and not predation in the technical antitrust sense of *Brooke Group*. This conclusion has been reached - after the *Brooke Group* decision - by the two District Courts in *Geneva Steel* and *Wheeling-Pittsburgh*. These cases are important because they are the only cases among those cited by the United States or of which the European Communities is aware in which

[236] The United States refers to *Brooke Group*, *Op. Cit.*, pp. 222-23.

courts were specifically called on to decide whether an action under the 1916 Act and based on specific intent to injure or destroy a US industry must plead and prove predation in the technical antitrust sense as opposed to the ordinary sense. The Court in *Geneva Steel* said the following:

> "Zenith Radio [referring to the opinions dealing with the comparability tests] did not reach the precise issue present in the instant case. However, to the extent Zenith Radio can be read to compel a finding that the 1916 Act has no protectionist aspects, as distinct from antitrust aspects, this court respectfully disagrees. Such a holding could only be reached by the judicial branch rewriting the statute, and thereby inappropriately invading the terrain of the legislative branch."[237]

3.325 The European Communities further recalls that the Court in *Wheeling-Pittsburgh* faced exactly the same issue and gave a similar response:

> "The Court finds that, under [the 1916 Act] [...] Wheeling-Pitt must show that the defendants sold their product at a price level prohibited by the statute with the intent to injure or destroy the domestic hot-rolled steel industry. The additional proof of 'predatory pricing' as the term is used in Brooke Group is not applicable to this case. [...] Under the domestic antitrust statutes, 'predatory pricing', after Brooke Group, means below-cost pricing established with the reasonable expectation that, through later acquired market share, recovery of the cost incurred by the earlier lower prices will occur. Under the Antidumping Act of 1916 [...] 'predatory pricing' means something different. The artificially low prices must be set with the goal of injuring, destroying, or preventing the establishment of an American industry. It is certainly within the purview of Congress to distinguish harm caused by domestic competitors from those caused by international ones. For example, dumping itself has long been noted to constitute a harmful international trade practice which may, through government, as opposed to market-driven action, cause sharp increases in imported goods, to the detriment of domestic producers."[238]

3.326 In the view of the European Communities, regardless of whether these two decisions are "final" or "conclusive", they are the most recent pronouncements of US courts on the 1916 Act. They appear to be the only judicial pronouncements, recent or otherwise, which deal specifically and narrowly with the question whether antitrust standards relating to predation apply to what must be pleaded and proved in 1916 Act claims based on an allegation of "intent to injure or destroy a US industry". While it is true that neither opinion was "final" in the sense of "appealable", they are both well reasoned opinions to which weight would be attributed by other courts confronted with the same issue - an issue which was not confronted by the cases on which the United States relies.

---

[237] *Geneva Steel*, *Op. Cit.*, p. 1219.

[238] *Wheeling-Pittsburgh*, *Op. Cit.*, pp. 603-04.

3.327 With respect to the suggestion of the United States that district court opinions, interlocutory or otherwise, do not have weight, the European Communities considers that it is sufficient to read the various opinions involved. All of the case law cited, except for two opinions of the Third Circuit Court of Appeals, consists of opinions of district courts. These opinions refer to and cite opinions of district courts, whether interlocutory or final, as well as the opinions of the circuit courts of appeals. The reasoning is very nuanced, paying particular attention to the precise issue dealt with in each case, but also showing a willingness, as illustrated by the opinions in *Geneva Steel* and *Wheeling-Pittsburgh*, to examine the logic applied by a circuit court of appeals other than the one having jurisdiction over the district court in question, and to disagree with it. This is consistent with the common law system as applied by US federal courts. In that system, opinions of circuit courts of appeals are binding on district courts located in the circuit in question which deal with the specific question before the district court, but otherwise district courts are free to, and do, consider the issues before them on the merits, considering all relevant authorities and arguments.

3.328 In summing up its position, the European Communities reiterates that it remains the case that, in respect of the difference between intent to injure under the 1916 Act and predatory intent under the Robinson-Patman Act, there are circumstances where facts caught by the former in respect of imported products would not be caught by the latter in respect of domestic products. To take a simple example, an internal memorandum of the defendant declaring the intention to take market share from a US competitor could, by itself, be evidence of intent to injure under the 1916 Act but would not suffice to show predation under the Robinson-Patman Act.

3.329 In response, the **United States** argues that the European Communities provides no support for the conclusion it draws from its hypothetical example involving the internal memorandum. According to the United States, there is credible evidence to support the opposite conclusion. For example, the European Communities' analysis squarely contradicts a comment by the District Court in *Geneva Steel*. In that case, the District Court observed that

> "mere knowledge on the part of the importer that his sales will capture business away from his United States competitor, standing alone, will not be sufficient to demonstrate an intent to injure the entire United States steel industry and will therefore be inadequate to establish a violation of the Act."[239]

3.330 The United States also notes that, in 1983, the Third Circuit Court of Appeals in *In re Japanese Electronic Products II* dismissed the plaintiffs' claims against Sony, Motorola and Sears because the plaintiffs' evidence was found to be legally insufficient. That evidence included that the defendants sold CEPs at substantially lower prices in the United States than the prices at which comparable CEPs were sold in Japan; that they knew that the other defendants were engaging in similar activity; and they knew that concerted dumping could injure or destroy the CEP industry in the United States. The court found that even this evidence did not rise to the level of showing a "specific predatory intent."

[239] *Geneva Steel, Op. Cit.*, p. 1224.

3.331 The United States thus considers it, at the very least, highly questionable that the internal memorandum example posed by the European Communities would result in liability under the 1916 Act.

3.332 In concluding, the United States recalls that the highest US court to have considered the issue of intent requirement, the Third Circuit Court of Appeals, has held that the showing of intent required by the 1916 Act is essentially the same as the showing of predatory intent required to establish primary line price discrimination under the Robinson-Patman Act, as interpreted by the Supreme Court in its *Brooke Group* decision.

3.333 The United States argues, however, that even if recoupment is not the requirement, the Panel should still conclude that the 1916 Act treats imports no less favourably than the Robinson-Patman Act treats domestic products. First, the European Communities does not offer an explanation or support for its opinion that it is more difficult to prove recoupment of losses than a specific intent to destroy an industry. The European Communities' opinion is also contradicted by the actual application of the 1916 Act as well as express statements by the courts and the Tariff Commission. Second, the case-law indicates that the specific predatory intent element is virtually impossible to satisfy. Thus, in no instance do importers receive less favourable treatment.

(ii) The Measurement of Price Discrimination

3.334 The **European Communities** notes a difference in the approach to establishment of price discrimination under the 1916 Act and the Robinson-Patman Act. According to the European Communities, the 1916 Act is applicable whenever goods are imported into the United States at prices *substantially below the prices charged in the country* of production or other countries where the goods are commonly exported. The statute reads in the relevant part:

> "It shall be unlawful [...] to import, sell or cause to be imported or sold such articles within the United States at a price substantially less than the actual market value or wholesale price of such articles, at the time of exportation to the United States."[240]

3.335 The European Communities recalls that, by contrast, to establish a primary line infringement under the Robinson-Patman Act, it must be shown that the defendant is *charging prices below a certain measure of its costs*. In the practice of the courts, that measure is the average variable cost of production. Where prices are above average variable cost of production, there is no infringement, even if the accused company is applying different prices to different customers.

3.336 In the view of the European Communities, in many if not most cases of international price discrimination, prices of imported products are still above average variable costs of production.[241] In such cases, importers may have to face legal proceedings under the 1916 Act for price practices above average variable cost while

---

[240] 15 U.S.C. § 72.

[241] According to the European Communities, the use of term 'substantially' in the 1916 Act does not change this conclusion, since there will be many cases where the price discrimination meets the "substantial" test without the price of the imported product falling below average variable costs.

domestic producers would not be at risk under the Robinson-Patman Act for sales made at similar levels.[242] The fact that sanctions can be imposed and damages awarded in situations involving foreign goods sold at a price which bears a given relation to cost of production, while the same price having the same relation to cost of production charged by domestic producers cannot be challenged under the Robinson-Patman Act, amounts to less favourable treatment of imported products prohibited under Article III:4 of the GATT 1994.

3.337 The **United States** asserts that, as regards the requisite price discrimination, the 1916 Act treats foreign products *more* favourably than the Robinson-Patman Act treats domestic products, because the 1916 Act requires a more difficult showing by the complainant in this area than does the Robinson-Patman Act.

3.338 The United States' first supporting argument is that the 1916 Act requires proof of a far larger number of illegal price differences - imposed in a systematic way - in order to establish liability. In particular, the complainant must show that the defendant "commonly and systematically" made the sales prohibited by the 1916 Act. By contrast, under the Robinson-Patman Act, liability can be established on the basis of as few as two consummated sales.[243]

3.339 The United States notes, as a second point, that the 1916 Act requires proof of a larger price difference than the Robinson-Patman Act in an absolute sense. In particular, under the 1916 Act the complainant must establish that the articles at issue are sold within the United States at a price "substantially less than actual market value or wholesale price of such articles [...] in the principal markets of the country of their production, or of other foreign countries to which they are commonly exported." By contrast, the Robinson-Patman Act simply requires a showing of a "cognizable" difference in price, which need only be greater than a *de minimis* difference. Thus, for example, a circuit court of appeals recently held that a 2.38 percent price difference provided a basis for liability under the Robinson-Patman Act.[244] Such a small difference would hardly satisfy the requirement that the price be "substantially less" under the 1916 Act.

3.340 The United States considers that the European Communities ignores these facts by focussing instead on what type of price practices will result in an award of damages under the two statutes. The United States further considers that the European Communities' argument is contradicted by US case law. According to the US Supreme Court, under the Robinson-Patman Act, the complainant only needs to "prove that the prices complained of are below an appropriate measure of the rival's cost."[245] Lower courts, meanwhile, have not agreed on what the appropriate measure of a rival's costs are. Some courts have held, for example, that the prices complained of need only be below average cost, while other courts have held that they need to be below average variable costs. In the 1916 Act context, on the other hand, the one

---

[242] The European Communities notes that the *Geneva Steel* and the *Wheeling-Pittsburgh* proceedings are two concrete examples.

[243] The United States refers to *International Telephone & Telegraph Corp. et al., Op. Cit.*, p. 417, citing E. Kinter, *A Robinson-Patman Primer*, 3rd ed. (1979), p. 35.

[244] The United States refers to *Chroma Lighting v. GTE Products Corp.*, 1997-1 Trade Cas (CCH) 71,836 (9th Cir. 1997) at 79,885.

[245] *Brooke Group , Op. Cit.*, pp. 222-23.

court that has squarely addressed this issue has only endorsed the more stringent standard of average variable costs. As that Court explained:

> "It is somewhat of a stretch to suggest the [1916] Act justifies damages when [the defendant's] prices equalled or exceeded average variable cost [...]. Therefore, this Court shall limit damages to those cases where [the defendant] set prices below average variable cost."[246]

3.341 The United States considers, therefore, that, in a 1916 Act case, the plaintiff may have to establish two elements: first, the price difference between the US market and the foreign market; and second, the price in the US market, which must be below average variable costs. In contrast, in a Robinson-Patman Act case, the plaintiff must only establish a certain measurement of below cost pricing. Thus, the 1916 Act actually affords more favourable treatment to imports than the Robinson-Patman Act does to domestic goods.

3.342 The United States thus concludes that the European Communities' argument overlooks or ignores the relevant case law, which confirms that on this difference as well the 1916 Act is applied more strictly than the Robinson-Patman Act.

3.343 In response to the US argument that there is some disagreement among US courts on what the appropriate measure of a rival's costs is, the **European Communities** recalls, first of all, how it comes about in the US federal court system that courts reach different results on the same issue of law. For federal court purposes, the United States is divided into circuits, each circuit having its own circuit court of appeals. Appeals from decisions of district courts lie to the circuit court of appeals of the circuit in which they are located. District courts are bound by the positions taken by their circuit court of appeals, which is in turn bound by positions taken by the US Supreme Court. So long as the Supreme Court has not spoken on a particular issue of law, it can happen that different and conflicting positions develop among the circuit courts.

3.344 Addressing the substantive aspects of the disagreement among US courts on what is the "appropriate measure of costs", the European Communities notes that at least two Circuits, the Second and the Fifth, have clearly and unequivocally adopted the "average variable cost" test. They have held that sales below the "average variable cost" level are conclusively presumed to be predatory while sales above it are conclusively presumed not to be.[247] Other Circuits have taken more nuanced positions, which allow of the possibility that predation may be established at prices above average variable costs but below average total costs, depending on the presence of other indicia of predatory intent.[248] However, according to the European Communities, what matters is that the test of the 1916 Act concerns differences in sales prices alone, whereas the Robinson-Patman Act after the Supreme Court's *Brooke Group* decision requires not only differences in price but also a price below costs. Whatever the "appropriate measure of costs" is, it is clear that there can be situations where a

---

[246] *Helmac II, Op. Cit.*, p. 583.

[247] The European Communities refers to *Northeastern Telephone Company v. AT&T, Op. Cit.*; *International Air Industries v. American Excelsior Co.*, 517 F.2d 714 (5th Cir. 1975).

[248] The European Communities refers to, e.g., *Mcgahee v. Northern Propane Gas Company, Op. Cit.*; *Chillicothe Sand & Gravel Co. v. Martin Marietta Corp., Op. Cit.*.

price in the United States is "substantially" below the sales price applied in the domestic market but is not below costs. In such a situation, the 1916 Act could apply, whereas in the comparable situation involving domestic products, the Robinson-Patman Act could not.

3.345 The European Communities is aware that a Michigan District Court in *Helmac II* declined to award damages under the 1916 Act absent a showing of prices below average variable costs. The Michigan District Court justified this with no other reasoning than the observation that "it is somewhat of a stretch" to allow damages for prices above this level. This decision was not appealed, and the Court's unsupported reasoning would have been a good issue on appeal if there had been one. Its implausibility is accentuated by the fact that the same Court, in the same case, a few months earlier, explicitly held that the other element of antitrust predation - reasonable prospect of recoupment of losses from sales below cost - did not have to be proved in claims under the 1916 Act.[249]

3.346 The European Communities notes, finally, that, even if on the basis of the court decision in *Helmac II* no remedy (damages) were available to a plaintiff if the price is not below costs, there would still be a difference between the Robinson-Patman Act and the 1916 Act. Under the Robinson-Patman Act, there is no liability at all if the price is not below cost. Under the 1916 Act, this would not prevent liability from arising but simply lead to only nominal damages being recovered. This is of only limited help to an importer who has had to suffer the expense and uncertainty of lengthy litigation in the US courts.

3.347 The **United States** replies that *Helmac II* is the only final decision to have considered the issue. The District Court applied precisely the same measure of discrimination to the 1916 Act claim as is applied in many primary line Robinson-Patman Act cases. The European Communities has no answer to this point other than that it believes that the Court's reasoning is "unsupported" or "implausible", which the United States disputes. The European Communities' opinion, however, is not relevant. It is not for the parties or the Panel to agree or disagree with the judicial interpretations of the 1916 Act. The question of the proper interpretation of the 1916 Act is a question of fact for the present Panel.

3.348 The United States argues that, in any event, there are a number of good reasons for the *Helmac II* Court's decision to measure price discrimination in the same way under both the 1916 Act and the Robinson-Patman Act. In particular, comparing the price charged by a particular firm to the cost structure of that firm can help establish whether the price represents competition on the merits or is instead intended to injure competition as part of a predatory strategy. For example, average variable cost constitutes the shut-down point, i.e. the price level below which it makes more sense to shut down completely than to continue operating. If a firm makes sales at prices below average variable cost for a significant period of time, that suggests that it in-

---

[249] The European Communities refers to *Helmac I*, *Op. Cit.*, p. 576 where the Court states the following: "Helmac alleges that Roth (plastics) attempted to injure Helmac, an industry in the United States. Such an allegation, if proven, would establish a violation of the Antidumping Act of 1916. It is not necessary, however, for Helmac to prove that Roth (plastics) had the ability to recoup the losses incurred in eliminating Helmac from competition".

tends to injure competition, because there is no pro-competitive reason for making sales at such prices.

(iii) Offering for Sale vs. Actual Sale as Threshold Requirements for Complaints

3.349 For the **European Communities**, another reason why dumping is easier to establish under the 1916 Act than under the Robinson-Patman Act is that under the former a simple *offer* to sell foreign goods is sufficient to entitle a request for treble damages, while cases against price discrimination under the Robinson-Patman Act require actual sales.[250]

3.350 The **United States** concedes that one district court has suggested that an offer to sell may be sufficient to support a claim under the 1916 Act, but recalls that the Act still requires that the offers to sell were made "commonly and systematically." Any significance this difference may have is more than offset by the greater difficulty of establishing the prevalence of price differences under the 1916 Act than under the Robinson-Patman Act. The 1916 Act requires the plaintiff to prove that the price differences at issue - whether in the form of offers or actual sales - are imposed "commonly and systematically." By contrast, the Robinson-Patman Act can be satisfied with as few as two consummated sales.

(iv) Defences Available under the Robinson-Patman Act, but not Expressly Provided for in the 1916 Act

3.351 The **European Communities** believes that price discrimination under the Robinson-Patman Act may be more easily justified, as specific and additional defences against a *prima facie* case of price discrimination are available under its provisions. Under the Robinson-Patman Act, a defence against a *prima facie* case of price discrimination exists when:

(a) the seller shows "that his lower price or the furnishing of services or facilities to any purchaser was made in good faith to meet an equally low price of a competitor, or the services furnished by a competitor" ("meeting competition" defence),

(b) the price changes occur "in response to changing conditions affecting the market for or the marketability of the goods concerned" ("changing market conditions" defence).[251]

3.352 The European Communities notes that none of the above defences is provided for in the 1916 Act. In the view of the European Communities, these two examples are an additional demonstration that sanctioning price discrimination under the Robinson-Patman Act is more difficult than under the 1916 Act.

3.353 The **United States** agrees that the 1916 Act, on its face, does not specifically authorize any defences. The Robinson-Patman Act, on the other hand, allows three defences namely, a "meeting competition" defence, a defence based upon "changing

250 The European Communities refers to *Helmac I*, *Op. Cit.*, pp. 575-76.

251 15 U.S.C. 13(a),(b) (emphasis added by the European Communities).

market conditions" and a "cost justification" defence.[252] The United States contends that these differences do not undermine the conclusion that the 1916 Act accords no less favourable treatment to foreign products than the Robinson-Patman Act accords domestic products because these defences are inherent in the 1916 Act's requirement that an intent to injure or destroy an industry be proven. This is also recognized in the following excerpt from a treatise on US and EC competition laws:

> "Unlike the Robinson-Patman Act, the 1916 Act does not expressly provide for meeting competition and cost justification defenses. These considerations would appear relevant to predatory intent and thus should implicitly be included in the 1916 Act."[253]

3.354 The United States therefore considers that, in a 1916 Act case, any evidence which would support the Robinson-Patman Act defences would be equally and directly relevant to whether the showing of predatory intent can be made in the first place. Evidence showing that the defendant's pricing practices were undertaken only with the intent of meeting competition, responding to changing market conditions or to account for cost savings would be used to show whether the defendant had the requisite predatory intent in the first place. This type of evidence would not have to be presented as a defence, but, rather would undermine any other available evidence tending to show that the defendant had a predatory intent. Indeed, a case upon which the European Communities relies, *Geneva Steel,* makes this point. There, the Court explained that one reason why it is difficult to prove the requisite intent under the 1916 Act is that "evidence of normal pricing cuts [...] would be insufficient to establish liability under the 1916 Act."[254] In a Robinson-Patman Act case, it is necessary to provide for these defences. Without them, conduct undertaken merely to meet competition or for other proper purposes could be punished.

3.355 In response to a question of the Panel regarding the implications for US law purposes of the distinction between codified and non-codified defences, the United States further notes that, as far as the defendant is concerned, there is no particular advantage to having a defence codified in a statute as opposed to arguing that the same evidence undermines the plaintiff's required showing. In fact, it would seem that the opposite is true. If a defence is codified, the defendant would bear the burden of pleading and proving the defence. On the other hand, if the same evidence is relevant to rebutting the plaintiff's required showing, the defendant may present this evidence without having to carry the ultimate burden.

3.356 The **European Communities** concedes that the same evidence may be relevant in many cases under both the Robinson-Patman Act and the 1916 Act. However, the European Communities asserts that it is evident that evidence which establishes the "meeting competition" or "changing market conditions" defence under the Robinson-Patman Act will not in all circumstances suffice to negate predatory intent under the 1916 Act. There are other circumstances in which liability under the 1916 Act would arise than predatory pricing, let alone predatory pricing in the antitrust sense.

---

252 15 U.S.C. 13(a),(b).

253 B. Hawk, *United States, Common Market and International Antitrust* (1996-1 Suppl.), p. 357

254 *Geneva Steel, Op. Cit.*, p. 1220.

3.357 The **United States** notes that the European Communities does not offer any examples, concrete or hypothetical, to support this allegation. The United States finds it impossible to imagine, for example, that any court would conclude that a particular defendant intended to destroy a particular industry if the defendant was simply matching the prices of competing firms in that industry or facilitating the sale of perishable merchandise.

H. Violation of Article XVI:4 of the Agreement Establishing the WTO

1. The Meaning and Scope of Article XVI:4

3.358 The **European Communities** considers that, since, in its view, the 1916 Act is an anti-dumping statute covered by the discipline of Article VI of the GATT 1994 and the Anti-Dumping Agreement, it should, pursuant to Article XVI:4 of the Agreement Establishing the WTO[255], have been brought into full conformity with the rules set forth in Article VI and in the Anti-Dumping Agreement.

3.359 The European Communities contends that Article XVI:4 lays down a new and additional obligation in the framework of the multilateral trading system. It imposes a positive obligation to ensure the conformity of a Member's domestic laws, regulations and administrative procedures with its WTO obligations. As a result of this obligation, in cases where pre-existing domestic legislation may be inconsistent with new WTO obligations, including those arising under Article VI of the GATT 1994, and Articles 1, 2.1, 2.2, 3, 4 and 5.5 of the Anti-Dumping Agreement, a Member was required to amend its domestic legislation so as to avoid any conflict as from 1 January 1995.

3.360 According to the European Communities, the new principle governing the relationship between domestic laws, regulations and administrative procedures and WTO obligations that is embodied in Article XVI:4 of the Agreement Establishing the WTO is a fundamental one.[256] Because it is laid down in the basic agreement of the system, it covers the whole set of the annexed agreements, whether or not they may contain specific expressions of the same principle. Furthermore, by virtue of Article XVI:3 of the Agreement Establishing the WTO it is a superior rule to provisions in the annexed agreements.

3.361 The **United States** takes the view that the meaning of the text of Article XVI:4 is straightforward. If a Member's law, regulation, or administrative procedure does not conform with its obligations as provided in the WTO agreements, that Member has an affirmative obligation to bring it into conformity. Conversely, if

[255] Article XVI:4 of the Agreement Establishing the WTO reads as follows:

> "Each Member shall ensure the conformity of its laws, regulations and administrative procedures with its obligations as provided in the annexed Agreements."

[256] The European Communities refers to the Award of the Arbitrator, *Japan - Taxes on Alcoholic Beverages*, Arbitration under Article 21.3(c) of the DSU (*"Japan - Alcoholic Beverages II*), WT/DS8/15, WT/DS10/15, WT/DS11/13, 14 February 1997, DSR 1997:I, 3, para 9, where it is stated that "[a]s a general and fundamental obligation imposed on all WTO Members, Article XVI:4 of the Marrakesh *Agreement Establishing the World Trade Organization* (the "*WTO Agreement*") requires that each Member shall ensure the conformity of its laws, regulations and administrative procedures with its obligations as provided in the *WTO Agreement*."

those laws, regulations and administrative procedures conform with its obligations, the Member need undertake no further action. Thus, as regards the instant case, Article XVI:4 is not relevant, unless the 1916 Act is shown to be inconsistent with a separate US obligation under a WTO agreement.

3.362 The United States further considers that the new so-called "obligations" asserted by the European Communities have been created out of whole cloth. Article XVI:4 of the Agreement Establishing the WTO provides that "[e]ach Member shall ensure the conformity of its laws, regulations and administrative procedures with its obligations *as provided in the annexed Agreements*."[257] By its terms, this provision does not provide a new and additional obligation beyond those provided in the annexed Agreements.

3.363 The **European Communities** adds that Article XVI:4 applies over and above similar obligations under general public international law as enshrined in Articles 26 and 27 of the Vienna Convention on the Law of Treaties. The Vienna Convention on the Law of Treaties, in Article 26, codifies the customary principle of good faith implementation of international treaty obligations and, in Article 27, spells out a negative obligation, i.e. to refrain from invoking domestic law in order to justify any departure from an international obligation undertaken by a state. The obligation to respect WTO obligations thus results directly from the presence of those rules in the WTO Agreement and Article XVI:4 of the Agreement Establishing the WTO would be reduced to redundancy if interpreted as not containing an additional and different obligation.

3.364 The European Communities further argues that the obligation in Article XVI:4 of the Agreement Establishing the WTO must go beyond merely revoking the "grandfather clause" of the Protocol of Provisional Application, which permitted the maintenance of mandatory legislation inconsistent with the GATT 1947. This is effected by the introductory text to the GATT 1994.

3.365 The **United States** is perplexed by the European Communities' argument regarding Articles 26 and 27 of the Vienna Convention because the Vienna Convention is not a covered agreement under the WTO. In fact, it is through the provisions of Article XVI:4 that the principles of Article 26 of the Vienna Convention became legally binding on all Members of the WTO, even though not all Members are parties to the Vienna Convention. For example, the United States is not a party.

3.366 With regard to the European Communities' argument based upon the introductory text of the GATT 1994, the United States argues that, by definition, Article 1(a) and (b) are applicable only to the GATT 1994, and not to other WTO agreements such as the General Agreement on Trade in Services (hereinafter the "GATS") and the Agreement on Trade-Related Aspects of Intellectual Property Rights (hereinafter the "TRIPS Agreement"). Article XVI:4 therefore provides an overarching statement in the Agreement Establishing the WTO, clearly applicable to all annexed agreements and not just the GATT 1994, that no measures are grandfathered. Article XVI:4 thus serves to remove any doubt which might have existed in its absence that all measures must be brought into conformity as from 1 January 1995. Indeed, it was precisely in this manner and for this purpose that the Appellate Body cited Article

[257] Emphasis added by the United States.

XVI:4 in *India - Patent.* In that case, India attempted to argue that it could delay changing its law as required by Article 70.9 of the TRIPS Agreement because of differences between the language of that provision and that of other Articles of the TRIPS Agreement. Specifically, India claimed that while other TRIPS Agreement provisions explicitly required changes to domestic laws, Article 70.9 did not. The Appellate Body rejected this argument, stating at the outset of its discussion that "India's arguments must be examined in the light of Article XVI:4 of the *WTO Agreement*".[258] Article XVI:4 thus assisted in clarifying that India could not rely on claimed differences in TRIPS Agreement language to delay compliance.

3.367 In the view of the United States, beyond serving this overarching function of providing context for provisions of the WTO agreements, Article XVI:4 imposed an obligation on Members to review existing legislation at the time the WTO Agreement was to enter into effect to make sure that existing laws, regulations and administrative procedures did, in fact, conform to the Members' WTO obligations, and where those laws did not, to bring them into conformity. In the United States, for example, a comprehensive review of US law was undertaken after the Uruguay Round Final Act to determine which laws, regulations or administrative procedures might need to be changed in order to comply with Article XVI:4. Where a statutory change was necessary, it was proposed to the US Congress and enacted as part of the Uruguay Round Agreements Act, which was signed into law on 8 December 1994. All changes in regulations and administrative procedures that were necessary to bring the United States into conformity with its obligations under the WTO Agreement were described in the Statement of Administrative Action which was submitted by the executive branch and approved by Congress as part of the Uruguay Round Agreements Act.

3.368 The US counter-arguments notwithstanding, the **European Communities** maintains its view that Article XVI:4 does not only contain an obligation to avoid violating the WTO agreements. According to the European Communities, it also contains an obligation to take positive action to ensure that nothing in a WTO Member's "laws, regulations and administrative procedures" is inconsistent with the WTO agreements, that nothing in them contains conditions or criteria or powers to take action which conflict with those agreements. This has already been recognised by the Appellate Body in the *India -Patent* case. In that case, both the panel and the Appellate Body upheld the United States' claim that domestic law can be inconsistent with WTO provisions not merely because it mandates WTO-inconsistent actions, but also because it fails to provide "a sound legal basis" for the administrative procedures or any other executive action required to implement WTO obligations.[259] The underlying rationale was that in the absence of a sound legal basis for mailbox patent applications in domestic law, the basic objective of WTO law, namely to create predictable conditions of competition, could not be achieved.

3.369 The European Communities submits that the 1916 Act also does not provide such a "sound legal basis" for implementation of Article VI of the GATT 1994 and

258 Appellate Body Report, *India - Patents, supra*, footnote 29, para. 79.

259 The European Communities refers to Appellate Body Report, *India - Patents, supra*, footnote 29, para 58.

the Anti-Dumping Agreement. Its wording conflicts with Article VI of the GATT 1994 and the Anti-Dumping Agreement in the ways that the European Communities has explained. The United States seeks to diminish this by arguing that certain courts have suggested that the 1916 Act may have some characteristics of antitrust legislation. It is clear that this case law, even taken together with the extrapolations thereof which the United States seeks to make and suggests may be adopted in the future, is a long way from "ensuring conformity" with Article VI of the GATT 1994 and the Anti-Dumping Agreement. The two most recent decisions of US courts, *Geneva Steel* and *Wheeling-Pittsburgh*, actually interpret and allow the 1916 Act to be applied in a way which would violate those provisions. In this regard, the European Communities notes that the applicability of Article XVI:4 is not limited to final judgements and that, in any event, the United States has done nothing to fulfil its obligation under Article XVI:4. It has neither amended the 1916 Act nor intervened in the cases referred to in order to ensure that the 1916 Act is not applied in a manner contrary to the United States' WTO obligations. Nor has it even said that it disagrees with the decisions adopted by the District Courts in these two cases.

3.370 In its response, the **United States** recalls that the discussion by the Appellate Body in *India-Patent* of a "sound legal basis" comes in the context of an analysis of the specific textual obligation at issue in that case, Article 70.8(a) of the TRIPS Agreement. That provision affirmatively requires Members to provide in their domestic legal systems a mechanism for the filing of applications for patents which protects their novelty and priority. India instead had on its books a law explicitly prohibiting such applications, that is, specifically mandating a violation of India's TRIPS Agreement obligations. India claimed that unwritten, unpublished "administrative instructions" never produced for the panel took priority over the mandatory law, but the panel and Appellate Body found nothing to support this claim. It was in this context, the context of Article 70.8(a) of the TRIPS Agreement with its requirement of a domestic legal mechanism accomplishing specific ends, that the panel and Appellate Body concluded that the "administrative instructions" failed to provide a sound legal basis.[260] The concept was not analysed in the abstract as somehow derived independently of Article 70.8(a). Furthermore, it is worth noting that the Appellate Body reversed panel findings relating to "legitimate expectations" generally and removal of "reasonable doubts" because these findings were not textually based. Likewise, the European Communities' theory that the 1916 Act violates Article XVI:4 because it does not provide a "sound legal basis" for implementation of Article VI has no textual basis and must therefore be rejected.

2. *The Relevance to an Article XVI:4 Inquiry of the Distinction Between Mandatory and Discretionary Legislation*

3.371 The **European Communities** argues that, even if it were possible to interpret the 1916 Act in a manner compatible with Article VI of the GATT 1994, Article XVI:4 of the Agreement Establishing the WTO would require a WTO Member to

[260] The United States refers to *India - Patents*, *supra*, footnote 29, paras. 56-58.

take positive measures to ensure compliance with its WTO obligations and eliminate even a potential incompatibility with WTO obligations. The United States cannot hide behind the excuse that action contrary to WTO obligations might one day not be allowed by the US Supreme Court. The fact that courts are regularly interpreting the 1916 Act in a manner contrary to Article VI of the GATT 1994, should require the United States to intervene and prevent this.

3.372 According to the **United States**, the European Communities' assertion that Members must take affirmative action to eliminate even a "potential" incompatibility suggests that the European Communities believes that WTO Members are under an affirmative obligation to include in their domestic law explicit limits on discretionary authority. This formulation of WTO obligations is diametrically opposed to the principle set forth in each and every panel report which has addressed the issue - that legislation must mandate, and not merely leave open the possibility, of GATT- or WTO-inconsistent action. Likewise, such a formulation is also inconsistent with the approach taken in other GATT 1947 contexts, for example, working parties examining the legislation of a contracting party or acceding country to determine whether that legislation *mandates* GATT-inconsistent results and not whether it *could* deliver such results.[261] Therefore, the analysis of whether the 1916 Act is inconsistent with Article XVI:4 must be based upon an analysis of whether the 1916 Act mandates a violation of the text of Article VI and the Anti-Dumping Agreement.

3.373 The **European Communities** responds that, even if on the basis of the GATT 1947 it could be argued that any aspect of the 1916 Act is discretionary and not a *per se* violation of the United States' obligations, the situation is in any event different under the WTO Agreement, since Article XVI:4 of the WTO Agreement now expressly requires Members to "ensure the conformity of its laws, regulations and administrative procedures with its obligations" under the WTO agreements. Article XVI:4 covers both domestic legislation *per se* and its application to specific cases.

3.374 The European Communities further notes that one effect of Article XVI:4 is to shift the borderline between discretionary and mandatory legislation so as to bring legislation with "less mandatory" character under WTO disciplines. Article XVI:4, whatever its other consequences may be, at least broadens the range of acts that can be classified as "mandatory". This is well illustrated by the decision of the GATT 1947 panel in the *EC - Audio Cassettes* case. The panel in that case applied the "shall ensure the conformity" clause of what was then Article 16.6(a) of the Tokyo Round Anti-Dumping Code to hold EC anti-dumping legislation as Code-infringing, despite the fact that the initiation of proceedings under the legislation was discretionary. It then examined particular rules within the legislation to see whether they mandated infringements of the Code or allowed administrators discretion to act in a legal way. The panel expressed itself as follows:

> "[T]he Panel did not consider in any event that its task in this case was to determine whether the EC's Basic Regulation in its totality was non-mandatory in the sense that the initiation of investigations and imposition of duties were not mandatory functions. Should panels ac-

[261] The United States refers to the *Report on The European Economic Community*, adopted on 29 November 1957, BISD 6S/70, p. 80, para.10.

cept this approach, they would be precluded from ever reviewing the content of a Party's anti-dumping legislation, a result that would undermine the requirement of Article 16:6 of the Agreement that Parties bring their legislation, regulations and administrative procedures into conformity with the provisions of the Agreement. Rather, the Panel considered that its task in this case was to determine whether the EC's Basic Regulation was mandatory in the sense that the EC was required by its legislation to use the averaging methodology complained of by Japan."[262]

3.375 The European Communities submits that the *EC - Audio Cassettes* case shows that the criteria and conditions set out in legislation whose overall application may be discretionary must also comply with WTO obligations. The same reasoning can be extended to the instant case. For example, the 1916 Act says that criminal prosecution is discretionary, but once a case is coming into prosecutions, the question arises whether there is an offence.

3.376 The European Communities is aware that the report of the panel in the *EC - Audio Cassettes* case was never adopted, but notes that the reason why the report was not adopted had nothing to do with the distinction between mandatory and discretionary measures. Moreover, the Appellate Body in *Japan - Alcoholic Beverages* noted on the legal status of an unadopted panel report that:

> "a panel could nevertheless find useful guidance in the reasoning of an unadopted panel report that it considered to be relevant."[263]

3.377 The European Communities adds that the panel in *United States - Definition of the Wine Industry* took the same position as the *EC - Audio Cassettes* panel. The report of that panel was adopted. In *United States - Definition of the Wine Industry*, the United States argued that the case should not proceed in the absence of an application of the law since the violation was purely "hypothetical". The panel rejected this argument and ruled on the compatibility of the US law stating:

> "The Panel noted that it had been called upon, in its terms of reference, to review the facts of the matter referred to the Committee by the EEC in document SCM/54, and that the issue raised in this document was the conformity of the US law in question (i.e. Section 612(a)(1) of the Trade and Tariff Act of 1984) *as such* with the provisions of the Code, as required by its Article 19:5(a)."[264]

3.378 The European Communities notes that Article 19:5(a) of the Tokyo Round Subsidies Agreement was virtually identical to Article 16:6(a) of the Tokyo Round Anti-Dumping Code which the *EC- Audio Cassettes* panel relied on. Both are equivalent to Article XVI:4 of the Agreement Establishing the WTO.

3.379 The European Communities further points out that one of the purposes of Article XVI:4 of the Agreement Establishing the WTO is to ensure security and predictability in the international trading system. Placing importers under the threat of draconian civil and criminal penalties can have a "chilling effect" on imports even if

---

262 *EC - Audio Cassettes*, *Op. Cit.*, para. 362.

263 Appellate Body Report, *Japan - Alcoholic Beverages*, *supra*, footnote 224, at 108.

264 *United States - Definition of the Wine Industry*, *Op. Cit.*, para. 4.1.

the legislation has for some reason not so far been applied to the point of imposing penalties.[265] Paradoxically, the more a law is effective as a deterrent, the less will be the evidence of actual rather than possible application. The following passage of the report of the panel in *United States - Malt Beverages* is pertinent:

> "[...] the measure continues to be mandatory legislation which may influence the decisions of economic operators".[266]

3.380 The European Communities submits that the report of the GATT 1947 panel in the *Japan - Trade in Semi-conductors* case[267] also illustrates this point. It makes clear that even a measure which is not formally binding can still be capable of constituting an infringement. The same can be said of binding measures that are not often enforced, such as the 1916 Act.

3.381 The **United States** maintains its view that, since the 1916 Act is susceptible to an interpretation that is fully consistent with all of the United States' WTO obligations and has been so interpreted to date, there is no requirement under Article XVI:4 that the United States take action to change the law. Moreover, the distinction is still being applied in cases brought under the WTO, as is evidenced by the report of the panel on *Canada - Aircraft.*

3.382 The **European Communities** responds that the US interpretation would reduce Article XVI:4 of the Agreement Establishing the WTO to inutility and redundancy. The US argument that the 1916 Act "is susceptible to an interpretation that is fully consistent with all US WTO obligations" is based on an alleged non-actionability of discretionary legislation under the GATT 1947 and ignores Article XVI:4 of the Agreement Establishing the WTO, which has at least significantly reduced the required degree of mandatoriness for actionability.

3.383 The European Communities concedes that the mandatory/discretionary distinction continues to be significant, for example, in cases where an administrative authority is given a general power to regulate trade and to adopt measures of commercial policies. This gives to the authority the possibility to take measures which are incompatible with WTO obligations but it can of course also choose to remain within the bounds of what would not violate WTO rules. The fact that the authority has the possibility to take measures which are incompatible is not of itself a violation of WTO obligations. A violation arises where incompatible measures are taken or where the administration is obliged to take into consideration criteria or apply conditions that are inconsistent with those prescribed in the WTO agreements. It is the latter situation that prevails in the case of the 1916 Act.

3.384 As regards the relevance of the panel report on *Canada - Aircraft*, the European Communities recalls that the panel in that case found that the measure authorising grants could not be an infringement of the SCM Agreement since the body in question was not required to subsidize, i.e. to infringe the SCM Agreement.[268] The

[265] The European Communities notes that the mere fact of non-application may be accidental, subject to change and completely out of a government's control.

[266] *United States - Malt Beverages*, *Op. Cit.*, para. 5.60.

[267] Panel Report on *Japan - Trade in Semi-conductors,* adopted on 4 May 1988, BISD 35S/116.

[268] The European Communities refers to Panel Report, *Canada - Aircraft*, *supra,* footnote 40, para. 9.127

panel then went on to consider whether that body actually did give subsidies. This case is not, however, of any guidance in the present case in view of the context in which the panel's reasoning occurs. The panel at that point in *Canada - Aircraft* was examining whether there were any subsidies in preparation for examining whether they were *de facto* export contingent and therefore prohibited. Subsidies are not as such inconsistent with the WTO Agreement, as indeed the SCM Agreement recognises in its footnote 23. They only violate the WTO Agreement if certain conditions are met, notably if they are export-contingent. Therefore, *a fortiori* the mere power to grant subsidies is not objectionable. Even if the *Canada - Aircraft* panel's overall conclusion may be correct, its reliance on the discretionary/mandatory distinction to arrive at its conclusion appears misplaced and inappropriate. In any event, this part of the report has not had the benefit of being reviewed by the Appellate Body.

3. Relationship with Article 18.4 of the Anti-Dumping Agreement

3.385 In response to a question of the Panel to both parties regarding the relationship between Article XVI:4 of the Agreement Establishing the WTO and Article 18.4 of the Anti-Dumping Agreement, the **European Communities** argues that Article 18.4 of the Anti-Dumping Agreement reiterates and confirms, for the specific area covered by that Agreement, the general obligation laid down in Article XVI:4 of the Agreement Establishing the WTO in respect of all its annexed agreements. Article XVI:4 is therefore broader in scope than Article 18.4 of the Anti-Dumping Agreement and also applies, for example, to Article VI of the GATT 1994.

3.386 The European Communities further notes that, as regards their respective content, there is essentially no difference between Article 18.4 and Article XVI:4. The only substantive difference results from the qualification in the Anti-Dumping Agreement "as [the WTO provisions] may apply for the Member in question". Apart from a historical explanation that this clause was carried forward from the Tokyo Round Code, in the new Anti-Dumping Agreement the scope for differential treatment of specific countries is rather limited. One example is provided by Article 15 as regards developing country Members. Moreover, the slight difference in wording does not remove the WTO dumping provisions from the scope of Article XVI:4. For example, in *Guatemala - Anti-Dumping Investigation Regarding Portland Cement From Mexico*, the panel reviewed a claim under Article 5.5 of the Anti-Dumping Agreement in the light of Article XVI:4.[269]

3.387 The European Communities adds that Article XVI:4 has generalised an obligation which was first set out in a more sectoral context and within a more limited group of GATT 1947 contracting parties, i.e. the parties to the Tokyo Round Anti-Dumping Code and the parties to the Tokyo Round Subsidies Code. If regard is had to the negotiating history of the Agreement Establishing the WTO, it is clear that it came at a relatively late stage of the Uruguay Round. At that stage, the negotiations

[269] The European Communities refers to the Panel Report on *Guatemala - Anti-Dumping Investigation Regarding Portland Cement From Mexico*, WT/DS60/R, adopted 25 November 1998, DSR 1998:IX, 3797, para 7.38.

of the Anti-Dumping Agreement were much more advanced and the reiteration of the old Code provision had not been questioned.

3.388 The **United States** is of the view that, like any other US law, regulation or administrative procedure, under Article XVI:4, anti-dumping laws, regulations and procedures, assuming they are mandatory, must conform with the requirements of the various WTO agreements.

3.389 With regard to Article 18.4 of the Anti-Dumping Agreement, the United States notes that, although the language is not identical to Article XVI:4, there were similar provisions in the Tokyo Round Codes on Anti-Dumping and Subsidies which have generally been interpreted as requiring the parties to those agreements to adopt laws, regulations and procedures that permit them to act in conformity with their obligations under those Agreements. Article 18.4 of the Anti-Dumping Agreement should be interpreted in the same way.

IV. THIRD PARTY SUBMISSIONS

A. India

4.1 According to **India**, Article VI of the GATT 1994 establishes the only GATT-compatible means of dealing with dumping. Three steps are envisaged in this Article. Firstly, what constitutes dumping; secondly, what conditions must be fulfilled for the application of remedial measures; and thirdly, what steps a Member can take once dumping has been established. As regards this third step, Article VI:2 provides for the levying of anti-dumping duties. It is therefore clear that Article VI lays down that, provided that there is material injury to the domestic industry and provided the relevant procedures are followed, WTO Members can levy anti-dumping duties. Hence, Article VI clearly establishes that the application of anti-dumping duties is the sole and only means authorized by the GATT 1994 to deal with the problem of dumped imports.

4.2 India notes, however, that, under the 1916 Act, the United States can apply measures other than anti-dumping duties.[270] Thus the very purpose and intent of Article VI and that of the Anti-Dumping Agreement is thwarted. The remedial measures provided for by the 1916 Act are treble damages and/or criminal penalties, including fines and/or imprisonment. These remedies are not duties and are not, therefore, the type of measures allowed under WTO anti-dumping rules to counter dumping practices. The United States has argued that the use of the phrase "may levy [...] an anti dumping duty" in Article VI:2 does not preclude the use of other remedies for dumping. This argument is not valid. Article VI of the GATT 1994 was specifically incorporated to address the problems of dumping and provides for the levying of anti-dumping duties as the sole remedy. It would be totally unacceptable if Members could not only impose anti-dumping duties, but also such other civil or criminal penalties as are prescribed by the 1916 Act. Clearly therefore, the 1916 Act violates Article VI:2 of the GATT 1994. Read in its proper context, the word "may" in Article

[270] India notes, in this regard, that the 1916 Act can be invoked and has been invoked over the years by complaining parties desirous of using the remedies offered by it as an alternative and, more importantly, as a supplement to the Antidumping Act of 1921 and later US anti-dumping legislation.

VI:2 appears to imply that the levying of an anti-dumping duty is not mandatory. However, it cannot under any circumstances, be interpreted as providing recourse to Members to resort to measures other than "anti-dumping duties".

4.3 Moreover, India does not agree with the US contention that the application of such measures, i.e. measures other than the application of anti-dumping duties, is justified on the grounds that the conduct to which the 1916 Act applies is defined in a manner which, while incorporating the essential elements of dumping, differs by the addition of one or more conditions. It is the view of India that, as long as the 1916 Act provides remedial action for dumping of products into the domestic market, it must be in conformity with the provisions of Article VI and the Anti-Dumping Agreement. Since this is not the case, the 1916 Act is inconsistent with the principles and objectives laid down in Article VI of the GATT 1994 and the Anti-Dumping Agreement.

4.4 India is also of the view that the 1916 Act is inconsistent with Article VI:1 of the GATT 1994 and Article 3 of the Anti-Dumping Agreement because it does not require there to be actual injury, let alone material injury to the domestic industry as a precondition for taking action. It only stipulates that action under the 1916 Act can be taken as long as there is intent to injure the domestic industry. Moreover, the absence of administrative procedures in the 1916 Act means that no investigation conforming to the requirements of the Anti-Dumping Agreement needs to be carried out when taking action under the 1916 Act. Thus, judicial decisions under the 1916 Act can be made without the procedural safeguards otherwise provided for in the Anti-Dumping Agreement. Finally, the 1916 Act fails to respect a number of procedural and due process requirements as set forth in the Anti-Dumping Agreement, including inter alia (i) the requirement that the competent authority verify the information given in any complaint before initiating an investigation; (ii) the requirement that notice be given to the government of the exporting country before such an investigation is started; (iii) the requirement that a complaint will be entertained only if it is supported by a minimum percentage of the domestic industry; (iv) the possibility for the governments of exporting countries to make comments on the proposed findings and (v) the requirement that the measures not be restrictive. The 1916 Act is therefore clearly violative of the procedural provisions of the Anti-Dumping Agreement.

4.5 As regards the US argument that the 1916 Act is not an anti-dumping law at all, but is an antitrust law, India does not agree. As accepted by the United States, the 1916 Act clearly targets products which are being sold within the United States allegedly at a price substantially less than the actual market value or wholesale price of the products. This is entirely in consonance with the definition of dumping given in Article VI. In accordance with Article VI, dumping occurs when "products of one country are introduced into the commerce of another country at less than the normal value of the products". Clearly therefore, the 1916 Act is a law which should be subject to the provisions of Article VI of the GATT 1994 and of the Anti-Dumping Agreement.

4.6 Furthermore, India entirely agrees with the averments by the European Communities relating to the 'grandfathering' of the 1916 Act. It is clear from the various statements made before US Senate Committees, including the testimony by the USTR General Counsel in 1986, that even in the United States the view was that without grandfathering the 1916 Act would be GATT-inconsistent. The failure of the United States to seek a grandfather exception under the GATT 1994, after admitting that the 1916 Act benefited from grandfathering under the GATT 1947, necessarily implies that the United States waived its grandfather rights on the 1916 Act. The United States cannot, therefore, keep in force domestic legislation which is clearly incompatible with the provisions of the GATT 1994.

4.7 India further argues that the 1916 Act cannot escape the discipline of Article VI simply because it requires the prohibited conduct to be "common and systematic". Article VI applies whether the dumping is limited in occurrence or sporadic, and whether the dumping is frequent or systematic. Once it is established that the relevant rule or law, in the present case the 1916 Act, is subject to Article VI, then the only remedy permitted is the imposition of anti-dumping duties, subject to a finding of dumping in accordance with the definition of Article VI and the existence of injury to the domestic industry, or threat thereof. Thus, any anti-dumping law which goes beyond providing relief in the form of anti-dumping duties, such as the 1916 Act, is inconsistent with the GATT 1994.

4.8 Finally, India recalls the United States' argument that the US courts' interpretation of the 1916 Act is dispositive as a factual matter of the nature of the 1916 Act and that the Panel cannot depend on its own interpretation. In this connection, India simply refers the Panel to the Appellate Body's decision in *India - Patents*.[271]

4.9 In conclusion, it is India's view that even though the 1916 Act provides relief against alleged dumping, it does not conform to the provisions of Article VI of the GATT 1994 and those of the Anti-Dumping Agreement. The 1916 Act thereby nullifies and impairs the benefits accruing to the United States' trading partners under those Agreements. India therefore urges the Panel to find the 1916 Act to be violative of the above-mentioned provisions and requests the Panel to direct the United States to bring its domestic law in conformity with its obligations under the GATT 1994.

B. Japan

4.10 **Japan** considers that it has a substantial trade interest in the present matter. In this regard, Japan recalls that, in November 1998, the Wheeling-Pittsburgh Steel Corporation filed a complaint under the 1916 Act against nine companies, including three Japanese trading firms. They are Mitsui & Co., Marubeni America Corp., and Itochu International Inc.. Japan is one of the major steel producing countries, and the US steel market was the largest market abroad for the Japanese steel makers in 1998. The Japan Iron and Steel Exporters Association and other exporters' associations asked the Japanese government to take appropriate action. They are concerned about the negative implications for trade in steel and the threat of substantial trade barriers for steel exports.

4.11 According to Japan, the pending litigation initiated by Wheeling-Pittsburgh Steel has serious negative trade implications. One is the "chilling effect" on exports from Japan. Even if no criminal or civil penalties are ever imposed, the potential liability under the 1916 Act discourages defendants - in the *Wheeling-Pittsburgh* case Japanese trading firms - from importing the relevant products at issue once legal proceedings have been initiated. Considering that litigation of this kind usually is

[271] Appellate Body Report, *India - Patents*, *supra*, footnote 29, paras. 65-66.

protracted and given the possibility of treble damages being imposed, the importers' risk when continuing to import without knowing the final outcome of the litigation is tremendous and prohibitive. The threat of retroactive imposition of treble damages is sufficient to deter imports. The eventual impact of the *Wheeling-Pittsburgh* litigation will not result from the final judgement of the District Court, but from the actual negative effect on imports due to the threat of civil liability or criminal sanctions.

4.12 Japan further argues that the three Japanese trading firms involved in *Wheeling-Pittsburgh* have found the litigation process to be extraordinarily expensive, burdensome as well as disruptive to their business. The effect of these burdens is already so obvious that four non-Japanese defendants in this litigation have reached out-of-court settlements. Although the precise terms of the settlements are not publicly available, these defendants settled with Wheeling-Pittsburgh Steel by agreeing to buy a certain quantity of steel from it at an agreed price. These settlements have obviously distorted sound, market-oriented trade practice, which has been an essential concept during successive rounds of multilateral trade negotiations.

4.13 Japan adds that it cannot be denied that this kind of litigation under the 1916 Act may occur again. So far, no judgement as to whether liability exists have been rendered in the *Geneva Steel* or *Wheeling-Pittsburgh* case. However, even at the present stage of litigation, the existence of the 1916 Act and the ongoing litigation have enormous adverse effects on trade, as shown above.

4.14 Japan also argues that, until and unless overturned by other court decisions, the decisions in *Geneva Steel* and *Wheeling-Pittsburgh* will prevail in the application of the 1916 Act. Even if they were to be overturned, similar cases may arise any time and repeatedly as long as the 1916 Act remains in force.

4.15 Turning to legal aspects, Japan considers that judicial decisions under the 1916 Act are made without the procedural safeguards provided for in the Anti-Dumping Agreement. Furthermore, Japan rejects the US assertion that the 1916 Act is not directed at dumping and therefore is not an anti-dumping statute. The 1916 Act is not only directed at antitrust, but also directed at dumping. The US assertion is not justified, considering recent US court findings, i.e. *Geneva Steel* and *Wheeling-Pittsburgh*, the previous testimonies and documents by US government officials, the legislative history as well as the wording of the 1916 Act.

4.16 Japan further notes that on 26 July 1999 the DSB established another panel in respect of the 1916 Act at Japan's request and pursuant to Article XXIII of the GATT 1994, Articles 4 and 6 of the DSU and Article 17 of the Anti-Dumping Agreement. In its panel request, Japan requests that the panel find that the 1916 Act is neither consistent with nor justified by the following relevant provisions:[272]

(a) Article III:4 of the GATT 1994;

(b) Article VI of the GATT 1994 and the Anti-Dumping Agreement, and in particular Article VI:2 of the GATT 1994 and Article 18.1 of the Anti-Dumping Agreement;

(c) Article XI of the GATT 1994;

(d) Article XVI:4 of the Agreement Establishing the WTO

---

[272] Japan refers to WT/DS162/3.

4.17 Japan also recalls that the subject of and the issues underlying Japan's panel request are the same as in the dispute before the present Panel. In relation to some relevant provisions, Japan has concerns similar to those set out by the European Communities before the present Panel. However, Japan has additional legal arguments which the panel established at its request will need to assess.

C. Mexico

4.18 **Mexico** is of the view that the present dispute concerns a law which violates the WTO agreements both in its letter and in its operation, regardless of the nature of that law within the US legal system. The 1916 Act has had real adverse effects and represents a risk for trade with the United States.

4.19 Mexico contends that the Panel should not follow the principles of interpretation of the United States courts, as the United States suggests, since its terms of reference are as follows:

> "To examine, in the light of the relevant provisions of the covered agreements cited by the European Communities in document WT/DS136/2, the matter referred to the DSB by the European Communities in that document and to make such findings as will assist the DSB in making the recommendations or in giving the rulings provided for in those agreements."[273]

4.20 In the view of Mexico, the terms of reference clearly require the Panel to examine the *matter* referred to the DSB by the European Communities *in the light of the relevant provisions of the WTO Agreement, of the GATT 1994 and of the Anti-Dumping Agreement.* It follows that the examination must be conducted in the light of those three Agreements only, and not of the domestic judicial decisions of the United States, which not only do not form part of the terms of reference of the Panel, but also concern an area of application that is different and independent of the WTO. Mexico agrees with the European Communities that the nature of the 1916 Act should be determined with reference to the provisions of the GATT 1994 and WTO law and not on the basis of the national legislation or case law of any particular Member.

4.21 Mexico notes, in this regard, that the trade practice regulated by the 1916 Act contains several of the elements of Article VI of the GATT 1994 and of the Anti-Dumping Agreement. Mexico agrees with the European Communities that in order to determine the applicability of the disciplines of Article VI of the GATT 1994 to the 1916 Act, it is necessary to compare the content of the two systems. Thus, Article VI contains two basic elements which also appear in the 1916 Act:

(i) It targets imports;

(ii) it is based on the difference between the prices of imports and a concept commonly known as "normal value".

4.22 Mexico further notes that there are additional elements common to the two systems, including the following:

(i) Both systems are based on price differentials;

[273] WT/DS136/3.

(ii) the calculations in both systems require adjustments;

(iii) both systems incorporate the concept of injury or material retardation;

(iv) both systems condemn the trade practice in question.

4.23 Mexico concludes, therefore, that the trade practice regulated by the 1916 Act comes under the definition of dumping, and consequently, it is a law that regulates dumping and the associated remedies. Both disciplines are provided for in Article VI of the GATT 1994 and the Anti-Dumping Agreement.

4.24 Mexico recalls that the United States asserts that there are a number of differences between the 1916 Act and the Anti-Dumping Agreement. However, for the following reasons, Mexico considers that these differences are irrelevant for the purposes of determining the nature of the 1916 Act:

(a) The price differential is irrelevant. The Anti-Dumping Agreement applies to small dumping margins and large dumping margins alike. In any case, the concept of "substantially less" coincides with the *de minimis* concept in the Anti-Dumping Agreement.

(b) The requirement that the differential should be "common and systematic" is also irrelevant. There is no requirement in Article VI of the GATT 1994 or in the Anti-Dumping Agreement that the trade practice should be sporadic.

(c) According to the United States, unlike the Anti-Dumping Agreement, the 1916 Act requires that there should be intent of destroying or injuring an industry in the United States, or of preventing the establishment of an industry in the United States. Mexico contends that the United States assertion is at best partial, since it fails to recognize that the purpose of both the GATT 1994 and the Anti-Dumping Agreement, on the one hand, and the 1916 Act, on the other, is to avoid injury or material retardation to the domestic industry.

(d) The United States argues that the 1916 Act requires that the complaining party suffer damages, while the Anti-Dumping Agreement requires that injury to a domestic industry must be found to exist. However, this argument fails to recognize that both systems provide for the initiation of the procedure at the request of a party when such party is affected by the trade practice in question.

4.25 Mexico notes that, in any case, none of the differences invoked by the United States mean that the 1916 Act does not regulate the trade practice known as dumping, and consequently, the United States has failed to substantiate its assertions that Article VI of the GATT 1994 and the Anti-Dumping Agreement are not applicable thereto. In fact, the only thing that the United States succeeds in showing by highlighting the differences between the two systems is that the 1916 Act does not meet the minimum WTO requirements for initiating and conducting procedures in respect of this kind of unfair international trade practice and for settling such cases.

4.26 Mexico considers, therefore, that the 1916 Act regulates the trade practice known as dumping and that it is subject to the disciplines of Article VI of the GATT

1994 and the Anti-Dumping Agreement. Mexico further considers that the 1916 Act violates certain provisions of Article VI of the GATT 1994 and the Anti-Dumping Agreement. The table below sets out the most important violations.[274]

Provisions of the 1916 Act	Provisions violated	Comments
"[A] price substantially less than the actual market value or wholesale price of such articles [...] in the principal markets of the country of their production, or of other foreign countries to which they are commonly exported [...]."	Article VI:1(a) and (b) of the GATT 1994 and Articles 2.1 and 2.2 of the Anti-Dumping Agreement	The 1916 Act does not respect the precedence of criteria for establishing normal value.
"*Provided*, That such act or acts be done with the intent of destroying or injuring an industry in the United States, or of preventing the establishment of an industry in the United States, or of restraining or monopolizing any part of trade and commerce in such articles in the United States".	Article VI:1 of the GATT 1994 and Article 3 of the Anti-Dumping Agreement	In order to condemn dumping, there must be injury, threat of injury or material retardation, while the 1916 Act merely requires the intent thereof.
"Any person who violates or combines or conspires with any other person to violate this section is guilty of a misdemeanour, and, on conviction thereof, shall be punished by a fine not exceeding $5,000, or imprisonment not exceeding one year, or both, in the discretion of the court."	Article VI:2 of the GATT 1994 and Article 1 of the Anti-Dumping Agreement.	WTO Members may only offset dumping through the imposition of duties not greater than the margin of dumping and only once they have initiated and conducted an investigation in accordance with the Anti-Dumping Agreement.
"[A]nd shall recover threefold the damages sustained, and the cost of the suit, including a reasonable attorney's fee."	Article VI:2 of the GATT 1994	Anti-dumping duties may not be greater than the margin of dumping of the product in question.
"The foregoing provisions shall not be construed to deprive the proper State courts of jurisdiction in actions for damages thereunder."	Article 1 of the Anti-Dumping Agreement, Article VI of the GATT 1994	The proper means of offsetting dumping consists in anti-dumping measures imposed pursuant to an investigation conducted in accordance with the Anti-Dumping Agreement.

4.27 Furthermore, Mexico agrees with the European Communities that since the 1916 Act is subject to the obligations of Article VI of the GATT 1994 and of the Anti-Dumping Agreement, and since the 1916 Act is not in conformity with the obligations imposed by those Agreements, it also violates Article XVI:4 of the Agreement Establishing the WTO.

274 Mexico points out that without prejudice to its view that there may be other provisions that are violated, the present examination will be limited to the provisions that are expressly set forth in the request for the establishment of a panel by the European Communities.

4.28 For these reasons, Mexico considers that the Panel should conclude that the 1916 Act violates the provisions of the WTO, in particular of the Anti-Dumping Agreement and of the GATT 1994, and that consequently, it violates Article XVI:4 of the Agreement Establishing the WTO. Similarly, the 1916 Act may also violate Article III of the GATT 1994, but Mexico does not see the need to dwell on this point.

V. INTERIM REVIEW[275]

A. Introduction

5.1 The interim report of the Panel was issued to the parties on 20 December 1999, in application of Article 15.2 of the DSU. On 7 January 2000, the European Communities and the United States submitted written requests to the Panel to review some aspects of the interim report. Neither the European Communities nor the United States requested that the Panel hold a further meeting with the parties.

5.2 As we were reviewing the comments of the parties, we noted that the United States raised an argument relating to the competence of the Panel to make some of the findings it had made under Article VI of the GATT 1994 and the Anti-Dumping Agreement. Without prejudice to the question whether the argument of the United States was procedurally or substantively justified, we considered that there were reasons to give further consideration to the issue raised by the US argument and to consult the parties on this matter. Since the issue was very specific and none of the parties had actually requested a hearing, we were of the view that such a consultation would be better carried out in writing. We therefore asked questions to both parties regarding the admissibility of the US argument. We also requested the United States to elaborate on its statement and asked the European Communities to comment on it.

B. Comments by the European Communities

5.3 The EC has made comments regarding the clarity of certain paragraphs. Whenever appropriate, we have clarified what we meant.

5.4 In that context, we have modified paragraph 6.60 by specifying that we considered the historical context and legislative history of the 1916 Act like US courts would do.

5.5 The EC also refers to our review of the statements of the US executive branch regarding "grandfathering" of the 1916 Act and our conclusion in paragraph 6.65 that we should use such statements only to the extent that they confirm established practice. The EC claims that we appear to have omitted to do so when we examined the historical context and legislative history of the 1916 Act. We did not refer to these confirmatory elements in the section on historical context and legislative history because that section related to how the notion of dumping in the 1916 Act was under-

---

[275] According to Article 15.3 of the Understanding on Rules and Procedures Governing the Settlement of Disputes (hereinafter "DSU"), "the findings of the final report shall include a discussion of the arguments made at the interim review stage". The following section entitled "Interim Review" is therefore part of the findings of our report.

stood at the time of its enactment. The confirmatory elements to which the EC refers relate more, in our opinion, to the question whether, as of 1947, the United States considered that the 1916 Act was inconsistent with its obligations under GATT 1947.

5.6 We addressed the arguments of the parties regarding the above-mentioned statements of the US executive branch because the parties discussed extensively the validity of those statements. We found that they were of limited use. The reason why we did not refer to them later was that, in our opinion, there was no related evidence to which they could be attached.

5.7 With respect to the comments of the EC on paragraphs 6.89 and 6.161 (now 6.164), we redrafted these two paragraphs to differentiate the present issue from that in the *United States - Tobacco* case. Since the 1916 Act had been applied in specific cases, there was no need to determine whether there was a possibility to interpret it in the future in a WTO-compatible manner. It was only necessary to determine whether the 1916 Act fell within the scope of Article VI or not.

5.8 In paragraph 6.106 (now 6.109), the EC suggested that the Panel replaces, in its comparison of the definitions of price discrimination in the 1916 Act and Article VI of the GATT 1994, the words "sufficiently different" by "qualitatively different". We agree that the question related to the nature of the requirements contained in the price discrimination test of the 1916 Act and we clarified the concept wherever appropriate.

5.9 The EC also requested the Panel to avoid using the term "affirmative defences" in paragraph 6.204 (now 6.206) and to modify paragraph 6.167 (now 6.170) and footnote 400 (now 424) because "affirmative defence" has a specific meaning and relates to a legal issue, in particular an exception, not to the initial question of fact. According to the EC, the US arguments on the mandatory/non-mandatory nature of the 1916 Act are factual arguments designed to rebut the EC's factual arguments.

5.10 We agree that the meaning to be given to the terms of the 1916 Act is of course a question of fact. However, in our opinion, the issue whether the 1916 Act as interpreted by US courts mandates or not a violation of the WTO Agreement is an issue of law. The Panel also considers the reference of the United States to the non-mandatory nature of the 1916 Act to be a legal defence advanced by the United States against the claims of violation made by the EC. As a result, we did not modify the related paragraphs which the EC requested us to amend.

5.11 With respect to our consideration of judicial economy in paragraph 6.205 (now 6.207), we made it clear that, in our opinion, findings under Article VI:1 and VI:2 addressed the essential features of the 1916 Act. We consider that our findings under the Anti-Dumping Agreement address secondary aspects of the 1916 Act. We nonetheless considered that it was useful to make such findings given the various ways in which the United States may decide to implement this report.

5.12 Finally, the EC requested the Panel to redraft paragraph 6.226(a) (now 6.228(a)) because the Panel did not need to make and, actually, had not made findings about the future developments of US case-law. We note that the United States also requested the Panel to delete that sub-paragraph as unnecessary to the Panel's finding and susceptible to foster misunderstanding of the role of panels in reviewing the domestic laws of Members.

5.13 As mentioned above, we do not intend to make findings on the potential or future evolution of the US case-law regarding the 1916 Act. On the contrary, since we found at present a violation of the WTO Agreement by the 1916 Act, we do not need to determine whether the 1916 Act could be found to be WTO consistent in the future. In addition, the question of the context in which the text of the 1916 Act should be addressed constitutes one of the issues on which the Panel expressly took position. We consequently decided to keep paragraph 6.228(a) in the final report, but we redrafted it to clarify it and address the concerns expressed by the parties, essentially with respect to the actual scope of our findings on this issue.

5.14 We also clarified paragraph 6.93 and 6.94, which related to arguments of the EC, and paragraph 6.167, regarding the finding of the panel on *United States - Definition of the Wine Industry*. However, we did not agree with the EC that that report actually stated what the EC said in its comments. The phrase "and [the panel] did not consider it necessary to examine whether the legislation was mandatory or discretionary" suggested by the EC seems to be more like an interpretation of the panel report. Moreover, we did not find it necessary to modify Article 6.134(a) since it seems clear to us that US court decisions in relation to the 1916 Act so far have only had legal effects within the US legal order.

C. *Comments by the United States*

5.15 The United States raised two main categories of comments. The first one addresses the alleged absence of "jurisdiction" of the Panel to make any findings with respect to any claim under the Anti-Dumping Agreement and, consequently, under Article VI of the GATT 1994. In support of its position, the United States relies on the findings of the Appellate Body in the case of *Guatemala - Anti-Dumping Investigation Regarding Portland Cement from Mexico*[276] and on those of the panel and of the Appellate Body in the case of *Brazil - Measures Affecting Desiccated Coconut.*[277] The second category of arguments relates to alleged misrepresentations of the United States' arguments by the Panel.

5.16 With respect to the first category, the United States contends that it continuously throughout the proceeding pointed out the failure of the EC to challenge any particular measure taken under the 1916 Act and that it argued on other grounds that the Panel had no right to address the 1916 Act under Article VI or the Anti-Dumping Agreement. We nevertheless note that, in practice, the United States framed its defence in the context of claims addressing the WTO-compatibility of the 1916 Act as such, by arguing that the 1916 Act was a non-mandatory law within the meaning of GATT 1947/WTO practice. Moreover, the preliminary issue it raised in its first submission related to the possibility of the EC to refer to Articles 1 and 18.1 of the Anti-Dumping Agreement as claims or as arguments in support of its claims. Such arguments are of a totally different nature than and totally unrelated to the argument raised by the United States at the interim review stage.

5.17 The United States also claims that its new argument is of a jurisdictional nature and had to be raised at this stage of the proceedings. We agree that some issues of jurisdiction may be of such a nature that they have to be addressed by the Panel at

---

[276] Appellate Body Report, *Guatemala Cement, supra,* footnote 26.

[277] Panel Report, *Brazil – Measures Affecting Desiccated Coconut* ("*Brazil – Desiccated Coconut*"), WT/DS22/R, adopted 20 March 1997, as upheld by the Appellate Body Report, WT/DS22/AB/R, DSR 1997:I, 189, hereinafter "*Brazil - Desiccated Coconut*".

any time. However, we consider that a distinction must be made between (i) issues of jurisdiction which occur exclusively as a result of the content of the interim report and could not be legitimately foreseen earlier in the process and (ii) jurisdictional issues that were already evident at the beginning of the proceedings. The fact that the EC challenged the 1916 Act as such and not one of the measures referred to in *Guatemala - Cement* was clear from the request of the EC for the establishment of a panel and was noted by the United States.[278] Consequently, we would have expected the United States to raise it at an early stage of the proceedings.

5.18 We agree that Article 15 of the DSU does not seem to prohibit a party from raising new arguments at the interim review stage, provided they are made in the context of a request for review of precise aspects of the interim report. However, we note that the DSU, in particular Appendix 3, provides for well defined steps in the proceedings, during which parties may raise arguments in support of their positions. The fact that the interim review takes place at the very end of those proceedings, once all submissions have been made, hearings have taken place and a draft report has been issued to the parties is evidence that this stage of the proceedings is not meant to address issues which could have been better addressed in the written and oral proceedings conducted by the Panel.[279] Moreover, Article 3.10 provides that parties must engage in dispute settlement in good faith. This implies that they should not withhold until the interim review stage arguments that they could be legitimately expected to have raised at a much earlier stage of the proceedings, in light of the claims developed in the first submissions. In this respect, we see no reasons why the United States could not have made the argument at issue at the very beginning of the proceedings, since it dealt with the admissibility of all the claims raised by the EC under Article VI of the GATT 1994 and the Anti-Dumping Agreement.

5.19 As a result, we consider that there would be a number of reasons to reject the US argument as untimely. However, since Article 15.3 of the DSU provides that the final report shall include a discussion of the arguments made at the interim review stage, and since our decision to address the EC claims under Article VI of the GATT 1994 and the Anti-Dumping Agreement may be subject to appeal, we consider that it is justifiable to explain why, in our view, the competence of the Panel to address a violation of Article VI and the Anti-Dumping Agreement is not affected by the findings of the Appellate Body in *Guatemala - Cement* and of the panel and Appellate Body in *Brazil - Desiccated Coconut*.

---

[278] See para. 3.27 above.

[279] The limited function of the interim review stage is confirmed by the existence of an appeal procedure, where parties may address issues of law covered in the panel report and challenge legal interpretations developed by the panel (Article 17.6 of the DSU). On the role of the interim review stage in panel proceedings, see, e.g., the views expressed by the panel in Panel Report, *India - Quantitative Restrictions on Imports of Agricultural, Textile and Industrial Products ("India – Quantitative Restrictions")*, WT/DS90/R, adopted 22 September 1999, as upheld by the Appellate Body Report, DSR 1999:V, 1799, para. 4.2. The Panel notes in this respect that the parties have not contested any of the factual findings made in the course of these proceedings, in particular those relating to the meaning of the 1916 Act, the context of its enactment and the interpretations made by the US courts, which would be the type of questions that a party may wish to raise at the interim review stage.

5.20 We first consider the provisions of the Anti-dumping Agreement on consultation and dispute settlement. Paragraphs 1 to 4 provide as follows:

> "17.1 Except as otherwise provided herein, the Dispute Settlement Understanding is applicable to consultations and the settlement of disputes under this Agreement.
>
> 17.2 Each Member shall afford sympathetic consideration to, and shall afford adequate opportunity for consultation regarding, representations made by another Member with respect to any matter affecting the operation of this Agreement.
>
> 17.3 If any Member considers that any benefit accruing to it, directly or indirectly, under this Agreement is being nullified or impaired, or that the achievement of any objective is being impeded, by another Member or Members, it may, with a view to reaching a mutually satisfactory resolution of the matter, request in writing consultations with the Member or Members in question. Each Member shall afford sympathetic consideration to any request from another Member for consultation.
>
> 17.4 If the Member that requested consultations considers that the consultations pursuant to paragraph 3 have failed to achieve a mutually agreed solution, and if final action has been taken by the administering authorities of the importing Member to levy definitive anti-dumping duties or to accept price undertakings, it may refer the matter to the Dispute Settlement Body ("DSB"). When a provisional measure has a significant impact and the Member that requested consultations considers that the measure was taken contrary to the provisions of paragraph 1 of Article 7, that Member may also refer such matter to the DSB."

5.21 We first note that Article 17 of the Anti-Dumping Agreement does not replace the DSU as a coherent system of dispute settlement for that Agreement.[280] In this respect, the Appellate Body in *Guatemala - Cement* explained that "the rules and procedures of the DSU [...] apply to disputes brought pursuant to the consultation and dispute settlement provisions contained in Article 17".[281]

5.22 We also note that nothing in the terms of either Article 17.2 or Article 17.3 limits the scope of possible consultations under the Anti-Dumping Agreement. Article 17.3 was not listed in Appendix 2 of the DSU because "it provides the legal basis for consultations to be requested by a complaining member under the *Anti-Dumping Agreement*. Indeed, it is the equivalent provision in the Anti-Dumping Agreement to Articles XXII and XXIII of the GATT 1994, which serves as the basis for consultation and dispute settlement under the GATT 1994 [and] under most of the other agreements in Annex 1A of the *Marrakesh Agreement Establishing the World Trade Organization*".[282]

[280] Appellate Body Report, *Guatemala - Cement, supra*, footnote 26, para. 67.

[281] *Ibid.*, para. 64.

[282] *Ibid.*

5.23 In contrast, Article 17.4 deals with a particular situation under the Anti-Dumping Agreement, hence its status of special or additional provision under the DSU. As stated by the Appellate Body in *Guatemala - Cement*:

> "We see the special or additional rules and procedures of a particular covered agreement as fitting together with the generally applicable rules and procedures of the DSU to form a comprehensive, integrated dispute settlement system for the *WTO Agreement*. The special or additional provisions listed in Appendix 2 of the DSU are designed to deal with the particularities of dispute settlement relating to obligations arising under a specific covered agreement, while Article 1 of the DSU seeks to establish an integrated and comprehensive dispute settlement system for all of the covered agreements of the *WTO Agreement* as a whole. It is, therefore, only in the specific circumstance where a provision of the DSU and a special or additional provision of another covered agreement are mutually inconsistent that the special or additional provision may be read to *prevail* over the provision of the DSU."[283]

5.24 Paragraph 66 of the Appellate Body report in *Guatemala - Cement* illustrates the function of Article 17.4. Article 17.4 deals with the particular issue of challenging *actions taken by anti-dumping authorities*. There is nothing in the provisions of Article 17.4 limiting the scope of application of the dispute settlement provisions applicable to anti-dumping, except in relation to the specific issue of Members' anti-dumping actions.[284]

5.25 Our reading of Article 17.4 is not only confirmed by the immediate context of that provision, i.e. Article 17.1, 17.2 and 17.3, but also by other provisions of the Anti-Dumping Agreement. Article 18.4 provides that:

> "Each Member shall take all necessary steps, of a general or particular character, to ensure, no later than the date of entry into force of the WTO Agreement for it, the conformity of its laws, regulations and administrative procedures with the provisions of this Agreement as they may apply for the Member in question."

We understand Article 18.4 of the Anti-Dumping Agreement as requiring the conformity of Members' anti-dumping laws as of the date of entry into force of the WTO Agreement for those Members. In other words, a Member's anti-dumping legislation must be compatible with the WTO Agreement continuously, whether that legislation is applied or not. If dispute settlement could be initiated in relation to anti-dumping *actions* only, i.e. if the conformity of a domestic anti-dumping law could only be reviewed when that law is applied, the provisions of Article 18.4 would be deprived of their meaning and useful effect, since a Member could maintain a WTO-

---

283 *Ibid.*, para. 66.

284 If the position of the United States that only the three types of measures referred to by the Appellate Body in *Guatemala – Cement, supra,* footnote 26, could be challenged under the DSU were correct, then any Member could escape the application of the disciplines of Article VI and the Anti-Dumping Agreement merely by taking other types of measures than those provided for in the Anti-Dumping Agreement.

incompatible law in total impunity as long as none of the measures referred to in Article 17.4 is adopted. Even if, on the occasion of the review of a particular action, the law on which the measure was based were found to be WTO-incompatible, the interpretation advocated by the United States would fail to give meaning and legal effect to the terms "no later than the date of entry into force of the WTO Agreement for [that Member]" in Article 18.4 and would be contrary to the principle of effectiveness.[285] Moreover, Article 18.4 requires that *all necessary steps*, of a general or particular nature, be taken. Those terms would be redundant if the anti-dumping laws of Members only had to be WTO-consistent when actually applied to a particular situation.

5.26 As could already be noticed from the previous paragraphs, the interpretation of Article 17 of the Anti-Dumping Agreement by the Appellate Body confirms our view. The argument of the United States is essentially based on an interpretation of paragraph 79 of the Appellate Body Report in *Guatemala - Cement* taken out of its context.[286] The facts at issue in the *Guatemala - Cement* case were different from those before us. In that case, Mexico contested a specific investigation carried out by Guatemala against imports of Portland cement from Mexico. If one reads the reasoning of the Appellate Body in the factual context to which it pertains, it is not possible to draw the extensive conclusion suggested by the United States. The specific scope of the findings in that case is confirmed by the Appellate Body itself in the paragraph following the one quoted by the United States:

> "80. For all of these reasons, we conclude that the Panel erred in finding that Mexico did not need to identify "specific measures at is-

---

285 *Ut res magis valeat quam pereat.* See, e.g., Appellate Body Report on *Argentina - Safeguard Measures on Imports of Footwear*), WT/DS121/AB/R, adopted 12 January 2000, DSR 2000:I, 515, para. 88 and Appellate Body Report on *United States - Standards for Reformulated and Conventional Gasoline*, adopted 20 May 1996, WT/DS2/AB/R, DSR 1996:I, 3, at 15.

286 Appellate Body Report, *Guatemala Cement, supra,* footnote 26, para. 79 referred to by the United States reads as follows:

> "79. Furthermore, Article 17.4 of the *Anti-Dumping Agreement* specifies the types of "measure" which may be referred as part of a "matter" to the DSB. Three types of anti-dumping measure are specified in Article 17.4: definitive anti-dumping duties, the acceptance of price undertakings, and provisional measures. According to Article 17.4, a "matter" may be referred to the DSB *only if* one of the relevant three anti-dumping measures is in place. This provision, when read together with Article 6.2 of the DSU, requires a panel request in a dispute brought under the *Anti-Dumping Agreement* to identify, as the specific measure at issue, either a definitive anti-dumping duty, the acceptance of a price undertaking, or a provisional measure. This requirement to identify a specific anti-dumping measure at issue in a panel request in no way limits the nature of the *claims* that may be brought concerning alleged nullification or impairment of benefits or the impeding of the achievement of any objective in a dispute under the *Anti-Dumping Agreement*. As we have observed earlier, there is a difference between the specific measures at issue - in the case of the *Anti-Dumping Agreement*, one of the three types of anti-dumping measure described in Article 17.4 - and the claims or the legal basis of the complaint referred to the DSB relating to those specific measures. In coming to this conclusion, we note that the language of Article 17.4 of the *Anti-Dumping Agreement* is unique to that Agreement."

sue" in this dispute. We find that in disputes under the *Anti-Dumping Agreement* relating to the initiation and conduct of anti-dumping investigations, a definitive anti-dumping duty, the acceptance of a price undertaking or a provisional measure must be identified as part of the matter referred to the DSB pursuant to the provisions of Article 17.4 of the *Anti-Dumping Agreement* and Article 6.2 of the DSU." (emphasis added)

Thus, the findings of the Appellate Body in *Guatemala-Cement* were limited to the taking of action in situations contemplated in Article 17.4. They could not be - and actually were not - intended to limit the scope of application of dispute settlement under the Anti-Dumping Agreement.

5.27 We therefore conclude that Article 17 of the Anti-Dumping Agreement does not prevent us from reviewing the conformity of laws as such under the Anti-Dumping Agreement. The same applies, *a fortiori*, with respect to Article VI of the GATT 1994. In that respect, we consider that the findings of the panel and the Appellate Body in *Brazil - Desiccated Coconut* referred to by the United States are not applicable to this case, since those findings referred to the non-applicability of the Agreement on Subsidies and Countervailing Measures to existing measures or investigations initiated pursuant to applications made before the entry into force of that Agreement.[287]

5.28 The second category of comments by the United States relates to allegedly factually misleading statements of the Panel or to alleged misrepresentations of the arguments of the United States in the findings.

5.29 Regarding the statement of the Panel in paragraph 6.42 concerning the fact that criminal prosecutions may have been initiated under the 1916 Act, the United States argues that, to its knowledge, no criminal prosecutions have ever been brought under the 1916 Act. In fact, we relied on a remark of the United States District Court, E.D. Pennsylvania, in its 1980 judgement in *Zenith Radio Corp. v. Matsushita Electric Industrial Co. Ltd.*, where the court stated that:

"apparently there have been four attempts to enforce the criminal provisions of the Act, but none of them has been successful and none has given rise to a reported judicial decision. Marks, *United States Anti-dumping Laws - A Government Overview* 43 Antitrust L.J. 580, 581 (1974)"[288]

We note, however, that the statement contested is not essential to our findings. Since the comment of the United States would tend to confirm that records are not clear on this point, we redrafted paragraph 6.42 in line with the general thrust of the paragraph, which was to specify in what context (criminal or civil proceedings) US courts had interpreted the 1916 Act.

5.30 Regarding the comments of the United States on paragraph 6.77, we clarified that the phrase in the fifth sentence of that paragraph quoted by the United States was the opinion of the Panel, not that of the United States. Moreover, the United States

[287] See Article 32.3 of the Agreement on Subsidies and Countervailing Measures.

[288] 494 F. Supp. 1190, at p. 1212.

asserts that its position was actually different from that summarised by the Panel. However, it is our understanding that, in the view of the United States, anti-dumping duties were not the exclusive remedy against injurious dumping allowed under Article VI. This is the only point that the Panel wishes to make in the sentence at issue. Consequently, we have added footnote 346 which refers to the arguments of the United States regarding the interpretation of Article VI:2 of the GATT 1994 in section III.E.2 of this report.

5.31 At the request of the United States, we also clarified paragraph 6.85, even though the terms contested were included in the opinion of the Panel, not in a summary of the position of the United States. What we meant was that, once a law has been found not to mandate a WTO-illegal action, any review of that law under the DSU must stop and it cannot be challenged as such. Since the EC does not contest specific instances of applications of the law, this appeared to the Panel to be the essence of the US argumentation.

5.32 The United States also argues that the Panel has misrepresented the US position in paragraph 6.195 (now 6.197) by stating that "the United States does not seem to contest the fact that Article 18.1 of the Anti-Dumping Agreement in the least states that duties are the only remedies allowed to counter certain forms of dumping under Article VI of the GATT 1994 and the Anti-Dumping Agreement". We do not see any contradiction between the interpretation of the US argument made by the Panel and the position of the United States as expressed in its comments. The United States alleges that a Member could counteract dumping with measures which are not explicitly set forth in Article VI or the Anti-Dumping Agreement. In the view of the Panel, this does not exclude that, *under Article VI and the Anti-Dumping Agreement*, the only remedy be anti-dumping duties. This is different from saying that anti-dumping duties are the only remedies allowed against injurious dumping *under the WTO Agreement*. Our understanding of the US arguments is also consistent with the position of the United States in this case that "Article 18.1 of the Anti-Dumping Agreement uses carefully crafted language to express the intended limitation regarding other remedies than duties."[289] We nevertheless redrafted paragraph 6.197 to make the elements of our deduction clearer.

5.33 Finally, we also clarified paragraph 6.112 (now 6.115) to make clear that the term "'effect' tests" originated in the Panel, not the United States.

5.34 In the light of the comments of the parties, the Panel considered that some aspects of its reasoning had to be further clarified. In this respect, the Panel found it useful to add paragraph 6.97 on the relationship between Article VI of the GATT 1994 and the Anti-Dumping Agreement. In addition, it reorganised its presentation of section C.2(b)(i) and (ii). The Panel also added footnote 293 to paragraph 6.1, footnote 310 to paragraph 6.32, footnote 313 to paragraph 6.34, footnote 352 to paragraph 6.84. We also modified footnote 344 to paragraph 6.76, as well as paragraph 6.79. These new or modified paragraphs or footnotes merely qualify or elaborate on statements already contained in the text. They neither change the reasoning of the Panel nor affect its findings.

---

[289] See para. 3.245 above.

VI. FINDINGS

A. *Facts at the Origin of the Dispute and Issues to be Addressed by the Panel*

1. *Facts at the Origin of the Dispute*

6.1 The law, the WTO-consistency of which is contested by the European Communities,[290] is a United States legislative text enacted under the heading of "Unfair Competition" in Title VIII of the Revenue Act of 1916.[291] It has been known since as the "Antidumping Act of 1916."[292] The 1916 Act, which provides for civil and criminal penalties by US federal courts for a certain form of transnational price discrimination[293] when conducted with specific intent,[294] reads as follows:

> "It shall be unlawful for any person importing or assisting in importing any articles from any foreign country into the United States, commonly and systematically to import, sell or cause to be imported or sold such articles within the United States at a price substantially less than the actual market value or wholesale price of such articles, at the time of exportation to the United States, in the principal markets of the country of their production, or of other foreign countries to which

[290] Throughout these findings, the European Communities as a WTO Member will be indifferently referred to as the "European Communities" or the "EC".

[291] Act of 8 September 1916. The Revenue Act can be found at 39 Stat. 756 (1916). Title VIII of the Revenue Act is codified at 15 U.S.C. §§ 71-74.

[292] A number of official documents published by the US authorities and a number of US court decisions refer to Title VIII of the Revenue Act of 1916 as the "Antidumping Act of 1916". Authors have also called it the "1916 Antidumping Act" or qualified it as an act dealing with certain forms of dumping, irrespective of whether they considered it to be an "anti-dumping" law or an "anti-trust" law. See, e.g., A. Paul Victor: *The Interface of Trade/Competition Law and Policy: An Overview*, 56 Antitrust L.J. 397, p. 401; John H. Jackson, *World Trade and the Law of GATT* (1968), p. 403, footnote 4. However, we note that the word "anti-dumping" does not appear as such in the text of the law. Since the question whether this law is an anti-dumping law within the meaning of Article VI of GATT 1994 is one of the issues that this Panel has to address, we find it more appropriate to refer to it in our discussion as the "1916 Act".

[293] Even though the word "discrimination" may have specific meanings in certain circumstances, it is used throughout the findings as meaning a differentiation, a distinguishing mark (see, e.g., *The New Shorter Oxford English Dictionary* (1993), p. 689). As a result, the term "transnational price discrimination" in these findings refers only to the existence of a difference in price between two markets located in different countries, irrespective of the intent of the exporter behind that price difference or the effects thereof. See also Jacob Viner's definition of "dumping" as a "price-discrimination between national markets" (*Dumping, A Problem in International Trade* (1923), p. 3).

[294] The 1916 Act was part of a legislative effort of the United States to address a number of practices perceived at that time as "unfair competition". A number of major anti-trust and trade laws of the United States still applicable today were adopted by the Congress of the United States (hereinafter the "US Congress") between the end of the 19th century and the 1930's. The Sherman Act (15 U.S.C. 1-7) dates back to 1890 and the Clayton Act to 1914 (15 U.S.C. 12, 13, 14-19, 20, 21, 22-27; 29 U.S.C. 52, 53). Subsequent to the 1916 Act came the 1921 Anti-Dumping Act, the 1930 Tariff Act (which has become since the basis of the current US anti-dumping legislation) and the 1936 Robinson-Patman Act, amending Section 2 of the Clayton Act of 1914.

they are commonly exported after adding to such market value or wholesale price, freight, duty, and other charges and expenses necessarily incident to the importation and sale thereof in the United States: *Provided*, That such act or acts be done with the intent of destroying or injuring an industry in the United States, or of preventing the establishment of an industry in the United States, or of restraining or monopolizing any part of trade and commerce in such articles in the United States.

Any person who violates or combines or conspires with any other person to violate this section is guilty of a misdemeanour, and, on conviction thereof, shall be punished by a fine not exceeding $5,000, or imprisonment not exceeding one year, or both, in the discretion of the court.

Any person injured in his business or property by reason of any violation of, or combination or conspiracy to violate, this section, may sue therefor in the district court of the United States for the district in which the defendant resides or is found or has an agent, without respect to the amount in controversy, and shall recover threefold the damages sustained, and the cost of the suit, including a reasonable attorney's fee.

The foregoing provisions shall not be construed to deprive the proper State courts of jurisdiction in actions for damages thereunder."

6.2 Two significant features of the 1916 Act are that:

(a) it provides for a review of the practices concerned by the judiciary branch of government[295] at the federal level, not by the executive branch of government; and

(b) it provides for two "tracks" of litigation before US federal courts: (i) civil proceedings through which a person may seek to recover damages, and (ii) criminal proceedings whereby the US Department of Justice may seek the imposition of a fine or imprisonment.

2. *Issues to be Addressed by the Panel*

6.3 The understanding of the Panel as to the claims and defences of the parties is, in a summarised form, as follows.[296]

6.4 The EC challenges the 1916 Act as such, not a particular instance of application. It claims that the 1916 Act violates Articles III:4, VI:1 and VI:2 of the GATT 1994, Articles 1, 2.1, 2.2, 3, 4, 5.5 of the Agreement on Implementation of Article VI

---

[295] The terms "judiciary branch of government", "executive branch of government" and "legislative branch of government" are, throughout this report, used within the meaning given to them in US constitutional law.

[296] The claims and arguments of the parties are reported in greater detail in Sections II and III of this Report.

of the General Agreement on Tariffs and Trade 1994[297] and Article XVI:4 of the Marrakesh Agreement Establishing the World Trade Organization.[298]

6.5 The EC claims that the 1916 Act falls within the scope of Article VI of the GATT 1994 because the 1916 Act targets certain practices defined as "dumping" in that Article. According to the EC, the 1916 Act applies (i) when imported products are sold on the United States market at a lower price than they are sold on the domestic market of the exporting country or of a third country and (ii) by reason of their importation. This corresponds to the definition of dumping under Article VI:1. The EC argues that recent court decisions and, in general, US case-law on the 1916 Act should be used by the Panel as factual guidance that the 1916 Act has been applied as an anti-dumping statute. Moreover, since the 1916 Act does not respect other requirements of Article VI:1 of the GATT 1994, the 1916 Act violates Article VI:1.

6.6 The EC also claims that, by providing for treble damages, fines or imprisonment, the 1916 Act violates Article VI:2 of the GATT 1994, which provides that the imposition of duties is the only remedy allowed to counteract dumping under the WTO Agreement.

6.7 Furthermore, the EC claims that the 1916 Act violates a number of requirements of the Anti-Dumping Agreement, *inter alia* by not respecting procedural requirements as to the determination of material injury and the initiation and conduct of the investigation leading to the imposition of measures.

6.8 The EC claims that since the 1916 Act is an anti-dumping statute covered by the disciplines of Article VI of the GATT 1994 and the Anti-Dumping Agreement, it should have been brought into conformity with the rules set forth in Article VI of the GATT 1994 and with the Anti-Dumping Agreement, pursuant to Article XVI:4 of the Agreement Establishing the WTO.

6.9 Finally, the EC claims, in the alternative or if the Panel were to find that the 1916 Act complies fully or in part with Article VI of the GATT 1994, that the 1916 Act violates Article III:4 of the GATT 1994 to the extent that it provides less favourable treatment to imported goods than is granted to US goods under the Robinson-Patman Act[299] in terms of the difference in (i) injury/predation standards, (ii) measurement of price discrimination, (iii) sales requirements and thresholds requirements for complaints and (iv) the statutory defences available under the Robinson-Patman Act and not expressly provided for in the 1916 Act.

6.10 The United States argues that the 1916 Act is an anti-trust statute.[300] It is not subject to the disciplines of Article VI since it does not address injurious dumping

[297] Referred to hereafter as the "Anti-Dumping Agreement".

[298] Throughout these findings, the Marrakesh Agreement Establishing the World Trade Organization, including its annexes, will be referred to as the "WTO Agreement". The Marrakesh Agreement Establishing the World Trade Organization, without its annexes, will be referred to as the "Agreement Establishing the WTO". In that context, Article XVI:4 of the Marrakesh Agreement Establishing the World Trade Organization will be referred to as "Article XVI:4 of the Agreement Establishing the WTO". The agreements annexed to the Agreement Establishing the WTO will be referred to as the "WTO agreements".

[299] See footnote 294 above.

[300] The Panel notes that the parties have used the terms "competition" and "anti-trust" to refer to the same rules and policies. We are aware of the fact that the term "anti-trust" is more frequently used in the United States. We also note that the term "competition" is used not only in EC law but also by

within the meaning of Article VI but a much narrower form of international price discrimination with an anti-trust objective, as demonstrated by the legislative history and the subsequent case-law relating to it. In this respect, the United States stresses that it is not the role of the Panel to interpret US law and case-law. It should consider it as facts to be proved. On that basis, the Panel should find that the 1916 Act, as an anti-trust statute, does not violate Article VI:1 of the GATT 1994. If one were to follow the EC interpretation of Article VI:1, all anti-trust laws of Members, including the EC competition rules under Article 82 of the Treaty of Amsterdam, would be subject to Article VI of the GATT 1994 to the extent that they rely on transnational price discrimination.

6.11 The United States further claims that Article VI:2 as such does not provide that duties are the sole remedy allowed to counteract dumping and that a Member is bound to respect the provisions of the Anti-Dumping Agreement only to the extent it intends to impose duties.

6.12 The United States argues that in any event the 1916 Act, to the extent that the US Department of Justice enjoys discretion to file - or not - a suit with a federal court, is a "non-mandatory" law within the meaning given to that concept by GATT 1947 panels and by panels and the Appellate Body under the WTO. The United States further argues that the 1916 Act is susceptible, and indeed has been interpreted in a WTO-compatible manner. In application of past GATT 1947 panel practice, this also makes the 1916 Act "non-mandatory" legislation. It is therefore for the EC to prove that the 1916 Act is not capable of a WTO-compatible interpretation.

6.13 The United States further argues that Article XVI:4 of the Agreement Establishing the WTO does not require Members to pre-empt any possible WTO-inconsistent interpretation of their domestic laws. It is the opinion of the United States that the 1916 Act is in conformity with its WTO obligations until it is ruled by the WTO that it is not.

6.14 Finally, the United States claims that the 1916 Act does not violate Article III:4 of the GATT 1994. Compared with the Robinson-Patman Act, the 1916 Act actually grants more favourable treatment to imported goods than to US goods. The 1916 Act requires an *intent* to destroy or injure an industry in the United States, or to prevent the establishment of an industry in the United States, or to restrain or monopolize any part of trade and commerce in the articles concerned in the United States. According to the United States, this requirement that an "intent" be demonstrated by the plaintiff has been considered to be the main reason for the very rare and generally unsuccessful application of the 1916 Act compared with the Robinson-Patman Act. Apart from this, the procedural requirements under the two statutes are either similar or more favourable to defendants under the 1916 Act.

6.15 From the above, it appears to the Panel that the two parties address the WTO-compatibility of the 1916 Act through approaches that are diametrically opposed. The European Communities, basing itself on the definition of "dumping" found in

certain international organizations, such as the OECD (see, e.g., *Competition and Trade Policy, Their Interaction* (1984)). However, since our examination of the matter requires us to deal with US statutes and case-law, it was found appropriate to use the term "anti-trust" when describing the practice that the parties consider to fall within the scope of "anti-trust" or "competition" law in general.

Article VI:1 of the GATT 1994 and the absence of express limitation of the scope of that article, seems to be of the view that any law which targets "dumping" within the meaning of Article VI is a "trade" law and is therefore subject to the relevant WTO disciplines. The approach of the United States, on the contrary, seems to be that the disciplines of Article VI of the GATT 1994 apply only to the extent that a law purports to address dumping as an international trade practice. If what the law targets is not "injurious dumping" within the meaning of Article VI of the GATT 1994, but the anti-trust effects (e.g., restraining or monopolising trade within the territory of a Member) of a narrower form of transnational price discrimination, WTO disciplines on anti-dumping do not apply to it.

6.16 On the basis of the arguments developed by the parties, the Panel considers that it needs to approach the matter before it as follows.

6.17 First, since we are called to determine the compatibility of a law of the United States with the WTO obligations of that Member, we should determine how to consider that law and its "surrounding", i.e. the circumstances of its enactment (including the legislative history)[301] and the subsequent interpretation(s). This is in our view important since both parties have substantially discussed those aspects, including the relevance of certain court decisions. Judicial interpretation, as evidence of the meaning given to the terms of a legal text, may affect the way we should understand the terms of the 1916 Act.

6.18 Second, we should proceed to address the issue whether we review the 1916 Act under Article VI or under Article III:4 of the GATT 1994 first, or if we review it under either provision at all. The reason for this is that, while the 1916 Act addresses transnational price discrimination, it imposes internal measures. Article VI relates to actions by Members *vis-à-vis* a particular practice whereas Article III:4 ensures that foreign products, once imported, are not subject to less favourable treatment than domestic products. We believe that it falls within our competence and duty to determine the applicability of Articles III:4 and VI as part of our review of the compatibility of the 1916 Act under the provision(s) found applicable, without prejudice to judicial economy.

6.19 On the basis of our conclusions on the application of Articles III:4 and VI to the 1916 Act, we shall address the compatibility of the 1916 Act under Article III:4 and/or Article VI of the GATT 1994 and the Anti-Dumping Agreement to the extent necessary to assist the WTO Dispute Settlement Body[302] in making its recommendations. We should do this having regard to the defence of the United States based on the alleged "mandatory/non-mandatory" nature of the 1916 Act.

6.20 Once this is done, we may also consider the claims of the EC under Article XVI:4 of the Agreement Establishing the WTO.

6.21 However, before reviewing the substantive issues of the case, we need to address the procedural issues raised by the parties in the course of the proceedings.

[301] Since the term "legislative history" is used throughout this report in relation to the preparation of US pieces of legislation, it will be given the meaning it has under US practice, i.e. "The background and events, including committee reports, hearings, and floor debates, leading up to the enactment of a law." *Black's Law Dictionary*, 6th Ed. (1990), p. 900.

[302] Hereinafter also referred to as the "DSB".

B. *Procedural Issues*

1. *Request for a Preliminary Ruling by the United States*

6.22 The United States, in its first written submission, requested the Panel to issue a preliminary ruling on two claims allegedly made by the EC in its first written submission. According to the United States, the EC claimed that the 1916 Act violates Articles 1 and 18.1 of the Anti-Dumping Agreement for the first time in its first submission. In the opinion of the United States, Articles 6.2 and 7 of the Understanding on Rules and Procedures Governing the Settlement of Disputes[303] and Article 17.4 and 17.5 of the Anti-Dumping Agreement preclude the Panel from considering these two claims because they were not included in the EC's request for the establishment of a panel.

6.23 At the request of the Panel, the European Communities addressed the request of the United States. The EC stated that the United States asked the Panel to exclude claims that the European Communities had not made. The EC claimed a violation of Article VI:2 of the GATT 1994, but it made no separate claims that the 1916 Act violates Articles 1 and 18.1 of the Anti-Dumping Agreement. These provisions were merely arguments in support of the EC claims.

6.24 The Panel recalls that in its report on *European Communities - Regime for the Importation, Sale and Distribution of Bananas*, the Appellate Body mentioned that

> "Article 6.2 of the DSU requires that the *claims*, but not the *arguments*, must all be specified sufficiently in the request for the establishment of a panel in order to allow the defending party to know the legal basis of the complaint."[304]

In light of the reply of the EC that Articles 1 and 18.1 of the Anti-Dumping Agreement "were only mentioned as arguments in support of [its] claims", the Panel considered that it was not necessary to address the issue any further.

6.25 However, the United States stressed, during the first meeting of the Panel with the parties, that the Panel should reject the EC's attempt to circumvent the requirements of the DSU by describing its references to Articles 1 and 18.1 of the Anti-Dumping Agreement as "mere arguments". Indeed, if the Panel were to analyse whether these newly invoked articles support the EC's other claims, the Panel would be required to determine whether those provisions provide an exclusive remedy for dumping.

6.26 We understand these arguments of the United States as an elaboration of its original request for a preliminary ruling, even though they were also made in relation to the EC claim of a violation of Article VI:2 of the GATT 1994. At this stage, we address them to the extent necessary to reply to the procedural aspect of the arguments of the United States. We note that panels in the past have faced similar situations where a complainant relied on a given provision to support a claim based on another provision. In *India - Quantitative Restrictions on Imports of Agricultural*

---

[303] Hereinafter the "DSU".

[304] Appellate Body Report on *European Communities - Regime for the Importation, Sale and Distribution of Bananas*, WT/DS27/AB/R, adopted 25 September 1997, (hereinafter "*European Communities -Bananas*"), DSR 1997:II, 591, para. 143 (emphasis in the original).

Textile and Industrial products, the United States discussed the applicability of both Article XVIII:B of the GATT 1994 and of the Understanding on Balance-of-Payments Provisions of the GATT 1994. The panel found that, while the United States had made a claim under Article XVIII:11 of the GATT 1994, it had not made any claim under other provisions of Article XVIII:B of the GATT 1994 or under the Understanding on Balance-of-Payments Provisions of GATT 1994. The panel concluded that it would not "address any claim of the United States based on the [Understanding on Balance-of-Payments Provisions of GATT 1994] or on other provisions of Article XVIII:B other than Article XVIII:11". The panel nonetheless held that these provisions were "part of the context of those provisions alleged by the United States to have been violated".[305]

6.27 We also recall that Article 31 of the Vienna Convention on the Law of Treaties (1969)[306] provides that the interpretation of a provision of a treaty should be made in its context, and that "context", for the purpose of the interpretation of a treaty, shall comprise, *inter alia,* the "text [of the treaty], including its preamble and annexes".[307] As a result, there are grounds to consider that other provisions of the WTO agreements than those referred to in the terms of reference can be considered by the Panel under certain conditions.

6.28 However, we limit ourselves at this stage to taking note of the fact that the EC does not make any separate claim under Article 18.1 of the Anti-Dumping Agreement. In light of the clarification by the EC, we also conclude that the EC claim under Article 1 of the Anti-Dumping Agreement[308] does not relate to its claim under Article VI:2 of the GATT 1994, but addresses a different aspect of the matter.

2. *Request for Enhanced Third Party Rights by Japan*

6.29 On 2 September 1999, Japan requested to be granted enhanced third party rights in this case. In particular, Japan requested to receive all the necessary documents, including submissions and written versions of statements of the parties and to attend all the sessions of the second substantive meeting of the Panel. At the request of the Panel, the EC and the United States commented on this request. The EC agreed to the request of Japan, provided that the EC's request of a similar nature in the case initiated by Japan concerning the same matter (WT/DS162) would also be accepted.

6.30 The United States strongly objected to the request of Japan. In the opinion of the United States, enhanced third party rights were not necessary in order to obtain access to the submissions of the parties. In *European Communities - Measures Con-*

---

305 Panel Report, *India - Quantitative Restrictions, supra*, footnote 279, paras. 5.18-5.19. These findings were not modified by the Appellate Body.

306 Hereinafter the "Vienna Convention". Article 3.2 of the DSU instructs us to clarify the existing provisions of the WTO Agreement "in accordance with customary rules of interpretation of public international law". From its very first decision and repeatedly thereafter, the Appellate Body has considered that these customary rules were embodied *inter alia* in Articles 31 and 32 of the Vienna Convention.

307 Article 31.2 of the Vienna Convention.

308 See WT/DS136/2.

cerning Meat and Meat Products ("Hormones"),[309] the panel had granted enhanced third party rights essentially because the panel had informed the parties that concurrent deliberations would be conducted in the case initiated by the United States and in the case initiated by Canada. The United States mentioned that it would not support concurrent deliberations in this case and that it could not agree to a request of which the apparent purpose was to provide the third parties with an opportunity to make an additional submission in their own panel process.

6.31 On 13 September 1999, the Panel, through its Chairman, informed the parties and Japan that it could not accede to the request of Japan. The Panel reserved its right to reconsider the issue in light of subsequent events and informed the parties and Japan that it would address the matter in detail in its findings.

6.32 The Panel carefully considered the arguments raised by the parties. It notes that, while the DSU does not provide for enhanced third party rights, neither Article 10 of the DSU nor any other provision of the DSU prohibits panels from granting third party rights beyond those expressly mentioned in Article 10.[310] The Appellate Body in the *EC - Hormones* case confirmed that granting enhanced third party rights was part of the discretion of panels under Article 12.1 of the DSU.[311]

6.33 The Panel notes, however, that the DSU differentiates in terms of rights between main parties and third parties and that this principle should be respected in order to keep with the spirit of the DSU in that respect. Enhanced third party rights have so far been granted for specific reasons only. In the *EC - Hormones* case, like in this case and the case initiated by Japan (WT/DS162), the two panels were composed of the same panelists and dealt with the same matter. While these elements appeared to play a significant role in the decisions taken by the panels and in their confirmation by the Appellate Body, we consider that they could not be decisive. Otherwise, enhanced third party rights would have to be granted in almost all cases where the same matter is subject to two or more complaints with the same panel composition.[312] We note that particular circumstances existed in the *EC - Hormones* case which certainly contributed to the decisions of the panels to review the two cases concurrently, such as their highly technical and factually intensive nature, as well as the fact that the panels had decided to hold one single meeting with the parties and the experts consulted pursuant to Article 11.2 of the Agreement on Sanitary and Phytosanitary Measures. These decisions were largely based on practical reasons and due process had to be preserved. We conclude from the reports in the *EC - Hormones*

---

[309] Panel Report, *EC Measures Concerning Meat and Meat Products* (Hormones) - *Complaint by Canada,* WT/DS48/R/CAN, adopted 13 February 1998, DSR 1998:II, 235, (hereinafter the "*EC - Hormones*" case). See also Panel Report, WT/DS26/R/USA, *EC Measures Concerning Meat and Meat Products* (Hormones) - *Complaint by the United States*, *supra*, footnote 38.

[310] The Panel considers that the provisions of Article 9 of the DSU, in particular Article 9.3 which addresses the situation of this Panel and the panel requested by Japan on the same matter WT/DS162) are of limited assistance in the present issue.

[311] Appellate Body Report, *EC Measures Concerning Meat and Meat Products,* WT/DS26/AB/R, DS48/AB/R, adopted 13 February 1998, DSR 1998:I, 135, para. 154.

[312] Our remark is based on our understanding of the current state of the WTO practice. It is without prejudice to the question whether enhanced third party rights would be advisable or not in general.

case that enhanced third party rights were granted primarily because of the specific circumstances.

6.34 We find that no similar circumstances exist in the present matter, which does not involve the consideration of complex facts or scientific evidence. Moreover, none of the parties requested that the panels harmonise their timetables or hold concurrent deliberations in the two procedures (WT/DS136 and WT/DS162). In fact, the European Communities was not in favour of delaying the proceedings in WT/DS136 and the United States objected to concurrent deliberations. We are of the view that, in such a context, we ought to conduct this case independently from the case initiated by Japan both in terms of procedure and of analysis of the substantive issues before us.[313]

6.35 We are of the view that respecting due process *vis-à-vis* Japan did not require the participation of Japan in the second substantive meeting of the Panel. This said, having regard to Article 18.2 of the DSU, we urged the EC and the United States, in the course of the proceedings, to communicate to Japan in due course meaningful non-confidential summaries of their submissions to the Panel, if requested to do so by Japan.

6.36 We therefore find that there was no reason to grant enhanced third party rights to Japan in these proceedings.

3. Burden of proof

6.37 We recall the Appellate Body Report on *United States - Measure Affecting Imports of Woven Wool Shirts and Blouses from India*,[314] which stated that:

> "the burden of proof rests upon the party, whether complaining or defending, who asserts the affirmative of a particular claim or defence. If that party adduces evidence sufficient to raise a presumption that what is claimed is true, the burden then shifts to the other party, who will fail unless it adduces sufficient evidence to rebut the presumption."

6.38 Applying this rule to the factual evidence submitted in the present case, the European Communities, as the complainant, should normally adduce sufficient evidence to raise a *prima facie* case that each of its claims has merit. If it were to do so, it would then be for the United States to adduce sufficient evidence to rebut that *prima facie* case. If the United States were to assert the affirmative of a particular defence, it would bear the burden of proving it. This rule however is only applicable to determine whether and when a party bears the burden of proof. Once both parties have submitted evidence meeting those requirements, it is up to the Panel to weigh the evidence as a whole. In cases where the evidence as a whole regarding a particu-

[313] Accordingly, while we assume that the United States may further elaborate on its argumentation or submit new arguments in the case initiated by Japan, this Panel shall consider only the arguments of the United States submitted in the course of the present case and exclusively as they were developed in the present case.

[314] Appellate Body Report, *United States - Measure Affecting Imports of Woven Wool Shirts and Blouses from India* ("*US - Wool Shirts and Blouses*"), WT/DS33/AB/R, adopted 23 May 1997, DSR 1997:I, 323, at 335.

lar claim or defence remains in equipoise, the issue must be decided against the party bearing the burden of proof on that claim or defence.

6.39 With respect to the interpretation of the covered agreements, the Panel will be aided by the arguments of the parties but will not be bound by them. Pursuant to Article 3.2 of the DSU, our decision on such matters must be in accord with the rules of treaty interpretation applicable to the WTO Agreement.

C. Preliminary Issues

1. Context in which the 1916 Act Should be Examined by the Panel

(a) Issue before the Panel

6.40 We note that the EC contests the compatibility of the 1916 Act as such - not of particular instances of application - with certain provisions of the WTO Agreement. While it is clear from the terms of Article 3.2 of the DSU that it falls within the competence of the Panel to "clarify the existing provisions of [the covered agreements] in accordance with customary rules of interpretation of public international law", the DSU does not expressly provide how panels should address domestic legislation. Article 11 of the DSU only specifies that panels "should make [...] an objective assessment of the facts of the case". However, both Article 3.2 of the DSU and the practice of the Appellate Body make it clear that we have, whenever appropriate, to develop our approach on the basis of that of international courts in similar circumstances. We will consequently take into consideration the practice of international tribunals in this respect.

6.41 This case has an additional dimension. Although panels often have to address domestic laws, in the present case we are called upon to review the consistency of a law which was enacted more than eighty years ago, and the historical, cultural, legal and economic context of the time undoubtedly influenced its terms. We also note that the parties seem to have diverging views regarding how the Panel should consider the court decisions relating to that law.

6.42 The 1916 Act was seldom applied since its enactment and no court judgement based on that law has so far imposed sanctions on the defendant. It is the understanding of the Panel, based on the information provided by the parties, that there was never any court decision based on criminal proceedings under the 1916 Act. Until the early 1970's, there was only one reported court decision addressing the civil procedure provided for in the 1916 Act.[315] Since 1975, there has been only a limited number of judicial interpretations of the provisions of the 1916 Act. All these interpretations come from US circuit courts of appeals or US district courts.[316] No claim

[315] *H. Wagner and Adler Co. v. Mali*, F.2d 666 (2d Cir. 1935).

[316] Federal courts (district courts and circuit courts of appeals) are competent to review cases brought under the 1916 Act, under the supervision of the Supreme Court of the United States.

under the 1916 Act was ever expressly reviewed by the Supreme Court of the United States.[317]

6.43 Therefore, we find it appropriate to clarify from the outset how we shall take into consideration the text of the 1916 Act itself, the historical context of its enactment (including the legislative history) and its subsequent interpretation as it results from the US case-law and any other relevant element of information.

(b) How should the Panel Consider the Text of the 1916 Act, the Context of its Enactment, the Case-Law Relating to it and other Relevant Pieces of Information

(i) Arguments of the Parties and Approach of the Panel

6.44 The European Communities claims that the 1916 Act is clear on its face. In its view, the Panel should not be influenced by the terms used by US courts when it characterises the 1916 Act under the WTO Agreement. The EC considers that judgements of national courts are relevant insofar as they offer guidance on the meaning or interpretation of national laws and it is appropriate for the Panel to take them into account for that purpose. The Panel should follow the reasoning of the Appellate Body in its report on *India - Patent Protection for Pharmaceutical and Agricultural Chemical Products*[318] and carry out an examination of the relevant aspects of US municipal law. The interpretation of the 1916 Act, i.e. determining what it means, including what must be pleaded and proved in order to establish a claim under it, is a matter of US law and therefore of fact before the Panel.

6.45 The EC also refers to letters or statements of US officials before the US Congress that the 1916 Act was "grandfathered" under GATT 1947 as "existing legislation" within the meaning of the Protocol of Provisional Application. For the EC, this is an admission by the United States of the GATT/WTO-incompatibility of the 1916 Act.

6.46 The United States argues that the role of the Panel is to assess the facts and then determine their conformity with the relevant WTO agreements, which generally entails interpreting the scope and applicability of those agreements to the facts. The proper interpretation of the 1916 Act is a question of fact to be established, as it is an accepted principle of international law that municipal law is a fact to be proven before international tribunals.

6.47 The United States also considers that the Congressional Record and other documents such as the 1915 *Annual Report of the* [US] *Secretary of Commerce* are evidence that the 1916 Act addresses unfair competition. Regarding the statements of US officials referred to by the EC, the United States considers that the Panel should

---

[317] In *United States v. Cooper Corporation* (312 U.S. 600, 1941), hereinafter the "*Cooper* case", at p. 745, the Supreme Court of the United States made a reference to the 1916 Act as "supplemental" to the Sherman Act. This decision is discussed further in section VI.D.2.(d)(ii) below.

[318] Appellate Body Report on *India - Patent Protection for Pharmaceutical and Agricultural Chemical Products,* WT/DS50/AB/R, adopted 16 January 1998, DSR 1998:I, 9 (hereinafter "*India - Patent (US)*").

attach no weight to them in light of the official US notifications to the GATT of its "grandfathered" laws, which did not include the 1916 Act.[319] Thus, those statements are mistaken as a matter of fact.

6.48 The understanding of a law the WTO-compatibility of which has to be assessed begins with an analysis of the terms of that law. However, we consider that we should not limit ourselves to an analysis of the text of the 1916 Act in isolation from its interpretation by US courts or other US authorities, even if we were to find that text to be clear on its face. If we were to do so, we might develop an understanding of that law different from the way it is actually understood and applied by the US authorities. This would be contrary to our obligation to make an objective assessment of the facts of the case, pursuant to Article 11 of the DSU. Therefore, we must look at all the aspects of the domestic legislation of the United States that are relevant for our understanding of the 1916 Act. However, looking at all the relevant aspects of the domestic law of a Member may raise some methodological difficulties, such as how much deference must be paid to that Member's characterisation of its legislation. In that context, we will determine first how to deal with that aspect of the examination of a domestic law and how we should consider the case-law related to it, since courts are, *inter alia*, responsible for interpreting the law. Moreover, in light of the fact that the law at issue was enacted more than eighty years ago and not regularly invoked, and since the parties have referred to other elements such as the historical context, the legislative history and subsequent declarations of US authorities made in relation to the 1916 Act, we shall also explain how we will consider them.

(ii) Consideration by Panels of Domestic Law in General

6.49 We note that in *India - Patent(US)*, the Appellate Body addressed in some detail the issue of how panels should consider municipal law. The Appellate Body stated that:

> "In public international law, an international tribunal may treat municipal law in several ways. Municipal law may serve as evidence of fact and may provide evidence of State practice."[320]
>
> "It is clear that the examination of the relevant aspects of Indian municipal law [...] is essential to determining whether India has complied with its obligations under Article 70.8(a) [of the TRIPS Agreement]. [...] To say that the Panel should have done otherwise would be to say that only India can assess whether Indian law is consistent with India's obligations under the *WTO Agreement*. This, clearly, cannot be so."[321]

6.50 The extent to which panels may examine the laws of Members was illustrated by the Appellate Body in the same report. Having to determine whether India pro-

---

[319] The United States refers to GATT document L/2375/Add.1 (19 March 1965).

[320] Op. Cit., para. 65. See also M.N. Shaw, *International Law* (1995), p. 106, mentioning that domestic law "can be utilised as evidence of compliance or non-compliance with international obligations".

[321] *Ibid.*, para. 66.

vided for legal protection commensurate with the requirements of Article 70.8 of the TRIPS Agreement, the Appellate Body asked itself the question of "what constitutes [...] a sound legal basis in Indian law".[322] Moreover, it agreed with the conclusion of the panel that "the current administrative practice [of India, based on so-called "administrative instructions" from the government] creates a certain degree of legal insecurity in that it requires Indian officials to ignore certain mandatory provisions of the Patent Act."[323] The Appellate Body also agreed that "it was necessary for the Panel in this case to seek a detailed understanding of the *operation* of the Patent Act as it relates to the 'administrative instructions' in order to assess whether India had complied with Article 70.8(a) [of the TRIPS Agreement.]"[324]

6.51 Thus, our understanding of the term "examination" as used by the Appellate Body is that panels need not accept at face value the characterisation that the respondent attaches to its law. A panel may analyse the operation of the domestic legislation and determine whether the description of the functioning of the law, as made by the respondent, is consistent with the legal structure of that Member. This way, it will be able to determine whether or not the law as applied is in conformity with the obligations of the Member concerned under the WTO Agreement.[325]

(iii) Consideration of the Case-Law Relating to the 1916 Act

6.52 In the present case, unlike India in the *India - Patent (US)* case, the United States does not claim that some administrative interpretations determine the meaning of the 1916 Act. The situation is different to the extent that both parties rely, in order to support their claims, on a number of judgements by US courts which have applied and interpreted the 1916 Act since the 1970's.[326] In many Members, final judicial

---

322 *Ibid..*, para. 59.

323 *Ibid.*, para. 63, Panel Report, para. 7.35.

324 *Ibid.*, para. 68 (emphasis added).

325 This is evidenced by the examples used by the Appellate Body (*Ibid.*, para. 67):

> "Previous GATT/WTO panels also have conducted a detailed examination of the domestic law of a Member in assessing the conformity of that domestic law with the relevant GATT/WTO obligations. For example, in *United States - Section 337 of the Tariff Act of 1930* [footnote omitted], the panel conducted a detailed examination of the relevant United States' legislation and practice, including the remedies available under Section 337 as well as the difference between patent-based Section 337 proceedings and federal district court proceedings, in order to determine whether Section 337 was inconsistent with Article III:4 of the GATT 1947."

326 The following - final or interlocutory - court decisions relate to claims made under the 1916 Act: *H. Wagner and Adler Co. v. Mali, Op. Cit.*; *In re Japanese Electronic Products Antitrust Litigation*, 388 F.Supp. 565 (Judicial Panel on Multidistrict Litigation, 1975) (hereinafter "*In re Japanese Electronic Products I*"); *Zenith Radio Corp. v. Matsushita Electric Industrial Co., Ltd.*, 402 F.Supp. 244 (E.D. Pa. 1975) (hereinafter "*Zenith I*"); *Zenith Radio Corp. v. Matsushita Electric Industrial Co., Ltd.*, 402 F.Supp. 251 (E.D. Pa. 1975) (hereinafter "*Zenith II*"); *Outboard Marine Corp. v. Pezetel*, 461 F. Supp. 384 (D. Del. 1978); *Schwimmer v. Sony Corp. of America*, 471 F. Supp. 793 (E.D.N.Y. 1979); *Schwimmer v. Sony Corp. of America*, 637 F.2d 41 (2nd Cir. 1980); *Jewel Foliage Co. v. Uniflora Overseas Florida*, 497 F. Supp. 513 (M.D. Fla. 1980); *Zenith Radio Corp. v. Matsushita Electric Industrial Co., Ltd.*, 494 F.Supp. 1190 (E.D. Pa. 1980) (hereinafter "*Zenith III*"); *In re Japanese Electronic Products Antitrust Litigation (Zenith Radio Corp. v. Matsushita Electric In-*

decisions regarding the interpretation of a given law may not be contested any further, whereas administrative interpretations of a law may generally be overruled by a domestic judge called upon to review that law. However, an administrative interpretation will normally provide one single interpretation. In contrast, depending on the judicial structure of a Member, judicial interpretations may emanate from several courts positioned at different levels in the judicial order. The diversity of the sources of the case-law may make it more difficult to assess the respective value of the judgements of which that case-law is composed.

6.53 We recall that the International Court of Justice, in the *Elettronica Sicula S.p.A (ELSI)* case, referred to the judgement of the Permanent Court of International Justice[327] in the *Brazilian Loans* case - to which the United States also refers in its submissions - and noted that:

> "Where the determination of a question of municipal law is Essential to the Court's decision in a case, the Court will have to weigh the jurisprudence of the municipal courts, and 'If this is uncertain or divided, it will rest with the Court to select the interpretation which it considers most in conformity with the law' (*Brazilian Loans*, PCIJ, Series A, Nos. 20/21, p. 124)." [328]

We are fully aware that our role is to clarify the existing provisions of the covered agreements so as to determine the compatibility of a domestic law with those agreements. We are also aware that, in the *Brazilian Loans* case, the PCIJ was asked to apply domestic legislation to a given case. We are nevertheless of the view that there is nothing in the text of the DSU, nor in the practice of the Appellate Body, that prevents us from "weigh[ing] the jurisprudence of municipal [US] courts" if it is "uncertain or divided". This would not require us to develop our own independent interpretation of US law, but simply to select among the relevant judgements the interpretation most in conformity with the US law, as necessary in order to resolve the matter before us.[329]

---

dustrial Co., Ltd.), 723 F.2d 319 (3d Cir. 1983) (hereinafter "*In re Japanese Electronic Products II*"); *Western Concrete Structures Co. v. Mitsui & Co.*, 760 F.2d 1013 (9th Cir. 1985); *Isra Fruit Ltd. v. Agrexco Agr. Export Co.*, 631 F. Supp. 984 (S.D.N.Y. 1986); *In re Japanese Electronic Products Antitrust Litigation (Zenith Radio Corp. v. Matsushita Electric Industrial Co., Ltd.)*, 807 F.2d 44 (3d Cir. 1986) (hereinafter "*In re Japanese Electronic Products III*") *Helmac Products Corp. v. Roth (Plastics) Corp.*, 814 F. Supp. 560 (E.D. Mich. 1992) (hereinafter "*Helmac I*"); *Helmac Products Corp. v. Roth (Plastics) Corp.*, 814 F.Supp. 581 (E.D. Mich. 1993) (hereinafter "*Helmac II*"); *Geneva Steel Company v. Ranger Steel Supply Corp.*, 980 F.Supp. 1209 (D. Utah 1997) (hereinafter "*Geneva Steel*"); *Wheeling-Pittsburgh Steel Corporation v. Mitsui Co.*, 35 F.Supp.2d. 597 (S.D. Ohio 1999) (hereinafter "*Wheeling-Pittsburgh*").

[327] Hereinafter "PCIJ".

[328] ICJ, *Case Concerning Elettronica Sicula S.p.A. (ELSI)* (United States of America v. Italy), ICJ Reports 1989, p. 15, at p.47, para. 62.

[329] We do not consider that this would be engaging into *interpreting* US law, with the risks highlighted by the United States in its submissions. Our approach is in line with the reasoning of the PCIJ in the *Brazilian Loans* case, which, even though it had to apply domestic law, was prudent in its approach of the domestic case-law:

> "It follows that the Court must pay the utmost regard to the decisions of the municipal courts of a country, for it is with the aid of their jurisprudence that it will be

6.54 We note that the 1916 Act is applied by US federal courts. Interpretations by the Supreme Court of the United States (hereinafter the "Supreme Court") prevail over interpretations made by the courts of appeals of the various circuits. Interpretations by courts of appeals, in turn, prevail over interpretations by district courts, but only within the same circuit.[330]

6.55 We understand from the submissions of the parties that the Supreme Court has yet to address the interpretation of specific provisions of the 1916 Act. It mentioned the 1916 Act in only one of its judgements.[331] Thus, the case-law submitted by the parties that would allow us to understand the actual meaning of the 1916 Act today essentially comes from district courts and courts of appeals of various circuits of the US federal judicial system. We also note that the parties in their submissions have relied on different judgments, which they claim support their interpretations of the 1916 Act.

6.56 We shall respect the formal hierarchy of court decisions in the US federal system to the extent that it is applicable. In that context, we shall allow a circuit court of appeals decision to prevail over a district court decision. However, applying such a formal approach may prove insufficient in some instances, for example when the decisions to be compared come from different circuits.[332] Therefore, in all instances, we shall first ascertain whether the judgements subject to our comparison address (i) the same issue, and (ii) at the same level of detail. In other words, we should always make sure that a comparison can reasonably be made, both in terms of fact and in terms of the legal issues addressed, before giving preference to the interpretation contained in one judgement compared with the interpretation contained in another judgement of a court belonging to another circuit.

6.57 Moreover, we should normally, with respect to a given issue, allocate more weight to a final judgement than to an interim or "interlocutory" decision, since the latter does not definitively determine a cause of action, but only "decides some intervening matter pertaining to the cause."[333] However, we should also determine which argumentation is more convincing. Again, we will not substitute our judgement for that of US courts. Our analysis should be based not only on the quality of the reasoning, but also on what we would perceive to be in line with the dominant interpretation, "paying utmost regard to the decision of the municipal courts". This is consistent with the US court practice that if a precedent is not binding, the weight afforded to it will depend on the persuasive value of the reasoning in the decision.

6.58 If, after having applied the above methodology, we could not reach certainty as to the most appropriate court interpretation, i.e. if the evidence remains in equi-

---

enabled to decide what are the rules which, in actual fact, are applied in the country the law of which is recognized as applicable in a given case" (PCIJ, Series A, Nos. 20/21, p. 124)

330 A description of the organization of the US federal judicial system is found in para. 2.14 and footnote 21 above.

331 *Cooper*, *Op. Cit.*

332 From the replies of the United States to our questions, we understand that the *stare decisis* effect which can be attached to precedents in common law does not apply between court decisions handed down in different circuits.

333 See *Black's Law Dictionary*, 6th Ed. (1990), p. 815.

poise, we shall follow the interpretation that favours the party against which the claim has been made, considering that the claimant did not convincingly support its claim.

6.59 Finally, we also consider that we should not accept at face value the use of certain terms such as "dumping", "antidumping", "antitrust", "protectionism" or "predatory pricing" in court decisions, in other administrative documents or in academic works, when those terms are not further substantiated. We recall that the mere description or categorisation of a measure by a Member should not be considered as a decisive factor for the application of the WTO Agreement to that measure.[334] In the present case, such descriptions or categorisations may be valid under US law but not necessarily in the WTO context. Likewise, having regard to the importance of the legislative history in the interpretation of statutes by the US judiciary branch, terms used in 1916 will have to be understood within the meaning they had at the time, not in light of the meaning they have today, unless we have evidence that US courts have done so.

(iv) Consideration of the Historical Context and Other Evidence of the Meaning of the 1916 Act

6.60 The historical context of the 1916 Act encompasses several elements. The first one, to which US courts also extensively refer in order to determine "the intent of Congress", is the legislative history as it appears, *inter alia*, from the Congressional Records. Since we have to examine the 1916 Act and understand its actual scope and operation, we should, as US courts do, pay attention to the legislative history of that statute, as appropriate. The political and economic context as it emerges from public declarations of the time or studies of the period may also be relevant. When considering this evidence, we should not lose sight of the degree of development of anti-trust and trade law concepts at the time of the enactment of the 1916 Act.

6.61 Regarding the statements of US officials referred to by the EC,[335] we note that the EC considers them as showing that, in the past, US Government bodies not only held the view that the 1916 Act concerns dumping practices, but also that, without "grandfathering", it would have been GATT illegal. For the European Communities, the US authorities admitted that the 1916 Act was "grandfathered" under the GATT 1947, even though the United States had not included the 1916 Act in its notification of "grandfathered" laws to the GATT 1947. We also note that the United States considers that the 1916 Act was not included in the survey of existing mandatory legis-

[334] See, Panel Report on *EEC - Regulation on Imports of Parts and Components*, adopted on 16 May 1990, BISD 37S/132 (hereinafter "*EC - Parts and Components*"), paras 5.6 and 5.7. In that report, the panel stated that:

> "if the description or categorization of a charge under the domestic law of a contracting party were to provide the required "connection with importation", contracting parties could determine themselves which of these provisions would apply to their charges."

[335] The arguments of the parties on this issue are reported in section III:D.2.(c) above.

lation not in conformity with part II of the GATT 1947[336] because the 1916 Act was GATT-legal and therefore did not require "grandfathering".

6.62 The consequences that the European Communities would like the Panel to draw from the above-mentioned statements are not clear. We are not supposed to "make the case for [the] complaining party".[337] However, we find it relevant to determine at this stage what consequences could, from a legal point of view, be drawn from these statements.

6.63 First, we should determine whether they could actually generate legal obligations for the United States under international law. For instance, since they are subsequent to the notification by the United States of its "grandfathered" legislation under the GATT 1947, it might be argued that they implicitly modified that notification by stating that the 1916 Act was "grandfathered". We recall that the International Court of Justice has developed, *inter alia* in its judgement in the *Nuclear tests* case,[338] criteria on when a statement by a representative of a State could generate international obligations for that State. In the present case, we are reluctant to consider the statements made by senior US officials in testimonies or letters to the US Congress or to members thereof[339] as generating international obligations for the United States. First, we recall that the constitution of the United States provides for a strict separation of the judicial and executive branches. With the exception of criminal prosecutions, the application of the 1916 Act falls within the exclusive responsibility of the federal courts. Under those circumstances, a statement by the executive branch of government in a domestic forum can only be of limited value. Second, with the possible exception of the statement of US Trade Representative Clayton Yeutter, they were not made at a sufficiently high level compared with the statements considered by the International Court of Justice in the *Nuclear Tests* case, where essentially declarations by a head of State and of members of the French government were at issue. Moreover, the statements referred to in the present case were not directly addressed to the general public. Finally, they were not made on behalf of the United States, but - at best - on behalf of the executive branch of government. This aspect would not be essential if the statements had been made in an international forum, where the executive branch represents the State.[340] However, in the present case, the statements were addressed to the US legislative branch. Therefore, we cannot consider them as creating obligations for the United States under international law.

6.64 A related issue is whether these statements should be treated as admissions of facts or of the legal nature of the 1916 Act under the WTO. We note that the factual accuracy of the statements mentioned in this case has been put in doubt by the United

---

[336] See GATT Doc. L/2375/Add.1 of 19 March 1965.

[337] Appellate Body Report on *Japan - Measures Affecting Agricultural Products*, WT/DS76/AB/R, adopted 19 March 1999, DSR 1999:I, 277, para. 129 (hereinafter "*Japan - Agricultural Products*").

[338] ICJ, *Nuclear Tests case*, judgements of 20 December 1974, ICJ Reports 1974, p. 253 (Australia v. France), p. 457 (New Zealand v. France). See, e.g., Patrick Daillier & Alain Pellet, *Droit International Public*, 5th edition (1994), p. 354-358.

[339] The statements or letters to which the EC refers are listed in para. 3.126 and footnotes 105 and 106 above.

[340] See also Article 7 of the Vienna Convention.

States before the Panel. While this is not sufficient to reject those statements out of hand, we are reluctant to consider them as "admissions" of the United States without prior verification of the context in which they were made.

6.65 For these reasons, we consider that these statements should be used only to the extent that they confirm other established evidence.

6.66 The United States has also referred to the codification system of its federal legislation and to a compilation made for the use of the Committee on the Judiciary of the US House of Representatives as evidence of the anti-trust nature of the 1916 Act. These documents are informative regarding the opinions of the authorities of the United States as to the classification of the 1916 Act as an anti-trust or as an anti-dumping statute. However, as such, the codification of the 1916 Act or its inclusion in a compilation for a committee of the US Congress cannot affect our determination of the compatibility of the 1916 Act with the WTO provisions.[341] With regard to the 1995 *Antitrust Enforcement Guidelines for International Operations* issued by the US Department of Justice and the US Federal Trade Commission referred to by the European Communities, we note their role as "antitrust guidance to business engaged in international operations". We therefore consider that they are indicative of the position of a particular department of the executive branch of the US government. Moreover, to the extent that these guidelines do not substantiate the reasons why the 1916 Act should be considered as a trade statute and, in fact, mention that "its subject-matter is closely related to the anti-trust rules regarding predation", we consider that we should refer to those guidelines only as a confirmation of other established evidence, if necessary.

6.67 Having clarified how we shall consider the materials before us in assessing the WTO-compatibility of the 1916 Act, we now proceed to discuss the preliminary issue of the applicability of Articles III:4 and VI of the GATT 1994

2. *Relationship between Article III and Article VI of the GATT 1994*

(a) Issue before the Panel

6.68 The European Communities primarily claims that the 1916 Act violates Article VI of the GATT 1994 and certain provisions of the Anti-Dumping Agreement. It also claims that the 1916 Act violates Article III:4 of the GATT 1994 *in the alternative* or "if [...] all or any portion of the 1916 Act is consistent with Article VI of the GATT 1994 and the Anti-Dumping Agreement". The United Sstates claims that the 1916 Act is not subject to the disciplines of Article VI essentially because it is not aimed at dumping.

6.69 Article III:4 of the GATT 1994 provides in relevant parts as follows:

---

[341] See Panel Report on *EC - Parts and Components*, Op. Cit., para. 5.7. That panel addressed the description or categorisation of a charge under domestic law and concluded that if the description or categorisation of a charge under the domestic law of a contracting party were to provide the required "connection with importation", contracting parties could determine themselves which of these provisions would apply to their charges. With such an interpretation the basic objective underlying Articles II and III could not be achieved. We consider that the same reasoning applies with respect to the application of Article VI.

> "The products of the territory of any contracting party imported into the territory of another contracting party shall be accorded treatment no less favourable than that accorded to like products of national origin in respect of laws, regulations and requirements affecting their internal sale, offering for sale, purchase, transportation, distribution or use...".

6.70 Article VI provides in relevant parts as follows:

> "1. The contracting parties recognize that dumping, by which products of one country are introduced into the commerce of another country at less that the normal value of the product, is to be condemned if it causes or threatens material injury to an established industry in the territory of a contracting party or materially retards the establishment of a domestic industry. [...]
>
> 2. In order to offset or prevent dumping, a contracting party may levy on any dumped product an anti-dumping duty no greater in amount than the margin of dumping in respect of such product. [...]"

6.71 The arguments of the parties raise the question whether the 1916 Act could, by its nature, fall within the scope of Article VI only, of Article III:4 only, or partly or wholly within the scope of both. This question is prompted by two considerations:

(a) from the arguments of the parties, it does not seem that the same provision of the 1916 Act could, at the same time, infringe Article III:4 and Article VI of the GATT 1994; and

(b) these articles seem to be based on different premises: Article III (entitled "National Treatment") operates on the basis of a comparison between the treatment granted to domestic and imported products respectively, once the latter have been cleared through customs. Thus Article III:4 applies to measures imposed by Members internally, irrespective of the objective of the measures. In contrast, Article VI does not compare the treatment of domestic and imported products. The basis for the applicability of Article VI to the law of a Member does not seem to be the type of *measures* which is imposed by that Member, since other reasons than dumping may lead to the imposition of duties, but the type of trade practice *at the origin* of the measure.

6.72 The Panel thus believes that the *nature* of the 1916 Act might be such as to affect the relevance of the EC claims under Article III:4 or Article VI. Irrespective of the question of judicial economy, the Panel considers that it has the "competence of its competence", i.e. that it may determine whether a given claim can be addressed, irrespective of the positions expressed by the parties on the issue.[342] The fact that the European Communities formulates its claims primarily under Article VI does not require the Panel to address the EC claims under Article VI if it were to find that that

[342] This is different from exercising judicial economy, which is based on the necessity to address a claim in light of findings made on another claim. It is also different from determining whether a claim is properly before the Panel on the basis of the request for establishment of a panel. It is a question of knowing whether the Panel can rule on two claims which, on the basis of a first consideration of the facts and arguments before it, might be mutually exclusive.

provision is not applicable because the *qualification juridique* made by the EC is not correct.[343] On the other hand, the Panel may not have to address the EC claims under Article III:4 if it were to find that the 1916 Act falls exclusively within the scope of Article VI.

6.73 Therefore, it would be relevant to consider whether Article III:4 or Article VI of the GATT 1994 - or both - are *applicable* to the 1916 Act, irrespective of whether the 1916 Act is *compatible* with those provisions or not.

(b) Approach to be Followed by the Panel

6.74 Having regard to paragraph 6.71(b) above, we note that the issue whether the 1916 Act should be addressed under Article III:4 only, Article VI only, or both, is not obvious from the outset. In our opinion, reaching conclusions on this matter requires that we address the substance of the case, since one of the issues before us is whether the 1916 Act can be subject to the disciplines of Article VI and the Anti-Dumping Agreement. It is therefore appropriate to address this question as part of the substantive issues of this case, but separately from the actual WTO-compatibility of the 1916 Act. Based on our findings regarding the applicability of Articles III:4 and VI to the 1916 Act, we shall proceed to review the compatibility of that law with either provision or both.

6.75 However, even though we do not reach yet any conclusion on the applicability of either provision, we need to decide at this stage whether to begin our analysis with Article VI or Article III:4.

6.76 It is a general principle of international law that, when applying a body of norms to a given factual situation, one should consider that factual situation under the norm which most specifically addresses it.[344] As a result, one way to reply to the question above is to determine which article more specifically addresses the 1916 Act. We agree that this will require us to touch upon the substance of the case, but we recall that this test is used here for purely procedural reasons, that is to determine the order of our review. Such a *prima facie* analysis is, of course, without prejudice to the final findings on the issue of the applicability of Articles III:4 and VI, to be reached after a more detailed review of the scope of each provision, as necessary.

6.77 As mentioned above, our understanding is that Article III:4 and Article VI are based on two different premises. The applicability of Article III:4 seems to depend primarily on whether the measure applied pursuant to the law at issue is an internal measure or not.[345] In contrast, the applicability of Article VI seems to be based on the

[343] For instance, if a complainant were to claim a violation of Article XI of GATT 1994 in relation to a small tariff increase, the panel called upon to address the issue may be entitled to reject the claim on the ground that the measure at issue is not a quantitative restriction within the meaning of Article XI, without addressing any further the claim and the related arguments.

[344] See Appellate Body Report, *European Communities - Bananas, supra,* footnote 29, para. 204, and the judgement of the Permanent Court of International Justice in the *Serbian Loans* case (1929), where the PCIJ stated that "the special words, according to elementary principles of interpretation, control the general expression" (PCIJ, Series A, No. 20/21, at p. 30). See also György Haraszti, *Some Fundamental Problems of the Law of Treaties* (1973), p. 191.

[345] See Panel Report on *United States - Restrictions on Imports of Tuna* (not adopted), DS21/R, 3 September 1991, para 5.12:

nature of the trade practice which is addressed. Under Article VI, the type of sanction eventually applied does not seem to be relevant for a measure to be considered as an anti-dumping measure, or not. We note in this respect that, for the EC, the fact that the 1916 Act imposes other sanctions than duties is insufficient to make that law fall outside the scope of Article VI and, for the United States, under Article VI, dumping does not have to be counteracted exclusively with duties.[346] Consequently, it seems to us that the fact that a law imposes measures that can be qualified as "internal measures", such as fines, damages or imprisonment, does not appear to be sufficient to conclude that Article VI is not applicable to that law.

6.78 We also note that the parties agree that the 1916 Act deals with transnational price discrimination. Furthermore, the United States argues that it does not merely address dumping, and that other requirements under the 1916 Act make that law fall outside the scope of Article VI. We note that Article III:4 states that imported products

> "shall be accorded treatment no less favourable than that accorded to like products of national origin in respect of laws, regulations and requirements affecting their internal sale, offering for sale, purchase, transportation, distribution or use."

Determining that damages, fines or imprisonment, which are imposed on persons, may accord less favourable treatment to imported products with respect to their internal sale, offering for sale, purchase, transportation, distribution or use, is not *a priori* impossible and has actually been done by previous panels.[347] However, a preliminary examination of the scope of application of Article III:4 (i.e. internal sale, offering for sale, purchase, transportation, distribution or use) would tend to show that the terms of Article III:4 are less specific than those of Article VI when it comes to the notion of transnational price discrimination.

6.79 In application of the principle recalled by the Appellate Body *in European Communities - Bananas* and by the Permanent Court of International Justice in the

---

> "Another panel had found that the words "treatment no less favourable" in Article III:4 call for effective equality of opportunities for imported products in respect of the application of laws, regulations or requirements affecting the sale, offering for sale, purchase, transportation, distribution or use of products [...]. It was apparent to the Panel that the comparison implied was necessarily one between the measures applied to imported products and the measures applied to like domestic products."

[346] See the arguments of the United States regarding the ordinary meaning of Article VI:2 of the GATT 1994, in section III.E.2 above.

[347] See, e.g., Panel Report on *United States - Section 337 of the Tariff Act of 1930*, adopted on 7 November 1989, BISD 36/345, para. 5.10. See also Panel Report on *Italian Discrimination Against Imported Agricultural Machinery*, adopted on 23 October 1958, BISD 7S/60, which mentioned at para. 12 that:

> "The selection of the word "affecting" [in Article III:4] would imply, in the opinion of the Panel, that the drafters of the Article intended to cover in para. 4 not only the laws and regulations which directly governed the conditions of sale or purchase but also any laws or laws or regulations which might adversely modify the conditions of competition between the domestic and imported products on the internal market."

Serbian Loans case,[348] there would be reasons to reach the preliminary conclusion that we should review the applicability of Article VI to the 1916 Act in priority, as that article apparently applies to the facts at issue more specifically. This preliminary conclusion is based on our understanding of the arguments of the parties and on a preliminary review of the terms of Articles III:4 and VI. Since the fact that the 1916 Act provides for the imposition of internal measures does not seem to be sufficient as such to differentiate the scope of application of Article III:4 and that of Article VI, we had to consider the other terms of these articles.

6.80 Our preliminary conclusion does not address the question whether the 1916 Act could fall within the scope of both provisions. If we determine that the 1916 Act actually falls within the scope of Article VI, we will continue with the EC claims of violation of Article VI:1, VI:2 and the Anti-Dumping Agreement, as necessary to enable the DSB to make sufficiently precise recommendations and rulings. Once this part of our terms of reference has been addressed, we shall also decide whether pursuing our review with an analysis of the applicability of Article III:4 would be necessary to enable the DSB to make sufficiently precise recommendations and rulings so as to allow for prompt compliance "in order to ensure effective resolution of disputes to the benefit of all Members."[349] If we do not find that the 1916 Act falls within the scope of Article VI of the GATT 1994, we will proceed to consider the applicability of Article III:4 to the 1916 Act and, if applicable, the compatibility of the 1916 Act with that provision.

6.81 Consequently, we proceed with a review of the applicability of Article VI to the 1916 Act.

D. *Applicability of Article VI of the GATT 1994 to the 1916 Act*

1. *Preliminary Remarks on the Possibility of Interpreting the 1916 Act in a WTO-Compatible Manner and on its "Mandatory/Non-Mandatory" Nature*

(a) Issue before the Panel

6.82 We recall that the United States has argued in the course of these proceedings that the 1916 Act is non-mandatory legislation within the meaning of the GATT/WTO practice essentially because (i) with respect to both civil and criminal proceedings, US courts have interpreted in the past and/or could in the future interpret the 1916 Act in a manner consistent with the WTO obligations of the United States and (ii) the US Department of Justice has discretion to initiate or not criminal proceedings under the 1916 Act.[350] The EC considers that the mandatory/non-mandatory doctrine applies only to the executive branch of government. Judges have no discretion in applying a law. Finally, pursuant to the panel practice under the Tokyo Round agreements on anti-dumping and on subsidies and countervailing meas-

---

[348] See footnote 344 above.

[349] Appellate Body Report, *Australia - Measures Affecting Importation of Salmon* ("*Australia - Salmon*"), WT/DS18/AB/R, adopted 6 November 1998, DSR 1998:VIII, 3327, para. 223.

[350] The United States does not seem to allege that a similar discretion exists in relation to the civil proceedings which would make the 1916 Act non-mandatory.

ures, the discretion of the US Department of Justice to initiate criminal proceedings is insufficient to make the 1916 Act a non-mandatory law.

6.83 We could treat these arguments as a question of admissibility of the EC claims. However, for the reasons presented below, we shall address them as part of our review of the EC claims under Article VI of the GATT 1994 and the Anti-Dumping Agreement and, if necessary, Article III:4 of the GATT 1994.[351]

6.84 As a preliminary remark, it should be noted that, even though the parties used the terms "mandatory/non-mandatory" or "discretionary" legislation in their arguments with respect to different aspects of the 1916 Act, we consider that we should differentiate the issues before us. We consider that the question whether the US Department of Justice has discretion to initiate or not criminal proceedings under the 1916 Act is indeed a question of application of the doctrine on mandatory/non-mandatory legislation within the meaning usually given to it in the GATT and in public international law.[352] The question whether the 1916 Act could be or has been interpreted in a way that would make it fall outside the scope of Article VI is, however, simply a question of assessing the current meaning of the law.

(b) The Possibility of Interpreting the 1916 Act in a WTO-Compatible Manner

6.85 Concerning the argument according to which US courts have interpreted in the past and/or could in the future interpret the 1916 Act in a manner consistent with the WTO obligations of the United States, the United States relies to a large extent on the panel report on *United States - Measures Affecting the Importation, Internal Sale and Use of Tobacco.*[353] In our opinion, the United States refers to that case for essentially two reasons. First, the United States relies on the *United States - Tobacco* case to argue that a law which can be interpreted in a WTO-consistent manner is a law that does not mandate a WTO-illegal action. Second, the United States claims that, in

[351] Such an approach is also consistent with the practice of other panels, which addressed this issue in the course of their review of the conformity of measures with GATT provisions. See *United States - Measures Affecting the Importation, Internal Sale and Use of Tobacco*, adopted on 4 October 1994, BISD 41S/131, para. 118. That report refers to the report of the panel on *United States - Taxes on Petroleum and certain Imported Substances*, adopted on 17 June 1987, BISD 34S/136, p. 160; the report of the panel on *EEC - Regulation on Imports of Parts and Components*, *Op. Cit.*, pp. 198-199; the report of the panel on *Thailand, Restrictions on Importation of and Internal Taxes on Cigarettes*, adopted on 7 November 1990, BISD 37S/200 pp. 227-228; the report of the panel *on United States - Measures Affecting Alcoholic and Malt Beverages*, adopted on 19 June 1992, BISD 39S/206, pp. 281-282, 289-290; and the report of the panel on *United States - Denial of MFN Treatment as to Non-Rubber Footwear from Brazil*, adopted on 19 June 1992, BISD 39S/128, p. 152. See also Panel Report on *Canada - Measures Affecting the Export of Civilian Aircraft*, WT/DS70/R, adopted 20 August 1999, DSR 1999:IV, 1443, para. 9.124.

[352] The Panel is mindful of the of the findings of the panel *in United States - Sections 301-310 of the Trade Act of 1974 ("US - Section 301 Trade Act")*, WT/DS152/R, adopted 27 January 2000, DSR 2000:II, 815, which was adopted after the issuance of the interim report in the present case. However, we do not consider that the reasoning of the panel in that case affects our reasoning in the present case.

[353] Op. Cit., hereinafter "*United States - Tobacco*".

accordance with that report, the EC bears the burden to prove that there is no possibility to interpret the 1916 Act in a WTO-consistent manner.

6.86 The issue here is primarily, like in the *United States - Tobacco* case, a question of interpretation of an ambiguous text. However, in our opinion, similarities are limited to that aspect. In the *United States - Tobacco* case, the panel had to deal with the question whether the ambiguous term at issue mandated a violation of Article VIII of the GATT 1947. In the present case, what is at issue is whether the terms of the 1916 Act are such as to make Article VI *applicable* to that law. We are consequently at an earlier stage of our analysis than the panel in the *United States - Tobacco* case. Moreover, in the *United States - Tobacco* case, the United States had as yet neither changed the fee structure nor promulgated rules implementing the law at issue. In the present case, the 1916 Act did not require any implementing measures from the US government and, contrary to the law at issue in the *United States - Tobacco* case, it has been applied in a number of instances by US courts. Consequently, the situations faced by this Panel and the panel in the *United States - Tobacco* case are factually different.

6.87 These differences have implications for the burden of proof. In the *United States - Tobacco* case, the extensive burden of proof imposed on the complainants was obviously related to the absence of any application of the ambiguous term by the executive branch of the US government at the time of the findings. Since the United States had so far applied its law in conformity with Article VIII of the GATT 1947 and since there was no evidence that the United States intended to apply the law in a GATT-incompatible manner, the principle *in dubio mitius* logically applied.[354]

6.88 In contrast, several courts have interpreted and applied the 1916 Act. In fact, reaching a decision on the US argument requires the Panel to determine whether the interpretation of the 1916 Act by US courts has been such as to actually make the 1916 Act WTO-compatible by making it fall outside the scope of Article VI of the GATT 1994. In such a context, the EC only needs to prove that the 1916 Act, as it has been interpreted and applied so far by US courts, meets the conditions to fall within the scope of Article VI. If the EC succeeds in proving it, we will proceed with a review of the compatibility of the 1916 Act with Article VI.

6.89 The question whether there could be a possibility to interpret the 1916 Act in the future so that it would fall outside the scope of Article VI would be relevant, according to the *United States - Tobacco* case, only if the 1916 Act had not yet been applied. Since the 1916 Act has actually been applied and has been subject to interpretation by US courts, the issue before us is (i) whether Article VI is found to be applicable to the 1916 Act on the basis of the current court interpretation and (ii) whether a violation of Article VI by the 1916 Act as currently applied is identified.

6.90 Even if we were to consider that the factual circumstances in the present case and in the *United States - Tobacco* case are comparable, we recall that, in *United States - Tobacco*, an important element in the finding of the panel had been the pres-

---

[354] See Appellate Body Report in *EC Measures Concerning Meat and Meat Products (Hormones)*, WT/DS/26/AB/R, WT/DS48/AB/R, adopted 13 February 1998, DSR 1998:I,135, footnote 154, where the Appellate Body held that this principle is widely recognised in international law as a "supplementary means of interpretation".

ence of an *ambiguity* in the text of the law under review. The term "comparable" could be interpreted in GATT-compatible as well as in GATT-incompatible ways. Assuming that the reasoning of the panel in the *United States - Tobacco* case could be extended to the present situation in spite of the differences highlighted above, if we find that no such ambiguity exists regarding the applicability of Article VI to the text of the 1916 Act itself or as interpreted by the US courts, (i) we will not have to apply the burden of proof which the United States alleges was applied in the *US - Tobacco* case and (ii) we will conclude that the 1916 Act falls within the scope of Article VI and will address it as any other legislation.[355]

(c) Mandatory/Non-Mandatory Nature of the 1916 Act

6.91 Concerning the discretion enjoyed by the US Department of Justice to initiate or not criminal proceedings under the 1916 Act, we recall that the European Communities have claimed that the discretion to initiate an investigation was found insufficient under the Tokyo Round Agreement on Interpretation and Application of Articles VI, XVI and XXIII of the General Agreement on Tariffs and Trade[356] and the Tokyo Round Agreement on Implementation of Article VI of the General Agreement on Tariffs and Trade[357] to consider as "non-mandatory" a law reviewed under those agreements.

6.92 We have undertaken a preliminary review of the panel reports referred to by the EC. [358] We note that the issue of the "mandatory/non-mandatory" nature of a law has apparently been addressed differently under Article VI of the GATT and the Tokyo Round subsidies and anti-dumping agreements than under Article III of the GATT. In order to avoid making unnecessary findings, we find it appropriate to address this issue once we have determined whether the 1916 Act falls within the scope of Article VI or not, a determination to be made in any event for the reasons mentioned in the previous paragraphs.

---

[355] If we conclude that the 1916 Act falls within the scope of Article VI, we will not need to take position on the issue whether the reasoning in the *United States - Tobacco* report, which was adopted under the GATT 1947, would still be valid after the entry into force of the WTO Agreement, in light of Article XVI:4 of the Agreement Establishing the WTO.

[356] Hereinafter the "Tokyo Round Subsidies Agreement".

[357] Hereinafter the "Tokyo Round Anti-Dumping Agreement".

[358] See *Panel on United States Definition of Industry Concerning Wine And Grape Products*, adopted on 28 April 1992, BISD 39S/436 (hereinafter "*United States - Definition of Wine Industry*") and the report of the panel on *EC - Anti-Dumping Duties on Audio Tapes in Cassettes Originating in Japan*, ADP 136, 28 April 1995 (hereinafter "*EC - Audio Cassettes*"). The latter was not adopted. However, we recall that in its report on *Japan - Taxes on Alcoholic Beverages*, *supra*, footnote 224, at 108, the Appellate Body confirmed that "a panel could nevertheless find useful guidance in the reasoning of an unadopted panel report that it considered to be relevant."

2. *Does the 1916 Act Fall Within the Scope of Article VI of the GATT 1994?*

(a) Issue before the Panel

6.93 The European Communities claims that the 1916 Act is an anti-dumping law subject to the disciplines of Article VI of the GATT 1994 because Article VI refers (i) to rules targeted at imports and by the fact of their importation; and (ii) to practices defined by reference to price discrimination in the form of lower prices in the market of the importing country than those practiced on the market of the country of export. It is only dumping meeting the definition in Article VI that is to be condemned, and then only in the stated circumstances of injury, threat of injury or material retardation of the establishment of a domestic industry.

6.94 The United States claims that Article VI does not state that its disciplines govern any law based upon the concept of price discrimination regardless of any other elements required to be proven under the law. Article VI only addresses actions taken for the purpose of offsetting or preventing injurious dumping, not actions that are not designed to offset or prevent injurious dumping, as is the case with the 1916 Act. According to the United States, the EC seems to read in Article VI the limitation that all laws with any type of international price discrimination component must conform to the anti-dumping rules. If it were to be the case, this would extend these rules into the realm of anti-trust and, therefore, Member's other anti-trust laws prohibiting various forms of discriminatory or low pricing would be WTO-inconsistent to the extent that those laws address attempted monopolization or an abuse of dominance undertaken through predatory, cross-border pricing practices. The negotiating history and subsequent practice under the GATT 1947 support the contention that Article VI of the GATT 1994 is not intended as a remedy for "predatory pricing".

6.95 The EC contends that one of the clearest targets of Article VI of the GATT 1994 is precisely "predatory" dumping. The EC does not argue that Article VI and the Anti-Dumping Agreement govern any international price discrimination regardless of the other elements of the law. The approach in Article VI is confirmed by the basic theory of anti-dumping which recognises a particular problem posed by price discrimination of this type, requiring an analysis distinct from that applying to price discrimination within the same market.

6.96 The United States contests that the distinction between anti-trust and anti-dumping should be based upon whether price discrimination occurs within a single market or across markets. Moreover, the United States considers that Article VI and the Anti-Dumping Agreement do not govern competition laws simply because those laws incorporate the element of price discrimination. The existence of an anti-trust objective in a law regulating cross-border price discrimination should remove it from the scope of Article VI of the GATT 1994.

6.97 Since the EC made claims of violation of Article VI and, separately, of the Anti-Dumping Agreement, we would like to clarify how we see the relationship between these provisions. Just as the panel in the *India - Quantitative Restrictions*[359] case did not analyse Article XVIII:B in isolation from the Understanding on Balance-

---

[359] Op. Cit., footnote 305 above.

of-payments Provisions of the General Agreement on Tariffs and Trade 1994, this Panel has no intention to address Article VI in isolation from the Anti-Dumping Agreement. In our opinion, Article VI and the Anti-Dumping Agreement are part of the same treaty or, as the panel and the Appellate Body put it in *Argentina - Safeguard Measures on Import of Footwear* with respect to Article XIX and the Agreement on Safeguards, an "inseparable package of rights and disciplines".[360] In application of the customary rules of interpretation of international law, we are bound to *interpret* Article VI of the GATT 1994 as part of the WTO Agreement and the Anti-Dumping Agreement is part of the context of Article VI.[361] This implies that Article VI should not be interpreted in a way that would deprive it or the Anti-Dumping Agreement of meaning. Rather, we should give meaning and legal effect to all the relevant provisions.[362] However, the requirement does not prevent us from making *findings* in relation to Article VI only, or in relation to specific provisions of the Anti-Dumping Agreement, as required by our terms of reference.

6.98 The Panel also considers that its role, pursuant to Article 3.2 of the DSU, is to clarify the meaning of Article VI in order to determine whether it applies, as claimed by the European Communities, to the type of measures addressed by the 1916 Act. For the sake of clarity, we will first address the applicability of Article VI to the terms of the 1916 Act as such, in isolation from subsequent interpretation(s). We will then review the circumstances of the enactment of the 1916 Act (including the legislative history) as well as the relevant US court case-law and determine to what extent they affect the conclusions that we will have reached on the basis of the text only.

(b) Does the 1916 Act, on the Basis of its Terms only, Fall within the Scope of Article VI of the GATT 1994?

(i) Approach of the Panel

6.99 We note that the views of the parties diverge as to the criteria that should be used to determine the applicability of Article VI of the GATT 1994 to the 1916 Act. For the EC, the 1916 Act should be subject to the norms of Article VI because Article VI applies to imports by the reason of their importation and addresses practices defined by reference to discrimination between the prices of the imported products and domestic prices in the country of export or, in the absence of such prices, export prices to a third country or cost of production. The United States considers that Article VI only addresses actions taken for the purpose of offsetting or preventing injurious dumping, not actions that are *not* designed to offset or prevent injurious dumping, as is the case with the 1916 Act.

---

360 Appellate Body Report on *Argentina - Safeguard Measures on Import of Footwear, supra,* footnote 285, para. 81.

361 See, in this respect, our reasoning in para. 6.195 below.

362 See, e.g., the reports of the Appellate Body on *Argentina - Safeguard Measures on Import of Footwear, supra,* footnote 285, para. 81, *Korea - Definitive Safeguard Measures on Import of Certain Dairy Products*, WT/DS98/AB/R, adopted 12 January 2000, DSR 2000:I, 3, para. 81 and *United States - Standards for Reformulated and Conventional Gasoline*, WT/DS2/AB/R, adopted 20 May 1996, DSR 1996:I, 3, at. 21.

6.100 We consider that, in order to determine whether the 1916 Act falls within the scope of Article VI of the GATT 1994, we need to define that scope by interpreting Article VI:1 on the basis of the relevant provisions of the Vienna Convention and then compare those requirements to those of the 1916 Act. However, we note that we are called upon to consider the compatibility of a specific law with Article VI of the GATT 1994, not to make an interpretation of the scope of that article in absolute terms. Thus, any assessment we may make of the scope of Article VI will be circumscribed to the specific issues raised by the terms of the 1916 Act.

6.101 Finally, as recalled in paragraph 6.59 above, the mere description or categorization of a measure under the domestic law as well as the policy purpose behind the measure cannot be a decisive factor in the categorization of that measure under the WTO Agreement. We therefore do not consider as decisive the classification of the 1916 Act under the US Code or the fact that it is generally called the "Antidumping Act of 1916". We consider that we should exclusively rely at this stage on what the text of the law expressly says. This does not mean that we should disregard the objective of the 1916 Act. However, for now we will consider it only to the extent that it results from the terms of the law itself, to the exclusion of the legislative history or the subsequent court practice, which we will address later.[363]

(ii) Scope of Article VI of the GATT 1994

6.102 Article VI:1 provides, in relevant parts, as follows:

> "The contracting parties recognize that dumping, by which products of one country are introduced into the commerce of another country at less than the normal value of the products, is to be condemned if it causes or threatens material injury to an established industry in the territory of a contracting party or materially retards the establishment of a domestic industry. For the purpose of this article, a product is to be considered as being introduced into the commerce of an importing country at less than its normal value, if the price of the product exported from one country to another
>
> (a) is less than the comparable price, in the ordinary course of trade, for the like product when destined for consumption in the exporting country, or,
>
> (b) in the absence of such domestic price, is less than either
>
> (i) the highest comparable price for the like product for export to any third country in the ordinary course of trade, or
>
> (ii) the cost of production of the product in the country of origin plus a reasonable addition for selling cost and profit.
>
> Due allowance shall be made in each case for differences in conditions and terms of sale, for differences in taxation, and for other dif-

[363] This also seems to be consistent with US court practice. In *Zenith I* (1975), Op. Cit., p. 246, Judge Higginbotham stated that "as always, when a court is called to construe a statute, it is wise to begin by reading the statute itself."

> ferences affecting price comparability." [notes *Ad Article VI:1* omitted]

6.103 Considering the terms of Article VI in their ordinary meaning, we note that Article VI does not regulate the practice of dumping itself, but the anti-dumping activities of Members. In other words, Article VI concentrates on what Members may do in order to counteract dumping. However, Article VI is based on a definition of dumping, found at the beginning of Article VI:1:

> " dumping, by which products of one country are introduced into the commerce of another country at less than the normal value of the products"[364]

The normal value is either the comparable price, in the ordinary course of trade, for the like product when destined for consumption in the exporting country, or, in the absence of such domestic price, the highest comparable price for the like product for export to any third country in the ordinary course of trade, or the cost of production of the product in the country of origin plus a reasonable addition for selling cost and profit.

6.104 Therefore, the conditions for "dumping" to exist are the following:

(i) there must be products imported and cleared through customs ("introduction into the commerce"); and

(ii) those imported products must be priced at a price lower than their normal value, i.e. their price in a foreign country, be it the country of production or another country of export, or a constructed value based on a calculation of cost and profits.

In other words, there must be a price difference between like products sold in two markets, one of which is not within the jurisdiction of the same Member, their price in the country of exportation being lower that their price in the country of production or in a third country to which they are exported. [365]

6.105 It is this practice that "is to be condemned", provided certain conditions are met. Thereafter follow certain substantive (i.e. material injury[366] and causality) and procedural requirements; but they do not qualify the original definition of "dumping".[367] While "dumping" can be subject to sanctions only if it causes material injury,

---

[364] We note that this definition is close to the definition of dumping given by Jacob Viner in *Dumping, A Problem in International Trade,* Op. Cit., p. 3, i.e. "price-discrimination between national markets." The court in *Zenith III, Op. Cit.*, p. 1213, refers to the 1966 edition which includes, at p. 4, a slightly revised definition: "price discrimination between purchasers in different national markets."

[365] The existence of a price difference between two markets *located in two different Members*, together with a *lower price in the importing country* than in the country of production are essential features to differentiate dumping from other forms of price discrimination and pricing practices. In this respect, see also Viner, Op. Cit., pp. 2-3.

[366] Throughout these findings, the term "material injury" shall be taken to refer to "material injury to an established industry in the territory of" a Member, threat thereof or material retardation of the establishment of a domestic industry, within the meaning of Article VI:1 of the GATT 1994.

[367] We do not read the language "For the purpose of this article, a product is to be considered as being introduced into the commerce of an importing country at less than its normal value, if the price of the product exported from one country to another..." as qualifying anything but the term "normal

this does not affect the fact that, on the basis of the structure of Article VI, "dumping" within the meaning of the definition of Article VI:1 has to be found in the first place.

6.106 Neither the context of Article VI, nor the object and purpose of the GATT 1994 or the WTO Agreement contradicts this assessment. On the contrary, Article VI:1(a) and (b) confirm that there is no requirement that the export price be above or below fixed or variable costs or that price undercutting, price suppression or price depression be identified for "dumping" to exist, even though they may be considered for injury purposes. Article VI:2 supports the view that Article VI is about what Members are entitled to do when they counteract dumping within the meaning of Article VI. So does Article 1 of the Anti-Dumping Agreement, by referring to "anti-dumping *measure[s]*" which may be applied by Members.[368] The supplementary means of interpretation of Article 32 of the Vienna Convention, in particular the *travaux préparatoires*, confirm that Article VI of the GATT was about what category of dumping could be subject to counteracting measures.[369]

6.107 We therefore reach the conclusion that a law that would counteract "dumping" as defined in Article VI:1 would fall within the scope of Article VI. However, as mentioned in paragraph 6.100 above, we are not called upon to make findings in the absolute. We therefore proceed to review more specifically the 1916 Act on the basis of the scope of Article VI as defined above.

(iii) Examination of the 1916 Act on the Basis of the Scope of Article VI

Similarities

6.108 We note that the 1916 Act contains a transnational price discrimination test:

> "It shall be unlawful for any person *importing or assisting in importing* any articles from any foreign country into the United States, commonly and systematically to import, sell or cause to be imported or sold such articles within the United States *at a price substantially less than the actual market value or wholesale price of such articles, at the time of exportation to the United States, in the principal markets of the country of their production, or of other foreign countries* to which they are commonly exported after adding to such market value

value". Additional conditions have been introduced in the Anti-Dumping Agreement, such as the *de minimis* requirement for the margin of dumping (Article 5.8 of the Anti-Dumping Agreement) but they do not affect the original definition to such an extent that they would change our conclusions.

[368] Article 1, first sentence, of the Anti-Dumping Agreement provides that:

> "An anti-dumping measure shall be applied only under the circumstances provided for in Article VI of GATT 1994 and pursuant to investigations initiated and conducted in accordance with the provisions of this agreement."

[369] See U.N. Doc. EPCT/C.II/48 (1946), p. 1, "the discussion had shown that there were four types of dumping: price, service, exchange and social. Article 11 permitted measures to counteract the first type. It would obligate members not to impose anti-dumping duties with respect to the other three types". See also Jackson: *World Trade and the Law of GATT*, p. 402 and 404.

or wholesale price, freight, duty, and other charges and expenses necessarily incident to the importation and sale thereof in the United States..." (emphasis added)

This test includes requirements similar to the introduction of the dumped product into the commerce of one Member since it refers to "import or sell or cause to be imported or sold [...] within the United States". We further note that the 1916 Act is premised on a comparison between two prices, one in the United States, the other one in the country of production of the product or in a third country where the product is also sold. There is consequently a very strong similarity between the definition of dumping in Article VI and the transnational price discrimination test found in the 1916 Act.

6.109 This said, would there be elements in the text of the 1916 Act that would lead us to conclude that the transnational price discrimination test in the 1916 Act nevertheless does not meet the definition of dumping in Article VI? We note that the 1916 Act relies not only on the actual market value but also on wholesale price. It also refers to the "principal markets of the country of [...] production [of the imported merchandise]" or of "other foreign countries to which they are commonly exported". We do not find the nature of these requirements to be different from those of Article VI:1 to such a degree as to make them fall outside the concept of "comparable price, in the ordinary course of trade, for the like product when destined for consumption in the exporting country" found in Article VI:1(a). The 1916 Act also refers to sales on the "principal markets" of "other foreign countries to which they are commonly exported". This may not be the "highest comparable price for the like product for export to any third country in the ordinary course of trade" found in Article VI:1(b) but, once again, its nature does not, in our view, depart to a significant degree from the criteria of Article VI:1 and it does not relate to other concepts which, by their nature, could be differentiated from those found in Article VI:1. Finally, we note that the 1916 Act does not provide for the possibility to use a "constructed" normal value, within the meaning of Article VI:1(b)(ii). However, this only makes the transnational price discrimination test in the 1916 Act "narrower" than the definition of "dumping" in Article VI:1, without making it fall outside its scope. We also note that the 1916 Act provides for adjustments. Even though these adjustments are not those found in the last sub-paragraph of Article VI:1, they do not affect the scope of the price discrimination test in the 1916 Act in relation to Article VI. On the contrary, they confirm the similarity of the two texts as far as the criteria for the identification of the practice at issue is concerned.

6.110 This does not mean that the criteria for establishing price discrimination under the 1916 Act would always be compatible with the requirements of Article VI of the GATT 1994. This means only that we do not find in these criteria anything that would make us consider that the 1916 transnational price discrimination test would partly or totally fall outside the definition of "dumping" found in Article VI:1.

Specific Arguments of the United States

6.111 The United States argues that the 1916 Act is not merely about dumping and has additional requirements compared with Article VI. In the first place, the 1916 Act requires the price difference to be "substantial" and the importation and sales to be done "commonly and systematically". Secondly, the 1916 Act includes additional requirements that are not found in Article VI, which make of it an instrument targeting specific forms of price discrimination in an anti-trust context.

6.112 We do not consider that conditions which make the establishment of dumping more difficult, such as the requirement of substantial price difference and of common and systematic dumping are such as to make the price discrimination test of the 1916 Act fall outside the scope of the definition of Article VI:1. As long as the test of the 1916 Act requires a price difference between two markets, each located in the territory of a different Member, the fact that additional requirements make a finding of dumping more difficult does not affect the applicability of Article VI. Members may not exempt themselves from the rules and disciplines of the WTO Agreement when counteracting dumping, but they remain free to apply requirements which make the imposition of measures more difficult.

6.113 With respect to the other requirements of the 1916 Act, we recall that the price discrimination addressed by the 1916 Act must be applied with the intent of (a) "destroying" or (b) "injuring an industry in the United States", or of (c) "preventing the establishment of an industry in the United States", or of (d) "restraining" or (e) "monopolizing any part of trade and commerce [in the goods concerned] in the United States." We note that the first three tests are quite similar to the material injury and retardation tests of Article VI:1, while the two last ones are more of the type used in an anti-trust context.[370] However, we found above that the existence of "dumping" within the meaning of Article VI:1 is a condition *sine qua non* for a Member to take action under Article VI. We note that, before identifying any intent under the 1916 Act, US judges would also have to establish that there has been importation or sales at discriminatory prices of the type required by that law.[371] We have been presented with no evidence that transnational price discrimination under the 1916 Act could be presumed when the court had only established the existence of an intent to destroy, injure or prevent the establishment of an industry in the United States, or to restrain or monopolise any part of the trade in the product concerned within the United States. Therefore, we conclude that the existence in the 1916 Act of additional requirements which are not found in Article VI does not *per se* suffice to make the 1916 Act fall outside the scope of Article VI.

6.114 Moreover, we recall that dumping "is to be condemned if it causes or threatens" to cause certain effects listed in Article VI:1. Even though Article VI:1 does not read "dumping is to be condemned *only* if" it causes those effects, we consider that it should be interpreted as limiting the use of anti-dumping measures to the

[370] See Robinson-Patman Act, which provides that the "effect of such discrimination may be substantially to lessen competition or tend to create a monopoly in any line of commerce, or to injure, destroy, or prevent competition with any person who either grants or knowingly receives the benefit of such discrimination or with customers of either of them."

[371] See the statement of the court in *In Re Japanese Electronic Products II* (1983), p. 324, that:

> "The first element necessary to a finding of dumping under the 1916 Act is proof that a price differential exists between two comparable products, one of which is imported or sold in the United States and the other of which is sold in the exporting country."

See also *Helmac II* (1993), p. 591,which recognised that "dumping: the pricing of goods on the American market at a price lower than on the home market" was "the key to liability under the [1916] Act".

situations expressly foreseen in Article VI.[372] In other words, whenever a Member addresses a practice that meets the definition of Article VI:1, it has to abide by the WTO rules governing anti-dumping.[373] If, as the United States seems to argue, a Member could decide to apply other tests or other sanctions to counteract "dumping" practices within the meaning of Article VI, this would be contrary to the terms of Article VI. Also, alleging that the disciplines of Article VI are only applicable to the extent a Member wants to address situations of material injury, threat thereof or material retardation of the establishment of a domestic industry would undermine the whole purpose of Article VI and the Anti-Dumping Agreement. From the terms of Article VI, we deduce that the purpose of that provision is to define the conditions under which counteracting dumping *as such* is allowed. This purpose is confirmed by Article 1, first sentence, of the Anti-Dumping Agreement, which provides that:

> "An anti-dumping measure shall be applied *only under the circumstances provided for in Article VI of GATT 1994* and pursuant to investigations initiated [footnote 1 omitted] and conducted in accordance with the provisions of this Agreement." (emphasis added)

Article 18.1 of the Anti-Dumping Agreement also confirms this understanding:

> "No specific action against dumping of exports from another Member can be taken *except in accordance with the provisions of GATT 1994*, as interpreted by this Agreement. [footnote 24 omitted][374]" (emphasis added)

This implies that, by adopting Article VI and the Anti-Dumping Agreement, Members have agreed to use only one approach against "dumping" as such. The interpretation suggested by the United States would undermine the useful effect of the provisions of Article VI and of the Anti-Dumping Agreement.

6.115 For these reasons, we cannot consider that the existence of other "effect" tests than those provided for under Article VI should be sufficient to exclude the 1916 Act from the scope of Article VI. The 1916 Act may be targeting particular effects of cross-border price discrimination, but to the extent that such price discrimination

---

[372] Such a limitation was clearly envisaged by the drafters of Article VI. The Report of the Sub-Committee at the Havana Conference which considered the provision which was to replace the original Article VI in the GATT 1947 noted that "The Article as agreed to by the Sub-Committee condemns *injurious 'price dumping'* as defined therein and does not relate to other types of dumping." (emphasis added) (Havana Reports, p. 74, para. 23, as reported in *GATT, Analytical Index: Guide to GATT Law and Practice, Updated 6th Edition* (1995), p. 222).

[373] This is without prejudice to a Member choosing to address the effects of dumping, e.g. increased imports, or its causes (e.g., subsidisation) through other legitimate means under the WTO Agreement, such as countervailing or safeguard measures. However, it cannot choose to address "dumping" as such with instruments or in ways that are different from those allowed in the WTO Agreement for that purpose. This is, in our view, the meaning of footnote 24 to Article 18.1 of the Anti-Dumping Agreement, which provides that "This is not intended to preclude actions under other relevant provisions of GATT 1994, as appropriate."

[374] We did not overlook the terms of footnote 24. Footnote 24, as we understand it, does not affect our conclusion that, when dealing with dumping as such, Members must comply with Article VI of the GATT 1994 and the Anti-Dumping Agreement.

meets the definition of "dumping" contained in Article VI:1, it has to be subject to the disciplines of Article VI and the Anti-Dumping Agreement.[375]

6.116 Finally, the United States argues that the existence of an anti-trust objective in a law regulating cross-border price discrimination removes it from the scope of Article VI of the GATT 1994. While we agree that Article VI applies when Members have recourse to a given trade policy instrument, i.e. anti-dumping action, we do not agree that the application of Article VI is dependent on the objective pursued by the Member concerned. As we have demonstrated in the previous paragraphs, Article VI is based on an objective premise. If a Member's legislation is based on a test that meets the definition of Article VI:1, Article VI applies. The stated purpose of the law cannot affect this conclusion.[376]

6.117 We therefore conclude that the fact that the 1916 Act may have an anti-trust objective or be categorized in US law as an anti-trust law does not *per se* make it fall outside the scope of Article VI, unless it is demonstrated that this objective and this categorisation have an impact on the operation of the 1916 Act. In light of our reasoning, this would require that the terms of the transnational price discrimination test of the 1916 Act be understood in such a way that it would not meet the definition of "dumping" of Article VI:1 of the GATT 1994.

(iv) Conclusion

6.118 We find that the 1916 Act, based on an analysis of its terms, objectively addresses a type of transnational price discrimination that meets the definition of "dumping" contained in Article VI:1 of the GATT 1994 and, thus, should be subject to the disciplines of Article VI.

6.119 However, our findings are based on the definition of dumping as found in Article VI:1 of the GATT 1994 and on the terms of the 1916 Act in their current ordinary meaning. As we recalled above,[377] we must pay due regard to the fact that we are dealing with a text drafted more than eighty years ago. If, by the time it was enacted, the 1916 Act was not designed to address "dumping", in other words if the terms found in the 1916 Act had a different meaning in 1916 than they appear to have today, this should be apparent from the legislative history and the context of its enactment. Since the United States refers to the legislative history of the 1916 Act as well as to the context of its enactment, this aspect needs to be addressed. The United States also claims that US courts have interpreted the 1916 Act consistently with its

---

[375] We understand that the United States did not argue that the tests at issue were less stringent than the material injury/material retardation tests of Article VI. Therefore, we do not address this point.

[376] See Panel Report on *EC - Parts and Components, Op. Cit.*, at para. 5.6, where the panel examined whether the policy purpose of a charge was relevant to determining the issue of whether the charge was imposed "in connection with importation", within the meaning of Article II:1(b) of GATT 1947. The panel noted that:

> "the policy purpose of charges is frequently difficult to determine objectively. Many charges could be regarded as serving both internal purposes and purposes related to the importation of goods. Only at the expense of creating substantial legal uncertainty could the policy purpose of a charge be considered to be relevant in determining whether the charge falls under Article II:1(b) or Article III:2."

[377] See section C.1. above.

anti-trust purpose, and in such a way that it is removed from the scope of application of Article VI. Having regard to our conclusions in paragraph 6.117 above that this would require that the price discrimination test of the 1916 Act be interpreted in such a way that it would no longer meet the definition of Article VI:1, we must also address this argument, as well as the EC argument that, in fact, US courts have applied the 1916 Act as an anti-dumping instrument.

(c) Impact of the Historical Context and of the Legislative History of the 1916 Act

(i) Approach of the Panel

6.120 The United States and, to a lesser extent, the European Communities have referred the Panel to the historical context of the law in general and its legislative history in particular, as it results, *inter alia*, from the Congressional Records. Our understanding is that the legislative history of an act of the US Congress is an important tool for US courts to identify the "intent of Congress".[378] The legislative history allows US courts to interpret a law in accordance with what they perceive to be the original intent of the US Congress when the text of that law is not clear. US courts may also use legislative history, when necessary, to confirm the clear meaning of a law.[379] Since, as mentioned above,[380] we have to identify how the 1916 Act is understood within the US legal system, we need to address the arguments of the parties based on the historical context and the legislative history of the 1916 Act, taking into account the use that US courts made of those interpretation tools in practice.

6.121 We have found that the key to the applicability of Article VI of the GATT 1994 to the 1916 Act is whether that law objectively addresses "dumping" within the meaning of that article. We have also found that the terms of the 1916 Act, on their face, showed that the transnational price discrimination test in that law met the definition of "dumping" in Article VI:1 of the GATT 1994. We consider that we now have to determine whether there is evidence in the legislative history or the historical context of the enactment of the 1916 Act that we should understand the price discrimination test of the 1916 Act differently than we have on the basis of the text of the law.

(ii) Review of the Historical Context and Legislative History

6.122 Having reviewed the materials submitted by the parties, we have found no indication that the terms of the price discrimination test found in the 1916 Act were understood differently at the time of its enactment than we understand them today. In

---

[378] In the *Zenith III* case, p. 1213, the court mentioned that the US Supreme Court had "recently observed that 'courts, in construing a statute, may with propriety recur to the history of the times when it was passed; and this is frequently necessary in order to ascertain the reason as well as the meaning of particular provisions in it.' Leo Sheep Co. v. United States, 440 U.S. 668, 669, 99 S.Ct. 1403, 1405, 59 L.Ed.2d 677 (1979)".

[379] US courts had recourse to the legislative history of the 1916 Act in a number of cases. See, e.g., the *Zenith I* (1975) and *Zenith III* (1980) judgements.

[380] See section C.1. above.

its 1919 *Information Concerning Dumping and Unfair Foreign Competition in the United States and Canada's Anti-Dumping Law*, at p. 9, the United States Tariff Commission included a definition of "dumping" identical in substance to the concept addressed by Article VI:

> "Dumping may be comprehensively described as the sale of imported merchandise at less than its prevailing market or wholesale price in the country of production. The definition derives particular importance from a not infrequent tendency to confuse with dumping [...] certain other trade practices which are generally considered unfairly competitive."

This statement of the Tariff Commission shows that dumping was probably not the only price practice which could be considered as unfairly competitive. However, the Tariff Commission added that

> "The anti-dumping act of Congress of September 8, 1916, [footnote omitted] somewhat modifies the above definition by condemning importation as well as sale, if commonly and systematically resorted to with the purpose specified in the law."

While not part of the legislative history of the 1916 Act as such, this document of the Tariff Commission indicates that the practice addressed by the 1916 Act was already clearly understood to be "dumping" as we define it today. The Tariff Commission definition of "dumping" is, with some exceptions which we found not to affect the applicability of Article VI:1 of the GATT 1994,[381] similar to the definition of transnational price discrimination in the 1916 Act. Therefore, it seems reasonable to conclude that the US Congress, when it passed the 1916 Act, was fully aware of the fact that that law addressed "dumping" and not another form of price discrimination.[382]

6.123 Moreover, even though the 1916 Act might pursue anti-trust objectives, we found no *express* indication in the legislative history that price discrimination in the 1916 Act should be understood in any particular anti-trust context.

6.124 The United States argues that the district court in *Zenith III* (1980) held that, to give rise to a violation of the 1916 Act, the products sold in the United States and the products sold in the foreign country had to be of "like grade and quality" as that phrase is used in Section 2 of the Clayton Act as amended by the Robinson-Patman Act. As a result, litigants under the 1916 Act were not "clothed with the same discretion as the US Treasury Department under the 1921 Antidumping Act"[383] in terms of the definition of the products to be compared.

6.125 First, in our opinion, the comparison with the 1921 Antidumping Act in *Zenith III* was not intended to differentiate the 1916 Act in terms of product comparison, since the range of products that can be compared under the 1916 Act as interpreted in *Zenith III* includes not only "identical" products, but also "similar" prod-

---

381 See para. 6.112 above.

382 In *Zenith II* (1975), p. 258, the court stated that "The practice [of dumping] itself long outdated the passage of the Antidumping Act of 1916 [...], which clearly implies that Congress knew whereof it wrote when it enacted the statute."

383 Op. Cit., p. 1197.

ucts. The comparison was meant to specify that the 1916 Act did not leave as much discretion as the 1921 Act in this respect.

6.126 Second, we also note that the conclusion in the *Zenith III* case to which the United States refers is only indirectly based on the legislative history of the 1916 Act. It is the result of the interpretation by the court of the intent of the US Congress that the purpose of the 1916 Act was to complement the existing anti-trust laws. It is from this "intent", not from specific statements relating to the meaning of the words "such articles" in the 1916 Act or in any anti-trust law that the court apparently deduced the application of the Clayton Act standard of "like grade and quality". A further examination of the court decision[384] shows that the court also relied on terms of the 1916 Act directly imported from the Tariff Act of 1913 to reject the narrow interpretation of "such articles" advocated by the defendants.

6.127 The court in the *Zenith III* case apparently used both justifications without any distinction as to their respective weight, even though it specified that it would hold that "there is no violation of the 1916 Act unless the standards of similarity of the customs appraisement law are met".[385] In any case, we note that neither affects the scope of the price discrimination test to such an extent that it would be removed from the scope of the definition of "dumping" in Article VI:1 of the GATT 1994. By accepting a comparison not only between "identical" products, but also between "similar" products, the court interpretation in the *Zenith III* case is probably broader than the Article VI comparison based on "like" products. However, whether broader or narrower in terms of product comparison, the transnational price discrimination test in the 1916 Act still meets the definition of Article VI:1 of the GATT 1994.

6.128 The United States also argues that the historical context and the legislative history show that the 1916 Act was intended to *supplement* or *complement* the rules applicable to US products in an anti-trust context. The United States deduces from this that the 1916 Act is an anti-trust law not subject to the disciplines of Article VI of the GATT 1994. The United States refers, *inter alia*, to the statement of Representative Claude Kitchin:

> "We believe that the same unfair competition law which now applies to the domestic trader should apply to the foreign import trader."[386]

6.129 We also note that the US Secretary of Commerce William Redfield explained in 1915 that

> "Unfair competition is forbidden by law in domestic trade, and the Federal Trade Commission exists to determine the facts and abate the evil wherever found. The door, however, is still open to "unfair competition" from abroad which may seriously affect American industry for the worse."[387]

The two statements refer to the extension of "unfair competition" rules applicable to US domestic commerce to imports. We have noted above that the US Congress had used in the 1916 Act a definition of transnational price discrimination which was

---

[384] See pp. 1229-1230.

[385] *Ibid.* p. 1197. See also *In re Japanese Electronic Products II* (1983), p. 324.

[386] 53 Cong. Rec. App. 1938 (1916), as quoted in *Zenith III*, p. 1222.

[387] *Annual Report of the Secretary of Commerce* 43 (1915), as quoted in *Zenith III*, p. 1219.

already at that time understood as "dumping". We have also concluded in paragraph 6.116 above that the fact that the 1916 Act had an anti-trust objective was not relevant and did not make the 1916 Act fall outside the scope of Article VI of the GATT 1994. Likewise, we are not convinced that the fact that the 1916 Act was presented at the time of its enactment as "supplementing" or "complementing" the existing anti-trust laws necessarily requires that the 1916 Act be interpreted as an anti-trust law. In our opinion, the argument of the United States is only valid if the United States can prove that the historical context and the legislative history of the 1916 Act give indications that anti-trust and anti-dumping were already separate legal concepts. If the two were not clearly identified but, rather, were still part of one single notion of "unfair competition", the US argument should be rejected.

6.130 We note that, at the time of the enactment of the 1916 Act, the current distinction between anti-trust and anti-dumping did not apply in the United States. We reviewed the materials submitted by the parties and the extensive analysis of the legislative history of the 1916 Act in the *Zenith III* case. While it appears, *inter alia* from the quotations above, that the US Administration and US lawmakers of that time considered that the 1916 Act "complemented" or "supplemented" the unfair competition rules applied to domestic products essentially under the Sherman Act and the Clayton Act,[388] it also seems that no clear legal distinction had yet been made in the United States between unfair competition resulting from dumping and unfair competition resulting from other practices, as it is made today.[389] Dumping as defined in Article VI:1 of the GATT 1994 was just one specific cause of action under anti-trust law,[390] as noted in 1923 by Jacob Viner:

---

[388] See J. Viner, *Dumping: A Problem in International Trade* (1923), Op. Cit.; pp. 242-243:

> "[The Wilson Administration] therefore recommended that any measure adopted to meet the problem should be divorced from customs legislation [in the sense of imposition of higher tariffs] and should take the form of a further extension to those engaged in the import trade of the restraints against unfair competition which had been imposed on domestic commerce."

See also the excerpt from the letter of Samuel J. Graham, Assistant Attorney General, to the New York Times, 4 July 1916, included in a footnote to the above quotation.

[389] Even though dumping is now subject to specific international disciplines and may have acquired other purposes, the origins of anti-trust and that of anti-dumping were essentially the same, as highlighted by the 1974 report of the *Ad Hoc* Committee on Antitrust and Antidumping of the American Bar Association Section on Antitrust Law, which stated as follows:

> "Both U.S. antidumping and antitrust law and policy have historic roots, and both were intended to protect and engender the fundamental U.S. economic policy of free and fair competition.
>
> [...] antidumping policy seeks to accommodate the legitimate need for legislation which protects American competition from unfair price discrimination by foreign concerns."

43 Antitrust L.J. 653, 691-93 (1974), as reproduced in J. H. Jackson & W. Davey, *Legal Problems of International Economic Relations*, 2d Ed. (1986). This is an additional reason for not deciding on the applicability of Article VI of the GATT 1994 to the 1916 Act on the basis of the general objective of the law.

[390] In that context, the statement of the court in the *Zenith III* case, at p. 1220, that "the political and legal history of the era supports our conclusion from the statutory text that the 1916 Act was an antitrust based unfair competition law, not a protectionist one" does not support the US position.

> "This antidumping provision, beyond the fact that it makes the participation of the importer both as to act and intent in predatory dumping *specifically unlawful and not merely unlawful by construction as a practice by which competition can be restrained or monopoly established*, adds nothing to the Sherman Act. Beyond the fact that it makes unnecessary the proof of conspiracy between the importer and others, it adds nothing to the Wilson Act of 1894" (emphasis added).[391]

6.131 Even if we were to agree with the United States that the objective of the law is decisive, the historical context and legislative history do not confirm that the 1916 Act had a purely "anti-trust" purpose, within the meaning of that concept today. Rather, it appears that anti-dumping as it is known today in international trade law and anti-trust laws dealing with predatory pricing were part of the same notion of "unfair competition."

(iii) Conclusion

6.132 We note that evidence from the historical context of the 1916 Act supports our finding that the 1916 Act transnational price discrimination test corresponds to "dumping" within the meaning of Article VI. We also note that, at the time of the enactment of the 1916 Act, there would have been no need to give any different meaning to that test in order to make it fall within the scope of US anti-trust law because, at that time, "dumping" had not yet been conceptually isolated from the body of US anti-trust laws. In any event, the United States has not submitted evidence from the historical context or the legislative history of the 1916 Act that the terms of the transnational price discrimination test of the 1916 Act were understood differently because of the anti-trust objective of the law or that that objective was such as to make the 1916 Act fall outside the scope of Article VI.

6.133 We therefore conclude that the historical context and the legislative history of the 1916 Act, while showing that there was an intent to parallel the rules applicable to US and foreign companies, do not lead us to conclude any differently than we have on the basis of the terms of the 1916 Act as such. Therefore, we proceed to review the impact of the US case-law relating to the 1916 Act.

(d) Impact of the US Case-Law Relating to the 1916 Act

(i) Approach of the Panel

6.134 We recall our findings under Section C.1 above on how we should consider the various court decisions regarding the 1916 Act and their interrelationship. We note that the United States claims that the case-law is evidence that the 1916 Act has been applied as an anti-trust statute. We would like to make two preliminary remarks in relation to this argumentation of the United States.

From the paras. preceding that conclusion, we understand it as meaning that the court opposed the use of selective "unfair competition" instruments to the application of higher tariffs as part of a protectionist policy.

[391] J. Viner, *Dumping: A Problem in International Trade* (1923), Op. Cit.; p. 244.

(a) First, as already mentioned, the categorisation of the 1916 Act as an anti-trust law or an anti-dumping law by the US courts should not be decisive in determining the WTO-compatibility of that law.[392] Since the point of our review of the US case-law is to ascertain the actual meaning of the 1916 Act in order to assess its conformity with the WTO Agreement, the classification of this law by US courts can only be of limited impact for the purpose of the present case. For the Panel, it is the reasoning, if any, behind the classification that matters.

(b) Second, we found that the 1916 Act price discrimination test met, on its face, the definition of Article VI:1 of the GATT 1994, and that the other tests of the 1916 Act based on the "intent" of the exporter engaged in "dumping" do not have any bearing on that conclusion. As a result, we are of the view that we need not consider any court interpretation of the 1916 Act relating to any other test than the transnational price discrimination test.

We must therefore identify the instances, if any, where US courts, in applying the 1916 Act, have addressed the "dumping" test contained in that law and determine whether those courts have applied/interpreted that test in such a way that it would no longer meet the definition of Article VI:1 of the GATT 1994.

6.135 Since we have already found that the text of the 1916 Act, on its own, supports the conclusion that Article VI is applicable to that law, we consider that, in order for that conclusion to be confirmed, it is not necessary for the EC to demonstrate that there was no court decision that applied the 1916 Act in a WTO-consistent manner. If we find that the US court practice is not sufficiently well established, or that there is no prevailing interpretation, or no sufficiently clear reasoning regarding the way the transnational price discrimination test of the 1916 Act should be applied, we shall rely on the text of the law itself. However, for the United States to prevail, it would be sufficient in our view to show that there is one definitive interpretation supporting its position. As a result, we first determine whether there is any relevant Supreme Court decision which would provide us with a definitive authority at the highest level of jurisdiction. If not, we will review the circuit court decisions.

(ii) The US Supreme Court and the 1916 Act

6.136 We first note that the US Supreme Court has not yet been called upon to interpret the text of the 1916 Act. However, as highlighted by the United States, in the *Cooper* case,[393] the Supreme Court described the 1916 Act as "supplemental" to the Sherman Act, as part of an illustration that "Congress had in mind the distinction between public and private remedies". The United States concludes from this that the 1916 Act is an anti-trust instrument. However, the Supreme Court also referred to the 1916 Act as "the antidumping provisions of the Revenue Act of 1916". Even if the

[392] See *EC - Parts and Components,* Op. Cit., para. 5.19. In that context, the statement of the court in *Zenith III* (1980) that the 1916 Act is an anti-trust, not a protectionist statute is for us of limited assistance if this statement is not followed by specific conclusions in terms of interpreting the price discrimination test of the 1916 Act.

[393] Op. Cit., p. 308.

Supreme Court regarded the 1916 Act as an anti-trust law, the fact that it refers to "anti-dumping provisions" leaves the issue of the interpretation of the price discrimination test of the 1916 Act open, since US courts may well apply the 1916 Act as an anti-trust law when it comes to the "intent" test, while applying the price discrimination test without any additional requirements than those contained in the text of the 1916 Act.

6.137 What the Supreme Court meant by "supplemental" is not clear in the absence of an agreed technical definition under US law. The 1916 Act could be "supplemental" to anti-trust statutes in a number of other ways than that suggested by the United States. For instance, an anti-dumping law could "supplement" a domestic predatory pricing law. The context of the statement in the decision is of limited use.[394]

6.138 Therefore, we are not in a position to draw any definitive conclusion from the US Supreme Court statements in the *Cooper* case. Even if the Supreme Court had expressly stated that the 1916 Act was an anti-trust or an anti-dumping law, this statement would have no relevance for this Panel as long as it was not supported by an explanation of the reasons why the Supreme Court thought that way, or of the implications of that statement on the interpretation of the transnational price discrimination test of the 1916 Act.

6.139 As a result, any conclusion on the basis of the US case-law becomes delicate because there is no unambiguous authority at the highest level of US jurisdiction. This does not mean that we will not find an unanimous interpretation, or even a prevailing interpretation that would be convincing. Indeed, many judgements are final as a practical matter at the level of the circuit court of appeals, *inter alia,* because the possibility to appeal before the Supreme Court is not automatically granted.

(iii) The Interpretation of the Transnational Price Discrimination Test of the 1916 Act at the Circuit Court Level

"Dumping" as an international trade concept applied in an anti-trust context

6.140 Considering the other cases mentioned by the parties and decided either at the district court level or at the court of appeals level, the Panel notes that the court in *Zenith III* (1980) stated that the 1916 Act

> "should be interpreted whenever possible to parallel the "unfair competition" law applicable to domestic commerce. Since the 1916 Act is a price discrimination law, it should be read in tandem with the price discrimination law, section 2 of the Clayton Act, which was amended by the Robinson-Patman Act of 1936 in 1936."

[394] The term "supplemental" was also used by US Secretary of Commerce Redfield in his legislative proposal of 1915 (*Annual Report of the Secretary of Commerce* (1915), Op Cit.) when he said "I also recommend that legislation supplemental to the Clayton Antitrust Act be enacted…" However, we already expressed the view when we addressed the historical context and the legislative history of the 1916 Act that the borderline between anti-dumping and anti-trust was not so clear at that time, if only because anti-dumping was at an early stage of development and because it was probably not yet perceived in the United States as a trade instrument separate from anti-trust.

6.141 The United States relies heavily on this and other similar statements[395] to argue that the 1916 Act should be interpreted similarly to the Robinson-Patman Act. However, as outlined above, the fact that the 1916 Act was adopted for anti-trust purposes and the fact that it mixes "dumping" with other tests which are typical of US anti-trust legislation are of no relevance in this case. What matters for us is the way transnational price discrimination has been addressed by US courts. At the district court level, the United States relied substantially on the 1980 *Zenith III* judgement. We note, with respect to price discrimination *stricto sensu*, that the court, after having recalled Viner's definition of dumping, stated that "to restate the obvious, the Antidumping Act of 1916 is a prohibition of international price discrimination." This would tend to confirm that the court applied the transnational price discrimination test of the 1916 Act without reading into it additional anti-trust-like requirements which would modify its meaning. The Court also recalled that "as a price discrimination statute, the Antidumping Act of 1916 is functionally similar to the price discrimination statutes which are applicable to domestic business." However, this was before the introduction - implicitly in the *In Re Japanese Electronic Products III* case or explicitly in the *Brooke Group* case - of the predatory pricing/recoupment test. We have no clear evidence that, before those judgements, the price discrimination test of the 1916 Act was applied differently from what is mentioned in the Act itself.

6.142 When examining the historical context and the legislative history, we addressed the conclusion of the court in *Zenith III* regarding product comparison to the effect that the products sold in the United States and the products sold in the foreign country had to be of "like grade and quality" as that phrase is used in Section 2 of the Clayton Act as amended by the Robinson-Patman Act. We note that the Court of Appeals in *In Re Japanese Electronic Products II* (1983) confirmed that the phrase "actual market value or wholesale price of such articles" was a term of art borrowed from the Tariff Act of 1913 and defined in that Act.[396] The conclusions we drew from the historical context when we addressed the product comparison aspect of the transnational price discrimination test of the 1916 Act[397] are not affected by the court decisions which subsequently addressed it.

6.143 We have not found in the decisions referred to by the United States other elements which would demonstrate that the price discrimination test of the 1916 Act, as such, was affected by attempts to parallel the Robinson-Patman Act. In fact, the court in *Zenith II* (1975) largely used "standard dictionary definitions" to interpret the terms of the 1916 Act that had been challenged by the defendants on grounds of vagueness. This was the case for the terms "commonly and systematically", and "other charges and expenses necessarily incident to the importation and sale". Regarding the term "substantially", the court only referred to the case-law regarding the Clayton Act to conclude that if the term "substantially" in "substantially to lessen competition" in the Clayton Act was not found unconstitutionally vague the term " substantially less" in the 1916 Act cannot be either. Finally, the court also referred to the 1913 Tariff Act to interpret the phrase "actual market value or wholesale price."

---

395 See *Zenith III*, p. 1223.

396 See *In Re Japanese Electronic Products II*, p. 324.

397 See paras. 6.124-6.126 above.

6.144 The United States also mentions that every final and conclusive US court decision has supported the *Zenith III* analysis. We note however that a number of these cases were concerned with the issue of *locus standi* in a 1916 civil action[398] or more generally with the problem of establishing a cause of action.[399] If they confirm *Zenith III*, it seems to be essentially by reason of not expressly objecting to its conclusions, which we have found not to affect our provisional findings based on the terms of the 1916 Act alone. In fact, it seems that courts have concentrated their efforts on other aspects of the 1916 Act, such as the standing and damages provisions, which were found "essentially the same as those applicable to the antitrust laws under section 4 of the Clayton Act" and the criminal penalty clause which is "virtually identical to, and specifies the same penalties as, the corresponding clauses of the Sherman Antitrust Act as then in force."[400]

6.145 Other elements tend to show that courts approached the transnational price discrimination test found in the 1916 Act as "dumping" within the meaning of Article VI of the GATT 1994. For instance, a number of those decisions, including the cases cited by the United States in support of its position, refer to the definition of dumping by Jacob Viner, i.e. "price discrimination between purchasers in different national markets"[401] and generally address the price discrimination test found in the 1916 Act as "dumping", without any further qualification. In this respect, the court in *Zenith II* did not find it necessary to look any further than that definition and the popular title of the 1916 Act to conclude that:

> "An economic regulatory statute could scarcely acquire the designation of an 'antidumping Act' unless the business community to which the statute was addressed knew what 'dumping' was."[402]

---

[398] See *Schwimmer v. Sony Corp. of America* (1979), Op. Cit.; *Schwimmer v. Sony Corp. of America* (1980), Op. Cit.; *Western Concrete Structures Co. v. Mitsui & Co.* (1985).

[399] *Jewel Foliage Co. v. Uniflora Overseas Florida* (1980), *Op. Cit.*; *Outboard Marine Corporation v. Pezetel* (1978), Op. Cit.

[400] *Zenith III*, p. 1214.

[401] J. Viner, *Dumping: A Problem in International Trade*, 1966 edition, p. 4. See, e.g., *Zenith II* (1975), *Outboard Marine Corporation v. Pezetel* (1978), p. 408; *Zenith III* (1980); *In re Japanese Electronic Products II* (1983), p. 321

[402] *Zenith II*, p. 258. See also the statement of the court in *Zenith III*, p. 1196:

> "We also have occasion to compare the 1916 Act, which creates a private right of action for treble damages and provides criminal penalties for dumping, with the Antidumping Act of 1921"

The terms used by the court and the subsequent developments in the judgement show that "dumping" in the 1916 Act and in the 1921 Act, which was the US anti-dumping law based on administrative investigations applied until the implementation of the Tokyo Round, were not understood differently. The fact that the understanding of the meaning of "dumping" by US courts corresponds to the definition of that concept in Article VI:1 of the GATT 1994 is confirmed by the following statement of the court in *In Re Japanese Electronic Products II*, at p. 324:

> "The first element necessary to a finding of dumping under the 1916 Act is proof that a price differential exists between two comparable products, one of which is imported or sold in the United States and the other of which is sold in the exporting country."

See also *Helmac II* (1993), p. 591, which recognised that the key to liability under the 1916 Act was "dumping: the pricing of goods on the American Market at a price lower than on the home market".

6.146 These examples are evidence that some US courts, irrespective of their interpretation of the other parts of the 1916 Act, considered that the transnational price discrimination test had to be interpreted as "dumping", as it is also understood in international trade, and on the basis of US trade law standards.

The *Brooke Group* recoupment test

6.147 The United States claims that, since the 1986 Third Circuit Court of Appeals decision *In Re Japanese Electronic Products III* and the 1993 Supreme Court decision in *Brooke Group Ltd. v. Brown & Williamson Tobacco Corporation*,[403] courts have applied to the 1916 Act the anti-trust predatory pricing/recoupment test developed in those cases.[404]

6.148 We understand the predatory pricing/recoupment test in the *Brooke Group* case to require that (i) the complainant establish that the prices complained of are below an appropriate measure of its rival's costs and that (ii) the complainant demonstrate that the competitor had a reasonable prospect of recouping its investment in below-cost prices.[405] The Supreme Court further held that evidence of below-cost pricing is not on its own sufficient to permit an inference of probable recoupment and injury to competition. Determining whether recoupment of predatory losses is likely requires an estimate of the cost of the alleged predation and a close analysis of both the scheme alleged by the plaintiff and the structure and conditions of the relevant market.[406]

6.149 It is not clear whether the recoupment test should be analysed as part of the transnational price discrimination test or as part of the "intent" test of the 1916 Act. As a result, in order to consider the applicability of the *Brooke Group* test to the price discrimination test of the 1916 Act, we have to assume that price recoupment is more related to the type/amount of price discrimination that can be achieved by the importer than to its intent to affect the US market. If the *Brooke Group* test relates to the "intent" test of the 1916 Act, it cannot affect the transnational price discrimination test of the 1916 Act.

6.150 This said, regarding the first criterion of the *Brooke Group* test, i.e. below cost prices, we do not consider that the introduction of a below-cost price test would make Article VI of the GATT 1994 no longer applicable to the 1916 Act, essentially because the definition of dumping in Article VI:1 does not incorporate a notion of magnitude of price difference. We are aware that Article 5.8 of the Anti-Dumping Agreement provides that there "shall be immediate termination in cases where the authorities determine that the margin of dumping is *de minimis*", i.e. that it is less than 2 per cent, expressed as a percentage of the export price. We have no evidence

---

[403] 509 U.S. 209, 118 S.Ct. 2578, hereinafter the "*Brooke Group* case".

[404] Even though the parties have discussed the implication of the court decision *In Re Japanese Electronic Products III*, we do not find it necessary to determine whether the court actually applied in that case the predatory pricing/recoupment test later established by the Supreme Court in the *Brooke Group* case. For the sake of our analysis, we will assume that the court in *In Re Japanese Electronic Products III* actually applied a standard similar to the *Brooke Group* test.

[405] *Op. Cit.*, pp. 2587-2588.

[406] *Ibid.*, p. 2589.

that this *de minimis* dumping margin bears any link with any kind of below-cost test as applied in anti-trust. The application of a below-cost price test in the 1916 Act may make the establishment of a transnational price difference more difficult, but it does not affect the basic requirement that a price difference has to be established under the 1916 Act, which is also the basic requirement of Article VI:1 of the GATT 1994.

6.151 As far as the cost recoupment criterion is concerned, we do not believe either that the introduction of a recoupment requirement under the 1916 Act would make Article VI of the GATT 1994 no longer applicable to the 1916 Act for essentially two reasons. First, the definition of dumping set out in Article VI:1 would still apply. Even if a cost recoupment were to be required in addition to a price difference, a price difference must always be found in the first place. The second reason is more of an economic nature. Since, in transnational price discrimination, an exporter may benefit from an isolated domestic market, which is often considered to be one of the reasons why dumping is possible in the first place, recoupment on the *export* market may not always occur in a situation of international predatory pricing. The recoupment requirement, which may be justified in cases of price discrimination within the United States, may be an economically questionable requirement in cases of transnational price discrimination, at least whenever the exporter does not need to recoup its costs on the US market.[407] Indeed, the company exporting at dumping prices may benefit from a simultaneous recoupment of its "dumping" costs through its sales on its domestic market.

6.152 However, this Panel is called on to clarify WTO provisions, not to discuss specific anti-trust issues. Therefore, having expressed the above-mentioned reservations, we proceed to consider if, effectively, the *Brooke Group* test has been actually and consistently applied by US courts in their interpretation of the 1916 Act.

6.153 If the Supreme Court decision in *Brooke Group* is applicable to the 1916 Act, one would expect the other courts which had to consider complaints under the 1916 Act to apply that test. We have no clear evidence that this has been the case, even if one assumes that the test was already applicable since *In Re Japanese Electronic Products III* (1986), as it would appear from the reaction of the courts in the *Geneva Steel* [408] and *Wheeling-Pittsburgh* cases.[409]

6.154 In that context, the parties have discussed the content of the *Helmac I* case (1992). We understand that the court in the *Helmac I* case concluded that the complainant did not have to establish recoupment. On the contrary, the court noted the importance of the difference in terminology between the 1916 Act and the US anti-trust statutes. According to the court, the 1916 Act

> "focuses upon intent while the antitrust statutes focus upon effect. Beside injury to competition, the Antidumping Act also provides a cause

---

[407] We find relevant the view expressed in *Note, Rethinking the 1916 Anti-Dumping Act*, Harvard Law Review, Vol. 110, No. 7, May 1997, p. 1555, at p. 1566, submitted by the EC.

[408] Op. Cit. See para. 6.158 below.

[409] Op. Cit. See para. 6.160 below.

> of action when the defendant attempts to, among other things, injure an industry in the United States."[410]

The court only stated as a possibility that the adoption of the recoupment theory would be appropriate if Helmac, the complainant in that case, had claimed that the defendant's conduct injured *competition*. Since Helmac alleged an attempt to injure an *industry* in the United States, the court concluded that proving ability to recoup losses was not necessary.[411] In the *Helmac II* decision (1993) the court differentiated between liability, of which a finding of dumping was the key, and the calculation of the harm caused to the domestic industry.[412]

6.155 Therefore, we consider that we do not have sufficient evidence of the actual application of the *Brooke Group* test to 1916 Act cases in relation to the establishment of the price discrimination required by that law.

The interlocutory decisions relied upon by the European Communities

6.156 The EC alleges that two interlocutory judgements in the *Geneva Steel* and the *Wheeling Pittsburgh* cases support its claims that the 1916 Act addresses dumping within the meaning of Article VI of the GATT 1994. The United States argues that these two decisions are neither final nor conclusive under US law. Therefore, they cannot, at the present time, be considered by the Panel as authoritative interpretations of US law.

6.157 We are fully aware of the fact that these decisions are only interlocutory judgements. We consider that our review of the other - final - judgements referred to by the parties already shows that US courts did not interpret the transnational price discrimination test of the 1916 Act in such a way that it would fall outside the scope of Article VI of the GATT 1994. However, we recall that we are required to make an objective assessment of the facts of the case. Since these two interlocutory judgements have, like the *Zenith* cases, actually discussed in detail the origin, objectives and practical operation of the 1916 Act, we found it relevant to consider also those cases. We also note that these two cases are subsequent to the *Zenith* cases and the Supreme Court decision in the *Brooke Group* case. Considering them is appropriate in light of the arguments of the United States based on those decisions. Finally, as mentioned in paragraph 6.134(a) above, we are interested in the *reasoning* followed by the US courts as a clarification of how the transnational price discrimination test of the 1916 Act operates. If this reasoning is convincing, we feel justified in taking it into account in our examination.

6.158 In *Geneva Steel*, the district court addressed the question whether the 1916 Act always requires evidence of antitrust-like predatory pricing. Since the intent of predatory pricing in our opinion does not affect the transnational price discrimination test of the 1916 Act, we do not consider that judgement to be directly relevant to our case. However, we note that the court considered that "By the words it chose, Con-

[410] *Helmac I*, Op. Cit., pp. 575-576.

[411] *Ibid.*, p. 575.

[412] *Helmac II*, Op. Cit., at p. 591.

gress protected United States industry from unfair dumping."[413] Having regard to our conclusions regarding the use of the word "dumping" in other judgements, we assume that the court consciously used the word "dumping" in the same meaning as this word is given in Article VI:1 of the GATT 1994.

6.159 Other reasonings of the court are relevant in so far as they seem to confirm our understanding of the case-law. For instance, the court in *Geneva Steel* considered the conclusion in *Zenith III* that the 1916 Act was "an antitrust, not a protectionist statute" and stated that such conclusion did not appear to be necessary for the finding of the court in the *Zenith III* case that the term "such articles" included also "similar" articles.[414] This view is close to that of this Panel that the finding of applicability of the Clayton Act "like-grade and quality" standard in *Zenith III* was not necessary when it had already been established that the relevant text in the 1916 Act had been imported from the 1913 Tariff Act, which provided for a "similarity" standard. We also note that the court in *Geneva Steel* found the terms of the 1916 Act unambiguous,[415] as we did when we considered the text of the 1916 Act in isolation.

6.160 The court in the *Wheeling-Pittsburgh* case did not address the price discrimination test of the 1916 Act as such, but the question whether predatory intent had to be demonstrated. Its reasoning is therefore less relevant for this case, except for its discussion of the inclusion of the predatory pricing/price recoupment test in the 1916 Act.[416] In that respect, like in the *Geneva Steel* case, the court in *Wheeling-Pittsburgh* rejected the application of this test with respect to certain circumstances of application of the 1916 Act because it created a double burden of proof for the complainants. Indeed, the court considered that, to the "intent" to injure or destroy or prevent the establishment of a domestic industry contained in the text of the 1916 Act, the court in *Zenith III* had added "an antitrust type of predatory pricing, including the reasonable prospect of resultant market control and price recoupment."[417]

6.161 The *Geneva Steel* and *Wheeling-Pittsburgh* cases shed additional light on the interpretation of the pricing/recoupment test because they have addressed quite specifically the question of its application. They also represent additional evidence that some district courts do not find themselves compelled, at least at an early stage of consideration of an issue, to apply the *Brooke Group* predatory pricing/price recoupment test to claims under the 1916 Act.

(iv) Conclusion

6.162 We conclude that the assessment made by courts of the price discrimination test of the 1916 Act was based essentially on the text of the 1916 Act itself, without

---

[413] *Geneva Steel, Op. Cit.* p. 1217.

[414] *Ibid.*, p. 1218.

[415] *Ibid.*, p. 1222-1223.

[416] The Court in *Wheeling-Pittsburgh* (1999) gave its views as to why the "predatory pricing" part of the *Brooke Group* test could not apply to cases under the 1916 Act. The court stated that "by requiring a plaintiff to prove 'intent to injure a domestic industry' by below-cost-pricing, the Anti-dumping Act of 1916 does require proof of predatory intent, albeit of a different kind." However, since its reasoning was based only on the "intent" requirement of the 1916 Act, we do not find it necessary to address it.

[417] *Wheeling-Pittsburgh, Op. Cit.*, p. 605.

any significant additions. We also conclude that, at best, we have no clear evidence of the relevance and of a consistent application of the cost recoupment test - or any other "anti-trust" standards, such as below-cost prices - in the implementation of the transnational price discrimination test of the 1916 Act. In accordance with our approach,[418] we find that the US case-law supports our original conclusion that the 1916 Act addresses "dumping" within the meaning of Article VI:1 of the GATT 1994.

3. *Conclusions on the Applicability of Article VI of the GATT 1994 to the 1916 Act*

(a) The 1916 Act Falls within the Scope of Article VI of the GATT 1994

6.163 Having interpreted Article VI of the GATT 1994 in accordance with the Vienna Convention, we have reached the conclusion that the rules and disciplines of that article apply to laws that address "dumping" as defined in Article VI:1. Having examined the text of the 1916 Act, we have found that the transnational price discrimination test incorporated in that law falls within the definition of "dumping" of Article VI:1 of the GATT 1994. On the basis of our interpretation of Article VI, we have also found that none of the additional conditions or requirements contained in the text of the 1916 Act is such as to make the transnational price discrimination test of the 1916 Act fall outside the scope of the definition of "dumping" in Article VI:1 or otherwise modify our conclusions. We found no convincing evidence in the legislative history that should lead us to understand the terms of the price discrimination test of the 1916 Act differently than we have. Finally, our review of the US court decisions submitted by the parties did not show that courts interpreted the transnational price discrimination test of the 1916 Act in such a way that it would no longer meet the definition of Article VI:1 of the GATT 1994.

6.164 This conclusion also disposes of the argument of the United States that the 1916 Act has been interpreted in such a manner that it falls outside the scope of Article VI of the GATT 1994.

6.165 Having found that Article VI of the GATT 1994 applies to the 1916 Act, we note that Article 1 of the Anti-Dumping Agreement provides that an anti-dumping measure shall be applied only pursuant to investigations initiated and conducted in accordance with the provisions of that Agreement. Article 1, second sentence, also provides that

> "the [provisions of the Anti-Dumping Agreement] govern the application of Article VI of GATT in so far as action is taken under anti-dumping legislation or regulations."

Given the link between Article VI of the GATT 1994 and the Anti-Dumping Agreement, we find that the applicability of Article VI to the 1916 Act also implies the applicability of the Anti-Dumping Agreement.

---

[418] See paras. 6.134-6.135 above.

* Footnote number 419 was skipped. Thus no text is missing.

(b) The 1916 Act is a Mandatory Law within the Meaning of GATT 1947/WTO Practice

6.166 With respect to the discretion enjoyed by the US Department of Justice which would, according to the United States, make the 1916 Act non-mandatory, we recall our reasoning in paragraph 6.92 above.

6.167 The EC claims that we should rely on the panel report on *United States - Definition of Wine Industry* and conclude that "trade remedy legislation" is not "non-mandatory" merely because the administration enjoys a discretion to initiate an investigation or not. We consider that, in *United States - Definition of Wine Industry*, the panel did not address the mandatory/non-mandatory nature of the United States countervailing duty legislation. However, it stated that its mandate instructed it to review the conformity of the legislation at issue with the provisions of the Tokyo Round Subsidies Agreement, "as required by its Article 19:5(a)."[420] On that basis, the panel proceeded to review Section 612(a)(1) of the Trade and Tariff Act of 1984 as such.

6.168 The EC also refers to the panel report in *EC - Audio Cassettes*, which was not adopted.[421] This report stated why the mere fact that the initiation of anti-dumping investigations was discretionary would not make the EC legislation non-mandatory. The panel stated that:

> "[it] did not consider in any event that its task in this case was to determine whether the EC's Basic Regulation was non-mandatory in the sense that the initiation of investigations and impositions of duties were not mandatory functions. Should panels accept this approach, they would be precluded from ever reviewing the content of a party's anti-dumping legislation."[422]

The *EC - Audio Cassettes* panel based its reasoning on the fact that this would undermine the obligation contained in Article 16.6 of the Tokyo Round Anti-Dumping Agreement. That provision provided that parties had to bring their laws, regulations and administrative procedures into conformity with the provisions of the Tokyo Round Anti-Dumping Agreement.[423] We note that almost identical terms are found in Article 18.4 of the WTO Anti-Dumping Agreement, which reads as follows:

---

420 Op. Cit., para. 4.1. Article 19.5(a) of the Tokyo Round Subsidies Agreement was the equivalent of Article 16.6(a) of the Tokyo Round Anti-Dumping Agreement (see footnote 423 below).

421 Op. Cit. On the legal value of unadopted panel reports, see footnote 358 above and its reference to the Appellate Body Report on *Japan - Alcoholic Beverages, supra,* footnote 224.

422 Op. Cit., para. 362.

423 Article 16.6(a) ("National Legislation") of the Tokyo Round Anti-Dumping Agreement provided as follows:

> "Each government accepting or acceding to this Agreement shall take all necessary steps, of a general or particular character, to ensure , not later than the date of entry into force of this Agreement for it, the conformity of its laws, regulations and administrative procedures with the provisions of this Agreement as they may apply to the Party in question."

> "Each Member shall take all necessary steps, of a general or particular character, to ensure, no later than the date of entry into force of the WTO Agreement for it, the conformity of its laws, regulations and administrative practices with the provisions of this Agreement, as they may apply to the Member in question."

Since we found that Article VI and the WTO Anti-Dumping Agreement are applicable to the 1916 Act, we consider that the reasoning of the panel in the *EC - Audio Cassettes* case should apply in the present case. Interpreting the provisions of Article 18.4 differently would undermine the obligations contained in that article and would be contrary to the general principle of useful effect by making all the disciplines of the Anti-Dumping Agreement non-enforceable as soon as a Member would claim that the investigating authority has discretion to initiate or not an anti-dumping investigation.

6.169 We therefore conclude that the discretion enjoyed by the US Department of Justice to initiate a case under the 1916 Act should not be interpreted as making the 1916 Act a non-mandatory law.

6.170 As a result, we consider that the United States, as the party having raised this defence, failed to supply convincing evidence that the 1916 Act should be considered as a "non-mandatory legislation" within the meaning of GATT 1947/WTO practice.[424] We therefore find that the 1916 Act cannot be considered to be a "non-mandatory law" which would have the effect that we would not be entitled to review its conformity as such with the relevant provisions of the WTO Agreement, but only to review its conformity in particular instances of application.[425]

(c) Concluding Remarks on the Applicability of Article VI to the Price Discrimination Test of the 1916 Act

6.171 The United States warned the Panel of the implications of an interpretation of the price discrimination test of Article VI that would be so broad that it could make Article VI applicable to all anti-trust laws when such laws address situations of transnational price discrimination. The EC considered that no such risk existed as long as the law did not apply only to imports and did not use a definition that copied that of Article VI of the GATT 1994.

6.172 We recall that we were requested to review the conformity of the 1916 Act with the provisions of the WTO Agreement, not to address the general issue of the relationship between trade law and anti-trust law. In order to assess the WTO-compatibility of the 1916 Act, we interpreted the provisions of Article VI:1 of the

---

[424] We recall that we found in para. 6.87 above that the burden of proof established by the *United States - Tobacco* panel was not applicable in the present case. We also note that, even though the issue originated in a question of the Panel, the United States developed it as a defence in its second submission and thereafter. In application of the rules on burden of proof recalled in paras. 6.37-6.39 above, we consider that it was up to the United States to provide sufficient evidence to establish a *prima facie* case of defence.

[425] Having found that the 1916 Act cannot be considered as "non-mandatory" legislation within the meaning of that concept under GATT1947/WTO practice, we do not find it necessary to address the arguments of the parties on the impact of Article XVI:4 of the Agreement Establishing the WTO on the application of that concept.

GATT 1994 in conformity with the general principles of interpretation of public international law, as embodied in the Vienna Convention. This exercise led us to conclude that the terms of Article VI, interpreted in their context and in the light of the object and purpose of the GATT 1994 and the WTO Agreement, applied to the form of transnational price discrimination targeted by the 1916 Act. The United States did not provide us with any evidence or argument that would demonstrate that we should have read in Article VI:1 a limitation addressing the risk highlighted by the United States in the previous paragraph.[426] As recalled by the Appellate Body, we are not to import into the text of the WTO Agreement conditions that do not appear from its terms interpreted in accordance with the Vienna Convention.[427] Our conclusion is, therefore, fully consistent with our mandate.

6.173 Furthermore, we are not convinced that our conclusion, if applied outside the context of this dispute, would generate the effect referred to by the United States.

6.174 First, we note that transnational price discrimination of the type covered by the definition of "dumping" in Article VI:1 of the GATT 1994 is only one narrowly defined type of price discrimination. Other types of price discrimination, beginning with primary-line price discrimination under the Robinson-Patman Act, do not fall within the scope of the definition of "dumping" in Article VI:1.[428] In particular, the definition of Article VI:1 does not address price discrimination within the territory of a given jurisdiction.

6.175 Second, under Article VI:1 of the GATT 1994, the identification of "dumping" is the starting-point of any determination of injurious dumping. It is the only possible basis for the initiation of an anti-dumping investigation by a Member. Injury not causally linked to the dumping cannot be addressed through anti-dumping.[429]

---

[426] We note that, in any event, the scope of the WTO Agreement does not exclude *a priori* restrictive business practices. Thus, the fact that the 1916 Act would be an anti-trust law would not *per se* be sufficient to exclude the application of WTO rules to that law. We note that panels under GATT 1947 and the WTO have addressed various aspects of restrictive business practices initiated by governments when such practices had the effect of impeding market access of foreign products or entry of foreign enterprises (see e.g., *Japan - Trade in Semiconductors,* adopted on 4 May 1988, BISD 35S/116; Panel Report, *Japan - Measures Affecting Consumer Photographic Films and Paper,* WT/DS44R, adopted 22 April 1998, DSR 1998:IV, 1179 and M. Matsushita: *Restrictive Business Practices and the WTO/GATT Dispute Settlement Process in International Trade Law and the GATT/WTO Dispute Settlement System,* E.-U. Petersmann Ed. (1997), p. 359. Consequently, we do not consider the dichotomy trade law/anti-trust law, to the extent that it would be based on the assumption that WTO disciplines are not intended to apply to business restrictive practices, to be a limitation to the application of WTO rules and disciplines.

[427] See, e.g., Appellate Body Report in *India - Patent (US), supra,* footnote 318, para. 45, where the Appellate Body stated that the principles of interpretation contained in Article 31 of the Vienna Convention "neither require nor condone the imputation into a treaty of words that are not there or the importation into a treaty of concepts that were not intended."

[428] At our request, the United States confirmed that in order for the Robinson-Patman primary-line price discrimination to apply, both commodities involved in the alleged price discrimination must be sold for use, consumption or resale in the United States (see also *Zenith I,* Op. Cit., p. 246).

[429] See Article 3.5 of the Anti-Dumping Agreement, which provides that injuries caused by certain factors must not be attributed to the dumped imports and includes among those factors "trade restrictive practices of and competition between the foreign and domestic producers". This provision would seem to imply that transnational price discrimination of the kind defined in Article VI:1 of the

Comparatively, under anti-trust law, the causes of a given market disruption can be several. When determining what could be at the origin of certain prices, anti-trust investigators will try to identify specific practices such as price conspiracy or abuse of dominant position. It is the understanding of the Panel that, under anti-trust law, transnational price discrimination of the type covered by the definition of "dumping" in Article VI:1 of the GATT 1994 is not sufficient as such to form the basis for a claim of violation of anti-trust law, even in the presence of a price-based disruption on the export market. It is necessary to demonstrate other specific practices, such as monopoly, abuse of dominant position, price agreement or concerted practices, of which international price discrimination may at most constitute supporting evidence.

6.176 We therefore conclude that the likelihood that our findings with respect to Article VI:1 of the GATT 1994 could affect the application of anti-trust laws of Members is very limited, since transnational price discrimination as defined in Article VI :1 of the GATT 1994 is only one limited form of price discrimination and it is unlikely to constitute by itself one of the practices which anti-trust law would consider to be a cause for imposition of sanctions.

6.177 Having found that Article VI is applicable to the 1916 Act, we proceed to address the EC claims of violation of Article VI:1 and VI:2 and the Anti-Dumping Agreement. On the basis of our findings, we will consider whether it is necessary to address the issue of the applicability and violation of Article III:4 of the GATT 1994.

E. Violation of Article VI:1 and VI:2 of the GATT 1994

1. Violation of Article VI:1 of the GATT 1994

(a) Issue before the Panel

6.178 The EC claims that the 1916 Act violates Article VI:1 because that Article provides that dumping is to be condemned if it causes or threatens to cause injury to a domestic industry. We note in that context that the EC makes a similar claim under Article 3 of the Anti-Dumping Agreement. The EC argues that Article 3 of the Anti-Dumping Agreement lays down a detailed definition of the notion of injury under that Agreement and how injury may be established and that there is nothing in the 1916 Act which ensures that the injury shown must correspond to the "material injury" standard of Article VI.1 of the GATT 1994 and Article 3 of the Anti-Dumping Agreement. The EC also argues that because other intents are relevant under the 1916 Act, in certain circumstances measures will be authorized under the 1916 Act without any inquiry into the effects on the domestic industry.

(b) Analysis

6.179 We note that Article VI:1 of the GATT 1994 requires the establishment of material injury or a threat thereof. We also note that Article 3 of the Anti-Dumping

GATT 1994 is not considered to be part of the "competition" practices between the foreign and domestic producers.

Agreement is part of the context of Article VI:1[430] which we are instructed to consider under Article 31 of the Vienna Convention when interpreting Article VI:1.

6.180 We note that Article VI:1 of the GATT 1994 requires the establishment of material injury or a threat thereof. The 1916 Act does not expressly refer to material injury or threat of material injury or material retardation of the establishment of a domestic industry but to "the *intent* of destroying or injuring an industry in the United States, or of preventing the establishment of an industry in the United States".[431] In certain circumstances, an intent may be more difficult to prove than actual injury. The United States executive branch early considered that the requirement of an "intent" made the imposition of remedies under the 1916 Act almost impossible.[432] However, identifying an "intent" may not always *require* a finding of actual injury or actual threat of injury. The Panel recalls that the Supreme Court in *Brooke Group* considered, with respect to corporate planning documents speaking of a desire to slow the growth of a given segment of industry, that "even an act of pure malice by one business competitor against another does not, without more, state a claim under the federal anti-trust law". Thus, assuming that the *Brooke Group* test applies to the 1916 Act, and assuming further that it relates to the "intent" aspect of the law,[433] evidence of predatory pricing and prospects of recoupment are necessary, in addition to a statement of aggressive policy in an internal corporate document. However, we are not convinced that such requirements could be interpreted as having replaced the "intent" test by an "actual effect" test in the 1916 Act. Interpreting the term "injuring an industry or [...] preventing the establishment of an industry in the United States" as meaning "causing material injury" might be possible under US law. However, reading the "intent" requirement out of the 1916 Act would be a *contra legem* interpretation of which we have seen no instance yet in relation to this case.

(c) Conclusion

6.181 For that reason we find that the 1916 Act, to the extent that it provides for the identification of an "intent" by the defendant rather than for the injury requirements of Article VI is not compatible with Article VI:1 of the GATT 1994.

6.182 We now proceed to determine whether anti-dumping duties are the only remedies allowed under Article VI.

---

[430] Footnote 9 to Article 3 provides that:

> "Under this Agreement the term "injury" shall, unless otherwise specified, be taken to mean material injury to a domestic industry, threat of material injury to a domestic industry or material retardation of the establishment of such an industry and shall be interpreted in accordance with the provisions of this Article."

[431] Emphasis added.

[432] See *Geneva Steel*, Op. Cit., p. 1220, quoting a statement recorded in 56 Cong. Rec. 346 (Dec. 9, 1919):

> "The Tariff Commission declares that [the 1916 Act] is not workable, for the reason that it is almost impossible to show the intent on the part of the importer to injure or destroy business in the United States by such importation or sale"

[433] See our opinion in this respect in paras. 6.147-6.155 above.

2. *Anti-Dumping Duties as Sole Remedy under Article VI*

(a) Issues before the Panel

6.183 The European Communities argues that duties are the only remedies allowed against dumping and that the United States reads Article VI:2 of the GATT 1994 out of context and contrary to its clear purpose. The only reason why the word "may" in Article VI:2 was used, is because it was not intended that WTO Members should be obliged to impose anti-dumping duties. For the EC, the negotiating history confirms that remedies under Article VI were intentionally limited to anti-dumping duties. The introduction of Article 16.1 in the Tokyo Round Anti-Dumping Agreement cannot be argued to have changed the meaning of Article VI. Indeed, it confirms it. The reason for this was that the Tokyo Round Anti-Dumping Agreement and the GATT 1947 were distinct sets of rules, with different membership and separate means of enforcement.

6.184 According to the EC, the adoption of the WTO Anti-Dumping Agreement has not changed the context of Article VI. Article 18.1 of the Anti-Dumping Agreement confirms the limitation of remedies under Article VI to duties. It is sufficient to rely on Article VI to claim that the 1916 Act violates WTO rules by providing for remedies other than duties in order to counter dumping. The EC only mentions Articles 1 and 18.1 of the Anti-Dumping Agreement as arguments. As held by the Appellate Body in *European Communities - Bananas,* claims, not arguments, need to be mentioned in a request for establishment of a panel. The Appellate Body statement in *Brazil - Measures Affecting Desiccated Coconut*[434] referred to by the United States rather supports the EC view that a separate citation of the Anti-Dumping Agreement together with Article VI is not necessary. Indeed, in that case the Appellate Body held that Article VI cannot be read independently from the Agreement on Subsidies and Countervailing Measures.

6.185 The United States argues that the terms of Article VI:2 do not support the claim of the EC that duties are the only remedies allowed to counteract dumping. Article VI:2 only states that a Member "may" levy an anti-dumping duty to offset or prevent dumping. The directive in Article VI:2 is permissive and unqualified. In other paragraphs of Article VI, such as paragraph 5 and 6(a), where express prohibitions are stated, the word "shall" is used. For the United States, the negotiating history is evidence that recourse to other remedies was allowed. It also notes that a paragraph similar to paragraph 7 of Article VI, which had been removed at the early stage of the GATT 1947, was reintroduced in Article 16.1 of the Tokyo Round agreement on anti-dumping. This inclusion and that of Article 18.1 in the WTO Anti-Dumping Agreement is evidence that Article VI:2 does not mean what the EC claims it says. The EC interpretation makes those provisions superfluous. Moreover, in application of the Appellate Body report in *Brazil - Desiccated Coconut*, any claim of violation must now include an invocation of a particular provision of the Anti-Dumping Agreement. For the United Statestates, the EC should not be allowed to bootstrap what are in reality new claims under Articles 1 and 18.1 to cure a defective

---

[434] Appellate Body Report, *Brazil - Measures Affecting Desiccated Coconut*, WT/DS22/AB/R, adopted 20 March 1997, DSR 1997:I, 167. (hereinafter " *Brazil - Desiccated Coconut*").

panel request. In accordance with the Appellate Body report in *India - Patent (US)*, the EC should have identified its claims under Articles 1 and 18.1 of the Anti-Dumping Agreement. In any event, the plain language of Articles 1 and 18.1 shows that these provisions do not merely interpret Article VI, but, rather, go beyond it by imposing a limitation on anti-dumping measures where Article VI:2 has none.

6.186 We note that, as instructed by Article 3.2 of the DSU, we shall endeavour to clarify the meaning of the relevant provisions by applying the general principles of interpretation of public international law as embodied in the Vienna Convention.

6.187 We are aware of the fact that Article 31 of the Vienna Convention provides for one "General Rule of Interpretation", as its title states. We will nevertheless, for the sake of clarity, address one after the other the factors to be reviewed pursuant to that Article. If necessary to confirm the meaning resulting from the application of Article 31 or to determine the meaning when the interpretation under Article 31 leaves the meaning ambiguous or obscure or leads to results manifestly absurd or unreasonable, we may have recourse to the supplementary means of interpretation under Article 32 of the Vienna Convention. However, in spite of the extensive reference of the parties to the negotiating history of Article VI, we do not find it appropriate to take it into account at this stage.

(b) Ordinary Meaning of the Terms of Article VI:2 of the GATT 1994

6.188 The first sentence of Article VI:2 of the GATT 1994 provides as follows:

> "In order to offset or prevent dumping, a contracting party may levy on any dumped product an anti-dumping duty not greater in amount than the margin of dumping in respect of such product."

6.189 In Article VI:2, the only term the meaning of which is actually debated by the parties is the verb "may". The ordinary meanings of the verb "may" as an auxiliary verb include "have ability or power to, can"[435] Taken on its own, this verb could mean that Members have the possibility only to impose duties or that they have a choice between duties and other types of measures. If the word "may" was used in the first meaning, it could be argued that the term "only" should have been added right after it so as to limit its meaning. However, such an argument disregards the immediate context of the word "may". The terms "in order to offset or prevent dumping" set up the framework in which the term "may" must be understood. By specifying that the purpose of anti-dumping measures is to "offset" dumping, not to impose punitive measures, Article VI:2, first sentence, limits the meaning of the word "may" to giving Members the choice between a duty equal to the dumping margin and a lower duty, not between anti-dumping duties and other measures.

6.190 In other words, the thrust of Article VI:2, first sentence, is to make the *imposition* of duties facultative and to limit in any event that amount to the dumping mar-

[435] See *The New Shorter Oxford English Dictionary* (1993), p. 1721. It is evident that while we review the ordinary meaning, our reading of the dictionary is already made selective by the broad context of the term. For instance, we left aside the definition of "may" as "have the possibility, opportunity or suitable conditions to..." or the definition of "may" which, in the interpretation of some statutes means "shall, must".

gin. If, as suggested by the United States, the sentence had been meant to allow other measures than anti-dumping duties, it is reasonable to expect that it would have been specified. As mentioned in paragraph 6.103 above, Article VI was meant to regulate the use of anti-dumping by WTO Members. It would have been logical to list the other possible sanctions, especially if those sanctions could be more severe than the imposition of offsetting duties.[436] We therefore conclude that the ordinary meaning of the terms of the first sentence of Article VI:2 support the view that anti-dumping duties are the only type of remedies allowed under Article VI.

(c) Context

6.191 The immediate context of Article VI:2 confirms our understanding of the word "may". The term "shall", as used in paragraphs 3 to 6 was not necessary in paragraph 2 if it was meant to be permissive, not mandatory to *impose* duties, and "shall" was not necessary either to express the idea that only anti-dumping duties could be imposed.

6.192 The parties argued at length on the possibility for the Panel to consider Articles 1 and 18.1 of the Anti-Dumping Agreement, since those provisions were not listed as claims in the request for establishment of the Panel. Article 1 provides as follows:

> "An anti-dumping measure shall be applied only under the circumstances provided for in Article VI of GATT 1994 and pursuant to investigations initiated [footnote 1] and conducted in accordance with the provisions of this Agreement. The following provisions govern the application of Article VI of GATT 1994 in so far as action is taken under anti-dumping legislation or regulations."

Footnote 1 to Article 1 reads as follows:

> "1 The term "initiated" as used in this Agreement means the procedural action by which a Member formally commences an investigation as provided in Article 5."

6.193 Article 18.1 provides as follows:

> "No specific action against dumping of exports from another Member can be taken except in accordance with the provisions of GATT 1994, as interpreted by this Agreement. [footnote 24]"

Footnote 24 to Article 18.1 reads as follows:

> "24 This is not intended to preclude action under other relevant provisions of GATT 1994, as appropriate."

6.194 We consider that it is our duty under Article 3.2 of the DSU and Article 31 of the Vienna Convention to look at any relevant context of Article VI:2. Indeed, our analysis would be incomplete if we were to stop at the ordinary meaning of the word "may" or if we were to disregard the context of the terms to address immediately the negotiating history of Article VI:2. As recalled in paragraph 6.26 above, other panels

[436] We note in that respect that Article 7.2 of the Anti-Dumping Agreement, which provides for the types of provisional measures that may be imposed, lists the measures that may be taken, i.e. "provisional duty or, preferably, a security".

have found it appropriate to rely on provisions mentioned by the parties as arguments in their analysis of the context of a given provision.[437] By following this approach, we do not think that we assist the EC in "curing a defective claim" under Article VI:2. A clear distinction must be made between a situation where a provision does not support at all the claim made in relation to it and the situation where, like in the present case, the ordinary meaning of the terms of the provision at issue could, on its own, already be interpreted as supporting the claim. In this case, we have reasonable grounds to believe that the terms of Article VI:2 could support the interpretation that duties are the only remedies allowed against dumping considered as such. We therefore find it relevant to review other provisions of the other covered agreements, in particular the Anti-Dumping Agreement, as context of Article VI:2.

6.195 The official title of the Anti-Dumping Agreement is "Agreement on Implementation of Article VI of the General Agreement on Tariffs and Trade 1994". This agreement is essential for the interpretation of Article VI. Articles 1 and 18.1 confirm the close link between Article VI and the Anti-Dumping Agreement. Moreover, as was recalled by the Appellate Body in the *Brazil - Coconuts* case, the WTO Agreement is a single treaty instrument which was accepted by the WTO Members as a single undertaking. As a result, Article 18.1 of the Anti-Dumping Agreement is part of the context of Article VI since Article 31.2 of the Vienna Convention provides that "the context for the purpose of the interpretation of a treaty shall comprise, [...] the text [of the treaty], including its preamble and annexes...". We are therefore not only entitled to consider Articles 1 and 18.1 of the Anti-Dumping Agreement even though the European Communities did not mention those provisions as part of its claims in its request for establishment of a panel, but we are also *required* to do so under the general principles of interpretation of public international law.[438]

6.196 In substance, we consider that the provisions of Articles 1 and 18.1 limit the anti-dumping instruments that may be used by Members to those expressly contained in Article VI and the Anti-Dumping Agreement. Except for provisional measures and price undertakings, the only type of measures foreseen by the Anti-Dumping Agreement is the imposition of duties. We also note that Article 9.1 of the Anti-Dumping Agreement[439] establishes an intimate link between the calculation of a dumping margin provided for in Article 2 of the Agreement and the final measures that may be imposed. We therefore conclude that the context of Article VI confirms the provisional conclusion we had reached on the basis of the ordinary meaning of that provision.

[437] See Panel Report, *India - Quantitative Restrictions, supra*, footnote 279.

[438] Like the panel in *India - Quantitative Restrictions*, our intention is not to make findings under Articles 1 and 18.1 of the Anti-Dumping Agreement in this context. As a result, the requirements of Article 6.2 and 7 of the DSU are not relevant in that situation.

[439] Article 9.1 provides as follows:

> "The decision whether or not to impose an anti-dumping duty in cases where all requirements for the imposition have been fulfilled, and the decision whether the amount of the anti-dumping duty to be imposed shall be the full margin of dumping or less, are decisions to be made by the authorities of the importing Member. It is desirable that the imposition be permissive in the territory of all Members, and that the duty be less than the margin if such lesser duty would be adequate to remove the injury to the domestic industry."

6.197 In our view, the argument of the United States does not seem to be incompatible with the fact that Article 18.1 of the Anti-Dumping Agreement in the least states that duties are the only remedies allowed to counter certain forms of dumping *under Article VI of the GATT 1994 and the Anti-Dumping Agreement.* Moreover, we understand that, in another dispute, the United States took the view that the Article VI remedies had been limited to offsetting duties.[440] Therefore, we take the US argumentation to be based on the premise that, if one looks at Article VI:2 exclusively, one cannot conclude that only duties are allowed to counteract injurious dumping. This may explain the opposition of the United States to the Panel even considering Articles 1 and 18.1 in its review of Article VI:2 of the GATT 1994. However, as mentioned above, the WTO Agreement is a single Agreement. Following the United States argument would not only have led to an unjustified interpretation of the function of a panel mandate, it would also have required us to disregard essential elements of interpretation of Article VI. It would have been contrary to the rule of interpretation of the Vienna Convention to make a finding based on Article VI:2 only, in isolation from its context.

6.198 The United States argues that footnote 24 to Article 18.1 of the Anti-Dumping Agreement, like footnote 16 to Article 16.1 of the Tokyo Round Anti-Dumping Agreement, does not lock a Member into levying anti-dumping duties when faced with a factual situation constituting injurious dumping. Footnote 24 leaves the option of taking other measures that are in accordance with the GATT 1994. According to the United States, if the measure is of a nature that is simply not regulated by the GATT 1994, as is the case for the 1916 Act, the measure is *a fortiori* consistent with the GATT 1994.

6.199 We consider that footnote 24 does not prevent Members from addressing the causes or effects of dumping through other trade policy instruments allowed under the WTO Agreement. Nor does it prevent Members from adopting other types of measures which are compatible with the WTO Agreement. Such a possibility does not affect our conclusion that, when a law of a Member addresses the type of price discrimination covered by Article VI and makes it the cause for the imposition of measures, that Member has to abide by the requirements of Article VI and the Anti-Dumping Agreement. In our opinion, the reason for the application of Article VI is not whether a Member wants to counteract *injurious* dumping or another effect of dumping. Nor is it whether a Member addresses dumping through the imposition of duties or another type of remedies, with the implication that Article VI applies only if a Member addresses dumping *through* the imposition of duties. It is whether the practice that triggers the imposition of the measures is "dumping" within the meaning of Article VI:1 of the GATT 1994. If the interpretation suggested by the United States were to be followed, Members could address "dumping" without having to respect the provisions of Article VI of the GATT 1994 and the Anti-Dumping Agreement. Such an interpretation would deprive Article VI of the GATT 1994 and the Anti-Dumping Agreement of their useful effect within the framework of rules and disciplines imposed by the WTO Agreement.

---

[440] See, e.g., *Panel Report on United States - Imposition of Anti-Dumping Duties on Imports of Fresh and Chilled Atlantic Salmon from Norway*, adopted on 28 April 1994, ADP/87, para. 75.

(d) Preparatory Work

6.200 We could conclude our analysis based on the rule of Article 31 of the Vienna Convention. However, since the parties have discussed the meaning of the negotiating history at length, we consider it in order to determine if it confirms the meaning of Article VI:2 of the GATT 1994 we identified under Article 31.

6.201 The parties have referred to a number of documents relating to the negotiation of the Havana Charter and the GATT.[441] We do not consider it necessary to review all these materials since our analysis under Article 31 of the Vienna Convention has not left the meaning of Article VI ambiguous or obscure and has not led to a manifestly absurd or unreasonable result. We recall, however, that the parties have more particularly discussed the Report of the Working Party on Modifications to the General Agreement, which was adopted by the CONTRACTING PARTIES on 1-2 September 1948. This report mentions at paragraph 12 that:

> "endorsing the views expressed by Sub-Committee C of the Third Committee of the Havana Conference, [footnote omitted] [it] agreed that measures other than compensatory anti-dumping and countervailing duties may not be applied to counteract dumping or subsidization except in so far as such other measures are permitted under other provisions of the General Agreement."[442]

6.202 We consider that the first part of the sentence ("measures other than compensatory anti-dumping and countervailing duties may not be applied to counteract dumping or subsidization") confirms our understanding of Article VI. The second part of the sentence ("except in so far as such other measures are permitted under other provisions of the General Agreement"), may be understood as allowing members to counter dumping through other measures than anti-dumping duties.[443] The United States argues that a number of measures could be legally applied against dumping, such as raising unbound tariffs, tariff renegotiation, safeguard measures or countervailing measures. We note, however, that even though those measures may be legally applied to address dumping, the basis for their imposition would not objectively be "dumping". Safeguard measures or the increase of unbound tariffs would apply on a most favoured nation basis. So would the results of a tariff renegotiation. Unless all Members were dumping, dumping could not be considered as the objective reason for the imposition of the measures or of the renegotiated tariff *vis-à-vis* each Member. Countervailing measures can only be imposed in relation to subsidies. The fact that those subsidies may allow their beneficiaries to dump is not as essential for the imposition of the countervailing measures as the existence of the subsidy it-

---

441 See section III.E.3. above.

442 BISD Vol. II, p. 41 (1952).

443 This seems to be the understanding of John H. Jackson in *World Trade and the Law of GATT* (1968), p. 411, where it is mentioned that:

> "Although Article VI carves out an exception to GATT obligations for anti-dumping or countervailing duties, nevertheless, measures that do not violate other GATT provisions can also be used to counteract dumping or subsidies. Thus, insofar as tariffs on a particular product are not bound in a GATT schedule, a country that found that the product was being dumped could raise its tariffs without limit to counteract the dumping, and go even further and punish the dumper."

self. Therefore, this sentence can only be understood as having the same meaning as footnote 24 to Article 18.1 of the Anti-Dumping Agreement.[444]

6.203 We conclude that the supplementary means of interpretation of Article 32 of the Vienna Convention confirm our interpretation of Article VI:2 of the GATT 1994 based on the ordinary meaning of its terms taken in their context.

(e) Conclusion on the Violation of Article VI:2 of the GATT 1994

6.204 We therefore find that Article VI:2 provides that only measures in the form of anti-dumping duties may be applied to counteract dumping as such and that, by providing for the imposition of fines or imprisonment or for the recovery of treble damages, the 1916 Act violates Article VI:2 of the GATT 1994.

6.205 We also recall our remark in paragraphs 6.89 and 6.164 above. Since we found a violation of Article VI, paragraph 1 and paragraph 2, we do not find it necessary to determine what would be the legal consequences of a consistent WTO-compatible interpretation of the 1916 Act by US courts *in the future*.

3. Concluding Remarks on Burden of Proof with Respect to the Violation of Article VI of the GATT 1994

6.206 In paragraph 6.99 above, we noted the difference of approach of the parties regarding the applicability of Article VI of the GATT 1994. Because of this difference, each party has concentrated its efforts in terms of submission of evidence on

---

[444] See para. 6.199 above. We also recall the reasons stated in the report of the Working Party established by Sub-Committee C of the Third Committee of the Havana Conference (E/CONF.2/C.3/C/18, 22 January 1948) for the deletion of para. 6 of Article 34 of the Geneva Draft Charter of the International Trade Organisation. Para. 6 was similar to para. 7 of the original Article VI of the GATT 1947 and read as follows:

> "No measures other than anti-dumping or countervailing duties shall be applied by any contracting party in respect of any product of the territory of any other contracting party for the purpose of offsetting dumping or subsidization."

The question had been prompted by the issue whether para. 6 should be deleted or amended in the event that it could be interpreted so as to limit action permitted under Articles 13 and 14 of the Geneva Draft. The report stated that:

> "The Working Party was evenly divided as to whether the terms of para. (6) could be construed as limiting the rights of Members under Articles 13 and 14. It was in agreement, however, that para. (6) was unnecessary and that its deletion would not effect any change in substance."

These statements confirm the intent to restrict the measures allowed to counteract dumping *as such* to offsetting duties. The fact that Article VI allows only for duties to counteract dumping practices as such is also confirmed by the Report of the Review Working Party on "Other Barriers to Trade", which mentions that:

> "With respect to para. 3 of Article VI, the Working Party considered a proposal submitted by New Zealand which would have permitted under certain circumstances the use of quantitative restrictions to offset subsidization or dumping. This proposal did not receive the support of the Working Party, and has not been recommended." (BISD 3S/223, as quoted in *GATT, Analytical Index: Guide to GATT Law and Practice, Updated 6th Edition* (1995), p. 238.)

different aspects, which sometimes did not correspond to the Panel's division of its analysis. However, we consider that the EC has established a *prima facie* case for each point addressed by the Panel in relation to the violation of Article VI. The United States did not sufficiently rebut them. Moreover, we consider that the United States did not establish such a *prima facie* case with respect to its defences, especially regarding its argumentation based on the possibility to interpret the 1916 Act in a WTO-compatible manner and on the non-mandatory nature of the 1916 Act.

F. Violation of Provisions of the Anti-Dumping Agreement

1. Preliminary Remarks

6.207 We have found a violation of Article VI:1 because the 1916 Act does not provide for an "injury" test. Moreover, we have found a violation of Article VI:2 because the 1916 Act imposes other remedies than anti-dumping duties. These findings address essential features of the 1916 Act. We could therefore consider exercising judicial economy at this stage. We are however of the view that findings under the Anti-Dumping Agreement would probably further assist the DSB in making sufficiently precise recommendations and rulings so as to allow for prompt compliance by the United States with those recommendations and rulings "in order to ensure effective resolution of disputes to the benefit of all Members."[445] Indeed, we are of the view that "adapting" the 1916 Act to the injury requirements of Article VI and replacing the sanctions currently provided for in that law with duties at the border may not be totally sufficient to make the 1916 Act WTO-compatible,[446] as will be seen from our findings below.

2. Review of the EC Claims under the Anti-Dumping Agreement

(a) General Comments Regarding the EC Claims under Article 1 and Article 2.1 and 2.2 of the Anti-Dumping Agreement

6.208 The EC argues that the 1916 Act prohibits dumping under different conditions than those laid down in Article VI of the GATT 1994 and the Anti-Dumping Agreement and applies different procedures and remedies than provided therein. The EC claims the violation of Articles 1, 2.1, 2.2, 3, 4 and 5.5 of the Anti-Dumping Agreement. As far as Article 1 is concerned, we note that if we find a violation of other provisions of the Anti-Dumping Agreement, it will be demonstrated that an anti-dumping investigation under the 1916 Act is not "initiated or conducted in accordance with the provisions of this Agreement" and a breach of Article 1 will be established.

---

[445] See Appellate Body Report on *Australia - Measures Affecting Importation of Salmon, supra*, footnote 349, para. 223.

[446] While this statement is not made under Article 19.1 of the DSU, we note that, pursuant to that provision, we are entitled to suggest ways in which the Member concerned could implement the Panel's recommendations.

6.209 Regarding the violation of Article 2.1 and 2.2 of the Anti-Dumping Agreement, we note that the European Communities simply states that "Articles 2.1 and 2.2 set forth amplified rules on the substantive definition of dumping." The EC did identify its claims under Article 2.1 and 2.2 in its request for the establishment of a panel. However, we do not consider that it precisely set out and progressively clarified its arguments on Article 2.1 and 2.2 during the proceedings. In particular, it did not submit any argument or evidence as to which specific aspects of Article 2.1 and 2.2 were violated, and why. We are of the view that we face a situation similar to that addressed by the Appellate Body in *Japan - Agricultural Products*.[447] In the present case, the EC did not establish a *prima facie* case of violation of Article 2.1 and 2.2 . The fact that we found a violation of Article VI:1 of the GATT 1994 is not as such sufficient to conclude that Articles 2.1 and 2.2 of the Anti-Dumping Agreement have been breached, in the absence of more specific arguments and evidence. Indeed, there could be several reasons to claim a violation of Article 2.1 and 2.2 which would be totally independent from those we relied upon with respect to Article VI.[448]

6.210 We therefore conclude that we are not in a position to address the claims of the EC under Articles 2.1 and 2.2 of the Anti-Dumping Agreement.

(b) Violation of Article 3

6.211 Since we found above that the 1916 Act violated Article VI:1 by not providing for an injury test compatible with the terms of that Article and since Article 3 simply addresses in more detail the requirement of "material injury" contained in Article VI:1, we do not find it necessary to make specific findings under Article 3 and therefore exercise judicial economy, as we are entitled to do under GATT panel practice and WTO panel and Appellate Body practice.[449]

(c) Violation of Article 4

6.212 The EC also claims that the 1916 Act fails to respect a number of procedural and due process requirements set forth in Article 4[450] of the Anti-Dumping Agreement-

---

[447] Op. Cit., para. 129. In that case, the complainant had not made a specific argument. The panel had actually deduced it from the experts' answers to its questions. The Appellate Body considered that, even though Article 13 of the DSU and Article 11.2 of the SPS Agreement suggest that panels have significant investigative authority, this authority cannot be used by a Panel to rule in favour of a complaining party which has not established a *prima facie* case of inconsistency based on specific legal claims asserted by it.

[448] For instance, the fact that the 1916 Act would not provide for the treatment of sales of the like product in the domestic market of the exporting country or sales to a third country at prices below per unit (fixed and variable) costs of production plus administrative, selling and general costs (Article 2.2.1).

[449] See, e.g., Panel Report on *Canada - Administration of the Foreign Investment Review Act*, adopted on 7 February 1984, BISD 30S/140, para. 5.16; Panel Report on *Brazil - Desiccated Coconut, supra*, footnote 277, para. 293; Appellate Body Report on *United States - Measures Affecting Imports of Woven Wool Shirts and Blouses from India, supra*, footnote 314, at 339.

[450] Article 4 provides as follows:

> "4.1 For the purposes of this Agreement, the term "domestic industry" shall be interpreted as referring to the domestic producers as a whole of the like products or

ment, in particular the requirement that a complaint be made on behalf of the domestic industry and be supported by a minimum proportion of the domestic industry.

6.213 We note that civil proceedings under the 1916 Act are available to "any person injured in his business or property" by reason of a violation of the 1916 Act. This term is nowhere qualified by a statement that this person should be sufficiently representative of the industry of the United States, within the meaning of Article 4 of the Anti-Dumping Agreement. We note that the 1916 Act refers to the intent of destroying or injuring an *industry* in the United States, or of preventing the establishment of an *industry* in the United States. However, we have no evidence that a minimum representation level for a given industry must be established by the complainant before filing a case before a federal court. On the contrary, we note that all cases so far have in fact been initiated by individual companies under their own responsibility. In light of the terms of the 1916 Act and, in particular, the term "any person injured in his business or property", which is particularly clear, we have no reason to believe that US federal courts will be in a position to interpret that provision consistently with Article 4 of the Anti-Dumping Agreement.

---

to those of them whose collective output of the products constitutes a major proportion of the total domestic production of those products, except that:

(i) when producers are related [footnote omitted] to the exporters or importers or are themselves importers of the allegedly dumped product, the term "domestic industry" may be interpreted as referring to the rest of the producers;

(ii) in exceptional circumstances the territory of a Member may, for the production in question, be divided into two or more competitive markets and the producers within each market may be regarded as a separate industry if *(a)* the producers within such market sell all or almost all of their production of the product in question in that market, and *(b)* the demand in that market is not to any substantial degree supplied by producers of the product in question located elsewhere in the territory. In such circumstances, injury may be found to exist even where a major portion of the total domestic industry is not injured, provided there is a concentration of dumped imports into such an isolated market and provided further that the dumped imports are causing injury to the producers of all or almost all of the production within such market.

4.2 When the domestic industry has been interpreted as referring to the producers in a certain area, i.e. a market as defined in para. 1(ii), anti-dumping duties shall be levied only on the products in question consigned for final consumption to that area. When the constitutional law of the importing Member does not permit the levying of anti-dumping duties on such a basis, the importing Member may levy the anti-dumping duties without limitation only if *(a)* the exporters shall have been given an opportunity to cease exporting at dumped prices to the area concerned or otherwise give assurances pursuant to Article 8 and adequate assurances in this regard have not been promptly given, and *(b)* such duties cannot be levied only on products of specific producers which supply the area in question.

4.3 Where two or more countries have reached under the provisions of para. 8(a) of Article XXIV of GATT 1994 such a level of integration that they have the characteristics of a single, unified market, the industry in the entire area of integration shall be taken to be the domestic industry referred to in para. 1.

4.4 The provisions of para. 6 of Article 3 shall be applicable to this Article."

6.214 For that reason, we find that the 1916 Act, because it does not require a minimum representation of a US industry, violates Article 4 of the Anti-Dumping Agreement.

(d) Violation of Article 5.5

6.215 The EC also claims that the 1916 Act fails to respect a number of procedural and due process requirements set forth in Article 5.5[451] of the Anti-Dumping Agreement, essentially because it fails to require that notice be given to the government of the exporting country before an anti-dumping case is launched under the 1916 Act.

6.216 We note that the text of the 1916 Act as such does not provide for the notification required by Article 5.5, neither under the "civil track", nor under the "criminal track". The Panel was not made aware of any other text or administrative practice which would imply a notification to the governments concerned, either by the courts or by the executive branch of the US government. We therefore conclude that the 1916 Act violates Article 5.5 of the Anti-Dumping Agreement.

3. Conclusion

6.217 For the reasons mentioned above, we find that the 1916 Act violates Articles 4 and 5.5 of the Anti-Dumping Agreement. In light of our findings and for the reasons mentioned in paragraphs 6.208 above, we also find that the 1916 Act violates Article 1 of the Anti-Dumping Agreement.

G. Violation of Article III:4 of the GATT 1994

6.218 We recall that the EC requested us to make a finding of violation of Article III:4 of the GATT 1994 in the alternative or "if the Panel considers that all or any portion of the Act is consistent with GATT Article VI and the *Anti-Dumping Agreement*". Such finding would apply to the "portion of the Act found to be consistent with GATT Article VI and the *Anti-Dumping Agreement*."[452]

6.219 We recall that we decided to proceed first with a review of whether Article VI applied to the 1916 Act because Article VI seemed to address more specifically the terms of the 1916 Act. We found that the 1916 Act, because it targets "dumping" within the meaning of Article VI of the GATT 1994, was fully subject to the provisions of Article VI of the GATT 1994 and the Anti-Dumping Agreement and could not evade the disciplines of Article VI by the mere fact that it had anti-trust objectives or included requirements of an anti-trust nature. We therefore find it unnecessary to determine whether some elements of the 1916 Act could be subject to Article III:4.

---

[451] Article 5.5 provides as follows:

> "The authorities shall avoid, unless a decision has been made to initiate an investigation, any publicizing of the application for the initiation of an investigation. However, after receipt of a properly documented application and before proceeding to initiate an investigation, the authorities shall notify the government of the exporting Member concerned."

[452] Emphasis in the original.

6.220 We also found that the 1916 Act violates the provisions of Article VI and certain provisions of the Anti-Dumping Agreement. We consider these findings sufficiently complete to enable the DSB to make sufficiently precise recommendations and rulings so as to allow for prompt compliance "in order to ensure effective resolution of disputes to the benefit of all Members."[453] Therefore, we are entitled to exercise judicial economy in accordance with WTO panel and Appellate Body practice[454] and decide not to review the EC claims under Article III:4.

H. Violation of Article XVI:4 of the Agreement Establishing the WTO

6.221 We note that the parties disagree as to the scope of Article XVI:4 of the Agreement Establishing the WTO as it relates to this dispute. However, both parties agree that if a Member's law, regulation, or administrative procedure does not conform with its obligations as provided in the WTO Agreement, that Member has an affirmative obligation to bring it into conformity.[456]

6.222 Article XVI:4 of the Agreement Establishing the WTO reads as follows:

> "Each Member shall ensure the conformity of its laws, regulations and administrative procedures with its obligations as provided in the annexed Agreements."

6.223 If Article XVI:4 has any meaning, it is that when a law, regulation or administrative procedure of a Member has been found incompatible with the WTO obligations of that Member under any agreement annexed to the WTO Agreement, that Member is also in breach of its obligations under Article XVI:4.[457] We found that the 1916 Act violates Article VI:1 and VI:2 of the GATT 1994. The GATT 1994 being one of the "annexed Agreements" within the meaning of Article XVI:4, we find that, by violating those provisions, the United States violates Article XVI:4 of the Agreement Establishing the WTO.

6.224 In light of our conclusion, we do not find it necessary to address the question of the violation of Article XVI:4 of the Agreement Establishing the WTO as a result of the violation of Articles 1, 4 and 5.5 of the Anti-Dumping Agreement.

6.225 We therefore find that, by violating Articles VI:1 and VI:2 of the GATT 1994, the 1916 Act violates Article XVI:4 of the Agreement Establishing the WTO.

I. Nullification or Impairment

6.226 The EC claims that, by violating Articles XVI:4 of the Agreement Establishing the WTO, Articles VI:1 and VI:2 of the GATT 1994, Articles 1, 2.1, 2.2, 3, 4 and

---

[453] See Appellate Body Report on *Australia - Measures Affecting Importation of Salmon*, *supra*, footnote 349, para. 223.

[454] See footnote 449 above.

[*] Footnote number 455 was skipped. Thus no text is missing.

[456] See arguments of the parties in paras. 3.358 and 3.361 above.

[457] We did not exercise judicial economy with respect to Article XVI:4 because, in that context, a violation of Article XVI:4 "automatically" results from the breach of another provision of the WTO Agreement.

5.5 of the Anti-Dumping Agreement and Article III:4 of the GATT 1994, the United States has nullified or impaired benefits accruing to the EC under those agreements.

6.227 We have found that the 1916 Act as such violates Article VI:1 and VI:2 of the GATT 1994, as well as Articles 1, 4 and 5.5 of the Anti-Dumping Agreement. We also concluded that, by not ensuring the conformity of the 1916 Act with its obligations as provided under the above-mentioned provisions, the United States violates Article XVI:4 of the Agreement Establishing the WTO. Since Article 3.8 of the DSU provides that "In cases where there is an infringement of the obligations assumed under a covered agreement, the action is considered *prima facie* to constitute a case of nullification or impairment" and as the United States has adduced no evidence to the contrary, we conclude that the 1916 Act nullifies or impairs benefits accruing to the European Communities under the WTO Agreement.

J. Summary of Findings

6.228 Our findings may be summarised as follows:

(a) in order to review the conformity of the 1916 Act with the provisions of the WTO Agreement, we were entitled, consistently with the practice of the Appellate Body and of other international tribunals, to carry out an examination of the US domestic law, including a review of the relevant legislative history and an analysis of the relevant case-law;

(b) Article VI:1 of the GATT 1994, interpreted in accordance with the Vienna Convention, must be understood as applying to any situation where a Member addresses the type of transnational price discrimination defined in that Article;

(c) on the basis of the terms of the 1916 Act, the transnational price discrimination test found in that law meets the definition of Article VI:1 of the GATT 1994. The legislative history of the 1916 Act and the subsequent interpretation by US courts do not lead us to reach a different conclusion;

(d) by not providing exclusively for the injury test[458] provided for in Article VI, the 1916 Act violates Article VI:1 of the GATT 1994;

(e) by providing for the imposition of treble damages, fines or imprisonment, instead of anti-dumping duties, the 1916 Act violates Article VI:2 of the GATT 1994;

(f) by not providing for a number of procedural requirements found in the Anti-Dumping Agreement, the 1916 Act violates Articles 1, 4, and 5.5 of the Anti-Dumping Agreement;

(g) by violating Articles VI:1 and VI:2 of the GATT 1994, the 1916 Act violates Article XVI:4 of the Agreement Establishing the WTO;

(h) since violations have been established that have not been rebutted by the United States, the United States nullifies or impairs benefits accruing to the European Communities under the WTO Agreement.

---

[458] See footnote 366 above.

VII. CONCLUSIONS AND RECOMMENDATIONS

7.1 We *conclude* that

(i) the 1916 Act violates Article VI:1 and VI:2 of the GATT 1994;

(ii) the 1916 Act violates Articles 1, 4 and 5.5 of the Anti-Dumping Agreement;

(iii) the 1916 Act violates Article XVI:4 of the Agreement Establishing the WTO;

(iv) as a result, benefits accruing to the European Communities under the WTO Agreement have been nullified or impaired.

7.2 We therefore *recommend* that the DSB request the United States to bring the 1916 Act into conformity with its obligations under the WTO Agreement.

UNITED STATES - ANTI-DUMPING ACT OF 1916

Complaint by Japan

Report of the Appellate Body

WT/DS136/AB/R
WT/DS162/AB/R

Adopted by the Dispute Settlement Body on 26 September 2000

United States, *Appellant/Appellee*
European Communities, *Appellant/Appellee/Third Participant*
Japan, *Appellant/Appellee/Third Participant*
India, *Third Participant*
Mexico, *Third Participant*

Present:
Lacarte-Muró, Presiding Member
Ehlermann, Member
Feliciano, Member

TABLE OF CONTENTS

I. INTRODUCTION

1. The United States, the European Communities and Japan appeal from certain issues of law and legal interpretations in the Panel Reports, *United States - Anti-Dumping Act of 1916,* complaint by the European Communities (the "EC Panel Report") [1] and *United States - Anti-Dumping Act of 1916,* complaint by Japan (the "Ja-

[1] Panel Report, *United States - Anti-Dumping Act of 1916 - Complaint by the European Communities*, WT/DS136/R, adopted 26 September 2000.

pan Panel Report").[2] These Panel Reports were rendered by two Panels composed of the same three persons.[3] The two Panel Reports, while not identical, are alike in all major respects.

2. The Panel was established to consider claims by the European Communities and Japan that Title VIII of the United States Revenue Act of 1916 (the "1916 Act")[4] is inconsistent with United States' obligations under the covered agreements. The 1916 Act allows, under certain conditions, civil actions and criminal proceedings to be brought against importers who have sold foreign-produced goods in the United States at prices which are "substantially less" than the prices at which the same products are sold in a relevant foreign market.[5]

3. The European Communities claimed that the 1916 Act is inconsistent with Articles VI:1 and VI:2 of the *General Agreement on Tariffs and Trade 1994* (the "GATT 1994"), Articles 1, 2.1, 2.2, 3, 4 and 5 of the *Agreement on Implementation of Article VI of the General Agreement on Tariffs and Trade 1994* (the "*Anti-Dumping Agreement* ") and Article XVI:4 of the *Marrakesh Agreement Establishing the World Trade Organization* (the "*WTO Agreement*"). In the alternative, the European Communities claimed that the 1916 Act is inconsistent with Article III:4 of the GATT 1994. Japan claimed that the 1916 Act is inconsistent with Articles III:4, VI and XI of the GATT 1994, Articles 1, 2, 3, 4, 5, 9, 11, 18.1 and 18.4 of the *Anti-Dumping Agreement* and Article XVI:4 of the *WTO Agreement*.

4. In the EC Panel Report, circulated to Members of the World Trade Organization (the "WTO") on 31 March 2000, the Panel concluded that:

(i) the 1916 Act violates Article VI:1 and VI:2 of the GATT 1994;

(ii) the 1916 Act violates Articles 1, 4 and 5.5 of the Anti-Dumping Agreement;

(iii) the 1916 Act violates Article XVI:4 of the Agreement Establishing the WTO;

(iv) as a result, benefits accruing to the European Communities under the WTO Agreement have been nullified or impaired.[6]

5. In the Japan Panel Report, circulated to Members of the WTO on 29 May 2000, the Panel concluded that:

(i) the 1916 Act violates Article VI:1 and VI:2 of GATT 1994;

(ii) the 1916 Act violates Articles 1, 4.1, 5.1, 5.2, 5.4, 18.1 and 18.4 of the Anti-Dumping Agreement;

---

[2] Panel Report, *United States - Anti-Dumping Act of 1916 - Complaint by Japan*, WT/DS162/R, adopted 26 September 2000.

[3] As the composition of both Panels was identical, we will refer to the Panels as "the Panel".

[4] Act of 8 September 1916, 39 Stat. 756 (1916); 15 U.S.C. § 72.

[5] Relevant factual aspects of the 1916 Act are set out at paras. 2.1 - 2.5 and 2.13 - 2.16 of the EC Panel Report, and at paras. 2.1 - 2.5 and 2.14 - 2.16 of the Japan Panel Report. Relevant portions of the 1916 Act are also reproduced in this Report, *infra*, para. 129.

[6] EC Panel Report, *supra*, footnote 1, para. 7.1.

(iii) the 1916 Act violates XVI:4 of the Agreement Establishing the WTO; and

(iv) as a result, benefits accruing to Japan under the WTO Agreement have been nullified or impaired.[7]

6. In both Panel Reports, the Panel recommended that the Dispute Settlement Body (the "DSB") request the United States to bring the 1916 Act into conformity with its obligations under the *WTO Agreement*.[8]

7. On 29 May 2000, the United States notified the DSB of its intention to appeal certain issues of law covered in the EC Panel Report and the Japan Panel Report and certain legal interpretations developed by the Panel, pursuant to paragraph 4 of Article 16 of the *Understanding on Rules and Procedures Governing the Settlement of Disputes* (the "DSU"), and filed two Notices of Appeal pursuant to Rule 20 of the *Working Procedures for Appellate Review* (the "*Working Procedures*"). In view of the close similarity of the issues raised in the two appeals, it was decided, after consultation with the parties, that a single Division would hear and decide both appeals. On 8 June 2000, the United States filed one appellant's submission for both appeals.[9] On 13 June 2000, the European Communities and Japan filed a joint other appellants' submission in respect of both appeals.[10] On 23 June 2000, the European Communities and Japan each filed an appellee's/third participant's submission[11], and the United States filed an appellee's submission.[12] On the same day, India and Mexico each filed a third participant's submission.[13]

8. The oral hearing in the two appeals was held on 19 July 2000. The participants and third participants presented oral arguments and responded to questions put to them by the Members of the Division hearing the appeals.

II. ARGUMENTS OF THE PARTICIPANTS AND THIRD PARTICIPANTS

A. Claims of Error by the United States - Appellant

1. Claims Against the 1916 Act as Such

(a) Jurisdiction of the Panel to Hear Claims Against the 1916 Act as Such

9. The United States argues that the Panel erred in failing to dismiss the claims raised by the European Communities and Japan under Article VI of the GATT 1994

---

[7] Japan Panel Report, *supra*, footnote 2, para. 7.1.

[8] EC Panel Report, *supra*, footnote 1, para. 7.2; Japan Panel Report, *supra*, footnote 1, para. 7.2.

[9] Pursuant to Rule 21 of the *Working Procedures*.

[10] Pursuant to Rule 23(1) of the *Working Procedures*.

[11] Pursuant to Rules 22 and 24 of the *Working Procedures*. The European Communities is an appellee in dispute WT/DS136 and a third participant in dispute WT/DS162. Japan is an appellee in dispute WT/DS162 and a third participant in dispute WT/DS136.

[12] Pursuant to Rule 23(3) of the *Working Procedures*.

[13] Pursuant to Rule 24 of the *Working Procedures*. India is a third participant in both disputes. Mexico is a third participant in dispute WT/DS136, but not in dispute WT/DS162.

and the *Anti-Dumping Agreement* for lack of jurisdiction. In each dispute, the complaining party invoked the jurisdiction of the Panel pursuant to Article 17 of the *Anti-Dumping Agreement*. However, when Article 17 of the *Anti-Dumping Agreement* is invoked as a basis for a panel's jurisdiction to determine claims made under that Agreement, it is necessary for the complaining party to challenge one of the three types of measure set forth in Article 17.4 of that Agreement, i.e., a definitive anti-dumping duty, a provisional measure or a price undertaking. In the view of the United States, a Member wishing to challenge another Member's anti-dumping law as such must wait until one of the three measures referred to in Article 17.4 is also challenged.

10. The United States considers that this rule is clearly established by the text and context of Article 17.4 of the *Anti-Dumping Agreement*, as well as by the Appellate Body Report in *Guatemala - Anti-Dumping Investigation Regarding Portland Cement from Mexico* ("*Guatemala - Cement* ").[14] In the present cases, the complainants only challenged the 1916 Act as such, and did not challenge any measure of the type identified in Article 17.4. For this reason alone, according to the United States, the Panel's findings must be vacated for lack of jurisdiction.

11. The United States also contends that the Panel erred in finding that it had jurisdiction to consider claims under Article VI of the GATT 1994. The United States considers that Article VI of the GATT 1994 and the *Anti-Dumping Agreement* form part of an inseparable package of rights and obligations and that, based on the reasoning of the Appellate Body in *Brazil - Measures Affecting Desiccated Coconut* [15], one part of such a package cannot be invoked independently of the other. The United States thus concludes that, since the Panel did not possess jurisdiction to consider the *Anti-Dumping Agreement* claims, and since Article VI cannot be invoked independently of the *Anti-Dumping Agreement*, it follows that the Panel also lacked jurisdiction to consider claims under Article VI of the GATT 1994.

(b) Mandatory and Discretionary Legislation

12. The United States requests the Appellate Body to reverse the Panel's analysis and findings regarding the distinction between mandatory and discretionary legislation. If the Panel found, or the Appellate Body finds, that the 1916 Act is ambiguous, then, the United States submits, the Panel should have asked, and the Appellate Body should ask, whether there is an interpretation of the 1916 Act that would permit the United States to act in conformity with its WTO obligations. Instead, according to the United States, the Panel interpreted and applied the distinction between mandatory and discretionary legislation in a way that has no basis in existing WTO/GATT jurisprudence, erred in treating the distinction as a "defence", and erred in its treatment of United States' municipal law relevant to this issue.

13. As regards the nature of the mandatory and discretionary legislation distinction, the United States considers that the Panel based its approach on a "gross mis-

---

[14] Appellate Body Report, *Guatemala – Anti-Dumping Investigation Regarding Portland Cement from Mexico* ("*Guatemala Cement*"),WT/DS60/AB/R, adopted 25 November 1998, DSR 1998:IX, 3767.

[15] Appellate Body Report, *Brazil - Measures Affecting Desiccated Coconut* ("*Brazil - Desiccated Coconut*"), WT/DS22/AB/R, adopted 20 March 1997, DSR 1997:I, 167.

reading" of the panel report in *United States - Measures Affecting the Importation, Internal Sale and Use of Tobacco* ("*United States - Tobacco*").[16] Contrary to the Panel's finding, whether or not a law has been applied in the past does not determine the applicability of the distinction between mandatory and discretionary legislation. The United States also asks the Appellate Body to reject the Panel's finding in the Japan Panel Report that Article 18.4 of the *Anti-Dumping Agreement* renders the distinction between mandatory and discretionary legislation "irrelevant". The cases cited by the Panel, *EC - Anti-Dumping Duties on Audio Tapes in Cassettes Originating in Japan* ("*European Communities - Audio Cassettes*") [17] and *United States - Definition of Industry Concerning Wine and Grape Products* ("*United States - Wine and Grape Products*") [18], do not support such a conclusion. Furthermore, the United States contends, the ordinary meaning and context of Article 18.4 demonstrate that this provision does not modify or otherwise limit the distinction between mandatory and discretionary legislation.

14. The United States also underlines that there is no legal basis for the Panel's finding that the distinction between discretionary and mandatory legislation is a "defence" which the United States bore the burden of proving. The burden of proving that a measure is inconsistent with a WTO provision rests with the complaining party, which must demonstrate that the law in question *mandates* a violation of the relevant provision. Since the European Communities and Japan have not met the burden of proof, properly applied, the United States asks the Appellate Body to reverse the Panel's findings that the 1916 Act violates the provisions at issue in this dispute.

2. *Applicability of Article VI of the GATT 1994 and the Anti-Dumping Agreement to the 1916 Act*

15. The United States claims that the principal substantive error made by the Panel was its finding that Article VI of the GATT 1994, as interpreted by the *Anti-Dumping Agreement*, applies to the 1916 Act.

16. According to the United States, this finding is erroneous because it is based on an erroneous test for determining the applicability of Article VI. The correct analysis, in the view of the United States, is that for a Member's law to fall within the scope of Article VI, it must satisfy two criteria. First, the law must impose a particular type of border adjustment measure, namely, duties on an imported product. Second, the duties imposed by the Member's law must specifically target "dumping" within the meaning of Article VI:1. Consequently, the United States concludes, if the Member's law imposes a type of measure other than duties, or if it does not specifically target dumping, it is not governed by Article VI.

17. The United States submits that, with respect to dumping, Article VI of the GATT 1994 simply provides Members with a right to use anti-dumping duties, and then sets forth rules regulating the manner in which Members may exercise this right. Article VI does not attempt to regulate other types of measure that a Member may

[16] Panel Report, adopted 4 October 1994, BISD 41S/131.

[17] Panel Report (unadopted), ADP/136, circulated 28 April 1995.

[18] Panel Report, adopted 28 April 1992, BISD 39S/436.

want to take in order to counteract dumping, as that task is left to other GATT provisions, including Article III:4 of the GATT 1994. The United States considers that the ordinary meaning of the terms used in Article VI - and, in particular, Article VI:2 - as well as the limited role of Article VI within the GATT framework, Articles 1 and 18.1 of the *Anti-Dumping Agreement*, the panel reports in *Japan - Trade in Semi-Conductors* ("*Japan - Semi-Conductors*") [19] and *EEC - Regulation on Imports of Parts and Components* ("*EEC - Parts and Components*")[20] and the negotiating history of Article VI, confirm such an interpretation of the scope of Article VI.

18. According to the United States, the word "may" in Article VI:2 of the GATT 1994 confirms that Article VI provides a right that Members would not otherwise have - the right to impose duties - but does not contain any prohibition on the use of other types of measure. Article 1 of the *Anti-Dumping Agreement* means that a Member's actions are governed by Article VI and the *Anti-Dumping Agreement* if a Member is applying one of the specified measures to counteract dumping, i.e., anti-dumping duties, provisional measures or price undertakings. Article 18.1 of the *Anti-Dumping Agreement* and its footnote 24 also make clear that when specific action taken against dumping is in the form of anti-dumping duties, provisional measures or price undertakings, such action must comply with Article VI, as interpreted by the *Anti-Dumping Agreement*, but that when specific action against dumping takes another form, such action is governed by the provisions of the GATT 1994 *other than* Article VI.

19. The United States claims that the Panel engaged in a flawed analysis of the scope of Article VI and, as a result, erroneously concluded that Article VI of the GATT 1994 and the *Anti-Dumping Agreement* apply to *all* anti-dumping measures. The United States reasons that, when the correct test is applied, it is clear that Article VI does not apply to the 1916 Act. The United States underscores that the 1916 Act does not impose any type of border adjustment, much less duties, on imported products: it is an internal law.

20. The United States adds that the 1916 Act is also not subject to Article VI because it does not specifically target "dumping" within the meaning of Article VI:1. Although one element of a 1916 Act claim is the existence of a price difference between two national markets, the United States argues that this element alone is not sufficient under the 1916 Act. Rather, the United States contends, such a price difference is simply one indicator, or supporting evidence, of the possible existence of the activity which the 1916 Act does target, i.e., predatory pricing by the importer in the United States' market, which consists of sales at predatorily low price levels with the intent to destroy, injure, or prevent the establishment of an American industry or to restrain trade in or monopolize a particular market. According to the United States, the existence of such predatory intent is the primary indicator of the anti-competitive conduct which is targeted by the 1916 Act, as the United States' courts have held.

---

[19] Panel Report, adopted 4 May 1988, BISD 35S/116.

[20] Panel Report, adopted 16 May 1990, BISD 37S/132.

3. *Articles VI:1 and VI:2 of the GATT 1994, Certain Provisions of the Anti-Dumping Agreement and Article XVI:4 of the WTO Agreement*

21. The United States observes that the Panel found that the 1916 Act violates various substantive and procedural requirements of Article VI of the GATT 1994 and the *Anti-Dumping Agreement*. The United States requests the Appellate Body to reverse these findings as they were all based on the Panel's erroneous view of the scope of Article VI and the *Anti-Dumping Agreement*.

22. The United States reiterates that the Panel found support for its broad view of the scope of Article VI in Article VI:1 even though the actual text of this provision does not address the issue of whether Article VI regulates all actions against dumping, or only the imposition of anti-dumping duties. The United States recalls that, on its interpretation of Article VI:2 of the GATT 1994 and Articles 1 and 18.1 of the *Anti-Dumping Agreement*, a Member may take specific action against dumping - other than the imposition of anti-dumping duties - so long as such action is in accordance with, or consistent with, the provisions of the GATT 1994 other than Article VI. If the Appellate Body accepts this interpretation, it follows that Article VI does not apply to the 1916 Act, the claims made by the European Communities and Japan under the various provisions of Article VI and the *Anti-Dumping Agreement* must fail, and the Panel's findings of violations of those provisions must be reversed. In addition, the United States submits, since the Panel's findings of violation of Article XVI:4 of the *WTO Agreement* are based on its findings of violation of Article VI, the Appellate Body must also reverse the findings of violation of Article XVI:4.

B. *Arguments by the European Communities - Appellee/Third Participant*

1. *Claims Against the 1916 Act as Such*

(a) Jurisdiction of the Panel to Hear Claims Against the 1916 Act as Such

23. The European Communities requests the Appellate Body to reject the United States' arguments on the issue of jurisdiction on the basis that this ground of appeal is both untimely and unfounded. The United States could have and should have raised this objection before the interim review stage of the panel proceedings in the case brought by the European Communities. Interim review is only intended to allow review of "precise aspects" of the report and not the presentation of new arguments. The European Communities relies in particular on the principle that procedural objections must be raised in a timely manner and in good faith, as confirmed by the Appellate Body in *Korea - Definitive Safeguard Measure on Imports of Certain*

Dairy Products ("*Korea - Dairy Safeguards*")[21] and *United States - Tax Treatment for "Foreign Sales Corporations"* ("*United States - FSC* ").[22]

24. The European Communities also argues that the jurisdictional arguments of the United States are misconceived since Article 17.4 of the *Anti-Dumping Agreement* only applies to proceedings involving the imposition of the measures identified in that provision and does not generally shelter anti-dumping legislation from scrutiny under the dispute settlement mechanism. Even if it did, the legislation would still have to comply with Article XVI:4 of the *WTO Agreement*, which has also been invoked in this proceeding and is properly before the Appellate Body.

(b) Mandatory and Discretionary Legislation

25. In relation to the issue of the relevance and meaning of the alleged distinction between mandatory and discretionary legislation in WTO law, the European Communities contests that any such general principle exists and refers the Appellate Body to the report of the panel in *United States - Sections 301-310 of the Trade Act of 1974* ("*United States - Section 301* ").[23]

26. The European Communities also considers that the existing GATT and WTO case law clearly demonstrates that the alleged distinction between mandatory and discretionary legislation would in any event not protect the 1916 Act from review in dispute settlement proceedings.

2. *Applicability of Article VI of the GATT 1994 and the Anti-Dumping Agreement to the 1916 Act*

27. On the central question of the scope of application of Article VI of the GATT 1994, the European Communities supports the view of the Panel that Article VI recognizes the existence of a specific problem in international trade - dumping - and establishes a specific discipline which must be followed by WTO Members in dealing with it. This discipline applies to rules and measures taken thereunder, which, viewed objectively, deal with dumping. The discipline is not limited to rules which provide for the imposition of duties at the frontier.

28. The European Communities bases its interpretation of the scope of Article VI of the GATT 1994 on the text of Article VI itself, as well as on Articles 1 and 18.1 of the *Anti-Dumping Agreement*. In particular, Article VI:1 establishes that Article VI applies to measures which: (i) are targeted at imports; and (ii) provide a remedy against trading practices defined by reference to price discrimination in the form of lower prices in the importing country than those in the country of export. When Article VI:2, on which the United States relies, is read in the context of Article VI:1, it is clear that the word "may" simply means that the imposition of duties is optional, and that the amount of any such duty may not be greater than the margin of dumping.

---

[21] Appellate Body Report, *Korea - Definitive Safeguard Measure on Imports of Certain Dairy Products* ("*Korea - Dairy Safeguards*"), WT/DS98/AB/R, adopted 12 January 2000, DSR 2000:I, 3.

[22] Appellate Body Report, *United States - Tax Treatment for "Foreign Sales Corporations"* ("*United States - FSC* "),WT/DS108/AB/R, adopted 20 March 2000, DSR 2000:III. 1619.

[23] Panel Report, *United States - Sections 301-310 of the Trade Act of 1974* ("*United States - Section 301* "), WT/DS152/R, adopted 27 January 2000, DSR 2000:II, 815.

Furthermore, according to the European Communities, Article 18.1 of the *Anti-Dumping Agreement* and footnote 24 make clear that "specific action" against dumping may only be taken in accordance with Article VI, but this does not prevent the application of safeguard measures or countervailing duties (pursuant to and in conformity with Articles XIX and VI of the GATT 1994, respectively) to conduct which may also involve dumping.

29. The European Communities considers that the arguments made by the United States on appeal mischaracterize the Panel's findings, and find no support in the text or context of Article VI, Articles 1 or 18.1 of the *Anti-Dumping Agreement*, or the panel reports in *Japan - Semi-Conductors* or *EEC - Parts and Components*. The European Communities cautions that the arguments of the United States as regards the scope of Article VI of the GATT 1994 would eviscerate the disciplines of Article VI and allow Members easily to circumvent their WTO obligations by modifying their legislation to provide for fines instead of anti-dumping duties.

3. Articles VI:1 and VI:2 of the GATT 1994, Certain Provisions of the Anti-Dumping Agreement and Article XVI:4 of the WTO Agreement

30. Since the European Communities believes that the Panel correctly interpreted the scope of Article VI of the GATT 1994 and the *Anti-Dumping Agreement*, the European Communities asks the Appellate Body also to uphold the Panel's related conclusions that the 1916 Act violates Article VI:1 and VI:2 of the GATT 1994 and Articles 1, 4.1, 5.4, 5.5, 18.1 and 18.4 of the *Anti-Dumping Agreement*.

31. The European Communities reasons that when an anti-dumping law, which falls within the scope of application of Article VI of the GATT 1994 and the *Anti-Dumping Agreement*, allows the imposition of sanctions other than duties, this is a breach of the discipline established by Article VI of the GATT 1994 and the *Anti-Dumping Agreement*. Likewise, if such a law provides for imposition of measures on the basis of criteria which do not fulfil the substantive requirements of the discipline, or pursuant to procedures which do not respect its procedural requirements, such measures also constitute breaches of the discipline. The European Communities contends that the 1916 Act breaches the discipline in all three respects.

C. Arguments by Japan - Appellee/Third Participant

1. Claims Against the 1916 Act as Such

(a) Jurisdiction of the Panel to Hear Claims Against the 1916 Act as Such

32. Japan argues that the Panel correctly concluded that it had jurisdiction. According to Japan, nothing in the text of Article 17 of the *Anti-Dumping Agreement* or its context takes away the well-established GATT/WTO right to challenge facially inconsistent legislation. Article 17.4 is a special and additional rule listed in Appendix 2 to the DSU. According to Japan, Article 17.4 is an exception to the general rule contained in Article 17.1 of the *Anti-Dumping Agreement* and, by its terms, Article 17.4 establishes special rules that apply only to challenges of actions taken by anti-dumping authorities.

(b) Mandatory and Discretionary Legislation

33. According to Japan the Panel correctly concluded that, in light of Article 18.4 of the *Anti-Dumping Agreement*, the distinction between mandatory and discretionary legislation is not relevant in this dispute. In any event, Japan contends, the 1916 Act is mandatory in character. When its substantive elements are established, the remedies (fines and/or imprisonment) prescribed by the 1916 Act must be imposed. Japan submits that the Panel also correctly concluded that the burden of proof was properly on the United States to substantiate its claim that the 1916 Act was not mandatory.

2. *Applicability of Article VI of the GATT 1994 and the Anti-Dumping Agreement to the 1916 Act*

34. In Japan's view, the Panel correctly concluded that the proper basis for applicability of Article VI of the GATT 1994 is the type of conduct addressed, not the remedies applied to the conduct. By its terms, the object of Article VI is to counteract "dumping". Japan underscores that anti-dumping duties are the instrument, not the object of Article VI.

35. Japan believes that its interpretation is supported by the plain meaning of Article VI, as well as Articles 1 and 18.1 of the *Anti-Dumping Agreement*. Japan also expresses concern that Members could easily circumvent WTO obligations if a Member could escape Article VI simply by enacting legislation providing for fines and/or imprisonment rather than anti-dumping duties.

36. Japan agrees with the Panel that the 1916 Act falls within the scope of Article VI of the GATT 1994. On its face, the 1916 Act addresses the same type of price discrimination as Article VI. The existence in the 1916 Act of certain additional requirements, which make the imposition of measures to counteract dumping more difficult than required by Article VI, do not make the Act fall outside the scope of Article VI. According to Japan, the historical context, legislative history and United States' case law regarding the 1916 Act all support this conclusion.

3. *Articles VI:1 and VI:2 of the GATT 1994, Certain Provisions of the* Anti-Dumping Agreement *and Article XVI:4 of the WTO Agreement*

37. Japan argues that since the Panel correctly determined that Article VI of the GATT 1994 and the *Anti-Dumping Agreement* were applicable to the 1916 Act, its findings and conclusions regarding violations of the GATT 1994 and *Anti-Dumping Agreement* provisions also were correct. In particular, the Panel correctly concluded that anti-dumping duties are the only permissible remedy to counteract dumping. The text of Article VI:2 of the GATT 1994 explicitly and unambiguously establishes that anti-dumping duties are the only authorized remedy for dumping, and Article 18.1 and footnote 24 of the *Anti-Dumping Agreement* confirm this conclusion. Japan adds that this conclusion is further supported by the object and purpose of Article VI:2, as well as by the negotiating history.

D. *Claims of Error by the European Communities and Japan - Appellants*

1. Third Party Rights

38. The European Communities and Japan contend that the Panel erred in not granting enhanced third party rights to Japan in the case brought by the European Communities, and in not granting enhanced third party rights to the European Communities in the case brought by Japan. They ask the Appellate Body to reverse the Panel's findings and reasoning in this regard, in particular with respect to the proper interpretation of Article 9.3 of the DSU and the appropriate standard for evaluating whether enhanced third party rights should be granted. The European Communities and Japan stress the similarity between the present cases and *EC Measures Concerning Meat and Meat Products (Hormones)* ("*European Communities - Hormones*").[24]

39. According to the European Communities and Japan, in *European Communities - Hormones* the Appellate Body identified three conditions for the granting of enhanced third party rights to a Member involved in a related dispute: (i) the two proceedings deal with the same matter; (ii) the same panelists serve in both disputes; and (iii) the proceedings are held concurrently. They add that, even if the treatment of the European Communities and Japan as third parties was simply a matter of the Panel's discretion under Article 12.1 of the DSU, such discretion should have been exercised on the basis of the principles reflected in Articles 9 and 10 of the DSU, taking account of the need to respect due process.

2. Conditional Appeals

(a) Articles III:4 and XI of the GATT 1994

40. If the Appellate Body finds the United States' arguments on the scope of Article VI of the GATT 1994 admissible and well-founded, then the European Communities and Japan request the Appellate Body to find that the 1916 Act violates Articles III:4 and XI of the GATT 1994. The European Communities and Japan incorporate by reference and to the extent necessary the arguments that they developed before the Panel in this regard.

(b) Article XVI:4 of the *WTO Agreement*

41. Should the Appellate Body find the United States' arguments regarding the Panel's jurisdiction and the "non-mandatory" character of the 1916 Act to be admissible and well-founded, the European Communities and Japan ask the Appellate Body to find that the 1916 Act violates Article XVI:4 of the *WTO Agreement*. The European Communities and Japan incorporate by reference and to the extent necessary all the arguments that they developed before the Panel in this connection.

[24] Appellate Body Report, *EC Measures Concerning Meat and Meat Products (Hormones)* ("*European Communities - Hormones*"),WT/DS26/AB/R, WT/DS48/AB/R, adopted 13 February 1998, DSR 1998:I, 135.

E. Arguments by the United States - Appellee

1. Third Party Rights

42. The United States urges the Appellate Body to affirm the Panel's decision to deny enhanced third party rights to the European Communities and Japan. As a preliminary matter, the United States contests the claim of the European Communities and Japan that they were "prejudiced" by such denial, given that they prevailed on every substantive argument on which the Panel made findings.

43. The United States contends that the Panel's denial of enhanced third party rights was correct as a matter of law. In the view of the United States, Articles 9.2 and 9.3 of the DSU are of no assistance to the European Communities and Japan. Rather, as the Panel correctly noted and as the Appellate Body found in *European Communities - Hormones*, the question of whether to grant enhanced third party rights is a matter within the sound discretion of a panel. Unlike that case, these proceedings did not involve the consideration of complex facts or scientific evidence or a joint meeting of the parties. There were no "concurrent deliberations" as that term was used in the context of *European Communities - Hormones*. Furthermore, the granting of enhanced third party rights in these proceedings might have prejudiced the United States. In view of these circumstances, the United States considers that the Panel correctly denied enhanced third party rights to the European Communities and Japan.

2. *Conditional Appeals*

(a) Articles III:4 and XI of the GATT 1994

44. The United States submits that the Appellate Body lacks the authority to consider the claims by the European Communities and Japan under Articles III:4 and XI of the GATT 1994. First, the European Communities cannot request the Appellate Body to make any findings regarding Article XI of the GATT 1994 since that provision was not included in the European Communities' request for a panel. Second, the Panel made no factual or legal findings relating to the claims under Article III:4 and XI of the GATT 1994. As the facts relevant to the assessment of these claims were disputed before the Panel, the United States concludes that the limits on appellate review contained in Article 17 of the DSU prevent the Appellate Body from making any determinations of the claims under Articles III:4 and XI of the GATT 1994.

(b) Article XVI:4 of the *WTO Agreement*

45. Should the Appellate Body reach this issue, the United States requests the Appellate Body to affirm the Panel's conclusion that the 1916 Act only violates Article XVI:4 of the *WTO Agreement* to the extent that the 1916 Act violates Article VI of the GATT 1994.

F. Arguments by India and Mexico - Third Participants

1. India

(a) Jurisdiction of the Panel to Hear Claims Against the 1916 Act as Such

46. India argues that the Panel correctly assumed jurisdiction in these disputes. The United States' argument amounts to a contention that a Member's anti-dumping law *as such* may not be challenged. If accepted, this position would deprive Article 18.4 of the *Anti-Dumping Agreement* of any meaning or legal effect, and allow a Member to maintain a WTO-incompatible law with impunity as long as none of the measures referred to in Article 17.4 of the *Anti-Dumping Agreement* were adopted. India considers that the Panel correctly held that the Appellate Body ruling in *Guatemala - Cement* applies only if the dispute is related to the initiation and conduct of an anti-dumping investigation, and does *not* exclude review of anti-dumping laws *as such*.

47. India also considers that the reasoning in *India - Patent Protection for Pharmaceutical and Agricultural Chemical Products* [25] is sufficient to dispose of the United States' argument that it is the interpretation by the United States' courts of the 1916 Act that is dispositive of the nature of the Act and whether it is mandatory or discretionary.

(b) Applicability of Article VI of the GATT 1994 and the *Anti-Dumping Agreement* to the 1916 Act

48. India does not accept the United States' contention that the 1916 Act is an anti-trust rather than an anti-dumping law. The 1916 Act clearly addresses transnational price discrimination and targets imported products sold in the United States. This is entirely consonant with the definition of dumping in Article VI of the GATT 1994. India underlines that Article VI applies whether the dumping is limited, sporadic, frequent or systemic. Accordingly, the 1916 Act cannot escape the disciplines of Article VI simply because it requires the prohibited conduct to be "common and systematic". India therefore agrees with the Panel that Article VI establishes that anti-dumping duties are the sole means authorized to deal with dumped imports.

2. Mexico

49. Mexico argues that the Panel correctly concluded that the key to the applicability of Article VI of the GATT 1994 to the 1916 Act is whether that law objectively addresses "dumping" within the meaning of that article, that the 1916 Act does address such "dumping", and that anti-dumping duties are the sole remedy authorized under Article VI of the GATT 1994.

---

[25] Appellate Body Report, *India - Patent Protection for Pharmaceutical and Agricultural Chemical Producs*, WT/DS50/AB/R, adopted 16 January 1998, DSR 1998:I, 41, paras. 65 - 66.

III. ISSUES RAISED IN THESE APPEALS

50. The following issues are raised in these appeals:

(a) Whether the Panel erred in its assessment of the claims against the 1916 Act as such, in particular:

(i) in concluding that it had jurisdiction to consider claims that the 1916 Act as such is inconsistent with United States' obligations under Article VI of the GATT 1994 and the Anti-Dumping Agreement; and

(ii) in its interpretation and application of the distinction between mandatory and discretionary legislation;

(b) Whether the Panel erred in concluding that Article VI of the GATT 1994 and the *Anti-Dumping Agreement* apply to the 1916 Act;

(c) Whether the Panel erred in concluding:

(i) in the EC Panel Report, that the 1916 Act is inconsistent with Articles VI:1 and VI:2 of the GATT 1994, Articles 1, 4 and 5.5 of the *Anti-Dumping Agreement* and Article XVI:4 of the *WTO Agreement*; and

(ii) in the Japan Panel Report, that the 1916 Act is inconsistent with Articles VI:1 and VI:2 of the GATT 1994, Articles 1, 4.1, 5.1, 5.2, 5.4, 18.1 and 18.4 of the *Anti-Dumping Agreement* and Article XVI:4 of the *WTO Agreement*;

(d) Whether the Panel erred in refusing to grant "enhanced" third party rights to Japan in the case brought by the European Communities, and to the European Communities in the case brought by Japan; and

(e) If the Appellate Body were to reverse the Panel's findings that Article VI of the GATT 1994 and the *Anti-Dumping Agreement* apply to the 1916 Act, whether the Appellate Body can or should find that the 1916 Act is inconsistent with Articles III:4 and XI of the GATT 1994, and, if the Appellate Body were to reverse the Panel's findings on jurisdiction or on the distinction between mandatory and discretionary legislation, whether the Appellate Body can or should find that the 1916 Act is inconsistent with Article XVI:4 of the *WTO Agreement*.

IV. CLAIMS AGAINST THE 1916 ACT AS SUCH

A. Jurisdiction of the Panel to Hear Claims Against the 1916 Act as Such

51. With respect to its jurisdiction to examine the claims of the European Communities and Japan, the Panel found that:

> ... Article 17 of the Anti-Dumping Agreement does not prevent us from reviewing the conformity of laws as such under

> the Anti-Dumping Agreement. The same applies, a fortiori, with respect to Article VI of the GATT 1994. ... [26]

52. The United States appeals the Panel's finding that it had jurisdiction to consider the claims that the 1916 Act as such is inconsistent with Article VI of the GATT 1994 and the *Anti-Dumping Agreement.*

53. In its appellee's submission, the European Communities argues that the United States' appeal relating to the Panel's finding on jurisdiction should be rejected because the United States' objection to the Panel's jurisdiction was both not timely raised before the Panel and not well founded. In the case brought by the European Communities, the United States did not raise this objection to the jurisdiction of the Panel until the stage of interim review. The Panel stated that "there would be a number of reasons to reject the US argument as untimely." [27] The European Communities agrees and argues before us that the jurisdictional objection by the United States could have and should have been raised before the interim review stage of the proceedings before the Panel. The European Communities invokes the principle that procedural objections must be made in a timely manner and in good faith and refers in this respect to the Appellate Body Reports in *Korea - Dairy Safeguards* [28] and *United States - FSC.* [29]

54. We agree with the Panel that the interim review was not an appropriate stage in the Panel's proceedings to raise objections to the Panel's jurisdiction for the first time. An objection to jurisdiction should be raised as early as possible and panels must ensure that the requirements of due process are met. However, we also agree with the Panel's consideration that "some issues of jurisdiction may be of such a nature that they have to be addressed by the Panel at any time."[30] We do not share the

---

[26] EC Panel Report, *supra*, footnote 1, para. 5.27. See also Japan Panel Report, *supra*, footnote 2, para. 6.91.

[27] EC Panel Report, *supra*, footnote 1, para. 5.19.

[28] Appellate Body Report, *Korea – Dairy Safeguards*, *supra*, footnote 21, paras. 127 - 131.

[29] Appellate Body Report, *United States – FSC, supra*, footnote 22, para. 166.

[30] EC Panel Report, *supra*, footnote 1, para. 5.17. We note that it is a widely accepted rule that an international tribunal is entitled to consider the issue of its own jurisdiction on its own initiative, and to satisfy itself that it has jurisdiction in any case that comes before it. See, for example, *Case Concerning the Administration of the Prince von Pless (Preliminary Objection)* (1933) P.C.I.J. Ser. A/B, No. 52, p. 15; Individual Opinion of President Sir A. McNair, *Anglo-Iranian Oil Co. Case (Preliminary Objection)* (1952) I.C.J. Rep., p. 116; Separate Opinion of Judge Sir H. Lauterpacht in *Case of Certain Norwegian Loans* (1957) I.C.J. Rep., p. 43; and Dissenting Opinion of Judge Sir H. Lauterpacht in the *Interhandel Case (Preliminary Objections)* (1959) I.C.J. Rep., p. 104. See also M.O. Hudson, *The Permanent Court of International Justice 1920-1942* (MacMillan, 1943), pp. 418-419; G. Fitzmaurice, *The Law and Procedure of the International Court of Justice*, Vol. 2 (Grotius Publications, 1986), pp. 530, 755-758; S. Rosenne, *The Law and Practice of the International Court* (Martinus Nijhoff, 1985), pp. 467-468; L.A. Podesta Costa and J.M. Ruda, *Derecho Internacional Público,* Vol. 2 (Tipográfica, 1985), p. 438; M. Diez de Velasco Vallejo, *Instituciones de Derecho International Público* (Tecnos, 1997), p. 759. See also the award of the Iran-United States Claims Tribunal in *Marks & Umman v. Iran,* 8 Iran-United States C.T.R., pp. 296-97 (1985) (Award No. 53-458-3); J.J. van Hof, *Commentary on the UNCITRAL Arbitration Rules: The Application by the Iran-U.S. Claims Tribunal* (Kluwer, 1991), pp. 149-150; and Rule 41(2) of the rules applicable to ICSID Arbitration Tribunals: International Centre for Settlement of Investment Disputes, Rules of Procedure for Arbitration Proceedings (Arbitration Rules).

European Communities' view that objections to the jurisdiction of a panel are appropriately regarded as simply "procedural objections". The vesting of jurisdiction in a panel is a fundamental prerequisite for lawful panel proceedings. We, therefore, see no reason to accept the European Communities' argument that we must reject the United States' appeal because the United States did not raise its jurisdictional objection before the Panel in a timely manner.

55. The United States appeals, on the basis of the wording of Article 17.4 of the *Anti-Dumping Agreement* and our Report in *Guatemala - Cement,* the Panel's finding that it had jurisdiction to examine the 1916 Act as such. According to the United States, Members cannot bring a claim of inconsistency with the *Anti-Dumping Agreement* against legislation as such independently from a claim of inconsistency of one of the three anti-dumping measures specified in Article 17.4, i.e., a definitive anti-dumping duty, a price undertaking or, in some circumstances, a provisional measure. The United States contends that:

> [When a Member has] a law which [provides for the imposition of] duties to counteract dumping and, under the *Anti-Dumping Agreement*, if [another Member wishes] to challenge that law, then [the other Member must] wait until one of the three measures [referred to in Article 17.4 of the *Anti-Dumping Agreement*] is in place.[31]

56. Since, in the present cases, the European Communities and Japan did not challenge a definitive anti-dumping duty, a price undertaking or a provisional measure, the United States concludes that the Panel did not have jurisdiction to examine the 1916 Act as such. Moreover, the United States contends that if the 1916 Act as such cannot be challenged under the *Anti-Dumping Agreement*, it cannot be challenged under Article VI of the GATT 1994 because Article VI and the *Anti-Dumping Agreement* are an inseparable package of rights and obligations.

57. In examining the legal basis for the Panel's jurisdiction to consider the claims of inconsistency made in respect of the 1916 Act as such, we begin with Article 1.1 of the DSU, which states, in relevant part:

> The rules and procedures of this Understanding shall apply to *disputes brought pursuant to the consultation and dispute settlement provisions of the agreements listed in Appendix 1* to this Understanding (referred to in this Understanding as the "covered agreements"). (emphasis added)

For the DSU to apply to claims that the 1916 Act as such is inconsistent with Article VI of the GATT 1994 and the *Anti-Dumping Agreement*, a legal basis to bring the claims must be found in the GATT 1994 and the *Anti-Dumping Agreement*, respectively.

58. We note that in the present cases, the European Communities and Japan both brought their claims of inconsistency with Article VI of the GATT 1994 and the

31 United States' response to questioning at the oral hearing.

Anti-Dumping Agreement pursuant to Article XXIII of the GATT 1994 and Article 17 of the *Anti-Dumping Agreement.*[32]

59. Articles XXII and XXIII of the GATT 1994 serve as the basis for consultations and dispute settlement under the GATT 1994 and, through incorporation by reference, under most of the other agreements in Annex 1A to the *WTO Agreement* .[33] According to Article XXIII:1(a) of the GATT 1994, a Member can bring a dispute settlement claim against another Member when it considers that a benefit accruing to it under the GATT 1994 is being nullified or impaired, or that the achievement of any objective of the GATT 1994 is being impeded, as a result of the failure of that other Member to carry out its obligations under that Agreement.

60. Prior to the entry into force of the *WTO Agreement*, it was firmly established that Article XXIII:1(a) of the GATT 1947 allowed a Contracting Party to challenge legislation as such, independently from the application of that legislation in specific instances. While the text of Article XXIII does not expressly address the matter, panels consistently considered that, under Article XXIII, they had the *jurisdiction* to deal with claims against legislation as such.[34] In *examining* such claims, panels developed the concept that mandatory and discretionary legislation should be distinguished from each other, reasoning that only legislation that mandates a violation of GATT obligations can be found as such to be inconsistent with those obligations. We consider the application of this distinction to the present cases in section IV(B) below.

61. Thus, that a Contracting Party could challenge legislation as such before a panel was well-settled under the GATT 1947. We consider that the case law articulating and applying this practice forms part of the GATT *acquis* which, under Article XVI:1 of the *WTO Agreement,* provides guidance to the WTO and, therefore, to panels and the Appellate Body. Furthermore, in Article 3.1 of the DSU, Members affirm "their adherence to the principles for the management of disputes heretofore applied under Articles XXII and XXIII of GATT 1947". We note that, since the entry into force of the *WTO Agreement*, a number of panels have dealt with dispute settlement claims brought against a Member on the basis of its legislation as such, independently from the application of that legislation in specific instances.[35]

---

[32] WT/DS/136/2, 12 November 1998; WT/DS162/3, 4 June 1999; and WT/DS162/3/Corr.1, 10 February 2000.

[33] We note, however, that, as discussed in our Report in *Guatemala - Cement*, the *Anti-Dumping Agreement* does not incorporate by reference Articles XXII and XXIII of the GATT 1994: Appellate Body Report, *supra,* footnote 14, para. 64 and footnote 43.

[34] See, for example, Panel Report, *United States - Taxes on Petroleum and Certain Imported Substances* (*"United States - Superfund"*), adopted 17 June 1987, BISD 34S/136; Panel Report, *United States - Section 337 of the Tariff Act of 1930*, adopted 7 November 1989, BISD 36S/345; Panel Report, *Thailand - Restrictions on Importation of and Internal Taxes on Cigarettes* ("*Thailand - Cigarettes*"), adopted 7 November 1990, BISD 37S/200; Panel Report, *United States - Measures Affecting Alcoholic and Malt Beverages* ("*United States - Malt Beverages*"), adopted 19 June 1992, BISD 39S/206; and Panel Report, *United States - Tobacco, supra*, footnote 16. See also Panel Report, *United States - Wine and Grape Products*, *supra*, footnote 18, examining this issue in the context of a claim brought under the Tokyo Round *Agreement on Interpretation and Application of Articles VI, XVI and XXIII of the General Agreement of Tariffs and Trade.*

[35] See, for example, Panel Report, *Japan - Taxes on Alcoholic Beverages*, WT/DS8/R, WT/DS10/R, WT/DS11/R, adopted 1 November 1996, as modified by the Appellate Body Report, WT/DS8/AB/R, WT/DS10/AB/R, WT/DS11/AB/R, DSR 1996:I, 125; Panel Report, *Canada - Cer-*

62. Turning to the issue of the legal basis for claims brought under the *Anti-Dumping Agreement*, we note that Article 17 of the *Anti-Dumping Agreement* addresses dispute settlement under that Agreement. Just as Articles XXII and XXIII of the GATT 1994 create a legal basis for claims in disputes relating to provisions of the GATT 1994, so also Article 17 establishes the basis for dispute settlement claims relating to provisions of the *Anti-Dumping Agreement*. In the same way that Article XXIII of the GATT 1994 allows a WTO Member to challenge *legislation* as such, Article 17 of the *Anti-Dumping Agreement* is properly to be regarded as allowing a challenge to legislation as such, unless this possibility is excluded. No such *express* exclusion is found in Article 17 or elsewhere in the *Anti-Dumping Agreement*.

63. In considering whether Article 17 contains an *implicit* restriction on challenges to anti-dumping legislation as such, we first note that Article 17.1 states:

> Except as otherwise provided herein, the Dispute Settlement Understanding is applicable to consultations and the settlement of disputes under this Agreement.

64. Article 17.1 refers, without qualification, to "the settlement of disputes" under the *Anti-Dumping Agreement*. Article 17.1 does not distinguish between disputes relating to anti-dumping legislation as such and disputes relating to anti-dumping measures taken in the implementation of such legislation. Article 17.1 therefore implies that Members can challenge the consistency of legislation as such with the *Anti-Dumping Agreement* unless this action is excluded by Article 17.

65. Similarly, Article 17.2 of the *Anti-Dumping Agreement* does not distinguish between disputes relating to anti-dumping legislation as such and disputes relating to anti-dumping measures taken in the implementation of such legislation. On the contrary, it refers to consultations with respect to "any matter affecting the operation of this Agreement".

66. Article 17.3 of the *Anti-Dumping Agreement* states, in wording that mirrors Article XXIII of the GATT 1994:

> If any Member considers that any benefit accruing to it, directly or indirectly, under this Agreement is being nullified or impaired, or that the achievement of any objective is being impeded, by another Member or Members, it may, with a view to reaching a mutually satisfactory resolution of the matter, request in writing consultations with the Member or Members in question. …

---

tain Measures Concerning Periodicals, WT/DS31/R, adopted 30 July 1997, as modified by the Appellate Body Report, WT/DS31/AB/R, DSR 1997:I, 481; Panel Report, *European Communities - Hormones*, WT/DS26/R, WT/DS48/R, adopted 13 February 1998, as modified by the Appellate Body Report, *supra*, footnote 24; Panel Report, *Korea - Taxes on Alcoholic Beverages*, WT/DS75/R, WT/DS84/R, adopted 17 February 1999, as modified by the Appellate Body Report, WT/DS75/AB/R, WT/DS84/AB/R, DSR 1999:I, 44; Panel Report, *Chile - Taxes on Alcoholic Beverages*, WT/DS87/R, WT/DS110/R, adopted 12 January 2000, as modified by the Appellate Body Report, WT/DS87/AB/R, WT/DS110/AB/R, DSR 2000:I, 303; Panel Report, *United States - FSC*, WT/DS108/R, adopted 20 March 2000, as modified by the Appellate Body Report, DSR 200:IV, 1677; and Panel Report, *United States - Section 110(5) of the US Copyright Act*, WT/DS160/R, adopted 27 July 2000.

67. In our Report in *Guatemala - Cement*, we described Article 17.3 as:

> ... the equivalent provision in the *Anti-Dumping Agreement* to Articles XXII and XXIII of the GATT 1994, which serve as the basis for consultations and dispute settlement under the GATT 1994 ...[36]

68. Article 17.3 does not explicitly address challenges to legislation as such. As we have seen above, Articles XXII and XXIII allow challenges to be brought under the GATT 1994 against legislation as such. Since Article 17.3 is the "equivalent provision" to Articles XXII and XXIII of the GATT 1994, Article 17.3 provides further support for our view that challenges may be brought under the *Anti-Dumping Agreement* against legislation as such, unless such challenges are otherwise excluded.

69. As indicated above, the United States bases its objection to the Panel's jurisdiction on Article 17.4 of the *Anti-Dumping Agreement* and our Report in *Guatemala - Cement*.

70. Article 17.4 of the *Anti-Dumping Agreement* provides:

> If the Member that requested consultations considers that the consultations pursuant to paragraph 3 have failed to achieve a mutually agreed solution, and if *final action* has been taken by the administering authorities of the importing Member to levy *definitive anti-dumping duties* or *to accept price undertakings*, it may refer the matter to the Dispute Settlement Body ("DSB"). When *a provisional measure has a significant impact* and the Member that requested consultations considers that the measure was taken contrary to the provisions of paragraph 1 of Article 7, that Member may also refer *such matter* to the DSB. (emphasis added)

We note that, unlike Articles 17.1 to 17.3, Article 17.4 is a special or additional dispute settlement rule listed in Appendix 2 to the DSU.

71. In *Guatemala - Cement*, Mexico had challenged Guatemala's *initiation* of anti-dumping proceedings, and its *conduct* of the investigation, without identifying any of the measures listed in Article 17.4. We stated that:

> ... Three types of anti-dumping measure are specified in Article 17.4: definitive anti-dumping duties, the acceptance of price undertakings, and provisional measures. According to Article 17.4, a "matter" may be referred to the DSB *only if* one of the relevant three anti-dumping measures is in place. This provision, when read together with Article 6.2 of the DSU, requires a panel request in a dispute brought under the *Anti-Dumping Agreement* to identify, as the specific measure at issue, either a definitive anti-dumping duty, the acceptance of a price undertaking, or a provisional measure. ... (original emphasis)

[36] Appellate Body Report, *Guatemala - Cement*, *supra*, footnote 14, para. 64.

> ... We find that in disputes under the *Anti-Dumping Agreement relating to the initiation and conduct of anti-dumping investigations*, a definitive anti-dumping duty, the acceptance of a price undertaking or a provisional measure must be identified as part of the matter referred to the DSB pursuant to the provisions of Article 17.4 of the *Anti-Dumping Agreement* and Article 6.2 of the DSU.[37] (emphasis added)

72. Nothing in our Report in *Guatemala - Cement* suggests that Article 17.4 precludes review of anti-dumping legislation as such. Rather, in that case, we simply found that, for Mexico to challenge Guatemala's initiation and conduct of the anti-dumping investigation, Mexico was required to identify one of the three anti-dumping measures listed in Article 17.4 in its request for establishment of a panel. Since it did not do so, the panel in that case did not have jurisdiction.

73. Important considerations underlie the restriction contained in Article 17.4. In the context of dispute settlement proceedings regarding an anti-dumping investigation, there is tension between, on the one hand, a complaining Member's right to seek redress when illegal action affects its economic operators and, on the other hand, the risk that a responding Member may be harassed or its resources squandered if dispute settlement proceedings could be initiated against it in respect of each step, however small, taken in the course of an anti-dumping investigation, even before any concrete measure had been adopted.[38] In our view, by limiting the availability of dispute settlement proceedings related to an anti-dumping investigation to cases in which a Member's request for establishment of a panel identifies a definitive anti-dumping duty, a price undertaking or a provisional measure[39], Article 17.4 strikes a balance between these competing considerations.

74. Therefore, Article 17.4 sets out certain conditions that must exist before a Member can challenge action taken by a national investigating authority in the context of an anti-dumping investigation. However, Article 17.4 does not address or affect a Member's right to bring a claim of inconsistency with the *Anti-Dumping Agreement* against anti-dumping legislation as such.

75. Moreover, as we have seen above, the GATT and WTO case law firmly establishes that dispute settlement proceedings may be brought based on the alleged inconsistency of a Member's legislation as such with that Member's obligations. We find nothing, and the United States has identified nothing, inherent in the nature of anti-dumping legislation that would rationally distinguish such legislation from other types of legislation for purposes of dispute settlement, or that would remove anti-dumping legislation from the ambit of the generally-accepted practice that a panel may examine legislation as such.

---

[37] *Guatemala - Cement, supra,* footnote 14, paras. 79 - 80.

[38] An unrestricted right to have recourse to dispute settlement during an anti-dumping investigation would allow a multiplicity of dispute settlement proceedings arising out of the same investigation, leading to repeated disruption of that investigation.

[39] Once one of the three types of measure listed in Article 17.4 is identified in the request for establishment of a panel, a Member may challenge the consistency of any preceding action taken by an investigating authority in the course of an anti-dumping investigation.

76. Our reading of Article 17 as allowing Members to bring claims against anti-dumping legislation as such is supported by Article 18.4 of the *Anti-Dumping Agreement.*

77. Article 18.4 of the *Anti-Dumping Agreement* states:

> Each Member shall take all necessary steps, of a general or particular character, to ensure, not later than the date of entry into force of the WTO Agreement for it, the conformity of its laws, regulations and administrative procedures with the provisions of this Agreement as they may apply for the Member in question.

78. Article 18.4 imposes an affirmative obligation on each Member to bring its legislation into conformity with the provisions of the *Anti-Dumping Agreement* not later than the date of entry into force of the *WTO Agreement* for that Member. Nothing in Article 18.4 or elsewhere in the *Anti-Dumping Agreement* excludes the obligation set out in Article 18.4 from the scope of matters that may be submitted to dispute settlement.

79. If a Member could not bring a claim of inconsistency under the *Anti-Dumping Agreement* against legislation as such until one of the three anti-dumping measures specified in Article 17.4 had been adopted and was also challenged, then examination of the consistency with Article 18.4 of anti-dumping legislation as such would be deferred, and the effectiveness of Article 18.4 would be diminished.

80. Furthermore, we note that Article 18.1 of the *Anti-Dumping Agreement* states:

> No specific action against dumping of exports from another Member can be taken except in accordance with the provisions of GATT 1994, as interpreted by this Agreement.

81. Article 18.1 contains a prohibition on "specific action against dumping" when such action is not taken in accordance with the provisions of the GATT 1994, as interpreted by the *Anti-Dumping Agreement.* Specific action against dumping could take a wide variety of forms. If specific action against dumping is taken in a form other than a form authorized under Article VI of the GATT 1994, as interpreted by the *Anti-Dumping Agreement*, such action will violate Article 18.1.[40] We find nothing, however, in Article 18.1 or elsewhere in the *Anti-Dumping Agreement,* to suggest that the consistency of such action with Article 18.1 may only be challenged when one of the three measures specified in Article 17.4 has been adopted. Indeed, such an interpretation must be wrong since it implies that, if a Member's legislation provides for a response to dumping that does *not* consist of one of the three measures listed in Article 17.4, then it would be impossible to test the consistency of that legislation, and of particular responses thereunder, with Article 18.1 of the *Anti-Dumping Agreement.*

82. Therefore, we consider that Articles 18.1 and 18.4 support our conclusion that a Member may challenge the consistency of legislation as such with the provisions of the *Anti-Dumping Agreement.*

83. For all these reasons, we conclude that, pursuant to Article XXIII of the GATT 1994 and Article 17 of the *Anti-Dumping Agreement*, the European Commu-

---

[40] See *infra*, paras. 122-126.

nities and Japan could bring dispute settlement claims of inconsistency with Article VI of the GATT 1994 and the *Anti-Dumping Agreement* against the 1916 Act as such. We, therefore, uphold the Panel's finding that it had jurisdiction to review these claims.

B. Mandatory and Discretionary Legislation

84. In the proceedings before the Panel, the United States invoked the distinction between mandatory and discretionary legislation[41] to make two types of argument:

> ... the 1916 Act is non-mandatory legislation within the meaning of the GATT/WTO practice essentially because (i) with respect to both civil and criminal proceedings, US courts have interpreted in the past and/or could in the future interpret the 1916 Act in a manner consistent with the WTO obligations of the United States and (ii) the US Department of Justice has discretion to initiate or not criminal proceedings under the 1916 Act.[42]

85. With respect to the first of these arguments, the Panel concluded:

> The question whether the 1916 Act could be or has been interpreted in a way that would make it fall outside the scope of Article VI is ... simply a question of assessing the current meaning of the law.[43]

86. As regards the second argument made by the United States, the Panel found:

> ... the discretion enjoyed by the US Department of Justice to initiate a case under the 1916 Act should not be interpreted as making the 1916 Act a non-mandatory law.[44]

87. On appeal, the United States asks us to reverse the Panel's interpretation and application of the distinction between mandatory and discretionary legislation.

88. As indicated above, the concept of mandatory as distinguished from discretionary legislation was developed by a number of GATT panels as a threshold consideration in determining when legislation as such - rather than a specific application of that legislation - was inconsistent with a Contracting Party's GATT 1947 obligations.[45] The practice of GATT panels was summed up in *United States - Tobacco*[46] as follows:

---

[41] While the Panel used the phrase "non-mandatory legislation" to describe legislation that does not mandate a violation of a relevant obligation, we prefer the phrase "discretionary legislation".

[42] EC Panel Report, *supra*, footnote 1, para. 6.82. See also Japan Panel Report, *supra*, footnote 2, para. 6.95.

[43] EC Panel Report, *supra*, footnote 1, para. 6.84. See also Japan Panel Report, *supra*, footnote 2, para. 6.97.

[44] EC Panel Report, *supra*, footnote 1, para. 6.169. See also Japan Panel Report, *supra*, footnote 2, para. 6.191.

[45] The reason it must be possible to find legislation as such to be inconsistent with a Contracting Party's GATT 1947 obligations was explained as follows:

> [the provisions of the GATT 1947] are not only to protect current trade but also to create the predictability needed to plan future trade. That objective could not be attained if contracting parties could not challenge existing legislation mandating

> ... panels had consistently ruled that legislation which mandated action inconsistent with the General Agreement could be challenged as such, whereas legislation which merely gave the discretion to the *executive authority* of a contracting party to act inconsistently with the General Agreement could not be challenged as such; only the actual application of such legislation inconsistent with the General Agreement could be subject to challenge.[47] (emphasis added)

89. Thus, the relevant discretion, for purposes of distinguishing between mandatory and discretionary legislation, is a discretion vested in the *executive branch* of government.

90. The 1916 Act provides for two types of actions to be brought in a United States federal court: a civil action initiated by private parties, and a criminal action initiated by the United States Department of Justice. Turning first to the civil action, we note that there is no relevant discretion accorded to the executive branch of the United States' government with respect to such action.[48] These civil actions are brought by private parties. A judge faced with such proceedings must simply *apply* the 1916 Act. In consequence, so far as the civil actions that may be brought under the 1916 Act are concerned, the 1916 Act is clearly mandatory legislation as that term has been understood for purposes of the distinction between mandatory and discretionary legislation.

91. The Panel, however, examined that part of the 1916 Act that provides for criminal prosecutions, and found that the discretion enjoyed by the United States Department of Justice to initiate or not to initiate criminal proceedings does not mean that the 1916 Act is a discretionary law.[49] In light of the case law developing and applying the distinction between mandatory and discretionary legislation[50], we believe that the discretion enjoyed by the United States Department of Justice is not discretion of such a nature or of such breadth as to transform the 1916 Act into discretionary legislation, as this term has been understood for purposes of distinguishing

---

> actions at variance with the General Agreement until the administrative acts implementing it had actually been applied to their trade.

Panel Report, *United States - Superfund, supra*, footnote 34, para. 5.2.2.

[46] Panel Report, *supra*, footnote 16.

[47] *Ibid.*, para. 118, referring in footnote to: Panel Report, *United States - Superfund, supra*, footnote 34, p. 160; Panel Report, *EEC - Parts and Components, supra*, footnote 20, pp. 198-199; Panel Report, *Thailand - Cigarettes, supra*, footnote 34, pp. 227-228; Panel Report, *United States - Malt Beverages, supra*, footnote 34, pp. 281-282 and 289-290; Panel Report, *United States - Denial of Most-Favoured Nation Treatment as to Non-Rubber Footwear from Brazil*, adopted 19 June 1992, BISD 39S/128, p. 152.

[48] The Panel noted that the United States did not allege that any discretion of the executive branch of government in relation to the civil proceedings would make the 1916 Act discretionary. EC Panel Report, footnote 350 to para. 6.82; Japan Panel Report, footnote 482 to para. 6.95.

[49] EC Panel Report, *supra*, footnote 1, para. 6.169; Japan Panel Report, *supra*, footnote 2, para. 6.191.

[50] See, in particular the reasoning in the Panel Report, *United States - Malt Beverages, supra*, footnote 34, para. 5.60.

between mandatory and discretionary legislation. We, therefore, agree with the Panel's finding on this point.

92. In any event, we note that, on appeal, the United States does not directly challenge the Panel's finding that the discretion to enforce the 1916 Act enjoyed by the United States Department of Justice does not mean that the 1916 Act is discretionary legislation, but instead takes issue with several aspects of the reasoning employed by the Panel in reaching this conclusion. First, according to the United States, the Panel erred by "creating" a rule that the mandatory/discretionary distinction can apply only if the challenged legislation has never been "applied". In response to our inquiries at the oral hearing, the United States identified the following statement by the Panel as "creating" such a rule:

> The question whether there could be a possibility to interpret the 1916 Act in the future so that it would fall outside the scope of Article VI would be relevant, according to the *United States - Tobacco* case, only if the 1916 Act had not yet been applied.[51]

93. Review of the context in which the above passage appears in the Panel Reports reveals that the Panel did not, as the United States argues, find that the distinction between mandatory and discretionary legislation is only relevant if the challenged legislation has never been applied. Rather, in response to the United States' argument that the circumstances of the present cases resemble those in *United States - Tobacco*, the Panel noted that these cases are factually different from *United States - Tobacco*, where no implementing measures had been adopted and the law had never been applied, and reasoned that "[t]hese differences have implications for the burden of proof."[52] We see no *finding* by the Panel that the distinction between mandatory and discretionary legislation is relevant only if the challenged legislation has never been applied.

94. The United States also takes issue with the Panel's identification and application of the burden of proof, in particular the Panel's statement that:

> ... the United States, as the party having raised this *defence*, failed to supply convincing evidence that the 1916 Act should be considered as "non-mandatory legislation" within the meaning of GATT 1947/WTO practice.[53] (emphasis added)

95. According to the United States, the Panel erred in characterizing the distinction between discretionary and mandatory legislation as a "defence" which the United States bore the burden of proving.

96. In our Reports in *United States - Measure Affecting Imports of Woven Wool Shirts and Blouses from India*[54] and *European Communities - Hormones*[55], we

[51] EC Panel Report, *supra*, footnote 1, para. 6.89; Japan Panel Report, *supra*, footnote 2, para. 6.103.

[52] EC Panel Report, *supra*, footnote 1, paras. 6.86 - 6.87; Japan Panel Report, *supra*, footnote 2, paras. 6.100 - 6.101.

[53] Japan Panel Report, *supra*, footnote 2, para. 6.192. See also EC Panel Report, *supra*, footnote 1, para. 6.170.

[54] Appellate Body Report, *United States - Measure Affecting Imports of Woven Wool Shirts and Blouses from India,'* WT/DS33/AB/R, adopted 23 May 1997, DSR 1997:I, 323, at 333-336.

found that a complaining Member bears the burden of bringing forth sufficient evidence and legal argument to demonstrate that, *prima facie*, another Member's measure is inconsistent with a relevant obligation of that other Member under the covered agreements. Once the complaining Member has done so, the burden shifts to the defending Member to introduce evidence and legal argument sufficient to rebut the *prima facie* case.

97. Our examination of the Panel Reports shows that the Panel correctly articulated [56] and applied[57] the burden of proof in the cases before it. The Panel, in its analysis, found that the European Communities and Japan had satisfied their respective burdens of proof by establishing a *prima facie* case that the 1916 Act is, on its face, inconsistent with Article VI of the GATT 1994 and the *Anti-Dumping Agreement.* Having so found, the Panel went on to examine the arguments and evidence presented by the United States to rebut this *prima facie* case. One such argument made by the United States was that the 1916 Act is discretionary legislation. The Panel found that the United States did not supply persuasive evidence in support of this argument. We are satisfied that, in these cases, the Panel correctly identified and applied the burden of proof.

98. The United States further claims that, in the Japan Panel Report, the Panel wrongly concluded, based on the reasoning of the panel in the unadopted *European Communities - Audio Cassettes* panel report, that:

> ... to the extent that Article 18.4 requires the conformity of the 1916 Act with the Anti-Dumping Agreement as of the date of entry into force of the WTO Agreement for the United States, *the notion of mandatory/non-mandatory legislation is no longer relevant* in determining whether the Panel can or cannot review the conformity of the 1916 Act with the Anti-Dumping Agreement.[58] (emphasis added)

99. We note that answering the question of the continuing relevance of the distinction between mandatory and discretionary legislation for claims brought under the *Anti-Dumping Agreement* would have no impact upon the outcome of these appeals, because the 1916 Act is clearly not discretionary legislation, as that term has been understood for purposes of distinguishing between mandatory and discretionary legislation. Therefore, we do not find it necessary to consider, in these cases, whether Article 18.4, or any other provision of the *Anti-Dumping Agreement*, has supplanted or modified the distinction between mandatory and discretionary legislation. [59] For

[55] Appellate Body Report, *European Communities - Hormones' supra*, footnote 24, para. 109.

[56] EC Panel Report, *supra*, footnote 1, paras. 6.37 - 6.38; Japan Panel Report, *supra*, footnote 2, paras. 6.24 - 6.25.

[57] EC Panel Report, *supra*, footnote 1, paras. 6.86 - 6.90; Japan Panel Report, *supra*, footnote 2, paras. 6.100 - 6.104.

[58] Japan Panel Report, *supra*, footnote 2, para. 6.189.

[59] We note that in a recent case, a panel found that even discretionary legislation may violate certain WTO obligations. See Panel Report, *United States - Section 301*, *supra*, footnote 23, paras. 7.53 - 7.54.

the same reasons, the Panel did not, in the Japan Panel Report, need to opine on this issue.[60]

100. Lastly, we note that, before the Panel and before us, the United States invoked the distinction between mandatory and discretionary legislation to argue that the 1916 Act cannot be mandatory legislation because United States' courts have interpreted or may interpret the 1916 Act in ways that would make it consistent with the WTO obligations of the United States. As we have seen, in the case law developed under the GATT 1947, the distinction between mandatory and discretionary legislation turns on whether there is relevant discretion vested in the *executive branch* of government. The United States, however, does not rely upon the discretion of the executive branch of the United States' government, but on the interpretation of the 1916 Act by the United States' courts. In our view, this argument does not relate to the distinction between mandatory and discretionary legislation.

101. On this point, we agree with the Panel that the question whether the 1916 Act could be or has been interpreted by the United States' courts in a way that would make it fall outside the scope of Article VI of the GATT 1994 is a matter of determining the meaning of the law in order to examine its consistency with the United States' obligations.[61] We review, to the extent that it is relevant in these appeals, the Panel's assessment of the meaning and consistency of the 1916 Act in the following sections of this Report.

102. As a result of the above reasoning, we uphold, to the extent that we have found it necessary to consider the issue, the Panel's interpretation and application of the distinction between mandatory and discretionary legislation.

V. APPLICABILITY OF ARTICLE VI OF THE GATT 1994 AND THE *ANTI-DUMPING AGREEMENT* TO THE 1916 ACT

103. The Panel found that Article VI of the GATT 1994 and the *Anti-Dumping Agreement* apply to the 1916 Act. With respect to the applicability of Article VI to the 1916 Act, the Panel concluded:

> Having interpreted Article VI of the GATT 1994 in accordance with the Vienna Convention, we have reached the conclusion that the rules and disciplines of that article apply to laws that address "dumping" as defined in Article VI:1. Having examined the text of the 1916 Act, we have found that the transnational price discrimination test incorporated in that law falls within the definition of "dumping" of Article VI:1 of the GATT 1994. ...[62]

The Panel further concluded that:

---

[60] We note that, in the EC Panel Report, the Panel reached the same results as in the Japan Panel Report without making any finding that the notion of mandatory/discretionary legislation "is no longer relevant".

[61] EC Panel Report, *supra*, footnote 1, para. 6.84; Japan Panel Report, *supra*, footnote 2, para. 6.97.

[62] EC Panel Report, *supra*, footnote 1, para. 6.163; Japan Panel Report, *supra*, footnote 2, para. 6.182.

> ... the applicability of Article VI to the 1916 Act also implies the applicability of the Anti-Dumping Agreement to the 1916 Act.[63]

104. The United States appeals these findings. According to the United States, Article VI of the GATT 1994 applies to a law of a Member only when two criteria are satisfied: first, the law must impose anti-dumping duties and, second, it must "specifically target" dumping within the meaning of Article VI:1. The United States emphasizes that the 1916 Act does not impose anti-dumping duties - it provides for imprisonment, the imposition of fines or an award of treble damages. Moreover, the United States argues that the 1916 Act does not "specifically target" dumping, but rather predatory pricing. The United States, therefore, maintains that Article VI and, by implication, the *Anti-Dumping Agreement*, do not apply to the 1916 Act.

105. Article VI of the GATT 1994 concerns "dumping". "Dumping" is defined in Article VI:1 of the GATT 1994 and further elaborated in Article 2 of the *Anti-Dumping Agreement*. The first sentence of Article VI:1 defines "dumping" as conduct:

> ... by which products of one country are introduced into the commerce of another country at less than the normal value of the products ...

106. The second and third sentences of Article VI:1 state:

> For the purposes of this Article, a product is to be considered as being introduced into the commerce of an importing country at less than its normal value, if the price of the product exported from one country to another
>
> (*a*) is less than the comparable price, in the ordinary course of trade, for the like product when destined for consumption in the exporting country, or,
>
> (*b*) in the absence of such domestic price, is less than either
>
> (i) the highest comparable price for the like product for export to any third country in the ordinary course of trade, or
>
> (ii) the cost of production of the product in the country of origin plus a reasonable addition for selling cost and profit.
>
> Due allowance shall be made in each case for differences in conditions and terms of sale, for differences in taxation, and for other differences affecting price comparability.

Article 2 of the *Anti-Dumping Agreement* further elaborates the definition of "dumping" in Article VI:1 by setting out detailed rules for the determination of dumping.

---

[63] Japan Panel Report, *supra*, footnote 2, para. 6.184. See also EC Panel Report, *supra*, footnote 1, para. 6.165.

107. We note that, under Article VI:1 of the GATT 1994 and Article 2 of the *Anti-Dumping Agreement*, neither the intent of the persons engaging in "dumping" nor the injurious effects that "dumping" may have on a Member's domestic industry are constituent elements of "dumping".

108. With regard to "dumping", Article VI of the GATT 1994 states, in relevant part:

> 1. The Members recognize that dumping ... is to be condemned if it causes or threatens material injury to an established industry in the territory of a Member or materially retards the establishment of a domestic industry. ...
>
> 2. In order to offset or prevent dumping, a Member may levy on any dumped product an anti-dumping duty not greater in amount than the margin of dumping in respect of such product. ...

109. Whether Article VI of the GATT 1994 is applicable to the 1916 Act depends, first of all, on whether Article VI regulates all possible measures Members can take in response to dumping. If Article VI regulates *only* the imposition of anti-dumping duties and neither prohibits nor regulates other measures which Members may take to counteract dumping, then, since the 1916 Act does not provide for anti-dumping duties, Article VI would not apply to the 1916 Act.

110. Article VI:1 of the GATT 1994 makes clear that dumping is "to be *condemned* if it causes or threatens material injury". (emphasis added) However, Article VI:1 does not address the remedies that Members may take against dumping.

111. Remedies are addressed in Article VI:2 of the GATT 1994. The only type of measure that Article VI:2 explicitly authorizes Members to impose "in order to offset or prevent dumping" is an anti-dumping duty. However, Article VI:2 does not specify that Members may impose *only* anti-dumping duties in order to offset or prevent dumping.

112. In arguing that Article VI of the GATT 1994 regulates only the imposition of anti-dumping duties and does not apply to other measures taken to counteract dumping, the United States emphasizes that Article VI:2 states that Members "*may* levy on any dumped product an anti-dumping duty ...". (emphasis added). For the United States, the verb "may" indicates that while Members "may" choose to impose anti-dumping duties and thereby be bound by the rules of Article VI, Members may also choose to impose other types of anti-dumping measures, in which case they are not bound by the rules of Article VI.

113. We agree with the first part of the United States' argument, namely, that the verb "may" indicates that it is permissive, rather than mandatory, to impose anti-dumping duties. However, it is not obvious to us, based on the wording of Article VI:2 alone, that the verb "may" also implies that a Member is permitted to impose a measure other than an anti-dumping duty.

114. We believe that the meaning of the word "may" in Article VI:2 is clarified by Article 9 of the *Anti-Dumping Agreement* on the "Imposition and Collection of Anti-Dumping Duties". Article VI of the GATT 1994 and the *Anti-Dumping Agreement* are part of the same treaty, the *WTO Agreement*. As its full title indicates, the *Anti-Dumping Agreement* is an "Agreement on Implementation of Article VI of the Gen-

eral Agreement on Tariffs and Trade 1994". Accordingly, Article VI must be read in conjunction with the provisions of the *Anti-Dumping Agreement*, including Article 9.

115. Article 9 of the *Anti-Dumping Agreement* states in relevant part:

> It is desirable that the imposition [of an anti-dumping duty] be permissive in the territory of all Members, and that the duty be less than the margin if such lesser duty would be adequate to remove the injury to the domestic industry.

116. In light of this provision, the verb "may" in Article VI:2 of the GATT 1994 is, in our opinion, properly understood as giving Members a choice between imposing an anti-dumping duty *or not*, as well as a choice between imposing an anti-dumping duty equal to the dumping margin or imposing a lower duty. We find no support in Article VI:2, read in conjunction with Article 9 of the *Anti-Dumping Agreement*, for the United States' argument that the verb "may" indicates that Members, to counteract dumping, are permitted to take measures other than the imposition of anti-dumping duties.

117. As a result of the above reasoning, it appears to us that the text of Article VI is inconclusive as to whether Article VI regulates all possible measures which Members may take to counteract dumping, or whether it regulates only the imposition of anti-dumping duties.

118. As we have stated, Article VI of the GATT 1994 must be read together with the provisions of the *Anti-Dumping Agreement*. Article 1 of that Agreement provides:

> An anti-dumping measure shall be applied only under the circumstances provided for in Article VI of GATT 1994 and pursuant to investigations initiated and conducted in accordance with the provisions of this Agreement. The following provisions govern the application of Article VI of GATT 1994 in so far as action is taken under anti-dumping legislation or regulations.

119. The first sentence of Article 1 states that "an anti-dumping measure" must be consistent with Article VI of the GATT 1994 and the provisions of the *Anti-Dumping Agreement*. However, as the United States concedes, the meaning of an "anti-dumping measure" in this sentence is "not immediately clear".[64] The United States argues, on the basis of the history of this provision, that the phrase "anti-dumping measure" refers *only* to definitive anti-dumping duties, price undertakings and provisional measures. However, the ordinary meaning of the phrase "an anti-dumping measure" seems to encompass all measures taken against dumping. We do not see in the words "an anti-dumping measure" any explicit limitation to particular types of measure.[65]

---

[64] United States' appellant's submission, para. 85.

[65] We consider that the second sentence of Article 1 merely indicates that the *Anti-Dumping Agreement* implements only those provisions of Article VI of the GATT 1994 that concern dumping, as distinguished from the provisions of Article VI of the GATT 1994 that concern countervailing duties imposed to offset subsidies.

120. Since "an anti-dumping measure" must, according to Article 1 of the *Anti-Dumping Agreement*, be consistent with Article VI of the GATT 1994 and the provisions of the *Anti-Dumping Agreement*, it seems to follow that Article VI would apply to "an anti-dumping measure", i.e., a measure against dumping.

121. We consider that the scope of application of Article VI is clarified, in particular, by Article 18.1 of the *Anti-Dumping Agreement*. Article 18.1 states:

> No *specific action against dumping* of exports from another Member can be taken except in accordance with the provisions of GATT 1994, as interpreted by this Agreement. (emphasis added)

122. In our view, the ordinary meaning of the phrase "specific action against dumping" of exports within the meaning of Article 18.1 is action that is taken in response to situations presenting the constituent elements of "dumping". "Specific action against dumping" of exports must, at a minimum, encompass action that may be taken *only* when the constituent elements of "dumping" are present.[66] Since intent is not a constituent element of "dumping", the *intent* with which action against dumping is taken is not relevant to the determination of whether such action is "specific action against dumping" of exports within the meaning of Article 18.1 of the *Anti-Dumping Agreement.*

123. Footnote 24 to Article 18.1 of the *Anti-Dumping Agreement* states:

> This is not intended to preclude action under other relevant provisions of GATT 1994, as appropriate.

We note that footnote 24 refers generally to "action" and not, as does Article 18.1, to "specific action against dumping" of exports. "Action" within the meaning of footnote 24 is to be distinguished from "specific action against dumping" of exports, which is governed by Article 18.1 itself.

124. Article 18.1 of the *Anti-Dumping Agreement* contains a prohibition on the taking of any "specific action against dumping" of exports when such specific action is not "in accordance with the provisions of GATT 1994, as interpreted by this Agreement". Since the only provisions of the GATT 1994 "interpreted" by the *Anti-Dumping Agreement* are those provisions of Article VI concerning dumping, Article 18.1 should be read as requiring that any "specific action against dumping" of exports from another Member be in accordance with the relevant provisions of *Article VI* of the GATT 1994, as interpreted by the *Anti-Dumping Agreement.*

125. We recall that footnote 24 to Article 18.1 refers to "*other* relevant provisions of GATT 1994" (emphasis added). These terms can only refer to provisions other than the provisions of Article VI concerning dumping. Footnote 24 thus confirms that the "provisions of GATT 1994" referred to in Article 18.1 are in fact the provisions of Article VI of the GATT 1994 concerning dumping.

126. We have found that Article 18.1 of the *Anti-Dumping Agreement* requires that any "specific action against dumping" be in accordance with the provisions of Article VI of the GATT 1994 concerning dumping, as those provisions are interpreted by the *Anti-Dumping Agreement*. It follows that Article VI is applicable to any "specific

[66] We do not find it necessary, in the present cases, to decide whether the concept of "specific action against dumping" may be broader.

action against dumping" of exports, i.e., action that is taken in response to situations presenting the constituent elements of "dumping".

127. We now turn to the question whether the 1916 Act provides for "specific action against dumping" of exports from another Member and, thus, falls within the scope of application of Article VI of the GATT 1994.

128. As mentioned above, the United States contends that the 1916 Act does not fall within the scope of application of Article VI of the GATT 1994 because it does not "specifically target" dumping. According to the United States, the activity targeted by the 1916 Act is "predatory pricing; that is, sales at predatorily low price levels with the intent to destroy, injure, or prevent the establishment of an American industry, or to restrain trade in or monopolize a particular market." [67] Although one element of liability under the 1916 Act is the existence of price differences between national markets, this element is, according to the United States, "simply one indicia of whether the U.S. importers pricing practices are predatory in nature." [68]

129. The 1916 Act states in relevant part:

> It shall be unlawful for any person importing or assisting in importing any articles from any foreign country into the United States, commonly and systematically to import, sell or cause to be imported or sold such articles within the United States at a price substantially less than the actual market value or wholesale price of such articles, at the time of exportation to the United States, in the principal markets of the country of their production, or of other foreign countries to which they are commonly exported after adding to such market value or wholesale price, freight, duty, and other charges and expenses necessarily incident to the importation and sale thereof in the United States: *Provided*, That such act or acts be done with the intent of destroying or injuring an industry in the United States, or of preventing the establishment of an industry in the United States, or of restraining or monopolizing any part of trade and commerce in such articles in the United States.
>
> Any person who violates or combines or conspires with any other person to violate this section is guilty of a misdemeanour, and, on conviction thereof, shall be punished by a fine not exceeding $5,000, or imprisonment not exceeding one year, or both, in the discretion of the court.
>
> Any person injured in his business or property by reason of any violation of, or combination or conspiracy to violate, this section, may sue therefor in the district court of the United States for the district in which the defendant resides or is found or has an agent, without respect to the amount in con-

67 United States' appellant's submission, para. 133.

68 *Ibid.*

> troversy, and shall recover threefold the damages sustained, and the cost of the suit, including a reasonable attorney's fee.[69]

130. On the basis of the wording of the 1916 Act, it is clear that the 1916 Act provides for civil and criminal proceedings and penalties when persons import products from another country into the territory of the United States, and sell or offer such products for sale at a price less than the price for which the like products are sold or offered for sale in the country of export or, in certain cases, a third country market. In other words, in the light of the definition of "dumping" set out in Article VI:1 of the GATT 1994, as elaborated in Article 2 of the *Anti-Dumping Agreement*, the civil and criminal proceedings and penalties contemplated by the 1916 Act require the presence of the constituent elements of "dumping". The constituent elements of "dumping" are built into the essential elements of civil and criminal liability under the 1916 Act. The wording of the 1916 Act also makes clear that these actions can be taken *only* with respect to conduct which presents the constituent elements of "dumping". It follows that the civil and criminal proceedings and penalties provided for in the 1916 Act are "specific action against dumping". We find, therefore, that Article VI of the GATT 1994 applies to the 1916 Act.

131. We note that the United States places much emphasis on the "intent" requirement of the 1916 Act, i.e., the stipulation that dumping is "unlawful" when it is:

> ... done with the intent of destroying or injuring an industry in the United States, or of preventing the establishment of an industry in the United States, or of restraining or monopolizing any part of trade and commerce in such Articles in the United States.[70]

132. This requirement of intent to destroy, injure, or prevent the establishment of an American industry, or to restrain or monopolize any part of trade, does not affect the applicability of Article VI of the GATT 1994 to the 1916 Act. As already noted, action may be taken under the 1916 Act only when the constituent elements of dumping are present. The fact that an importer can only be found to have violated the 1916 Act when the sales of dumped products in the United States were carried out with a certain intent does not mean that the actions under the 1916 Act are not "specific action against dumping". Proof of a requisite intent under the 1916 Act only constitutes an additional requirement for the imposition of the civil and criminal penalties set out in that Act. Even if the 1916 Act allowed the imposition of penalties *only* if the intent proven were an intent to monopolize or an intent to restrain trade (i.e., an "antitrust"-type intent), this would not transform the 1916 Act into a statute which does not provide for "specific action against dumping", and, thus, would not remove the 1916 Act from the scope of application of Article VI.

133. For all these reasons, we agree with the Panel's conclusion that Article VI of the GATT 1994 applies to the 1916 Act. We also agree with the Panel that, having regard to the relationship between Article VI and the *Anti-Dumping Agreement*, "the

---

[69] *Supra*, footnote 4.

[70] *Supra*, footnote 4.

applicability of Article VI to the 1916 Act also implies the applicability of the Anti-Dumping Agreement" to the 1916 Act.[71]

VI. ARTICLES VI:1 AND VI:2 OF THE GATT 1994, CERTAIN PROVISIONS OF THE *ANTI-DUMPING AGREEMENT* AND ARTICLE XVI:4 OF THE *WTO AGREEMENT*

134. With regard to the EC Panel Report, the United States argues that the Panel erred in finding that the 1916 Act was inconsistent with Articles VI:1 and VI:2 of the GATT 1994, Articles 1, 4 and 5.5 of the *Anti-Dumping Agreement* and Article XVI:4 of the *WTO Agreement*. With regard to the Japan Panel Report, the United States argues that the Panel erred in finding that the 1916 Act was inconsistent with Articles VI:1 and VI:2 of the GATT 1994, Articles 1, 4.1, 5.1, 5.2, 5.4, 18.1 and 18.4 of the *Anti-Dumping Agreement* and Article XVI:4 of the *WTO Agreement*.

135. With the exception of the finding of inconsistency with Article VI:2 of the GATT 1994, the United States appeals these findings of inconsistency on the sole basis that the 1916 Act does not fall within the scope of application of Article VI and the *Anti-Dumping Agreement* and that the Panel, therefore, erred in making these findings of inconsistency. These findings of inconsistency, thus, stand or fall along with the Panel's findings regarding the scope of application of Article VI of the GATT 1994 and the *Anti-Dumping Agreement*. Since we have upheld the Panel's conclusion that the 1916 Act falls within the scope of application of Article VI and the *Anti-Dumping Agreement*, we also uphold these findings of inconsistency of the Panel.

136. As regards the Panel's finding that the 1916 Act is inconsistent with Article VI:2 of the GATT 1994, the United States argues that Article VI:2 only regulates the imposition of anti-dumping duties, and that other measures to counteract dumping are not addressed by Article VI:2.

137. As we have concluded above, Article VI of the GATT 1994 and the *Anti-Dumping Agreement* apply to "specific action against dumping". Article VI, and, in particular, Article VI:2, read in conjunction with the *Anti-Dumping Agreement*, limit the permissible responses to dumping to definitive anti-dumping duties, provisional measures and price undertakings. Therefore, the 1916 Act is inconsistent with Article VI:2 and the *Anti-Dumping Agreement* to the extent that it provides for "specific action against dumping" in the form of civil and criminal proceedings and penalties.

---

[71] EC Panel Report, *supra*, footnote 1, para. 6.165. See also Japan Panel Report, *supra*, footnote 1, para. 6.184. We note that the Panel frequently referred to the concept of "transnational price discrimination". It should be stressed that "transnational price discrimination", i.e., a difference in price between two markets, is a broader concept than "dumping" as defined in Article VI:1 of the GATT 1994. Unlike transnational discrimination, "dumping" requires *importation*, and a lower price in the *import market* than in the export market or relevant third country market. Dumping is always transnational price discrimination, but transnational price discrimination is not always dumping. We are, therefore, of the opinion that the Panel's use of the term "transnational price discrimination" in its findings is problematic, and deserves specific mention.

138. With the caveat that Article VI:2 must be read together with the relevant provisions of the *Anti-Dumping Agreement*, we, therefore, agree with the conclusion of the Panel that:

> ... by providing for the imposition of fines or imprisonment or for the recovery of treble damages, the 1916 Act violates Article VI:2 of the GATT 1994.[72]

VII. THIRD PARTY RIGHTS

139. The European Communities and Japan contend that the Panel erred in refusing to grant "enhanced" third party rights to Japan in the case brought by the European Communities, and to the European Communities in the case brought by Japan.

140. The rules relating to the participation of third parties in panel proceedings are set out in Article 10 of the DSU, and, in particular, paragraphs 2 and 3 thereof, and in paragraph 6 of Appendix 3 to the DSU.

141. Article 10.2 of the DSU states:

> Any Member having a substantial interest in a matter before a panel and having notified its interest to the DSB (referred to in this Understanding as a "third party") shall have an opportunity to be heard by the panel and to make written submissions to the panel. These submissions shall also be given to the parties to the dispute and shall be reflected in the panel report.

142. Article 10.3 of the DSU states:

> Third parties shall receive the submissions of the parties to the dispute to the first meeting of the panel.

143. Paragraph 6 of Appendix 3 to the DSU provides:

> All third parties which have notified their interest in the dispute to the DSB shall be invited in writing to present their views during a session of the first substantive meeting of the panel set aside for that purpose. All such third parties may be present during the entirety of this session.

144. Although the European Communities and Japan invoke Article 9 of the DSU, and, in particular, Article 9.3, in support of their position, we note that Article 9 of the DSU, which concerns procedures for multiple complaints related to the same matter, does not address the issue of the rights of third parties in such procedures.

145. Under the DSU, as it currently stands, third parties are only entitled to the participatory rights provided for in Articles 10.2 and 10.3 and paragraph 6 of Appendix 3.

146. Article 12.1 of the DSU states:

> Panels shall follow the Working Procedures in Appendix 3 unless the panel decides otherwise after consulting the parties to the dispute.

---

[72] EC Panel Report, *supra*, footnote 1, para. 6.204; Japan Panel Report, *supra*, footnote 2, para. 6.230.

Pursuant to Article 12.1, a panel is required to follow the Working Procedures in Appendix 3, unless it decides otherwise after consulting the parties to the dispute.

147. In support of their argument that the Panel should have granted them "enhanced" third party rights, the European Communities and Japan refer to the considerations that led the panel in *European Communities - Hormones* to grant third parties "enhanced" participatory rights, and stress the similarity between *European Communities - Hormones* and the present cases.

148. The Panel in the present cases gave the following reasons for refusing to grant the European Communities and Japan "enhanced" participatory rights in the panel proceedings:

> ... We conclude from the reports in the *EC - Hormones* cases that enhanced third party rights were granted primarily because of the specific circumstances in those cases.
>
> We find that no similar circumstances exist in the present matter, which does *not* involve the *consideration of complex facts or scientific evidence*. Moreover, *none* of the parties *requested* that the panels *harmonise their timetables or hold concurrent deliberations* in the two procedures (WT/DS136 and WT/DS162). In fact, the European Communities was not in favour of delaying the proceedings in WT/DS136 and the United States objected to concurrent deliberations. ... (emphasis added)[73]

149. In our Report in *European Communities - Hormones*, we stated:

> Although Article 12.1 and Appendix 3 of the DSU do not specifically require the Panel to grant ... ["enhanced" third party rights] to the United States, we believe that this decision falls within the sound discretion and authority of the Panel, particularly if the Panel considers it necessary for ensuring to all parties due process of law.[74]

150. A panel's decision whether to grant "enhanced" participatory rights to third parties is thus a matter that falls within the discretionary authority of that panel. Such discretionary authority is, of course, not unlimited and is circumscribed, for example, by the requirements of due process. In the present cases, however, the European Communities and Japan have not shown that the Panel exceeded the limits of its discretionary authority. We, therefore, consider that there is no legal basis for concluding that the Panel erred in refusing to grant "enhanced" third party rights to Japan or the European Communities.

---

[73] EC Panel Report, *supra*, footnote 1, paras. 6.33 - 6.34. See also Japan Panel Report, *supra*, footnote 2, paras. 6.33 - 6.34.

[74] Appellate Body Report, *European Communities – Hormones*, *supra*, footnote 24, para. 154.

VIII. ARTICLES III:4 AND XI OF THE GATT 1994 AND ARTICLE XVI:4 OF THE *WTO AGREEMENT*

151. Before the Panel, the European Communities and Japan submitted that the 1916 Act is inconsistent with Article III:4 of the GATT 1994 and Article XVI:4 of the *WTO Agreement*. Japan also claimed that the 1916 Act is inconsistent with Article XI of the GATT 1994. The Panel found that:

> ... we are entitled to exercise judicial economy and decide not to review the claims of [the European Communities and] Japan under Article III:4 of the GATT 1994.[75]
>
> ...
>
> ... we are entitled to exercise judicial economy and decide not to review the claims of Japan under Article XI.[76]

152. With respect to the alleged violations of Article XVI:4 of the *WTO Agreement*, the Panel held, in the EC Panel Report:

> We therefore find that, by violating Articles VI:1 and VI:2 of the GATT 1994, the 1916 Act violates Article XVI:4 of the Agreement Establishing the WTO.[77]

In the Japan Panel Report the Panel found:

> ... that by violating provisions of Article VI of the GATT 1994, the United States violates Article XVI:4 of the WTO Agreement.[78]

153. In their joint other appellant's submission, the European Communities and Japan ask us to rule that the 1916 Act is inconsistent with United States' obligations under Articles III:4 and XI of the GATT 1994 and Article XVI:4 of the *WTO Agreement*. With respect to Articles III:4 and XI of the GATT 1994, their requests are conditioned on our reversal of the Panel's findings that the 1916 Act falls within the scope of Article VI of the GATT 1994 and the *Anti-Dumping Agreement*. With respect to Article XVI:4 of the *WTO Agreement*, their requests are conditioned on our reversal of the Panel's findings with respect to jurisdiction and the distinction between mandatory and discretionary legislation. Since, however, the conditions on which these requests are predicated have not been fulfilled, there is no need for us to examine the conditional appeals of the European Communities and Japan.

154. For these reasons, we decline to rule on the conditional appeals of the European Communities and Japan relating to Articles III:4 and XI of the GATT 1994 and Article XVI:4 of the *WTO Agreement*.

IX. FINDINGS AND CONCLUSIONS

155. For the reasons set out in this Report, the Appellate Body:

---

75 Japan Panel Report, *supra*, footnote 2, para. 6.272. See also EC Panel Report, *supra*, footnote 1, para. 6.220.

76 Japan Panel Report, *supra*, footnote 2, para. 6.281.

77 EC Panel Report, *supra*, footnote 1, para. 6.225.

78 Japan Panel Report, *supra*, footnote 2, para. 6.288.

(a) upholds the Panel's conclusion that it had jurisdiction to consider claims that the 1916 Act as such is inconsistent with United States' obligations under Article VI of the GATT 1994 and the *Anti-Dumping Agreement*;

(b) upholds, to the extent it found it necessary to consider the issue, the Panel's interpretation and application of the distinction between mandatory and discretionary legislation;

(c) upholds the Panel's findings that Article VI of the GATT 1994 and the *Anti-Dumping Agreement* apply to the 1916 Act;

(d) upholds the Panel's findings in the EC Panel Report that the 1916 Act is inconsistent with Articles VI:1 and VI:2 of the GATT 1994, Articles 1, 4 and 5.5 of the *Anti-Dumping Agreement* and Article XVI:4 of the *WTO Agreement*;

(e) upholds the Panel's findings in the Japan Panel Report that the 1916 Act is inconsistent with Articles VI:1 and VI:2 of the GATT 1994, Articles 1, 4.1, 5.1, 5.2, 5.4, 18.1 and 18.4 of the *Anti-Dumping Agreement* and Article XVI:4 of the *WTO Agreement*;

(f) upholds the Panel's refusal to grant "enhanced" third party rights to Japan in the case brought by the European Communities, and to the European Communities in the case brought by Japan; and

(g) declines to rule on the conditional appeals of the European Communities and Japan relating to Articles III:4 and XI of the GATT 1994 and Article XVI:4 of the *WTO Agreement*.

156. The Appellate Body *recommends* that the DSB request the United States to bring the 1916 Act into conformity with its obligations under Article VI of the GATT 1994 and the *Anti-Dumping Agreement*.

UNITED STATES - ANTI-DUMPING ACT OF 1916

Complaint by Japan

Report of the Panel

WT/DS162/R

Adopted by the Dispute Settlement Body
on 26 September 2000
as Upheld by the Appellate Body Report

TABLE OF CONTENTS

I. INTRODUCTION

1.1 On 10 February 1999, Japan requested consultations with the United States pursuant to Article 4 of the Understanding on Rules and Procedures Governing the Settlement of Disputes (hereinafter the "DSU"), Article XXII:1 of the General Agreement on Tariffs and Trade 1994 (hereinafter the "GATT 1994") and Article 17.2 of the Agreement on Implementation of Article VI of the General Agreement on Tariffs and Trade 1994 (hereinafter the "Anti-Dumping Agreement") regarding Title VIII of the US Revenue Act of 1916, also known as the US Anti-Dumping Act of 1916 (hereinafter the "1916 Act").[1]

1.2 Consultations were held on 17 March 1999, but did not lead to a mutually satisfactory resolution of the matter.

1.3 On 3 June 1999, Japan requested the Dispute Settlement Body (hereinafter the "DSB") to establish a panel pursuant to Article XXIII of the GATT 1994, Articles 4 and 6 of the DSU and Article 17 of the Anti-Dumping Agreement.[2] Japan claimed that the 1916 Act was inconsistent with Article III:4 of the GATT 1994; Article VI of the GATT 1994 and the Anti-Dumping Agreement, in particular Article VI:2 of the GATT 1994 and Article 18.1 of the Anti-Dumping Agreement as well as Articles 1, 2, 3, 4, 5, 9 and 11 of the Anti-Dumping Agreement; Article XI of the GATT 1994; and Article XVI:4 of the Marrakesh Agreement Establishing the World Trade Organization (hereinafter the "WTO Agreement") and Article 18.4 of the Anti-Dumping Agreement.

---

[1] See WT/DS162/1.

[2] See WT/DS162/3.

1.4 On 26 July 1999, the DSB established a panel pursuant to the request made by Japan, in accordance with Article 6 of the DSU. In document WT/DS162/4, the Secretariat reported that the parties had agreed that the panel would have the standard terms of reference. The terms of reference are the following:

> "To examine, in the light of the relevant provisions of the covered agreements cited by Japan in document WT/DS162/3, the matter referred to the DSB by Japan in that document and to make such findings as will assist the DSB in making the recommendations or in giving the rulings provided for in those agreements."

1.5 Document WT/DS162/4 also reported that, on 11 August 1999, the Panel was constituted as follows:

Chairman:	Mr. Johann Human
Members:	Mr. Dimitrij Grčar
	Professor Eugeniusz Piontek

1.6 The European Communities and India reserved their rights to participate in the Panel proceedings as third parties. Both of them presented arguments to the Panel.

1.7 The Panel met with the parties on 3 and 4 November 1999 as well as 8 and 9 December 1999. It met with third parties on 4 November 1999. The Panel issued its interim report to the parties on 28 February 1999. The Panel issued its final report to the parties on 31 March 2000.

II. FACTUAL ASPECTS

A. *Description of the 1916 Act*

2.1 The 1916 Act at issue in the present dispute was enacted by the US Congress under the heading of "Unfair Competition" in Title VIII of the Revenue Act of 1916.[3] It provides as follows:

> "It shall be unlawful for any person importing or assisting in importing any articles from any foreign country into the United States, commonly and systematically to import, sell or cause to be imported or sold such articles within the United States at a price substantially less than the actual market value or wholesale price of such articles, at the time of exportation to the United States, in the principal markets of the country of their production, or of other foreign countries to which they are commonly exported after adding to such market value or wholesale price, freight, duty, and other charges and expenses necessarily incident to the importation and sale thereof in the United States: *Provided*, That such act or acts be done with the intent of destroying or injuring an industry in the United States, or of preventing the establishment of an industry in the United States, or of restraining or monopolizing any part of trade and commerce in such articles in the United States.

[3] Act of 8 September 1916. The Revenue Act of 1916 can be found at 39 Stat. 756 (1916).

> Any person who violates or combines or conspires with any other person to violate this section is guilty of a misdemeanour, and, on conviction thereof, shall be punished by a fine not exceeding $5,000, or imprisonment not exceeding one year, or both, in the discretion of the court.
>
> Any person injured in his business or property by reason of any violation of, or combination or conspiracy to violate, this section, may sue therefor in the district court of the United States for the district in which the defendant resides or is found or has an agent, without respect to the amount in controversy, and shall recover threefold the damages sustained, and the cost of the suit, including a reasonable attorney's fee.
>
> The foregoing provisions shall not be construed to deprive the proper State courts of jurisdiction in actions for damages thereunder." [4]

2.2 Thus, the business activity which the 1916 Act prohibits is a form of international price discrimination, which has two basic components:

(a) An importer[5] must have sold a foreign-produced product[6] within the United States at a price which is "substantially less" than the price at which the same product is sold in the country of the foreign producer.

(b) The importer must have undertaken this price discrimination "commonly and systematically."

2.3 It is a condition for criminal or civil liability under the 1916 Act that the importer must have undertaken this price discrimination with "an intent of destroying or injuring an industry in the United States, or of preventing the establishment of an industry in the United States, or of restraining or monopolizing any part of trade and commerce in such articles in the United States."

2.4 Another characteristic of the 1916 Act is that it provides for a private right of action in a federal district court and the remedy of treble damages for a private complainant, based on the injury sustained by that complainant in its business or property, as well as for criminal penalties in an action brought by the US government.

2.5 The 1916 Act is codified in Title 15 of the United States Code, entitled "Commerce and Trade".[7]

B. Description of other Relevant US Acts

1. Antidumping Act of 1921 and Tariff Act of 1930

2.6 In 1921, the United States enacted the "Antidumping Act of 1921".[8] It empowered the Secretary of the Treasury to impose duties on dumped goods without regard to the dumper's intent. Whereas the Antidumping Act of 1921 was later re-

---

4 15 U.S.C. § 72.

5 The importer may be a domestic US company.

6 The 1916 Act does not apply to sales of domestic goods.

7 See 15 U.S.C. §§ 71-74.

8 The Antidumping Act of 1921 was codified at 19 U.S.C. §§ 160-71 (repealed).

pealed, it is on this Act that the United States' Tariff Act of 1930, as amended (hereinafter the "Tariff Act of 1930"), is built.[9] The Tariff Act of 1930 is implemented through proceedings governed by regulations promulgated by the US Department of Commerce and the US International Trade Commission[10].

2.7 The 1921 Antidumping Act was, and the 1930 Tariff Act, as amended, is, codified in Title 19 of the United States Code, entitled "Customs Duties".

2.8 The United States has notified Title VII of the Tariff Act of 1930, as amended, and its implementing regulations to the WTO Committee on Anti-Dumping Practices in accordance with Articles 18.4 and 18.5 of the Anti-Dumping Agreement.

2. *Robinson-Patman Act*

2.9 Section 2(a) of the Clayton Act, as amended by the Robinson-Patman Act in 1936, provides in pertinent part:

> "It shall be unlawful for any person engaged in commerce, in the course of such commerce, either directly or indirectly, to discriminate in price between different purchasers of commodities of like grade and quality, where either or any of the purchasers involved in such discrimination are in commerce, where such commodities are sold for use, consumption, or resale within the United States [...] and where the effect of such discrimination may be substantially to lessen competition or tend to create a monopoly in any line of commerce, or to injure, destroy, or prevent competition with any person who either grants or knowingly receives the benefit of such discrimination or with customers of either of them."[11]

2.10 Section 2(f) of the Clayton Act, as amended by the Robinson-Patman Act, applies the same principles to the conduct of a buyer, by making it unlawful for a buyer "knowingly to induce or receive discrimination in price" prohibited by other parts of the Act.[12]

2.11 A violation of either of these provisions is subject to criminal penalties and also is actionable in a private right of action, where treble damages and injunctive relief are available, and in administrative or federal court actions initiated by the Federal Trade Commission.

2.12 To establish price discrimination in an action under the Robinson-Patman Act, there first must be evidence of two actual sales at different prices, with each sale occurring in interstate commerce.[13] Thus, the Robinson-Patman Act does not apply to cross-border price discrimination.[14] In addition, a successful price discrimination

---

[9] The Tariff Act of 1930 is codified at 19 U.S.C. §§ 1671 et seq.

[10] See 19 C.F.R. Part 200.

[11] 15 U.S.C. 13(a).

[12] See 15 U.S.C. 13(f).

[13] See *International Telephone & Telegraph Corp. et al.*, 104 F.T.C. 280, 417, citing E. Kinter, *A Robinson-Patman Primer*, 3rd ed. (1979), p. 35.

[14] However, imported goods that have become a part of domestic commerce may be subject to the Robinson-Patman Act. Accordingly, the Robinson-Patman Act applies in a situation where a foreign

claim requires a showing of an anti-competitive effect. Case law has established that, if the claim is directed at so-called "primary line injury", meaning injury to the price discriminator's rivals, which corresponds to the situation addressed by the 1916 Act, the requisite anti-competitive effect can be demonstrated through a showing of (i) pricing below an appropriate measure of cost and (ii) the likelihood that the predator will recoup its losses in the future.[15] If the claim is directed at "secondary line injury", meaning injury to disfavoured buyers from the price discriminator, the requisite anti-competitive effect can be inferred, subject to rebuttal, from substantial price differences between competing purchasers over time.[16]

2.13 The Robinson-Patman Act is codified in Title 15 of the United States Code, entitled "Commerce and Trade".[17]

C. *Instances of Application of the 1916 Act*

2.14 The 1916 Act has been invoked infrequently. Accordingly, there is a limited number of judicial interpretations of its specific provisions.[18] In this regard, it should be noted that, under the US legal system, the judicial branch of the government is the

---

producer makes two sales of the same imported product within the United States at a different price, assuming that all other requirements under the Act are met.

[15] See *Brooke Group Ltd. v. Brown & Williamson Tobacco Corp.*, 509 U.S. 209, 222-23 (1993) (hereinafter "*Brooke Group*").

[16] See, e.g., *Falls City Industries v. Vanco Beverage, Inc.*, 460 U.S. 428, 436 (1983); *FTC v. Morton Salt*, 334 U.S. 37, 50-51 (1948); *Chroma Lighting v. GTE Products Corp.*, 111 F.3d 653, 657 (1997).

[17] Also located in Title 15 are the Sherman Act (15 U.S.C. §§ 1-7, to be found at 26 Stat. 209 (1890)), the Clayton Act (15 U.S.C. §§ 12-27, to be found at 38 Stat. 730 (1914)) and the Federal Trade Commission Act (15 U.S.C. §§ 41-58, to be found at 38 Stat. 717 (1914)).

[18] Most of those interpretations can be found in the following - final or interlocutory - court decisions referenced by the parties: *In re Japanese Electronic Products Antitrust Litigation*, 388 F.Supp. 565 (Judicial Panel on Multidistrict Litigation, 1975) (hereinafter "*In re Japanese Electronic Products I*"); *Zenith Radio Corp. v. Matsushita Electric Industrial Co., Ltd.*, 402 F.Supp. 244 (E.D. Pa. 1975) (hereinafter "*Zenith I*"); *Zenith Radio Corp. v. Matsushita Electric Industrial Co., Ltd.*, 402 F.Supp. 251 (E.D. Pa. 1975) (hereinafter "*Zenith II*"); *Outboard Marine Corp. v. Pezetel*, 461 F. Supp. 384 (D. Del. 1978); *Schwimmer v. Sony Corp. of America*, 471 F. Supp. 793 (E.D.N.Y. 1979); *Schwimmer v. Sony Corp. of America*, 637 F.2d 41 (2nd Cir. 1980); *Jewel Foliage Co. v. Uniflora Overseas Florida*, 497 F. Supp. 513 (M.D. Fla. 1980); *Zenith Radio Corp. v. Matsushita Electric Industrial Co., Ltd.*, 494 F.Supp. 1190 (E.D. Pa. 1980) (hereinafter "*Zenith III*"), affirmed in part and reversed in part, 723 F.2d 319 (3d Cir. 1983), reversed and remanded, 475 U.S. 574, 106 S. Ct. 1348 (1986), District Court decision affirmed on remand, 807 F. 2d 44 (3d Cir. 1986); *In re Japanese Electronic Products Antitrust Litigation (Zenith Radio Corp. v. Matsushita Electric Industrial Co., Ltd.)*, 723 F.2d 319 (3d Cir. 1983) (hereinafter "*In re Japanese Electronic Products II*"); *Western Concrete Structures Co. v. Mitsui & Co.*, 760 F.2d 1013 (9th Cir. 1985); *Isra Fruit Ltd. v. Agrexco Agr. Export Co.*, 631 F. Supp. 984 (S.D.N.Y. 1986); *In re Japanese Electronic Products Antitrust Litigation (Zenith Radio Corp. v. Matsushita Electric Industrial Co., Ltd.)*, 807 F.2d 44 (3d Cir. 1986) (hereinafter "*In re Japanese Electronic Products III*") *Helmac Products Corp. v. Roth (Plastics) Corp.*, 814 F. Supp. 560 (E.D. Mich. 1992) (hereinafter "*Helmac I*"); *Helmac Products Corp. v. Roth (Plastics) Corp.*, 814 F.Supp. 581 (E.D. Mich. 1993) (hereinafter "*Helmac II*"); *Geneva Steel Company v. Ranger Steel Supply Corp.*, 980 F.Supp. 1209 (D. Utah 1997) (hereinafter "*Geneva Steel*"); *Wheeling-Pittsburgh Steel Corporation v. Mitsui Co.*, 35 F.Supp.2d. 597 (S.D. Ohio 1999) (hereinafter "*Wheeling-Pittsburgh*").

final authority regarding the meaning of federal laws, such as statutes passed by the legislative branch, i.e. the US Congress. It should also be noted, however, that no claims under the 1916 Act have ever been reviewed by the US Supreme Court, which is the highest federal court in the United States.[19] All court decisions so far have been rendered by US circuit courts of appeals or US district courts.[20]

2.15 All of the court decisions addressing the meaning of the 1916 Act and its various provisions to date also have involved private civil complaints rather than criminal prosecutions. No complainant in a civil suit has yet recovered treble damages and the cost of the suit. However, in one recent civil case involving a 1916 Act claim, *Wheeling-Pittsburgh*, some defendants have elected to settle rather than proceed to trial.[21]

2.16 The US Department of Justice, the agency responsible for prosecuting criminal violations of the 1916 Act, has never successfully prosecuted a criminal case under the 1916 Act.[22] Accordingly, no criminal sanctions have ever been imposed pursuant to the 1916 Act.

III. CLAIMS AND MAIN ARGUMENTS

A. *Request by the European Communities for Enhanced Third Party Rights*

3.1 The **European Communities**, which is a third party in the present case and has requested the establishment of another panel in respect of the 1916 Act,[23] re-

---

[19] The only reported case in which the US Supreme Court has considered the 1916 Act was *United States v. Cooper Corp.*, 312 U.S. 600 (1941), although the issue in that case was whether the United States is a "person" within the meaning of Section 7 of the US Sherman Act entitled to sue for treble damages thereunder.

[20] In the United States, the judicial branch is established on three levels. Generally, the lowest level is the trial court level, consisting of the various US district courts. At least one district court can be found in each of the 50 States. The next level consists of the US circuit courts of appeals, which are intermediate appellate courts responsible for reviewing district court decisions. There are 12 federal court circuits. At the highest level of the federal court system is the US Supreme Court, which, at its discretion, hears appeals from decisions of the circuit courts.

[21] Up until the Panel's second substantive meeting with the parties, the case was still pending while the remaining litigants conducted discovery. Since the Panel's second substantive meeting with the parties there have, according to the United States, been further developments in the *Wheeling-Pittsburgh* case. According to the United States, the plaintiff in that case, Wheeling-Pittsburgh Steel Corporation, has voluntarily dismissed its claims against the remaining defendants at the trial court level so that all that remains is an appeal of an interlocutory opinion regarding injunctive relief currently pending before the US Court of Appeals for the Sixth Circuit.

[22] The United States notes that, to its knowledge, the US Department of Justice has never prosecuted a criminal case under the 1916 Act. In *Zenith III*, *Op. Cit.*, p. 1212, the following is stated regarding enforcement of the 1916 Act's criminal provisions until the early 1970s:

> "Apparently there have been four attempts to enforce the criminal provisions of the Act, but none of them has been successful and none has given rise to a reported judicial decision. Marks, *United States Antidumping Laws - A Government Overview* 43 Antitrust L.J. 580, 581 (1974)."

[23] See WT/DS162/3. That panel was established on 26 July 1999 and composed on 11 August 1999 (WT/DS162/4).

quests to be granted enhanced third party rights.[24] In particular, the European Communities requests to be present throughout both substantive meetings of the Panel and be able to make a submission on each occasion.

3.2 In response, **Japan** states that it accepts the European Communities' request that it be accorded enhanced third party rights. On the same basis, Japan requests that it in turn receive all the necessary documents, including submissions, and written versions of statements by the parties in the case initiated by the European Communities in respect of the 1916 Act (WT/DS136).

3.3 The **United States**, in reply to the a request by the Panel, notes that it strongly objects to expanded third party rights for the European Communities in the present case, since the circumstances of the case do not warrant it.

3.4 For the United States, expanded third party rights are not needed in order to obtain access to the parties' submissions. The United States supports full transparency in the WTO and will be making its submissions and oral statements available to the public. Furthermore, the United States recalls that it has requested in both panel proceedings dealing with the 1916 Act (WT/DS136 and WT/DS162) that each party provide a non-confidential summary of the information contained in each submission that could be disclosed to the public unless the party has made the submission public. The United States further recalls that the DSU provides that parties shall make such non-confidential versions available upon request. Accordingly, both the European Communities and Japan will have access to each others' submissions as soon as they comply with the requirements of the DSU in this regard.

3.5 The United States argues, moreover, that, as individual complaining parties, Japan and the European Communities have more than adequate opportunity to present their views and respond to the arguments of the United States. In *EC Measures Concerning Meat and Meat Products (Hormones)*[25], the panel allowed expanded third party rights because the panel had stated that it intended to conduct concurrent deliberations in those cases meaning that its deliberations were going to be based upon the arguments and presentations in both cases, including presentations by experts made jointly to both panels. The panel proceeded with this approach despite the fact that the United States had expressed its unequivocal concern with the panel's "concurrent deliberations" approach. Thus, because the panel was going to consider arguments made in one case in the course of deciding another case, the United States requested and was allowed enhanced third party rights. Otherwise, without an opportunity for the United States to respond, the panel would have been considering what would have been, in effect, *ex parte* submissions.

3.6 The United States notes that, in the present case, the Panel has not stated that it intends to conduct concurrent deliberations, and for the reasons expressed in the *European Communities - Hormones* proceeding, the United States would not support concurrent deliberations. Accordingly, the European Communities will not be denied

---

[24] As stated in the European Communities' letter to the Chairman of the Panel, dated 25 August 1999.

[25] Panel Report on *EC Measures Concerning Meat and Meat Products (Hormones)*, WT/DS26/R/USA, WT/DS48/R/CAN, adopted 13 February 1998, DSR 1998:III, 699 and DSR 1998:II, 235, respectively (hereinafter "Panel Report on *European Communities - Hormones*").

an opportunity to respond to arguments of the United States that will be considered by the Panel in making its decision in the case initiated by the European Communities. The same holds true for Japan in its case. The apparent purpose for the request for expanded third party rights is to provide the third parties with an opportunity to make an additional submission in their own panel process. There is no provision in the DSU for such additional submissions.

3.7 The position taken by the Panel in the course of the proceedings *vis-à-vis* the European Communities' request is reflected in section VI.B.1 of this report.

B. Overview of the Claims of the Parties and Findings Requested

3.8 **Japan** contests the maintenance and application of the 1916 Act by the United States. Specifically, the maintenance and enforcement of the 1916 Act violates the following US obligations under the WTO agreements:

(a) Article VI:2 of the GATT 1994 and Article 18.1 of the Anti-Dumping Agreement by allowing the application of penalties other than anti-dumping duties to remedy dumping;

(b) Article VI of the GATT 1994 and Article 1 of the Anti-Dumping Agreement by applying an anti-dumping measure without conducting the requisite investigation and establishing the requisite facts;

(c) Article VI of the GATT 1994 and Article 2 of the Anti-Dumping Agreement, *inter alia*, by specifying a comparison for normal value that is not compatible with the comparison set forth in those articles;

(d) Article VI of the GATT 1994 and Article 3 of the Anti-Dumping Agreement by providing for application of an anti-dumping measure without establishing material injury or threat thereof;

(e) Article VI of the GATT 1994 and Articles 4 and 5 of the Anti-Dumping Agreement, *inter alia*, by not limiting the parties that may pursue an anti-dumping claim;

(f) Article VI of the GATT 1994 and Article 9 of the Anti-Dumping Agreement by providing for the imposition of impermissible penalties outside the scope and directives of Article 9;

(g) Article VI of the GATT 1994 and Article 11 of the Anti-Dumping Agreement by not limiting the duration of an anti-dumping measure and not providing for periodic reviews of the need for its continued imposition;

(h) Articles 1 and 18.1 of the Anti-Dumping Agreement by failing to comply with Article VI of the GATT 1994 and Articles 2, 3, 4, 5, 9 and 11 of the Anti-Dumping Agreement;

(i) Article III:4 of the GATT 1994 by providing less favourable treatment to imports via the 1916 Act versus domestic goods, which are subject to the far less restrictive, nearly moribund, Robinson-Patman Act;

(j) Article XI of the GATT 1994 by providing for, via the 1916 Act, the improper application of an impermissible prohibition or restriction; and

(k) Article XVI:4 of the WTO Agreement and Article 18.4 of the Anti-Dumping Agreement by failing to conform its laws to WTO provisions.

3.9 For these reasons, Japan requests that the Panel find that the 1916 Act is neither consistent with nor justified by Articles III:4, VI and XI of the GATT 1994, the provisions of the Anti-Dumping Agreement and the WTO Agreement[26], and to recommend that the United States bring 1916 Act into conformity with these provisions. Japan further requests that the Panel recommend that the United States repeal the 1916 Act in order to bring the Act into conformity with US obligations under these provisions.

3.10 The **United States** requests that the Panel rule that Japan has failed to show that Article VI:2 of the GATT 1994 and Article 18.1 of the Anti-Dumping Agreement mandate that anti-dumping duties are the exclusive remedy for dumping.[27] If the Panel rejects this claim, Japan's entire challenge under Article VI and the various provisions of the Anti-Dumping Agreement would fail and the Panel would not need to reach the question of whether Article VI and the Anti-Dumping Agreement govern the 1916 Act.

3.11 According to the United States, if the Panel reaches the question of whether the 1916 Act is subject to Article VI:2 and the Anti-Dumping Agreement, it should conclude that Japan, as the complaining party, has failed to show that the 1916 Act is not susceptible to an interpretation that would permit action consistent with US WTO obligations. In contrast, the United States has demonstrated that the 1916 Act is clearly susceptible to an interpretation that would parallel domestic competition law and, in fact, has been so interpreted to date. As a competition law, the 1916 Act is not subject to Article VI:2 of the GATT 1994 or the Anti-Dumping Agreement.

3.12 The United States also requests that the Panel rule that the 1916 Act is consistent with Article III:4 because interpreting the 1916 Act to parallel domestic competition law does not raise any national treatment concerns as parallel treatment obviously does not constitute less favourable treatment. The United States reiterates that the Panel's decision in this regard should be informed by the fact that the 1916 Act establishes a standard for relief which has *never* been met in the case of importers and imported goods.

3.13 The United States requests, furthermore, that the Panel rule that the 1916 Act is consistent with Article XI of the GATT 1994 because, in light of the fact that the only relief available under the 1916 Act is monetary in nature, the Act does not fall within the purview of the prohibition on quantitative restrictions as set out in Article XI of the GATT 1994.

---

[26] Japan notes that, even if the 1916 Act were not an anti-dumping law (which it is), the United States still would be in violation of Articles III:4 and XI of the GATT 1994 and Article XVI:4 of the WTO Agreement.

[27] The United States recalls that Japan, as the complainant in the present dispute, has the burden of establishing a violation of a provision of the WTO Agreement. The United States refers to the Appellate Body Report on *United States - Measure Affecting Imports of Woven Wool Shirts and Blouses from India*, WT/DS33/AB/R, adopted 23 May 1997, DSR 1997:I, 323, at 335 (hereinafter Appellate Body Report on "*United States - Shirts and Blouses*").

3.14 The United States asserts, finally, that because the 1916 Act is susceptible to an interpretation that is fully consistent with all US WTO obligations and, in fact, has been so interpreted to date, there is no requirement under Article XVI:4 of the WTO Agreement that the United States take action to change the law.

C. *Trade Effects of the 1916 Act and their Relevance to the Present Case*

3.15 **Japan** asserts that the 1916 Act has a substantial negative impact on Japan-US trade. One is the "chilling effect" on exports from Japan. Even if the *Wheeling-Pittsburgh* case does not result in criminal or civil penalties, the potential threat and liability under the 1916 Act discourages defendants (in the present case Japanese trading firms) from importing products once litigation begins. Litigation of this kind is protracted and costly. Also, apart from fines and attorneys' costs, the potential of treble damage[28] or criminal sanctions is very threatening. The risk an importer bears if it continues to import is tremendous and prohibitive. Thus, the greatest impact on trade of the 1916 Act, and litigation under it, is not necessarily the risk of a negative judicial judgement, but the significant deterrent of *potential* legal action and the possibility of very substantial civil and/or criminal liability.

3.16 Japan argues that, to completely avoid the potential for paying treble damages, defendants are likely to cease any activity that possibly could be construed as violating the law. Because the amount of treble damages a defendant faces in a 1916 Act claim depends on the amount of sales it makes, an importer named in litigation under the 1916 Act that continues to import goods increases its potential liability. Given the punitive nature of the remedy in the 1916 Act, Japanese companies naturally have decreased shipments of steel into the United States.[29]

3.17 Japan contends that the chilling effect of the 1916 Act is magnified by the exceedingly lax pleading and proof requirements of the Act, which prevent the Japanese steel companies from assessing if they are engaged in an activity prohibited under the law. Rather than estimate the threshold price that triggers liability (and face treble damages if they are incorrect), the companies chose to significantly decrease or stop their imports.

[28] Japan notes that the theory behind providing for treble damages in any law is to make the penalty for violating the law so severe that people will refrain from any activity that *potentially* could violate the law. As the US Supreme Court has acknowledged, "[t]he very idea of treble damages reveals an intent to punish past, and to deter future unlawful conduct, not to ameliorate the liability of wrongdoers." Japan refers to *Texas Indus. v. Radcliff Materials*, 451 U.S. 630, 639 (1981).

[29] Japan states that, according to data provided by the companies, the total volume (in thousand MT) of exports from Japan to the United States of the three Japanese defendants declined as follows:

April to September 1998:	149/month (average)
October 1998:	154
November 1998 (petition filed):	39
December 1998:	0.4
January 1999:	0.7
February 1999:	0.0

3.18 Japan recalls, second, that the three defendant Japanese trading firms[30] have found the litigation process to be extraordinarily expensive, burdensome and otherwise disruptive to their businesses. Indeed, the effect of this burden is so substantial that six non-Japanese defendants in this litigation conceded to out-of-court settlements with Wheeling-Pittsburgh. Although the precise terms of the settlements are not publicly available, it is known that the defendants settled with the plaintiff, Wheeling-Pittsburgh, by agreeing, among other things, to:

- buy a certain amount of steel from the plaintiff during 1999; and
- restrict their imports of foreign steel.[31]

3.19 In the view of Japan, these settlements demonstrate the third type of negative impact of the 1916 Act. The Act is being used by US companies to extort settlements from foreign companies. The settlements disrupt free trade and further undermine the world trading order. If left unchecked, the practice will compromise the WTO regime.

3.20 Japan argues, in addition, that litigation under the 1916 Act is likely to multiply. This is because individual US companies can initiate cases (without the majority support of the remaining industry or evidence of dumping and material injury, as required under the WTO and the other US anti-dumping law) and because US companies have seen how easily Wheeling-Pittsburgh and Geneva Steel were able to burden and extract settlements from their foreign competitors.

3.21 Japan considers that, for these reasons, the lack of a determination of liability by the courts at the present moment is beside the point. Injury has accrued and is continuing and the mere existence of the 1916 Act does great damage to Japan's legitimate trading interests.

3.22 The **United States** considers that Japan's allegations that the 1916 Act is having a "negative impact on Japanese companies" are unsubstantiated. These allegations should be disregarded by the Panel as they are without proof and, in any event, are not relevant to the legal questions before the Panel. First, Japan has presented no evidence that the 1916 Act is the actual cause of the decrease in steel exports from Japan to the United States. In fact, a dumping petition involving Japanese steel was filed with the Department of Commerce in September 1998 with the Commerce Department making a preliminary finding of critical circumstances in November 1998. This meant that if the injury finding were confirmed by the International Trade Commission (which it was), the imports would be subject to anti-dumping duties from November 1998. Thus, the decline in steel imports is more likely attributable to this injury finding than the 1916 Act case. Furthermore, there are many

---

[30] Japan notes that, on 20 November 1998, Wheeling-Pittsburgh Steel Corporation, a US company, filed a complaint under the 1916 Act against nine companies, including three Japanese trading firms, Mitsui & Co., Marubeni America Corp., and Itochu International Inc. Japan is a major steel-producing country, and, in 1998, the US steel market was the largest export market for Japanese steel. The Japan Iron and Steel Exporters Association and other exporters' associations requested the Japanese government to take appropriate action. They are concerned not only with the Act's inconsistency with relevant WTO provisions, but also about the negative impact on trade in steel products, including "hot-rolled steel", and the possibility that the 1916 Act will remain a substantial barrier to Japan's steel exports to the United States.

[31] Japan refers to Wheeling-Pittsburgh Steel Corporation press releases.

factors that go into the business decision of how much to export to another country. Japan simply has not shown that the 1916 Act was the factor that caused the Japanese trading firms to decrease their imports into the United States.

3.23 The United States notes, second, that even if it is assumed for the sake of argument that the allegations are credible, they are not material to the Panel's determination in the present case. Even if the 1916 Act were affecting trade between Japan and the United States, that is not relevant to whether the 1916 Act is inconsistent with the WTO obligations raised by Japan in its panel request. Whether or not there are any trade effects would only be relevant in the event that Japan was in the position of seeking compensation for failure of the United States to implement an adverse panel finding. Outside of that context, the trade effects are not relevant in the present case.

D. The Distinction Between Discretionary and Mandatory Legislation and its Relevance to the Present Case

3.24 The **United States** argues that if the complaining party is challenging a statute, *as such*, as Japan is doing in the present case, the first question for the Panel is whether the statute is mandatory or discretionary. It is well established under GATT 1947 and WTO jurisprudence that only legislation which mandates WTO-inconsistent action can itself be WTO-inconsistent. In this regard, the panel in *Canada - Measures Affecting the Export of Civilian Aircraft* recently stated:

> "We recall the distinction that GATT/WTO panels have consistently drawn between discretionary legislation and mandatory legislation. For example, in *United States - Tobacco*, the panel "recalled that panels had consistently ruled that legislation which mandated action inconsistent with the General Agreement could be challenged as such, whereas legislation which merely gave the discretion to the executive authority [...] to act inconsistently with the General Agreement could not be challenged as such; only the actual application of such legislation inconsistent with the General Agreement could be subject to challenge"[citation omitted]."[32]

3.25 According to the United States, this settled distinction between mandatory and discretionary legislation was the basis for the panel's decision in *EEC - Regulation on Imports of Parts and Components.*[33] In that case, the panel found that "the mere existence" of the anti-circumvention provision of the European Communities' anti-dumping legislation was not inconsistent with the European Communities' GATT 1947 obligations, even though the European Communities had taken GATT-

---

[32] Panel Report on *Canada - Measures Affecting the Export of Civilian Aircraft,* WT/DS70/R, adopted 20 August 1999, DSR 1999:IV,1443, para. 9.124 (hereinafter "Panel Report on *Canada - Aircraft*"), citing the Panel Report on *United States - Measures Affecting the Importation, Internal Sale and Use of Tobacco*, adopted on 4 October 1994, BISD 41S/131, para. 118 (hereinafter "*United States - Tobacco*").

[33] Panel Report on *EEC - Regulation on Imports of Parts and Components*, adopted on 16 May 1990, BISD 37S/132 (hereinafter "*EEC - Parts and Components*").

inconsistent measures under that provision.[34] The panel based its finding on its conclusion that the anti-circumvention provision "does not mandate the imposition of duties or other measures by the EEC Commission and Council; it merely authorizes the Commission and the Council to take certain actions."[35]

3.26 The United States notes that, in applying the discretionary-mandatory distinction, panels have even found that legislation explicitly directing action inconsistent with GATT 1947 principles does not mandate inconsistent action so long as it provides the possibility for authorities to avoid such action. For example, in *United States - Taxes on Petroleum and Certain Imported Substances.*[36] The Superfund Act required importers to supply sufficient information regarding the chemical inputs of taxable substances to enable the tax authorities to determine the amount of tax to be imposed; otherwise, a penalty tax would be imposed in the amount of five percent *ad valorem* or a different rate to be prescribed in regulations by the Secretary of the Treasury by a different methodology. The regulations in question had not yet been issued. Nevertheless, the panel concluded:

> "[W]hether [the regulations] will eliminate the need to impose the penalty tax and whether they will establish complete equivalence between domestic and imported products, as required by Article III:2, first sentence, remain open questions. From the perspective of the overall objectives of the General Agreement it is regrettable that the Superfund Act explicitly directs the United States tax authorities to impose a tax inconsistent with the national treatment principle but, since the Superfund Act also gives them the possibility to avoid the need to impose that tax by issuing regulations, the existence of the penalty rate provisions as such does not constitute a violation of the United States obligations under the General Agreement."[37]

3.27 The United States points out that, similarly, in *Thailand - Restrictions on Importation of and Internal Taxes on Cigarettes*[38] the panel examined Thailand's Tobacco Act, which established a higher ceiling tax rate for imported cigarettes than for domestic cigarettes. While the Act explicitly gave Thai officials the authority to implement discriminatory tax rates, this did not render the statute mandatory. The panel concluded that "the possibility that the Tobacco Act might be applied contrary to Article III:2 was, by itself, not sufficient to make it inconsistent with the General Agreement."[39]

3.28 The United States recalls, finally, that in *United States - Tobacco*, a case of which the facts more closely resemble those in the present dispute, the panel found

---

[34] *Ibid.*, paras. 5.9, 5.21, 5.25-5.26.

[35] *Ibid.*, para. 5.25.

[36] Panel Report on *United States - Taxes on Petroleum and Certain Imported Substances*, adopted on 17 June 1987, BISD 34S/136 (hereinafter "*United States - Superfund*").

[37] *Ibid.*, para. 5.2.9.

[38] Panel Report on *Thailand - Restrictions on Importation of and Internal Taxes on Cigarettes*, adopted on 7 November 1990, BISD 37S/200 (hereinafter "*Thailand - Cigarettes*").

[39] *Ibid.*, para. 86. The United States further notes that the panel found, at para. 88, that the actual implementation of the tax rates through regulations was also consistent with Thailand's obligations, since these rates were non-discriminatory.

that a law did not mandate GATT-inconsistent action where the language of that law was susceptible of a range of meanings, including ones permitting GATT-consistent action. The panel examined the question of whether a statute requiring that "comparable" inspection fees be assessed for imported and domestic tobacco mandated that these fees had to be identical for each, without respect to differences in inspection costs. If so, the statute would be inconsistent with Article VIII:1(a) of the GATT 1947, which prohibits the imposition of fees in excess of services rendered.[40] The United States argued that the term "comparable" need not be interpreted to mean "identical", and that the law did not preclude a fee structure commensurate with the cost of services rendered.[41] The panel agreed with the United States:

> "[T]he Panel noted that there was no clear interpretation on the meaning of the term "comparable" as used in the 1993 legislative amendment. It appeared to the Panel that the term "comparable", including the ordinary meaning thereof, was susceptible of a range of meanings. The Panel considered that this range of meanings could encompass the interpretation advanced by the United States in this proceeding, an interpretation which could potentially enable USDA to comply with the obligation of Article VIII:1(a) not to impose fees in excess of the cost of services rendered, while at the same time meeting the comparability requirement of [the U.S. law]."[42]

3.29 The Panel therefore found that the complaining party had "not demonstrated that [the US law] *could not* be applied in a manner ensuring that fees charged for inspecting tobacco were not in excess of the cost of services rendered."[43]

3.30 The United States submits that the distinction in GATT 1947/WTO jurisprudence between discretionary and mandatory legislation is not based upon a particular provision of any WTO agreement or upon which branch of government enforces the law, nor is it limited in its application to a particular WTO provision. In the cases discussed above, for example, this distinction was applied in both the Article III and Article VIII context. This distinction is a general principle developed by panels that most likely has its origin in the presumption against conflicts between national and international law. It is both general international practice and that of the United States that statutory language is to be interpreted so as to avoid conflicts with international obligations. There is thus a presumption against a conflict between international and national law. In general,

> "[a]lthough national courts must apply national laws even if they conflict with international law, there is a presumption against the existence of such a conflict. As international law is based upon the common consent of the different states, it is improbable that a state would intentionally enact a rule conflicting with international law. A rule of national law which ostensibly seems to conflict with international law

---

40 *Ibid.*, para. 118.

41 *Ibid.*, para. 122.

42 *Ibid.*, para. 123.

43 *Ibid.* (emphasis added by the United States)

must, therefore, if possible always be so interpreted as to avoid such conflict."[44]

3.31 The United States further argues that, under US law, it is an elementary principle of statutory construction that "an act of Congress ought never to be construed to violate the law of nations if any other possible construction remains."[45] While international obligations cannot override inconsistent requirements of domestic law, "ambiguous statutory provisions [...] [should] be construed, where possible, to be consistent with international obligations of the United States."[46] Thus, GATT 1947 jurisprudence distinguishing between mandatory and discretionary legislation does no more than apply the general principle that there is a presumption against conflicts between national and international law. If a law is susceptible to an interpretation that is WTO-consistent, there is a presumption that domestic authorities will interpret that law so as to avoid a conflict with WTO obligations. This presumption may be seen as underlying the *United States - Tobacco* panel's finding that a domestic law susceptible of multiple interpretations would not violate a party's international obligations so long as one possible interpretation permits action consistent with those obligations.[47]

3.32 In the view of the United States, this principle applies with equal force in the instant case. In the present dispute, Japan is not challenging a specific application of the 1916 Act. Rather, it is challenging the mere existence of the 1916 Act. Thus, for that challenge to succeed, Japan must demonstrate not only that the 1916 Act authorizes WTO-inconsistent action, but that it mandates such action. In other words, it must show that this legislation is *not* susceptible to an interpretation that would permit the US government to comply with its WTO obligations.

3.33 The United States asserts that Japan has failed to meet that burden. The 1916 Act is clearly susceptible to an interpretation that is WTO-consistent and, in fact, all final judicial decisions that have considered the 1916 Act have interpreted it as such.[48] Indeed, US courts have repeatedly admonished that the 1916 Act "should be interpreted whenever possible to *parallel the unfair competition law applicable to domestic commerce*."[49] Interpreting the 1916 Act to parallel domestic unfair competition law is clearly consistent with WTO obligations - particularly, Article VI of the GATT 1994 and the Anti-Dumping Agreement - because the WTO does not govern

---

[44] *Oppenheim's International Law*, 9th ed., pp. 81-82 (footnote omitted).

[45] *Murray v. Schooner Charming Betsy*, 6 U.S. (2 Cranch) 64, 118 (1804) (hereinafter "*Charming Betsy*").

[46] *Footwear Distributors and Retailers of America v. United States*, 852 F. Supp. 1078, 1088 (CIT), appeal dismissed, 43 F.3d 1486 (Table) (Fed. Cir. 1994), citing *DeBartolo Corp. v. Florida Gulf Coast Building and Trades Council*, 485 U.S. 568 (1988). The United States also refers to the Restatement (Third) of the Foreign Relations of the United States, s. 114 (1987).

[47] The United States refers to *United States - Tobacco*, Op.Cit., para. 123.

[48] In response to a question of Japan, the United States notes that in making this argument it is not implicitly admitting that the 1916 Act is capable of being interpreted in a manner that is WTO-inconsistent.

[49] 494 F. Supp. at 1223 (emphasis added by the United States).

competition laws.[50] In addition, a law regarding imports that "parallels" a domestic law would not raise any national treatment concerns under Article III of the GATT 1994.

3.34 The United States points out that the elements of the 1916 Act and the relevant case law, which demonstrate the anti-trust nature and purpose of the Act are discussed more fully below. The point here is that the statute is susceptible to an interpretation that is consistent with WTO obligations. Again, because Japan has challenged the 1916 Act *as such* and not any specific application of the Act, Japan must demonstrate that there is no interpretation of the 1916 Act that would be WTO-consistent. This has not been the case. Not only have the US courts interpreted the 1916 Act consistently as an anti-trust statute whose elements are not the same as the "dumping" and "injury" elements of the Anti-Dumping Agreement, but also any susceptibility that particular elements of a 1916 Act claim may have to a range of possible meanings is ultimately of no consequence because the 1916 Act remains different from an anti-dumping statute under the entire range of conceivable interpretations.

3.35 **Japan** considers that, contrary to what the United States may assert, the 1916 Act is "mandatory" in the sense that the term is used in the WTO. If a court finds that a plaintiff has established the elements of the offence (the dumping element and the injury element[51]), the court "shall" impose penalties under the Act. It must impose sanctions. This is required by the text of the Act, and is not contested by the United States.

3.36 Japan notes that the fact that a US court has stated that the 1916 Act has anti-trust as well as anti-dumping elements is inapposite. The 1916 Act applies to conduct commonly understood to be dumping and it mandates that a court finding a violation impose penalties specified in the 1916 Act. The court has no discretion; once it has found the defendant guilty, it must impose penalties.

3.37 Japan recalls the recent statement by the panel in *Canada - Measures Affecting the Export of Canadian Aircraft* that in contrast to legislation granting executives authority to act inconsistently with the WTO

> "[...] panels had consistently ruled that legislation which mandated action inconsistent with the General Agreement could be challenged as such [...]."[52]

Thus, the 1916 Act is mandatory.

3.38 Japan contests the US claim that the 1916 Act is not mandatory because it is susceptible to WTO-consistent interpretation. In Japan's view, the United States implies that if there is room for interpreting the 1916 Act in a GATT/WTO-consistent manner, the 1916 Act is not WTO-inconsistent. Making use of this mandatory or discretionary argument, the United States seems to insist that a domestic law suscep-

---

[50] In this regard, the United States notes that even Japan acknowledges that the *Zenith III* court "applied anti-trust standards to determine liability". Japan does not dispute that the WTO agreements do not prohibit anti-trust measures.

[51] In response to a question of the United States, Japan explains that by "injury element" it means "the intent of destroying or injuring an industry in the United States, or of preventing the establishment of an industry in the United States" as set forth in the text of the 1916 Act.

[52] Panel Report on *Canada - Aircraft*, *supra*, footnote 32, para. 9.124.

tible to multiple interpretations would not violate GATT 1947/WTO obligations. The United States tries to justify its inconsistent application of the 1916 Act, using as a disguise an argument regarding whether the 1916 Act is mandatory or discretionary in nature.[53]

3.39 Japan argues, first, that the terms of the 1916 Act are quite clear. The 1916 Act penalises a certain type of international price discrimination. Regardless of whether a US court calls the 1916 Act an anti-trust measure or an anti-dumping measure, the conduct the Act regulates remains the same. No court has interpreted the 1916 Act so that the 1916 Act did not apply to international price discrimination in which an importer sells at a lower price in the United States than in its home markets, i.e. dumping.

3.40 Japan argues, second, that the United States emphasizes the conclusion of the court in *Zenith III* that, for a limited purpose, the 1916 Act should be treated as an anti-trust law. But, far from exonerating the United States, this US assertion is additional proof of the US violation. The conduct regulated - that subset of international price discrimination commonly called dumping - did not change. But the court applied anti-trust standards to determine liability. This, of course, is the core of Japan's case. To regulate and remedy dumping, a Member must follow the standard for determining and remedying liability set out in the Anti-Dumping Agreement. A Member may not import standards from other sources.

3.41 Japan asserts that, contrary to the US assertion, the instant case does not closely resemble *United States - Tobacco.*[54] The text of the 1916 Act is not susceptible to a range of meanings. It requires WTO-inconsistent action. Thus, the US claim that the 1916 Act is susceptible to WTO-consistent interpretation is completely without merit.

3.42 Japan further argues that, even if the US assertion were correct - which it is not - it would be irrelevant and would not justify the WTO inconsistency of the 1916 Act. The United States cannot hide its WTO violations behind inconsistent enforcement of one of its laws by US courts. The position urged by the United States would completely undermine the goals of consistency and predictability which the GATT 1947/WTO system seeks to achieve.

3.43 Japan notes, moreover, that it contradicts Article XVI:4 of the WTO Agreement and, in the present proceedings, Article 18.4 of the Anti-Dumping Agreement. Each Member must conform its laws, regulations and administrative procedures to the provisions of the WTO agreements. The US courts' inconsistent interpretations of the 1916 Act is a blatant challenge to this important, systemic WTO principle.

3.44 Japan considers that the United States has not conformed its laws to its WTO obligations. Thus, it is in violation of Article XVI:4 of the WTO Agreement and Article 18.4 of the Anti-Dumping Agreement, which establish similar and specific obligations. Article XVI:4 sets forth Members' obligation to ensure the consistency of

---

[53] Japan considers that this argument is inapposite. According to Japan, it would allow a Member to avoid its WTO obligations simply by wording a law so that it could be interpreted in a WTO-consistent fashion, even though the Member always or usually applied it in a WTO-inconsistent fashion.

[54] Japan refers to *United States - Tobacco, Op. Cit.*, para. 118.

domestic laws, regulations and administrative procedures with the WTO agreements. This Article is general in scope, applying to all WTO agreements, including the GATT 1994 and the Anti-Dumping Agreement. Article 18.4 is reflective of the general obligation set out by Article XVI:4 as it applies to anti-dumping. In addition to the general obligation to "ensure the conformity" of domestic laws, regulations and administrative procedures, Article 18.4 imposes an additional obligation to ensure conformity by "tak[ing] all necessary steps, of a general or particular character".

3.45 According to Japan, the 1916 Act is inconsistent with US obligations under WTO provisions and, thus, the United States has violated Article XVI:4 of the WTO Agreement and Article 18.4 of the Anti-Dumping Agreement by failing to conform the Act to its WTO obligations. The fact that a law provides for WTO-inconsistent action is sufficient to establish a violation, even if there is a possibility of WTO-consistent action. If the Panel for some reason were to find that the 1916 Act is not mandatory, then this obligation, rather than the mandatory/discretionary dichotomy drawn from GATT 1947 precedent, should apply in the present dispute.

3.46 Japan asserts, furthermore, that the US position contradicts previous GATT 1947 and WTO panel and Appellate Body judgements. In this connection, the "sound legal basis" principle set forth in the *India - Patents* Appellate Body Report is instructive. In *India - Patents*, the panel and the Appellate Body upheld the US claim that a domestic law can violate a WTO provision not simply because it mandates WTO-inconsistent action, but also because it fails to provide "a sound legal basis" for the administrative procedure required to implement WTO obligations.[55] The panel and Appellate Body found that Members' laws and regulations must have "sound legal basis" for enforcement that creates the predictability needed to plan future trade. The Appellate Body reversed portions of the panel report on the issue of legitimate expectations, but clearly upheld the "sound legal basis" principle.[56]

3.47 Japan claims that its position is supported not only by *India - Patents*, but also by the *United States - Superfund* proceeding.[57] The fact that the US courts have interpreted the 1916 Act in a WTO-inconsistent fashion demonstrates the absence of a "sound legal basis". Accordingly, the mere potential of WTO-inconsistency is sufficient to establish a violation in the context of the WTO's provisions relating to anti-dumping.[58]

---

[55] Japan refers to the Panel Report on *India - Patent Protection for Pharmaceutical and Agricultural Chemical Products*, WT/DS50/AB/R, adopted 16 January 1998, DSR 1998:I, 41, para. 7.28; and the Appellate Body Report on *India - Patent Protection for Pharmaceutical and Agricultural Chemical Products*, WT/DS50/AB/R, adopted 16 January DSR 1998:I, 9, para. 36 (hereinafter "Appellate Body Report on *India - Patents*").

[56] Japan refers to the Appellate Body Report on *India - Patents, supra*, footnote 55, paras. 56-57.

[57] Japan refers to *United States - Taxes on Petroleum and Certain Imported Substances*, adopted on 17 June 1987, BISD 34S/136, para. 5.2.2. Japan notes that the panel emphasized the need for certainty and predictability.

[58] In response to a question of the United States regarding what is the legal basis for Japan's statement that "the mere potential of WTO inconsistency is sufficient to establish a violation [...]," Japan notes that the legal basis can be found in the panel and the Appellate Body reports on *India - Patents* (on "sound legal basis") and *United States - Tobacco* (and panel reports cited therein) as well as Article XVI:4 of the WTO Agreement and Article 18.4 of the Anti-Dumping Agreement. The mere

3.48 Japan reminds the Panel and the United States of the fact that the United States itself successfully advanced a similar argument in *India - Patents*. The panel noted that, in that proceeding, the United States argued as follows:

> "[...] The *Superfund* case was thus relevant to this matter because it clarified that Members were obligated "to protect expectations" of other Members as to the "competitive relationship" between their respective products. [...] [T]here was no need to wait for a violation to take place or speculate on whether it would take place, since the present case concerned a failure to take an affirmative action to implement a specific obligation in a WTO agreement."[59]

3.49 The **United States** notes that both Japan and the European Communities argue that the 1916 Act mandates a violation of WTO obligations. Although Japan did not further elaborate on this point, the European Communities argues in its third party submission that "several panel reports under GATT 1947 have found domestic legislation to run afoul of Article III GATT even before it had actually been applied, and, therefore, before any actual discrimination had taken place."

3.50 The United States considers that the European Communities misses the point with this argument. The European Communities is confusing an unenforced mandatory measure with a non-mandatory measure. The United States does not dispute that a mandatory measure may be found to be WTO-inconsistent before actual application or enforcement. The key question is whether the measure is mandatory or non-mandatory.

3.51 The United States recalls that the European Communities also argues that "mandatory measures are those which, under national law, require the executive authority to impose a measure" implying that only measures enforced through the executive branch could ever be considered under the mandatory/non-mandatory distinction. The European Communities cites the *United States - Denial of Most-Favoured-Nation Treatment As to Non-Rubber Footwear from Brazil* case as support.[60]

3.52 The United States argues that, although the panel report in *United States - Non-Rubber Footwear* mentions the "executive authority", the panel's decision did not turn on which branch of government enforced the measure.[61] In fact, the United States is not aware of any panel report having considered this question. Neither Japan nor the European Communities offer any reason why the mandatory/non-mandatory distinction should not apply to measures which are enforced through the judicial branch. The European Communities argues that courts are charged with interpreting legislation, not with exercising discretion in respect of legislation. However, the EC

---

potential of WTO-inconsistency establishes a violation in light of these WTO provisions and precedents.

[59] Panel Report on *India - Patents*, *supra, footnote 55*, para. 4.28.

[60] The United States refers to the Panel Report on *United States - Denial of Most-Favoured-Nation Treatment As to Non-Rubber Footwear from Brazil*, adopted on 19 June 1992, BISD 39S/128 (hereinafter "*United States - Non-Rubber Footwear*").

[61] The United States notes that the panel mentions the executive authority in the context of explaining that legislation may be challenged *as such* (before actual application) if it mandates inconsistent action.

does not address the fact that, in interpreting legislation, the court is applying the legislation just as the executive branch would had it been charged with the legislation's enforcement (putting aside the criminal provisions of the 1916 Act for which the executive branch is charged with enforcing).

3.53 Thus, for the United States, the question again becomes: is there room in the application of the law for the government authority to act in a WTO-consistent manner? This is the fundamental test that has been applied in all cases considering the mandatory/discretionary distinction and there is no reason not to apply it when the judicial branch is charged with the application of a measure.[62] Indeed, in applying the discretionary/mandatory distinction in *United States - Superfund,* the panel found that legislation explicitly directing action inconsistent with GATT 1947 principles did not mandate inconsistent action so long as it provided the possibility for authorities to avoid such action.

3.54 The United States recalls that the European Communities attempts to distinguish the *United States - Tobacco* case as involving domestic legislation that was "incomplete", (meaning that the agency had not yet promulgated its regulations). In that case, the panel considered whether a term in a statute could be interpreted by the relevant government authorities (which happen to be executive branch authorities) in a WTO-consistent manner. Thus, the only distinction is again that executive branch authorities were involved instead of judicial branch authorities.

3.55 In the view of the United States, there is no reason not to apply the same principle in the present case. The focus in a mandatory/discretionary analysis should not be on which branch of government is applying the law, but whether there is room in the application of the law for the relevant government authorities to act in a WTO-consistent manner. This is consistent with the presumption against conflicts between international and national laws. In the instant case, the United States has shown that, not only is there room for such an interpretation, as a matter of fact, the law has been so interpreted. Accordingly, the present Panel should find that the 1916 Act, *as such*, is WTO-consistent.[63]

3.56 The United States also points out that there is a separate reason, solely applicable to the criminal context, for viewing the 1916 Act as non-mandatory legislation. The Department of Justice, an executive branch agency, has the discretion to decide whether or not to bring a criminal prosecution under the 1916 Act. In other words, while the 1916 Act authorizes the Department of Justice to bring a criminal prosecu-

[62] In response to an observation by Japan that in the present case the US Administration does not appear to possess the power to secure uniform, WTO-consistent interpretation of the 1916 Act because the enforcement mechanism is up to US courts, the United States argues that the relevant question is not which branch of government is acting, but whether the law mandates a violation.

[63] In response to a question of Japan regarding what measures are available for the US Administration to secure that all domestic laws be interpreted in line with international treaties in the US court system, the United States notes that in cases where the United States is itself a party to a civil or criminal litigation (acting through the Department of Justice), it has direct responsibility for ensuring that its own claims and actions comport with US laws and obligations, including international obligations, and for informing the court of such considerations. In addition, where appropriate, the Department of Justice can seek to intervene in a private civil litigation in order to protect a federal government interest. The Department of Justice does not routinely intervene in private civil litigation, however, and it remains a matter of judgment when and before which courts it should be done.

tion, it does not mandate it. In fact, there is no record of the Department of Justice as having filed, or even considered, a criminal case under the law.

3.57 **Japan** maintains that, despite continued US protestations, the 1916 Act is a mandatory law. The United States cannot rebut the critical fact that the 1916 Act requires punitive action where a US court finds that the elements of the offence (the dumping element and the injury element) have been established. Since the 1916 Act clearly regulates dumping (international price discrimination), there is no room for interpretation in line with international obligation (in this case Article VI of the GATT 1994 and the Anti-Dumping Agreement). Doctrines such as that established by *Murray v. The Schooner Charming Betsy*[64] can provide no succour to the United States. The *Charming Betsy* doctrine stands for the proposition that where "fairly possible", courts should construe legislation to avoid conflicts with US treaty obligations. The doctrine does not apply to the present case for two reasons. First, the 1916 Act is clear; the court has no discretion under the 1916 Act. Once the elements of the Act are proven, the court must impose the statutory sanctions. The court lacks any discretion in this situation to fulfill the *Charming Betsy* directive that, "where fairly possible", courts will construe an Act of Congress so as not to conflict with a treaty of the United States. It is not "fairly possible" for a US court to construe the 1916 Act to conform to the United States' WTO obligations.[65]

3.58 Japan notes, second, that the *Charming Betsy* doctrine does not apply, because the Uruguay Round Agreements Act (hereinafter the "URAA" - the US implementing legislation) expressly precludes US courts from altering US laws to conform them to US WTO obligations. According to Section 102(a)(1) of the URAA:

> "No provision of any of the Uruguay Round Agreements, nor the application of any such provision, to any person or circumstance, that is inconsistent with the law of the United States shall have effect."

3.59 According to Japan, this language is underscored by the decision of the US Court of Appeals for the Federal Circuit in *Suramericana de Aleaciones Laminadas, C.A. v. United States* where the court found that:

> "The GATT is not controlling. [...] The GATT does not trump domestic legislation; if the statutory provisions at issue are inconsistent with the GATT, it is a matter for Congress and not this court to decide and remedy." [66]

3.60 Japan submits, finally, that regardless of these telling points, the Panel should reject the US invitation to mire itself in the various judicial opinions. Instead, the Panel should base its decision on the unambiguous text of the 1916 Act.

---

64 Japan refers to *Murray v. The Schooner Charming Betsy*, 6 U.S. (2 Cranch) 64 (1804) (hereinafter "*Charming Betsy*").

65 Japan notes, in this context, that the United States attempts to characterize Japan's position on the mandatory/discretionary issue as being based on whether the judicial branch or the executive branch is enforcing the measure. This statement is not Japan's position. Japan's position is that neither the US executive branch nor US courts have any discretion in applying the WTO-inconsistent remedy that the 1916 Act mandates.

66 Japan refers to *Suramericana de Aleaciones Laminadas, C.A. v. United States*, 966 F.2d 660, 667-68 (Fed. Cir. 1992) (citations omitted by Japan).

3.61 The **United States** disagrees with Japan's contention that the 1916 Act is a "mandatory" measure because, if the requirements of the law are fulfilled, the court must impose a remedy. This argument misses the point. The relevant question for determining whether there is a WTO violation when a measure is challenged as such is: does the measure mandate a violation of any WTO obligations? The question is not: does the measure mandate the imposition of a remedy? To answer the question of whether the measure mandates a violation of any WTO obligations, the Panel must ask: what are the requirements of the law? The United States has shown that the requirements of the 1916 Act are subject to interpretation by the courts and that the courts have interpreted and applied the law as an anti-trust statute. In other words, the discretionary nature of the 1916 Act is found in how the elements of a violation of the 1916 Act can be interpreted, not in the remedy that must be imposed once such a violation has been established. That is enough for the present Panel to find that the law is susceptible to an interpretation that is WTO-consistent.

3.62 **Japan** considers that the United States attempts to mischaracterise its position as being that the 1916 Act is mandatory for purposes of the WTO simply because it "mandates the imposition of a remedy." This statement does not reflect Japan's argument. Japan's argument is that the question before the Panel is whether the measure mandates a violation of a WTO obligation. The answer to this question is "yes". The 1916 Act mandates the imposition of a remedy - a remedy that violates a WTO obligation.

3.63 The **United States** adds that Japan contradicts itself in arguing that the 1916 Act is a mandatory measure. First, it argues that the 1916 Act is not susceptible of differing interpretations. However, Japan also argues that the *Zenith III* court's interpretation is different and should be disregarded in favour of two recent preliminary district court opinions. This argument just serves to underscore the point that the 1916 Act is susceptible to a range of interpretations and any differences between the *Zenith III* decision and the two preliminary decisions demonstrate how much discretion the courts retain in applying the law.

3.64 With regard to the *Charming Betsy* doctrine, the United States notes that Japan's statement that it does not apply to the Uruguay Round Agreements is incorrect. The *Charming Betsy* doctrine holds that, absent express congressional language to the contrary, statutes should not be interpreted to conflict with international obligations. This time-honoured canon of statutory interpretation was first applied in *Charming Betsy*, wherein the Supreme Court explained:

> "It has also been observed that an act of Congress ought never to be construed to violate the law of nations, if any other possible construction remains, and consequently, can never be construed to violate neutral rights, or to affect neutral commerce, further than is warranted by the law of nations as understood in this country."[67]

3.65 The United States points out that the Uruguay Round Agreements have been held to be international obligations for purposes of the *Charming Betsy* doctrine.[68] In

[67] *Charming Betsy*, *Op. Cit.*, 2 L.Ed. 208 (1804).

[68] The United States refers to *Federal Mogul Corp. v. United States*, 63 F.3d 1572, 1581 (Fed. Cir. 1995) (hereinafter "*Federal Mogul*").

applying this doctrine, the court first must determine whether there is an express conflict between the US law and the international obligation. If there is an express conflict, then US law prevails. This is exactly what section 102(a)(1) of the URAA provides, and no more. However, if there is no express conflict, then the court will apply the *Charming Betsy* doctrine to adopt an interpretation of the statute that is consistent with the international obligation. Thus, the *Charming Betsy* doctrine is perfectly consistent with Section 102(a)(1) of the URAA. For instance, in *Federal Mogul*, the court of appeals ascertained that the statute permitted alternative interpretations and that there was no express statutory language conflicting with the relevant international obligation. The court then held that the interpretation by the Commerce Department of the relevant statute as allowing a tax neutral methodology for calculating dumping margins was consistent with GATT principles and therefore permissible.

3.66 The United States submits that, in another case, *Caterpillar Inc. v. United States*[69], the Court of International Trade applied the *Charming Betsy* doctrine in holding that the Customs Service's interpretation of a statute was impermissible because it conflicted with Article VII:3 of the GATT. The court first determined that there was no express language in the statute conflicting with this GATT provision. The court then held that, in accordance with the *Charming Betsy* doctrine, the statute should be construed in a manner consistent with international obligations. Because the Customs Service's interpretation was inconsistent, it was held to be impermissible.

3.67 The United States considers, finally, that, even without regard to judicial interpretations, the plain language of the 1916 Act is WTO-consistent. Although the Third Circuit has held that the possibility of recoupment must be established under the 1916 Act, that is not the only WTO-consistent interpretation. A review of the plain language of the 1916 Act shows that it is not a specific action against dumping. Rather, it is a measure directed at private predatory pricing practices. This reading of the plain language is confirmed by the statute's legislative history.

3.68 In response to a question of the Panel to both parties regarding whether there would be reasons to distinguish between, on the one hand, the situation where the terms of a law would make that law fall within the scope of a given provision of the WTO Agreement (e.g. Article VI of the GATT 1994) depending on the interpretation of those terms and, on the other hand, the situation where the applicability of a WTO provision is not in question (as was the case in *United States - Tobacco*), but where the law could be interpreted in such a way that it would violate that WTO provision, **Japan** notes that there would be.[70]

3.69 In Japan's view, "the situation where the terms of a law would make that law fall, or not, within the scope of a given provision of the WTO Agreement depending on the interpretation of those terms," is the situation where the authorities cannot apply the law in line with WTO obligations, because the terms of the law are so ambiguous that authorities cannot consistently interpret the law in line with WTO obligations. In this situation, since the law lacks the "sound legal basis" needed for do-

69 The United States refers to *Caterpillar Inc. v. United States*, 941 F. Supp. 1241 (CIT 1996).

70 Japan notes, however, that the present case falls under neither of the situations hypothesized by the Panel.

mestic legislation to create the predictability to plan future trade, the law violates provisions of the WTO Agreement, as the Appellate Body found in *India - Patents* regarding the TRIPS Agreement.

3.70 Japan submits that, on the other hand, "the situation where the applicability of a WTO provision is not in question, but where that law could be interpreted in such a way that it would violate that WTO provision," is the situation that the authorities may have some discretion to apply the law in line with WTO obligations, because a range of meaning of the law is susceptible of WTO-consistent interpretation, as was the case with the *United States - Tobacco* panel's finding regarding Article VIII of the GATT 1947.

3.71 Japan recalls that, in the *United States - Tobacco* case, the panel found no violation because, due to the ambiguity in the terms of the law, the US Administration was not mandated to act in a manner that was inconsistent with the GATT 1947. However, this situation should be distinguished from "the situation where the terms of a law would make that law fall, or not, within the scope of a given provision of the WTO Agreement depending on the interpretation of those terms," particularly if that WTO provision relates to the positive obligations of a WTO Member to provide for a certain procedural mechanism, such as in the TRIPS Agreement or the Anti-Dumping Agreement. In Japan's view, the refusal to comply with those obligations would *per se* constitute a violation of the WTO Agreement.

3.72 In its reply to the Panel's question, Japan also recalls, however, that the hypothesized situations in the Panel's question do not apply to the present case and that the question has no relevance in the present proceedings. The 1916 Act is clearly mandatory legislation that requires the US government to act in a manner that is inconsistent with its obligation under the WTO Agreement. According to Japan, the present case should be distinguished from the *United States - Tobacco* case, in that the text of the 1916 Act is quite clear and not at all vague.

3.73 The **United States**, in reply to the same question of the Panel, agrees with Japan that there is a reason to differentiate between the two situations. In the first scenario, the Panel should be guided by the interpretative principle of *in dubio mitius*. In *EC Measures Concerning Meat and Meat Products (Hormones)*, the Appellate Body applied this principle in finding that the panel erred in adopting a "far-reaching" interpretation of the SPS Agreement.[71] The Appellate Body, quoting Oppenheim's International Law, described this principle in footnote 154 as follows:

> "The principle of *in dubio mitius* applies in interpreting treaties, in deference to the sovereignty of states. If the meaning of a term is ambiguous, that meaning is to be preferred which is less onerous to the party assuming an obligation, or which interferes less with the territorial and personal supremacy of a party, or involves less general restrictions upon the parties."

3.74 The United States notes that, as a result, if the 1916 Act can be interpreted so as to fall outside the scope of Article VI and the Anti-Dumping Agreement, accord-

[71] Report of the Appellate Body on *EC Measures Concerning Meat and Meat Products (Hormones)*, WT/DS26/AB/R, WT/DS48/AB/R, adopted 13 February 1998, DSR 1998:I, 135, para.165 (hereinafter "Appellate Body Report on *European Communities - Hormones*").

ing to the principle *in dubio mitius*, that is the interpretation that should be adopted by the Panel. The 1916 Act can be and has been interpreted as an anti-trust statute. There is no dispute in the present case that Article VI and the Anti-Dumping Agreement do not apply to anti-trust measures.

3.75 The United States considers that the second scenario should be governed by the principle laid down in the *United States - Tobacco* case.

3.76 In response to another question of the Panel regarding the relationship between the GATT 1947/WTO practice in respect of mandatory/non-mandatory legislation and Article XVI:4 of the WTO Agreement, **Japan** notes that the obligation set out at Article XVI:4 "to ensure [...] the conformity" of laws, regulations and administrative procedures, rather than the mandatory/discretionary dichotomy drawn from GATT 1947 practice, should apply in the present dispute. Article XVI:4 establishes that Members must alter laws, regulations and administrative procedures that do not conform to WTO provisions. The 1916 Act has been applied in a manner that has been applied in a manner that is inconsistent with US WTO obligations and, thus, the United States has violated Article XVI:4 by failing to conform the law the 1916 Act to its WTO obligations.[72]

3.77 In reply to the same question, the **United States** submits that Article XVI:4 did not affect the distinction between mandatory and non-mandatory measures that existed under GATT 1947 jurisprudence and continues to exist under WTO practice. Article XVI:4 provides an overarching statement in the WTO Agreement, applicable to all annexed agreements and not just the GATT 1994, that no measures are grandfathered. Article XVI:4 imposed an obligation on Members to review whether existing laws, regulations and administrative procedures did, in fact, conform to the Members' WTO obligations, and where those laws did not, to bring them into conformity. Article XVI:4 thus served to remove any doubt that may have existed in its absence that all measures must be brought into conformity as from 1 January 1995.

3.78 In response to a follow-up question of the Panel regarding the relationship between the GATT 1947/WTO practice in respect of mandatory/non-mandatory legislation and the GATT 1947/WTO practice concerning the protection of expectations of the contracting parties/Members as to the competitive relationship between their products[73] and the "security and predictability of the WTO system"[74], **Japan** notes first of all that it does not see the relevance of this question to this dispute. As made most clear in Paragraph 5.2.2 of *United States - Superfund*, the issue of protection of expectations versus the need to prove actual trade effects arose in the context of "mandatory" legislation. Japan does not see the relevance of this question to this dis-

---

[72] In reply to a similar question of the United States, Japan states that, depending on the specific circumstances, the mandatory/non-mandatory distinction can still be a useful tool for analysing the WTO consistency of a domestic law or regulation. Japan considers that, in the present proceeding, it is not required to establish a general guideline as to the circumstances in which the distinction could be properly considered by the Panel.

[73] The Panel refers to, e.g., *United States - Superfund* and the Panel Report on *Japanese Measures on Import of Leather*, adopted on 15/16 May 1984, BISD 31S/113.

[74] The Panel refers to, e.g., the Panel Report on *Argentina - Measures Affecting Imports of Footwear, Textiles, Apparel and Other Items*, WT/DS56/R, adopted 22 April 1998, DSR 1998:III, 1033 (hereinafter "Panel Report on *Argentina - Footwear*").

pute. In any event, Japan considers that and the obligation to ensure the conformity of US laws set out in Article XVI:4 of the WTO Agreement and Article 18.4 of the Anti-Dumping Agreement, rather than the mandatory/discretionary dichotomy applicable to the GATT 1947, applies in the present dispute.

3.79 Japan is of the view, moreover, that even if the mandatory/discretionary dichotomy were to apply, the 1916 Act is mandatory. It requires action inconsistent with US WTO obligations.

3.80 The **United States**, in its response to the same question of the Panel, submits, first, that it is important to note that the panel in *United States - Superfund* refers to the objective of the "protection of the expectations of contracting parties as to the competitive relationship between products" in the context of two specific provisions, Article III and Article XI of the GATT 1947. The panel reasoned that "that objective could not be attained if contracting parties could not challenge existing legislation mandating actions at variance with the General Agreement until the administrative acts implementing it had actually been applied to their trade."[75] Obviously, the panel considered that the concepts were compatible because it based its conclusion that mandatory legislation is actionable even if not yet in effect in part on helping to achieve that objective.

3.81 The United States considers that, similarly, in more general terms, the mandatory/non-mandatory distinction is consistent with the "legitimate expectations of parties." The Appellate Body explained in *India - Patents* that "the legitimate expectations of the parties to a treaty are reflected in the language of the treaty itself."[76] Thus,

> "[…] the duty of a treaty interpreter is to examine the words of the treaty to determine the intentions of the parties. This should be done in accordance with the principles of treaty interpretation set out in Article 31 of the Vienna Convention. But these principles neither require nor condone the imputation of a treaty of words that are not there or the importation into a treaty of concepts that were not intended."[77]

3.82 The United States contends that, likewise, the mandatory/non-mandatory distinction is consistent with the "security and predictability of the WTO system." First, it is important to note that the "security and predictability of the WTO system" is not an obligation, but an objective of Article 3.2 of the Dispute Settlement Understanding. Article 3.2 provides, in pertinent part, that: "The dispute settlement system of the WTO is a central element in providing security and predictability to the multilateral trading system." Security and predictability are thus the objective which the DSU itself helps to achieve. In other words, the substantive obligations in the text of the WTO Agreement and its annexes, enforced through the DSU, provide security and predictability.

3.83 In the view of the United States, to discard a fundamental principle of jurisprudence and create uncertainty as to the WTO consistency of an indeterminate number of domestic laws heretofore considered discretionary would seriously undermine

---

[75] *United States - Superfund*, *Op. Cit.*, para. 5.2.2.

[76] Appellate Body Report on *India - Patents*, *supra*, footnote 55, para. 45.

[77] *Ibid.*

the security and predictability of the WTO system. As the Appellate Body noted in *Japan - Taxes on Alcoholic Beverages*, "[a]dopted panel reports are an important part of the GATT *acquis*. They are often considered by subsequent panels. They create legitimate expectations among WTO members, and, therefore, should be taken into account where they are relevant to any dispute."[78]

3.84 The United States notes, finally, that, in *Argentina - Footwear*, the panel does no more than affirm that mandatory legislation is actionable. The panel states, "GATT/WTO case law is clear that a mandatory measure can be brought before a panel, even if such an adopted measure is not yet in effect."[79] The panel refers to "security and predictability" in the context of the aim of tariff bindings and Article II of the GATT 1994, which are not at issue in the present case.

E. Role of the Panel in the Present Case

3.85 **Japan** recalls that Article 11 of the DSU requires panels to conduct an "objective assessment" of the facts of each dispute. Panels have found that panels cannot meet this obligation if they defer to a Member's findings in this regard.[80]

3.86 Japan also notes the Appellate Body opinion in *European Communities - Hormones*, which makes clear that the existence and characteristics of domestic law are questions of fact that are "left to the discretion of a panel as a trier of facts". In contrast, the "consistency or inconsistency of a given fact or set of facts" (the 1916 Act in the present case) with the requirements of a given treaty provision (relevant WTO Articles in the present case) would be a legal question.[81]

3.87 Japan recalls, furthermore, that, in *India - Patents*, the Appellate Body concluded that:

> "It is clear that an examination of the relevant aspects of Indian municipal law [...] is essential to determining whether India has complied with its obligations."[82]

3.88 In the view of Japan, this quoted passage reflects the position consistently taken by the Appellate Body and panels that, in order to fulfil the obligation under Article 11 of the DSU to make an objective assessment of the facts and to assess the conformity of the challenged measure with the relevant WTO agreements, a panel must conduct its own examination of the challenged law.[83]

---

[78] Appellate Body Report on *Japan - Taxes on Alcoholic Beverages,* WT/DS11/AB/R, adopted 1 November 1996, DSR 1996:I, 97, at 108.

[79] Panel Report on *Argentina - Footwear, supra*, footnote 74, para. 6.45.

[80] Japan refers to the Panel Report on *Korea - Definitive Safeguard Measure on Imports of Certain Dairy Products*, WT/DS98/R, adopted 12 January 2000, DSR 2000:I, 49, para. 7.30 (hereinafter "Panel Report on *Korea - Safeguards*", where the Panel states as follows: "We consider that for the Panel to adopt a policy of total deference to the findings of the national authorities could not ensure an 'objective assessment' as foreseen by Article 11 of the DSU."

[81] Japan refers to *EC Measures Concerning Meat and Meat Products* (*Hormones*), *supra*, footnote 71, para. 132 .

[82] Appellate Body Report on *India-Patents, supra*, footnote 55, para. 66.

[83] Japan refers to the Appellate Body Report on *European Communities - Hormones, supra*, footnote 71, paras. 110-119; Panel Report, *Korea - Safeguards, supra, footnote 80*, paras. 7.26-7.31;

3.89 Japan considers that it is also very instructive that the Appellate Body in *India - Patents* cites *United States - Section 337 of the Tariff Act of 1930* for the proposition that a panel must conduct "a detailed examination of the domestic law" in order to assess its WTO/GATT conformity.[84] Thus, the word "examination" indicates that the Panel must analyse the law to determine its substance and import. "Examination" encompasses all the aspects of the "objective assessment of the matter" provided in Article 11 of the DSU. Thus, it falls to the Panel, not the United States, to interpret the 1916 Act and determine whether it is WTO-inconsistent. The Panel should not accept the US judicial interpretation of the 1916 Act as binding. Any other position would allow the Member defending against a complaint simply to declare its law WTO-consistent, which would be an absurd result.

3.90 The **United States** notes that Japan acknowledges that the "characteristics" of the 1916 Act are questions of fact for the present Panel. The United States agrees. It is an accepted principle of international law that municipal law is a fact to be proven before an international tribunal.[85] In *India - Patents*[86] the Appellate Body directly addressed the proper review of municipal law. In that case, the Appellate Body affirmed the panel's review of India's domestic law as a question of fact, citing the Permanent Court of International Justice (hereinafter "PCIJ") decision in *Certain German Interests in Polish Upper Silesia*. The Appellate Body held that it was proper for the panel to conduct an extensive review of the Indian law at issue to determine whether India had met its obligations under the TRIPS Agreement. The Appellate Body noted approvingly that the panel had not interpreted Indian law *as such*, but, rather, had reviewed the law to determine whether it was WTO-consistent.

3.91 The United States argues that, likewise, in the present case, the Panel is not called upon to interpret or opine upon the meaning of the 1916 Act itself. Rather, the Panel must determine the fact of the 1916 Act under US law, which includes US judicial decisions interpreting the Act. The danger in the Panel interpreting the 1916 Act is that the Panel might adopt an interpretation that does not match the true application of the law in the United States. To do so would result in a panel report based upon hypothetical facts. In order to avoid such an outcome, the Panel should deem the case law interpreting the 1916 Act as dispositive for purposes of determining the fact of US law.[87]

Panel Report on *Argentina - Safeguard Measures on Imports of Footwear*, WT/DS121/R, adopted 12 January 2000, DSR 2000:I, 515, paras. 8.117-8.121.

[84] Japan refers to Appellate Body Report, *India - Patents*, *supra*, footnote 55, para. 67.

[85] The United States refers to *Case Concerning Certain German Interests in Polish Upper Silesia* [1926], PCIJ Rep., Series A, No. 7, p. 19; *Case Concerning the Payment in Gold of Brazilian Federal Loans Contracted in France*, PCIJ Rep., Series A, No. 21, pp. 124-25 (hereinafter "*Brazilian Loans*").

[86] The United States refers to Appellate Body Report on *India - Patents*, footnote 55, paras. 65-66.

[87] The United States refers to Judge Lauterpacht, *Case Concerning the Guardianship of an Infant* [1958], ICJ Rep., Sep. Op., p. 91. According to the United States, it is settled practice among States that international judicial bodies should accept, and treat as binding, questions of municipal law and practice decided by competent municipal courts. The United States refers to *Case Concerning the Payment of Various Serbian Loans Issued in France* [1929], PCIJ Rep., Series A, No. 20, p. 46; *Brazilian Loans*, *Op. Cit.*, pp. 124-25.

3.92 The United States recalls that, for example, in the *Brazilian Loans* case, the PCIJ attached controlling weight to the manner in which French courts had interpreted French legislation. The PCIJ admonished that a tribunal of international law should "pay the utmost regard to the decisions of the municipal courts of a country, for it is with the aid of their jurisprudence that it will be enabled to decide what are the rules which in actual fact, are applied in the country the law of which is recognized as applicable in a given case."[88] This principle "rests in part on the concept of the reserved domain of domestic jurisdiction, and in part on the practical need of avoiding contradictory versions of the law of a state from different sources."[89]

3.93 In response to a question of the Panel regarding the import of the Appellate Body report in *India - Patents* in terms of the Panel's consideration of domestic law and case law, the United States notes that the term "examination" as used by the Appellate Body in *India - Patents* means that the Panel must review the domestic law (including relevant court decisions law interpreting the law) to determine the fact of domestic law. The Appellate Body's statement on this point was in response to India's argument that the panel should have "sought guidance" from India as a party to the dispute on matters relating to the interpretation of Indian law implying that the panel should have deferred to India and not examined the law itself. The Appellate Body rejected this argument and noted approvingly that the panel examined Indian law to determine the fact of the law and that "the Panel was not interpreting Indian law 'as such.'"[90]

3.94 The United States considers that, similarly, in the present case, it is not for the Panel to interpret the 1916 Act itself, but the Panel must examine the domestic law and relevant case law to determine how the law is interpreted and applied in the United States. The United States is not advocating that the Panel refrain from "examining" US law and accept the US interpretation as a party in the present dispute. To the contrary, the United States provided copies of the relevant decisions and other materials to assist the Panel in examining the 1916 Act and the US case law interpreting the Act. However, it is not the role of the Panel to agree or disagree with the final judicial decisions interpreting and applying the Act.

3.95 The United States emphasizes, however, that it is not suggesting that the Panel has no interpretative role. As noted by the Appellate Body in *India - Patents*, once the Panel has determined the interpretation of the municipal law as a factual matter, it is the Panel's function to determine the applicability of the relevant WTO agreements to those facts. These determinations are questions of WTO law to be made by the Panel in the first instance.

3.96 **Japan** recalls the US assertion that the Panel should defer to the US characterisation of the 1916 Act in the present case. This is incorrect. A WTO Panel must conduct its own examination and assessment of a challenged law (in the instant case the 1916 Act) to fulfill its obligation under Article 11 of the DSU. The present Panel

---

88 The United States refers to *Brazilian Loans*, *Op. Cit.*, pp. 124-25.

89 The United States refers to I. Brownlie, *Principles of Public International Law*, 4th ed., Clarendon Press (1990), p.41.

90 The United States refers to the Appellate Body Report on *India - Patents*, *supra*, footnote 55, para. 66.

should not accept US unilateral assertions or interpretations about this law and its WTO-consistency. It must itself determine the conformity of the challenged law with the relevant WTO agreements. The present Panel's role is clear. It is to examine the 1916 Act's WTO-consistency; to accept the US characterisation would be to ignore this duty.

3.97 In response to the same question of the Panel regarding the import of the Appellate Body report in *India - Patents* in terms of the Panel's consideration of domestic law and case law, Japan states that *India - Patents* calls upon a WTO panel, at the very least, to analyse the text of a national law in question. A WTO panel should not accept a nation's judicial interpretations of a law as binding, but must review the text of the law itself. In doing so, a WTO panel may also analyse how courts and administrative agencies have applied the law and the effects the law's existence and/or application has on imports. Case law may inform a panel about possible interpretations of a statute. Again, however, case law should not be taken as the final word of a statute's effect on imports, particularly if other evidence (the statute's text and its real world effects) outweighs the prior contrary judicial interpretation of the statute.

3.98 The **United States** maintains its view that it is not the function of the present Panel to interpret US law. The United States submits that it is not advocating either that the Panel accept its interpretation of the 1916 Act as a party in the present dispute. It is the role of the Panel to determine as a matter of fact how the law is applied in the United States. Because the 1916 Act is applied through the judicial branch, the Panel must look to the judicial interpretations. Otherwise, the Panel runs the risk of basing its decision upon hypothetical facts if it should adopt its own interpretation of the 1916 Act that does not comport with how the law is actually applied in the United States. It is not for the Panel to decide the manner in which it believes that the 1916 Act *should* be applied which would entail interpreting the Act itself. Even if the Panel might disagree with how the courts have interpreted the text of the 1916 Act, it should not affect the Panel's decision in the present dispute. In the US legal system, the 1916 Act means what the courts say it means, and this is the relevant fact for purposes of the present dispute.

F. Applicability of Article VI of the GATT 1994 and the Anti-Dumping Agreement

1. Introduction

3.99 **Japan** considers that the 1916 Act is an anti-dumping statute and, thus, must comply with Article VI of the GATT 1994 and with the provisions of the Anti-Dumping Agreement.

3.100 Japan notes that, as indicated by its short-form title, the 1916 Act regulates dumping. This fact is confirmed by the text of the Act, the conduct the Act targets and the effect and impact of the 1916 Act when applied. Moreover, the fact that the 1916 Act is an anti-dumping law is further confirmed by its legislative history, US court decisions that have interpreted it and the views of the US executive branch, including the current Administration. Apparently, only before the present Panel does the US executive branch argue that the 1916 Act is not an anti-dumping law.

3.101 The **United States** considers that Japan's formulation of the statute's legislative history and relevant case law is distorted and misleading. A review of the relevant case law and the statute's legislative history demonstrates that the 1916 Act can be and, in fact, has been interpreted as a predatory pricing statute with anti-trust objectives, not an anti-dumping measure within the purview of Article VI and the Anti-Dumping Agreement.

3.102 According to the United States, Article VI simply does not govern the 1916 Act. Japan's various claims under Article VI and the Anti-Dumping Agreement therefore must be rejected.

2. *The Text of the 1916 Act*

3.103 In the view of **Japan**, analysis of the text of the 1916 Act demonstrates that the Act regulates dumping. The text of the Act provides as follows:

> "It shall be unlawful for any person importing or assisting in importing any Articles from any foreign country into the United States, commonly and systematically to import, sell or cause to be imported or sold such Articles within the United States *at a price substantially less than the actual market value or wholesale price of such articles, at the time of exportation to the United States, in the principal markets of the country of their production, or of other foreign countries to which they are commonly exported* after adding to such market value or wholesale price, freight, duty, and other charges and expenses necessarily incident to the importation and sale thereof in the United States: *Provided*, That such act or acts be done with the intent of *destroying or injuring an industry in the United States, or of preventing the establishment of an industry in the United States,* or of restraining or monopolizing any part of trade and commerce in such Articles in the United States."[91]

3.104 Japan recalls that under Article VI of the GATT 1994, dumping occurs when "products of one country are introduced into the commerce of another country at less than the normal value of the products", and "normal value" means the home market prices, third country prices, or the constructed cost of the product at issue.[92] These requirements are the core concept of dumping as prescribed in Article VI of the GATT 1994.[93] Article VI of the GATT 1994 prohibits Members from taking measures against dumping other than the anti-dumping duties prescribed by this Article, irrespective of "intent to injure" or "material injury". As the text of the 1916 Act quoted above shows, the 1916 Act targets precisely this conduct.

3.105 Japan notes that the 1916 Act sets out two basic elements that trigger a violation. First, the US price must be lower than the benchmark price (normal value), which can be based either on home market prices or on third country prices. Second, the price discrimination must be accompanied by an intent to injure, destroy or prevent the establishment of a US industry. Thus, the 1916 Act targets imports and is designed to protect US industries. The conduct which it prohibits or regulates is

---

91 15 U.S.C. § 72 (1999) (emphasis added by Japan).

92 Japan notes that this is the core of the concept of international price discrimination.

93 Japan notes in this regard that material injury is a necessary additional requirement to take measures against dumping, but that dumping is defined only in terms of price differentials.

dumping, defined as a "substantial" difference between US prices and home market or foreign market prices. Therefore, the Act is intended to regulate dumping every bit as much as would a law that complied with Article VI of the GATT 1994 and the Anti-Dumping Agreement.

3.106 Japan argues that the provisions of the 1916 Act show that the conduct the Act targets is the same as dumping as defined by Article VI of the GATT 1994 and by the Anti-Dumping Agreement:

(a) The US price must be lower than normal value (the comparison price).

(b) The US price must be adjusted for freight, customs duty and other expenses incident to importation to ensure comparability to the comparison price.

(c) The comparison price can be based either on home market prices or on third country prices.

3.107 Japan further submits that beyond the core concept of dumping, the 1916 Act also mirrors expressions stipulated in Article VI of the GATT 1994 by requiring injury to a domestic industry to warrant relief.

3.108 Japan considers that this comparison shows that the precise wording used in the 1916 Act and in Article VI:1 of the GATT 1994 may vary, but their essential concepts are identical. The addition of other qualifying elements on the core features of the law does not alter the fundamental nature of the 1916 Act as an anti-dumping law.[94] For example, requiring the US price to be "substantially" less than the comparison price does not change the fundamental nature of the international price discrimination targeted.[95] Likewise, whether the "injury" to the domestic industry is intentional or not, the fundamental requirement of injury to the US industry remains the same. The 1916 Act may reach only a subset of commercial instances of dumping - that is why the US Congress later passed other laws - but the Act provides for action against that subset and, thus, constitutes a remedy against dumping.

3.109 Japan argues, moreover, that if such additional qualifications could somehow change the fundamental nature of the law, then virtually no anti-dumping law in the world could be considered an anti-dumping law. Many national anti-dumping laws vary from Article VI of the GATT 1994 and the Anti-Dumping Agreement. These variations, however, do not change their fundamental nature as anti-dumping remedies.

3.110 The **United States** submits that Japan cannot dispute that there are significant differences between the 1916 Act and the anti-dumping rules. As a trade remedy, the

---

94 Japan argues that, just as a WTO Member can choose not to have a domestic anti-dumping law, it can choose to limit its ability to impose anti-dumping duties by including in its national law criteria and conditions stricter than those required by the GATT 1994 and the Anti-Dumping Agreement. Thus, the fact that the 1916 Act addresses only dumping that occurs "commonly and systematically" at a "substantially less" price does not alter the conclusion that the Act is an anti-dumping law and is subject to the requirements of Article VI of the GATT 1994 and the Anti-Dumping Agreement.

95 Japan argues, moreover, that the Anti-Dumping Agreement has an analogous concept. The Anti-Dumping Agreement clarifies that insubstantial price differences - those that produce only *de minimis* dumping margins - do not constitute dumping. Japan refers to Article 5.8 of the Anti-Dumping Agreement. The Anti-Dumping Agreement thus includes the requirement that the margin be substantial, just like the 1916 Act.

anti-dumping rules are triggered only in response to the practice of "dumping", i.e. a situation where an exporter sells its product abroad at lower prices than it does at home or at prices that are below cost, which causes "material injury" to producers of the product in the importing country. Once these facts are established, the investigating authorities may impose duties to offset prospectively the injurious dumping.

3.111 The United States argues that, in contrast, under the 1916 Act, mere dumping is not enough.[96] The complainant must show price discrimination which is common and systematic as well as substantial, and the complainant must demonstrate a predatory intent.[97] There is also no requirement that actual or threatened "material injury" to a domestic industry be shown. The complainant instead is required to show damages to its business or property. Thus, while an importer may violate the 1916 Act, it cannot be said that the same facts would satisfy the requirements for the imposition of anti-dumping duties.

3.112 In response to a question of the Panel regarding which criteria other than the "commonly and systematically" and "price substantially below" requirements are different from the Article VI definition of dumping, the United States notes that the 1916 Act addresses a particular type of price discrimination, namely, predatory pricing. For that reason, the price discrimination test in the 1916 Act includes not just the language quoted by the panel, but also the additional language describing the predatory intent that is required to be shown.

3.113 The United States concedes that the 1916 Act, like the Article VI definition of dumping, requires a showing that the product at issue has been sold in the United States at a price that is lower than the price at which that product has been sold abroad. However, the US price and the foreign price under the 1916 Act are not the

---

[96] The United States notes, in addition, that neither the heading of the 1916 Act nor its text uses the word "dumping".

[97] In response to a question of Japan regarding whether the United States would still consider Title VII of the Tariff Act of 1930 to be an anti-dumping law within the meaning of Article VI and the Anti-Dumping Agreement if the phrases "commonly and systematically" and "substantially" were added to the pertinent para. of Section 731, the United States notes that the hypothetical amendment would not seem to remove that law, as amended, from the coverage of Article VI. According to the United States, it would still be an anti-dumping law, as it requires findings of "dumping" and "injury," and it would still impose a border adjustment in the form of a duty. A Member may impose, as some Members currently do, requirements for the imposition of anti-dumping duties which go beyond the minimum requirements of "dumping" and "injury" set forth in Article VI, provided that those additional requirements serve to limit, rather than expand, the availability of anti-dumping duties, without necessarily removing the law from the coverage of Article VI. In response to a follow-up question of Japan regarding whether the answer would be the same if the requirement of intent is further added, the United States notes that, if the hypothesized intent is simply an intent to "dump" and cause "injury" within the meaning of Article VI, then the hypothesized law would seem to remain within the coverage of Article VI for the reasons discussed above. If the hypothesized intent is a predatory intent, the answer depends on how the inquiry into predation is incorporated into the law. If, for example, the law now required a finding of injury to competition instead of a finding of "injury" within the meaning of Article 3 of the Anti-Dumping Agreement, it would no longer seem to be an anti-dumping measure governed by Article VI. If, on the other hand, the law somehow retained the finding of "injury" within the meaning of Article 3 of the Anti-Dumping Agreement and did not require any finding of injury to competition, it would seem to remain within the coverage of Article VI for the reasons discussed above.

same as the US price and the foreign price under the Article VI definition of dumping. The basic differences are as follows:

(a) As to the US price, the 1916 Act provides only that the US price is the "price" at which the product at issue is imported or sold "within" the United States. In contrast, the US price found in the Article VI definition of dumping, as further described in Article 2 of the Anti-Dumping Agreement, is normally the price in the United States that is "made at the same level of trade, normally at the ex-factory level, and in respect of sales made at as nearly as possible the same time" as the price used for the foreign price, known as "normal value," with "[d]ue allowance [...] made [...], on its merits, for differences which affect price comparability, including differences in conditions and terms of sale, taxation, levels of trade, quantities, physical characteristics, and any other differences which are also demonstrated to affect price comparability."[98] In certain circumstances, however, a "constructed export price" is used to determine US price, and in that event "allowances for costs, including duties and taxes, incurred between importation and resale, and for profits accruing, should [...] be made" in addition to the allowances described above.[99]

(b) As to the foreign price, the 1916 Act provides that it is "the actual market value or wholesale price of such articles, at the time of exportation to the United States, in the principal markets of the country of their production, or of other foreign countries to which they are commonly exported after adding to such market value or wholesale price, freight, duty, and other charges and expenses necessarily incident to the importation and sale thereof in the United States." This price is similar to, but nevertheless different from, the foreign price found in the Article VI definition of dumping, as further described in Article 2 of the Anti-Dumping Agreement. This foreign price, or "normal value," the price in the exporting country that is "made at the same level of trade, normally at the ex-factory level, and in respect of sales made at as nearly as possible the same time" as the price used for the US price, with "[d]ue allowance [...] made [...], on its merits, for differences which affect price comparability, including differences in conditions and terms of sale, taxation, levels of trade, quantities, physical characteristics, and any other differences which are also demonstrated to affect price comparability."[100] In certain circumstances, however, instead of the price in the exporting country, "normal value" is based on the price in "an appropriate third country, provided that this price is representative, or with the cost of production in

---

98 The United States refers to Article 2.4 of the Anti-Dumping Agreement.

99 The United States refers to Articles 2.3 and 2.4 of the Anti-Dumping Agreement.

100 The United States refers to Article 2.4 Anti-Dumping Agreement.

the country of origin plus a reasonable amount for administrative, selling and general costs and for profits."[101]

3.114 The United States further argues that a review of the various substantive and procedural requirements of the 1916 Act confirms that they are the same as, or similar to, the requirements applicable under US anti-trust statutes.[102] In particular, a comparison of the 1916 Act with US anti-trust statutes shows, either on the basis of the plain language of the statutes or as interpreted by the courts, as follows:

(a) The 1916 Act requires a finding of price differences, like the Robinson-Patman Act.[103] The price differences under the 1916 Act, of course, must be "substantial" in amount and undertaken "commonly and systematically", while the Robinson-Patman Act only requires two sales to different buyers at different prices.[104]

(b) The 1916 Act requires a finding that the pricing at issue be undertaken with a specific predatory intent. This predatory pricing requirement is similar to that found in Section 2 of the Sherman Act and in so-called primary line cases under the Robinson-Patman Act.[105]

(c) The 1916 Act applies to Articles of "like grade and quality", just as that term is used in the Robinson-Patman Act.[106]

(d) The statute of limitations for bringing a lawsuit under the 1916 Act is the same as that under the Clayton Act and the Robinson-Patman Act, i.e. 4 years.[107]

(e) The 1916 Act provides for enforcement through either a civil lawsuit brought by a private party before a US court or a criminal prosecution brought by the US Department of Justice. These remedies mirror those available under the anti-trust laws including the Sherman Act, the Clayton Act and the Robinson-Patman Act.

[101] The United States refers to Article 2.2 of the Anti-Dumping Agreement.

[102] In response to a question of Japan, the United States answers, however, that the 1916 Act is not among those laws regularly enforced by the Department of Justice and the Federal Trade Commission. Hence the United States sometimes uses the term "anti-trust-type statute" when referring to the 1916 Act.

[103] The United States refers to 15 U.S.C. 13(a).

[104] The United States refers to *International Telephone & Telegraph Corp. et al.*, 104 F.T.C. 280, p. 417, citing E. Kintner, *A Robinson-Patman Primer*, 3d ed. (1979), p. 35.

[105] The United States notes that neither of those Acts normally requires proof of intent, at least in civil cases. There is an intent requirement in some anti-trust (Sherman Act) criminal cases. The United States refers to ABA, *Anti-trust Law Developments (Fourth)*, p. 662-64.

[106] The United States refers to *Zenith III, Op. Cit.*, p. 1223. The United States recalls that the *Zenith III* court explained that "we find that the same standard of 'like grade and quality' limited product comparisons under section 2 of the Clayton Act prior to the Robinson-Patman amendments. Since the Clayton Act was passed in 1914, the same standard is applicable under the Antidumping Act of 1916." The United States refers to ibid., pp. 1226-27.

[107] The United States refers to *Helmac I, Op. Cit.*, pp. 566-67, where, according to the United States, the court relied on the purpose of US Congress in enacting the 1916 Act to interpret the 1916 Act as having same statute of limitations as other anti-trust statutes, where the 1916 Act did not set forth applicable statute of limitations.

(f) The issue of whether a private party has the requisite standing to bring a 1916 Act lawsuit is determined by reference to anti-trust standing principles.[108]

(g) The 1916 Act authorizes the award of treble damages to a successful private litigant. This remedy is somewhat unusual under US civil law, but it is a common remedy for violations of US anti-trust statutes. Indeed, in the third paragraph of the 1916 Act, the US Congress basically replicated the then-existing language of Section 4 of the Clayton Act[109] and Section 7 of the Sherman Act[110] which authorized treble damages for "any person who shall be injured in his business or property" by reason of any conduct proscribed by US anti-trust laws.

(h) With regard to its criminal provisions, the 1916 Act is virtually identical to, and specifies the same penalties as, the criminal provisions of the Sherman Act in force in 1916.

3.115 **Japan** considers that the addition of qualifying elements to the core features of the law does not alter the fundamental nature of the 1916 Act as a anti-dumping law. The fact that the 1916 Act addresses only dumping that occurs "commonly and systematically" at a "substantially less" price does not alter the conclusion that the 1916 Act is an anti-dumping law and is subject to the requirements of Article VI of the GATT 1994 and the Anti-Dumping Agreement. Just as a WTO Member can choose not to have a domestic anti-dumping law, it can choose to restrict its ability to impose anti-dumping duties beyond the limits imposed by the Anti-Dumping Agreement. Any Member is free to include in its national law criteria and conditions stricter than those required by Article VI and the Anti-Dumping Agreement. However, a Member may not, as the United States has done, depart from Article VI and the Anti-Dumping Agreement to make it easier to impose anti-dumping duties or to allow other remedies.

3.116 Japan is of the view that the text of the 1916 Act is unequivocal. That is why Japan believes that the United States intentionally avoids a textual interpretation of the 1916 Act. However, as the Appellate Body has made clear on numerous occasions, under the rules of treaty interpretation, the Panel's primary focus should be the text.

3.117 The **United States** considers that Japan makes several unsupportable statements with regard to the text of the 1916 Act. At one point, Japan states that "[t]he issue is not what US courts say [...]." Japan even states that the text of the 1916 Act is "unequivocal," despite the fact that it later discusses the differing interpretations of that text reached by US courts in the *Zenith* line of cases and the preliminary decisions in *Geneva Steel* and *Wheeling-Pittsburgh.*

---

[108] The United States refers to, e.g., *Isra Fruit Ltd. v. Agrexco Agr. Export Co., Op. Cit.*, pp. 988-89; *Jewel Foliage Co. v. Uniflora Overseas Florida, Op. Cit.*, p. 516; *Schwimmer v. Sony Corp., Op. Cit.*, pp. 796-97.

[109] The United States notes that the relevant Clayton Act language can be found at 38 Stat. 731 (1914).

[110] The United States notes that the relevant Sherman Act language can be found at 26 Stat. 210 (1890). The US Congress later amended this part of the Sherman Act.

3.118 In the United States' view, an examination of the text of the 1916 Act is sufficient to show that the 1916 Act is outside the scope of Article VI. First, at the very least, the 1916 Act can be seen from its text to be an "internal" law. It imposes damages on importers; it does not impose a border adjustment in the form of a duty on imported products. That aspect of the 1916 Act - the nature of the measure imposed in application of the law - removes any doubt as to whether Article VI governs the 1916 Act. An "internal" law is only subject to Article III of the GATT 1994. It cannot be subject to Article VI. Article VI only governs a Member's use of a border adjustment in the form of an anti-dumping duty. Second, the text of the 1916 Act also indicates, very plainly, that it is not an anti-dumping law or measure attempting to counteract injurious dumping based on findings of "dumping" and "injury". The true nature of the 1916 Act, as an anti-trust statute, may be more difficult to discern simply from the text of the 1916 Act, but the case law interpreting the 1916 Act removes any doubt on this point.

3.119 The United States recalls that Japan attempts to characterise the 1916 Act as an anti-dumping law not by addressing the distinctions between anti-trust and anti-dumping, but rather by arguing that the "essential concepts" of the 1916 Act and Article VI are "identical". According to Japan, both the 1916 Act and Article VI regulate international price discrimination. In making this argument, Japan never addresses the obvious absence of the essential Article VI requirement of "injury" from the 1916 Act. Furthermore, in attempting to characterise the 1916 Act as simply a law addressing international price discrimination, Japan tries to minimise the significance of the predatory intent element of the 1916 Act, among others. It states that "the addition of qualifying elements on the core features of the law does not alter the fundamental nature of the Anti-Dumping Act of 1916 as an anti-dumping law." Nevertheless, however it is characterised, the fact remains that to succeed under the 1916 Act, a plaintiff must plead and prove many elements that make it qualitatively different from a measure designed to remedy injurious dumping. Foremost among these elements is the required showing of predatory intent.

3.120 The United States notes that, essentially, Japan is reading into Article VI the limitation that all laws with any kind of international price discrimination component must conform to the anti-dumping rules. If this were true, it would extend the anti-dumping rules far into a realm which pre-dated them and whose objectives, underlying principles and targeted conduct are quite different, namely, the realm of anti-trust laws.

Japan notes that, although the United States now asserts that the textual interpretation of the Act is important, the United States persists in arguing that the Panel is bound by one particular interpretation of the 1916 Act by one of its courts. This is inconsistent.

3.122 Japan also recalls the 1916 Act's proviso that its sanctions apply only when the dumping is undertaken with the intent to injure or destroy or prevent the establishment of a US industry. The dumping element is the exclusive criterion for determining whether the 1916 Act falls under the scope of Article VI of the GATT 1994 and the Anti-Dumping Agreement. Injury is an additional element that is required in order to impose anti-dumping duties when dumping exists. The 1916 Act indisputably is directed at protection of competitors rather than protection of competition. It is clear that the 1916 Act regulates dumping, not anti-trust. The United States seems to argue that "intent to injure" is different from "injury to domestic industry", and therefore the 1916 Act is not an anti-dumping law but an anti-trust law. This is incorrect. "Predatory intent" is a concept that exists in anti-trust laws; it is not a 1916 Act concept.

3.123 Japan also notes that in reply to Japan's questions, the United States concedes that anti-dumping laws do not cease to be anti-dumping laws merely because they contain "additional requirements [that] serve to limit, rather than expand, the availability of antidumping duties [...]."

3.124 The **United States** submits that Japan's assertion that "predatory intent" is not a 1916 Act concept, is clearly contradicted not only by the US court decisions such as *Zenith III* and the legislative history they discuss, but even by the preliminary *Geneva Steel* and *Wheeling-Pittsburgh* decisions on which Japan relies. Judge Sargus in *Wheeling-Pittsburgh* characterised the intent required under the 1916 Act as a "predatory intent". And, Judge Benson in *Geneva Steel*, recognized that proof of a monopolistic "recoupment" scenario would be sufficient and relevant, but decided that other sorts of injurious "intent" might also be shown.

3. *The Distinction Between Anti-Dumping Laws and Anti-Trust Laws*

3.125 **Japan** contends that in the United States, as elsewhere, anti-trust (or competition policy) statutes protect "competition, not competitors".[111] In the landmark US anti-trust case *Brown Shoe*, Supreme Court Chief Justice Earl Warren opined that the Cellar-Kefauver Amendment to the Clayton Act was created to "restrain mergers only to the extent that such mergers may tend to lessen competition."[112] The Chief Justice looked to the legislative history of the Amendment and found that Congress had intended to protect competition in markets, not companies competing in the markets (much less domestic industries). In *Brunswick*[113] the Supreme Court reaffirmed 25 years later that anti-trust laws protect "competition not competitors"[114].

3.126 Japan argues that anti-dumping statutes, on the other hand, protect domestic industries from the unfair trade practice of dumping by foreign competitors.[115] For example, under Article VI of the GATT 1994, the Anti-Dumping Agreement and the US Tariff Act of 1930, anti-dumping duties cannot be imposed unless the dumping is causing material injury or threat thereof to (or is retarding the establishment of) a US

[111] Japan refers to *Brown Shoe Co., Inc. v. United States*, 370 US 294, p. 319 (1962) (hereinafter "*Brown Shoe*"), where the court upheld action to enjoin merger of two shoe corporations. Japan also refers to *Brunswick Corp. v. Bowl-O-Mat, Inc.*, 429 US 477, p. 490 (1977) (hereinafter "*Brunswick*")

[112] Japan refers to *Brown Shoe, Op. Cit.*, p. 319.

[113] Japan refers to *Brunswick, Op. Cit.*, p. 488, where the court rejected as not cognizable under US anti-trust law Pueblo Bowl-O-Mat's claim of injury (reduced profits) due to Brunswick's purchase and reinvigoration of a near-bankrupt competitor.

[114] Japan refers to ibid.

[115] Japan refers to *J.C. Penney Co. v. Department of the Treasury*, 319 F. Supp. 1023, 1024 (S.D.N.Y 1970), aff'd, 439 F.2d 63 (2d Cir.), cert. denied, 404 US 869 (1971) where it is stated that anti-dumping laws prevent "actual or threatened injury to a domestic industry resulting from the sale in the United States market of merchandise at prices lower than in the home market." Japan also refers to *Timken v. Simon*, 539 F. 2d 221, 223 (1976).

industry. The International Trade Commission, in evaluating claims under the Tariff Act, follows the statutory test and bases its decision on whether there is material injury to the relevant US industry.[116]

3.127 Japan considers that, like the Tariff Act of 1930 and its predecessor, the Antidumping Act of 1921, the 1916 Act was enacted to protect domestic industries from dumping by foreign companies. As discussed above, this is evident from the plain language of the statute, which forbids the dumping of products "with the intent of destroying or injuring an industry in the United States, or of preventing the establishment of an industry in the United States."[117] The text of the 1916 Act text confirms that the Act protects domestic industries and this fact, in turn, confirms that the 1916 Act is an anti-dumping law.

3.128 The **United States** notes that Japan draws a complete dichotomy between anti-trust laws and their pursuit of consumer welfare, and trade laws and their focus on producer welfare in an apparent attempt to argue that any hint of US Congressional concern for the welfare of individual enterprises removes a law from the anti-trust ambit. Such a dichotomy exaggerates and distorts reality. The United States agrees entirely that the principal aim of United States anti-trust laws is to protect competition, not competitors or particular industries.[118] However, while the purpose of many, if not most, anti-trust laws is to preserve the competitive process in order to enhance economic efficiency and increase consumer welfare, it is also true that quite a number of anti-trust laws, in the United States and other countries, may have additional purposes, including the protection of small enterprises or other individual competitors. Anti-trust laws that pursue objectives other than just economic efficiency are not thereby deprived of their "anti-trust" character.

3.129 The United States states that one example of alternative anti-trust purposes can be found in the United States' Robinson-Patman Act, where, in the "secondary line" context (in which certain distributors of a good receive less advantageous sales terms than other distributors), the statutory concern is for adverse effects on individual competitors rather than competition itself.

3.130 The United States argues that other examples can readily be found in Japan's own anti-trust laws and enforcement guidelines. Section 19 of the Anti-Monopoly Act prohibits "unfair business practices", including price discrimination and "unjust low-priced sales" or "unfair price-cutting". The Japan Fair Trade Commission (hereinafter "JFTC") has defined these terms as:

> "Without proper justification, supplying a commodity or service continuously at a price which is excessively below cost incurred in the said supply, or otherwise unjustly supplying a commodity or service at a low price, thereby tending to cause difficulties to the business activities of other entrepreneurs."[119]

---

[116] Japan refers to, e.g., *Copperweld v. United States*, 682 F. Supp. 552 (Ct. Int' l Trade 1988). Japan also refers to *Gerald Metals v. United States*, 937 F. Supp. 930 (Ct. Int'l Trade 1996).

[117] Japan refers to 15 U.S.C. § 72 (1999).

[118] The United States refers to, e.g., *Brooke Group*, *Op. Cit.*, and *Brown Shoe*, *Op. Cit.*, p. 320.

[119] JFTC, Executive Bureau, Guidelines Concerning Unfair Price Cutting (Nov. 20, 1984).

3.131 According to the United States, the JFTC further defined "tending to cause difficulties to other entrepreneurs" to include "a recognized possibility of such disruption"; an "actual disruption" is not necessarily required. In FY 1998 the JFTC reported that it had issued one warning and 506 "cautions" to enterprises regarding "unjustified" low prices. These rules apply to imported as well as domestic goods; in addition, the JFTC is now applying the Anti-Monopoly Act to cross-border transactions.[120] Clearly, some provisions of Japan's anti-trust law seem to be designed to protect competitors as well as competition.[121]

3.132 **Japan** maintains its view that there are clear and fundamental differences between anti-dumping laws and anti-trust laws.[122] Anti-trust statutes protect competition, not competitors, and regulate competition within a country.[123] In contrast, anti-dumping statutes protect domestic industries from the unfair practice of dumping by foreign competitors. More particularly, anti-dumping regulates price differentials between sales in two countries.

3.133 Japan considers that anti-trust laws have the primary and essential concern of protecting competition in the single domestic market. "International price discrimination", or price differentials between goods in the exporting country's market and the importing country's market (here, the United States) does not fall within the scope of this concern. Anti-trust laws prohibit domestic price discrimination in order to protect competition in the domestic market only. And, as discussed below regarding the United States' Article III:4 violations, this is true regardless of whether goods are imported or domestic. A careful comparison of the differences between anti-dumping and anti-trust laws demonstrates that the 1916 Act does not address anti-trust concerns.

---

[120] The United States refers to BNA, Int'l Trade Reporter, Vol.15 No. 26, p. 1131 (1 July 1998), entitled "US, Canadian Companies Involved in Cases Launched Under Japan's Antimonopoly Law".

[121] The United States notes that a similar example is provided by the very recent decision of the German Supreme Court to uphold a German agency's ban on "unfair" US exports of consumer goods by the Lands End catalogue operation to Germany that were accompanied by the company's usual unconditional refund guarantee, a guarantee that the German authorities reportedly found "economically irrational." The United States refers to The Washington Post ("Business Digest"), September 25, 1999; Associated Press, "US Retailer's Advertisements Banned," September 24, 1999.

[122] In response to a question of the United States regarding whether there is a commonly accepted international standard for what constitutes an anti-trust law, Japan notes that such a standard is being developed, as shown by the discussions on trade and competition in the WTO. Whatever the precise terms of the standard eventually agreed upon, it is clear from the current state of discussions that the 1916 Act is a trade law and will not fall within the standard. More importantly, there *is* a commonly accepted international standard for an anti-dumping law - Article VI of the GATT 1994 and the Anti-Dumping Agreement.

[123] Japan considers that the United States attempts further to cloud this issue by calling attention to Japan's Anti-Monopoly Law. First, the topic of how Japan determines and enforces its anti-trust laws is irrelevant to the present proceeding. Second, the US presentation is factually inaccurate. Japan's law is designed to protect competition, not competitors. Specifically, as stated in Section 1 of the Law, the Law is intended to "promote fair and freer competition, [...] to assure the interests of Japan's consumers." Moreover, it does not apply to "cross-border price discrimination" or dumping. Also, for the record, Japan notes that in FY1998 the JFTC issued 599 cautions to enterprises regarding unjust low-price sales, not 506, as the US claims.

3.134 In the view of Japan, the 1916 Act clearly focuses on "international price discrimination"[124]; therefore, in no way can it be interpreted as an anti-trust law. It is very clear that the conduct addressed by the 1916 Act includes the essential concepts of dumping; therefore, the 1916 Act must comply with Article VI of the GATT 1994 and the provisions of the Anti-Dumping Agreement.

3.135 Japan submits that, in any event, the present proceeding does not require the Panel to promulgate a rule of general application or otherwise burden itself by trying to elucidate the distinction between anti-trust laws and anti-dumping laws.[125] Japan clarifies these distinctions only to help the Panel better understand the 1916 Act's inconsistency. When one focuses on the conduct regulated by the clear, unambiguous text of the 1916 Act, the character of the Act is manifest. It regulates dumping. The issue is not one of anti-trust, and this Panel's judgement in Japan's favour will have no bearing on Members' anti-trust laws.

3.136 The **United States** considers that Japan's conclusion that competition laws never protect competitors, but only the competitive process is simplistic. First, the Robinson-Patman Act arguably addressed the protection of competitors, as well as competition, in "primary line" cases prior to the 1993 *Brooke Group* decision, and still does so in the "secondary line" context. Second, the United States finds it difficult to grasp how the Japan Fair Trade Commission's "Guidelines Concerning Unfair Price Cutting" protect competition rather than competitors, as Japan claims. This one measure led to 599 "cautions" to enterprises in FY 1998 alone, according to Japan. The Guidelines themselves state at Section 3(2) that

> "[...] the second characteristic of unfair price-cutting is the fact that it "tend[s] to cause difficulties to the business activities of other entrepreneurs."

3.137 In response to a question of the Panel regarding the basic features of anti-dumping laws as opposed to anti-trust laws, **Japan** reiterates its view that anti-trust statutes protect competition, not competitors and regulate competition within a country. In contrast, anti-dumping statutes protect domestic industries from the unfair practice of dumping by foreign competitors. More particularly, anti-dumping laws regulate the price differential between sales in two countries. Careful comparison of those fundamental differences between anti-dumping and anti-trust laws enables one to conclude that the 1916 Act is not intended for anti-trust purposes.

---

[124] Japan refers to, e.g., "Overview and Compilation of U.S. Trade Statutes", US House of Representatives, US Government Printing Office (Washington: 1997), p. 65.

[125] Japan refers to the Appellate Body Report on *United States - Shirts and Blouses*, *supra*, footnote 27, at 340, where it is stated that "Article 3.2 of the DSU states that the Members of the WTO "recognize" that the dispute settlement system "serves to preserve the rights and obligations of Members under the covered agreements, and *to clarify the existing provisions of those agreements* in accordance with customary rules of interpretation of public international law" (emphasis added). Given the explicit aim of dispute settlement that permeates the DSU, we do not consider that Article 3.2 of the DSU is meant to encourage either panels or the Appellate Body to "make law" by clarifying existing provisions of the WTO Agreement outside the context of resolving a particular dispute. A panel needs only address those claims which must be addressed in order to resolve the matter in issue in the dispute." (emphasis in original).

3.138 The **United States**, in reply to the same question of the Panel, considers that anti-dumping rules and competition laws have different objectives, are founded on different principles, and seek to remedy different problems. Anti-dumping rules are not based on the economic assumptions that underlie most Members' competition laws, nor are they intended as a remedy for the predatory pricing practices of firms or as a remedy for any other private anti-competitive practices typically condemned by competition laws. Rather, the anti-dumping rules are a trade remedy which WTO Members have agreed is necessary to the maintenance of the multilateral trading system. Without this and other trade remedies, there could have been no agreement on broader GATT 1947 and later WTO packages of market-opening agreements, especially given the imperfections which remain in the multilateral trading system.

3.139 The United States argues that, as a trade remedy, the anti-dumping rules are triggered only in response to the practice of "dumping," i.e. a situation where an exporter sells its product abroad at lower prices than it does at home or at prices that are below cost, which causes "material injury" to producers of the product in the importing country. Once these facts are established, the investigating authorities may impose duties to offset prospectively the injurious dumping.

3.140 The United States considers that, while this simple definition of injurious dumping may suggest comparisons with competition laws addressing price discrimination, any careful analysis shows major differences between the anti-dumping rules and the competition laws.

3.141 The United States notes, first of all, that the relatively straightforward nature of the test for injurious dumping contrasts with the complexities of the imperfections in the multilateral trading system which give rise to the need for the anti-dumping rules in the first place. Although some dumping may be due to business advantages and market segmentation which have arisen in response to commercial forces, more typically it is a government's industrial policies or key aspects of the national economic system which a government has created, promoted or tolerated that enables injurious dumping to take place.

3.142 The United States contends that principally of concern in this regard are certain government industrial policies or practices which in most instances are not directly or fully subject to any type of WTO prohibitions or disciplines. In other instances, these policies or practices may not fully conform to WTO disciplines or, even if they do, may not leave all Members on an equal footing. These policies still are objectionable because they distort market structures or processes and, as a result, provide artificial advantages to home market producers (often at the expense of home market consumers). These artificial advantages generally translate into increased profits for these producers in their home market, which make it possible and, for various reasons, may encourage these producers to engage in injurious dumping abroad.

3.143 The United States submits that one broad category of objectionable policies can be found in government industrial policies which combine limits on domestic competition with market access barriers that keep out foreign competitors. Here, the possible combinations are quite extensive. On the one hand, the existence of only limited domestic competition may be due to many different types of industrial policies falling under the umbrella of government actions intended to influence the structure of the home market with the aim of affecting the number or type of producers, including (1) government policies limiting the number of producers in a particular industry, such as through the restrictive award of licenses, (2) state monopolies, (3) government policies favouring a "national champion" firm within an industry, (4) government policies which divide up and stabilize market shares, and (5) any of a variety of other government policies which regulate commerce by creating, promoting or tolerating monopolies or oligopolies or by favouring some domestic competitors over other domestic (and foreign) competitors. Protection against foreign competition, meanwhile, may be due to either high tariffs or any number of non-tariff barriers, such as (1) import charges, quantitative restrictions, import licensing and customs barriers; standards, testing, labelling and certification, including, for example, the acquiescence of a government in unwarranted regulations sought by industry, a government's unnecessarily restrictive application of sanitary and phytosanitary standards, and a government's refusal to accept foreign manufacturers' self-certification of conformance to home market product standards, (2) investment barriers, such as limitations on foreign equity participation and on access to government-funded research and development programs, local content and export performance requirements, and restrictions on transferring earnings and capital, (3) State trading rights, (4) services barriers, such as limits on the range of financial services offered by home market financial institutions, regulation of international data flows and restrictions on the use of foreign data processing, (5) lack of intellectual property protection, including inadequate patent, copyright and trademark regimes, (6) government procurement practices such as closed bidding and (7) bribery and corruption. Other general categories of objectionable policies include domestic price controls, government subsidization and certain state trading arrangements.

3.144 In the view of the United States, the anti-dumping rules are a practical, albeit indirect, response to these trade-distorting policies. The anti-dumping rules allow Members to respond through the imposition of offsetting duties when confronted with one harmful result of these policies, namely, injurious dumping in export markets by the producers that benefit from these policies. From this perspective, the anti-dumping rules represent an effort to maintain a "level playing field" among producers in different countries. Anti-dumping duties are designed to offset, quantitatively, the artificial advantages realized by the exporting country's producers so that producers in the importing country may compete, at least in the importing country's market, on equal footing with the exporting country's producers.

3.145 The United States considers that anti-dumping rules also help to neutralize inequities that may arise from differences in national economic systems, even as international trade liberalises. For example, differing social and legal arrangements for employment and under-employment, or differing debt-equity structures and debt burdens, often made possible by indirect government intervention in the banking system, can favour the exporting country's producers over the importing country's producers and lead to injurious dumping. Other circumstances that can lead to injurious dumping can include certain competition-inhibiting private conduct, cross-subsidization that can result from the legal organization and operation of foreign business groupings and, in the case of non-market economies or some economies in transition, export directives and prices and costs not entirely based on market principles.

3.146 The United States notes, therefore, that the anti-dumping rules implicitly recognize that there is an accepted norm for the behaviour of governments in the broad multilateral trade context, i.e. a government should not pursue industrial policies which distort market structures or processes and thereby provide artificial advantages to domestic producers to the detriment of producers in other countries. The anti-dumping rules also recognize that there should be a remedy for certain harms caused when different economic systems interact.

3.147 According to the United States, competition laws, on the other hand, appropriately do not take these matters into consideration, and they do not address the underlying problems at which the anti-dumping rules are directed. Instead, competition laws remedy private pricing practices which, in themselves, are objectionable because they are anti-competitive in an anti-trust sense.

3.148 The United States points out that the primary objectives of competition policy, as expressed in competition laws, are to promote economic efficiency and to maximize consumer welfare through the optimal allocation of resources in competitive markets. Through the protection of the competitive process, competition law helps to ensure productive, allocative, and distributional efficiencies throughout the economy. Healthy competition, including potential competition, results in pressures to reduce costs and prices (static efficiency) and to introduce new and better products on the market (dynamic efficiency).

3.149 The United States argues that competition laws therefore are largely directed at the competitive practices of private firms and market structures, with the objective of assuring a competitive market. In some countries, the competition laws have additional, less central objectives, such as the preservation of a decentralized economy, support of small businesses or maintenance of economic and social stability.

3.150 The United States acknowledges that the anti-dumping rules address certain private pricing practices as do the competition laws. However, dumping practices are not anti-competitive in an anti-trust sense. The anti-dumping rules provide a remedy against injurious dumping as an indirect response to a foreign government's market-distortive industrial policies or differences in national economic systems. As a result, although dumping by foreign producers can, for example, send false signals to the importing country's market that distort investment patterns, dumping practices will not normally qualify as "anti-competitive" when analysed under the distinct rules of most national competition laws.

3.151 The United States recalls that, in the Working Group on the Interaction between Trade and Competition Policy in 1998, the European Communities addressed the distinction between anti-dumping and competition rules:

> "Anti-dumping law and competition law apply in different economic, legal and institutional contexts. Competition law prohibits and subjects to strict penalties certain forms of pricing behaviour by firms. While competition law applies in principle within the context of an integrated market, Antidumping law applies in an economic setting which is still characterized by border measures and other regulatory obstacles and distortions of trade."[126]

3.152 The United States notes that, in addition, during the meeting at which the Working Group considered these papers, a representative of the European Commu-

[126] The United States refers to document WT/WGTCP/W/78.

nities "reiterated that the submission by his delegation argued that anti-dumping rules and competition rules applied in different economic, legal and institutional contexts and that therefore there could be no question of the replacement of one set of rules for the other, and no question of simply making a mechanical transposition from competition law into anti-dumping law of concepts which were intended to deal with a totally different kind of problem and underlay a totally different type of instrument."[127]

4. *The Reach of Article VI of the GATT 1994 and the Anti-Dumping Agreement*

3.153 According to the **United States**, there is no support in the text of Article VI or the Anti-Dumping Agreement for Japan's implicit contention that those disciplines govern any measure based in any respect on the concept of international price discrimination. Nowhere does the text of Article VI or the Anti-Dumping Agreement state that its disciplines govern *any* law based upon the concept of price discrimination *regardless* of any other elements required to be proven under the law.

3.154 The United States argues, moreover, that to read into the text of Article VI the limitation that all laws with any kind of international price discrimination component must conform to the anti-dumping rules would extend the anti-dumping rules far into a realm which pre-dated them and whose objectives, underlying principles and targeted conduct are quite different - namely, the realm of anti-trust (or competition) laws.

3.155 The United States considers that the anti-dumping rules and anti-trust laws have different objectives, are founded on different principles, and seek to remedy different problems. The anti-dumping rules are not intended as a remedy for the predatory pricing practices of firms or for any other private anti-competitive practices typically condemned by anti-trust laws.

3.156 The United States argues that, in contrast, anti-trust laws remedy, among other things, private pricing practices which are objectionable because they are instruments of cartelization, monopolisation or abuse of dominant position. Broadly speaking, anti-trust laws target conduct which restricts economic freedom for consumers and competitors.[128] While it is true that the anti-dumping rules address certain private pricing practices, it is not because these pricing practices - that is, injurious dumping practices - are anti-competitive in an anti-trust sense. Injurious dumping practices will not normally qualify as "anti-competitive" when analysed under the distinct rules of most national anti-trust laws.

3.157 The United States notes, in summary, that a review of the text and the objectives of the two sets of rules confirms that Article VI and the Anti-Dumping Agreement do not govern every single rule that references price discrimination regardless of the law's other requirements. The 1916 Act is not directed at the simple price differences that constitute dumping under the anti-dumping rules, nor is it based on the notion of material injury to a domestic industry. Therefore, because the 1916 Act is

---

[127] Report on the Meeting of 27-28 July 1998, WT/WGTCP/M/5, 25 September 1998, para. 71.

[128] The United States refers to *Northern Pacific Railway v. United States*, 356 US 1, p. 4 (1958).

an anti-trust-type statute, it is not governed by Article VI and the Anti-Dumping Agreement.

3.158 The United States considers, furthermore, that if the Panel were to accept Japan's argument and rule that Article VI and the Anti-Dumping Agreement apply to all forms of international price discrimination, and regardless of the nature of the injury sustained, the 1916 Act would not be the only casualty. Such a ruling would seem to mean that other Members' attempted monopolisation or abuse of dominance laws, such as those in Japan and the European Communities, would be WTO-illegal to the extent that those laws address attempted monopolisation or an abuse of dominance undertaken through predatory, cross-border pricing practices. That result could not have been intended by Article VI or the Anti-Dumping Agreement.

3.159 In reply to a request of the Panel for clarification of its argument, the United States notes that the broad interpretation of Article VI advocated by Japan and the European Communities would seem to preclude any legal remedies whatsoever against international price discrimination other than the imposition of offsetting duties particularly described in the WTO agreements. Logically, this would render inoperative any aspect of a Member's anti-trust/competition law applicable to cross-border predatory pricing practices. In the United States this would include at least Sections 1 and 2 of the Sherman Act[129], or perhaps even predatory pricing claims under the Robinson-Patman Act, if the goods in question were imports (and sold at predatory levels by US affiliates or agents of the exporters). In the EU it would encompass Article 82 of the Treaty of Amsterdam and similar Member State legislation (German and French law, for example), and, in Japan, aspects of the Anti-Monopoly Act. Even where low prices in the enforcing state's territory are not expressly and consistently compared with higher prices in the exporting state, an anti-trust law might proscribe predatory selling prices for imported (as well as domestic) goods.[130] If "anti-dumping duties" are suddenly deemed to be the exclusive remedy in all circumstances against low-priced imports, then the future of these kinds of anti-trust remedy is questionable.

3.160 The United States further notes that, to the extent that its Anti-Monopoly Act proscribes low-pricing of imported goods, Japan's own competition enforcement policies could be jeopardized by arguments for the exclusivity of Article VI. This could include enforcement of the Act's provisions against monopolisation and "unfair trade practices." According to the Japan Fair Trade Commission, such unfair trade practices include "refusal to deal, discriminatory pricing, dumping and resale price

---

[129] In response to a question of the Panel, the United States notes that the Sherman Act does not expressly mention price discrimination, but it indirectly addresses international price discrimination when it is a factual element in a monopolisation case based upon predatory pricing (including cases involving attempts or conspiracies to monopolise).

[130] The United States considers that the enforcement concern necessarily would be upon adverse economic effects within the enforcing state, not outside of it. As the Panel is aware, monopolisation (and abuses of dominance) cases require the identification of an appropriate relevant market within national anti-trust jurisdiction. Such a market could, in geographic terms, encompass a part of the enforcing state's territory, or all of it, or even a broader area in which the enforcing state would be a part (e.g., "regional" or "global" markets).

maintenance."[131] The exclusive scope argued for Article VI of the GATT 1994 might also prevent continued use of the JFTC's "Guidelines Concerning Unfair Price Cutting" insofar as they are applied against low-priced imported goods.

3.161 The United States argues that, likewise, European Union "abuse of dominance" cases such as *TetraPak II*[132] or even actions such as the Commission's 1997 decision on Boeing's acquisition of McDonnell Douglas[133] could be suspect, since they included allegations that foreign enterprises used dominant positions in international markets to engage in predation within the EU. Given the motivations of the European Communities to integrate previously separate national markets, geographic price-discrimination is often regarded with concern by Brussels.[134]

3.162 **Japan** responds that, regardless of precisely where anti-trust laws begin and end, the global trading community has decided where anti-dumping law begins and ends and the two types of laws are distinct. When one focuses on the conduct regulated by the clear, unambiguous text of the 1916 Act, the character of the 1916 Act is manifest. It regulates dumping.[135] The issue is not one of anti-trust, and this Panel's judgement in Japan's favour will have no bearing on Members' anti-trust laws.[136]

3.163 Japan also recalls that the issue in the present proceeding is not the scope of other Members' anti-trust laws, but whether the 1916 Act is inconsistent with WTO provisions. The United States attempts to once again shift the Panel's attention to Japan's and the EU's anti-trust or competition laws. This is irrelevant and, moreover, is not within the present Panel's terms of reference.

3.164 Japan notes, finally, that the United States claims, in its answer to a question of the Panel, that Japan's own competition policies could be jeopardised by Japan's argument for the exclusivity of Article VI. The United States quotes the word

---

131 The United States refers to the "Overview of the Anti-Monopoly Act," found at "www.jftc.admix.go.jp/e-page/ama.htm").

132 The United States refers to [1997] 4 CMLR 662 (ECJ 1996).

133 The United States refers to Decision of 30 July 1997, C (97) 2598.

134 The United States refers to Springer, *Borden and United Brands Revisited: a Comparison of the Elements of Price Discrimination under E.C. and U.S. Law*, 1 ECLR 42 (1997).

135 Japan notes, in response to a question of the Panel regarding the scope of Article VI and the Anti-Dumping Agreement, that they address international price discrimination where prices in the importing market are lower than prices in the exporting market. Where these conditions giving rise to this type of international price discrimination are met, a law, whatever it may be called, is an anti-dumping measure and must conform to Article VI and the Anti-Dumping Agreement. In response to a similar question of the United States regarding whether Article VI and the Anti-Dumping Agreement would apply to any law based upon the concept of international price discrimination regardless of any other elements to be proven under the law, Japan notes that Article VI of the GATT 1994 and the Anti-Dumping Agreement govern any and all laws and regulations that are aimed at countering international price discrimination as defined under those provisions. Requiring that other elements be proven does not change whether a law is governed by Article VI and the Anti-Dumping Agreement. A Member cannot avoid its obligations under Article VI and the Anti-Dumping Agreement simply by adding, altering or deleting an element. In addition, a Member cannot avoid its obligations by adding impermissible penalty provisions different from or more stringent than that allowed by Article VI and the Anti-Dumping Agreement.

136 In response to a question of the United States, Japan notes that "predatory pricing practices" as that phrase is used in anti-trust laws need not comport with the requirements of Article VI and the Anti-Dumping Agreement.

"dumping" completely out of the context in which it is used in the Japan Fair Trade Commission's unofficial English language home page and makes a misguided assertion. Examination of the authentic Japanese version of "'Unfair Trade Practices' Fair Trade Commission Notification No.15, June 18, 1982" demonstrates with absolute clarity that Japan's Anti-Monopoly Act regulates "unfair low price sales" and not "international price discriminations" as alleged by the United States. The word "dumping" is used in the alleged home page of the Japan Fair Trade Commission only in a generic sense to denote "unfair low price sales" for the sake of ease of understanding by the general public.[137]

3.165 The **United States** rejects Japan's attempt to downplay the necessary implications of its position in the present case with regard to other anti-trust laws. Japan's argument seems to boil down to its contention that anti-trust laws govern only *domestic* price discrimination and therefore no anti-trust rules would be affected by a finding by this Panel that *international* price discrimination measures must comport with Article VI and the Anti-Dumping Agreement.

3.166 The United States notes that it cannot agree. Japan's broad statement that anti-trust rules govern only domestic price discrimination does not comport with reality. In the United States, the Sherman Act and parts of the Clayton Act clearly apply to foreign conduct with direct and foreseeable anti-competitive effects in the United States. This has been the case for many years and is no longer particularly controversial. For example, the US Sherman and Clayton Acts have long been applied - when appropriate - to international pricing conduct by American and foreign parties. Two early Sherman Act cases are *United States v. American Tobacco Co.*[138] and *United States v. Pacific and Arctic Ry. Co.*[139]. Other examples are the Justice Department's

[137] In response to a question of the United States regarding whether Japan agrees that the word "dumping" may be used in a context that does not fall within Article VI or the Anti-Dumping Agreement, Japan notes that the word "dumping" can include various concepts and does not necessarily mean "international price discrimination" under Article VI of the GATT 1994. For example, in the panel report on *United States - Standards for Reformulated and Conventional Gasoline*, adopted on 20 May 1996, WT/DS2/R, the term "dumping" refers to the act of a refiner, blender or importer mixing into conventional gasoline fuel components that are restricted in reformulated gasoline. Japan refers to para. 2.4 of the panel report. However, here Japan is focusing on the issue of dumping as defined by Article VI of the GATT 1994 and the Anti-Dumping Agreement. Thus, all other definitions of "dumping" are irrelevant. In response to another question of the United States, regarding whether the JFTC is responsible for the content of the English language web site, Japan confirms that this is the case. However, the reference to "dumping" occurs only once in its English home page, where the JFTC gives a very general overview of the Anti-Monopoly Act of Japan for the sake of ease of understanding by the general public. In any event, Japan considers the type of semantic debate the United States has initiated here is totally irrelevant to the present case and only serves to cloud the important issues the present proceeding raises. Japan argues that in order to ascertain the legal meaning and connotation of a Japanese Act, one must always refer to the authentic copy of the Act and the Notification, which is available only in Japanese. Thus, the US assertion is misguided and unwarranted.

[138] The United States refers to 221 U.S. 106 (1911).

[139] The United States refers to 228 U.S. 87 (1913).

complaint in *United States v. United Fruit Company*[140] and the private case *Laker Airways Ltd. v. Pan American World Airways*[141].

3.167 The United States notes that, more recently, in its 1986 *Matsushita Electrical* decision, the US Supreme Court evaluated Sherman Act claims against Japanese television exporters that were based on the same facts as the plaintiffs' unsuccessful 1916 Act claims. The Supreme Court rejected the Sherman Act claims for a failure to provide evidence that predatory losses would be recouped through future monopoly rents, not for a lack of anti-trust jurisdiction over such conduct. Perhaps the most recent example is the anti-trust consent decree that the Department of Justice obtained in 1995 against the planned joint venture of an American and two European telecom firms. That decree settled concerns based upon those firms' possible use of foreign monopoly facilities to engage in exclusionary and discriminatory conduct in international telecom markets.[142] Similarly, in *Silicon Graphics, Inc.*, the Federal Trade Commission approved a consent order settling allegations in an accompanying complaint that a proposed acquisition would violate Section 7 of the Clayton Act and Section 5 of the Federal Trade Commission Act. The complainant alleged, *inter alia*, that the proposed acquisition would facilitate the unilateral exercise of market power through price discrimination by the acquiring firm in the world-wide market for entertainment graphics workstations.[143] As these cases demonstrate, dealing with international price-discrimination is not an aberration from other anti-trust concerns.

3.168 The United States submits that many other Members' anti-trust laws have a similar international jurisdiction - for example, the anti-trust Articles of the Treaty of Amsterdam. The United States recognizes that Japan for many years considered its Anti-Monopoly Act to have no international scope, but the United States understand that that policy is now changing. Japan will now apply the Act to some conduct beyond its borders, such as the use of exclusive dealing contracts by foreign suppliers and foreign mergers with significant consequences in Japan. There is no obvious reason why anti-trust rules regarding price discrimination or predatory conduct should stop "at the water's edge" either. Indeed, the United States reminds the Panel that on its web site the Japan Fair Trade Commission defines "unfair trade practices" to include "dumping". It is interesting that in trying to explain away the use of the word "dumping" by the Fair Trade Commission, Japan now apparently concedes that the word "dumping" may be used in a context that does not fall within Article VI and the Antidumping Agreement.

3.169 **Japan** disagrees with the US contention that "Japan for many years considered its Anti-Monopoly Act to have no international scope, but the policy is now changing". This is not only mischaracterizing Japan's position, but irrelevant. Japan has never asserted that Japan's Anti-Monopoly Act has no international dimension.[144]

---

140 The United States refers to E.D. La., Civ. Action No. 4560, 1954; amended complaint, 1956, consent decree, 1958.

141 The United States refers to 559 F.Supp. 1124 (D.D.C. 1983).

142 The United States refers to *United States v. Sprint Corporation*, Competitive Impact Statement (D.D.C. 1995), available at "www.usdoj.gov/atr/cases/".

143 The United States refers to *Silicon Graphics, Inc.*, 120 F.T.C. 928, 930, 933 (1995).

144 In response to a question of the United States regarding whether anti-trust laws may apply to conduct outside their borders but affect competition inside their borders, Japan notes that some WTO

5. *The Historical Context and Legislative History of the 1916 Act*

3.170 According to Japan, the historical context and legislative history of the 1916 Act show that Congress sought to enact an anti-dumping law to address the commercial problem of dumping, i.e. international price discrimination.[145] US government officials, legislators and industries feared that the end of World War I would wreak injury on US companies and industries as foreign companies and industries sought to revive themselves and recapture or increase their former share of the US market through unfair methods of competition, including dumping. Some Senators and Congressmen proposed higher tariffs to fend off the threat. The Wilson Administration advocated free, but fair, trade and proposed anti-dumping legislation instead.

3.171 Japan points out that the formal legislative history of the 1916 Act is sparse. The hearings records do, however, contain correspondence regarding the 1916 Act and the correspondence confirms that the legislation was considered to be anti-dumping legislation. For example, US hosiery manufacturers wrote that "[w]e are very anxious to have some anti-dumping law that will protect our hosiery manufacturers from an expected flood of cheap hosiery following the foreign war [...]."[146] The manufacturers cautioned, however, that they were "confident that the proposed section [601] as written in H.R. 16763 will have no effect whatever in controlling such low priced importations."[147]

3.172 Japan further notes that the records of the Congressional floor debates on the 1916 Act also are sparse. Certain legislators, however, indicated that the 1916 Act was a protectionist trade measure added to the larger Revenue Act to attract Republican votes. For example, Representative Denison stated:

> "I consider as childish that provision of this bill prohibiting what is called "unfair competition": it is commonly referred to as "anti-dumping", and pretends to protect American industries [...]. The democratic leader [...] in making his statement to the House said that the Republicans should support this bill because this provision against

---

Members' anti-trust laws may apply to conduct that occurs outside their borders but affects competition inside their borders. However, any so-called "anti-trust" law that addresses anti-competitive international business practices, as that conduct is also regulated by Article VI of the GATT 1994 and the Anti-Dumping Agreement, must be consistent with Article VI of the GATT 1994 and the Anti-Dumping Agreement if the relevant government is a WTO Member. Thus, Article VI of the GATT 1994 and the Anti-Dumping Agreement apply to the 1916 Act. Even though the United States is now attempting to characterize the 1916 Act as a pure anti-trust statute (despite many official remarks to the contrary), the 1916 Act is inconsistent with these obligations as Japan has demonstrated. However, Japan does not deny the possibility that there may be laws addressing anti-competitive international business practices to which Article VI of the GATT 1994 and the Anti-Dumping Agreement might not apply. No such laws are at issue in the present case.

[145] Japan refers to, e.g., *Geneva Steel*, *Op. Cit.*, pp. 1223-24.

[146] Japan refers to the Hearings on H.R. 16763 Before the Senate Comm. on Finance, 64th Cong., 1st Sess. at 274 (1916).

[147] Japan refers to ibid.

unfair competition is a protective measure and is a Republican policy."[148]

3.173 Japan states that other Members looked to the anti-dumping laws of other countries for guidance in how to address dumping in the United States. During Congressional debate on the "anti-dumping clause" of the Revenue Act (the 1916 Act), Senator Penrose argued that a "more effective dumping law is that one which has proved the test of time and experience and is contained in the tariffs laws of Canada."[149] Arguing that the anti-dumping legislation should contain no intent requirement, the Senator explained how the Canadian anti-dumping law operated and noted that South Africa and Australia had similar anti-dumping laws.[150] Senator Penrose's comments demonstrate that Congress was familiar with and sought to remedy the problem of dumping when it passed the 1916 Act.

3.174 Japan argues that events following passage of the 1916 Act confirm that it is an anti-dumping law. A number of parties opposed the Act's intent requirement; they were vindicated by subsequent developments. The US Tariff Commission (now the US International Trade Commission) issued a report in 1919 which concluded that the 1916 Act was not deterring dumping. The Commission recommended addressing the problem by adopting a statute modelled on the 1904 Canadian anti-dumping law (providing for the assessment of dumping duties on imported goods comparable to Canadian goods if the imports were sold below their foreign market value).

3.175 Japan notes that a bill providing for the assessment of anti-dumping duties was subsequently introduced and passed by the House of Representatives in 1919.[151] The House bill "provided for the imposition, on all imported merchandise sold by the exporter at a price less than the foreign home value and of a class or kind produced in the United States or competing with American products, of dumping-duties equal to the difference between the foreign home value and the export price."[152] Representative Kitchin, who sponsored the 1916 Act, stated: "[i]n the act of 1916 [...] we have as stringent and as drastic an anti-dumping proposition as is contained in this bill."[153]

3.176 Japan further recalls that the Senate Finance Committee substituted another measure for the House provision. The Senate version provided that anti-dumping duties should apply only after the Secretary of the Treasury found that a US industry was being or was likely to be injured or was prevented from being established by

148 53 Cong. Rec. App. 1475 (1916). Japan notes that others also perceived the 1916 Act as a concession to protectionist Republicans. Japan refers to, e.g., 53 Cong. Rec. 10761 (1916), where Rep. Fess described the anti-dumping clause as one of "many specific sops" in the larger Revenue Act to gain Republican votes needed to implement a controversial income tax; ibid., p. 10751, where Rep. Green stated that "the purpose and object of an anti-dumping clause embodies good Republican doctrine"); ibid., p. 10616, where Rep. Bailey complained that the clause would "shut[] out [...] competition from abroad" and was "contrary to Democratic doctrine [and] a concession to Republicanism".

149 Japan refers to 53 Cong. Rec. S13080 (1916) (statement of Senator Penrose).

150 Japan refers to ibid.

151 Japan refers to 59 Cong. Rec. 351.

152 J. Viner, *Dumping: A Problem in International Trade*, University of Chicago Press (1979 ed.), p. 259.

153 59 Cong. Rec. 346.

dumping.[154] The measure was not voted on by the Senate. The Senate version, however, served as the model for legislation that later became the Antidumping Act of 1921.

3.177 Japan points out that the 1921 Act was a comprehensive administrative statute designed to address price discrimination between foreign and US markets that caused or threatened injury to a US industry. Unlike the 1916 Act, the 1921 Act did not include an intent requirement and relief took the form of the assessment of special anti-dumping duties instead of treble damages in a private civil action or criminal prosecution.

3.178 Japan notes that, in 1975, when defendants in a US court proceeding argued that the 1916 Act should be struck down as an unconstitutionally vague criminal statute, a US court used the common understanding of the concept of dumping as one of the major reasons for rejecting the argument:

> "[...] the phenomenon described by the terms of the [1916 Act] has a meaningful referent in business usage and practice. [...] The practice itself long predated the passage of the Antidumping Act of 1916 [...] which clearly implies that Congress knew whereof it wrote when it enacted the statute. The popular title of the Act itself is a further indication that the conduct described has a meaningful business referent. An economic regulatory statute could scarcely acquire the designation of an "anti-dumping" act unless the business community to which the statute was addressed knew what "dumping" was."[155]

3.179 The **United States** submits that the 1916 Act was one of a series of anti-trust-related statutes enacted by the US Congress between 1914 and 1916 in order to supplement the United States' then existing anti-trust laws, principally the Sherman Act, which had been enacted in 1890 and represents the United States' first, and most basic anti-trust law.[156] In 1914, Congress enacted the Clayton Act[157] and the Federal Trade Commission Act[158]. Two years later, Congress enacted the 1916 Act.

3.180 The United States further points out that when the 1916 Act was later codified in the United States Code, it was placed under title 15, entitled "Commerce and Trade." Also located in title 15 are the Sherman Act, the Clayton Act and the Federal Trade Commission Act, which are all anti-trust laws. In contrast, anti-dumping laws are codified in title 19.[159]

---

[154] Japan refers to Viner, *Op. Cit.*, p. 259.

[155] *Zenith II*, *Op. Cit.*, pp. 258-59, aff'd, 723 F.2d 319, p. 326 (3d Cir. 1983) (citations omitted by Japan)

[156] The United States refers to 26 Stat. 209 (1890) (codified at 15 U.S.C. §§ 1-7).

[157] The United States refers to 38 Stat. 730 (1914) (codified at 15 U.S.C. §§ 12-27).

[158] The United States refers to 38 Stat. 717 (1914) (codified at 15 U.S.C. §§ 41-58).

[159] In response to a question of Japan regarding the significance of the placement of a statute under a certain title in the US Code system and whether the codification actually reflects the legislative intent, the United States notes that, ordinarily, when a bill has passed the US Congress and been enacted into law, the law itself does not provide under which title of the US Code it should be placed. The task of placing the new law in the proper title falls to the Office of the Law Revision Counsel, which was created pursuant to section 285 of title 2 of the US Code (2 U.S.C. § 285). The person who heads this office, known as the Law Revision Counsel, is appointed by the Speaker of the US House of Representatives on a non-partisan basis (See 2 U.S.C. § 285c, where it is stated that

3.181 The United States considers that Japan's description of the 1916 Act's legislative history is incomplete and misleading. Japan chooses to rely upon isolated fragments of Congressional and even private industry testimony that go against the clear weight of the record. Some of Japan's historical references date from years after the Act was passed, amounting to *post hoc* commentary, not the actual legislative history of the Act.

3.182 The United States argues that the history of the 1916 Act actually dates back to 1912. In that year, President Woodrow Wilson was elected on a party platform that promised major reductions in tariffs; reductions to a level adequate to generate sufficient revenue for the functions of government, but not so high as to provide unnecessary protection to domestic industry. His party, the Democratic party, also promised

"[...] the Law Revision Counsel [...] shall be appointed by the Speaker without regard to political affiliation and solely on the basis of fitness to perform the duties of the position."; 2 U.S.C. 285a, where it is stated that the Office of Law Revision Counsel "shall maintain impartiality as to issues of legislative policy to be determined by the House."). The duties of the Office of the Law Revision Counsel, which are overseen by the Committee on the Judiciary of the US House of Representatives, are set out in section 285. These duties include the preparation of "a complete compilation, restatement, and revision of the general and permanent laws of the United States which conforms to the understood policy, intent and purpose of the Congress in the original enactments [...] with a view to the enactment of each title as positive law," and "[t]o prepare and submit periodically such revisions in the titles of the code which have been enacted into positive law as may be necessary to keep such titles current." (2 U.S.C. § 285b) In addition, the Office of the Law Revision Counsel is "[t]o classify newly enacted provisions of law to their proper positions in the code where the titles involved have not yet been enacted into positive law." (ibid.) By way of background, the distinction between whether a particular title of the US Code is or is not "positive law" largely has relevance only for technical legislative drafting purposes and to establish, as a matter of legal evidence, the exact wording of a statute. A title of the US Code is the "positive law" when the title itself has been enacted into law. A title of the US Code is not the "positive law" when it is a collection of certain general and permanent laws of the United States placed there by the Office of the Law Revision Counsel, acting under the supervision of the House Judiciary Committee. In that event, the "positive law" is each of the general and permanent laws of the United States that have been placed in the title. For example, both title 15 and title 19 currently are not "positive law." This means simply that, for example, with regard to the 1916 Act, sections 71-74 of title 15 of the US Code are not "positive law"; rather, the "positive law" is sections 801-04 of the Revenue Act of 1916. Similarly, with regard to the Tariff Act of 1930, as amended, the United States' current anti-dumping law, sections 1671 *et seq.* of title 19 of the US Code are not the "positive law"; rather, the "positive law" is sections 701 *et seq.* of the Tariff Act of 1930, as amended. Currently, the Office of the Law Revision Counsel is engaged in a continuing, comprehensive project authorized by law to revise and codify, for enactment into "positive law," each title of the US Code. So far, twenty-two of fifty titles of the US Code have been converted into "positive law." The United States notes that, for purposes of the present dispute, the US Code itself first came into existence in 1926, ten years after the enactment of the 1916 Act and well before the creation of the Office of the Law Revision Counsel. Up until that point, the laws of the United States had simply been set forth in a compilation known as the Statutes at Large, which was organized by the chronological order of enactment. The creation of the US Code in 1926 was undertaken by the House Committee on the Revision of the Laws, with assistance from a Senate Select Committee. It was then that the laws of the United States were first assembled and classified. The United States also notes that the House Judiciary Committee more recently, in 1994, issued a "Compilation of Selected Anti-trust Laws," which expressly lists the 1916 Act as one of the principal anti-trust laws. The House Judiciary Committee is the same committee that oversees the work of the Office of the Law Revision Counsel.

more vigorous anti-trust enforcement.[160] During President Wilson's first term in office, the Tariff Act of 1913, known as the Underwood Tariff Act, was enacted along with the Clayton Act (15 U.S.C. §§ 12 *et seq.*) and the Federal Trade Commission Act (15 U.S.C. §§ 41 *et seq.*).

3.183 The United States notes that, in 1915, the Secretary of Commerce, a member of President Wilson's Cabinet, concluded that additional competition legislation was needed.[161] He stated that while "[u]nfair competition" was forbidden by law in domestic trade, "[...] [t]he door, however, is still open to 'unfair competition' from abroad which may seriously affect American industries for the worse. It is not normal competition of which I speak, but abnormal. [...] If it shall pass beyond fair competition and exert or seek to exert a monopolistic power over any part of our commerce, we ought to prevent it." The Secretary concluded that he would "prefer [...] to deal with it by a method other than tariffs, classing it rather as an offense similar to the unfair domestic competition we now forbid." Specifically, he

> "recommend[ed] that legislation supplemental to the Clayton Anti-trust Act be enacted which shall make it unlawful to sell or purchase Articles of foreign origin or manufacture where the prices to be paid are materially below the current rates for such Articles in the country of production or from which shipment is made, in case such prices substantially lessen competition on the part of the American producers or tend to create a monopoly in American markets in favour of the foreign producer."[162]

3.184 The United States recalls that, in 1916, Congress enacted legislation implementing the suggestion of the Secretary of Commerce[163] that the Clayton Act should be extended to import trade. On 1 July 1916, Representative Claude Kitchin introduced H.R. 16763, an extensive piece of legislation designed to raise additional revenue through expansion of the income tax and inauguration of a federal estate tax. It also contained, in a section entitled "Unfair Competition", the provision which became 15 U.S.C. § 72. During debate of the bill in the House of Representatives, Representative Kitchin described this provision in terms that made it clear that the section was intended as a supplement to existing anti-trust laws, and not as a form of protection for individual industries:

> "Then there is an unfair competition provision in this bill which ought to be good Republicanism and good Democracy. The Republican Party, in all of its 50 years of tariff writing, never had the wisdom and the judgment and the patriotism to incorporate in any of its legislation an unfair competition proposition. We believe that the same unfair

[160] The United States refers to *Zenith III*, *Op. Cit.*, p. 1218.

[161] The United States refers to the Annual Report of the Secretary of Commerce 1915 40-41 (1915).

[162] *Ibid.*

[163] The United contends that Congress was aware of the Secretary's recommendation. The United States refers to 53 Cong. Rec. 13,079 (1916)(Sen. Penrose); 53 Cong. Rec. App. 1475 (1916)(extension of remarks of Rep. Denison).

competition law which now applies to the domestic trader should apply to the foreign import trader."[164]

3.185 The United States further recalls that Representative Kitchin's bill was reported favourably to the whole House by the House Committee on Ways and Means. The Committee's report affirmed that the bill applied the same unfair competition law to the foreign import trader as to the domestic trader. The report stated that the bill "place[s] [...] persons, partnerships, corporations, and associations in foreign countries, whose goods are sold in this country [...] in the same position as our manufacturers with reference to unfair competition."[165]

3.186 The United States notes that, during debate on H.R.16763, numerous Republican congressmen criticized the approach taken by the anti-dumping provision, insisting that entire industries needed protection and that higher tariffs were the only adequate method of protecting American industry from the expected post-war competition.[166] Thus, the critics of the legislation recognized that it was not directed at protecting particular US industries, as tariffs and duties would be, but rather at unfair competition. Indeed, one Republican Congressman suggested that his colleagues should rewrite the provision "as a protective measure", incorporating a provision debated (but not enacted) in a previous Congress that assessed duties for dumping.[167] As previously stated, the provision that became 15 U.S.C. § 72, a Democratic initiative, was intended to protect competition.[168]

---

[164] 53 Cong. Rec. App. 1938 (1916).

[165] H.R. Rep. 922, 64th Cong., 1st Sess. 9-10 (1916).

[166] The United States refers to, e.g., 53 Cong. Rec. 10,531 (1916) (Rep. Longworth) (arguing, according to the United States, that provision should be coupled with a protective tariff); ibid., p. 10,587 (Rep. Green) (arguing, according to the United States, that higher tariffs were needed); ibid., p. 10,607 (Rep. Meeker) (arguing, according to the United States, the same); ibid., p. 10,619 (Rep. Switzer) (arguing, according to the United States, that the provision should be supplemented by higher tariffs); ibid., pp. 13,079-80 (Sen. Penrose) (arguing, according to the United States, that the provision is make-shift and that a protective tariff is needed); ibid., p. 13,490 (Sen. Colt) (arguing, according to the United States, that only duties can safeguard American industries; provision is "manifestly inadequate").

[167] The United States refers to ibid., p. 10,761 (Rep. Fess). The United States notes that, in the previous Congress, anti-dumping legislation based on a Canadian statute, which presaged modern anti-dumping laws by providing for an administrative process, with duties assessed without inquiry into the importer's intent, had been considered and rejected. The United States refers to *Zenith III, Op. Cit.*, p. 1217; 53 Cong. Rec. 10,619 (1916) (Rep. Switzer); ibid., p. 13,077 (Sen. Penrose); ibid., p. 13,080 (text of Canadian statute). The United States contends, therefore, that the Congress was aware of the possibility of such an approach, and chose instead to enact Section 72 - which requires anti-competitive intent, and provides for judicial, not administrative, remedies.

[168] The United States concedes that it is also true that some congressmen characterised the provision as "protectionist" or a "sop" to the protectionist Republicans, which was intended to get them to vote for the unpalatable revenue provisions of the bill. The United States refers to, e.g., 53 Cong. Rec. 10,588, pp. 10,594-95, 10,619, 10,747, 10,749-50, 10,761 (1916). However, in the view of the United States, these comments do not outweigh the characterisation of the bill by the Administration that proposed it, by its sponsor, and by the House Report, as a bill intended only to prevent unfair competition. The United States refers to *Zenith III, Op. Cit.*, p. 1223, where the court collects cases concerning greater weight to be given reports of Congressional committees and statements of the bill's sponsor.

3.187 The United States argues that Japan's description of events in 1919-1921 is correct insofar as it shows that the Tariff Commission found that the 1916 Act had no protectionist effects and that the 1921 Antidumping Act was very much "unlike" the 1916 Act. Japan, however, also quotes a 1919 floor statement from Representative Kitchin, as proof that he believed the Act was an "anti-dumping proposition". The quote is, however, three years after the fact, and taken out of context. Other remarks by Representative Kitchen in the same floor debate show that he believed that the 1916 Act only dealt with anti-competitive conduct.[169] For example, he stated that:

> "We tried to guard against unfair competition by the foreigner by the passage of the Act of 1916. We are willing to have foreign goods coming over here in competition with American-made goods, but there must not be such a competition that will destroy the American industry and thus give the foreigner the monopoly.
>
> In the Clayton Anti-trust Act, which we Democrats passed, we provided against unfair competition among our domestic industries.
>
> Now, if it be proper and just to protect our domestic industries against unfair competition by other domestic industries, why is it improper and unjust to protect our domestic industries against the unfair competition of foreign industries."[170]

3.188 The United States notes that, during the same House debate, another Congressman, Rep. Fordney gave as an example of unfair foreign competition German exports of a particular chemical:

> "Take the case of oxalic acid, which sold at 6.5 cents a pound when our producers at home were compelled to go out of business because of that unfair competition. When that was accomplished, the Germans immediately put the price up to 9 cents a pound - higher than ever before."[171]

3.189 The United States points out that a similar example was used during the 1921 Senate debates over the 1921 Antidumping Act, where Senator Simmons asserted that the "German dye monopoly" had "deliberately, purposefully and intentionally" pursued a course to destroy the US dye industry:

> "The [1916 Act] provision was to meet a case like that, where a foreign monopoly or a foreign industry was selling its products in this country, not for the purpose of profit, nor in the ordinary course and way of business, but with a view to destroying an industry already established in the United States or so as to prevent the establishment of a business in the United States. That was entirely different from the situation as we find it in connection with this bill."[172]

3.190 The United States notes, furthermore, that the agency responsible for prosecuting criminal violations of the 1916 Act, the US Department of Justice, made a

---

[169] The United States refers to 59 Cong. Rec., p. 346 (not p. 351).

[170] *Ibid.*

[171] *Ibid.*, p. 346.

[172] 61 Cong. Rec., pp. 1100-1101 (May 6, 1921).

public announcement regarding the nature of the 1916 Act at the time of its passage. Assistant Attorney General Samuel J. Graham stated that the "purpose" of the 1916 Act "should be to prevent unfair competition. Just as we have said to our own people by the Clayton Act that they should not indulge in unfair competition, so we propose to say the same to the foreigner."[173]

3.191 The United States notes, finally, and controlling for the United States' purposes, the fact that the 1916 Act's legislative history shows that it was intended as competition legislation is also confirmed by judicial decisions construing the 1916 Act. For example, the court in *Zenith III* specifically found that its conclusion that the 1916 Act was an anti-trust statute was "strongly corroborated by the political and legal history of the relevant era, and the legislative history of the 1916 Act."[174]

6. *US Judicial Interpretations of the 1916 Act*

(a) Relevance of Judicial Interpretations of the 1916 Act

3.192 In the view of **Japan**, the text of the 1916 Act is unambiguous. The Panel's analysis thus should end with the text.[175] What a US court has labelled the Act is irrelevant.[176] In any event, if the Panel considers US judicial interpretations, it will find that they confirm that the 1916 Act is a protectionist dumping remedy.

3.193 The **United States** considers that it is the role of the Panel to determine as a matter of fact how the law is applied in the United States. Because the 1916 Act is applied through the judicial branch, the Panel must look to the judicial interpretations. Even if the Panel might disagree with how the courts have interpreted the text of the 1916 Act, it should not affect the Panel's decision in the present dispute. In the US legal system, the 1916 Act means what the courts say it means, and this is the relevant fact for purposes of the present dispute.

---

[173] Letter from Samuel J. Graham, Assistant Attorney General, US Department of Justice, dated 30 June 1916 (published in *N.Y. Times*, 4 July 1916, p. 10).

[174] The United States refers to *Zenith III*, *Op. Cit.*, p. 1215.

[175] Japan notes that the United States may assert that the Panel should defer to the US characterisation of the Act as an anti-trust remedy. According to Japan, this is incorrect. The existence and characteristics of the Act are questions of fact that are "left to the discretion of a panel as a trier of facts." Japan refers to the Appellate Body Report on *European Communities - Hormones*, *supra*, footnote 71, para. 132. Japan notes that, in contrast, the "consistency or inconsistency of a given fact or set of facts" with the requirements of the Act would be a legal question. Japan refers to ibid. Japan also refers to *Korea - Definitive Safeguard Measure on Imports of Certain Dairy Products*, *supra*, footnote 80, para. 7.30, where the panel stated that "[w]e consider that for the Panel to adopt a policy of total deference to the findings of the national authorities could not ensure an 'objective assessment' as foreseen by Article 11 of the DSU." Japan notes that, obviously, if the United States were to advance such an argument and the Panel were to accept it, the result would be absurd - any Member complained against would have nearly complete control of the outcome of the case. Its law would be found to conform to the WTO agreements merely because the Member said it did.

[176] Japan further notes that US courts generally use interpretative guidelines very much akin to those in Articles 31 and 32 of the Vienna Convention on the Law of Treaties. The primary focus is the express words of the statute in their context. Only when the meaning is unclear, may a court resort to legislative history or other secondary means of ascertaining meaning. Japan refers to, e.g., *Connecticut National Bank v. Germain*, 503 US 250, 254 (1992).

(b) Statutory Interpretation under US Law

3.194 In response to a question of the Panel to the United States regarding the relative weight to be accorded - by a US court and the present Panel - to the legislative history of a statute compared to the case law interpreting the statute, the **United States** notes that legislative history is something that US courts look to in interpreting a statute. However, courts vary in their use of legislative history. Generally, where the statutory language is ambiguous or the plain meaning of the statutory language leads to absurd results, a court will look to the statute's legislative history.[177] Nonetheless, some courts have considered legislative history regardless of the clarity of the statute to ensure that the perceived clarity is not superficial.[178] The weight such history is given in construing a statute may vary according to such factors as whether the legislative history is sufficiently specific, clear and uniform to be a reliable indicator of intent.[179] With regard to statements made by the sponsor of the legislation, the Supreme Court has held that, although they are neither controlling nor dispositive, they are "entitled to weight" and considered "an authoritative guide to the statute's construction."[180]

3.195 The United States notes that the relative weight of legislative history compared to the case law interpreting the statute depends upon whether the case law is binding precedent. For instance, if an appellate court has opined upon the statute, a district court in that circuit is bound by that decision. If the precedent is not binding, the weight afforded to the case law will depend upon the persuasive value of the opinion's reasoning.

3.196 The United States contends that the role of a statute's legislative history is different for the present Panel. Here, the legislative history has been cited only as confirmation or to help explain the courts' holdings. Because the interpretation of the 1916 Act is a question of fact for the present Panel, it is not the role of the present Panel to consider and weigh the statute's legislative history itself. The present Panel must look to the judicial case law in determining how the 1916 Act is interpreted and applied in the United States because the law is applied through the judicial branch.

3.197 The United States further notes that usually, US courts give more weight to the meaning of the term at the time the law was passed. But sometimes laws are written expansively to give courts more discretion in interpreting the meaning of terms because Congress realizes that the meaning can evolve over time. This is generally true of US anti-trust laws. The Court of Appeals for the First Circuit has aptly described the "special interpretative responsibility" placed upon the judiciary in the anti-trust context:

> "The broad, general language of the federal anti-trust laws and their unilluminating legislative history place a special interpretative respon-

---

[177] The United States refers to *American Trucking Associations, Inc. v. Interstate Commerce Comm'n*, 669 F.2d 957 (5th Cir. 1982); *United States v. Smith*, 957 F.2d 835, p. 836 (11th Cir. 1992).

[178] The United States refers to *Hunt v. Nuclear Regulatory Comm'n*, 611 F.2d 332, p. 336 (10th Cir. 1979).

[179] The United States refers to *Miller v. C.I.R.*, 836 F.2d 1274, p. 1282 (10th Cir. 1988).

[180] The United States refers to *Simpson v. United States*, 435 U.S. 6, p. 13 (1978); *North Haven Board of Education v. Bell*, 456 U.S. 512, pp. 526-27 (1982).

sibility upon the judiciary. The Supreme Court has called the Sherman Act a 'charter of freedom' for the courts, with a 'generality and adaptability comparable to that found [...] in constitutional provisions.' *Appalachian Coals Inc. v. United States*, 288 U.S. 344, 359-60 (1933). [T]he federal courts have been invested 'with a jurisdiction to create and develop an 'anti-trust law' in the manner of the common law courts.' [citation omitted] The courts are aided in this task by canons of statutory construction, such as the presumption against violating international law, which serve as both guides and limits in the absence of more explicit indicia of congressional intent."[181]

3.198 **Japan**, replying to the same question of the Panel, notes that the US Supreme Court is the final arbiter of a statute's meaning. Where it has not addressed an issue, a subsidiary court generally must follow the precedent set by the appellate court overseeing it or risk reversal. Where no binding appellate court precedent exists, a court uses interpretive guidelines very much akin to those in Articles 31 and 32 of the Vienna Convention on the Law of Treaties. The primary focus is the express words of the statute in their context. Only when the statute's text is unclear or ambiguous, may a court resort to other elements such as legislative history as a supplementary means of ascertaining meaning.

3.199 Japan also contends that, if the statute's text is ambiguous, US courts may refer to supplementary means of interpretation. If necessary, both the meaning of that term at the time the law was passed and at the time the interpretation takes place may be considered. It depends upon the court, the statute and the circumstances of the case. Often, as is the case in the WTO[182], US courts interpret statutory terms based on contemporary concerns.

(c) United States v. Cooper Corp.

3.200 **Japan** contends that the US Supreme Court has never addressed the substance of the 1916 Act, but has described it as "[t]he anti-dumping provisions of the Revenue Act of 1916"[183]. Thus, to the extent the Supreme Court has said anything about the 1916 Act, it recognized the 1916 Act as an anti-dumping measure.

3.201 The **United States** argues that, contrary to Japan's assertion, the US Supreme Court has never recognized "the [1916] Act as an antidumping measure." In fact, *United States v. Cooper Corp.*, a 1941 Supreme Court decision construing the Clayton Act, expressly described the 1916 Act and the Clayton Act as "supplemental" to the original, 1890 Sherman Act.[184] Moreover, in the same decision, the Supreme Court also described the Clayton Act as supplemental to the Sherman Act.[185] Thus, this 58 year old Supreme Court decision supports, not refutes, the points that the United States has made here.

---

181 *United States v. Nippon Paper Industries*, 109 F.3d 1, 9 (1st Cir. 1997) (Lynch, concurring).

182 Japan refers to, e.g., the Appellate Body Report on *United States - Import Prohibition of Certain Shrimp and Shrimp Products*, adopted on 6 November 1998, WT/DS58/AB/R, para. 129.

183 Japan refers to *United States v. Cooper Corp.*, 312 U.S. 600, p. 609 (1941).

184 The United States refers to ibid., pp. 608-10.

185 The United States refers to ibid.

(d) Zenith Radio Corp. v. Matsushita Electric Industrial Co. and In re Japanese Electronic Products Anti-trust Litigation

3.202 **Japan** notes that the United States no doubt will characterise *Zenith III* and perhaps other, even more dated cases, as evidence that the 1916 Act is an anti-trust law. In *Zenith III*, the court concluded that the 1916 Act should be thought of as a competition law statute, not an anti-dumping statute. However, in *Geneva Steel* and *Wheeling-Pittsburgh*, the judges carefully considered the reasoning of *Zenith III* and rejected that reasoning as ignoring the text of the Act.

3.203 Japan recalls that, in *Geneva Steel*, the judge made several observations about *Zenith III*. First, the court noted that *Zenith III* did not focus on the nature of the 1916 Act itself, whereas the court in *Geneva Steel* had no other issues before it: the entire focus of the court's attention was the nature of the 1916 Act. Second, the court noted that *Zenith III* actually sought only to interpret a single phrase in the 1916 Act - the phrase "such articles" - and decided that the Robinson-Patman Act provided a useful context in which to interpret this phrase. Third, the court noted that the critical statement in *Zenith III* - that the 1916 Act "is an anti-trust, not a protectionist statute" - was at most *dictum* and not a persuasive legal statement.[186]

3.204 Japan also notes that the court in *Wheeling-Pittsburgh* concluded that *Geneva Steel* was correct, and *Zenith III* was wrong. Like the court in *Geneva Steel*, the court in *Wheeling-Pittsburgh* rejected the logic of *Zenith III* as flawed and inconsistent with the plain meaning of the statutory language at issue. The court characterised *Zenith III* as an effort to rewrite, rather than interpret, the statutory text.[187]

3.205 Japan argues, moreover, that *Zenith III* is not unequivocal. The court noted that "Congress borrowed language from contemporary customs appraisement law" to draft the 1916 Act and that Congress specifically incorporated into the 1916 Act provisions of the Tariff Act of 1913.[188] One of the court's holdings expressly recognized the importance of customs laws in the 1916 Act. The court stated that "[b]ecause of the use of language taken from the 1913 Tariff Act in the 1916 Anti-Dumping Act, we will hold that there is no violation of the 1916 Act unless the standards of similarity of customs appraisement law are met."[189] Despite its conclusion that the 1916 Act was meant to complement anti-trust statutes, the court declined to use anti-trust standards in evaluating claims brought under the 1916 Act. Instead, the court used standards from customs law, which are protectionist in nature.[190]

---

[186] Japan refers to *Geneva Steel, Op. Cit.*, pp. 1218-19. Japan notes that *dictum* refers to an opinion expressed by a court concerning a particular rule, principle, or application of law that is not relevant to the case or essential to its determination. Japan refers to *Black's Law Dictionary*, 6th ed. (1991), p. 313.

[187] Japan refers to *Wheeling-Pittsburgh, Op. Cit.*, p. 605.

[188] Japan refers to *Zenith III, Op. Cit.*, p. 1197.

[189] *Ibid.*

[190] Japan notes that, in *Zenith III*, the court used customs appraisement law to determine that the term "such" as used in the 1916 Act means "similar" which in turn means commercially interchangeable. The court reasoned that "by incorporating in the 1916 Act a phrase from contemporary customs law, Congress must have intended to direct that the appraisement of imported merchandise under the

3.206 Japan points out, finally, as the court in *Geneva Steel* noted, the court in *Zenith III* even admitted that the 1916 Act is not exclusively an anti-trust statute, but has anti-dumping elements.[191]

3.207 The **United States** argues that *Zenith III* is the leading lower court case addressing how specific provisions of the 1916 Act should be interpreted. There, the US District Court for the Eastern District of Pennsylvania described in detail the anti-trust origins of the 1916 Act and explained how these origins should affect the interpretation of specific 1916 Act provisions.

3.208 The United States notes that the *Zenith III* court provided its views during the course of ruling on summary judgment motions challenging the sufficiency of the complainants' 1916 Act allegations. As part of this exercise, the district court specifically considered the character of the 1916 Act because, according to the court, "the character of the statute is of salient concern in its construction." The court expressly stated that its threshold task was "to ascertain whether the 1916 Act was intended to be part of the corpus of anti-trust law, or whether the 1916 Act was intended to be 'protectionist' legislation, as that term is used in discussion of tariff barriers to free trade."[192]

3.209 The United States considers, therefore, that, far from being *dicta*, the *Zenith III* court obviously considered that an analysis of the character of the 1916 Act was necessary to its holding. After reviewing the provisions of the 1916 Act and comparing them in detail to US anti-trust statutes such as the Clayton Act and the Robinson-Patman Act, the *Zenith III* court "conclude[d] [...], on the basis of the statutory text, that *the 1916 Act is an anti-trust, not a protectionist statute.*"[193] The court also explained that "[t]hat conclusion is strongly corroborated by the political and legal history of the relevant era, and the legislative history of the 1916 Act," which the court also discussed at length.[194]

3.210 The United States points out that the court also quoted the relevant congressional report, which states that the purpose of the 1916 Act was to adopt a provision "[i]n order that persons, partnerships, corporations, and associations in foreign countries, whose goods are sold in this country, may be placed in the same position as our manufacturers with reference to unfair competition [...].[195]The court recounted that Representative Kitchin, the chairman of the House Committee on Ways and Means and the House sponsor of the 1916 Act, stated "in unambiguous terms" that the 1916 Act was "intended to do no more than to impose on importers the same pricing restrictions which had already been imposed on domestic businesses by the Clayton Anti-trust Act of 1914."[196] The court stated that:

> "Representative Kitchin, explaining his bill at the outset of its consideration by the full House of Representatives, explained:

1916 Act follow the principles set forth in the Tariff Act of 1913." Japan refers to *Zenith III, Op. Cit.*, p. 1216.

[191] Japan refers to *Geneva Steel, Op. Cit.*, p. 1218.

[192] *Zenith III, Op. Cit.*, p. 1212.

[193] *Ibid.*, p. 1215 (emphasis added by the United States).

[194] *Ibid.*

[195] *Ibid.*, p. 1221 (quoting H.R. Rep. No. 922, 64th Cong., 1st Sess. 9-10 (1916)).

[196] *Ibid.*, p. 1222.

> We believe that the *same* unfair competition law which now applies to the domestic trader should apply to the foreign import trader."[197]

3.211 The United States further notes that the *Zenith III* court also explained that, at the time of the enactment of the 1916 Act, "unfair competition" - which also is the caption of the title under which the 1916 Act was enacted - referred to the activities addressed by the anti-trust laws of the era. As the Secretary of Commerce, William Redfield, explained in 1915:

> "'Unfair competition' is forbidden by law in domestic trade, and the Federal Trade Commission exists to determine the facts and takes steps to abate the evil wherever found. The door, however, is still open to 'unfair competition' from abroad which may seriously affect American industries for the worse. It is not normal competition of which I speak, but abnormal. [...] If it shall pass beyond fair competition and exert or seek to exert a monopolistic power over any part of our commerce, we ought to prevent it."[198]

3.212 The United States points out that the *Zenith III* court ultimately concluded that it would be guided by the following principles when interpreting the 1916 Act:

> "The principal lesson which we draw from the legislative history of the 1916 Act, viewed against the historical background of the first [Woodrow] Wilson Administration, is that the statute should be interpreted whenever possible to parallel the 'unfair competition' law applicable to domestic commerce. Since the 1916 Antidumping Act is a price discrimination law, it should be read in tandem with the domestic price discrimination law, section 2 of the Clayton Act, which was amended by the Robinson-Patman Act in 1936. And, in order to be faithful to the intention of Congress to subject importers to the 'same unfair competition law,' *we should not interpret the 1916 Act to impose on importers legal strictures which are more rigorous than those applied to domestic enterprises.*"[199]

3.213 The United States notes that the *Zenith III* court's analysis was affirmed on appeal in 1983.[200] In that opinion, the appellate court stated that the 1916 Act was enacted "to do with unfair competition" and the court then held that "we will interpret the Act in light of its motivating purpose."[201]

3.214 The United States recalls that, in 1986, the Third Circuit Court of Appeals again had an opportunity to consider the plaintiffs' 1916 Act claims in *Zenith III* when the case was remanded from the US Supreme Court. Some background information is helpful to fully understand the Third Circuit's 1986 decision.

3.215 The United States points out that Zenith (and another US company named NEU) commenced litigation against Japanese television set manufacturers in the

---

197 *Ibid.*, p. 1222 (footnote omitted by the United States) (quoting 53 Cong. Rec. App. 1938 (1916)) (emphasis added by the United States).

198 *Ibid.*, p. 1219 (quoting Annual Report of the Secretary of Commerce 43 (1915).

199 *Ibid.*, p. 1223 (footnote omitted and emphasis added by the United States).

200 The United States refers to *In re Japanese Electronic Products Litigation II*, *Op. Cit.*

201 *Ibid.*, p. 325, n.4.

early 1970s, complaining of Sherman Act, Robinson-Patman Act, 1916 Act and other violations of federal law. During a series of decisions by the district court and the court of appeals in the years 1980-83, which are discussed above, the Sherman Act and 1916 Act claims were first dismissed by the district court for lack of evidentiary support and then reinstated by the Third Circuit. The US Supreme Court then accepted the Sherman Act anti-trust claims for review. Those claims were based on the theory that defendants had conspired to monopolise the US market by using excess profits in the Japanese home market to launch a predatory pricing attack on the United States.

3.216 The United States notes that the Supreme Court reversed the court of appeals and remanded, stating that the plaintiff had not developed any credible proof of an illegal conspiracy to monopolise. The Supreme Court held that claims under the Sherman Act for conspiracies or attempts to monopolise through predatory low pricing could only be established by proof that such prices were below some appropriate measure of costs as well as evidence of a realistic expectation of recouping prior losses through future monopoly rents.[202]

3.217 The United States recalls that the court of appeals was ordered to consider its prior orders in the *In re Japanese Electronic Products II* case in light of the Supreme Court's decision. On remand, the Third Circuit dismissed the plaintiffs' 1916 Act claims upon the basis that, like the Sherman Act claims, there was no evidence of the possibility of recoupment. The court reasoned that "[s]ince the Sherman Act conspiracy charge failed in the Supreme Court, our holding on the Antidumping [1916] Act conspiracy claim must fail with it."[203]

3.218 The United States notes that the Supreme Court's decision in *Matsushita Electrical* actually laid the groundwork for the high court's decision in *Brooke Group*[204] some 7 years later. In *Brooke Group*, the Supreme Court re-examined the so-called "primary line"[205] price discrimination provisions of the Robinson-Patman Act and held that proof of both sales at prices below an appropriate measure of cost and the likelihood of recoupment were required in order to establish the requisite predatory pricing needed to create primary line liability. In doing so, the Supreme Court relied heavily upon its decision in *Matsushita Electrical*.

3.219 The United States submits, therefore, that, in *In re Japanese Electronic Products III*, the 1916 Act claims were dismissed by the court of appeals based upon the same predatory pricing/recoupment standards that were established for the Robinson-Patman Act by *Brooke Group* some years later.[206] The Supreme Court's 1986 *Matsu-*

---

202 The United States refers to *Matsushita Electrical Industrial Co., Ltd. v. Zenith Radio Corp.*, 475 U.S. 574 (hereinafter "*Matshushita Electrical*"). The United States notes that the Supreme Court reiterated this standard that same year in another anti-trust case, *Cargill, Inc. v. Monfort of Colorado, Inc.*, 479 U.S. 104 (1986), where it decided, according to the United States, what constitutes proof of injury to competition in the Clayton Act context of mergers and acquisitions.

203 *In re Japanese Electronic Products III, Op. Cit.*, pp. 48-49.

204 *Brooke Group Ltd. v. Brown & Williamson Tobacco Corporation*, 509 U.S. 209 (1993) (hereinafter "*Brooke Group*").

205 The United States recalls that "primary line" price discrimination refers to adverse effects upon direct competitors of the defendant seller, while "secondary line" price discrimination refers to adverse effects upon competitors of the defendant seller's favoured downstream customers.

206 *In re Japanese Electronic Products III, Op. Cit.*, pp. 48-49.

shita Electrical decision was and remains a foundation of US anti-trust jurisprudence on predatory pricing issues.

3.220 In response to a question of the Panel regarding whether the predatory pricing recoupment test of *Brooke Group* would be applied in all instances of international price discrimination which are alleged to constitute a violation of the 1916 Act, the United States notes that this would seem to be the case. The same recoupment requirements that apply to Sherman Act Section 2 and primary line Robinson-Patman Act cases apply to the 1916 Act as well.[207]

3.221 The United States argues that, as a consequence, even a firm that possesses predatory intent and engages in predatory conduct would not be found to have violated the 1916 Act without proof, *inter alia*, that its predatory campaign is likely to succeed, because anti-competitive intent and conduct without a likelihood of success will not produce the anti-competitive effects which the 1916 Act is intended to prevent. Thus, for example, mere incantations in internal memoranda of an intent to injure or destroy a United States industry are meaningless unless the defendant at issue actually has a reasonable expectation of recouping its losses within a particular relevant geographic market in the United States. As the Supreme Court concluded in *Brooke Group*:

> "Even an act of pure malice by one business competitor against another does not, without more, state a claim under the federal anti-trust laws [...] [a]lthough some of [the defendant's] corporate planning documents speak of a desire to slow the growth of the [generic cigarette] segment, no objective evidence of its conduct permits a reasonable inference that it had any real prospect of doing so through anti-competitive means."[208]

3.222 The United States notes that the first step in determining whether recoupment is likely both to be feasible and to occur is to establish the relevant geographic market within which the product at issue under the 1916 Act is sold. Because the 1916

[207] At the request of the Panel, the United States further clarifies its position in this regard. The United States notes that its statement that the *Brooke Group* predation requirement "would" be applied in all instances was really addressing whether there is a factual situation where the *Brooke Group* predation test would be inapplicable. The United States meant to convey that it can think of no factual situation where the test would be inapplicable. The United States has not taken a position on whether *Brooke Group* predation *should* be required under the 1916 Act as that is a matter for the courts to decide. If a court were not to apply the *Brooke Group* predation test in a particular case, the United States cannot predict what the test would be. However, the only other articulation provided by the courts is that the plaintiff must prove a specific intent and that standard has been described as virtually impossible to satisfy. The United States further notes that there were almost no 1916 Act decisions taken after the Supreme Court's 1993 *Brooke Group* decision until the recent *Geneva Steel* and *Wheeling-Pittsburgh* decisions. In those two cases, the courts made preliminary decisions not to require use of the recoupment test. In 1995, a US federal court dismissed a 1916 Act claim for failure by the plaintiff to prosecute it, not reaching the merits of that claim (the United States refers to *Geneva Steel*, *Op. Cit.*, footnote 2, referring to the case of *Consolidated Inter. Automotive, Inc. v. Chen*). A recoupment test was applied by the Third Circuit in its 1986 *In re Japanese Electronic Products III* decision. It was the recoupment test previously announced by the Supreme Court in the same case, not the later *Brooke Group* version of the test, which was based in large part on the high court's earlier *Matsushita Electrical* opinion.

[208] *Brooke Group*, *Op. Cit.*, p. 241.

Act also requires a showing of price discrimination - that is, that the allegedly predatory price charged within the United States is also substantially lower than the prices charged by the same firm in its home country - the relevant geographic market must also be the market within the United States within which the lower prices are charged. Recoupment will be possible only if this geographic area is in fact a relevant geographic market; that is, it is sufficiently insulated from competition from firms operating in other geographic areas so that a small but significant increase in prices within that area will not produce new entry sufficient to defeat the price increase. The same standard is in general used to define relevant geographic markets under the Sherman Act, the Clayton Act, and the Federal Trade Commission Act.

3.223 The United States points out that the second step is to determine whether recoupment is in fact likely both to be feasible and to occur within this relevant market. The crucial question is whether there is evidence of a realistic expectation of recouping prior losses through future monopoly rents.[209] In general, a firm can expect to recoup prior losses only if it possesses substantial market power within the relevant market within the United States, so that it can sell its products at prices substantially above competitive levels without losing sales to competing firms. The fact that a firm exporting to the United States may charge higher prices in a foreign market because it possesses market power in that market ordinarily would not be necessary to establishing the possibility of recoupment under the 1916 Act. Of course, the price in the foreign market would be necessary to establishing - as the 1916 Act requires - that the prices charged in the United States are "substantially less" than the prices the firm charges in the foreign market.

3.224 With regard to the *Zenith III* decision, the United States further argues that the court's analysis in the seminal *Zenith III* case has been supported by other US courts which have considered the nature of the 1916 Act.[210]

3.225 The United States also argues that Japan's characterisation of an early decision in the *Zenith II* litigation is equally misleading. In that case, the district court determined that the 1916 Act was not unconstitutionally vague because, *inter alia*, it achieved definitional specificity from related terms like "dumping" which have commonly used meanings.[211] The court found the common meaning of "dumping" to be "price discrimination between purchasers in different national markets". This is, of course, a colloquial definition of "dumping", not one based on examination of "fair value" and "material injury" concepts. More importantly for present purposes, the district court went on to stress that the Act contains the additional element of "specific, predatory, anti-competitive intent". In this regard, the court stated:

---

[209] The United States refers to *Matsushita Electrical, Op. Cit.* The United States recalls that the Supreme Court reiterated this standard that same year in another anti-trust case, *Cargill, Inc. v. Monfort of Colorado, Inc., Op. Cit.*

[210] The United States refers to *Western Concrete, Op. Cit.*, p. 1019 (9th Cir. 1985); *Helmac I*, pp. 590-91; *Helmac II, Op. Cit.*, pp. 565-66; *Isra Fruit Ltd. v. Agrexco Agr. Export Co.*, 631 F. Supp. 984, pp. 988-89 (S.D.N.Y. 1986); *Jewel Foliage Co. v. Uniflora Overseas Florida*, 497 F. Supp. 513, p. 516 (M.D. Fla. 1980); *Schwimmer v. Sony Corp.*, 471 F. Supp. 793, pp. 796-97 (E.D.N.Y. 1979). The United States also refers to *Outboard Marine Corp. v. Pezetel*, 461 F. Supp. 384, pp. 408-09 (D. Del. 1978).

[211] The United States recalls that, in fact, the 1916 Act itself nowhere uses the word "dumping".

> "As I read the Act, it forbids regular, continued price discrimination between purchasers in different national markets whenever the discrimination is motivated by a desire to destroy *competition*. This, I submit, is a more than adequate definition of the conduct proscribed by the Act."[212]

3.226 **Japan** argues that, with the exception of a single, dated and rejected opinion - *Zenith III* - the US court precedents support Japan's position. Ironically, the analysis of the court in *Zenith III* has been most heavily criticised for failing to follow the tenets of statutory interpretation.[213] In US jurisprudence, as in the WTO, the analysis begins with the text and ends with the text, wherever (as with the 1916 Act) the text is unambiguous.

3.227 In this connection, Japan points out that *Zenith III*'s judgement has limited binding effect in the US judicial system. It is at most a non-binding decision except perhaps in subsidiary district courts in its circuit[214] (though, given the criticisms of other courts, it might very well be reversed in the Third Circuit if the issue arises again). Also, modern courts have heavily criticised the court's analysis in *Zenith III*, noting, in particular, that it ignores the text of the Act (as the United States does in the present proceeding).

3.228 The **United States** submits that Japan provides no support for its assertion that the relatively recent and extensively researched *Zenith III* decisions are "discredited", other than to point out that the District Courts in *Geneva Steel* and *Wheeling-Pittsburgh* disagreed with some aspects of *Zenith III*. It is not the function of the present Panel to interpret US law, but only to ascertain what US courts and other relevant authorities understand it to be. Moreover, there is simply no basis for such a negative characterisation of the *Zenith III* precedents, which include not one but three decisions by a court of appeals and a very important Supreme Court construction of the Sherman Act. The District Court decision in *Zenith III* was cited and followed by the District Court in *Helmac I* and the Supreme Court based its 1993 *Brooke Group* decision in part on its own 1986 decision in *Matsushita Electrical*.

(e) Western Concrete Structures v. Mitsui & Co.

3.229 With regard to the treatment of the 1916 Act by the US Circuit Courts of Appeal, **Japan** recalls that, in 1985, the Ninth Circuit noted that the "express purpose of

---

212 *Zenith II, Op. Cit.*, p. 259 (emphasis added by the United States).

213 Japan refers to *Geneva Steel, Op. Cit.*, pp. 1218-19; *Wheeling-Pittsburgh, Op. Cit.*, p. 605.

214 In this regard, Japan notes that, although the United States claims the decision is a Third Circuit opinion, the US discussion focuses on a District Court case which was affirmed in part and reversed in part by the Third Circuit. Thus, most of the US argument on this point is based on dicta from a 20-year-old, much criticised District Court opinion, not a 3rd Circuit opinion. The Third Circuit never found that the 1916 Act has only anti-trust elements; rather, it found that it has both anti-trust and anti-dumping elements, and that its "primary aim" is to prohibit anti-competitive pricing. Japan refers to *In re Japanese Electronic Products II, Op. Cit.*, p. 325. Thus, according to Japan, the United States juggles the two (actually three) opinions and confuses the issue.

the Act is to protect domestic industries from dumping by their foreign competitors."[215]

3.230 The **United States** considers that the Ninth Circuit's 1985 *Western Concrete* decision limiting who has "standing" to bring a 1916 Act claim does not establish that the Act is an "antidumping" law. The court of appeals cited the Clayton Act as analogous to the 1916 Act[216] and noted that plaintiff had alleged that defendants intended to injure their preferred customers' competitors and to drive them out of the market. The court stated that "in every reported case, the statute has been applied or restricted to domestic producers (or importers [...] where there were no domestic producers [...]) of the dumped good, prohibiting restraint or monopolization of the dumped good."[217]

3.231 The United States also recalls that, in 1983, the Third Circuit Court of Appeals similarly concluded that the "primary aim of the 1916 Act is to prohibit *anti-competitive pricing*" and held that the plaintiff must show a specific, not just general, *predatory* intent to injure or destroy an industry.[218]

3.232 The United States further recalls that, in 1986, on remand from the Supreme Court, the Third Circuit Court of Appeals in *In re Japanese Electronic Products III* dismissed the plaintiffs' 1916 Act claims upon the basis that, like the Sherman Act claims, there was no evidence of the possibility of recoupment. The court reasoned that "[s]ince the Sherman Act conspiracy charge failed in the Supreme Court, our holding on the Anti-Dumping [1916] Act conspiracy claim must fail with it."[219] In other words, the Third Circuit Court of Appeals has held that the 1916 Act is a predatory pricing statute requiring, among other things, proof of the possibility of recoupment and is aimed at anti-competitive behaviour.

3.233 The United States considers, therefore, that, contrary to Japan's statement, US appellate courts (including the Ninth Circuit) have not uniformly treated the 1916 Act as an anti-dumping measure.[220] Indeed, the facts show that quite the opposite is true.

---

[215] *Western Concrete, Op. Cit.*, p. 1019. Japan notes that the Third Circuit twice addressed issues arising from the district court decision in *Zenith III* (both before and after the case went to the Supreme Court), but in neither decision did the Circuit Court address the specific issue of whether the law should be construed as an anti-dumping or anti-trust statute. Japan refers to *In re Japanese Electronic Products II, Op. Cit.*; *In re Japanese Electronic Products III, Op. Cit.* The Second Circuit once addressed the issue of who would have standing under the 1916 Act. Japan refers to *Isra Fruit Ltd. v. Agrexco Agr. Export Co., Op. Cit.*

[216] The United States refers to *Western Concrete, Op. Cit.*, p. 1019.

[217] *Ibid.*

[218] The United States refers to *In re Japanese Electronic Products II, Op. Cit.*, p. 325.

[219] *In re Japanese Electronic Products III, Op. Cit.*, pp. 48-49.

[220] The United States notes that Japan quotes a line from *Western Concrete*, stating that the 1916 Act's "express purpose [...] is to protect domestic industries from dumping by their foreign competitors." Yet, in the view of the United States, the Ninth Circuit also expressly cited the Clayton Act as context for the 1916 Act. The United States refers to *Western Concrete, Op. Cit.*, p. 1019. The court noted that the plaintiff had alleged that defendants had an "intent to injure [their preferred customer's] competitors and to drive them out of the market." The court stated that "in every reported case, the statute [1916 Act] has been applied or restricted to domestic producers (or importers [...] where there were no domestic producers [...]) of the dumped good, prohibiting restraint or monopolization of the dumped good." *Ibid.*

(f) Geneva Steel Co. v. Ranger Steel Supply Corp. and Wheeling-Pittsburgh Steel Corp. v. Mitsui & Co.

3.234 **Japan** submits that several federal district courts have addressed to varying degrees the specific issue of whether the 1916 Act should be considered a protectionist anti-dumping remedy or a competition-oriented anti-trust remedy. In the two most recent decisions, each of the courts concluded that the 1916 Act is a protectionist anti-dumping law, based on an analysis of its text. These cases rely explicitly on the plain meaning of the text of the 1916 Act to reject limitations imported from US anti-trust law that defendants sought to graft onto the 1916 Act. In *Geneva Steel*, the judge summarized his views succinctly:

> "The [1916 Act] means what its plain language says. [...] the Act has a protectionist component that prohibits dumping designed to injure the domestic industry [...]."[221]

3.235 Japan notes that the judge analysed the five forms of harm the statute contemplates, and noted that only the last two - to "restrain" or to "monopolize" trade and commerce in the United States - were in the nature of competition law harms. The first three - to "destroy", to "injure", or to "prevent the establishment of" a US industry - were all in the nature of dumping harms.[222] The judge could have bolstered this point by noting that the notions of "to injure" and "to prevent the establishment of" a US industry are precisely parallel to the definition of dumping set forth in Article VI:1 of the GATT 1994 and the Anti-Dumping Agreement. In reaching the decision, the judge considered and rejected the analysis and holding of the court in *Zenith III*.

3.236 Japan recalls that in *Wheeling-Pittsburgh* the court reached the same conclusion, explaining that:

> "In this Court's view, the conclusion reached by the district court in *Geneva Steel* was correct. The Court held that the Anti-dumping Act of 1916 did not require the type of predatory intent defined in [competition law] because the statute 'has a protectionist reach beyond anti-trust and traditional predatory price-discrimination pleading requirements.'"[223]

Like the court in *Geneva Steel*, the court in *Wheeling-Pittsburgh* stressed the five specific harms enumerated by the statute. The court confirmed that the first three of them protected competitors (as an anti-dumping statute).[224]

3.237 Japan points out that, although *Geneva Steel* and *Wheeling-Pittsburgh* are still in litigation, the district judges have clearly and unequivocally expressed their views on the characteristic of the 1916 Act, and that issue, if not the issue of liability,

---

221 *Geneva Steel, Op. Cit.*, p. 1215. Japan considers that this passage also serves to demonstrate that, like WTO panels and the Appellate Body, the United States interprets laws and agreements on the basis of their text, whenever possible.

222 Japan refers to *Geneva Steel, Op. Cit.*, p. 1215. Indeed, they mirror the provisions of the US Tariff Act of 1930, as amended (19 U.S.C. § 1673d(b) (1999)).

223 *Wheeling-Pittsburgh, Op. Cit.*, p. 604 (citations omitted by Japan).

224 Japan refers to ibid., p. 603.

has been finally resolved. Moreover, a review of these decisions indicates that each is thoughtful and well reasoned.

3.238 The **United States** recalls that in *Geneva Steel* the US District Court for the District of Utah addressed the elements of the 1916 Act in the course of ruling on the defendants' motion for dismissal of the complaint. Its decision viewed the requisite intent element of the 1916 Act differently from the *Zenith III* court. In the *Geneva Steel* court's view, a complainant could show *either* the traditional anti-trust type predatory intent or an intent to injure an US industry.[225] However, the court did observe regarding the requirement of intent:

> "[T]he burden of proving such improper intent may not be easy. Absent some compelling evidence, it may be *nearly impossible.*"[226]

3.239 The United States notes that in *Wheeling-Pittsburgh*, the US District Court for the Southern District of Ohio recently ruled on a motion to dismiss a civil complaint. In the course of its ruling, it stated that the 1916 Act does require proof of predatory intent, albeit of a different kind than is required under the Sherman Act or the Robinson-Patman Act. Like *Geneva Steel*, the court held that a complainant must prove an intent to injure, destroy or prevent the establishment of a domestic industry, but does not have to establish the reasonable prospect of resultant market control and price recoupment. Although some defendants have elected to settle rather than proceed to trial, the case is still pending while the remaining litigants conduct discovery.[227]

3.240 The United States points out that, under US law, neither the *Geneva Steel* decision nor the *Wheeling-Pittsburgh* decision is considered "final" or "conclusive." Both cases are currently in the discovery stage which means that no trial has taken place.[228] A district court decision on a motion to dismiss is "final" only once all of the claims in the case have been tried or otherwise adjudicated and the district court has entered judgment.[229] At that point, the district court decision becomes "appeal-

---

[225] The United States refers to *Geneva Steel, Op. Cit.*, p. 1217, 1224

[226] The United States refers to ibid., p. 1224 (emphasis added by the United States).

[227] It should be noted that, since the second substantive meeting of the Panel with the parties, there have, according to the United States, been further developments in the *Wheeling-Pittsburgh* case. According to the United States, the plaintiff in *Wheeling-Pittsburgh* has voluntarily dismissed its claims against the remaining defendants at the trial court level so that all that remains is an appeal of an interlocutory opinion regarding injunctive relief currently pending before the US Court of Appeals for the Sixth Circuit.

[228] In response to a question of the Panel regarding the current status of the *Geneva Steel* case and the *Wheeling-Pittsburgh* case as far as the non-settled cases are concerned, the United States notes that the cases are still pending in the discovery stage and no final decisions have been issued, although an appeal of the decision in *Wheeling-Pittsburgh* that the 1916 Act does not allow for injunctive relief was taken. Wheeling-Pittsburgh's appeal of that decision is pending in the Court of Appeals for the Sixth Circuit. It should be noted that, after the second substantive meeting of the Panel with the parties, there have, according to the United States, been further developments in the *Wheeling-Pittsburgh* case. According to the United States, the plaintiff in *Wheeling-Pittsburgh* has voluntarily dismissed its claims against the remaining defendants at the trial court level so that all that remains is the above-mentioned appeal of an interlocutory opinion regarding injunctive relief currently pending before the US Court of Appeals for the Sixth Circuit.

[229] The United States refers to *Cohen v. Beneficial Industrial Loan Corp.*, 337 U.S. 541, pp. 545-47 (1949) which interprets 28 U.S.C. § 1291; also *International Society for Krishna Consciousness,*

able," meaning that a party to the case may take an appeal to a circuit court of appeals. If no party appeals the case, the district court's decision becomes "conclusive" and therefore binding on the parties. However, even a final district court decision is not binding on other district courts or appellate courts; it does not even have persuasive value unless it has been soundly reasoned.[230] If a party does appeal the case, the appellate court, in turn, will conduct a review and either affirm, modify or reverse the district court's decision. The appellate court's decision then is the "conclusive" decision in the case (assuming that it is not subsequently reviewed by the US Supreme Court).[231]

3.241 The United States argues, moreover, that Japan's discussion of the holdings in *Geneva Steel* and *Wheeling-Pittsburgh* are in any event irrelevant to the present Panel's analysis. Japan seems to take the position that those two decisions are "right" and that the *Zenith* line of cases are "wrong". Yet, it is not the role of Japan, the United States or the present Panel to agree or disagree with any particular judicial decision.[232] Rather, the present Panel must determine whether the 1916 Act is susceptible to an interpretation that is WTO-consistent. In the view of the United States, in the present case, the Panel need not struggle with speculating regarding possible WTO-consistent interpretations of the 1916 Act. There are judicial decisions already

---

Inc. v. Air Canada, 727 F.2d 253, pp. 254-55 (2d Cir. 1984) which states, according to the United States, that a motion to dismiss for failure to state a claim is not a final decision.

230 The United States refers to *Threadgill v. Armstrong World Industries Inc.*, 928 F.2d 1366, p. 1371 (3d Cir. 1991).

231 The United States refers to *Metropolitan Water Co. v. Kaw Valley Drainage District*, 223 U.S. 519, p. 524 (1912) where, having failed to seek review from a higher court, the judgment was "conclusive" and binding on the parties. In this context, Japan asks the United States to respond to the following observation: Since the *Zenith III* case - which the United States claims is the authoritative interpretation of the 1916 Act - involved the 3d and 9th circuits, it does not appear to be a binding precedent in other circuits. Since the State of Utah belongs to the 10th circuit and the State of Ohio belongs to the 6th circuit, there is no reason to believe that courts in *Geneva Steel* and *Wheeling-Pittsburgh* will be guided by the *Zenith III* precedent. The United States responds that this observation is irrelevant because the question is whether the 1916 Act is susceptible to a WTO-consistent interpretation.

232 In response to a question of Japan regarding whether the United States disagrees with the views expressed in *Geneva Steel* and *Wheeling-Pittsburgh* and whether it has taken any action in the two court cases to influence their decisions, the United States notes, first of all, that, as a general matter, it is not the role of the United States (or the Panel) in the present dispute to agree or disagree with any US judicial decision relevant to the interpretation of the 1916 Act. In any event, the preliminary decisions in *Geneva Steel* and *Wheeling-Pittsburgh* are not even part of the relevant case law, given that they are neither final nor conclusive under the US legal system. Furthermore, the United States is not a party to the *Geneva Steel* case or the *Wheeling-Pittsburgh* case, and it has taken no action in terms of intervening or filing briefs in either case. In fact, the United States does not agree that these decisions are inconsistent with US WTO obligations. In response to a follow-up question of Japan, the United States further notes that in cases where the United States is itself a party to a civil or criminal litigation (acting through the Department of Justice), it has direct responsibility for ensuring that its own claims and actions comport with US laws and obligations, including international obligations, and for informing the court of such considerations. In addition, where appropriate, the Department of Justice can seek to intervene in a private civil litigation in order to protect a federal government interest. The Department of Justice does not routinely intervene in private civil litigation, however, and it remains a matter of judgment when and before which courts it should be done.

applying the 1916 Act to parallel the domestic anti-trust laws in the US. The series of decisions in *Zenith* demonstrate that the 1916 Act is clearly susceptible to an interpretation that is WTO-consistent and, in fact, has been so interpreted.

3.242 **Japan** notes that, in an interesting twist, after attempting to eviscerate *Wheeling-Pittsburgh* and *Geneva Steel en route* to elevating the dated and rejected *Zenith* analysis over them, the United States later raises *Wheeling-Pittsburgh* from the dead as controlling precedent. The United States relies on *Wheeling-Pittsburgh* for the proposition that US courts have held that the 1916 Act does not provide for injunctive relief. Japan never argued that it did and, to be sure, the point in any case is irrelevant to Japan's Article XI argument. However, the United States' reliance on *Wheeling-Pittsburgh* highlights the inability of the United States to mount a consistent defence.

3.243 The **United States** considers it noteworthy that Japan has placed itself in the position of defending the legal reasoning of precisely those preliminary trial court decisions in *Geneva Steel* and *Wheeling-Pittsburgh* that it claims threaten WTO-illegal injury to its interests.

7. *Statements by US Executive Branch Officials*

3.244 **Japan** argues that the US government's denial in this proceeding that the 1916 Act is an instrument to counter dumping directly contradicts many official statements and positions of US executive branch officials, including officials of the current Administration.

3.245 Japan notes that several telling statements focus on the issue of whether the 1916 Act would be "grandfathered" under the WTO agreements, as it was under the GATT 1947. In a 1997 letter to Representative Ralph Regula, current USTR Charlene Barshefsky stated:

> "In responding to one of your questions at the March 14 hearings, I mistakenly indicated that the 1916 Act is 'grandfathered' under WTO rules. This is not the case. Under the GATT 1947, the United States was permitted to maintain practices that were inconsistent with the GATT in 1947 when the United States signed the GATT Protocol of Provisional Application, which 'grandfathered' pre-existing mandatory legislation. However, with entry into force of the GATT 1994, the GATT 1947 'grandfather clause' became no longer applicable."[233]

3.246 Japan notes that this issue had been addressed in 1986 by then-USTR Clayton Yeutter, who acknowledged in a letter to Congress that the 1916 "act was 'grandfathered' upon US accession to the GATT and is therefore GATT-legal."[234] These

[233] Letter from USTR Charlene Barshefsky to Rep. Ralph Regula, dated 4 Apr. 1997, p. 1.

[234] Japan refers to the Letter from USTR Clayton Yeutter to Sen. Strom Thurmond, dated 18 Feb. 1986, p. 10 (emphasis added by Japan). Japan also references the letter from Assistant Attorney General John Bolton to Sen. S. Thurmond, dated 4 February 1986, which states that "[t]o the extent that any provisions of the current 1916 Act are inconsistent with the GATT, they are protected by the 'grandfather clause,' para. 1(b) of the 1947 Protocol of Provisional Application of the GATT." Japan further refers to the Testimony of USTR General Counsel Alan Holmer to the US Senate Finance Committee, dated 18 July 1986, p. 5, which states that "the Anti-Dumping Act of 1916 [...] was

statements clarify that, prior to the WTO agreements, the United States could maintain the 1916 Act only because of the grandfather clause.

3.247 According to Japan, these statements demonstrate that the United States, for years, has viewed the Act as GATT-inconsistent and as requiring grandfathering. Coupled with the statements discussed below, they confirm that, for years, the US executive branch has considered the Act to be an anti-dumping law.

3.248 Japan submits that other relevant statements were made during the 1985 and 1987 attempts by some Congressmen to amend the 1916 Act. S. 236 and S. 1655, which were not adopted, would have weakened the criteria for applying the 1916 Act. USTR Clayton Yeutter and Assistant Attorney General John Bolton confirmed that the provisions of the 1916 Act establish liability against foreign companies that dump goods, as described in the 1916 Act, i.e. dumping calculated as the difference between the price in the US and the price in a foreign country.[235]

3.249 For Japan, the statements quoted above show that the US government consistently has viewed the Act as an anti-dumping law and that, absent grandfathering, it would have been GATT-illegal. In this connection, the analysis of the 1916 Act presented by USTR General Council Alan Holmer to the US Senate Finance Committee (18 July 1986) is useful:

> "We believe that our reading flows logically from the letter and spirit of the GATT and the Anti-Dumping Code. It also follows that S. 1655 would violate the Code by imposing additional sanctions on top of normal anti-dumping duties. *While the same criticism can be levelled at the 1916 Act, the Act was "grandfathered"* by the Protocol of Provisional application when the US joined the GATT in 1947. Because of this legal technicality, the 1916 Act in its present form is legal under the GATT."[236]

3.250 In the view of the **United States**, the statements of various government officials regarding whether the 1916 Act was "grandfathered" under the GATT 1947 and whether proposed amendments to the 1916 Act would be GATT-consistent as evidence that the 1916 Act is an anti-dumping statute deserve no weight in the Panel's consideration for two reasons. First, statements with respect to whether an amendment to the 1916 Act would be GATT-consistent are not relevant to the instant case because the amendments were never enacted. Second, with respect to the statements on the "grandfather" exception, the simple answer to Japan's argument is that these government officials were mistaken as a matter of fact as to whether the 1916 Act was "grandfathered" under the GATT 1947.[237]

---

grandfathered by the Protocol of Provisional Application when the US joined the GATT in 1947. Because of this legal technicality, the 1916 Act in its present form is legal under the GATT."

[235] Japan refers to the letter from Assistant Attorney General John Bolton to Sen. Strom Thurmond, dated 4 February 1986.

[236] Testimony of USTR General Counsel Alan Holmer to the US Senate Finance Committee, dated 18 July 1986, p. 5 (emphasis added by Japan).

[237] In response to a question of Japan whether the United States is negating the veracity of these statements, the United States notes that it is not negating the truthfulness of the statements in question; the officials who made them believed them to be correct. The United States is simply saying

3.251 According to the United States, GATT 1947 document L/2375/Add. 1 (19 March 1965) shows that the United States government did not include the 1916 Act anywhere in the survey of existing mandatory legislation not in conformity with Part II of the GATT 1947. Indeed, at one point, the United States government specifically notified statutes that were not in conformity with Articles III and VI - the two Articles which Japan claims the 1916 Act violates - and the 1916 Act was not among them. The plain import of L/2375/Add.1 is that, in the United States' view, the 1916 Act was *GATT-legal* and therefore did not require "grandfathering".

3.252 The United States argues that its notification in L/2375/Add.1 is an official statement of the United States government's position regarding the GATT-legality of the 1916 Act in a GATT 1947 forum. The United States did not have the occasion to address the GATT-legality of the 1916 Act in the only other possible GATT 1947 forum, i.e. a dispute resolution proceeding, because no contracting party challenged the 1916 Act under the GATT 1947 (despite the fact that the United States had never invoked the "grandfathering" protection made available by the Protocol of Provisional Application).

3.253 The United States submits that, because this notification by the United States contained in L/2375/Add.1 (19 March 1965), which is an official statement of the US government, contradicts, as a factual matter, the statements cited by Japan, the Panel should attach no weight to those statements when deciding whether the 1916 Act is WTO-consistent. The present Panel must review the current weight of judicial authority and decide for itself whether the 1916 Act is inconsistent with any WTO obligations.

3.254 **Japan** considers that the US contention that the US statement cited by Japan "deserve no weight" is unbelievable and wrong as a matter of law. It is simply not credible for the United States to assert that the authors of these statements are "mistaken" and that they do not reflect the official opinion of the United States. These statements were made by senior US government officials with unmatched expertise in the matter. Obviously, the statements of senior US government officials and US government documents reflect the official US interpretations of the 1916 Act.

3.255 In response to a question of the Panel to the United States regarding in which circumstances the statement of a US government official could be considered as the expression of the opinion of the United States, the **United States** notes that, generally, if the US government official is speaking on behalf of the whole United States in a capacity in which he or she has the authority to do so, then the statement would reflect the opinion of the United States. In the present case, the statements cited by Japan reflect the only opinion of the official's respective agency.

3.256 The United States considers that the International Court of Justice (hereinafter the "ICJ") cases referenced by the Panel, however, address a different issue. In those cases, the issue was whether a declaration by a government official created a binding legal obligation, not whether the declaration could be considered an expression of an opinion of a party to the dispute. In the *Nuclear Test* case, the ICJ held that repeated declarations by, among other high-ranking officials, the President of France that it

---

that, to the extent that those statements may be construed as inconsistent with the positions taken by the United States in the instant dispute, those statements are mistaken as a matter of fact.

would cease conducting atmospheric nuclear tests was a unilateral act creating a binding legal obligation. In a later case, *Frontier Dispute*, the ICJ held that a declaration by the Head of State of Mali did not constitute a unilateral act creating a binding legal obligation for purposes of the dispute. The ICJ explained that

> "[...] since it has to determine the frontier line on the basis of international law, it is of little significance whether Mali's approach may be construed to reflect a specific position towards, or indeed to signify acquiescence in, the principles held by the Legal Sub-Commission to be applicable to the resolution of the dispute. If those principles are applicable as elements of law, they remain so whatever Mali's attitude."

3.257 According to the United States, there is no question that the statements relied upon by Japan (and the European Communities) do not constitute a unilateral act by the United States creating a binding legal obligation in the present dispute. Like the statements at issue in *Frontier Dispute*, these statements do not purport to commit the United States to undertake or refrain from undertaking any kind of action. Rather, they are statements regarding whether, in the opinion of the particular author, the 1916 Act was grandfathered under the GATT 1947, and whether the 1979 Anti-Dumping Code and Article VI of the GATT 1947 provide that anti-dumping duties are the exclusive remedy for dumping. In both instances, statements by government officials cannot determine or change whether the 1916 Act was in fact grandfathered under GATT 1947 or whether, as a legal matter, Article VI of the GATT 1947 and the 1979 Anti-Dumping Code provided that anti-dumping duties were the exclusive remedy for dumping. These are questions that the Panel must determine pursuant to the mandate set forth in Article 11 of the Dispute Settlement Understanding. Article 11 requires that a panel "make an objective assessment of the facts of the case and the applicability of and conformity with the relevant covered agreements." If a panel were legally bound by statements of the parties concerning the facts in dispute or the conformity of their measures, it would be not be able to carry out its mandate under Article 11.

8. *Statements in Relevant US Government Documents*

3.258 **Japan** recalls that the US Department of Justice's and the US Federal Trade Commission's "Anti-trust Enforcement Guidelines for International Operations" expressly state: "the 1916 Act is not an anti-trust statute [...]. It is a trade statute that creates a private claim against importers [...]."[238] Thus, the two US government agencies that enforce US anti-trust law agree that the Act is not an anti-trust law, but is an anti-dumping law.

3.259 In response to a question of Japan regarding how the US position in the present proceeding can be reconciled with the statement in the above-mentioned Anti-trust Enforcement Guidelines for International Operations, according to which "the 1916 Act is not an anti-trust statute," the **United States** notes that, first of all, the

[238] Japan refers to US Department of Justice and US Federal Trade Commission, Anti-trust Enforcement Guidelines for International Operations, April 1995, Section 2.82.

quote excerpted by Japan is incomplete and misleading. The full quote is as follows: "The Revenue Act of 1916, better known as the Antidumping Act, 15 U.S.C. §§ 71-74, is not an anti-trust statute, *but its subject matter is closely related to the anti-trust rules regarding predation*."[239] Secondly, the United States notes that the Guidelines are not regulations with the force of law but rather "are intended to provide anti-trust guidance to businesses engaged in international operations on questions that relate specifically to the [enforcement] Agencies' international enforcement policy."[240] The Justice Department and the Federal Trade Commission continue to refer to them in speeches and policy statements, and to refer practitioners to them. They have not been withdrawn or superseded by any later guidelines.

3.260 **Japan** notes, in addition, that the Panel correctly points out that the 1916 Act is listed as an anti-dumping measure in the US government's "Overview and Compilation of U.S. Trade Statutes". The inclusion and explanation of the 1916 Act in the US government's Overview is telling.[241] The Overview is prepared for the US House of Representatives by the US Government Printing Office. The text of the 1916 Act is included in Section A, "Authorities to respond to foreign subsidy and dumping practices", of Chapter 9, "Trade Remedy Laws".[242] Of even greater relevance to the present proceeding is the discussion of the 1916 Act in Chapter 2 of the Overview. There, the Overview cites three provisions of US law which address dumping practices. The 1916 Act and Title VII of the Tariff Act of 1930 are two of the three.

3.261 According to Japan, this serves as a clear statement of the nature of the 1916 Act. In the words of the US government, the 1916 Act regulates "dumping practices" or "international price discrimination, whereby goods are sold in one export market (such as the United States) at prices lower than the prices at which comparable goods are sold in the home market of the exporter."[243] Japan cannot imagine how the United States possibly can try to explain away this clear statement.

3.262 In response to a question of the Panel regarding the fact that the 1916 Act figures both in the "Compilation of Selected Anti-trust Laws" of 20 December 1994 and in the "Overview and Compilation of U.S. Trade Statutes" of 4 August 1995, the **United States** notes that the Committee on the Judiciary of the US House of Representatives periodically issues a Compilation of Selected Anti-trust Laws. It has done so in 1950, 1959, 1965, 1978 and, most recently, 1994. The 1994 compilation is an official document of the House Judiciary Committee, and it includes an Introduction by the Chairman of the House Judiciary Committee describing it as "a reference source for the official text of our Nation's anti-trust laws." It also expressly lists the 1916 Act as one of the "principal" anti-trust laws.

3.263 The United States notes that the House Judiciary Committee is the same committee that is responsible for the "[r]evision and codification of the Statutes of the United States" under Rule 10 of the Rules of the US House of Representatives and for the supervision of the work of the Office of the Law Revision Counsel re-

[239] Emphasis added by the United States.

[240] Anti-trust Enforcement Guidelines for International Operations, April 1995, p. 1.

[241] Japan refers to the Overview and Compilation of US Trade Statutes, pp. X, 65 and 519.

[242] Japan refers to ibid., pp. X and 519.

[243] Japan refers to ibid., p. 65.

garding the placement of laws in their proper titles of the US Code, as set out in section 285 of title 2 of the US Code (2 U.S.C. § 285). The 1916 Act has been placed in title 15 of the US Code, along with the United States' other anti-trust laws.

3.264 With regard to the Overview and Compilation of U.S. Trade Statues, the United States notes that, on its cover, this compilation explains that it has been "[p]repared for the use of Members of the Committee on Ways and Means [of the US House of Representatives] by members of its staff." It adds that "[t]his document has not been officially approved by the committee and may not reflect the views of its Members." The Ways and Means Committee staff has prepared this unofficial compilation biannually since 1987, with the most recent unofficial compilation being issued on 25 June 1997 (without relevant amendments to the 1995 unofficial compilation). As the Panel notes, this unofficial compilation does list the 1916 Act as a trade statute. The United States also notes, however, that, on page 63, the unofficial compilation describes the 1916 Act in relation to the United States' first anti-dumping law, enacted in 1921[244], which forms the basis of the United States' current antidumping law. The unofficial compilation states that the two statutes address "*different* types of dumping practices."[245] In other words, unlike the United States' anti-dumping law, the 1916 Act does not address the dumping addressed by Article VI of the GATT 1994 and the Anti-Dumping Agreement. The unofficial compilation also explains that Congress found "the need for a different type of AD law" from the 1916 Act because "[t]he requirements under [the 1916 Act], particularly the need to show evidence of intent, are difficult to meet [...]."

3.265 According to the United States, the reason why the 1916 Act appears in two different compilations, in all likelihood, relates to the jurisdiction of House committees. A House committee normally would place in its compilation those statutes over which it has jurisdiction under the House Rules, and the House Judiciary Committee and, very possibly, the House Ways and Means Committee would seek to have a bill to amend the 1916 Act referred to them.[246]

3.266 The United States notes that, in the case of a bill to amend the 1916 Act, the House Judiciary Committee would certainly have jurisdiction, given that the 1916 Act is an anti-trust statute, included in title 15 of the US Code, and Rule 10 of the House Rules gives the House Judiciary Committee jurisdiction over the "[p]rotection of trade and commerce against unlawful restraints and monopolies." While the House Ways and Means Committee would normally not have jurisdiction over a bill proposing or amending an anti-trust statute, whether international in scope or solely domestic, it may have jurisdiction over a bill to amend the 1916 Act (along with the House Judiciary Committee) because of the circumstances surrounding the 1916

[244] The United States refers to the Antidumping Act of 1921, 19 U.S.C. §§ 160-71 (repealed).

[245] The United States refers to the Overview and Compilation of US Trade Statutes (emphasis added by the United States).

[246] The United States notes, in this regard, that when a bill is first introduced in the House, it is often referred to more than one House committee for consideration and review before there is a vote on the House floor regarding its passage. The House committees to which the bill is referred are those which are considered to have jurisdiction over one or more provisions of the bill under Rule 10 of the House Rules. The decision regarding which House committees to refer a bill to is made by the Speaker of the House, and sometimes it can be contentious.

Act's enactment. In this regard, the 1916 Act was passed at a time when the House Rules only allowed a bill to be referred to one House committee. Because the provisions that were to become the 1916 Act were one part of a much larger bill proposing the Revenue Act of 1916, and the House Ways and Means Committee was the House committee that had jurisdiction over all Revenue Acts under the House Rules at that time (as it is today), the House Ways and Means Committee was the House committee to which the entire bill was referred, even though the provisions that were to become the 1916 Act, if proposed in a separate bill by themselves, would have been referred to the House Judiciary Committee. It is possible but not definite that, because of the role that the House Ways and Means Committee played in the enactment of the 1916 Act, the Speaker of the House today might refer a bill to amend the 1916 Act to the House Ways and Means Committee (along with the House Judiciary Committee). It is for these same reasons, in all likelihood, that the House Ways and Means Committee staff placed the 1916 Act in its unofficial compilation.

3.267 In the United States' view, the House Judiciary Committee compilation confirms that the 1916 Act is an anti-trust statute, and it is noteworthy that this compilation was put together by the House committee most familiar with US anti-trust laws. The unofficial House Ways and Means Committee compilation is not necessarily inconsistent with the House Judiciary Committee's characterisation of the 1916 Act as an anti-trust statute because it also includes the 1916 Act among US trade statutes. For one thing, the unofficial House Ways and Means Committee compilation expressly states that the 1916 Act is a "different type" of statute from the United States' antidumping law. Moreover, if this unofficial compilation is understood from the standpoint of House committee jurisdiction, it can be seen that the inclusion of the 1916 Act by the House Ways and Means Committee staff is likely based on its view of the House Ways and Means Committee's jurisdiction, not based on a view that the 1916 Act is not an anti-trust statute. Indeed, the unofficial House Ways and Means Committee compilation discusses the 1916 Act (at page 63) in the context of historical background.

G. Violations of Article VI:2 of the GATT 1994 and Article 18.1 of the Anti-Dumping Agreement

3.268 **Japan** argues that Article VI of the GATT 1994 and the many provisions of the Anti-Dumping Agreement set forth the only WTO-consistent means of addressing dumping. They define dumping and set out the investigation a Member must conduct and the specific findings and determinations which a Member must make before it may impose an anti-dumping measure. Also, they narrowly define the measure a Member may take.

3.269 Japan considers that Article VI of the GATT 1994 authorizes *only one* measure in response to dumping: the imposition of an anti-dumping duty.[247] Thus, assuming a Member has followed the requirements of Article VI:2 of the GATT 1994

247 Japan refers to the text of Article VI:2 which reads:

> "In order to offset or prevent dumping, a contracting party may levy on any dumped product an anti-dumping duty not greater in amount than the margin of dumping in respect of such product [...]."

and the Anti-Dumping Agreement, a Member has two options: (i) it "may levy" an anti-dumping duty less than or equal to the margin of dumping on the dumped product; or (ii) it may decide to take no action. Any other action would violate Article VI of the GATT 1994.[248]

3.270 Japan argues that its view is also supported by the negotiating history of Article VI of the GATT 1994. After the close of the Havana Conference, at the second session of the contracting parties, the relevant Working Party in its Report "agreed that measures other than compensatory anti-dumping and countervailing duties may not be applied to counteract dumping or subsidization except insofar as such other measures are permitted under other provisions of the General Agreement."[249]

3.271 Japan submits that the overall purpose of the GATT 1994 bolsters this interpretation of Article VI:2 of the GATT 1994. One of the main purposes of the GATT 1994 regime is to eliminate trade barriers among countries and to promote free trade. Article VI of the GATT 1994 allows Members to do what they would not normally be allowed to do - to impede trade by imposing duties on imports in contravention of Article II of the GATT 1994. Because Article VI of the GATT 1994 gives Members the right to impede trade in specified circumstances, it is only logical that Article VI of the GATT 1994 establishes the right to restrict dumped imports only by a single authorized remedy, namely imposing an "anti-dumping duty".

3.272 Japan considers that the text of Article 18.1 of the Anti-Dumping Agreement reaffirms the understanding that Article VI of the GATT 1994 is the sole GATT-authorized remedy for dumping.[250] The plain meaning of this provision could not be more explicit. "No specific action" can be taken to address dumping except action that follows the requirements of Article VI of the GATT 1994.

3.273 Japan notes that senior US officials recognize that the imposition of an anti-dumping duty is the only permissible means of remedying dumping. In his 18 February 1986 letter to Senate Judiciary Committee Chairman Strom Thurmond, then-USTR Clayton Yeutter unambiguously declared:

> "Both the [Tokyo Round Anti-Dumping] Code and the GATT authorize a signatory to impose antidumping duties to counteract foreign dumping. This remedy represents a special exception to normal GATT rules regarding tariffs. The Code, however, expressly limits this remedy to the prospective collection of antidumping duties to off-

---

248 In response to a question of the Panel regarding how the parties understand the phrase "[i]n order to offset dumping [...]" in Article VI:2 of the GATT 1994, Japan notes that this term informs the purpose of and rationale behind anti-dumping duty procedures. The phrase and its context establish the reason why the measure to counter dumping is limited to a duty not greater than the dumping margin. An anti-dumping duty not exceeding the margin of dumping is the sole authorized remedy for dumping.

249 Japan refers to the Report of the Working Party on "Modifications to the General Agreement," adopted on 1 and 2 September 1948, BISD II/39, para. 12.

250 Japan recalls that Article 18.1 provides as follows:

> "No specific action against dumping of exports from another Member can be taken except in accordance with the provisions of GATT 1994, as interpreted by this Agreement."

> set the margin of dumping. *It prohibits the use of additional sanctions, such as anti-trust damages.*"[251]

3.274 Japan recalls that, similarly, in a 4 February 1986 letter to the Chairman Strom Thurmond, then Assistant Attorney General John Bolton stated:

> "Thus any private remedy for dumping must also be consistent with GATT. The Code permits a signatory to impose, in response to dumping, only antidumping duties limited to the margin of dumping."[252]

3.275 Japan submits further that it can scarcely improve on the analysis of the 1916 Act presented by USTR General Counsel Alan Holmer to the US Senate Finance Committee (18 July 1986):

> "The Antidumping Code, however, expressly *limits* the remedy for dumping to the prospective collection of antidumping duties *to offset the margin* of dumping. Article 16 of the Code [now Article 18.1 of the Anti-Dumping Agreement] states: "No specific action against dumping of exports from another Party can be taken except in accordance with the provisions of the General Agreement, as interpreted by this Agreement." *This language prohibits the use of additional sanctions, such as fines, embargoes, imprisonment or other draconian measures.*
>
> It has also been argued that "the Code also does not affect other actions that are not in the nature of 'duties' that may affect goods that are 'dumped'." The thrust of this argument is that if a government chooses to address dumping through the imposition of duties, it must do so under the procedures set out in the Anti-Dumping Code, but at the same time, a government is free to use any other means that it chooses to punish dumping. This interpretation of Article 16, however, appears rather implausible if one considers its consequences. Under this view, *a foreign government would be perfectly within its rights to convict an American businessman of dumping and imprison him for a period of 10 years, since the government would have a right to use whatever alternative sanctions for dumping it pleased.*
>
> *It follows that Article 16 must stand for the proposition that a government can provide its citizens one, and only one, remedy for dumping. That remedy is the collection of duties in a manner consistent with the Anti-Dumping Code."*[253]

3.276 Japan considers that this simple explanation demonstrates the obviousness of the many inconsistencies of the 1916 Act with the WTO anti-dumping regime. The

[251] Japan refers to the letter from USTR Clayton Yeutter to Sen. Thurmond, dated 18 February 1986, p. 9-10 (emphasis added by Japan).

[252] Japan refers to the letter from Assistant Attorney General John Bolton to Sen. Thurmond, dated 4 February 1986, p. 17.

[253] Japan refers to the testimony by Alan F. Holmer, General Counsel Office of the USTR, before the Subcommittee on International Trade of the US Senate, dated 18 July 1986, p. 4 (emphases added by Japan).

1916 Act is an anti-dumping law. Thus, it must comply with Article VI of the GATT 1994 and the provisions of the Anti-Dumping Agreement. However, it quite obviously does not.

3.277 Japan asserts, therefore, that the 1916 Act violates US obligations under Paragraph 2 of Article VI of the GATT 1994 and Article 18.1 of the Anti-Dumping Agreement because it provides that various penalties, including fines, imprisonment and treble damages, may be imposed for violations of the Act. Article VI:2 limits the remedy applicable to dumping to one remedy - anti-dumping duties of a specified amount.[254] In contrast, the 1916 Act provides for fines, treble damages and imprisonment and, thus, violates paragraph 2 of Article VI and Article 18.1 of the Anti-Dumping Agreement.

3.278 The **United States** argues that Article VI of the GATT 1994 and the Anti-Dumping Agreement do not govern all measures directed at dumping. Japan's interpretation that Article VI:2 of the GATT 1994 and Article 18.1 of the Anti-Dumping Agreement establish that anti-dumping duties are the exclusive remedy for injurious dumping is contradicted by the ordinary meaning of the terms used by the two Articles in question. In addition, Japan conveniently ignores the footnote to Article 18.1 of the Anti-Dumping Agreement. These Articles - and, in particular, Article 18.1 - provide that a Member may take a measure against injurious dumping even when such measures are not explicitly set forth in Article VI of the GATT 1994 or the Anti-Dumping Agreement, as long as the measure is not inconsistent with other provisions of the GATT 1994.

3.279 In the view of the United States, nothing in Article VI:2 of the GATT 1994 addresses whether anti-dumping duties are the exclusive remedy for dumping. Japan itself argues that Article VI was meant to provide an exception to the prohibition on tariffs above the bound rate as laid down in Article II of the GATT 1994 - i.e. not to provide the only remedy for dumping. Moreover, paragraph 2 simply states that a Member "may" levy an anti-dumping duty to offset or prevent dumping. It does not in any way suggest that remedies for dumping other than anti-dumping duties are prohibited. For example, it does not state that a Member "may only" levy anti-dumping duties. If the word "only" had been intended, the text could and would have said so.

3.280 The United States contends that, contrary to Japan's argument, the negotiating history of Article VI does not support its position that anti-dumping duties are the exclusive remedy for dumping. The negotiating history shows that the GATT 1947 originally included a paragraph in Article VI - paragraph 7 - providing in pertinent part:

> "No measures other than anti-dumping [...] duties shall be applied by any contracting party [...] for the purpose of offsetting dumping [...]."[255]

[254] Japan also refers to Article 18.1 of the Anti-Dumping Agreement which states that "[n]o specific action against dumping of exports from another Member can be taken except in accordance with the provisions of GATT 1994, as interpreted by this agreement." (footnote omitted by Japan)

[255] Reproduced in GATT, *Analytical Index: Guide to GATT Law and Practice*, 6th ed. (1995), p. 238.

However, paragraph 7 lasted only about one year. Article VI was modified soon after the GATT 1947 came into force, with the initial relevant discussions on this matter taking place in early 1948 during the "Havana Conference", which addressed the draft charter of the International Trade Organization ("ITO"), a document which was similar in many respects to GATT 1947.

3.281 The United States notes that at that time, members of the Subcommittee on Article 34 considered a provision in the draft ITO charter, identical to the original paragraph 7 of GATT 1947 Article VI, and decided to remove it. The record of these discussions explains:

> "The Subcommittee agreed to the deletion of paragraph 6 of the Geneva draft which expressly prohibited the use of measures other than anti-dumping or countervailing duties against dumping or subsidization. It did so with the definite understanding that measures other than compensatory anti-dumping [...] duties may not be applied to counteract dumping [...] *except insofar as such other measures are permitted under other provisions of the Charter.*"[256]

3.282 The United States further recalls that, later that year, during the Second Session of the GATT 1947, the Working Party on Modifications to the General Agreement referenced the work of the ITO Subcommittee on Article 34 and agreed, *inter alia*, to replace the entire then-existing Article VI with its counterpart under the draft ITO charter, which in final form contained no provision like paragraph 7 of Article VI of the GATT 1947. In a report, the Working Party explained:

> "The working party, endorsing the views expressed by [the ITO Subcommittee on Article 34], agreed that measures other than compensatory anti-dumping [...] duties may not be applied to counteract dumping [...] *except insofar as such other measures are permitted under other provisions of the General Agreement.*"[257]

3.283 The United States notes that, many years later, a paragraph similar in many respects to the original paragraph 7 of Article VI of the GATT 1947 appeared in Article 16.1 of the Tokyo Round Anti-Dumping Code. It provided:

> "No specific action against dumping of exports from another Party can be taken except in accordance with the provisions of the General Agreement, as interpreted by this Agreement."

In an accompanying footnote, Article 16.1 added that this provision "is not intended to preclude action under other relevant provisions of the General Agreement, as appropriate."

3.284 The United States recalls that a provision virtually identical to Article 16.1 of the Tokyo Round Anti-Dumping Code now appears in the Anti-Dumping Agreement, in Article 18.1, except that now it refers to the GATT 1994 instead of the GATT 1947. Article 18.1 and its footnote provide as follows:

---

[256] Reports of Committees and Principal Sub-Committees, ICITO I/8, p. 74, para. 25 (Geneva, September 1948), quoted in GATT, *Analytical Index: Guide to GATT Law and Practice*, 6th ed. (1995), p. 238 (emphasis added by the United States).

[257] BISD II/41, 42, para. 12 (emphasis added by the United States).

"18.1 No specific action against dumping of exports from another Member can be taken except in accordance with the provisions of GATT 1994, as interpreted by this Agreement.[24]

[...]

[24] This is not intended to preclude action under other relevant provisions of GATT 1994, as appropriate."

3.285 The United States points out that, in the "Dunkel Draft" text of the Anti-Dumping Agreement dated 20 December 1991, the Article on final provisions was left blank. In the course of the work of the Legal Drafting Group in April 1992, the Secretariat then inserted a new Article on final provisions, paragraph 1 of which was constituted of the text of former Article 16.1, with the words "General Agreement" mechanically transposed to "GATT 1993".[258] "GATT 1993" was then later mechanically transposed to "GATT 1994".

3.286 The United States submits that, in the context of the 1979 Anti-Dumping Code, the meaning of the footnote to Article 16.1 was clear. No action against dumping could be taken except consistently with the General Agreement. This merely restates the basic principle of *pacta sunt servanda*: every treaty in force is binding on the parties to it and must be performed by them in good faith. However, it is also clear that there was never any intention to eliminate the other GATT-consistent options available to address a factual situation that constituted a case of injurious dumping.[259] Thus, for example, a contracting party that was a Party to the 1979 Anti-Dumping Code retained the option to address such dumping by eliminating the injury, for instance by raising the duty on the product concerned on an MFN basis to a level not in excess of the relevant tariff binding. Or it could renegotiate the duty on the product consistent with Article XXVIII. Or it could provide adjustment assistance for the industry or workers injured by the dumping. Or, if the factual situation also supported the taking of a safeguard action under Article XIX or a countervailing duty under Article VI, the contracting party concerned could pursue those avenues.

3.287 The United States argues that, read literally, Article 16.1 alone might have been misinterpreted to lock any government into levying anti-dumping duties whenever it was faced with a factual situation constituting injurious dumping. The footnote preserved flexibility to take any other measure that was otherwise GATT-consistent.

3.288 The United States considers that the same conclusions hold today. If a Member is faced with a factual situation constituting injurious dumping, it is not locked into levying anti-dumping duties, but has the option of taking other measures that are in accordance with the GATT 1994. If the measure is of a nature that is simply not

[258] The United States refers to room document no. 625, dated 6 April 1992, p. 30.

[259] The United States refers to J. H. Jackson, *World Trade and the Law of GATT*, The Bobbs-Merrill Co. (1969), p. 411 where it is stated that "although Article VI carves out an exception to GATT obligations for antidumping and countervailing duties, nevertheless, measures that do not violate other GATT provisions can also be used to counteract dumping or subsidies."

regulated by the GATT 1994, as is the case for the 1916 Act, the measure is *a fortiori* consistent with the GATT 1994.

3.289 It is the United States' position in the present case, of course, that the 1916 Act should not be viewed as an action against dumping in the first place. Rather, under US law, the 1916 Act has been interpreted as an anti-trust statute. More fundamentally, it is a statute whose elements are not the same as the "dumping" and "injury" elements of Article VI of the GATT 1994 and the Anti-Dumping Agreement and therefore is not subject to Article VI:2 and Article 18.1.

3.290 **Japan** maintains its view that Article VI of the GATT 1994 and the Anti-Dumping Agreement set forth the only WTO-consistent means of addressing dumping. First of all, the US interpretation of footnote 24 is incorrect. The text of Article 18.1 and footnote 24 of the Anti-Dumping Agreement reaffirm the understanding that Article VI of the GATT 1994 is the sole GATT-authorized remedy for dumping. The plain meaning of Article 18.1 could not be more explicit. "No specific action" can be taken to address dumping except action that follows the requirements of Article VI of the GATT 1994. Footnote 24 provides that "appropriate" action under other provisions of the GATT 1994, such as a safeguard remedy, may be imposed where the WTO requirements for doing so are met. In other words, a Member may affect imports through actions authorized by other provisions of the GATT 1994. For example, in a situation involving dumping (i.e. where the requirements for imposing an anti-dumping duty were met), a Member could impose a safeguard measure after complying with the provisions of the WTO Safeguards Agreement.[260]

3.291 Japan notes, however, that the footnote does not authorize remedies other than anti-dumping duties to counteract dumping. The only "specific action" permitted "in accordance" with Article VI is imposition of anti-dumping duties after certain requirements have been met. In the instant case, no provision of the GATT 1994 justifies the procedures and penalties provided for by the 1916 Act. If the US interpretation were correct, a Member could take any measure in addition to anti-dumping duties after completing an investigation in accordance with the Anti-Dumping Agreement.[261]

3.292 Japan considers that the US interpretation in the present proceeding clearly departs from previous official US positions. The analysis by USTR General Counsel Alan Holmer to the US Senate Finance Committee clearly supports Japan's position. He testified that "the use of additional sanctions, such as fines, embargoes, imprisonment or other draconian measures" was not permitted, and that Article 16 (now Article 18.1 of the Anti-Dumping Agreement) allows a government to provide its citizens only one remedy for dumping - the collection of anti-dumping duties.

---

[260] In response to a question of the Panel regarding the interpretation of footnote 24, Japan notes that, for example, safeguard action consistent with Article XIX of the GATT 1994 might well have the incidental effect of stopping "dumped" imports as a result of the action, but the objective of the action itself would not be to address the dumping. According to Japan, footnote 24 thus simply avoids the possible conflict between other WTO actions against imports and the obligation under Article 18.1 of the Anti-Dumping Agreement not to take other actions against dumping.

[261] Japan notes, in this regard, that, under the US interpretation, footnote 24 would completely contradict the main point of Article 18.1 - that countries may not take any action against dumping other than the imposition of anti-dumping duties.

3.293 The **United States** responds that, first of all, Article VI does not govern all laws and measures that impose border adjustments or even all laws and measures that impose border adjustments in the form of duties. It only governs laws and measures that attempt to counteract injurious dumping through the imposition of duties, based on findings of "dumping" and "injury", as is clear from the GATT 1947 panel report in *United States - Countervailing Duties on Fresh, Chilled and Frozen Pork from Canada.*[262] There, the panel report first discusses one of two basic GATT 1947 provisions that prohibits duties from being imposed. That provision is Article I:1, and it provides that duties and charges of any kind imposed in connection with importation must meet the most-favoured-nation standard. The other one, according to the panel report, is Article II:1, which provides that an importing Member shall not impose duties on another Member's products in excess of the rate set forth in the importing Member's Schedule of Concessions, i.e. the bound rate. Specifically, Article II:1(b) provides that a Member's products

> "[...] shall [...] be exempt from ordinary customs duties in excess of those set forth and provided [in the importing Member's Schedule of Concessions]. Such products shall also be exempt from all other duties or charges of any kind imposed on or in connection with the importation in excess of those imposed on the date of this Agreement or those directly and mandatorily required to be imposed thereafter by legislation in force in the importing territory on that date."

3.294 According to the United States, Article II:2 does recognize certain situations where duties may be imposed in excess of the bound rate, and one of them is "any anti-dumping or countervailing duty applied consistently with the provisions of Article VI". Otherwise, according to the panel report, duties in excess of the bound rate (or duties provided on a non-most-favoured-nation basis) are prohibited.[263]

3.295 The United States argues that, when Article VI is read in the context of Article I:1 and Article II:1, it can be seen how the coverage of Article VI is limited. Article VI itself applies only to laws or measures that attempt to counteract injurious dumping through the imposition of anti-dumping duties.

3.296 The United States submits that, given the limited coverage of Article VI and, in particular, its status as a carve-out from the most-favoured-nation obligation of Article I:1 and Article II:1, it does not follow that Article VI (or Article 18.1 of the

---

[262] The United States refers to the Panel Report on in *United States - Countervailing Duties on Fresh, Chilled and Frozen Pork from Canada*, adopted on 11 July 1991, BISD 38S/30, para. 4.4 (hereinafter "*United States - Pork*").

[263] In response to the question of the Panel regarding how the parties understand the phrase "In order to offset dumping [...]" in Article VI:2 of the GATT 1994, the United States argues that the phrase "[i]n order to offset dumping [...]" is used in Article VI:2 of the GATT 1994 in order to differentiate the type of duty that a Member may impose under Article VI from the types of duty that would run afoul of Article I:1 and Article II:1 of the GATT 1994. As explained by the panel report in *United States - Pork*, Article I:1 prohibits duties on imported products that do not meet the most-favoured-nation standard. Article II:1 prohibits duties in excess of the bound rate. Within this context, the phrase "In order to offset dumping [...]" in Article VI:2 can be seen as an attempt to specify a situation in which it is proper for a Member to impose duties in excess of the bound rate and on a non-most-favoured-nation basis.

Anti-Dumping Agreement) would itself act as a prohibition against actions that a Member may take. Rather, Article VI is properly viewed as establishing a right that a Member has, and that is the right to impose duties to counteract injurious dumping. Article VI and the Anti-Dumping Agreement do require a Member to follow the rules set forth in the Anti-Dumping Agreement when imposing anti-dumping duties. But, they do not prohibit the imposition of other measures to counteract injurious dumping. Indeed, Article VI does not even address that issue. It is Article 18.1 of the Anti-Dumping Agreement that addresses that issue, and it makes clear that a Member may take whatever other action is consistent with other GATT 1994 provisions.

3.297 In the view of the United States, it is for precisely this reason that Professor Jackson opined that "although Article VI carves out an exception to GATT obligations for antidumping and countervailing duties, nevertheless, measures that do not violate other GATT provisions can also be used to counteract dumping or subsidies."[264]

3.298 In reply to the Japanese argument that "[i]f the US interpretation were correct, a Member could take any measure in addition to antidumping duties after completing an investigation in accordance with the Anti-Dumping Agreement", the United States maintains its position that Article 18.1 allows remedies for dumping other than duties as long as those remedies do not run afoul of other GATT 1994 provisions. However, that requirement poses a severe limitation on the actions available to a Member. For example, the national treatment obligation of Article III, by itself, substantially restricts the actions that a Member might take. If a law imposed damages on an importer based on findings of "dumping" and "injury", it would not be governed by Article VI, given that it did not impose duties. Instead, it would be an internal law, governed by Article III:4, and the treatment accorded to imported products by that law would have to be no less favourable than the treatment accorded to domestic products by any comparable domestic law. In all likelihood, moreover, that law would violate Article III:4, given that national anti-trust regimes generally base liability for low pricing on factors such as the possession of a large market share and predation.

3.299 The United States argues that, for these reasons, even if the Panel somehow were to rule that the 1916 Act was governed by Article VI of the GATT 1994, it should nevertheless find that nothing in Article VI or Article 18.1 of the Anti-Dumping Agreement makes anti-dumping duties the exclusive remedy for injurious dumping. Rather, the only requirement emanating from Article VI and the Anti-Dumping Agreement is that any other action taken by a Member with respect to injurious dumping must be consistent with other GATT 1994 provisions. As Article III:4 is the only other GATT 1994 provision under which Japan makes a claim in the present proceeding, any violation of Article VI and the Anti-Dumping Agreement in the present proceeding would have to be predicated on a violation of Article III:4, and that is not something that Japan has established.[265]

---

[264] The United States refers to J. H. Jackson, *Op. Cit.*, p. 411.

[265] In response to a question of Japan regarding whether the 1916 Act would be a GATT-consistent measure if sanctions against injurious dumping included capital punishment or life-term imprisonment, the United States notes that the question wrongly implies that the 1916 Act is a sanction

3.300 **Japan** argues that Article III is irrelevant in this context. It does not enable a Member to take specific measures against dumping. A Member may take measures permitted under other WTO provisions in a situation where there exists dumping. However, the United States does not and cannot identify any other WTO provision to justify the imposition of imprisonment, treble damages etc. The United States again attempts to escape from its burden to prove that imposition of imprisonment, treble damages, etc. are WTO-consistent and that anti-dumping duties are not the exclusive remedy for dumping. The United States refers to Professor Jackson's assertion that "measures that do not violate other GATT provisions can also be used to counteract dumping". This statement is in line with Japan's statement and does not support the US argument.

3.301 Japan notes that, in a contorted new argument in support of its contention, the United States asserts that the 1916 Act is not within the scope of Article VI of the GATT 1994 and the Anti-Dumping Agreement, but rather is governed by Article III:4 of the GATT 1994. Thus, since it would be a measure permitted by another WTO provision, anti-dumping duties are not the exclusive remedy for dumping. The logical fallacy is obvious.[266] If a law is not an anti-dumping law, the fact that other provisions may be violated is not relevant to the issue of whether measures other than anti-dumping duties are permitted in order to offset dumping. In all of its argumentation, the United States has been unable to explain how the 1916 Act's penalties - imprisonment, treble damages, fines and costs - are measures permitted under other WTO provisions. In answer to Japan's question, the United States says that if there is an analogous domestic statute providing capital punishment or life-term imprisonment, a Member can provide such remedies against dumping. This US interpretation runs counter not only to relevant WTO provisions but also to the objectives of the WTO regime.

3.302 The **United States**, in reaction to Japan's hypothetical examples of capital punishment or life imprisonment as remedies for 1916 Act violations, states that these are not among the (unused) criminal remedies provided in the 1916 Act itself. If they were, they would violate the national treatment provisions of Article III of the GATT 1994 unless and until the United States began to execute domestic price discriminators. The United States does not do that.

3.303 In response to a question of the Panel regarding the meaning of the word "measure" in Article 1 of the Anti-Dumping Agreement as opposed to that of the word "action" in Article 18.1 of the Anti-Dumping Agreement and footnote 24 attached thereto, **Japan** notes that the term "measure" in Article 1 of the Anti-Dumping Agreement refers to provisional measures pursuant to Article 7, price undertakings pursuant to Article 8, and anti-dumping duties pursuant to Article 9 of the Anti-Dumping Agreement. All of these types of actions must comply with the Anti-Dumping Agreement.

---

against injurious dumping. Apart from this, if those remedies were allowed under the 1916 Act, it would be inconsistent with Article III:4 as there is no analogous domestic statute providing for those remedies.

[266] In response to a question of the United States, Japan confirms its view that Article VI governs any and all measures taken in order to offset dumping regardless of whether the measure is applied at the border or within the border.

3.304 Japan argues that the term "action" in Article 18.1, in contrast, is intentionally broader. Because "action" is not defined in the Anti-Dumping Agreement, its meaning should be determined by "reference to its ordinary meaning, read in light of its context, and the object and purposes" of the Anti-Dumping Agreement.[267] The drafters recognized that countries might be tempted to take other actions targeted at "dumping," and therefore drafted a clear statement that any such actions were not permitted. "Action" thus covers any type of border measures, internal measures, procedural steps, or any other conduct to discipline dumping. This distinction also is echoed by the use of the narrower term "applied" in Article 1 versus the broader term "taken" in Article 18.1.

3.305 The **United States**, in reply to the same question of the Panel, submits that, in interpreting the term "measure" in Article 1 of the Anti-Dumping Agreement, it is first necessary to consider that this term is modified by the term "anti-dumping." When the term "anti-dumping measure" is read together with the plain meaning of the remainder of Article 1, it becomes clear that it means any of the measures provided for under the Anti-Dumping Agreement, which includes (1) provisional measures under Article 7, (2) price undertakings under Article 8 and (3) the imposition of anti-dumping duties under Article 9. A review of the history of Article 1 further confirms this meaning. In this regard, Article 1 of the 1979 Tokyo Round Anti-Dumping Code only expressly addressed a measure in the form of an anti-dumping duty. It provided that "[t]he imposition of an anti-dumping duty is a measure to be taken only" in the circumstances provided in Article VI and pursuant to the rules set forth in the Anti-Dumping Code. As a technical correction, Article 1 of the Anti-Dumping Agreement was subsequently clarified to read that any measure provided for by the Anti-Dumping Agreement could be taken only in the circumstances provided in Article VI and pursuant to the rules set forth in the Anti-Dumping Agreement. It is for this reason that it now refers to "[a]n anti-dumping measure" instead of only an anti-dumping duty.

3.306 The United States further notes that, with this meaning given to the term "anti-dumping measure," Article 1 of the Anti-Dumping Agreement can properly be interpreted as providing that if a Member takes a measure provided for by the Anti-Dumping Agreement, it may only do so in the circumstances provided in Article VI - which means that findings of "dumping" and "injury" must be made - and if it follows the rules set forth in the Anti-Dumping Agreement. Article 1 does not explain what a Member can do if it takes action against dumping other than by resorting to one of the measures provided for under Article VI and the Anti-Dumping Agreement. However, it plainly implies that measures other than those provided for in the Anti-Dumping Agreement can be taken against dumping. That is why the second sentence of Article 1 explains that it is only addressing what can happen "in so far as action is taken under anti-dumping legislation or regulations."

3.307 The United States points out that Japan has not challenged the United States' taking of any of the three types of measures set forth in the Anti-Dumping Agree-

---

[267] Japan refers to the Appellate Body Report on *Guatemala - Anti-Dumping Investigation Regarding Portland Cement from Mexico*, WT/DS60/AB/R, adopted 25 November 1998, DSR 1998:IX, 3767, para.70 (hereinafter Appellate Body Report on "*Guatemala - Cement*").

ment. It has only challenged the 1916 Act as such. What this means is that in the absence of a challenge to one of the three specific measures identified in the Anti-Dumping Agreement, the Panel has no jurisdiction to make any findings with respect to any claims under the Anti-Dumping Agreement. As the Appellate Body has made clear in *Guatemala - Cement*, the only matters that may be challenged under the Anti-Dumping Agreement are the three types of anti-dumping measures set forth in the Anti-Dumping Agreement. In the Appellate Body's words:

> "According to Article 17.4, a "matter" may be referred to the DSB *only if* one of the relevant three anti-dumping measures is in place. This provision, when read together with Article 6.2 of the DSU, requires a panel request in a dispute brought under the *Anti-Dumping Agreement* to identify, as the specific measure at issue, either a definitive anti-dumping duty, the acceptance of a price undertaking, or a provisional measure. This requirement to identify a specific anti-dumping measure at issue in a panel request in no way limits the nature of the *claims* that may be brought concerning alleged nullification or impairment of benefits or the impeding of the achievement of any objective in a dispute under the *Anti-Dumping Agreement.* As we have observed earlier, there is a difference between the specific measure at issue - in the case of the *Anti-Dumping Agreement*, one of the three types of anti-dumping measure described in Article 17.4 - and the claims or the legal basis of the complaint referred to the DSB relating to those specific measures. In coming to this conclusion, we note that the language of Article 17.4 of the *Anti-Dumping Agreement* is unique to that Agreement."[268]

3.308 The United States argues that, similarly, in light of the reasoning of the panel in *Brazil - Measures Affecting Desiccated Coconut* which was affirmed by the Appellate Body, the Panel has no jurisdiction to decide a claim under Article VI of the GATT 1994. The panel in that case found that: "Article VI of GATT 1994 is not independently applicable to a dispute to which the SCM Agreement is not applicable,"[269] relying on language parallel to Article 1 of the Anti-Dumping Agreement.

3.309 **Japan** considers that the particular finding of the Appellate Body in *Guatemala - Cement* cited by the United States has no relevance to the present panel proceeding. The *Guatemala - Cement* case dealt with the issue of whether a provisional or definitive anti-dumping *duty* had been levied before the relevant panel process was initiated. In the present case, however, the subject of the deliberations is not an anti-dumping duty or a price undertaking, but action other than anti-dumping duties or price undertakings. Thus, the findings of the panel or the Appellate Body in *Guatemala-Cement* on this particular issue do not apply here.

---

[268] The United States refers to the Appellate Body Report on *Guatemala - Cement, supra,* footnote 267, para. 79. (emphasis added by the United States).

[269] The United States refers to the Panel Report on *Brazil - Measures Affecting Desiccated Coconut*, WT/DS22/R, adopted 20 March 1997, DSR 1997:I, 189, para. 278 (hereinafter "*Brazil - Desiccated Coconut*").

3.310 With regard to the term "action" in Article 18.1 and footnote 24 of the Anti-Dumping Agreement, the **United States** notes that, like the term "measure" in Article 1 of the Anti-Dumping Agreement, the term "action" in Article 18.1 and footnote 24 of the Anti-Dumping Agreement is modified. In particular, Article 18.1 refers to a "specific action against dumping." A "specific" action against dumping is one that regulates particular import transactions, such as can take place through the imposition of duties, an injunction, a quantitative restriction or valuation procedures. An action is one that is "against dumping," meanwhile, if it is designed to counteract dumping.

3.311 The United States considers that, when Article 18.1 and footnote 24 are read together, it can be seen that they mean that a Member can take a specific action against dumping if it is consistent with, and not in violation of, the provisions of the GATT 1994.

3.312 The United States argues that it should be clear that Article 18.1 and footnote 24 do not even purport to address or place any limitation on a measure like the 1916 Act. First, the 1916 Act does not regulate particular import transactions or even imports generally; it only imposes liability on an importer. Second, the 1916 Act is not directed at dumping; it is directed at private anti-competitive conduct typically condemned by anti-trust laws. Of course, the Panel need not reach any of these issues because the 1916 Act, in the first place, is not even subject to Article VI of the GATT 1994 or the Anti-Dumping Agreement.

H. *Violations of Article VI:1 of the GATT 1994 and Articles 1, 2, 3, 4, 5, 9 and 11 of the Anti-Dumping Agreement*

3.313 Japan asserts that the 1916 Act violates the requirements set forth in Article VI of the GATT 1994 and in numerous provisions of the Anti-Dumping Agreement because it requires the imposition of impermissible anti-dumping remedies in situations where the procedural requirements for applying the one permitted remedy are not met.

3.314 Japan asserts, first, that the 1916 Act provides for the application of remedies against dumping outside the circumstances specified at Article VI:1 of the GATT 1994 and Article 1 of the Anti-Dumping Agreement. Specifically, the 1916 Act provides for the imposition of measures in the absence of an investigation (i) initiated and conducted in accordance with the provisions of and (ii) which establishes facts required by Article 1 of the Anti-Dumping Agreement.[270] Therefore, the Act is inconsistent with Article VI of the GATT 1994 and Article 1 of the Anti-Dumping Agreement.

3.315 Japan recalls, second, that the 1916 Act prohibits importation of a product at a price "substantially less" than the "actual market value or wholesale price of [the product] [...] in the principal markets of the country of their production, or of other foreign countries to which they are commonly exported [...]." Article VI:1(a) of the

[270] Japan refers to the Panel Report on *New Zealand - Imports of Electrical Transformers from Finland*, adopted on 18 July 1985, BISD 32S/55, para. 4.4, where it is stated that "it was clear from the wording of Article VI that no anti-dumping duties should be levied until certain facts had been established".

GATT 1994 and Articles 2.1 and 2.2 of the Anti-Dumping Agreement, in contrast, require that the first benchmark against which the price of the imported product is compared be the actual price of the product in the exporting country.[271]

3.316 Japan notes that, in addition, Article 2.4.1 of the Anti-Dumping Agreement provides those against whom dumping is alleged, protection against currency fluctuations. The 1916 Act provides no such protection. Japan considers, therefore, that the 1916 Act is inconsistent with Article VI:1(a) of the GATT 1994 and Article 2 of the Anti-Dumping Agreement, because it deviates from their requirements.

3.317 Japan argues, third, that Articles VI:1 and VI:6(a) of the GATT 1994, and Article 3 of the Anti-Dumping Agreement, require a Member to find that the dumping has caused or threatens to cause material injury to its domestic industry (or retards the establishment of a domestic industry) before applying an anti-dumping measure.[272] These Articles also set forth criteria which define and govern the determination of injury. For example, paragraphs 1, 2 and 4 of Article 3 of the Anti-Dumping Agreement set forth factors which a Member must examine in determining whether injury has occurred-volume and impact of prices of dumped imports, etc..

3.318 Japan notes that, in contrast, the 1916 Act requires only a showing of *intent*. Moreover, the intent requirement is defined as an intent to destroy or injure a United States industry or to prevent its establishment; thus, the 1916 Act has no "materially" requirement. The 1916 Act also provides for the application of penalties based merely upon a showing of the price differential discussed above and intent, a requirement that differs substantially from that set forth in the WTO agreements. This directly contravenes the United States' obligations under Article VI of the GATT 1994 and Article 3 of the Anti-Dumping Agreement.

3.319 Japan points out, fourth, that Articles 4 and 5 of the Anti-Dumping Agreement set forth requirements limiting the party or parties that properly may pursue an anti-dumping claim. Specifically, they require that a request be made "by or on behalf of the domestic industry".[273] In contrast, as shown by *Geneva Steel* and *Wheeling-Pittsburgh*, a single United States producer of a like product may advance a claim under the Anti-Dumping Act of 1916.[274] Japan notes, in addition, that Article 5

---

[271] Japan recalls that, under Article VI:1(a) and Article 2.1, the primary and preferred benchmark for comparison is "the comparable price, in the ordinary course of trade, for the like product when destined for consumption in the exporting country."

[272] Japan refers to the Panel Report on *Swedish Anti-Dumping Duties*, adopted on 26 February 1955, BISD 3S/81, para. 8, where it is states that "[t]he importing country is only entitled to levy an anti-dumping duty when there is material injury to a domestic industry [...].".

[273] Japan refers to Article 5.1 of the Anti-Dumping Agreement. Japan also notes that Article 4.1 defines "domestic industry" as "the domestic producers as a whole of the like products or [...] those of them whose collective output of the products constitutes a major proportion of the total domestic production of those products" and that Article 5.4 requires authorities to determine that a petition is supported by "those domestic producers whose collective output constitutes more than 50 per cent of the total production of the like product" of those producers supporting or opposing the petition. Japan notes that under no circumstances can an investigation be initiated if those supporting it account for less than 25 per cent of total domestic production of the like product.

[274] Japan refers to the 1916 Act which states that "[*a*]*ny* person injured [...] may sue therefor in the district court [...]" (emphasis added by Japan). Japan notes the contrast with the Report of the Group of Experts on 'Anti-Dumping and Countervailing Duties,' adopted on 13 May 1959, BISD 8S/145,

requires that petitions contain evidence of the three elements of dumping, injury and causation, and set a *de minimis* threshold applicable to the dumping element. The 1916 Act contains none of these requirements. Rather, an 1916 Act plaintiff needs only to present a "short and plain statement" of its claim.[275] Finally, Article 5.10 of the Anti-Dumping Agreement requires Members to complete their investigations and decide whether or not to impose duties within 18 months. The 1916 Act contains no such deadline. Therefore, the Act is inconsistent with Article VI of the GATT 1994 and Articles 4 and 5 of the Anti-Dumping Agreement.

3.320 Japan submits, fifth, that Article 9 of the Anti-Dumping Agreement sets forth the regime which Members must apply when imposing and collecting anti-dumping duties. The 1916 Act, however, ignores this regime. It provides for the US government to collect fixed monetary penalties and for private litigants to collect treble damages and attorneys costs without complying with any of the requirements of Article 9. Moreover, it ignores the Article 9.3 command that the penalty not exceed the margin of dumping and, further, imposes imprisonment as a penalty. In addition, the 1916 Act violates Article VI and Article 9 because it imposes retroactive, punitive penalties on importers, including treble damages and imprisonment. In contrast, Article 9, and especially Article 9.2, specifies that the remedy of anti-dumping duties is a prospective measure. A review of Article 11 of the Anti-Dumping Agreement further confirms this fact. Thus, the Act violates Article VI of the GATT 1994 and Article 9 of the Anti-Dumping Agreement.

3.321 Japan argues, finally, that Article 11 of the Anti-Dumping Agreement limits the duration of anti-dumping measures and requires periodic reviews of the need for continued imposition of anti-dumping duties. The 1916 Act has no provisions regarding either duration or review. Thus, the Act violates Article VI of the GATT 1994 and Article 11 of the Anti-Dumping Agreement.

3.322 The **United States** argues that the claims raised by Japan under various other provisions of Article VI of the GATT 1994 and the Anti-Dumping Agreement rest on the assumption that the Panel has already found the 1916 Act to be in violation of Article VI:2 of the GATT 1994 and Article 18.1 of the Anti-Dumping Agreement. Thus, each of these claims has the same mistaken premise, namely, that Article VI:2 of the GATT 1994 and Article 18.1 of the Anti-Dumping Agreement make anti-dumping duties the exclusive remedy for dumping and, further, that the 1916 Act is an anti-dumping statute that provides remedies for dumping other than anti-dumping duties.

3.323 The United States contends that Japan has failed to establish that Article VI and the Anti-Dumping Agreement govern anti-trust measures such as the 1916 Act, or that these provisions even govern all anti-dumping measures. Japan's various claims under Article VI and the Anti-Dumping Agreement therefore must be rejected.

---

para. 18 where it is stated that "the use of anti-dumping duties to offset injury to a single firm within a large industry [...] would be protectionist [...]".

[275] Japan refers to the US Federal Rule of Civil Procedure 8(a)(2).

I. Violations of Articles 1 and 18.1 of the Anti-Dumping Agreement

3.324 **Japan** contends that, by applying the 1916 Act without meeting the requirements of Article VI of the GATT 1994 and Articles 2, 3, 4, 5, 9 and 11 of the Anti-Dumping Agreement, the United States also has violated its obligation under Articles 1 and 18.1 of the Anti-Dumping Agreement.

3.325 Japan recalls that Article 1 of the Anti-Dumping Agreement provides as follows:

> "An anti-dumping measure shall be applied only under the circumstances provided for in Article VI of GATT 1994 and pursuant to investigations initiated and conducted in accordance with the provisions of this Agreement. The following provisions govern the application of Article VI of GATT 1994 in so far as action is taken under anti-dumping legislation or regulations."[276]

3.326 Japan also recalls that Article 18.1 reads as follows:

> "No specific action against dumping of exports from another Member can be taken except in accordance with the provisions of GATT 1994, as interpreted by this Agreement."

3.327 Japan recalls, finally, that, as previously demonstrated, the United States has violated many provisions of Article VI of the GATT 1994 and Articles, 2, 3, 4, 5, 9 and 11 of the Anti-Dumping Agreement. Thus, the United States has violated Articles 1 and 18.1 of the Anti-Dumping Agreement.

3.328 The **United States** argues that the claims raised by Japan under various other provisions of Article VI of the GATT 1994 and the Anti-Dumping Agreement rest on the assumption that the Panel has already found the 1916 Act to be in violation of Article VI:2 of the GATT 1994 and Article 18.1 of the Anti-Dumping Agreement. Thus, each of these claims has the same mistaken premise, namely, that Article VI:2 of the GATT 1994 and Article 18.1 of the Anti-Dumping Agreement make anti-dumping duties the exclusive remedy for dumping and, further, that the 1916 Act is an anti-dumping statute that provides remedies for dumping other than antidumping duties.

3.329 The United States contends that Japan has failed to establish that Article VI and the Anti-Dumping Agreement govern anti-trust measures such as the 1916 Act, or that these provisions even govern all anti-dumping measures. Japan's various claims under Article VI and the Anti-Dumping Agreement therefore must be rejected.

J. Violation of Article III:4 of the GATT 1994

1. The Relationship between Article III:4 and Article VI of the GATT 1994

3.330 In response to a question of the Panel to both parties regarding the relationship between Article III:4 and Article VI of the GATT 1994, **Japan** argues that Articles III:4 and VI are not related in the sense of necessarily being either dependent

[276] Footnote omitted by Japan.

upon one another or mutually exclusive. Thus, as in the present case, a domestic measure can violate both Articles. More specifically, if a measure conforms with Article VI, it is a permitted border measure (a measure imposed on or in connection with importation) and so is not within the scope of Article III. In the instant case, however, the measure violates Article VI as an anti-dumping law not in conformity therewith; it also violates Article III by regulating imported products under a separate, less favourable regime than is applicable to domestic products.

3.331 The **United States**, in reply to the Panel's question, considers that a specific law or measure falls under Article III:4 of GATT 1994 when it can be characterised as an "internal" law or measure. Basically, an "internal" law or measure is one, like the 1916 Act, that affects the internal sale, offering for sale, purchase, transportation, distribution or use of an imported product. Although it is possible for an internal charge or regulation to be collected or enforced in the case of an imported product at the time or point of importation and still be subject to Article III[277], an "internal" law or measure nevertheless does not include a law or measure making a border adjustment, such as the imposition of duties on an imported product.

3.332 In the view of the United States, for a specific law or measure to fall under Article VI of the GATT 1994, two requirements must be satisfied. First, it must involve a particular type of border adjustment, not just any border adjustment; it must be one that imposes duties on an imported product. Second, it must also be an anti-dumping law or measure, in the sense that it attempts to counteract injurious dumping based on findings of "dumping" and "injury."

3.333 The GATT 1947 panel report in *United States - Pork*[278] confirms that Article VI does not govern all laws and measures that impose border adjustments or even all laws and measures that impose border adjustments in the form of duties, but rather only laws and measures that attempt to counteract injurious dumping through the imposition of duties, based on findings of "dumping" and "injury." As the panel report explains, one of two basic GATT provisions that prohibits duties from being imposed is Article I:1 of the GATT 1994, which provides that duties and charges of any kind imposed in connection with importation must meet the most-favoured-nation standard. The other one, according to the panel report, is Article II:1, which provides that an importing Member shall not impose duties on another Member's products in excess of the rate set forth in the importing Member's Schedule of Concessions, i.e. the bound rate. Specifically, Article II:1(b) provides that a Member's products "shall [...] be exempt from ordinary customs duties in excess of those set forth and provided [in the importing Member's Schedule of Concessions]. Such products shall also be exempt from all other duties or charges of any kind imposed on or in connection with the importation in excess of those imposed on the date of this Agreement or those directly and mandatorily required to be imposed thereafter by legislation in force in the importing territory on that date." Article II:2 does recognize certain situations where duties may be imposed in excess of the bound rate, such as "any anti-dumping or countervailing duty applied consistently with the provisions of Article VI," but otherwise duties in excess of the bound rate (or duties provided on

[277] The United States refers to the Interpretative Note *ad* Article III.

[278] The United States refers to *United States - Pork*, *Op. Cit.*, para. 4.4.

a non-most-favoured-nation basis) are prohibited. When Article VI therefore is read in the context of Article I:1 and Article II:1, it can be seen how the coverage of Article VI is limited. Article VI itself applies only to laws or measures that attempt to counteract injurious dumping through the imposition of duties, based on findings of "dumping" and "injury."

3.334 The United States further argues that an anti-trust law or measure addressing private anti-competitive conduct, such as predatory pricing, through the imposition of treble damages - as does the 1916 Act - is not governed by Article VI for two independent reasons. First, it is not a law or measure that imposes any type of border adjustment; it is an internal law or measure. Second, it is not an anti-dumping law or measure; it addresses private anti-competitive conduct rather than injurious dumping.

3.335 The United States asserts that, if an anti-trust law or measure addressed private anti-competitive conduct, such as predatory pricing, through the imposition of duties on the imported product, it still would not be governed by Article VI, given that it is not an anti-dumping law or measure. It would, however, be governed by - and inconsistent with - Article II:1(b), which provides that an importing Member shall not impose duties on another Member's products in excess of the bound rate. Article II:2 does recognize certain situations where duties may nevertheless be imposed, as discussed above, such as "any anti-dumping [...] duty applied consistently with the provisions of Article VI," but there is no provision that would apply to an anti-trust law or measure addressing private anti-competitive conduct.

3.336 The United States contends, finally, that, if an anti-dumping law or measure addressed injurious dumping through the imposition of damages, it, too, would not be governed by Article VI, given that it did not impose duties and therefore would not even be any type of border measure. Instead, it would be governed by Article III:4, and the treatment accorded to imported products by that anti-dumping law or measure would have to be no less favourable than the treatment accorded to domestic products by any comparable domestic law or measure. In all likelihood, moreover, the anti-dumping law or measure would violate Article III:4, given that national anti-trust regimes generally base liability for low pricing on factors such as the possession of a large market share and predation.

3.337 In summing up, the United States notes that, in the case of Article III:4, it is the nature of the measures imposed in application of the law that is dispositive as to whether or not Article III:4 governs. As discussed above, a specific law or measure falls under Article III:4 when it can be characterised as an "internal" law or measure, and an "internal" law or measure is one that affects the internal sale, offering for sale, purchase, transportation, distribution or use of an imported product. An "internal" law or measure is not one that imposes duties at the border. The fact that the law may target specific practices, such as in the anti-dumping sense or the anti-trust sense, is irrelevant under Article III:4.

3.338 The United States notes that, in contrast, in the case of Article VI, both the nature of the measures imposed in application of the law and the fact that the law may target specific practices must be considered to determine whether or not Article VI governs. As discussed above, Article VI governs a particular type of law or measure, namely, one that makes a border adjustment, and then only if it is in the form of the imposition of duties on an imported product. Second, the law or measure must also be an anti-dumping law or measure, in the sense that it attempts to counteract injurious dumping based on findings of "dumping" and "injury."

2. *The 1916 Act Standing Alone and in Comparison to the Robinson-Patman Act*

3.339 **Japan** considers that the 1916 Act regulates prices of imported products under a regime separate from the analogous US law regulating prices of domestic products, i.e. the Robinson-Patman Act. The resulting differential and less favourable treatment is inconsistent with the United States' national treatment obligation under Article III:4 of the GATT 1994.[279]

3.340 Japan notes that, to establish a violation of Article III:4, the complaining party must demonstrate that the 1916 Act (i) is a "law, regulation or requirement", (ii) "affecting" the "internal sale, offering for sale, purchase, transportation, distribution or use" of imported products, and (iii) which accords less favourable treatment to imports than is accorded to domestic like products.

3.341 Japan considers that these three criteria are met in the present case. Japan notes, first of all, that the 1916 Act is a statute, i.e. a law, of the United States. The 1916 Act affects the sale of imported products within the United States because it regulates, by prohibiting, the sale or causing to be sold of imported products below the price threshold set out in the 1916 Act (home market price or third market price). The fact that the 1916 Act applies also to importers is inapposite. The 1916 Act applies not merely to the importing of products but also to the domestic US sale ("internal sale") of imported products.[280]

3.342 Japan recalls, moreover, that panels commonly apply Article III:4 of the GATT 1994 in cases where conditions of competition are affected. For years, panels have interpreted Article III:4 to have an exceedingly broad scope by virtue of its use of "affecting" - "[...] all laws, regulations and requirements *affecting* the internal sale, offering for sale, purchase, transportation distribution or use of products [...]." For example, in the 1958 Report on *Italian Discrimination Against Imported Agricultural Machinery*, the panel said:

> "The selection of the word 'affecting' would imply, in the opinion of the Panel, that the drafters of the Article intended to cover in paragraph 4 not only the laws and regulations which directly governed the conditions of sale or purchase but also any laws or regulations which might adversely modify the *conditions of competition between the domestic and imported products* on the internal market."[281]

---

[279] The first sentence of Article III:4 of the GATT 1994:

> "The products of the territory of any contracting party imported into the territory of any other contracting party shall be accorded treatment no less favourable than that accorded to like products of national origin in respect of all laws, regulations and requirements affecting their internal sale, offering for sale, purchase, transportation, distribution or use."

[280] Japan also refers to the Panel Report on *United States - Section 337*, adopted on 7 November 1983, BISD 36S/345, para. 5.10 (hereinafter "*United States - Section 337*"), which according to Japan, found inconsistent with Article III:4 a US measure that applied to importers, concluding that it nonetheless affected imported products within the meaning of Article III:4.

[281] Panel Report on *Italian Discrimination Against Imported Agricultural Machinery*, adopted on 23 October 1958, BISD 7S/60, para. 12 (emphasis added by Japan).

This is precisely the case in the present dispute; the 1916 Act sets minimum price levels on a product-specific basis that are applicable *only* to imports.

3.343 Regarding the "no less favourable treatment" standard laid down in Article III:4 of the GATT 1994, Japan argues that the situation in the present case is very similar to that resolved by the panel in *United States - Section 337*. In *United States - Section 337*, the panel found that the United States was in violation of its obligations under Article III:4 of the GATT 1994. Section 337 is a US law administered by the US International Trade Commission that provides a remedy for US patent holders against imported goods (but not domestic goods) infringing on US patents. A US patent holder also may pursue an infringement claim against imported (and domestic) goods in a federal district court.

3.344 Japan recalls that the panel found this scheme to be inconsistent with Article III:4 of the GATT 1994 in several ways. First, the panel found that:

> "[...] to provide the complainant with the choice of forum where imported products are concerned and to provide no corresponding choice when domestically-produced products are concerned is in itself less favourable treatment of imported products and therefore is inconsistent with Article III:4."[282]

Second, the panel found that several differences between the Section 337 and federal district court proceedings disadvantaged or treated less favourably, foreign patent holders defending against Section 337 claims.[283] Among the differences noted by the panel as significant were:

(i) a foreign Section 337 defendant could not raise counterclaims, but a defendant in a federal district court proceeding could;

(ii) Section 337 provides for penalties (exclusion orders) that are not available against US-origin products; and

(iii) a foreign patent holder could be subject to two claims, one under Section 337 and one in federal district court, but a domestic patent holder could be sued only in federal district court.[284]

3.345 Japan argues that, as in *United States - Section 337*, in the present case, the United States is in violation of Article III:4 of the GATT 1994 because it has established a separate legal regime solely for imports, in addition to the regime that applies to imports and domestic goods. Imports are required to meet a legal requirement, the 1916 Act, which does not apply to domestic US products. Thus, US law permits a US entity, but not a foreign entity, to engage in international price discrimination.

3.346 Japan further notes that the United States consistently has argued that the 1916 Act is the equivalent of the Robinson-Patman Act, which is the basic US price-discrimination statute. It prohibits sellers from discriminating in price between or among purchasers of goods so as to substantially limit competition or tend to create a

[282] *United States - Section 337*, *Op. Cit.*, para. 5.18.

[283] Japan refers to ibid., para. 5.19.

[284] Japan refers to ibid., paras. 5.19-5.20.

monopoly. The existence of the Robinson-Patman Act cannot, however, be invoked to establish that domestic products are treated in the same way.[285]

3.347 Japan recalls that imported products are *also* subject to the Robinson-Patman Act in the same way as domestic products. This Act, like any legitimate competition or anti-trust measure, does not distinguish between imported and domestic products. Discriminatory sales are prohibited by the Act whether they involve US products or products of foreign origin. The Robinson-Patman Act is entirely origin-neutral, unlike the 1916 Act, which is entirely origin-specific. Japan acknowledges that the Robinson-Patman Act only applies to price discrimination committed in the United States and that the 1916 Act may be considered to complement it in that it applies to *dumping,* which is a price discrimination practiced between the domestic market of the producer and an export market.

3.348 According to Japan, this complementarily does not avoid a violation of Article III:4 of the GATT 1994. The complementarily does not relate to the origin of the goods, but to the discrimination. Japan considers that the situation is similar to that addressed by the panel in *United States - Section 337.* Less favourable treatment is inherent because, due to the two avenues for liability, the importer or seller of imports is regulated by a separate regime. The seller of domestic goods need comply only with the Robinson-Patman Act.

3.349 Japan argues that subjecting US goods to no more favourable treatment than imported goods receive under the 1916 Act would require that the United States apply similar penalties and make available similar remedies for equivalent cases involving US goods. This would require legislation which would render US producers liable for equivalent penalties when they sold their goods in the United States at lower prices than on foreign markets under similar conditions to those set out in the 1916 Act. In its third party statement, the European Communities explained that this would require legislation along the following lines:

> "It shall be unlawful for any person producing any Articles in the United States, commonly and systematically to sell such Articles within the United States at a price substantially less than the actual market value or wholesale price of such Articles in the market of any foreign country to which they are commonly exported, after deducting from such market value or wholesale price, freight, duty, and other charges and expenses necessarily incident to the importation and sale thereof in the United States: *Provided,* That such act or acts be done with the intent of destroying or injuring an industry in the United States, or of preventing the establishment of an industry in the United States, or of restraining or monopolising any part of trade and commerce in such Articles in the United States."

3.350 Japan notes that the 1916 Act does not apply to such acts of US producers and nor does the Robinson-Patman Act. Such acts may in fact be conducted with impunity by producers of US goods (or at least not be subject to any other than the generally applicable laws). In other words, producers of US goods may do what pro-

[285] Japan notes that in its discussion of the Robinson-Patman Act, it focuses on "primary-line cases", where the plaintiff is a competitor of the defendant (as in a 1916 Act case).

ducers of foreign goods may not. They may seek to use isolated non-US markets to obtain the high profits needed to allow them to sell at low prices in the United States. Imported goods are therefore treated less favourably than US goods and this is contrary to Article III:4 of the GATT 1994.

3.351 Japan argues, furthermore, that the 1916 Act violates Article III:4 of the GATT 1994 because it otherwise causes imported products to be treated less favourably than domestic products with respect to the US regulation of price discrimination. As the court in *Wheeling-Pittsburgh* succinctly stated, "there is no requirement under the Constitution or elsewhere that Congress impose the same standards of conduct on the importers of goods as it does on domestic producers of goods".[286] The quick comparison below of the 1916 Act with the Robinson-Patman Act demonstrates that the US Congress has not hesitated to take advantage of this rule.

3.352 Specifically, Japan contends that:

(a) bringing a 1916 Act claim is easier than bringing a Robinson-Patman Act claim because of the differing pleading requirements;

(b) establishing and winning a 1916 Act claim is easier than establishing a Robinson-Patman Act claim, because the standards for obtaining relief under the 1916 Act are much lower than those for obtaining relief under the Robinson-Patman Act;

(c) the conduct subject to penalties under the 1916 Act exceed the conduct under the Robinson-Patman Act; and

(d) because a plaintiff can more easily prove a violation of the 1916 Act than of the Robinson-Patman Act, a domestic competitor can more easily impose significant litigation costs and business burdens on foreign producers than on domestic competitors.

3.353 Japan argues that even if the United States could establish (which, Japan believes, it cannot) that in some respects treatment under the 1916 Act is more favourable than under the Robinson-Patman Act, it would not prevail. As ruled by the panel in *United States - Section 337*, more favourable treatment of imported products in some areas cannot offset less favourable treatment in other areas.[287] Moreover, whether less favourable treatment actually has been suffered in a particular instance is irrelevant. As was the case in *European Economic Community - Payments and Subsidies Paid to Processors and Producers of Oilseeds and Related Animal-Feed Proteins*, a regulation which does not necessarily discriminate against imported products but is capable of doing so violates Article III of the GATT 1994.[288] Thus, the mere possibility that a measure may in some circumstances result in less favourable treatment of imported products is sufficient to establish a violation. Such is clearly the case in the present case.[289]

---

[286] Japan refers to *Wheeling-Pittsburgh*, *Op. Cit.*, p. 602.

[287] Japan refers to *United States - Section 337*, *Op. Cit.*, para. 5.14.

[288] Japan refers to the Panel Report on *European Economic Community - Payments and Subsidies Paid to Processors and Producers of Oilseeds and Related Animal-Feed Proteins*, adopted on 25 January 1990, BISD 37S/86, para. 141 (hereinafter "*EEC - Oilseeds*").

[289] In response to a question of the United States regarding how Japan reconciles its position that the mandatory/non-mandatory distinction may be applied to a measure under Article III:4 of the

3.354 The **United States** argues that, in order to determine whether the 1916 Act violates the national treatment guarantee of Article III:4, Japan must establish that the 1916 Act treats foreign products less favourably than any similar domestic statute treats like domestic products. Japan correctly recognizes that the comparable statute applicable to domestic goods is Section 2 of the Clayton Act, as amended by the Robinson-Patman Act.[290]

3.355 The United States notes that Japan suggests, however, that "the mere possibility that a measure may in some circumstances result in less favourable treatment of imported products is sufficient to establish a violation". Moreover, Japan suggests that "[l]ess favourable treatment is inherent" because the 1916 Act purportedly creates "a separate regime" for importers and sellers of imports. In short, Japan argues in effect that the mere existence of the 1916 Act - which of course was enacted years before Article III:4 of the GATT 1994, and has never been amended since then - is sufficient to establish a violation of that Article.

3.356 The United States submits that these arguments, and the standard of liability under Article III:4 of the GATT 1994 that they appear to suggest, are not correct. Article III:4 does not require every statute of every Member that applies in any way to imported products to apply in exactly the same way to domestic products as well. It rather requires WTO Members to accord products of foreign origin no less favourable treatment than products of domestic origin. In short, Article III:4 focuses on the treatment of imported products across the whole spectrum of the "laws, regulations and requirements" of WTO Members. Thus, in order to establish that the 1916 Act violates the national treatment guarantee of Article III:4, it is not sufficient to estab-

GATT 1994 with its reading of the *EEC - Oilseeds* case, Japan argues that, when a law or a regulation is mandatory, the simple fact that it merely exposes imported products to a risk of discrimination constitutes less favourable treatment and thus is in violation of Article III:4. Since the 1916 Act is clearly mandatory on its face, the mere possibility of discrimination is sufficient to establish an Article III:4 violation. In the *EEC - Oilseeds* case, the panel made the following findings: "[...] the Panel examined whether a purchase regulation which does not necessarily discriminate against imported products but is capable of doing so is consistent with Article III:4. The Panel noted that the exposure of a particular imported product to a *risk* of discrimination constitutes, by itself, a form of discrimination. The Panel therefore concluded that purchase regulations creating such a risk must be considered to be according less favourable treatment within the meaning of Article III:4." (*EEC - Oilseeds, Op. Cit.*, para. 141; emphasis in original). The panel report on *United States - Tobacco*, citing this precedent, also notes that "an internal regulation which merely exposed imported products to a risk of discrimination had previously been recognized by GATT panels to constitute, by itself, a form of discrimination, and therefore less favourable treatment within the meaning of Article III" (*United States - Tobacco, Op. Cit.*, para. 96). Thus, Japan's proposition that the mere possibility of discrimination is enough to establish an Article III:4 violation is confirmed by well-established GATT 1947 precedents. Where, as in the present case, the legislation at issue is mandatory, there can be no other conclusion. This proposition is fully compatible with the mandatory/non-mandatory distinction. In fact, the panel report on *United States - Tobacco* applied both principles to the case. As noted above, regarding Article III, the panel found a violation because of the mere possibility of discrimination. It did so because the regulation at issue was of a mandatory nature. However, regarding Article VIII, it applied the mandatory/non-mandatory distinction, and ultimately concluded that there was no violation. Thus, there is no conflict between mandatory/non-mandatory distinction and "the mere possibility" theory in Japan's argument.

[290] The United States refers to *Zenith III, Op. Cit.*, pp. 1213-14.

lish simply that the 1916 Act exists and that it does not apply to domestic products. Japan must establish that the United States relies on the 1916 Act to treat foreign products less favourably than any similar domestic statute treats like domestic products.[291]

3.357 The United States notes that, consistent with this standard, the panel report in *United States - Section 337* specifically rejected the argument that different treatment necessarily translates into unfavourable treatment. Thus, the panel explained that

> "[...] the mere fact that imported products are subject under Section 337 to legal provisions that are different from those applying to products of national origin is in itself not conclusive in establishing inconsistency with Article III:4. In such cases, it has to be assessed whether or not such differences in the legal provisions applicable do or do not accord to imported products less favourable treatment."[292]

3.358 The United States notes, second, that if Japan's arguments were accepted, any statute or portion of a statute in any country that expressly applied just to importers - regardless of when and under what circumstances it was enacted - could be found to violate Article III:4 of the GATT 1994 without any review or analysis whatsoever. These arguments cannot and should not be accepted as a substitute for the type of careful review and analysis that should be conducted under Article III:4 of the GATT 1994.[293]

3.359 In the view of the United States, a careful review and analysis of the historical applications of the 1916 Act and the Robinson-Patman Act conclusively demonstrate that the 1916 Act raises no national treatment concerns under Article III:4 of the GATT 1994. The 1916 Act has rarely been invoked by private parties, and has never been invoked by the US government. More importantly, the 1916 Act establishes a standard for relief which has *never* been met in the case of importers and imported goods. The Robinson-Patman Act, by contrast, has been successfully invoked in thousands of federal court and administrative cases, including a substantial number pursued administratively by the Federal Trade Commission. In short, the historical applications record clearly establishes that the 1916 Act treats importers and imported goods *more favourably* than the Robinson-Patman Act treats US sellers and their goods.

---

[291] The United States recalls that the European Communities suggests a reversal of this burden of proof; that is, that the United States must "show that [the 1916 Act] prevents less favourable treatment of imported products." This is not correct; the burden of proof rests with Japan.

[292] *United States - Section 337*, *Op. Cit.*, para.5.11.

[293] In this connection, the United States disagrees with Japan's argument (as well as the European Communities' similar argument) that US law permits a US enterprise, but not a foreign one, to engage in international price discrimination. The United States argues that, even setting aside the question whether this perspective is the right one under Article III, such conduct would in fact be prohibited by the Sherman Act whenever it has a predatory effect in a relevant US market. The Sherman Act has a very broad but flexible mandate for courts to prevent anti-competitive conduct in the foreign commerce as well as the domestic commerce of the United States. Also, Japan fails to recognize that the 1916 Act does apply to US companies that import goods. For example, one of the defendants in the *Geneva Steel* case is a US company headquartered in Houston, Texas.

3.360 The United States recalls, furthermore, that the 1916 Act is intended to prevent unfair competition by extending the prohibitions of unfair competition in domestic commerce embodied in Section 2 of the Clayton Act of 1914 to importers.[294] Consistent with that construction, the prevailing interpretation among the courts that have considered the 1916 Act is either an explicit or implicit endorsement of the following principles enunciated by the District Court in *Zenith III*:

> "The principal lesson which we draw from the legislative history of the 1916 Act, viewed against the historical background of the first Wilson administration, is that the statute should be interpreted whenever possible to parallel the "unfair competition" law applicable to domestic commerce. Since the 1916 Antidumping Act is a price discrimination law, it should be read in tandem with the domestic price discrimination law, section 2 of the Clayton Act, which was amended by the Robinson-Patman Act in 1936."[295]

3.361 According to the United States the prevailing judicial interpretation therefore is that the 1916 Act should not be applied to importers and imported goods more rigorously than the Clayton Act - as amended by the Robinson-Patman Act - is applied to domestic sellers and goods. Thus, for example, in *Zenith III*, the District Court expressly determined:

> "[The 1916 Act] was intended to complement the anti-trust laws by imposing on importers substantially the same legal strictures relating to price discrimination as those which had already been imposed on domestic businesses by the Clayton Anti-trust Act of 1914.[296]
>
> [...]
>
> [I]n order to be faithful to the intention of Congress to subject importers to "the same unfair competition law" [that is applicable to domestic commerce], we should not interpret the 1916 Act to impose on importers legal strictures which are more rigorous than those applied to domestic enterprises."[297]

[294] The United States notes that the European Communities recognizes that the Robinson-Patman Act "only applies to price discrimination committed in the US", and that the 1916 Act "may be considered to complement it" by virtue of its applicability to "price discrimination practised between the domestic market of the producer and an export market". In fact, with respect to imported products, the 1916 Act and the Robinson-Patman Act do address different sets of factual circumstances in a complementary way. The 1916 Act applies only to imported products that are, *inter alia,* sold in the United States at prices "substantially less" than their prices in certain foreign markets. As a consequence, establishing liability under the 1916 Act requires, *inter alia,* comparing prices in foreign markets with prices in the US market. By contrast, the Robinson-Patman Act applies only to domestic and imported products that are sold at different prices within the United States; the prices of these products in foreign markets are irrelevant.

[295] *Zenith III*, *Op. Cit.*, p. 1223; the United States also refers to ibid., p. 1214 where it is stated that "[a]s a price discrimination statute, the Antidumping Act of 1916 is functionally similar to the price discrimination statutes which are applicable to domestic business."

[296] *Ibid.*, p. 1197.

[297] *Ibid.*, p. 1223.

3.362 The United States notes that, on appeal, the Third Circuit Court of Appeals noted that under Article XVI of the 1953 Treaty of Friendship, Commerce, and Navigation with Japan, "national treatment" was defined as "treatment accorded within the territories of a Party upon terms no less favourable than the treatment accorded therein, in like situations, to [...] products [...] of such Party." The Court of Appeals concluded that:

> "[...] application of the 1916 Act to goods imported into or sold in the United States [did not violate] the mandate of Article XVI to accord "national treatment" to Japanese products sold in the United States. [...] For the reasons stated above, we hold that application of the 1916 Act to Japanese-made [consumer electronics products] sold in the United States does not violate Article XVI of the Treaty."[298]

3.363 The United States argues that, consistent with these pronouncements, comparing the provisions of the 1916 Act with those of the Robinson-Patman Act clearly establishes that the 1916 Act actually provides *more* favourable treatment than the Robinson-Patman Act in many ways - which Japan fails to address - and, in any event, does not in any instance provide less favourable treatment.

3.364 **Japan** points out, first of all, that the United States has the burden to prove that national treatment for imported products is secured even though there is a separate regime for imported goods. The United States, however, fails to prove why a separate legal scheme is necessary in spite of the fact that both domestic and imported goods are subject to the Robinson-Patman Act.

3.365 In response to a question of the United States regarding the basis for the Japanese assertion that the United States carries the burden of proof, Japan argues that it has demonstrated that, as a textual matter, the 1916 Act constitutes a *prima facie* violation of Article III:4 of the GATT 1994. Under the rules on burden of proof established by the Appellate Body in *United States - Shirts and Blouses*[299], the onus of disproving Japan's claim has shifted to the United States. Unfortunately, rather than accepting and attempting to meet this burden, the United States has tried to mire both Japan and the Panel in an unnecessary procedural debate. This is yet another attempt by the United States to avoid the important issues of the instant dispute.

3.366 Japan further considers the US argument regarding the historical applications of the 1916 Act to be irrelevant. As stated in the *EEC - Oilseeds* panel report, the mere possibility that a measure may in some circumstances result in less favourable treatment of imported products is sufficient to establish a violation.[300] Such is clearly the case in the instant case. Japan also notes that if the US assertions are correct, there should be no obstacle to repeal the 1916 Act.

3.367 Japan also argues that the issue is not which law plaintiffs use more often - the two laws are not interchangeable and do not even apply to the same conduct. Rather, the issues are: (i) does the 1916 Act provide a separate form of liability applicable to foreign but not todomestic traders? and (ii) if a company were to proceed

[298] *In re Japanese Electronic Products II, Op. Cit.*, p. 324.

[299] Japan refers to the Appellate Body Report on *United States - Shirts and Blouses*, supra, footnote 27.

[300] Japan refers to *EEC - Oilseeds, Op. Cit.*, para. 141.

with equivalent claims under each law, which would be easier to prove? The 1916 Act does impose additional liability on foreign traders and a plaintiff more easily can establish a claim under the 1916 Act. Moreover, in regard to the second issue, the US logic is confused. The 1916 Act historically has not been used a great deal because industries relied on the Tariff Act of 1930 to address dumping. Now, however, interest in using the 1916 Act is increasing as companies realise its many advantages. And, of course, analogous primary-line Robinson-Patman Act cases have ground to a halt since *Brooke Group*, due to the added pleading and proof requirements.

3.368 The **United States** notes that it has *not* argued in the present dispute that Japan's claim under Article III:4 should be dismissed because the 1916 Act has not had any trade effects. Although there may be some merit to that argument, the United States has chosen not to make it. With regard to Japan's suggestion that "there should be no obstacle to repeal the 1916 Act", the United States considers that it should be summarily rejected. Japan has failed to establish that the 1916 Act violates Article III:4, either on its face or as applied. In the complete absence of such a showing, there is no reason to consider what, if any remedy, might otherwise be appropriate.

3.369 The United States also insists that it is not arguing, contrary to what Japan attempts to suggest, that the 1916 Act on the whole treats imported goods more favourably than the Robinson-Patman Act treats domestic goods and only in a few instances treats imported goods less favourably than the Robinson-Patman Act treats domestic goods. In the instant dispute, the United States is arguing essentially that one element of a 1916 Act claim - the requirement of a malicious or predatory intent - renders the 1916 Act more favourable to importers and imported goods than is the Robinson-Patman Act to US sellers and their goods in every instance. The courts have interpreted this requirement as virtually impossible to satisfy, and the historical applications of the 1916 Act squarely support this view, as there has never been a successful case brought under the 1916 Act. The Robinson-Patman Act, in contrast, has been successfully invoked on innumerable occasions to obtain relief involving US sellers and their goods. When this factor is taken into account to the extent that it might be capable of exerting an offsetting influence in each individual case, as it should be, the only reasonable conclusion is, again, that the 1916 Act treats importers and imported goods *more favourably* than the Robinson-Patman Act treats US sellers and their goods.

3.370 The United States notes, moreover, that this approach was followed by the panel in the *United States - Section 337* case. There, the panel explained that "an element of more favourable treatment would only be relevant if it would always accompany and offset an element of differential treatment causing less favourable treatment".[301] The panel found that some of the procedural advantages given to foreign respondents under Section 337 operate in all cases, and therefore it "took these factors into account to the extent that they might be capable of exerting an offsetting influence in each individual case of less favourable treatment resulting from an element cited by the Community".[302]

[301] The United States refers to *United States - Section 337, Op. Cit.*, para. 5.16.

[302] The United States refers to ibid., para. 5.17.

3.371 Thus, in the view of the United States, it would be entirely appropriate for the Panel to begin and end its analysis of Japan's Article III claim based upon the fact that the intent requirement is virtually impossible to satisfy.

3.372 Finally, the United States disagrees with Japan inasmuch as Japan claims that the panel report in *EEC - Oilseeds* stands for the proposition that "the mere possibility that a measure may result in less favourable treatment of imported products is sufficient to establish a violation of Article III:4 of GATT 1994". This case does not stand for such a broad proposition. If that were the test, that would mean that the mandatory/non-mandatory distinction could not apply in Article III cases. By definition, the mandatory/non-mandatory distinction asks the question whether a WTO-consistent application is *possible.* As we have pointed out, however, this distinction has been applied by panels considering Article III claims - including, for example, *United States - Superfund* and *Thailand - Cigarettes.* In the *EEC - Oilseeds* case, the question was one of *de facto* discrimination under Article III. The panel considered whether the facts could result in less favourable treatment even though on its face the measure treated imported products no less favourably. In the present case, there is no possibility that the facts may result in unfavourable treatment because, as the United States has repeatedly explained, the legal standards for recovery under the 1916 Act are more stringent than, or at least as stringent, as those applicable under the Robinson-Patman Act. And those standards would be applicable in every factual scenario. Indeed, that is why there have been no recoveries under the 1916 Act.

3. Element-by-Element Comparison of the 1916 Act and the Robinson-Patman Act

(a) The Pleading Requirements

3.373 **Japan** asserts that an easier pleading burden is imposed on a 1916 Act plaintiff than on a Robinson-Patman Act plaintiff. This translates to a greater burden on a 1916 Act defendant. For example, as reflected in the *Geneva Steel* and *Wheeling-Pittsburgh* cases, a typical plaintiff alleging predatory pricing under the Robinson-Patman Act must satisfy special, more particularized pleading and proof requirements. These requirements address whether, through below-cost pricing, a defendant could reasonably expect to gain market dominance to the point that it could later raise prices and recoup its earlier losses. Under the 1916 Act, in contrast, a plaintiff need only allege and prove that a defendant is engaged in systematic dumping with the intent of injuring, destroying, or preventing the establishment of a domestic industry, or of restraining or monopolising trade or commerce.

3.374 Japan argues, moreover, that in a Robinson-Patman Act case, a plaintiff's general allegations of a traditional anti-trust violation and injury are insufficient; an anti-trust complaint must include enough hard data so that each element of an alleged violation can be identified.[303] Thus, a 1916 Act plaintiff faces a lower hurdle in filing

[303] Japan refers to, e.g., a case from the Federal District Court in Ohio, *The Zeller Corp. v. Federal-Mogul Corp.*, 3:95CV7501, 1996 US Dist. LEXIS 21198 (N.D. Ohio) (hereinafter "*Zeller Corp.*"). In *Zeller Corp.*, the court granted defendants' motion to dismiss a Robinson-Patman claim because plaintiff had not adequately pled a "reasonable expectation" of recoupment. (*Ibid.*, p. *8). The court

its initial complaint because the pleading requirements not only are fewer, but also are less particular.

3.375 Japan notes that a federal district court in the state of Ohio - the same state in which a federal district court is handling the *Wheeling-Pittsburgh* case - recently dismissed a primary-line Robinson-Patman Act claim. The court granted the defendants' motion to dismiss the Robinson-Patman claim because a "reasonable expectation" of recoupment had not been adequately pleaded.[304] In addition, the court held that the plaintiff had failed to plead that the defendant will recoup more than the losses it originally incurred with its allegedly below-cost pricing.[305]

3.376 According to Japan, the lower pleading threshold for a 1916 Act action makes it easier to bring such an action. Regardless of the likelihood of the plaintiff ultimately succeeding in the case, this makes the 1916 Act a tool for harassment. For these reasons, the United States is in violation of Article III:4 of the GATT 1994.

3.377 The **United States** considers that there are two reasons to reject Japan's argument. First, with respect to comparative pleading requirements, it is important to note that under the Federal Rules of Civil Procedure, complaints filed in all federal district courts in the United States are notice pleadings. This means that a particular complaint need simply recite allegations which - if proven - would be sufficient to establish the violations of law the complaint alleges. As the Supreme Court has indicated, "the liberal system of 'notice pleading' set up by the Federal Rules of Civil Procedure" simply requires "a short and plain statement of the claim that will give the defendant fair notice of what the plaintiff's claim is and the grounds upon which it rests"[306]. As a consequence, from the perspective of the content of the pleadings, it is no more difficult to file a complaint alleging one or more violations of the Robinson-Patman Act than to file a complaint alleging one or more violations of the 1916 Act. In either situation, it is sufficient for the complaint to recite the facts which, if proven, would establish the violations of law alleged.

3.378 The United States contends that the conclusion that pleading requirements have not in any way discouraged the filing of complaints under the Robinson-Patman Act is borne out by the relative numbers of 1916 Act and Robinson-Patman Act cases filed in the recent past. Since the issuance of the Supreme Court decision in *Brooke Group* in 1993, more than forty reported Court of Appeals and District Court opinions in more than forty different cases have addressed allegations that the price discrimination provisions of the Robinson-Patman Act have been violated, including cases leading to more than ten Court of Appeals and District Court decisions in 1998 alone. Moreover, during that same time period there have been fourteen federal dis-

held that plaintiff had "pled only conclusory allegations in support of its claim that Neapco is capable of obtaining sufficient market power to allow it to recoup alleged below-cost sales." (*Ibid.*, p. *6). In addition, the court held that plaintiff had "failed to plead that Neapco will recoup more than the losses it originally incurred with its allegedly below-cost pricing." (*Ibid.*, p. *8). In contrast, in *Wheeling-Pittsburgh*, another Ohio district court judged the conclusory allegations contained in Wheeling-Pittsburgh's 1916 Act complaint sufficient to withstand a motion to dismiss. (*Wheeling-Pittsburgh, Op. Cit.*, p. 603).

304 Japan refers to *Zeller Corp., Op. Cit.*, n. 74.

305 Japan refers to ibid.

306 The United States refers to *Leatherman v. Tarrant County NICU*, 507 US 163, p. 168 (1993).

trict court decisions addressing allegations of primary line Robinson-Patman Act violations. By contrast, only two complaints under the 1916 Act have been filed during that same period. In short, these data strongly support the conclusion that it is far easier for a plaintiff to satisfy the pleading requirements under the Robinson-Patman Act than those under the 1916 Act.

3.379 In response to this US argument in respect of the US Federal Rules of Procedure, **Japan** notes that the issue is not the similarity of the form of the "notice of claim" but the difference of burden of pleading imposed on complainants.

3.380 The **United States** notes further that its second reason for rejecting Japan's argument is that, with respect to the comparative difficulty of defeating a motion to dismiss or for summary judgment, the case law establishes that it is no easier for a plaintiff to do so under the 1916 Act than under the Robinson-Patman Act. Indeed, since the *Brooke Group* decision, four Court of Appeals decisions - arising from three cases addressing allegations of primary line price discrimination - have been issued.[307]

3.381 The United States recalls that, for example, in *Rebel Oil v. Atlantic Richfield*, two gasoline retailers alleged that ARCO had, *inter alia*, engaged in primary line price discrimination

> "by executing a pricing policy in Las Vegas of charging predatory prices in an attempt to increase its market share and eventually monopolise the Las Vegas gasoline market."[308]

The District Court granted a motion for summary judgment against ARCO, but the Court of Appeals for the Ninth Circuit reversed.[309] The Court noted the distinction in *Brooke Group* between the "reasonable prospect" of recoupment needed to show primary line discrimination and the "dangerous probability" of recoupment needed to show attempted monopolisation.[310] The Court relied on this distinction to reverse the grant of summary judgment as to the primary line discrimination allegation, concluding that:

> "Rebel's evidence is sufficient, however, to raise a disputed question of material fact as to whether ARCO achieved sufficient market power to enforce supracompetitive oligopoly pricing. This showing is sufficient to allow Rebel to survive summary judgment on the issue of anti-trust injury resulting from price discrimination under the Clayton Act."[311]

---

[307] The United States refers to *Kentmaster Manufacturing Co. v. Jarvis Products Corp.*, 146 F.3d 691, p. 694-95 (9th Cir. 1998), amended, No. 96-56341, 1999 WL 19636 (9th Cir. Jan. 20, 1999); *Coastal Fuels of Puerto Rico, Inc. v. Caribbean Petroleum Corp.*, 79 F.3d 182, p. 188 (1st Cir. 1996); *Rebel Oil Co. v. Atlantic Richfield Co.*, 146 F.3d 1088, p. 1091 (9th Cir. 1998), cert. denied, 119 S.Ct. 541 (1998), and 51 F.3d 1421, p. 1429 (9th Cir. 1995).

[308] *Rebel Oil Co., Inc. v. Atlantic Richfield Co.*, 957 F.Supp. 1184, p. 1192 (D. Nev. 1997), aff'd, 146 F.3d 1088 (9th Cir.), cert. denied, 119 S. Ct. 541 (1998).

[309] The United States refers to *Rebel Oil Co., Inc. v. Atlantic Richfield Co.*, 51 F.3d 1421 (9th Cir. 1995).

[310] The United States refers to ibid., pp. 1442, 1445, 1447.

[311] The United States compares ibid., pp. 1432-43 with ibid., pp. 1444-48. The United States notes that the court sustained the grant of summary judgment as to the attempted monopolisation allega-

3.382 The United States also recalls a second case, *Anti-Monopoly, Inc. v. Hasbro, Inc.*, in which the District Court considered allegations that Hasbro had, *inter alia*, engaged in primary line price discrimination by

> "providing substantial discounts, terms and services to major family board game retailers which are not made available on equal terms to competing smaller family board game retailers and wholesalers and which are not either cost justified or otherwise permitted under § 2 [of the Clayton Act]."[312]

The Court noted the *Brooke Group* standard for primary line liability; noted that the plaintiff had alleged, *inter alia*, that Hasbro "prices its products below an appropriate measure of its costs [...]"; concluded that the plaintiff "has stated a claim for a primary-line injury [...]"; and therefore denied Hasbro's motion to dismiss the primary line discrimination allegation.[313]

3.383 The United States notes that, in a third case, *En Vogue v. UK Optical, Ltd., the District Court* denied a motion by one of the defendants to dismiss the plaintiff's primary line price discrimination allegations.[314]

3.384 In conclusion, the United States notes that in each of these three cases - decided after *Brooke Group* - allegations of primary line price discrimination survived motions to dismiss or motions for summary judgment. The fact that such motions may have been granted in other cases cited by Japan - such as *Zeller Corp.* - does not in any way reduce the respective risks of liability bestowed by the 1916 Act and the Robinson-Patman Act. It rather simply reflects the fact that every case is different, and while some plaintiffs may be able to adduce evidence sufficient to ensure that they can move from the preliminary phase of a trial to the trial itself, other plaintiffs are not able to do so.

(b) Intent Requirement vs. Effect Requirement

3.385 **Japan** argues that another key difference between the 1916 Act and the Robinson-Patman Act is the burden of proving intent versus effect. The 1916 Act

---

tion, concluding that "Rebel has failed to provide sufficient evidence to support a jury verdict on the issue of ARCO's "market power" under the Sherman Act [...]." (*Ibid.*, p. 1448). On remand, the District Court granted a new motion for summary judgment filed by ARCO, noting that "[i]n order to meet the requirements of predatory pricing, the plaintiff must present some evidence that the defendant priced below *its* costs," and that Rebel had made "no showing of ARCO's actual costs of producing gasoline." The Court of Appeals affirmed that decision on the same basis. (*Rebel Oil Co., Inc. v. Atlantic Richfield Co.*, 957 F.Supp. 1184, 1196, 1197, 1203 (D. Nev. 1997), aff'd, 146 F.3d 1088 (9th Cir.), cert. denied, 119 S. Ct. 541 (1998).

312 *Anti-Monopoly, Inc. v. Hasbro, Inc.*, 1995-2 Trade Cas. ¶ 71,095 (S.D.N.Y. 1995), p. 75,241.

313 The United States refers to ibid. The United States notes that, subsequently, the plaintiff reached a settlement with two retailer defendants, Toys R Us and K Mart Corporation. Two years later, the District Court granted a motion by Hasbro for summary judgment, concluding, *inter alia*, that the plaintiff "has not provided factual support for either element of a below-cost pricing anti-trust claim." The United States refers to *Anti-Monopoly, Inc. v. Hasbro, Inc.*, 958 F.Supp. 895, pp. 897-98 note 1, 906 (S.D.N.Y. 1997), aff'd per curiam, 130 F.3d 1101 (3d Cir. 1997), cert. denied, 119 S. Ct. 48 (1998).

314 The United States refers to *En Vogue v. UK Optical, Ltd. and British Optical Import Company*, 843 F.Supp. 838, pp. 845-47 (E.D.N.Y. 1994).

requires a plaintiff to prove that discriminatorily low prices are set with the *intent* to injure, destroy, or prevent the creation of a domestic industry or to restrain or monopolise commerce in the United States.[315] In contrast, the Robinson-Patman Act prohibits price discrimination "where the *effect* of such discrimination may be substantially to lessen competition or tend to create a monopoly [...] or to injure, destroy or prevent competition with any person who grants or knowingly receives the benefit of such discrimination"[316]. US courts, including the Supreme Court, have interpreted this to require proof, not merely of intent, but of *effect.*[317] Thus, where a foreign defendant has intent *but* is unsuccessful in injuring, destroying or preventing competition, it could not be successfully prosecuted under the Robinson-Patman Act, but could be successfully prosecuted under the 1916 Act.[318]

3.386 Japan notes that US government officials themselves have concurred with this analysis, acknowledging that proving a 1916 Act claim is easier than proving a Robinson-Patman Act claim. In 18 July 1986 testimony before the US Senate Finance Committee, USTR General Counsel Alan Holmer said:

> "Under the rules in S. 1655 [a legislative proposal to amend the 1916 Act], the same conduct by two firms, one domestic and one foreign, could be deemed unfair competition subject to treble damages in the case of a foreign firm [under the 1916 Act], and not punishable at all in the case of the domestic firm [under the Robinson-Patman Act]. This is a denial of national treatment."[319]

3.387 Japan argues that apart from the differences in the substance of the standards, proving intent to injure under the 1916 Act is easier because the subjective intent standard is easier to prove than the objective effect standard. For example, a single internal memorandum stating that prices should be lowered to capture market share from a competitor could be sufficient evidence of an intent to injure; but, proving effect (and reasonable probability of recoupment) requires a complex economic inquiry into the competitive dynamics of the market in question. Indeed, in *Brooke Group*, the plaintiffs had shown subjective intent, but not effect, and the Supreme Court ruled that the subjective proof, alone, is insufficient.

---

[315] Japan refers to the text of the 1916 Act. Japan further notes that, in *Geneva Steel*, the court held that "by its express language, the 1916 Act is not limited only to anti-trust injury or predatory price discrimination." (*Geneva Steel*, *Op. Cit.*, p. 1215) Therefore, claimants need not prove actual predatory pricing, but only that "defendants acted as importers for the systematic dumping of [a product] with the intent of injuring, by any means, the domestic [...] industry." (*Ibid.*) Japan also refers to *Wheeling-Pittsburgh*, *Op. Cit.*, pp. 604-606.

[316] Emphasis added by Japan.

[317] Japan contends that, in *Brooke Group*, *Op. Cit.*, p. 225, the US Supreme Court confirmed the comparatively high proof requirements of the Robinson-Patman Act by specifically rejecting the notion that proof of bad "intent" or "malice" might, by itself, establish predatory pricing. The Court required, in addition, proof of *effect*, i.e. proof that competition has been injured.

[318] According to Japan, this fact, in and of itself, establishes a US violation of Article III:4. Japan refers to, e.g., *United States - Section 337*, *Op. Cit.*, paras. 5.13-5.14, where the panel finds that the key to an Article III:4 violation is whether the differential treatment "may" lead to less favourable treatment, based on an analysis of the "potential impact" of the laws.

[319] Testimony of USTR General Counsel Alan Holmer, *Op. Cit.*, p. 4.

3.388 According to Japan, this distinction establishes that the United States is violating its national treatment obligation under Article III:4 of GATT 1994.

3.389 The **United States** notes that the need to prove the requisite intent under the 1916 Act has for more than 80 years made it virtually impossible to establish violations of the 1916 Act. Thus, as the Tariff Commission stated in 1921:

> "[The 1916 Act] is not workable, for the reason that it is almost impossible to show the intent on the part of the importer to injure or destroy business in the United States by such importation and sale."[320]

Similarly, in *Geneva Steel*, on which Japan relies extensively for other arguments, the district court noted that it may be "'nearly impossible' to prove the requisite intent given that evidence of normal pricing cuts [...] would be insufficient to establish liability under the 1916 Act."[321]

3.390 For the United States it is clear from the history of litigation under the 1916 Act that the anti-competitive intent required to establish a violation of the Act is at least as difficult to prove as the corresponding anti-competitive intent required to establish the offences of monopolisation and attempted monopolisation under Section 2 of the Sherman Act. Contrary to Japan's contention that the basis of the US position is that US courts "should or will" read predation into the 1916 Act, as shown above in the factual section, the courts that have considered the intent element of the 1916 Act have already read precisely those requirements into the statute. As a factual matter, it is the US case law interpreting the 1916 Act that is dispositive in determining the nature of the 1916 Act.

3.391 The United States notes, moreover, that the case law indicates that it is even more difficult to establish that a particular defendant intended to destroy, injure, or prevent the establishment of an industry in the United States. Thus, in *Zenith II*, the district court concluded that satisfying the 1916 Act intent requirement requires establishing that the defendant possesses a "specific, predatory, anti-competitive intent"; that is, an intent "to destroy competition".[322]

3.392 The United States points out that Japan's only response to this argument is to suggest that proving "intent to injure" under the 1916 Act is "easier to prove than the objective effect standard. For example, a single internal memorandum stating that prices should be lowered to capture market share from a competitor could be sufficient evidence of an intent to injure [...]." Japan does not, however, provide any evidence or case analysis to support this suggestion.

3.393 The United States submits that, in fact, it is highly unlikely that any court would find such an internal memorandum to be particularly relevant to the intent issue under the 1916 Act. In general, United States courts have been reluctant to rely on inflammatory statements at meetings or in internal memoranda as a basis for establishing predatory intent precisely because such statements are of little or no relevance if the individual or firm making them is not likely to succeed in the purportedly predatory campaign. As the Supreme Court indicated in *Brooke Group*:

---

320 56 Cong. Rec. 346 (Dec. 9, 1919).

321 *Geneva Steel, Op. Cit.*, p. 1220.

322 The United States refers to *Zenith II, Op. Cit.*, p. 259.

> "Even an act of pure malice by one business competitor against another does not, without more, state a claim under the federal anti-trust laws [...] [a]lthough some of [the defendant's] corporate planning documents speak of a desire to slow the growth of the [generic cigarette] segment, no objective evidence of its conduct permits a reasonable inference that it had any real prospect of doing so through anti-competitive means."[323]

Moreover, even if such a campaign might conceivably succeed, such statements are frequently ambiguous because they are frequently made to convey perfectly competitive objectives. Thus, for example, in *Geneva Steel*, the district court noted:

> "Mere knowledge on the part of the importer that his sales will capture business away from his United States competitors, standing alone, will not be sufficient to demonstrate an intent to injure the entire United States steel industry and will therefore be inadequate to establish a violation of the Act."[324]

3.394 The United States argues that, by contrast, establishing civil liability under the Robinson-Patman Act does not require proving that the defendant intended to injure competition or competitors. As a consequence, the same conduct by two different firms could be found to violate the Robinson-Patman Act but not the 1916 Act. In short, the 1916 Act's intent requirement - because it is so difficult to satisfy - without more, serves to render the 1916 Act considerably more favourable to importers than the Robinson-Patman Act is to domestic firms. This conclusion is supported by the fact that there has *never* been a successful case brought under the 1916 Act in its 82-year history, while plaintiffs have secured relief in thousands of cases filed under the Robinson-Patman Act.

(c) The Recoupment Requirement

3.395 **Japan** notes that, in a landmark decision, *Brooke Group*, the US Supreme Court substantially increased the evidentiary burden on plaintiffs seeking to demonstrate violations of the Robinson-Patman Act in primary-line cases. The Supreme Court abolished the long-standing ability of a plaintiff to demonstrate that the "lessening of competition" requirement was satisfied by offering evidence of the defendant's intent and imposed a much higher evidentiary threshold for proving a violation requiring in addition proof of effect and recoupment.

3.396 Japan recalls that, with respect to primary line cases, the Supreme Court adopted a market-based analysis in which a plaintiff must prove "that the competitor had a reasonable prospect [...] of recouping its investment in below-cost prices".[325] The Court concluded that to prove recoupment, a plaintiff must show that the below-cost pricing must be capable: (i) of achieving its intended effects on the defendant's rivals (i.e. putting them out of business); and (ii) restraining competition long enough

323 *Brooke Group*, *Op. Cit.*, p. 225, 241.

324 *Geneva Steel*, *Op. Cit.*, p. 1224.

325 Japan refers to *Brook Group*, *Op. Cit.*, pp. 222-24.

for the defendant to raise its prices and recapture the profits it lost during the period of price cutting.[326]

3.397 According to Japan, this imposes on Robinson-Patman Act plaintiffs a requirement that is exceedingly difficult, indeed, nearly impossible, to meet. Japan notes that since *Brooke Group*, not one primary-line price discrimination lawsuit under the Robinson-Patman Act has succeeded. Of the twelve cases adjudicated, five were dismissed because the plaintiff had proven neither below cost sales nor possibility for recoupment[327], two were dismissed because the plaintiff had failed to show below cost sales[328], two were dismissed for failure to plead sales below cost or possibility of recoupment[329], one was dismissed for failure to plead possibility of recoupment[330], and two were dismissed for lack of standing[331].

3.398 Japan points out that a federal district court in the state of Ohio recently dismissed a primary-line Robinson-Patman Act claim. The Robinson-Patman Act case, *Zeller Corp.*, underscores the nearly insurmountable obstacles facing plaintiffs in such cases. Indeed, the court intimated that the predatory pricing requirements established by *Brooke Group* are extremely difficult to meet: "'the standard announced in Brooke Group has presented almost an impregnable fortress to [a] plaintiff claiming injury by reason of his rival's low prices.'"[332]

---

[326] Japan refers to ibid., pp. 225-26 (citations omitted by Japan). Japan notes that several US Circuit Courts of Appeal have observed that proving competitive injury through predatory pricing under *Brooke Group* is exceedingly difficult. The Court of Appeals for the Eighth Circuit has noted that the sales below cost and possibility of recoupment requirements "make it extremely difficult for plaintiffs to prove predatory pricing in anti-trust cases. That difficulty, however, reflects the economic reality that predatory pricing schemes are rarely tried, and even more rarely successful." Japan refers to *International Travel Arrangers v. NWA, Inc.*, 991 F.2d 1389, p. 1396 (8th Cir. 1993) (quoting *Matsushita Elec. Indus. Co.*, 475 U.S., p. 589). The Court of Appeals for the First Circuit has similarly observed that "the requisites for proving predatory pricing are demanding because the conditions under which it is plausible are not common, and because it can easily be confused with merely low prices which benefit consumers." Japan refers to *Tri-State Rubbish Waste, Inc. v. Waste Management, Inc.*, 998 F.2d 1073, p. 1080 (1st Cir. 1993). This is inconsistent with the national treatment obligation of Article III:4.

[327] Japan refers to *Taylor Publishing Company v. Jostens, Inc.*, 36 F. Supp. 2d 360, p. 369 (E.D.Tex. 1999); *Sally Bridges v. Maclean-Stevens Studios, Inc.*, 35 F. Supp. 2d 20, p. 28 (D.C. Maine 1998); *Anti-Monopoly, Inc. v. Hasbro, Inc.*, 958 F. Supp. 895, p. 906 (S.D.N.Y. 1997); *Clark. v. Flow Measurement, Inc.*, 948 F. Supp. 519, p. 529 (D.S.C. 1996); *C.B. Trucking, Inc. v. Waste Management, Inc.*, 944 F. Supp. 66, p. 69 (D. Mass. 1996).

[328] Japan refers to *Stearns Airport Equipment Co. v. FMC Corp.*, 977 F. Supp. 1269, p. 1273 (N.D. Tex. 1997); *Rebel Oil Co. v. Atlantic Richfield Company*, 957 F. Supp. 1184, p. 1204 (D.C. Nev. 1997).

[329] Japan refers to *Malek Wholesaler, Inc. v. First Film Extruding, Ltd.*, 97 C 7087, 1998 U.S. Dist. LEXIS 3674, p. *9 (N.D. Ill.); *Cardinal Indus. Inc. v. Pressman Toy Corp.*, 96 Civ. 4590 (MBM), 1996 U.S. Dist. LEXIS 18714, p. *18 (S.D.N.Y.) .

[330] Japan refers to *Zeller Corp., Op. Cit.*, pp. *6-8 (N.D. Oh.).

[331] Japan refers to *The City of New York v. Coastal Oil New York, Inc.*, 96 Civ. 8667 (RPP), 1998 U.S. Dist. LEXIS 2049, p. *19 (S.D.N.Y.); *Lago & Sons Dairy, Inc. v. H.P. Hood, Inc.*, Civ. No. 92-200-SD, 1994 U.S. Dist. LEXIS 12909, pp. *13-14 (D.N.H.).

[332] Japan refers to *Zeller Corp., Op. Cit.*, p. *6 (quoting defendants' motion to dismiss).

3.399 Japan asserts that, in contrast, claims under the 1916 Act, as in *Geneva Steel* and *Wheeling-Pittsburgh*, have a much better chance of success. A 1916 Act plaintiff need not prove recoupment. This differential treatment violates Article III:4.

3.400 The **United States** denies that recovery under the Robinson-Patman Act has ceased following the 1993 Supreme Court decision in *Brooke Group*. The evidence is to the contrary. While liability for an importer under the 1916 Act can arise only from injury to the firms with which it competes, domestic firm liability under the Robinson-Patman Act can arise both from that type of injury and from injury to one or more downstream purchasers. As a consequence, cases involving secondary line liability - as well as those involving primary line liability - are relevant to any comparison of the Robinson-Patman Act to the 1916 Act. Since the 1993 Supreme Court decision in *Brooke Group*, there have been more than forty reported Court of Appeals and District Court opinions in more than forty different cases that have addressed allegations that the price discrimination provisions of the Robinson-Patman Act have been violated, including cases leading to more than ten Court of Appeals and District Court decisions in 1998 alone.[333] By comparison, only two District Court decisions - at very early stages in their respective proceedings - have during that same period addressed allegations that the 1916 Act has been violated. This vast disparity alone establishes that the price discrimination proscriptions of the Robinson-Patman Act create far more danger of liability for domestic firms than the 1916 Act creates for importers, and therefore treat domestic firms less favourably than the 1916 Act treats importers.

3.401 The United States maintains that that conclusion remains valid even if one considers only the number of primary line price discrimination cases since *Brooke Group*. In particular, since that decision, four Court of Appeals decisions - arising from three cases addressing allegations of primary line price discrimination - have been issued.[334] To the extent that the success of a particular case can be measured by the level of the federal court system to which it rises, all of these lawsuits alleging primary line discrimination were more successful than either of the two 1916 Act

---

[333] The United States refers to, e.g., *Godfrey v. Pulitzer Publishing Co.*, 161 F.3d 1137 (8th Cir. 1998); *George Haug Co. v. Rolls Royce Motor Cars, Inc.*, 148 F.3d 136 (2d Cir. 1998); *Kentmaster Manufacturing Co. v. Jarvis Products Corp.*, 146 F.3d 691 (9th Cir. 1998), amended, No. 96-56341, 1999 WL 19636 (9th Cir. Jan. 20, 1999); *Metro Ford Truck Sales, Inc. v. Ford Motor Co.*, 145 F.3d 320 (5th Cir. 1998); *Sally Bridges v. MacLean-Stevens Studios, Inc.*, 35 F.Supp. 2d 20, p. 28 (D. Me. 1998); *Malek Wholesaler, Inc. v. First Film Extruding, Ltd.*, 1998 U.S.Dist. LEXIS 3674 (N.D. Ill. Mar. 20, 1998); *City of New York v. Coastal Oil New York, Inc.*, 1998-1 Trade Cas. (CCH) ¶ 72,087 (S.D.N.Y. 1998); *Liberty Lincoln-Mercury v. Ford Motor Co.*, 134 F.3d 557 (3d Cir. 1998); *Hoover Color Corp. v. Bayer Corp.*, 24 F. Supp. 2d 571 (W.D. Va. 1998); *Bell v. Fur Breeders Agricultural Cooperative*, 3 F. Supp. 2d 1241 (D. Utah 1998); *Precision Printing Co. v. Unisource Worldwide, Inc.*, 993 F. Supp. 338 (W.D. Pa. 1998); *Rebel Oil Co., Inc. v. Atlantic Richfield Co.*, 957 F.Supp. 1184, p. 1192 (D. Nev. 1997), aff'd, 146 F.3d 1088 (9th Cir.), cert. denied, 119 S. Ct. 541 (1998).

[334] *Kentmaster Manufacturing Co. v. Jarvis Products Corp.*, 146 F.3d 691, 694-95 (9th Cir. 1998), amended, No. 96-56341, 1999 WL 19636 (9th Cir. Jan. 20, 1999); *Rebel Oil Co. v. Atlantic Richfield Co.*, 146 F.3d 1088, p. 1091 (9th Cir. 1998), *cert. denied*, 119 S.Ct. 541 (1998), and 51 F.3d 1421, p. 1429 (9th Cir. 1995); *Coastal Fuels of Puerto Rico, Inc. v. Caribbean Petroleum Corp.*, 79 F.3d 182, p. 188 (1st Cir. 1996).

lawsuits. Moreover, fourteen District Court decisions addressing primary line discrimination - in addition to those which led to some of the above Court of Appeals decisions - have been issued.[335] Although most of these cases remain pending and have not yet been finally resolved, these figures suggest that allegations of primary line discrimination under the Robinson-Patman Act - even without considering allegations of secondary line discrimination - have continued to pose far more of a threat of liability to domestic firms than the 1916 Act poses to foreign firms.

3.402 The United States argues, in addition, that a number of cases establish, either directly or by implication, that the same predatory pricing and recoupment requirements applicable to Sherman Act Section 2 and primary line Robinson-Patman Act cases apply to the 1916 Act as well. Thus, in *Brooke Group* itself, the Supreme Court determined that for predatory pricing to constitute either a violation of Section 2 of the Sherman Act or a violation of the Robinson-Patman Act (under a primary line injury theory), (1) the challenged prices must lie "below an appropriate measure of [the defendant's] costs", and (2) the defendant must have a "reasonable prospect" [for Robinson-Patman Act liability] or a "dangerous probability" [for Sherman Act liability] of "recouping its investment in below-cost prices".[336] This determination derived, in part, from the Supreme Court's 1986 decision in *Matsushita Electrical*, in which the Court held that conspiracies or attempts to monopolise through predatorily low prices could only be established by proof that such prices were below some appropriate measure of costs, and that the defendants possessed a realistic expectation of recouping prior losses through future monopoly rents.[337] On remand, the court of appeals in *In re Japanese Electronic Products III* applied precisely this predatory pricing standard to the plaintiff's 1916 Act claims - which were based on an alleged "intent to injure or destroy an industry in the United States" - and found that they had to be dismissed based on the same failure to adduce proof of recoupment which led to dismissal of the Sherman Act claims.[338]

3.403 In response, **Japan** notes that the Supreme Court in its 1986 decision in the *Zenith* litigation expressly states that its ruling did not apply to the petitioners' 1916

---

[335] The United States refers to *J&S Oil, Inc. v. Irving Oil Corp.*, 1999-2 Trade Cas. (CCH) ¶ 72,615 (D Me. August 4, 1999), paras. 85551-54; *Wynn ex rel. Alabama v. Philip Morris Inc.*, 51 F.Supp. 2d 1232, p. 1247 (N.D. Ala. 1999); *Malek Wholesaler, Inc. v. First Film Extruding, Ltd.*, 1998 U.S. Dist. LEXIS 3674 (N.D. Ill. March 24, 1998); *Taylor Publishing Company v. Jostens, Inc.*, 36 F.Supp. 2d 360, pp. 372-73 (E.D. Tex. 1999); *Sally Bridges v. MacLean-Stevens Studios, Inc.*, 35 F.Supp. 2d 20, pp. 27-28 (D. Me. 1998); *City of New York v. Coastal Oil New York,* Inc., 1998-1 Trade Cas. (CCH) ¶ 72,087 (S.D.N.Y. 1998); *Stearns Airport Equip. Co. v. FMC Corp.*, 977 F.Supp. 1269, p. 1273 (N.D. Tex. 1997); *Cardinal Indus., Inc. v. Pressman Toy Corp.*, 1997-1 Trade Cas. (CCH) ¶ 71,738 (S.D.N.Y. Dec. 17, 1996); *Zeller Corp.*, 1997-1 Trade Cas. (CCH) ¶ 71,805 (N.D. Ohio June 25, 1996); *Anti-Monopoly, Inc. v. Hasbro, Inc.*, 958 F.Supp. 895, p. 906 (S.D.N.Y. 1997), and 1995-2 Trade Cas. ¶ 71,095 (S.D.N.Y. 1995), para. 75,241; *Clark v. Flow Measurement, Inc.*, 948 F.Supp. 519, pp. 522-29 (D. S.C. 1996); *C.B. Trucking, Inc. v. Waste Management, Inc. and WMX*, 944 F.Supp. 66, pp. 68-69 (D. Mass. 1996); *En Vogue v. UK Optical, Ltd. and British Optical Import Company*, 843 F.Supp. 838, pp. 845-47 (E.D.N.Y. 1994); *Lago & Sons Dairy, Inc. v. H.P. Hood, Inc.*, 1994 U.S. Dist. LEXIS 12909 (D. N.H. 1994).

[336] *Brooke Group*, 509 U.S., p. 224.

[337] The United States refers to *Matsushita Electrical, Op. Cit.*, p. 574; the United States also refers to *Cargill, Inc. v. Monfort of Colorado, Inc.*, 479 U.S. 104 (1986).

[338] The United States refers to *In re Japanese Electronic Products III, Op. Cit.*, pp. 48-49.

Act claims and the Court of Appeals decision was based on the petitioners' failure to prove its conspiracy claim. Thus, there is no support for the US assertion.

3.404 The **United States** concedes that the Supreme Court only decided the plaintiffs' Sherman Act claims (because those were the claims upon which the Supreme Court granted *certiorari*, or in other words, those were the only claims that the petitioner requested that the Supreme Court review). However, the Supreme Court remanded the entire case, including the 1916 Act claims, for the Court of Appeals' consideration in light of its decision. The Court of Appeals acted upon the Supreme Court's instructions by deciding that a failure to show a possibility of recoupment under the Sherman Act also constituted a failure to make out a 1916 Act claim, thus equating the two. Had the 1916 Act claim required lesser, or different evidence, it would not have been dismissed.

3.405 The United States recalls, moreover, that in the one instance in which a plaintiff was able to reach the question of what, if any damages, it might be entitled to - in *Helmac II*, as the consequence of a default discovery determination - the court indicated that damages would be available only for sales at prices below average cost. This determination and the other court decisions under the 1916 Act indicate that even if a plaintiff has extensive evidence on the subject of predatory intent, it is not likely to be able to establish a 1916 Act violation, to the satisfaction of a US court, without also being able to provide the same type of evidence of anticompetitive conduct and effects required in Sherman Act monopolisation and Robinson-Patman Act cases.

(d) The Available Defences

3.406 **Japan** contends that a Robinson-Patman defendant that has engaged in price discrimination has available several affirmative defences. In contrast, no defences are provided to 1916 Act defendants. The Robinson-Patman defences include:

(a) "cost justification", i.e. the price difference can be based on differences in the cost of manufacture, sale, or delivery where those differences result from differing methods or quantities in the sale or delivery of products to various purchasers[339];

(b) "changing conditions", i.e. price changes are permitted in response to changing conditions affecting the market for, or marketability of, a product (e.g. deterioration of perishable goods, obsolescence of seasonal goods, distress sales, outdated or damaged goods)[340]; and

(c) "meeting competition", i.e. a seller may reduce its prices to meet an equally low price of a competitor[341].[342]

---

[339] Japan refers to 15 U.S.C. § 13a (1997).

[340] Japan refers to 15 U.S.C. § 13(a) (1997).

[341] Japan refers to 15 U.S.C. § 13(b) (1997).

[342] In addition, Japan notes that under long-standing court decisions, two other affirmative defences are available to a defendant in a Robinson-Patman case. There is the judicially recognized "availability defense," according to which it is not an act of price discrimination for a seller to offer two prices, one normal and the other reduced on certain reasonable terms being met, where both prices are realistically available to the allegedly disfavoured customer. Japan refers to, e.g., *Boise Cascade*

3.407 Thus, according to Japan, even where a plaintiff has met the Robinson-Patman Act's stricter pleading and proof requirements, a defendant still can avoid liability simply by establishing any of these defences. In stark contrast, a 1916 Act defendant has no such escapes available. If the plaintiff meets the comparatively loose pleading and proof requirements, the defendant is liable under the 1916 Act. The provision by the United States of affirmative defences to domestic but not to foreign price discrimination defendants, is inconsistent with Article III:4 of the GATT 1994.

3.408 The **United States** concedes that the 1916 Act, on its face, does not specifically authorize any defences. The Robinson-Patman Act, on the other hand, allows three principal defences: a "meeting competition" defense, a defense based upon "changing market conditions", and a "cost justification" defence.[343] The defences are designed to ensure that pricing differentials employed for pro-competitive reasons are not prevented or discouraged. Nevertheless, these differences do not undermine the conclusion that the 1916 Act accords no less favourable treatment to foreign products than the Robinson-Patman Act accords domestic products because these defences are inherent in the 1916 Act's requirement that an intent to injure, destroy, or prevent the establishment of an industry in the United States - or to restrain or monopolise any part of trade and commerce - must be proven.

3.409 The United States asserts that, in a 1916 Act case, any evidence which would support the Robinson-Patman Act defences would be equally and directly relevant to determining whether the showing of the requisite predatory intent can be made in the first place. Thus, as Professor Hawk recognized in his treatise on US and EC competition laws, while the 1916 Act does not expressly provide for meeting competition and cost justification defences, "[t]hese considerations would appear relevant to predatory intent and thus should implicitly be included in the 1916 Act".[344] In particular, if the defendant charged the prices at issue with the intent of meeting competition in the form of comparable prices charged by other sellers, it is unlikely that a court would conclude that the defendant nevertheless intended to restrain or monopolise the line of commerce at issue, or intended to injure, destroy, or prevent the establishment of an US industry. Similarly, if the defendant charged the prices at issue in order to respond to changing market conditions, such as the deterioration of perishable commodities, it is unlikely that the requisite level of predatory intent could be established. In addition, if the defendant charged the prices at issue in order to account for cost savings, and in effect to pass those cost savings on to consumers, it is unlikely that a court would nevertheless conclude that the defendant acted with predatory intent. Indeed, in *Geneva Steel*, the court explained that one reason why it is difficult to prove the requisite intent under the 1916 Act is that "evidence of nor-

---

Corp. v. Federal Trade Commission, 837 F.2d 1127, p. 1163 (D.C. Cir. 1988). There also is the judicially recognized "functional discount" defence, according to which sellers are permitted to use price differentials to compensate certain classes of customers (e.g., wholesalers) for distributional services they perform. Japan refers to, e.g., *Texaco, Inc. v. Hasbrouck*, 496 U.S. 543, p. 561 (1990).

[343] The United States refers to 15 U.S.C. 13(a),(b).

[344] The United States refers to B. Hawk, *United States, Common Market and International Antitrust* (1996-1 Suppl.), p. 357.

mal pricing cuts [...] would be insufficient to establish liability under the 1916 Act".[345]

3.410 In short, the United States considers that the affirmative defences to which Japan refers, which are available to defendants in Robinson-Patman Act cases, are also, in effect, available to defendants in 1916 Act cases. The evidence establishing these defences does not, however, have to be presented as a defence. It instead can be presented to rebut any evidence the plaintiff may otherwise have on the subject of the defendant's intentions in charging the prices at issue.

3.411 **Japan** replies that, as a factual matter, the US arguments are incorrect. Evidence which establishes the "meeting competition" or "changing conditions" defences under the Robinson-Patman Act will not be sufficient to negate the "intent requirement" under the 1916 Act. In addition, the US assertion is mere speculation. There is a huge difference between explicit provision of stipulated defences under the Robinson-Patman Act and the speculative possibility of asserting defences under the 1916 Act.

3.412 The **United States** maintains its view that the affirmative defences which are available to defendants in Robinson-Patman Act cases are also, in effect, available to defendants in 1916 Act cases.

(e) The Conduct Subject to Penalties

3.413 **Japan** asserts that the conduct subject to penalties under the 1916 Act exceed those conduct under the Robinson-Patman Act. Both the 1916 Act and US anti-trust laws (through section 4 of the Clayton Act) provide for treble civil damage actions and recovery of the cost of the suit, including reasonable attorney's fees. However, the 1916 Act provides for *all types of violations* criminal fines of up to $5,000 or imprisonment not more than one year, or both. Section 3 of the Robinson-Patman Act, in contrast, provides the same penalties *only for a limited subset* of price discrimination practices that overlap with Section 2(a) of the Robinson-Patman Act and for "selling at unreasonably low prices" for the purpose of destroying competition or eliminating a competitor.[346]

3.414 According to Japan, the application by the US of criminal penalties to a broader range of foreign than domestic conduct is inconsistent with Article III:4 of the GATT 1994.

3.415 The **United States** recalls that the Robinson-Patman Act, like the 1916 Act, contains a criminal liability provision. In brief, Section 3 of the Act, 15 U.S.C. § 13a, prohibits

> "(1) territorial price discrimination 'for the purpose of destroying competition, or eliminating a competitor;' (2) charging 'unreasonably low prices for the purpose of destroying competition or eliminating a competitor'; and (3) granting discounts, rebates, or allowances that are

---

[345] *Geneva Steel, Op. Cit.*, p. 1220.

[346] The United States refers to 15 U.S.C. § 13a (1997).

> not made available to a recipient's competitors in the sale 'of goods of like grade, quality, and quantity.'"[347]

3.416 The United States notes that the Supreme Court has determined that "unreasonably low prices" are prices "below cost" and Section 3 thus prohibits sales at prices "below cost" that are made with the requisite predatory intent.[348] Both statutes provide that one who violates the criminal proscriptions can be fined up to $5,000, imprisoned for up to one year, or both. Moreover, as the District Court in *Zenith* stated:

> "The clause of the 1916 Act which creates criminal penalties is virtually identical to, and specifies the same penalties as, the corresponding clauses of the Sherman Anti-trust Act as then in force."[349]

Thus, from the perspective of both substantive scope and penalties, the criminal component of the 1916 Act treats importers no less favourably than the criminal provisions of the Robinson-Patman Act. That conclusion is further strengthened by the fact that the United States has never pursued a criminal case under the 1916 Act. By contrast, there have been a number of criminal prosecutions under Section 3 of the Robinson-Patman Act.

3.417 The United States notes that Japan nevertheless argues that the criminal component of the 1916 Act is less favourable, based on its suggestion that Section 3 of the Robinson-Patman Act covers only "a limited subset of price discrimination practices that overlap with Section 2(a) [...] and for selling at unreasonably low prices [...]." There does not, however, appear to be any basis for this suggestion. In fact, as the language of Section 3 itself indicates, it applies to "territorial price discrimination"; to charging "unreasonably low prices"; and to granting discounts, rebates, or allowances that are not made available to a recipient's competitors in the sale "of goods of like grade, quality, and quantity". In short, the coverage of this section actually appears to be broader than that of both the 1916 Act and of Section 2(a) of the Robinson-Patman Act, clearly establishing that the criminal provisions of the 1916 Act are, at a minimum, no less favourable to importers than the criminal provisions of Section 3 of the Robinson-Patman Act.

(f) The Litigation Costs and Business Burdens

3.418 **Japan** contends that, because plaintiffs more easily can prevail in lawsuits against importers and imported products under the 1916 Act than against domestic

---

[347] Section of Anti-trust Law, American Bar Association, *Anti-trust Law Developments (Fourth)* (1997), p. 490, quoting 15 U.S.C. § 13a.

[348] The United States refers to *United States v. National Dairy Products Corp.*, 372 U.S. 29, pp. 36-37 (1963). The Court also determined that such sales do not violate Section 3 of the Act:

> "when made in furtherance of a legitimate commercial objective, such as the liquidation of excess, obsolete or perishable merchandise, or the need to meet a lawful, equally low price of a competitor."

The United States further notes that, earlier, the Tenth Circuit had determined that such sales do not violate Section 3 of the Act if they are made "to increase volume and decrease unit cost in order to retain [one's] proportionate share of a diminishing market." (*Ben Hur Coal Co. v. Wells*, 242 F.2d 481, p. 486 (10th Cir.), cert. denied, 354 U.S. 910 (1957)).

[349] *Zenith III*, *Op. Cit.*, p. 1214.

competitors under the Robinson-Patman Act, they are more likely to file suit against importers than against domestic competitors for the same alleged conduct. As a consequence, importers face a higher risk of legal and business harassment under the 1916 Act than domestic producers face under the Robinson-Patman Act.[350]

3.419 Japan notes that these transaction and business costs take the form of legal expenses, disrupted business, uncertainty in the marketplace and a chilling effect on imports. In addition, using the threat of protracted lawsuits to seek to force defendants to accept out-of-court settlement is commonplace in the United States. The defendants in the *Geneva Steel* case have incurred the expense and uncertainty of being involved in litigation for nearly three years. The defendants in the *Wheeling-Pittsburgh* litigation have suffered even more dramatic consequences. Of the nine defendants in the case, six have reached out-of-court settlements.[351] Although these settlements remain confidential, most of them include certain restrictions on the importation of foreign steel and agreements to purchase undisclosed amounts of steel from the plaintiff.[352] According to statements from the plaintiff in that case, one defendant even agreed to pay it an undisclosed amount of money to settle the litigation.[353]

3.420 Japan argues that the settlements themselves distort trade. Importers have been forced to purchase steel from an US producer.[354] They have been forced to agree to curb their purchases of imported steel all to the benefit of an US steel producer.[355] Touting the successes of the 1916 Act actions brought by *Geneva Steel* and *Wheeling-Pittsburgh*, one even agreed to simply pay the plaintiff to end the legal harassment.[356]

3.421 In the view of Japan, what is perhaps even more troubling is that these recent cases and resulting settlements raise the potential for similar lawsuits and class action suits. Touting the success of *Geneva Steel* and *Wheeling-Pittsburgh*, at least one American law firm has solicited plaintiffs to bring a class action lawsuit under the 1916 Act against steel importers.[357]

3.422 The **United States** disagrees with Japan's argument that domestic firms can "more easily impose significant litigation costs and business burdens on foreign producers [through lawsuits under the 1916 Act] than on domestic competitors [through lawsuits under the Robinson-Patman Act]". Japan offers no support for this bald statement and none exists. The cases described establish that this theory is not valid; clearly, the far greater number of Robinson-Patman Act cases imposes far more sig-

---

[350] Japan notes that litigation under Robinson-Patman has come to a virtual standstill since the US Supreme Court handed down its ruling in *Brooke Group*. By comparison, the 1916 Act has seen a recent revival in activity, imposing trade-inhibiting transaction and business costs on the defendants named in recent cases.

[351] Japan notes that only three defendants, all Japanese, remain active in the litigation, opting thus far to continue to bear the costs and uncertainty associated with the litigation rather than the costs of settling.

[352] Japan refers to Wheeling-Pittsburgh Steel Corporation press releases.

[353] *Ibid.*

[354] *Ibid.*

[355] *Ibid.*

[356] *Ibid.*

[357] Japan refers to advertising material of a San Francisco law-firm.

nificant litigation costs and business burdens on domestic firms than the two 1916 Act cases could ever impose on foreign firms.

3.423 The United States recalls in this regard that the 1916 Act has rarely been invoked by private parties, and has never been invoked by the US government. More importantly, the 1916 Act establishes a standard for relief which has *never* been met in the case of importers and imported goods. The Robinson-Patman Act, by contrast, has been successfully invoked in thousands of federal court and administrative cases, including a substantial number pursued administratively by the Federal Trade Commission.

3.424 Finally, in respect of Japan's complaints that the fact that the ongoing *Geneva Steel* and *Wheeling-Pittsburgh* cases have compelled the defendants in both cases to incur the "expense and uncertainty" of litigation and that six of the nine defendants in the *Wheeling-Pittsburgh* case have reached "out-of-court settlements" (presumably voluntarily), the United States argues that these two complaints have nothing to do with the issues at hand. They are rather a product of the fact that if firms of one country choose to do business in another country, they must comply with the laws of that country, as well as their own.

(g) The Requisite Price Differences and Relative Price Levels

3.425 According to the **United States**, when it comes to establishing the requisite price discrimination - as a function of both price differences and price levels relative to costs - the 1916 Act treats foreign products more favourably than the Robinson-Patman Act treats domestic products, because it is more difficult to establish price discrimination that violates the 1916 Act than to establish price discrimination that violates the Robinson-Patman Act.

3.426 The United States argues, first, that the 1916 Act requires proof of a far larger number of illegal price differences - imposed in a systematic way - in order to establish liability. In particular, the plaintiff must show that the defendant "commonly and systematically" made the sales prohibited by the Act. By contrast, under the Robinson-Patman Act, liability can be established on the basis of as few as two consummated sales.[358]

3.427 The United States further argues that the 1916 Act requires proof of a larger price difference than the Robinson-Patman Act in an absolute sense. In particular, under the 1916 Act the plaintiff must establish that the Articles at issue are sold within the United States at a price "substantially less than actual market value or wholesale price of such Articles [...] in the principal markets of the country of their production, or of other foreign countries to which they are commonly exported".

3.428 The United States notes that, by contrast, the Robinson-Patman Act simply requires a showing of a "cognizable" difference in price, which need only be greater than a *de minimis* difference. Thus, for example, one circuit court of appeals recently held that a 2.38 per cent price difference provided a basis for liability under the

---

[358] The United States refers to *International Telephone & Telegraph Corp. et al.*, 104 F.T.C. 280, p. 417, citing E. Kintner, *A Robinson-Patman Primer*, 3d ed. (1979), p. 35.

Robinson-Patman Act.[359] Such a small difference would hardly satisfy the requirement that the price be "substantially less" under the 1916 Act.

3.429 The United States asserts, third, that even if the 1916 Act requirements with respect to price levels relative to costs are compared only to the corresponding requirements for establishing primary line liability under the Robinson-Patman Act - and such an approach ignores the substantial and far-reaching risk of liability for secondary line discrimination under the Robinson-Patman Act that domestic firms must confront under that statute - the 1916 Act is more favourable to importers than the Robinson-Patman Act is to domestic firms. Under the Robinson-Patman Act, the US Supreme Court has only stated that the plaintiff needs to "prove that the prices complained of are below an appropriate measure of the rival's cost".[360] Lower courts, meanwhile, have not agreed on what the appropriate measure of a rival' s costs should be. For example, while some courts have held that the prices complained of need only be below average cost, other courts have held that they must be below average variable cost.

3.430 The United States notes that, in the 1916 Act context, on the other hand, the one court that has squarely addressed this issue - in the context of establishing possible damages - required the plaintiff to prove that the defendant sold the products at issue at prices below its own average variable costs. As this court explained:

> "It is somewhat of a stretch to suggest the [1916] Act justifies damages when [the defendant's] prices equaled or exceeded average variable cost [...]. Therefore, this Court shall limit damages to those cases where [the defendant] set prices below average variable cost."[361]

3.431 The United States points out that Japan has failed to address any aspect of these arguments, presumably because it has recognized that the price difference and relative price level components of establishing liability under the 1916 Act are more difficult to satisfy than the corresponding components of the Robinson-Patman Act. Indeed, Japan's only reference to price differences and relative price levels arises in its discussion of dumping margins, where it recognizes that the "substantial" price differences required to establish liability under the Anti-Dumping Agreement and the 1916 Act are greater than the "*de minimis*" dumping margins that do not constitute dumping under the Anti-Dumping Agreement.

3.432 **Japan** argues that, to establish infringement under the Robinson-Patman Act in a so-called primary line case, it must be shown that the defendant is charging a price below the average variable cost of production. If prices are above the average variable cost of production, there is no infringement under the Robinson-Patman Act regardless of the existence of price discrimination. However, the 1916 Act is applicable whenever goods are imported into the United States at "a price substantially less than the actual market value [...]", regardless of the average variable cost of

---

[359] The United States refers to *Chroma Lighting v. GTE Products Corp.*, 1997-1 Trade Cas (CCH) 71,836 (9th Cir. 1997), para. 79,885.

[360] The United States refers to *Brooke Group, Op. Cit.*, pp. 222-23.

[361] *Helmac II, Op. Cit.*, p. 583.

production.[362] This difference presents the potential for 1916 Act defendants to face liability for prices above average variable cost. In contrast, domestic producers face no such risk under the Robinson-Patman Act. As the United States itself admits, "some lower courts [in Robinson-Patman Act cases] have held that the prices complained of need only be below average cost, while other courts have held that they must be below average variable cost". With this concession, the United States acknowledges that establishing price discrimination in Robinson-Patman Act cases can be more difficult than establishing a 1916 Act violation. Under the *Oilseeds* decision, this is all that is necessary to establish a violation of Article III:4 of the GATT 1994.

3.433 The **United States** disagrees with Japan's suggestion that sales at prices below average variable cost are a prerequisite to a finding of liability under the Robinson-Patman Act but not under the 1916 Act.[363] Under the Robinson-Patman Act, proof of sales at prices below some measure of the defendant's costs is not a prerequisite to a finding of secondary line liability. Moreover, with respect to primary line liability, the Supreme Court has expressly declined to require a showing of sales at prices below average variable cost. Instead, the Court stated, in *Brooke Group*, that the plaintiff needs to "prove that the prices complained of are below an appropriate measure of the rival's cost"[364], without specifying any particular measure. By contrast, in *Helmac II*, the only case that proceeded anywhere near a finding of liability under the 1916 Act - and only on a default basis, as a consequence of discovery problems - the District Court concluded that the defendant would be liable only for sales at prices below its own average variable costs.[365] Thus, as these cases establish, a showing that a defendant made sales at prices below average variable cost is required in order to establish 1916 Act liability, but is not required to establish primary line liability under the Robinson-Patman Act.[366]

---

[362] Japan notes that the *Helmac II* case says the liability standard under the 1916 Act is sales at prices below average variable cost and the *Brooke Group* standard for Robinson-Patman Act cases is sales below an appropriate measure of cost. However, other cases, including *Geneva Steel* and *Wheeling-Pittsburgh*, did not require that sales at prices below average variable cost be established for there to be liability under the 1916 Act.

[363] The United States notes that, similarly, the European Communities suggests that sales at prices below average variable costs are a prerequisite to Robinson-Patman Act liability but not to liability under the 1916 Act.

[364] *Brooke Group, Op. Cit.*, pp. 222-23.

[365] The United States refers to *Helmac II, Op. Cit.*, p. 583. The United States notes that the European Communities "contests the importance given by the US to the *Helmac II* case." For the United States, this position is somewhat surprising, inasmuch as requiring a showing of sales at prices below average variable cost in 1916 Act cases helps to ensure that the 1916 Act is more favourable to importers than the Robinson-Patman Act is to domestic firms. In any event, the European Communities does not provide any support for this position other than the suggestion that requiring a showing of sales at prices below average variable costs is not consistent with the court's decision in *Helmac I.*

[366] The United States notes that, as the European Communities indicates, in *Helmac I* the District Court indicated that the 1916 Act applies to offers to sell, as well as to consummated sales, while the Robinson-Patman Act applies to consummated sales. Contrary to the view of the European Communities, however, that determination does not diminish the difficulty of establishing liability under the 1916 Act, relative to the Robinson-Patman Act. Under the 1916 Act, the plaintiff still must show

K. Violation of Article XI of the GATT 1994

3.434 **Japan** contends that the 1916 Act violates the United States' obligations under Article XI of the GATT 1994 because it establishes impermissible import "prohibitions or restrictions other than duties, taxes or other charges".[367]

3.435 According to Japan, to establish a violation of Article XI, the complaining party must show (i) that the 1916 Act is an "other measure" maintained by the United States, (ii) that the measure makes "restrictions other than duties, taxes or other charges" effective, and (iii) that the measure is applied on the "importation" of products into the United States. Each of these elements is demonstrated below.

3.436 Japan asserts, first, that the 1916 Act unquestionably is a measure within the meaning of Article XI of the GATT 1994. It is a statute of the United States with binding effect.[368]

3.437 Japan argues, second, that the 1916 Act imposes "restrictions other than duties, taxes or other charges", thereby making the restrictions effective. Specifically, the 1916 Act provides for "a fine not exceeding $5,000, or imprisonment not exceeding one year, or both" as penalties. In addition, a person injured by a violation may recover treble damages and the cost of the suit, including a reasonable attorney's fee. Obviously, "imprisonment not exceeding one year" is neither a tax, nor a duty, nor a type of other charge. Equally obvious is the fact that the fine, treble damages and cost recovery are not duties or taxes. Likewise, they are not the type of "other charges" contemplated by Article XI:1.[369] Thus, this second element is satisfied, not merely by the imprisonment penalty, but also by the other impermissible penalties.

3.438 Japan submits, third, that the 1916 Act applies to the importation of products into the United States. The 1916 Act makes it unlawful to "import or cause to be imported or sold" any goods "from any foreign country into the United States" under certain conditions.

3.439 Japan notes, moreover, that one of the conditions for the importation to be unlawful is that the goods be dumped, or imported or sold in the United States at a price substantially less than their "actual market value or wholesale price". Specifically, the Act applies to goods

> "[...] imported or sold [...] within the United States at a price substantially less than the actual market value or wholesale price [...] in the principal markets of the country of their production, or of other

---

that the offers to sell were made "commonly and systematically," while as few as two sales may serve as a basis for liability under the Robinson-Patman Act.

[367] Article XI:1 states:

> "No prohibitions or restrictions other than duties, taxes or other charges, whether made effective through quotas, import or export licenses or other measures, shall be instituted or maintained by any contracting party on the importation of any product of the territory of any other contracting party or on the exportation or sale for export of any product destined for the territory of any other contracting party."

[368] Japan refers to, e.g., *Japan - Trade in Semi-conductors*, adopted on 4 May 1988, BISD 35S/116, paras. 104-09 (hereinafter "*Japan - Semi-conductors*") (finding, according to Japan, that "measure" as used in Article XI is a broad word encompassing not only laws and regulations, but also certain "non-mandatory requests").

[369] Japan points out that Article VIII of the GATT 1994 enumerates the types of permissible charges contemplated by Article XI, as well as Articles I and II, of the GATT 1994.

> foreign countries to which they are commonly exported after adding to such market value or wholesale price, freight, duty, and other charges and expenses necessarily incident to the importation and sale [...]."

This requirement highlights the fact that the 1916 Act is a measure applying to the importation of products into the United States. In essence, the 1916 Act establishes product-specific minimum price levels to protect US industries. Thus, it functions similarly to the minimum import price system declared inconsistent with Article XI of the GATT 1994 by the panel in *EEC - Programme of Minimum Import Prices, Licenses and Surety Deposits for Certain Processed Fruits and Vegetables.*[370] Furthermore, the application of the Act is not limited to a specific product, but is open to any product. The 1916 Act is a restriction that applies to imports within the meaning of Article XI of the GATT 1994.

3.440 Japan argues that the fact that the 1916 Act applies to "any person importing or assisting in importing any articles" is immaterial. As held by the panel in *United States - Section 337*, in the context of Article III of the GATT 1994, a measure applied to importers by imposing penalties on them also affects imported products.[371] In the context of Article XI, it does so by imposing restrictions on them.

3.441 Japan considers, therefore, that, as demonstrated above, the 1916 Act violates Article XI:1 of the GATT 1994.

3.442 The **United States** notes that, in general, Article XI prohibits, with certain exceptions, quantitative restrictions on imports or exports. Because the 1916 Act contains no provision which would enable a court to impose any sort of prohibition or restriction upon the importation of products, the Panel should reject this claim. In fact, the only court to have specifically considered whether the 1916 Act authorizes the imposition of a quantitative restriction on imports, *Wheeling-Pittsburgh*[372] held that no injunctive relief is available under the 1916 Act.

3.443 According to the United States, at most, a court may enter a *monetary judgment* (or impose a criminal sentence) against the particular *defendants* in a case for the amount of damage that the plaintiff's business has sustained. A monetary judgment (or a criminal sentence) against a party obviously does not apply to any particular product. In fact, the defendants in the case are free to continue importing their product. Furthermore, the judgment obviously does not apply to persons importing the same product that are not a party to the lawsuit. Thus, there is no basis for Japan's unsupported assertion that the 1916 Act "establishes product-specific minimum price levels".

---

[370] Japan refers to the Panel Report on *EEC - Programme of Minimum Import Prices, Licenses and Surety Deposits for Certain Processed Fruits and Vegetables*, adopted on 18 October 1978, BISD 25S/68, para. 4.9 (hereinafter "*EEC - Minimum Import Prices*") (holding, according to Japan, that the EEC's minimum import price system was a "restriction 'other than duties, taxes or other charges' within the meaning of Article XI:1"). Japan also refers to *Japan - Semi-conductors*, para. 29 (extending, according to Japan, the principle that restrictions on *imports* of goods *below* certain prices violate Article XI:1 to a situation in which restrictions applied to *exports* of goods *below* certain prices.).

[371] Japan refers to *United States - Section 337, Op. Cit.*, para. 5.10.

[372] The United States refers to *Wheeling-Pittsburgh, Op. Cit.*

3.444 The United States is of the view that even a cursory review of the panel report in *EEC - Minimum Import Prices* shows that there is no similarity between the 1916 Act and the minimum import pricing scheme at issue in that case. There, the questioned measure *prohibited* the importation of specific products (tomato concentrates) below a certain price. As such, it easily fell within the ambit of Article XI. Indeed, the EEC did not even dispute that the scheme was covered by Article XI.[373] Thus, the only real issue in that case was the application of the exceptions in Article XI:2.

3.445 The United States considers that Japan's reliance upon the panel report in *United States - Section 337* is similarly misplaced. At issue in that case was whether Article III:4 applied to the Section 337 proceedings. The panel found that the application of Article III:4 could not be avoided based upon the fact that Section 337 proceedings applied to persons rather than products.

3.446 In the present case, the United States does not dispute that Article III applies to the 1916 Act. However, the analysis under Article III is wholly different from an Article XI analysis. As noted by Japan, Article III has been interpreted to have an exceedingly broad scope based upon whether the measure "affects" the conditions of competition between the domestic and imported product. There is no language in Article XI concerning whether the measure "affects" the imported product nor any basis to conduct an analysis comparable to the changing conditions of competition analysis under Article III.

3.447 **Japan** replies that the fact that the 1916 Act does not provide for injunctive relief is irrelevant. The United States asserts that the 1916 Act is consistent with Article XI because, the United States claims, the 1916 Act does not allow a court to impose a "prohibition or restriction" on trade. However, the 1916 Act is a measure that applies to and restricts the importation of products. Because it allows for the imposition of fines, imprisonment, treble damages and costs, it violates Article XI.

3.448 Japan also notes that imprisonment is not "monetary" in nature. In Japan's view, imprisonment obviously has serious restriction on imports and imposes even more severe effect on imports than monetary punishment or administrative guidance. In a previous panel case - *Japan - Semiconductors* - the panel affirmed that in certain special circumstances such a soft instrument as administrative guidance could be regarded as a "governmental measure" enforcing trade policies. Japan does not believe that Article XI allows Members to take such measures as imprisonment with stronger enforcement effect and implication.

3.449 The **United States** reiterates its argument that a judgment under the 1916 Act against a party defendant (civil or criminal) does not apply to and therefore cannot restrict any particular product. The United States also notes that Japan did not address the distinctions raised by the United States between this case and the measures and claims at issue in *EEC - Minimum Import Prices* and *United States - Section 337*. Rather, Japan cites a different panel report - *Japan - Semiconductors* - for the proposition that, "in certain special circumstances such a soft instrument as administrative guidance could be regarded as a 'governmental measure' enforcing trade policies".

3.450 In the view of the United States, like *EEC - Minimum Import Prices* and *United States - Section 337*, the issues in *Japan - Semiconductors* are distinguishable

373 The United States refers to *EEC - Minimum Import Prices*, *Op. Cit.*, para. 3.3.

from this case. At issue in *Japan - Semiconductors* was whether the legal status of the practices in question rendered Article XI inapplicable. The panel concluded that:

> "[...] the complex of measures exhibited the rationale as well as the essential elements of a formal system of export control. The only distinction in this case was the absence of formal legally binding obligations in respect of exportation or sale for export of semi-conductors. However, the Panel concluded that this amounted to a difference in form rather than substance because the measures were operated in a manner equivalent to mandatory requirements. The Panel concluded that the complex of measures constituted a coherent system restricting the sale for export of monitored semi-conductors at prices below company-specific costs to markets other that the United States, inconsistent with Article XI."[374]

3.451 The "complex of measures" in question included "such measures as repeated direct requests by MITI, combined with the statutory requirement for exporters to submit information on export prices, the systematic monitoring of company and product-specific costs and export prices and the institution of the supply and demand forecasts mechanism and its utilization in a manner to directly influence the behaviour of private companies"[375].

3.452 The United States considers that it is obvious that the 1916 Act cannot be compared to the measures at issue in *Japan - Semiconductors* or *EEC - Minimum Import Prices.*[376]

L. Violation of Article XVI:4 of the WTO Agreement and Article 18.4 of the Anti-Dumping Agreement

3.453 **Japan** contends that the United States is in violation of its obligations under Article XVI:4 of the WTO Agreement and Article 18.4 of the Anti-Dumping Agreement. According to Article XVI:4 of the WTO Agreement:

> "Each member shall ensure the conformity of its laws, regulations and administrative procedures with its obligations as provided in the annexed Agreements."

3.454 Japan recalls that paragraph 4 of Article 18 of the Anti-Dumping Agreement sets forth a similar obligation that applies specifically to obligations under the Anti-Dumping Agreement:

> "Each Member shall take all necessary steps, of a general or particular character, to ensure, not later than the date of entry into force of the WTO Agreement for it, the conformity of its laws, regulations and administrative procedures with the provisions of this Agreement as they may apply for the Member in question."

3.455 In the view of Japan, these provisions clarify that the WTO agreements extend to all "laws, regulations and administrative procedures". Inconsistent future leg-

---

[374] *Japan - Semiconductors, Op. Cit.*, para. 117.

[375] The United States refers to *Japan - Semiconductors, Op. Cit.*, para. 117.

[376] In this regard, the United States refers to its earlier arguments.

islation is prohibited; inconsistent existing legislation must be amended so as to conform to the obligations under the WTO agreements.[377]

3.456 Japan asserts that the United States is in violation of each of these provisions because, as demonstrated above, it has failed to conform the 1916 Act to the obligations under the relevant provisions of the GATT 1994 and the Anti-Dumping Agreement.

3.457 The **United States** considers that, because the 1916 Act is susceptible to an interpretation that is fully consistent with all US WTO obligations and, in fact, has been so interpreted to date, there is no requirement under Article XVI:4 of the WTO Agreement that the United States take action to change the law.

3.458 In response to a question of the Panel to the United States regarding how the obligations contained in Article XVI:4 of the WTO Agreement are transposed into the US legal order, the United States notes that when the United States prepared its negotiating positions in the Uruguay Round, this preparation included a review of whether US law could be affected by those positions or by the proposals made by other Uruguay Round participants. In addition, after the Uruguay Round Final Act the United States undertook a comprehensive review of US law to determine which laws, regulations or administrative procedures might need to be changed in order to comply with US obligations under the WTO Agreement (including Article XVI:4). Where a statutory change was necessary, it was proposed to Congress and enacted as part of the Uruguay Round Agreements Act, which was signed into law on December 8, 1994. All changes in regulations and administrative procedures that were necessary to bring the United States into conformity with its obligations under the WTO Agreement were described in the Statement of Administrative Action which was submitted by the executive branch and approved by Congress as part of the Uruguay Round Agreements Act.

3.459 In reply to the same question of the Panel, **Japan** states that, in the United States, there is no direct application of international obligations. This is especially true in the context of WTO obligations. The obligations are transposed if and only if the US Congress decides to do so in passing a new law or an amendment to an existing law which then is enacted into law by the President.

3.460 In response to another question of the Panel to both parties regarding whether the requirements of Article XVI:4 of the WTO Agreement differ from those under Article 18.4 of the Anti-Dumping Agreement, Japan argues that they differ in two relevant respects. First, Article XVI:4 is more general in scope, applying to all WTO agreements, including the GATT 1994 and the Anti-Dumping Agreement. In other words, Article 18.4 is reflective of the general obligation set out by Article XVI:4 as it applies to anti-dumping. Second, in addition to the general obligation to "ensure the conformity" of laws, regulations and administrative procedures, Article 18.4 imposes an additional obligation to do so by "tak[ing] all necessary steps, of a general

---

[377] Japan notes that, under the GATT 1947, existing laws, including the 1916 Act, were "grandfathered." Under the WTO agreements, in contrast, only specified laws are exempted. The United States did not specify the 1916 Act for exemption and, thus, it is not grandfathered. The only measure grandfathered by the United States was the Jones Act, relating to exclusion of foreign-built vessels in US commerce. Japan refers to the introductory language of the GATT 1994, para. 3(a).

or particular character." These differences bolster Japan's view that the mere potential of WTO inconsistency is sufficient to establish a violation in the context of provisions relating to anti-dumping.

3.461 The **United States**, in response to the same question, submits that, like any other US law, regulation or administrative procedure, under Article XVI:4, anti-dumping laws, regulations and procedures (assuming they are mandatory) must conform with the requirements of the covered agreements. With regard to Article 18.4 of the Anti-Dumping Agreement, the United States notes that, although the language is not identical to Article XVI:4, there were similar provisions in the Tokyo Round Agreements on Anti-Dumping and Subsidies which have generally been interpreted as requiring the Parties to those agreements to adopt laws, regulations and procedures that permit them to act in conformity with their obligations under those Agreements. The United States submits that Article 18.4 of the Anti-Dumping Agreement should be interpreted in the same way.

3.462 In reply to yet another question of the Panel to both parties regarding whether, in light of Article 18.4 of the Anti-Dumping Agreement, there are grounds under the WTO provisions relating to anti-dumping for making a distinction between mandatory and non-mandatory laws, **Japan** notes that each Member must conform its laws, regulations and administrative procedures to the provisions of the WTO agreements. The United States has not done so and, thus, is in violation of Article 18.4. The WTO obligation is "to ensure [...] the conformity," by taking "all necessary steps, of a general or particular character." Given the ordinary meaning of these terms in their context, and in light of their object and purpose, that a law provides for WTO-inconsistent action is sufficient, even if there is the possibility of WTO-consistent action. This obligation, rather than the mandatory/discretionary dichotomy drawn from GATT 1947 precedent, should apply in the present dispute.

3.463 Japan argues that, in any case, the 1916 Act is mandatory. Japan has demonstrated that the 1916 Act mandates action inconsistent with Article VI and the Anti-Dumping Agreement.

3.464 The **United States**, in its answer to the Panel's question, argues that there is nothing inherent in the anti-dumping context that renders the generally applicable distinction between mandatory and non-mandatory legislation inapplicable. The distinction in GATT 1947/WTO jurisprudence between discretionary and mandatory legislation is not based upon a particular provision of any WTO agreement, nor is it limited in its application to a particular WTO provision. For example, this distinction has been applied in the Article III context and the Article VIII context. It has also been applied in the context of Article XI[378] and also, it appears, in the context of Articles I, II and X.[379]

3.465 According to the United States, this distinction is consistent with the presumption against conflicts between national and international laws. It is both general

[378] The United States refers to the Panel Report on *United States - Restrictions on Imports of Tuna*, dated 3 September 1991 (unadopted), BISD 39S/155.

[379] The United States refers to the Panel Report on *EEC - Parts and Components*, *Op. Cit.*, paras. 5.25-5.26.

international practice and that of the United States that statutory language is to be interpreted so as to avoid conflicts with international obligations. In general:

> "[a]lthough national courts must apply national laws even if they conflict with international law, there is a presumption against the existence of such a conflict. As international law is based upon the common consent of the different states, it is improbable that a state would intentionally enact a rule conflicting with international law. A rule of national law which ostensibly seems to conflict with international law must, therefore, if possible always be so interpreted as to avoid such conflict."[380]

Thus, GATT 1947 jurisprudence distinguishing between mandatory and discretionary legislation does no more than apply the general principle that there is a presumption against conflicts between national and international law. If a law is susceptible to an interpretation that is WTO-consistent, there is a presumption that domestic authorities will interpret that law so as to avoid a conflict with WTO obligations. This presumption may be seen as underlying the finding of the panel in *United States - Tobacco* that a domestic law susceptible of multiple interpretations would not violate a party's international obligations so long as one possible interpretation permits action consistent with those obligations.[381]

3.466 The United States also notes that two cases cited by the Panel, *EEC - Parts and Components* and *EC - Anti-Dumping Duties on Audio Tapes in Cassettes Originating in Japan*[382], support the conclusion that the 1916 Act is a non-mandatory measure and, therefore, the existence of the 1916 Act *as such* does not constitute a violation of any WTO obligation.

3.467 The United States recalls that, in *EEC - Parts and Components*, the panel noted that the anti-circumvention provision at issue did not mandate the imposition of duties or other measures by the EEC Commission and Council; it merely authorized the authorities to take certain actions.[383] The panel recalled that in a prior panel report adopted by the contracting parties (*United States - Superfund*), the panel had concluded that "legislation merely giving the executive authorities the possibility to act inconsistently with Article III:2 cannot, by itself, constitute a violation of that provision."[384] Thus, the panel concluded that the mere existence of the anti-circumvention provision was not inconsistent with the EEC's obligations under the General Agreement.

3.468 The United States points out that, similarly, the panel report in *EC - Audio Cassettes* concludes that the regulatory provision at issue was non-mandatory because the term "normally" was ambiguous and therefore left room for the EEC to act in a consistent manner.[385] The panel declined to base its finding upon the fact that

---

[380] *Oppenheim's International Law*, 9th ed., pp. 81-82 (footnote omitted by the United States).

[381] The United States refers to *United States - Tobacco, Op. Cit.*, para. 123.

[382] Panel Report on *EC - Anti-Dumping Duties on Audio Tapes in Cassettes Originating in Japan*, ADP/136 (unadopted), dated 28 April 1995 (hereinafter "*EC - Audio Cassettes*").

[383] The United States refers to *EEC - Parts and Components, Op. Cit.*, para. 5.25.

[384] The United States refers to ibid., para. 5.25.

[385] The United States refers to the Panel Report on *EC - Audio Cassettes, Op. Cit.*, paras. 362-364.

obligations under the anti-dumping legislation were dependent on whether certain factual prerequisites were fulfilled.

3.469 The United States argues that, likewise, the mere existence of the 1916 Act does not run afoul of any WTO obligations because the 1916 Act does not mandate that government authorities act in an inconsistent manner. The 1916 Act is clearly susceptible to an interpretation that is WTO-consistent and, in fact, all final judicial decisions that have considered the 1916 Act have interpreted it as such. Indeed, US courts have repeatedly admonished that the 1916 Act "should be interpreted whenever possible to *parallel the unfair competition law applicable to domestic commerce*."[386] Interpreting the 1916 Act to parallel domestic unfair competition law is clearly consistent with WTO obligations - particularly, Article VI of the GATT 1994 and the Anti-Dumping Agreement - because the WTO does not govern competition laws. In addition, a law regarding imports that "parallels" a domestic law would not raise any national treatment concerns under Article III of the GATT 1994.

IV. THIRD PARTY SUBMISSIONS

A. *The European Communities*

1. *Violation of Article VI of the GATT 1994 and the Anti-Dumping Agreement*

(a) The Applicability of Article VI of the GATT 1994 and the Anti-Dumping Agreement

4.1 As concerns the meaning and scope of Article VI of the GATT 1994, the **European Communities** considers that Article VI clearly goes beyond creating an exception from other provisions of the GATT 1994; it has a broader scope. It is clear from its opening words[387] that its purpose is to provide a body of rules for dealing with the problem of dumping in international trade.

4.2 The European Communities notes that Article VI of the GATT 1994 acknowledges the existence of a particular problem in international trade and then proceeds to provide the solution. Three steps are envisaged in this respect: First, Article VI defines the practice of dumping. Second, it sets out certain other conditions that need to be fulfilled for the application of remedial measures, such as the existence of injury. And third, it authorizes the remedial measures which can be taken to deal with dumping.

4.3 Concerning the definition of dumping, the European Communities notes that its essential feature is that it is defined as relating exclusively to imports and to price discrimination in the form of higher prices on the market of the exporting country

---

[386] The United States refers to 494 F. Supp., p. 1223.

[387] The European Communities refers to the following language used in Article VI:

> "The contracting parties recognize that dumping, by which products of one country are introduced into the commerce of another country at less than the normal value of the products, is to be condemned if it causes or threatens material injury to an established industry in the territory of a contracting party or materially retards the establishment of a domestic industry [...]"

than on the market of the importing country. As concerns the pre-conditions for taking action against dumping, the most important one is stated to be injury. Article VI:1 provides that dumping as defined is "to be condemned" *if* it "causes or threatens material injury to an established industry in the territory of a contracting party or materially retards the establishment of a domestic industry [...]". Thereafter Article VI :2 proceeds to authorize the measure that can be taken against dumping:

> "In order to offset or prevent dumping, a contracting party may levy on any dumped product an anti-dumping duty not greater in amount than the margin of dumping in respect of such product. For the purposes of this Article, the margin of dumping is the price difference determined in accordance with the provisions of paragraph 1."

4.4 According to the European Communities, this language establishes the application of anti-dumping duties as the sole means authorized by the GATT 1994 by which a contracting party can seek to deal with the problem of dumped imports.

4.5 The European Communities further points out that it is only dumping meeting the definition in Article VI:1 of the GATT 1994 that is to be condemned, and then only in the stated circumstances of injury, threat of injury or material retardation. Anti-dumping duties may be applied "in order to offset or prevent dumping", but only in an amount no greater than the margin of dumping as defined. The reference to "offsetting" as well as "preventing" also makes clear that anti-dumping duties are the sole remedy established by the GATT 1994 for dealing with the problem of dumping, whether past, present or future.

4.6 The European Communities considers that the Anti-Dumping Agreement is fully consistent with this scheme of Article VI and defines in greater detail the conditions and in particular the requirements for an investigation that need to be fulfilled to allow anti-dumping action to be taken. Article 1 of the Agreement confirms that an anti-dumping measure can be applied only under the circumstances provided for in Article VI of the GATT 1994 and pursuant to investigations conducted in accordance with the Agreement, while Article 18 of the same Agreement (which says that "no specific action against dumping of exports from another Member can be taken except in accordance with the provisions of GATT 1994 as interpreted by this Agreement") confirms that action can be taken against the import of dumped products from another GATT 1994 Member *only if* the dumping causes or threatens material injury, and that no other measures can be taken than those provided for by Article VI of the GATT 1994 and the Anti-Dumping Agreement.

4.7 The European Communities notes that the purpose of Article VI and the Anti-Dumping Agreement would be thwarted if parties were allowed to apply measures other than anti-dumping duties - for example, civil liability for damages or criminal penalties - to deal with the problem for which Article VI establishes anti-dumping duties as the sole remedy. Likewise it would be thwarted if the Members could justify the application of such other measures on the basis that the conduct to which they are applied is defined in a manner which, while incorporating the essential elements of the definition of dumping, differs by the addition of one or another additional condition - for example, providing that the additional remedy is available in case of aggravated or "predatory" dumping. This is exactly what the 1916 Act does. Of course it was not enacted in order to circumvent the discipline of Article VI of the GATT 1994, which was only adopted three decades later. But to accept that the 1916

Act is compatible with Article VI of the GATT 1994 would entail accepting that Article VI can be circumvented by national legislation simply by resorting to the expedient of "bolting on" a few additional definitional elements or providing a remedy other than anti-dumping duties.

4.8 Separately, the European Communities notes that the GATT 1994 contains rules on anti-dumping (Article VI) and that these rules establish the sole system of remedies authorized by the GATT for dealing with the problem of dumping. By contrast, the GATT 1994 does not contain any specific discipline on anti-trust matters. The question posed by the 1916 Act is therefore: is the 1916 Act of such a nature as to be subject to the rules of Article VI and the Anti-Dumping Agreement?

4.9 The European Communities considers that this question is to be answered by the Panel by reference to the principles of GATT 1994 and WTO law. It is not to be determined on the basis of national legislation or case law of any particular Member. The Panel cannot be bound by the views of national courts of WTO Members on this question. Words like "anti-trust", "unfair competition", and "predatory" may have different meanings in different Member States. They may be used in different ways at different times. Allowing their use to determine the scope of application of the discipline of Article VI would effectively invite Members themselves to choose to withdraw their legislation from WTO disciplines simply by choosing the right label. On the other hand, judgments of national courts are relevant insofar as they offer guidance on the meaning or interpretation of national laws as distinct from the legal categorisation for WTO purposes, and it is appropriate for the Panel to take them into account for that purpose.

4.10 Thus, according to the European Communities, it is Article VI itself which gives the answer as to whether the 1916 Act is subject to its provisions or not. It provides a definition of dumping "by which products of one country are introduced into the commerce of another country at less than the normal value of the products". A first essential feature of the definition is that it refers to rules *relating exclusively to imports*. The definition is based on the concept of price discrimination in the form of higher prices on the market of the exporting country than on the market of the importing country.[388] This analysis yields the definition of the kinds of rules which are anti-dumping rules subject to the discipline of Article VI of the GATT 1994:

(a) The rules are targeted at imports and by the fact of their importation.

(b) The practice is defined by reference to discrimination which takes the form of higher prices in the domestic market of the exporter than in the import market.

4.11 For the European Communities the 1916 Act is clearly a law which is subject to Article VI of the GATT 1994:

(a) It is targeted at imports. Its prohibition is directed to "any person importing or assisting importing any Articles in the United States". Such persons who breach the prohibition are guilty of a misdemeanour, and

[388] The European Communities points out, in this connection, notably in light of the US argument that Japan's and the European Communities' claim under Article VI would entail bringing all regulation of international price discrimination under Article VI, that dumping as defined in Article VI constitutes only a subcategory of international price discrimination.

are liable for treble damages to persons who are injured by the prohibited conduct.

(b) The regulated conduct is defined by reference to discrimination between the price of the imported products and "the actual market value or wholesale price of such Articles [...] in the principal markets of the country of their production, or of other foreign countries to which they are commonly exported".

4.12 The European Communities argues that the 1916 Act does not escape the discipline of Article VI because it requires the prohibited conduct to be "common and systematic", or because the price differential must be "substantial". Article VI applies whether the dumping is limited in occurrence and sporadic, or frequent and systematic; whether the dumping margin is large or small. It takes into account the magnitude and frequency of the dumping only through the rule that the level of anti-dumping duty imposed may not exceed the level of dumping found.

4.13 Moreover, in the view of the European Communities, the 1916 Act does not escape the discipline of Article VI because sanctions can only be imposed under the 1916 Act if one or more of the enumerated specific intents are found. The discipline of Article VI applies to any rule directed at dumping. Once it is established that the rule or law is subject to Article VI, then the sole remedy permitted by Article VI (the imposition of anti-dumping duties) is conditional on a finding of (i) dumping in accordance with the definition of Article VI and (ii) injury, threat of injury, or material retardation. Substituting the specific intent tests incorporated in the 1916 Act for the injury tests required by Article VI in no way serves to take the 1916 Act out of the discipline of Article VI; quite the contrary, it is one of the grounds which cause the 1916 Act to infringe Article VI, since the 1916 Act permits the application of sanctions in circumstances other than the only ones envisaged by Article VI - namely where there is injury, threat of injury or material retardation.

4.14 With respect to the relevance of US case law, the European Communities reiterates its view that the legal categorisation of the 1916 Act is a matter of WTO law and therefore it should be made by the Panel and not by national (in the present case, US) courts. In any event, courts' views on the matter are far from consonant.[389] It is sufficient to note that while some judgments (i.e. those of the District Court and the Circuit Court of Appeals in the *Zenith III* case) suggest that the 1916 Act is an anti-trust law and not a trade law, this view has been strongly contested. For example, the District Court in *Geneva Steel* held:

[389] In this respect, the European Communities draws attention to a pronouncement by the ICJ, which, referring to an earlier judgment by the PCIJ, noted the following:

> "Where the determination of a question of municipal law is essential to the Court's decision in a case, the Court will have to weigh the jurisprudence of the municipal courts, and 'If this is uncertain or divided, it will rest with the Court to select the interpretation which it considers most in conformity with the law' (*Brazilian Loans*, PCIJ, Series A, Nos. 20/21, p. 124)" (*Elettronica Sicula S.p.A. (ELSI)*, Judgment, ICJ Reports 1989, p. 47, para. 62).

The European Communities claims that it has shown throughout its argumentation, and that the United States has not denied, that the views of US courts which have interpreted the 1916 Act are far from consonant.

> "The 1916 Act means what its plain language says. In addition to its anti-trust prohibitions, the Act has a protectionist component that prohibits conduct designed to injure the domestic steel industry".

4.15 But, in the view of the European Communities, even those Courts that claim that the 1916 Act is solely an anti-trust statute acknowledge that establishing that dumping took place remains the first prerequisite to apply the 1916 Act. For instance, in the *In re Japanese Electronic Products II* case, which is described as "complex anti-trust litigation", the Court of Appeals for the Third Circuit held that:

> "[t]he 1916 Act makes it illegal to *dump* imported goods on the US market with the purpose of destroying or injuring US industry [...]. The first element necessary to a finding of *dumping* under the 1916 Act is proof that a price differential exists between two comparable products, one of which is imported or sold in the US and the other of which is sold in the exporting country."[390]

4.16 The European Communities argues that the fact that the conduct targeted by a statute is defined by reference to discrimination between the price of the imported products and a benchmark which is (generally) the price of the product in the exporting country, is sufficient to determine that the statute is directed at dumping and is subject to the disciplines of Article VI of the GATT 1994. While the European Communities does not accept that applicability of Article VI of the GATT 1994 requires examination of the question whether the law protects competitors as distinct from competition, or whether the specific intent requirement relates to an intent to injure industry as opposed to an intent to injure competition, the language just quoted makes clear that US courts themselves have taken sharply different positions on these questions, and there is nothing to suggest that greater clarity will be brought in the foreseeable future.

4.17 Finally, the European Communities agrees with Japan that the United States' denial in the present proceeding that the 1916 Act is an instrument to counter dumping directly contradicts many official statements and positions of US executive branch officials, including officials of the current Administration.

(b) Violation of Article VI:2 of the GATT 1994

4.18 The European Commnities submits that the WTO anti-dumping rules, laid down in Article VI of the GATT 1994 and in the Anti-Dumping Agreement, establish a comprehensive and complete multilateral regime to define and address the issue of dumping in international trade. This comprehensive character also pertains to the regulation of the measures that can be taken once injurious dumping within the meaning of Article VI of the GATT 1994 is found. In that case, "[i]n order to offset or prevent dumping, a contracting party may levy on any dumped product an anti-dumping duty not greater in amount than the margin of dumping in respect of such product", as made clear already by Article VI:2 of the GATT 1994. This exclusive character cannot but be clearer if the several provisions included in Article VI are

390 *In re Japanese Electronic Products II, Op. Cit.*, p. 322 and 324 (emphasis added by the European Communities); the European Communities also refers to, e.g., *Zenith I, Op. Cit.*; *Wheeling-Pittsburgh, Op. Cit.*; *Geneva Steel, Op. Cit.*, pp. 1212-14.

examined together. That Article *inter alia* assigns a specific function to anti-dumping measures and repeatedly sets precise maximum quantitative limits to their permissible level. The function of anti-dumping measures is to "offset" dumping (or "prevent" in the case of threat of material injury). This is then further emphasized in Article 9.1 of the Anti-Dumping Agreement, where it is suggested to limit the duty to the amount necessary to offset the *injury* suffered by the domestic industry, which may be less than the full dumping margin. The imposition of duties is additionally limited in those paragraphs of Article VI of the GATT 1994 that prohibit parties from cumulating anti-dumping and countervailing duties to counter the same practice. It cannot go unnoticed that all those limitations and qualifications applying to the imposition of anti-dumping duties would have absolutely no purpose and absolutely no result if WTO Members were free to choose any other type of measure and then with no maximum limits as to amount and impact.

4.19 The European Communities recalls that the remedial measures provided for by the 1916 Act are treble damages and/or criminal penalties (fines and/or imprisonment). These remedies are not duties. As made clear above, they do not fall into the only type of measures allowed under multilateral anti-dumping rules to counter dumping practices, nor are they authorized by other WTO provisions.

4.20 In the view of the European Communities, recognition of the foregoing was again made by the US authorities. In that respect, the European Communities simply refers the Panel to the testimony of USTR General Counsel Alan Holmer to the US Senate Finance Committee, dated 18 July 1986. The only comment that may be added to this eminently clear statement made by Mr. Holmer is that Article 16 of the 1979 Anti-Dumping Code is identical to Article 18 of the WTO Anti-Dumping Agreement.

4.21 The European Communities considers that the compensatory, remedial objective (in economic terms) of the measure authorized in Article VI assumes that only a quantifiable price measure offsetting a precisely quantified dumping margin (or possibly, lower injury level) may be adopted. In other words, only a measure increasing the costs of the exporters up to the point of somehow forcing them to raise prices on their export markets where they have been found to dump is really fit to "offset" dumping (in the sense of a dumping margin, or possibly an injury level). On the other hand, this remedial objective can certainly not be served by criminal liability. The presence of pecuniary criminal sanctions bears no relation to the margin of dumping.

4.22 In the view of the European Communities, the United States is reading Article VI:2 of the GATT 1994 out of context and contrary to its clear object and purpose. A provision in an Agreement such as the GATT 1994 stating that something "may" be done does not necessarily mean that any alternative action, which could be more or less restrictive of trade, is in no way restricted. Whether it has this meaning or whether it implies on the contrary that no other action may be taken depends on the context in which the word "may" is being used. The context of Article VI comprises the structure of the GATT 1994. It is important to note that Articles III to XIX of the GATT 1994 regulate problems in international trade. Thus, Article VI regulates the action that Members may take against dumping and the conditions under which they may take this action. Article VI:2 expressly states that the action which may be taken is to levy an anti-dumping duty. When read in context and in the light of its object and purpose, Article VI prevents Members to take other action than duties to counter dumping, for example imprisoning the importers.

4.23 Addressing the negotiating history of Article VI, the European Communities notes that, despite attempts by some contracting parties to the GATT 1947 to provide for other types of offsetting measures than duties, both during the preparatory work and the Review Session of 1955, Article VI was intentionally limited to anti-dumping duties. The European Communities notably recalls that the 1948 Working Party on "Modifications to the General Agreement" noted, in respect of the current text of Article VI (corresponding to Article 34 Havana Charter):

> "While agreeing that there is no substantive difference between Article VI of the General Agreement and Article 34 of the Charter, the working party recommends the replacement of that article, as the text adopted at Havana contains a useful indication of the principle governing the operation of that Article and constitutes a clearer formulation of the rules laid down in that article. The working party, endorsing the views expressed by [the Subcommittee on Article 34 at the Havana Conference] agreed that measures other than compensatory anti-dumping and countervailing duties may not be applied to counteract dumping or subsidization except in so far as such other measures are permitted under other provisions of the General Agreement."[391]

4.24 According to the European Communities, by expressly stating that there was no substantive change, the Working Party has made it quite clear that there was no intention, in changing the text of Article VI of the GATT 1947, to allow other remedies than duties against dumping.

4.25 The European Communities also points out that the Working Party further noted that it:

> "[...] agreed that measures other than compensatory anti-dumping and countervailing duties may not be applied to counteract dumping or subsidization except insofar as such other measures are permitted under other provisions of the General Agreement."[392]

4.26 The European Communities adds that, in doing so, the Working Party confirmed the "definite understanding" of the relevant Subcommittee of the Havana Conference, from which the text of Article VI was taken. Therefore, it results not only from the negotiating history of the GATT 1947, but also from subsequent interpretation that duties are the only authorized remedy to counter dumping practices under Article VI of the GATT 1994.

4.27 The European Communities argues, in addition, that the adoption of the WTO Anti-Dumping Agreement has not changed the content of Article VI in respect of the limitation to duties because it includes no derogation or conflicting rule on this point. To the contrary, the WTO Anti-Dumping Agreement, and specifically Article 18.1 thereof, does nothing but confirm Article VI in this respect. Therefore, it is sufficient

---

391 BISD II/41, 42, para. 12.

392 Reprinted in GATT, *Analytical Index: Guide to GATT Law and Practice* (1994), pp. 216-217.

to rely on Article VI to claim that the 1916 Act violates WTO rules by providing for remedies other than duties in order to counter dumping practices.

4.28 On the interpretation of the footnote to Article 18.1 of the Anti-Dumping Agreement, the European Communities notes that the ordinary meaning of the footnote to Article 18.1 and of its predecessor in Article 16.1 of the Tokyo Round Anti-Dumping Code is that the Anti-Dumping Agreement does not prevent Members from taking appropriate action under other trade defence instruments provided for in the GATT 1994, such as countervailing duty action and safeguard action.

4.29 According to the European Communities, this interpretation is confirmed by the negotiating history. The factors taken into account by the negotiators in deciding to delete a corresponding provision when drafting the Havana Charter, and when amending the GATT 1947, were exactly the same. It is true that in the first case the negotiators used the phrase "other provisions of the Charter" whereas those in the second spoke of "other provisions of the General Agreement". However, it is clear that the Charter negotiators had in mind the Charter provisions that were incorporated in the General Agreement. The Report of the Working Party established by Sub-Committee C of the Third Committee of the Havana Conference further supports this conclusion. Paragraphs 3(iv) and 6 clearly show that the express prohibition of other measures against dumping was agreed to be unnecessary, removed and replaced by a statement to the minutes that other measures were not allowed because of concerns that some parties had about the implications for enforcing their rights under Articles 13 and 14 which correspond to what is now Article XVIII of the GATT 1994.[393] Moreover, even if it could be argued that the Charter negotiators intended to preserve a wider range of possible measures, those who negotiated the 1948 amendments to the GATT 1947 clearly did not, since they explicitly refer to "other provisions of the General Agreement". The GATT 1947 negotiators were prepared to refer to the Havana Charter where that was their intention, as is apparent, for instance, from the Note *ad* Article II:4 of the GATT 1947.

4.30 In conclusion, for the European Communities, the fact that this footnote was considered necessary merely confirms that alternative action against dumping such as treble damages, fines and imprisonment is not compatible with WTO rules.

2. *Violation of Article III:4 GATT 1994*

(a) The Robinson-Patman Act as an Equivalent Measure Applying to US Goods

4.31 The European Communities considers that to the extent that the 1916 Act is not inconsistent with Article VI of the GATT 1994 and the Anti-Dumping Agreement, the 1916 Act infringes Article III:4 of the GATT 1994 since it accords to products of WTO Members imported into the United States treatment less favourable that that accorded to like products of US origin.

4.32 The European Communities notes that there is no dispute about the fact that the 1916 Act is a "law" within the meaning of Article III:4 "affecting the internal sale of products" because it prohibits, *inter alia*, the sale or offering for sale of products

[393] The European Communities refers to document E.CONF.2/C.3/C/18, paras. 3(iv) and 6.

below a certain price. Also, although the 1916 Act nominally applies to importers, this does not prevent the applicability of Article III:4.[394] Furthermore, the circumstances under which a product is imported do not affect the characterization of domestic and imported products as "like".

4.33 As regards the "less favourable treatment" accorded by the United States to imported products, the European Communities submits that the very fact that the 1916 Act applies exclusively to imported products already establishes a *prima facie* breach of Article III:4, since domestic products are not subject to the requirements of the Act. Therefore, the European Communities agrees with Japan that the 1916 Act violates Article III:4 by establishing a separate and additional legal regime for imports and subjecting imports to separate legal requirements not applicable to domestic goods.

4.34 The European Communities notes that the United States seeks to defend the 1916 Act by claiming that domestic products are subject to a comparable legislation regulating price discrimination on the US market and therefore imported products are not treated "less favourably". In this respect the United States refers to the Robinson-Patman Act. However, the United States has failed to show that this Act prevents less favourable treatment of imported products.

4.35 In this regard, the European Communities argues, first of all, that imported products are *also* subject to the Robinson-Patman Act in the same way as domestic products. This Act, like any legitimate competition or anti-trust measure, does not distinguish between imported and domestic products. It is true that the Robinson-Patman Act only applies to price discrimination committed in the United States and that in the 1916 Act may be considered to complement it in that it applies to *dumping,* which is a price discrimination practised between the domestic market of the producer and an export market. It is not however possible to say that the 1916 Act and the Robinson-Patman Act are complementary in a manner which could possibly avoid a violation of Article III:4 of the GATT 1994. The complementarity does not relate to the origin of the goods, but to the discrimination. Subjecting US goods to no less favourable treatment than imported goods would therefore require that the United States apply similar penalties and make available similar remedies for equivalent cases involving US goods. This would require legislation which would render US producers liable for equivalent penalties when they sold their goods in the US at lower prices than on foreign markets under similar conditions to those set out in the 1916 Act, for example, along the following lines:

> "It shall be unlawful for any person producing any Articles in the United States, commonly and systematically, to sell such Articles within the United States at a price substantially less than the actual market value or wholesale price of such Articles in the market of any foreign country to which they are commonly exported, after deducting from such market value or wholesale price, freight, duty, and other charges and expenses necessarily incident to the importation and sale thereof in the United States: *Provided*, That such act or acts be done

[394] The European Communities refers to the Panel Report on *United States - Section 337, Op. Cit.*, para. 5.10 in particular.

with the intent of destroying or injuring an industry in the United States, or of preventing the establishment of an industry in the United States, or of restraining or monopolizing any part of trade and commerce in such Articles in the United States."

4.36 The European Communities points out that the 1916 Act does not apply to such acts and nor does the Robinson-Patman Act. Such acts may in fact be conducted with impunity by producers of US goods (or at least not be subject to any other than the generally applicable laws). In other words, producers of US goods may do what producers of foreign goods may not. They may seek to use isolated non-US markets to obtain the high profits needed to allow them to sell at low prices in the United States. Imported goods are therefore treated less favourably than US goods and this is contrary to Article III:4 of the GATT 1994.[395]

(b) Element-by-Element Comparison of the 1916 Act and the Robinson-Patman Act

4.37 The European Communities considers that even if the Robinson-Patman Act were considered to be an equivalent measure applying to US goods, imported products are still treated "less favourably" than domestic products.[396] A careful comparison of the two laws, taking into account not only the respective texts but also the additional requirements read into the Robinson-Patman Act as a condition for finding primary line violations, demonstrates that it is substantially more difficult to prove a violation of the Robinson-Patman Act than it is to prove a violation of the 1916 Act. As a consequence, the 1916 Act allows the application of measures (like awarding damages) under less favourable conditions for imported products than those resulting for domestic products from the application of the Robinson-Patman Act. Therefore, less favourable treatment is accorded to imported products in violation of Article III:4 of the GATT 1994.

4.38 The European Communities submits that the reason why the application of the "no less favourable treatment" standard requires an element-by-element comparison of the laws at issue rather than of the frequency of their concrete applications lies in the purpose of Article III. It is longstanding practice that Article III protects competitive opportunities. Hence, in order to establish a violation of Article III:4 it is not

---

[395] The European Communities asserts in this connection that its arguments also demonstrate the fallacy of the US argument that the 1916 Act is properly regarded as an "anti-trust" measure. Even if there were some basis for saying that once a measure is classified as an "anti-trust" measure it falls outside certain GATT 1994 disciplines, for the European Communities it is clear that a *bona fide* "anti-trust" measure would not apply only to imported products.

[396] As a preliminary point, the European Communities recalls that among Robinson-Patman Act cases a distinction is made between the probable impact of price discrimination (i) on direct competitors of the discriminating seller (primary line injury), (ii) on the favoured and disfavoured buyers of the discriminating seller (second-line injury) and (iii) on the customers of either of them (third-line injury). Primary line discrimination is the only direct domestic analogue of international price discrimination as condemned in the 1916 Act. The US Supreme Court has held in the *Brooke Group* case that in order for the requisite effect on competition to be present in primary line cases, it must be shown that (i) the defendant charged prices below an appropriate measure of cost, and (ii) it had a reasonable prospect of recouping its investment in below cost prices.

necessary to show that the measure challenged has had any actual effects. The mere *possibility* that a measure may result in some circumstances in less favourable treatment being afforded to imported products is already sufficient to establish a violation of Article III:4. Thus, in the *EEC - Oilseeds* case:

> "[...] the Panel examined whether a purchase regulation which does not necessarily discriminate against imported products but is *capable* of doing so is consistent with Article III:4. The Panel noted that the exposure of a particular imported product to a *risk* of discrimination constitutes, by itself, a form of discrimination. The Panel therefore concluded that purchase regulations creating such a risk must be considered to be according less favourable treatment within the meaning of Article III:4"[397]

4.39 On the other hand, the European Communities contests the value and relevance to the present case of the US contention that the 1916 Act has rarely been invoked by private parties and has never been invoked by the US government. The analysis of the "no less favourable treatment" standard must be carried out on the basis of the two sets of rules, and reference to the history of the application of one of them is therefore irrelevant. Taking into account the history of the application of the 1916 Act could suggest that less favourable treatment resulting from the application of the 1916 Act at one point in time[398] could be offset by more favourable treatment resulting from the application of it at another point in time. Such a reasoning was clearly rejected by the Panel in the *United States - Gasoline* case and the same conclusion should apply to the present case.[399]

4.40 The European Communities argues that, in any event, the difficulties of practical application have been recognized in respect of predatory pricing generally and precisely in connection with a claim under the Robinson-Patman Act. In its *Brooke Group* judgment, the Court held that "predatory pricing schemes are rarely tried and even more rarely successful" and "the costs of erroneous liability are high"[400]. In addition, the European Communities considers that the fact that the 1916 Act has not often been invoked is due to a number of factors which do nothing to demonstrate that it provides more favourable treatment to imports than the Robinson-Patman Act does to domestic goods. More importantly, the 1916 Act has (i) a "harassment value" because it gives to complainants (i.e. competitors of the importer in the domestic market) a private right of action in federal district courts and (ii) a "chilling effect" on importers because of its own terms, including the nature of the remedies which it provides (i.e., imprisonment and treble damages).

397 Panel Report on *EEC - Oilseeds*, *Op. Cit.*, para. 141 (emphasis added by the European Communities).

398 The European Communities refers to the *Geneva Steel*, *Op. Cit.*, and *Wheeling-Pittsburgh*, *Op. Cit.*, cases.

399 For the European Communities it is therefore clear that an analysis under Article III:4 has to be carried out at the level of an individual product, not at the level of the application of the law to all possible products. Any individual product must be treated no less favourably than a like domestic product - and this in all cases.

400 *Brooke Group*, *Op. Cit.*

4.41 The European Communities submits further that a comparison between the texts of the Robinson-Patman Act and the 1916 Act reveals that they differ as regards the elements which must be proved in order for an infringement of the law to be present, which results in unfavourable treatment being afforded to imported products in violation of Article III:4 of the GATT 1994. They concern, *inter alia*, (i) the intent requirements under each Act, (ii) the measurement of price discrimination, (iii) the sufficiency of offers for sale for supporting claims under each Act.

4.42 With regard to the intent requirements, the European Communities notes that, under the Robinson-Patman Act, a primary line complainant, in order to successfully demonstrate predatory pricing, must establish that (i) the defendant is charging prices below an appropriate measure of cost, namely, average variable costs and (ii) that it has a reasonable prospect to recoup its investment in below cost price.[401] These two conditions and especially the second one represent a burden of proof which is very difficult to be sustained by the plaintiff as the Supreme Court itself has recognized.[402]

4.43 The European Communities argues that the intent requirements under the Robinson-Patman Act are not present in the framework of a 1916 Act case. Under the 1916 Act, discriminatory pricing must rather be conducted with the intent of injuring, destroying or preventing the establishment of a US industry. The practical result of the difference between the "predatory pricing" test under the Robinson-Patman Act and the "intent to injure" test under the 1916 Act is that the same conduct by two firms, one selling imported products and the other selling domestic products, could be deemed to infringe the 1916 Act in the case of the imported products, and not to infringe the Robinson-Patman Act in the case of the domestic products. This was recognized by the US Court in the *Helmac I* case.

4.44 Furthermore, the European Communities agrees with Japan that the subjective intent standard under the 1916 Act is easier to prove than the objective effect standard under the Robinson-Patman Act. As Japan correctly points out, in *Brooke Group*, the plaintiffs had shown subjective intent, but not effect, and the Supreme Court ruled that the subjective proof, alone, is insufficient.

4.45 With regard to the measurement of price discrimination, the European Communities notes that the 1916 Act is applicable whenever goods are imported into the United States at prices *substantially below the prices charged in the country* of production or other countries where the goods are commonly exported. By contrast, under the Robinson-Patman Act, it must be shown that the defendant *is charging prices below a certain measure of its costs.* In the practice of the courts, that measure is the average variable cost of production. Where prices are above average variable cost of production, there is no infringement, even if the accused company is applying different prices to different customers.

4.46 In the view of the European Communities, in many if not most cases of international price discrimination, prices of imported products are still above average variable costs of production. In such cases, importers may have to face legal proceedings under the 1916 Act for price practices above average variable cost while domestic producers would not be at risk under the Robinson-Patman Act for sales

---

401 The European Communities refers to *Brooke Group, Op. Cit.*

402 The European Communities refers to *Matsushita Electrical, Op. Cit.*

made at similar level.[403] The fact that sanctions can be imposed and damages awarded in situations involving foreign goods sold at a price which bears a given relation to cost of production, while the same price having the same relation to cost of production charged by domestic producers cannot be challenged under the Robinson-Patman Act, amounts to less favourable treatment of imported products prohibited under Article III:4 of the GATT 1994.

4.47 What matters, in the opinion of the European Communities, is that the test of the 1916 Act concerns differences in sales prices alone, whereas the Robinson-Patman Act after the Supreme Court's *Brooke Group* decision requires not only differences in price but also a price below costs. Whatever the "appropriate measure of costs" is, it is clear that there can be situations where a price in the United States is "substantially" below the sales price applied in the domestic market but is not below costs. In such a situation, the 1916 Act could apply, whereas in the comparable situation involving domestic products, the Robinson-Patman Act could not.

4.48 Finally, the European Communities contests the importance given by the United States to the *Helmac II* case, essentially because the same Court, in the same case, a few months earlier, explicitly held that the other element of anti-trust predation - reasonable prospect of recoupment of losses from sales below cost - did not have to be proved in claims under the 1916 Act.[404]

4.49 The European Communities submits that another reason why dumping is easier to establish under the 1916 Act than under the Robinson-Patman Act is that under the former a simple offer to sell foreign goods is sufficient to entitle a request for treble damages, while cases against price discrimination under the Robinson-Patman Act require actual sales. As observed in the *Helmac I* case:

> "It is obvious that a sale must take place to state a Robinson-Patman Act claim. It is a requirement born from the type of conduct that is being prohibited by the statute, one supplier giving a competitive edge to one competitor by charging a lower price. There is no way the favoured purchaser could gain the competitive advantage until that sale from the supplier to the favoured purchaser takes place. Without the sale the favoured purchaser has received no cost benefit, and no competitive advantage. This explains the sales requirement of a claim under Robinson-Patman [sic] claim."[405]

4.50 The European Communities considers that for the reasons set out above, by maintaining the 1916 Act in effect, the United States accords "less favourable treatment" to foreign products than to its own domestic products.

[403] According to the European Communities, the *Geneva Steel, Op. Cit.*, and the *Wheeling-Pittsburgh, Op. Cit.*, proceedings are two concrete examples.

[404] The European Communities refers to *Helmac I, Op. Cit.*

[405] *Helmac I, Op. Cit.*, p. 15.

3. *The Distinction between Discretionary and Mandatory Legislation and its Relevance to the Present Case*

(a) Claims against Domestic Legislation as Such

4.51 The European Communities takes issue with the US contention that in order to challenge a Member's legislation as such as WTO-inconsistent there would be a general requirement to show that legislation is mandatory. This is refuted by the text of WTO provisions as well as by GATT 1947 and WTO practice. Both elements have now made abundantly clear that legislation can be declared *per se* inconsistent with WTO provisions, and the European Communities submits that this in particular applies to the WTO obligations at issue in the instant dispute. For example, several panel reports under GATT 1947 have found domestic legislation to run afoul of Article III of the GATT 1947 even before it had actually been applied, and therefore before any actual discrimination had taken place.[406] Additionally, that domestic measures may be challenged as such has also been confirmed by WTO practice.

4.52 The European Communities submits that the fact that laws as such may be inconsistent with WTO provisions is further confirmed by Article XVI:4 of the WTO Agreement.[407] The types of provisions referred to in Article XVI:4, and certainly laws, like the one at issue in the present dispute, are by definition measures of general application. Therefore, Article XVI:4 recognizes in general terms that laws must *per se* conform with WTO provisions - and may thus be challenged as *per se* inconsistent if Members fail to bring them into conformity. In doing so, Article XVI:4 draws no distinction between mandatory or "non-mandatory" and "discretionary" laws.

4.53 The European Communities argues that in the present case the possibility to challenge the 1916 Act regardless of its concrete applications also results from the very nature of the WTO obligations on which Japan's claims are based. As regards the WTO provisions on dumping, the European Communities has already pointed out that they constitute a complete regulation of whether and under which conditions action against dumping can be taken. Within that regulation, in view of the dangerous impact on the market of a practice that the WTO drafters have, under certain conditions, considered objectionable and therefore "to be condemned", the same drafters have also authorized individual Members to react and *unilaterally* sanction a

---

[406] The European Communities refers to, for example, the Panel Reports on *United States - Superfund, Op. Cit.*, para. 5.2.2, where the legislation imposing the tax discrimination only had to be applied by the tax authorities at the end of the year after the panel examined the matter, and *United States - Measures Affecting Alcoholic and Malt Beverages*, adopted on 19 June 1992, BISD 39S/206, paras. 5.39, 5.57, 5.60 and 5.66, where the legislation imposing the discrimination was, for example, not being enforced by the authorities. The European Communities also refers to Panel Reports on *EEC - Parts and Components, Op. Cit.*, paras. 5.25-5.26, and *Thailand - Cigarettes, Op. Cit.*, para. 84, and *United States - Tobacco, Op. Cit.*, para. 118.

[407] The European Communities refers to the text of Article XVI:4 of the WTO Agreement. The text reads as follows:

> "Each Member shall ensure the conformity of its *laws*, regulations and administrative procedures with its obligations as provided in the annexed Agreements." (emphasis added by the European Communities)

violation of those provisions.[408] The WTO Members have however committed not to take anti-dumping action outside the conditions laid down in the relevant WTO provisions, including those relied upon in the present dispute. Approving or maintaining legislation which is *per se* contrary to this commitment effectively removes the guarantee, offered by the United States when accepting Article VI of the GATT 1994 and the Anti-Dumping Agreement, that it will not take anti-dumping action outside the conditions laid down in such rules.[409]

4.54 The European Communities further contends that the US approach according to which "Japan must demonstrate that there is no interpretation of the 1916 Act that would be WTO-consistent" and "the Panel must determine whether the 1916 Act is susceptible to an interpretation which is WTO-consistent" is fundamentally flawed. Even if it is possible to imagine an interpretation of the 1916 Act which is WTO-consistent (*quod non*), the European Communities contests that this disposes of the matter. The United States has not sought to argue that the interpretation given to the 1916 Act in *Geneva Steel* and *Wheeling-Pittsburgh* is consistent with the WTO, only that these are not "final decisions" and that other courts have expressed different views. For the European Communities, the mere fact that the 1916 Act *is susceptible to* an interpretation that is contrary to Article VI of the GATT 1994 would be sufficient to establish its inconsistency with that provision because it removes the commitment not to take anti-dumping action outside the conditions laid down in WTO provisions.

4.55 In the view of the European Communities, this is in particular the case of measures such as the 1916 Act, which have enormous harassment value in the hands of domestic producers who wish to intimidate importers. The *Geneva Steel* and *Wheeling-Pittsburgh* cases illustrate this eloquently. These cases which will take years, if not decades, to complete present importers with the prospect of enormous but uncertain potential liability - treble damages plus attorney fees. In these cases, the more unclear the law is, that is the more interpretations it is susceptible of, the more disruptive it is for importers. Indeed, as Japan has explained, many importers prefer to settle than go through this process. But they pay a high price.[410]

---

[408] The European Communities notes that this, however, constitutes a departure from the general rule that violations of the WTO agreements, and therefore their sanctioning, should not be done unilaterally. In this regard, the European Communities refers to Article 23.1 of the DSU which states the following:

"When Members seek the *redress of a violation of obligations* or other nullification or impairment of benefits under the covered agreements or an impediment to the attainment of any objective of the covered agreements, they shall *have recourse to* and abide by, the rules and procedures of this Understanding." (emphasis added by the European Communities).

[409] The European Communities notes, with regard to Article III of the GATT 1994, that the reason why a law as such can result in a violation have already been sufficiently clarified in GATT 1947 and WTO practice. The European Communities recalls that Article III protects competitive opportunities and the expectations not to be put at a disadvantage on the market.

[410] On the same issue, the European Communities queries what would be the position if a WTO Member were to adopt an anti-dumping law that was so outrageous or unclear that no importer or exporter ever bothered to defend itself but stopped selling its products immediately it was threatened with action. According to the United States, no WTO action could be taken unless a duty is actually imposed (which does not happen) or another Member can prove that there is no possible way of

4.56 In view of the foregoing the European Communities submits that the 1916 Act, as such, precludes compliance with WTO anti-dumping provisions relied upon in the present dispute as well as with Article III:4 of the GATT 1994.

(b) The Nature of the 1916 Act

4.57 The European Communities considers that the 1916 Act is mandatory legislation within the meaning of GATT 1947 and WTO practice. According to that practice, mandatory measures are those which, under national law, require the executive authority to impose a measure. For example, in the *United States - Non-Rubber Footwear* case:

> "[...] the Panel examined whether this legislation as such is consistent with Article I:1. The Panel noted that the CONTRACTING PARTIES had decided in previous cases that legislation mandatorily *requiring the executive authority to impose a measure* inconsistent with the General Agreement was inconsistent with that Agreement *as such*, whether or not an occasion for the actual application of the legislation had arisen. The Panel recalled that the backdating provisions of the two Acts *are mandatory legislation*, that is *they impose on the executive authority requirements which cannot be modified by executive action*, and it therefore found that these provisions *as such*, *not merely their application in concrete cases*, have to be consistent with Article I:1."[411]

4.58 For the European Communities, it is apparent from the foregoing that the definition of mandatory legislation in WTO practice does not correspond to the really extraordinary one which the United States has repeatedly put forward in its submissions. In other words, not only it is not necessary for legislation to be "mandatory" to be challenged *per se* as inconsistent with WTO obligations. The "mandatory legislation" class is also not limited to laws "susceptible to no interpretation which would be consistent with U.S. WTO obligations".

4.59 In the view of the European Communities, the United States appears to be invoking (and confusing) two different issues. The first is the *discretion in the application of legislation* and the second is the pretended *ambiguity in the interpretation of the legislation*. On the second issue, the simple truth is that not even one of the possible interpretations referred to by the United States is curing the WTO incompatibility of the 1916 Act. On the first issue the United States relies in particular on the case *EEC - Parts and Components*. However, that case concerned authorising provisions in respect of which there was discretion for the administration to take or not to take measures. Whether these provisions produced any effects in practice depended on the discretion of an administration. There is no such discretion for the administration in the case of the 1916 Act.

---

interpreting or applying the law that would be compatible with WTO provisions. In the view of the European Communities, not only is this result unacceptable as such, it is also completely contrary to Article XVI:4 of the WTO Agreement.

[411] *United States - Non-Rubber Footwear*, *Op. Cit.*, para. 6.13 (emphasis added and footnote omitted by the European Communities).

4.60 The European Communities contends that the reasons why the 1916 Act is mandatory legislation are manifold. A first reason is that the 1916 Act is simply not applied by the US executive authorities. Its administration is conferred to the judiciary. It is the courts, and only the courts that can take measures under the law at issue in the present dispute. Additionally, the 1916 Act does not "impose on the executive authority requirements", and in any event its requirements "cannot be modified by executive action".

4.61 According to the European Communities, courts by definition are charged with interpreting legislation, not with exercising discretion in respect of legislation. Their mission is to tell what the law is and in doing so they are subjected to the law and to the law only. Moreover, if it is true, as the United States submits, that the actual meaning of the 1916 Act depends on courts' interpretation of its provisions, it is even clearer that the government has no discretion at all to influence courts' decisions nor can it modify the 1916 Act's legal requirements. In other words, even if courts could apply the 1916 Act consistently with WTO obligations, *quod non*, the US government can do nothing to force recalcitrant courts to do so when they do not. This further confirms that the 1916 Act is "mandatory".

4.62 The European Communities further submits that a court does not have discretion to dismiss a well-founded case under the 1916 Act. This results from the language of the 1916 Act and applies to any claim brought under the 1916 Act. The type of remedy which is requested has no bearing on this. For example, in respect of criminal liability, the 1916 Act states:

> "Any person who violates or combines or conspires with any other person to violate this section is guilty of a misdemeanour, and, *on conviction thereof*, *shall* be *punished* by a fine not exceeding $5,000, or imprisonment not exceeding one year, or both, in the discretion of the court."[412]

The European Communities considers therefore that it is mandatory for courts to take action against dumping under the 1916 Act once a case has been properly established.

4.63 The European Communities notes that, likewise, in respect of civil liability, the 1916 Act states:

> "Any person injured in his business or property by reason of any violation of, or combination or conspiracy to violate, this section, may sue therefor in the district court of the United States for the district in which the defendant resides or is found or has an agent, without respect to the amount in controversy, and *shall recover threefold the damages* sustained, and the cost of the suit, including a reasonable attorney's fee."[413]

For the European Communities, therefore, a court does not have discretion not to award treble damages that had been properly established.

---

[412] Emphasis added by the European Communities.
[413] Emphasis added by the European Communities.

4.64 The European Communities considers that, as a result, both the civil and criminal provisions of the 1916 Act create legal effects and in neither case does this depend on the administration taking some discretionary action. These legal effects are contrary to the provisions invoked by the European Communities in the present case. In both cases courts are required to take measures.

4.65 The European Communities submits that, contrary to what the United States pretends, there is no basis even under the old GATT 1947 to defend legislation which is on its face GATT-inconsistent on the ground that courts might one day interpret it in a GATT-consistent manner. The only GATT 1947 case in which there is any reference to *interpretation* is *United States - Tobacco* which the United States claims is particularly pertinent to the present dispute.

4.66 According to the European Communities, the *United States - Tobacco* case involved a situation in which domestic legislation was *incomplete.*[414] There was a requirement to promulgate fees for the inspection of imported tobacco at a level "comparable" to that for domestic tobacco but at the same time power to adjust the level of fees for the inspection of domestic tobacco. The Panel therefore understandably held that there was no basis to hold that the administration in fixing the level of fees for imported tobacco would do so at a level inconsistent with Article VIII:1(a) of the GATT 1947 - in other words, that at such stage there was no mandatory legislation inconsistent with the GATT 1947. In the present case, there is of course no power for the US administration to complete or amend the 1916 Act, in particular so as to make it compatible with the WTO. All the requirements are already laid down in the 1916 Act.

(c) The Content of the Obligation Laid Down in Article XVI:4 of the WTO Agreement

4.67 The European Communities submits that Article XVI:4 of the WTO Agreement lays down a new and additional obligation in the framework of the multilateral trading system. It imposes a positive obligation to ensure the conformity of a Member's domestic laws, regulations and administrative procedures with its WTO obligations. As a result of this obligation, in cases where pre-existing domestic legislation may be inconsistent with new WTO obligations, including those arising under Article VI of the GATT 1994, and Articles 1, 2.1, 2.2, 3, 4 and 5.5 of the Anti-Dumping Agreement, a Member was required to amend its domestic legislation so as to avoid any conflict as from 1 January 1995.

4.68 The European Communities notes that the new principle governing the relationship between domestic laws, regulations and administrative procedures that is embodied in Article XVI:4 of the WTO Agreement is a fundamental one.[415] Because

[414] The European Communities refers to *United States - Tobacco*, paras. 114-118.

[415] The European Communities refers to the Report of the Arbitrator on *Japan - Taxes on Alcoholic Beverages*, Arbitration under Article 21(3)(c) of the DSU, 14 February 1997, WT/DS11/13, para. 9, where it is stated at para. 9 that "[a]s a general and fundamental obligation imposed on all WTO Members, Article XVI:4 of the *Marrakesh Agreement Establishing the World Trade Organization* (the "*WTO Agreement*") requires that each Member shall ensure the conformity of its laws, regulations and administrative procedures with its obligations as provided in the *WTO Agreement*."

it is laid down in the basic agreement of the system, it covers the whole set of the annexed agreements, whether or not they may contain specific expressions of the same principle. Furthermore, by virtue of Article XVI:3 it is a superior rule to provisions in the annexed agreements.

4.69 In the view of the European Communities, Article XVI:4 applies over and above similar obligations under general public international law as enshrined in Article 26 and 27 of the Vienna Convention on the Law of Treaties. The Vienna Convention on the Law of Treaties codifies the customary principle of good faith implementation of international treaty obligations (Article 26) and spells out a negative obligation, i.e. to refrain from invoking domestic law in order to justify any departure from an international obligation undertaken by a State (Article 27). The obligation to respect WTO rules thus results directly from the presence of those rules in the Agreement and its annexes and Article XVI:4 of the WTO Agreement would be reduced to redundancy if interpreted as not containing an additional and different obligation. The European Communities further contends that Article XVI:4 of the WTO Agreement also goes beyond the elimination of the "grandfather clause" of the Protocol of Provisional Application (PPA), since this is effected in the introductory text of the GATT 1994.

4.70 For the European Communities, Article XVI:4 of the WTO Agreement is not simply an obligation to avoid violating the WTO agreements. It is also an obligation to take positive action to ensure that nothing in the "laws, regulations and administrative procedures" is not in conformity with the WTO agreements, that is nothing in them contains conditions or criteria or powers to take action which conflict with those agreements.[416]

4.71 According to the European Communities, this has already been recognized by the Appellate Body in the *India patent* case. In that case both the Panel and the Appellate Body upheld an US claim that domestic law can be inconsistent with WTO provisions not merely because it mandates WTO-inconsistent actions, but also because it fails to provide "a sound legal basis"[417] for the administrative procedures (or any other executive action) required to implement WTO obligations. The underlying rationale was that in the absence of a sound legal basis for mailbox patent applications in domestic law, the basic objective of WTO law, namely to create predictable conditions of competition, could not be achieved.

4.72 For the European Communities, it is clear that the 1916 Act also does not provide such "sound legal basis" for implementation of Article VI of the GATT 1994 and the Anti-Dumping Agreement. Its wording conflicts with Article VI of the GATT 1994 and the Anti-Dumping Agreement in the ways that the European Communities has explained. The United States seeks to deflect attention from this obvious fact by arguing that certain courts have suggested that the 1916 Act may have some characteristics of anti-trust legislation. However, this kind of categorisation is

---

[416] The European Communities again refers to the text of Article XVI:4 which reads:
"Each Member *shall ensure the conformity* of its laws, regulations and administrative procedures with its obligations as provided in the annexed Agreements." (emphasis added by the European Communities)

[417] The European Communities refers to Appellate Body Report, *India - Patents*, *supra*, footnote 55, para 58.

irrelevant because it does not address - let alone solve - the basic issue in the present dispute: whether the price discrimination practice described in the 1916 Act is also covered by WTO rules on dumping and whether the discipline of that practice laid down in the 1916 Act is consistent with WTO obligations.

4.73 The European Communities considers that the above-mentioned case law, even taken together with the extrapolations thereof which the United States seeks to make and suggest may be adopted in the future, are a long way from "ensuring conformity" with Article VI of the GATT 1994 and the Anti-Dumping Agreement. On the contrary, by granting remedies which are not allowed by WTO anti-dumping rules and under conditions which are not those established in WTO anti-dumping rules, that case law is in itself a violation of US obligations.

4.74 The European Communities further contends that the two most recent decisions of US courts[418] actually interpret and allow the 1916 Act to be applied in a way which even the United States implicitly accepts would violate those provisions (since its only defence of them is to suggest that they do not represent the prevailing weight of US judicial interpretation). These decisions constitute, for the time being, the final expression of the judicial authority in the cases in which they have been pronounced. Up until their reversal by a contrary decision, they stand.

4.75 The European Communities notes that the cases that the United States portrays as prevailing weight of US judicial interpretation are witnesses of the legal insecurity and unpredictability resulting from the 1916 Act. On the contrary, in these latter decisions one is not even any longer in the realm of lack of security and predictability for the respect of WTO obligations. One has entered the realm of secure and predictable violations of those obligations.

4.76 The European Communities argues that Article XVI:4 of the WTO Agreement makes clear that the United States has an obligation to ensure that such conflicts cannot arise by amending the 1916 Act and intervening to correct interpretations which it considers to be erroneous and in conflict with WTO obligations. The United States has taken no steps to fulfil its obligation under Article XVI:4. It has not amended the 1916 Act, it has not intervened in the cases referred to to ensure that the 1916 Act is not applied in a manner contrary to the United States' WTO obligations. It has not even said that it disagrees with the decisions adopted by its courts in these two cases. Its very defence is to deny that there is any step to take.

4.77 For the European Communities, this is even more evident since the 1916 Act is definitely a mandatory piece of legislation within the meaning of GATT 1947 and WTO practice. But even aside from this, Article XVI:4 confirms what was already made clear by GATT 1947 panel practice, i.e. that a Member's legislation may breach GATT 1947/WTO obligations independent of concrete applications (this is precisely why Article XVI:4 requires the elimination of inconsistencies which are already on Members' statute books). Article XVI:4 provides this confirmation on a general basis. It draws no distinction between mandatory and discretionary legislation. It makes no exception for discretionary legislation. It is not limited to final judgments.

---

[418] The European Communities refers to *Geneva Steel, Op. Cit.*; *Wheeling-Pittsburgh, Op. Cit.*

4. *Good Faith Application of Treaty Obligations*

4.78 The European Communities first of all recalls that the fundamental rule of treaty interpretation in Article 31 of the Vienna Convention on the Law of Treaties starts off by providing that "[a] treaty shall be interpreted in good faith [...]".

4.79 Second, the European Communities notes that Article VI of the GATT 1994 is not a prohibition in the same way as most other GATT 1994 provisions, such as Article III or Article XI or even Article I. Article VI acknowledges the existence of a particular problem in international trade and then proceeds to provide the solution. It regulates what may be done about it by defining the conditions that need to be fulfilled for the application of remedial measures, such as the existence of injury and authorising the remedial measures which can be taken to deal with dumping.

4.80 The European Communities asserts that, as a consequence, the rationale for the mandatory/discretionary distinction, assuming it still to be valid, does not apply to regulatory measures as opposed to prohibitions. When a provision regulates behaviour, it is not a good faith interpretation of the text to claim that if a Member's measure deviates from it in one important respect, or allows its authorities to take alternative measures on a discretionary basis, then the other disciplines automatically do not apply. Yet this is exactly what the United States is claiming.

4.81 For this reason the European Communities considers that both the US claim that the 1916 Act escapes the disciplines of Article VI and the Anti-Dumping Agreement because it specifies a remedy other than duties, as well as the US claim that it escapes WTO inconsistency because it is in some sense discretionary, must fail.

4.82 The European Communities also argues that when a text regulates a certain problem, there is a legitimate expectation by a party that other parties will not reserve for themselves the option of taking non-infringing measures. The US approach to the interpretation of its obligations under Article VI of the GATT 1994 and the Anti-Dumping Agreement is not in good faith and it is therefore wrong.

5. *Conclusion*

4.83 For the reasons set out above, the European Communities supports Japan's claims that the 1916 Act is neither consistent with nor justified by any of the WTO provisions mentioned above.

B. *India*

1. *Violation of Article VI of the GATT 1994 and the Anti-Dumping Agreement*

4.84 According to **India**, Article VI of the GATT 1994 establishes the only GATT-compatible means of dealing with dumping. Three steps are envisaged in this Article. Firstly, what constitutes dumping; secondly, what conditions must be fulfilled for the application of remedial measures; and thirdly, what steps a Member can take once dumping has been established. As regards this third step, Article VI:2 provides for the levying of anti-dumping duties. It is therefore clear that under Article VI the concerned Members can levy anti-dumping duties provided that the material injury to the domestic industry is established and the procedures as laid down are followed. Hence Article VI clearly establishes that the application of anti-dumping duties shall be the sole and only means authorized by the GATT 1994 to deal with the problem of dumped imports.

4.85 India notes, however, that, under the 1916 Act, the United States can apply measures other than anti-dumping duties - for example, civil liability for damages and/or criminal penalties.[419] Thus the very purpose and intent of Article VI and that of the Anti-Dumping Agreement is thwarted. The remedial measures provided for by the 1916 Act are treble damages and/or criminal penalties, including fines and/or imprisonment. These remedies are not duties and do not therefore fall into the type of measures allowed under the multilateral anti-dumping rules to counter dumping practices.

4.86 India recalls that the United States has tried to justify these 1916 Act remedies under footnote 24 of Article 18.1 of the Anti-Dumping Agreement. The footnote provides: "This is not intended to preclude action under other relevant provisions of GATT 1994, as appropriate." But the United States has failed to cite any GATT 1994 provision under which the 1916 Act remedies could be justified. It has merely stated that the 1916 Act "measure is *a fortiori* consistent with the GATT 1994", if it is not regulated by the GATT 1994. It may be noted that a footnote cannot override the main provision. The provision in this case, Article 18.1, is so worded that the Members cannot take any "specific action [...] except in accordance with the provisions of GATT 1994 [...]". Thus the US argument that the GATT 1994 does not regulate the measure is not correct. The GATT 1994 in fact prohibits any measure (including the measures under the 1916 Act) other than the anti-dumping duty, unless it is in accordance with the GATT 1994 and the Anti-Dumping Agreement.

4.87 India notes that the United States has also argued that the use of the phrase "may" levy an anti-dumping duty in Article VI:2 does not preclude the use of other remedies for dumping. This argument is not valid. Article VI of the GATT 1994 was specifically incorporated to address the problems of dumping and provides for the levying of anti-dumping duties as the sole remedy. It would be totally unacceptable if Members could not only impose anti-dumping duties, but also such other civil or criminal penalties as are prescribed by the 1916 Act. The word "may" in Article VI:2 endows the Members with discretionary authority whether or not to invoke the remedial action in case of dumping. However, if the Member concerned decides to take action, it must be by way of imposing anti-dumping duties only. Clearly therefore, the 1916 Act violates Article VI:2 of the GATT 1994 as well as Article 18.1 of the Anti-Dumping Agreement.

4.88 India does not agree with the US contention that the application of measures other than anti- dumping duties is justified on the grounds that the conduct to which the 1916 Act applies is defined in a manner which, while incorporating the essential elements of dumping, differs by the addition of one or more conditions. It is India's view that as long as the 1916 Act provides remedial action for dumping of products into the domestic market, it must be in conformity with the provisions of Article VI

---

[419] India notes, in this regard, that the 1916 Act can be invoked and has been invoked over the years by complaining parties desirous of using the judicial remedies offered by it as an alternative and/or supplement to the Antidumping Act of 1921 and later US anti-dumping legislation.

of the GATT 1994 and the Anti-Dumping Agreement. Since this is not the case, the 1916 Act is inconsistent with the principles and objectives laid down in Article VI of the GATT 1994 and the Anti-Dumping Agreement.

4.89 India is also of the view that the 1916 Act is inconsistent with Article VI:1 of the GATT 1994 and Article 3 of the Anti-Dumping Agreement because it does not require there to be actual injury, let alone material injury, to the domestic industry as a precondition for taking action. It only stipulates that action under the 1916 Act can be taken as long as there is intent to injure the domestic industry. Moreover, the absence of administrative procedures within the 1916 Act means that no investigation conforming to the requirements of the Anti-Dumping Agreement needs to be carried out when taking action under the 1916 Act. Thus, judicial decisions under the 1916 Act can be made without the procedural safeguards otherwise provided for in the Anti-Dumping Agreement. Finally, it is India's view that the 1916 Act fails to respect a number of procedural and due process requirements as set forth in the Anti-Dumping Agreement, *inter alia* including (i) the requirements that the competent authority verify the information given in any complaint before initiating an investigation; (ii) the requirement that notice be given to the government of the exporting country before such an investigation is started; (iii) the requirement that only a complaint supported by a minimum percentage of the domestic industry will be entertained; (iv) the possibility for the governments of exporting countries to make comments on the proposed findings; and (v) the requirement that the measures not be restrictive. The 1916 Act is therefore clearly violative of the procedural provisions of the Anti-Dumping Agreement.

4.90 As regards the alternative US argument that the 1916 Act is not an anti-dumping law at all, but is an anti-trust law, India does not agree. As accepted by the United States, the 1916 Act clearly targets products which are being sold within the United States allegedly at a price substantially less than the actual market value or wholesale price of the products. This is entirely in consonance with the definition of dumping given in Article VI, according to which dumping is said to occur when "products of one country are introduced into the commerce of another country at less than the normal value of products". Clearly therefore, the 1916 Act is a law which deals with "dumping" and as a result should be subject to the disciplines of Article VI of the GATT 1994 and of the Anti-Dumping Agreement.

4.91 India further argues that the 1916 Act cannot escape the discipline of Article VI simply because it requires the prohibited conduct to be "common and systematic". Article VI applies whether the dumping is limited in occurrence or sporadic, and whether the dumping is frequent or systemic. Once it is established that the concerned rule or law, in this case the 1916 Act, is subject to Article VI, then the only remedy permitted is the imposition of anti-dumping duties subject to a finding of dumping in accordance with the definition of Article VI and the existence of injury, or threat of injury, to the domestic industry. Thus, any anti-dumping law which goes beyond providing relief in the form of anti-dumping duties, such as the 1916 Act, is inconsistent with the GATT 1994.

4.92 Finally, India recalls the US argument that the US courts' interpretation of the 1916 Act is dispositive as a factual matter of the nature of 1916 Act and that the

Panel cannot depend upon its own interpretation. In this connection, India would simply like to invite the attention of the Panel to the Appellate Body's decision in *India - Patents*.[420]

2. *Violation of Article III of the GATT 1994*

4.93 Regarding the requirement of national treatment under Article III of the GATT 1994, India notes that the United States has argued that the 1916 Act is the equivalent of the Robinson-Patman Act. India considers that these two Acts establish two different regimes for pursuing claims against imported products and domestic products, respectively. The United States has, however, argued that treatment under the 1916 Act in certain aspects is more favourable than under the Robinson-Patman Act. But a comparison of these Acts and their operation reveals the following differences:

(a) Bringing a 1916 Act claim is easier than bringing a Robinson-Patman Act claim because of the differing pleading requirement;

(b) establishing and winning a 1916 Act claim is easier than establishing a Robinson-Patman Act claim because the standards for obtaining relief under the 1916 Act are much lower than those for obtaining relief under the Robinson-Patman Act;

(c) the conduct subject to penalties under the 1916 Act exceeds the conduct under the Robinson-Patman Act; and

(d) because a plaintiff can more easily prove a violation of the 1916 Act than of the Robinson-Patman Act, a domestic competitor can more easily impose significant litigation costs and business burdens on foreign producers than on domestic competitors.

4.94 India further argues that, even if the US argument that the 1916 Act is more favourable in certain respects is true, it is not justified. As ruled by the GATT 1947 Panel in *United States - Section 337*, a more favourable treatment of imported products in some areas cannot be justified by less favourable treatment in other areas. Moreover, whether any less favourable treatment has actually been suffered in a particular instance is irrelevant. In *EEC - Oilseeds*, the GATT 1947 panel held that a regulation which does not necessarily discriminate against imported products, but is capable of doing so, is violative of Article III of the GATT 1994. The comparison of the 1916 Act and the Robinson-Patman Act shows that imported products could get less favourable treatment under the regime of the 1916 Act than domestic products. Therefore, the 1916 Act should be held to be violative of Article III of the GATT 1994.

3. *Conclusion*

4.95 In conclusion, it is India's view that the 1916 Act is a statute providing relief against alleged dumping and that it does not conform to the provisions of Articles III and VI of the GATT 1994 and those of the Agreement on Anti-Dumping. The 1916

[420] Appellate Body Report , *India - Patents*, *supra*, footnote 55, paras. 65-66.

Act thereby nullifies and impairs the benefits accruing to the United States' trading partners under the above Agreements. India therefore urges the Panel to find the 1916 Act to be violative of these provisions and requests the Panel to recommend that the United States bring its domestic law in conformity with its obligations under the GATT 1994.

V. INTERIM REVIEW[421]

A. *Introduction*

5.1 The interim report of the Panel was issued to the parties on 28 February 2000, in application of Article 15.2 of the DSU. On 6 March 2000, Japan and the United States submitted written requests to the Panel to review some aspects of the interim report. Neither Japan nor the United States requested that the Panel hold a further meeting with the parties.

5.2 As a preliminary remark, the Panel notes that the parties did not comment on the factual assessments made in its interim report, with the exception of the factual error in footnote 552 to paragraph 6.192, which related to when in the proceedings the United States raised a particular argument.[422]

B. *Comments by Japan*

5.3 Japan requested that we review paragraphs 6.52, 6.76, 6.103 and 6.170 of the interim report.

5.4 Regarding paragraph 6.52, Japan is critical of the last sentence of the paragraph. While we agree with Japan that the starting-point of our analysis was the text of the 1916 Act, we acknowledge that court interpretations could substantially elaborate on such a concise text as that of the 1916 Act, as was apparently the case with the Sherman Act, for instance. We therefore used the term "US law" as meaning US law in general, not the 1916 Act. We also used the term "select" in order to confirm that we would not interpret US law in general or judgements of US courts in particular. We would only compare the court decisions with what we perceived to be the current status of US law in that field. We therefore did not find it appropriate to modify the last sentence of paragraph 6.52.

---

[421] According to Article 15.3 of the Understanding on Rules and Procedures Governing the Settlement of Disputes (hereinafter "DSU"), "the findings of the final report shall include a discussion of the arguments made at the interim review stage". The following section entitled "Interim Review" is therefore part of the findings of our report.

[422] The Panel is of the view that if it had misunderstood or misrepresented some factual aspects of the case in its findings, the parties would need the opportunity of the interim review stage to make the appropriate corrections or clarifications because, contrary to errors of law, errors of fact normally cannot be corrected on appeal. Parties should seize this last opportunity to correct factual assessments by the Panel because, otherwise, the Panel could needlessly be exposed to the risk of being accused of not having made an objective assessment of the facts. It could be argued that for a party not to inform the Panel of a factual error in its findings may be contrary to the obligation laid down in Article 3.10 of the DSU, which provides *inter alia* that "all Members will engage in these [DSU] procedures in good faith in an effort to resolve the dispute".

5.5 We clarified paragraph 6.76 to address Japan's concern. However, we did not consider it necessary to modify paragraph 6.103 along the line suggested by Japan, since the issue addressed in that paragraph was the interpretation of the 1916 Act by courts, currently or in the future.

5.6 Regarding paragraph 6.170, the Panel did not take position on the issue to which Japan refers. It simply noted that an isolated domestic market has *often* been considered as *one of the reasons* why dumping is possible in the first place. Second, the fact that the issue is very controversial among WTO Members is not as such a reason for removing that statement from a panel report. However, the Panel considered that the statement at issue was not essential for its reasoning. It consequently redrafted the sentence concerned to focus more precisely on its actual purpose.

C. *Comments by the United States*

5.7 The United States commented on the content of paragraph 6.36, footnote 552 to paragraph 6.192, and footnote 599 to paragraph 6.292 of the interim report.

5.8 Regarding paragraph 6.39, we do not read the statement at issue ("both Article 3.2 of the DSU and the practice of the Appellate Body make it clear that we have, whenever appropriate, to develop our approach on the basis of that of international courts in similar circumstances") in the interim report as stating that panels have an *obligation* under the DSU to take other international court's practice into consideration. First, we note that the verb "have to" is qualified by the terms "whenever appropriate" and "on the basis of". Second, we recall that the Appellate Body in its report on *European Communities - Regime for the Importation, Sale and Distribution of Bananas* considered whether certain judgements of the International Court of Justice "establish[ed] a general rule that in all international litigation, a complaining party must have a legal interest in order to bring a case." The Appellate Body determined that the judgements referred to by the parties did not deny the need to consider the question of standing under the dispute settlement provisions of any multilateral treaty, by referring to the terms of that treaty.[423] We assume from that report that if the judgements of the International Court of Justice had established a general rule on demonstration of legal interest, and the terms of the WTO Agreement did not prevent its application to dispute settlement, the Appellate Body would have applied that principle. However, in order to avoid misunderstanding, we clarified the phrase at issue.

5.9 We also modified the factual error relating to the stage at which the United States raised a particular argument in these proceedings.

5.10 Regarding footnote 599 to paragraph 6.292, we agree with the United States that no specific claim was raised by Japan in relation to the settlements reached between parties in the *Wheeling-Pittsburgh* case. The footnote was intended to complement the phrase according to which the 1916 Act "has never led to the imposition of any remedies by courts." The Panel meant to show that it had considered carefully all the potential aspects of the factual situation, including the situation where the

[423] Appellate Body Report, *European Communities - Regime for the Importation, Sale and Distribution of Bananas*, WT/DS27/AB/R, adopted 25 September 1997, DSR 1997:II, 591, para. 133.

court concerned would have formally sanctioned the settlements reached by Wheeling-Pittsburgh Steel Corporation, with the consequence that such settlements might be enforced if necessary by the US authorities, such as courts or the customs or competition authorities. In this respect, the Panel recalls that the responsibility of the Members under international law applies irrespective of the "branch of government" at the origin of the action having international repercussions. Footnote 599 was only intended to clarify that "remedies" in the form of a settlement sanctioned by a court had not been the subject of a claim of Japan. We therefore modified footnote 599 in the final report in order to make our purpose clearer.

VI. FINDINGS

A. *Issues to be Addressed by the Panel*

1. *Facts at the Origin of the Dispute*

6.1 The law, the WTO-consistency of which is contested by Japan, is a United States legislative text enacted under the heading of "Unfair Competition" in Title VIII of the Revenue Act of 1916.[424] It has been known since as the "Antidumping Act of 1916."[425] The 1916 Act, which provides for civil and criminal penalties by US federal courts for a certain form of transnational price discrimination[426] when conducted with specific intent,[427] reads as follows:

[424] Act of 8 September 1916. The Revenue Act can be found at 39 Stat. 756 (1916). Title VIII of the Revenue Act is codified at 15 U.S.C. §§ 71-74.

[425] A number of official documents of the United States government and a number of US court decisions refer to Title VIII of the Revenue Act of 1916 as the "Antidumping Act of 1916". Authors have also called it the"1916 Antidumping Act" or qualified it as an act dealing with certain forms of dumping, irrespective of whether they considered it to be an "anti-dumping" law or an "anti-trust" law. See, e.g., A. Paul Victor. *The Interface of Trade/Competition Law and Policy: An Overview*, 56 Antitrust Law Journal 397, at p. 401; John H. Jackson, *World Trade and the Law of GATT* (1968), at p. 403, footnote 4. However, we note that the word "anti-dumping" does not appear as such in the text of the law. Since the question whether this law is an anti-dumping law within the meaning of Article VI of GATT 1994 is one of the issues that this Panel has to address, we find it more appropriate to refer to it in our discussion as the "1916 Act".

[426] Even though the word "discrimination" may have specific meanings in certain circumstances, it is used throughout the findings as meaning a differentiation (see, e.g., *The New Shorter Oxford English Dictionary* (1993), p. 689). As a result, the term "transnational price discrimination" in these findings refers only to the existence of a difference in price between two markets located in different countries, irrespective of the intent of the exporter behind that price difference or the effects thereof. See also Jacob Viner's definition of "dumping" as a "price-discrimination between national markets" (*Dumping, A Problem in International Trade* (1923), p. 3).

[427] The 1916 Act was part of a legislative effort of the United States to address a number of practices perceived at that time as "unfair competition". A number of major anti-trust and trade laws of the United States still applicable today were adopted by the Congress of the United States (hereinafter the "US Congress") between the end of the 19th century and the 1930's. The Sherman Act (15 U.S.C. 1-7) dates back to 1890 and the Clayton Act to 1914 (15 U.S.C. 12, 13, 14-19, 20, 21, 22-27; 29 U.S.C. 52, 53). Subsequent to the 1916 Act came the 1921 Anti-Dumping Act, the 1930 Tariff Act (which has become since the basis of the current US anti-dumping legislation) and the 1936 Robinson-Patman Act, amending Section 2 of the Clayton Act of 1914.

> "It shall be unlawful for any person importing or assisting in importing any articles from any foreign country into the United States, commonly and systematically to import, sell or cause to be imported or sold such articles within the United States at a price substantially less than the actual market value or wholesale price of such articles, at the time of exportation to the United States, in the principal markets of the country of their production, or of other foreign countries to which they are commonly exported after adding to such market value or wholesale price, freight, duty, and other charges and expenses necessarily incident to the importation and sale thereof in the United States: *Provided*, That such act or acts be done with the intent of destroying or injuring an industry in the United States, or of preventing the establishment of an industry in the United States, or of restraining or monopolizing any part of trade and commerce in such articles in the United States.
>
> Any person who violates or combines or conspires with any other person to violate this section is guilty of a misdemeanour, and, on conviction thereof, shall be punished by a fine not exceeding $5,000, or imprisonment not exceeding one year, or both, in the discretion of the court.
>
> Any person injured in his business or property by reason of any violation of, or combination or conspiracy to violate, this section, may sue therefor in the district court of the United States for the district in which the defendant resides or is found or has an agent, without respect to the amount in controversy, and shall recover threefold the damages sustained, and the cost of the suit, including a reasonable attorney's fee.
>
> The foregoing provisions shall not be construed to deprive the proper State courts of jurisdiction in actions for damages thereunder."

Two significant features of the 1916 Act are that:

(a) it provides for a review of the practices concerned by the judiciary branch of government[428] at the federal level, not by the executive branch of government; and

(b) it provides for two "tracks" of litigation before US federal courts: (i) civil proceedings through which a person may seek to recover damages, and (ii) criminal proceedings whereby the US Department of Justice may seek the imposition of a fine or imprisonment, or both.

---

[428] The terms "judiciary branch of government", "executive branch of government" and "legislative branch of government" are, throughout this report, used within the meaning given to them in US constitutional law.

2. *Issues to be Addressed by the Panel*

(a) Summary of Issues before the Panel

6.2 The understanding of the Panel as to the claims and defences of the parties is, in a summarized form, as follows.[429]

6.3 Japan challenges the 1916 Act as such, not a particular instance of application. It claims that the 1916 Act violates Article III:4, Article XI of the GATT 1994, Article VI:2 of the GATT 1994 and Article 18.1 of the Agreement on Implementation of Article VI of the General Agreement on Tariffs and Trade 1994[430], Article VI of the GATT 1994 and Article 1 of the Anti-Dumping Agreement, Article VI of the GATT 1994 and Article 3 of the Anti-Dumping Agreement, Article VI of the GATT 1994 and Articles 4 and 5 of the Anti-Dumping Agreement, Article VI of the GATT 1994 and Article 9 of the Anti-Dumping Agreement, Article VI of the GATT 1994 and Article 11 of the Anti-Dumping Agreement, Articles 1 and 18.1 of the Anti-Dumping Agreement by failing to comply with Article VI of GATT 1994 and Articles 2, 3, 4, 5, 9 and 11 of the Anti-Dumping Agreement, Article XVI:4 of the Agreement Establishing the World Trade Organization[431] and Article 18.4 of the Anti-Dumping Agreement. Finally, Japan requests that the Panel recommend that the United States repeal the 1916 Act in order to bring its legislation into conformity with US obligations under the WTO Agreement.

6.4 Japan claims that the 1916 Act falls within the scope of Article VI of the GATT 1994 and the Anti-Dumping Agreement because the 1916 Act targets a form of international price discrimination defined as "dumping" in that Article. Japan argues that recent US court decisions support the view that the 1916 Act has been applied as an anti-dumping law. The anti-dumping nature of the 1916 Act has also been recognised by officials of the US executive branch.

6.5 Japan also claims that, by providing for treble damages, fines or imprisonment, the 1916 Act violates Article VI:2 of the GATT 1994 and Article 18.1 of the Anti-Dumping Agreement, which provide that the imposition of duties is the only remedy allowed to counteract dumping under the WTO Agreement.

6.6 Furthermore, Japan claims that the 1916 Act violates a number of requirements of Article VI and the Anti-Dumping Agreement, *inter alia* by not providing for the same elements in terms of comparison for the purpose of establishing the dumping margin, regarding the determination of material injury and with respect to procedural requirements regarding the initiation and conduct of the investigation and the imposition and duration of measures.

---

429 The claims and arguments of the parties are reported in greater detail in sections II and III of this Report.

430 Referred to hereafter as the "Anti-Dumping Agreement".

431 Throughout these findings, the Marrakesh Agreement Establishing the World Trade Organization, including its annexes, will be referred to as the "WTO Agreement". The Marrakesh Agreement Establishing the World Trade Organization, without its annexes, will be referred to as the Agreement Establishing the WTO. In that context, Article XVI:4 of the Marrakesh Agreement Establishing the World Trade Organization will be referred to as "Article XVI:4 of the Agreement Establishing the WTO". The agreements annexed to the Agreement Establishing the WTO will be referred to as the "WTO agreements".

6.7 In addition, Japan claims that the 1916 Act violates Article III:4 of the GATT 1994 to the extent that it provides less favourable treatment to imported goods than is granted to US goods under the Robinson-Patman Act[432] in terms of the difference in (i) pleading requirements, (ii) the use of the intent requirement in the 1916 Act instead of a requirement of "effect" under the Robinson-Patman Act, (iii) cost recoupment requirement, (iv) the statutory defences available under the Robinson-Patman Act and not expressly provided for in the 1916 Act, and (v) the conducts subject to penalties.

6.8 Moreover, Japan claims that the 1916 Act violates Article XI because it establishes impermissible import prohibitions or restrictions other than duties, taxes or other charges.

6.9 Japan finally claims that the United States, because it has failed to conform the 1916 Act with the provisions of the Anti-Dumping Agreement and the provisions of the GATT 1994 referred to above, also violates Article 18.4 of the Anti-Dumping Agreement and Article XVI:4 of the Agreement Establishing the WTO.

6.10 The United States argues that the Panel has no jurisdiction to address the compatibility of the 1916 Act with the Anti-Dumping Agreement since, pursuant to Article 17.4 of that agreement, and as confirmed by the Appellate Body in *Guatemala - Anti-Dumping Investigation Regarding Portland Cement From Mexico*,[433] a panel may consider a violation of the Anti-Dumping Agreement only when one of three specific measures have been adopted. The Panel cannot review the compatibility of the 1916 Act as such with the Anti-Dumping Agreement. Moreover, given the relationship between the Anti-Dumping Agreement and Article VI of the GATT 1994, the Panel cannot make a finding under Article VI separately from the Anti-Dumping Agreement.[434]

6.11 The United States also argues that the 1916 Act, to the extent that the US Department of Justice enjoys discretion to file - or not - a suit with a federal court, is a "non-mandatory" law within the meaning given to that concept by GATT 1947 panels and by panels and the Appellate Body under the WTO. The United States further argues that the 1916 Act is susceptible to, and indeed has been interpreted in, a WTO-compatible manner. In application of past GATT 1947 panel practice, this also makes the 1916 Act "non-mandatory" legislation.

6.12 The United States also argues that the 1916 Act is an anti-trust statute. It is not subject to the disciplines of Article VI of the GATT 1994 since it does not address injurious dumping within the meaning of Article VI but a specific form of international price discrimination with predatory intent. The United States considers that Article VI applies only to laws purporting to impose border measures in the form of anti-dumping duties against dumping causing injury. Members are free to address dumping, including injurious dumping, through other WTO-consistent means. The 1916 Act, because it imposes damages on importers rather than border measures in

[432] See footnote 279 above.

[433] Appellate Body Report, WT/DS60/AB/R, adopted 25 November 1998, DSR 1998:IX, 3767, hereinafter "*Guatemala - Cement*".

[434] The United States refers to the Panel and Appellate Body Reports on *Brazil - Measures Affecting Desiccated Coconut*, WT/DS22/R, DSR 1997:I, 167, WT/DS22AB/R, DSR 1997:I, 189, adopted on 20 March 1997, hereinafter "*Brazil - Desiccated Coconut*".

the form of anti-dumping duties, is an internal measure subject to Article III, but not to Article VI. On that basis, the Panel should find that the 1916 Act does not violate Article VI of the GATT 1994. If the Panel were to follow Japan's arguments on Article VI and the Anti-Dumping Agreement, all anti-trust laws of Members, including Japan's legislation and the EC competition rules (under Article 82 of the Treaty of Amsterdam), would be subject to Article VI of the GATT 1994 to the extent that they rely on transnational price discrimination.

6.13 The United States also contends that Article VI:2 of the GATT 1994 and the Anti-Dumping Agreement do not provide that duties are the sole remedy allowed to counteract dumping. A Member is bound to respect the provisions of the Anti-Dumping Agreement only to the extent it intends to impose duties.

6.14 Finally, the United States claims that the 1916 Act does not violate Article III:4 of the GATT 1994. Compared with the Robinson-Patman Act, the 1916 Act actually grants more favourable treatment to imported goods than to US goods. The 1916 Act requires an *intent* to destroy or injure an industry in the United States, or to prevent the establishment of an industry in the United States, or to restrain or monopolize any part of trade and commerce in the articles concerned in the United States. According to the United States, this requirement that an "intent" be demonstrated by the plaintiff has been considered to be the main reason for the very rare and generally unsuccessful application of the 1916 Act compared with the Robinson-Patman Act. Apart from this, the procedural requirements under the two statutes are either similar or more favourable to defendants under the 1916 Act.

6.15 The United States also states that the 1916 Act does not violate Article XI of the GATT 1994, since none of the remedies provided in the 1916 Act are of such a nature as to fall within the scope of Article XI:1.

6.16 The United States further argues that, since the 1916 Act is susceptible to an interpretation that is fully consistent with all WTO obligations of the United States and, in fact, has been so interpreted to date, there is no requirement under Article XVI:4 of the Agreement Establishing the WTO that the United States change that law.

(b) General Approach of the Panel

6.17 From the above, it appears to the Panel that the two parties address the WTO-compatibility of the 1916 Act through approaches that are diametrically opposed. Japan, basing its arguments on the definition of "dumping" found in Article VI:1 of the GATT 1994, seems to be of the view that any law which targets "dumping" within the meaning of Article VI is a "trade" law and is therefore subject to the relevant WTO disciplines. The approach of the United States, on the contrary, seems to be that the disciplines of Article VI of the GATT 1994 apply only to the extent that a law purports to address "injurious dumping" through the imposition of duties. If what the law targets is not "injurious dumping" within the meaning of Article VI of the GATT 1994, and if the measures imposed are not border measures in the form of anti-dumping duties, the WTO disciplines on anti-dumping do not apply to it.

6.18 On the basis of the arguments developed by the parties, the Panel considers that it needs to approach the matter before it as follows.[435]

6.19 First, since we are called to determine the compatibility of a law of the United States with the WTO obligations of that Member, we must determine how we should consider that law and its "surrounding", i.e. the circumstances of its enactment (including the legislative history)[436] and the subsequent interpretation(s) by the judiciary branch of the US government. This is in our view important since both parties have substantially discussed the role of the Panel in that respect. How we consider judicial interpretation, as evidence of the meaning given to the terms of a legal text, may affect the way we should understand the terms of the 1916 Act.

6.20 Second, we should proceed to address the issue whether we review the 1916 Act under Article VI of the GATT 1994 and the Anti-Dumping Agreement or under Article III:4 of the GATT 1994 first, or if we review it under either provision or agreement at all. The reason for this is that, while the 1916 Act addresses transnational price discrimination, it imposes internal measures. Article VI of the GATT 1994 and the Anti-Dumping Agreement relate to actions by Members *vis-à-vis* a particular practice whereas Article III:4 ensures that foreign products, once imported, are not subject to less favourable treatment than domestic products. We believe that it falls within our competence and duty to determine the applicability of Article III:4 of the GATT 1994 on the one hand and Article VI and the Anti-Dumping Agreement on the other hand as part of our review of the compatibility of the 1916 Act under the provision(s) found applicable, without prejudice to judicial economy.

6.21 On the basis of our conclusions, we shall address the compatibility of the 1916 Act under Article III:4 and/or Article VI of GATT 1994 and the Anti-Dumping Agreement to the extent necessary to assist the WTO Dispute Settlement Body[437] in making its recommendations. We should do this having first dealt with the "jurisdictional" argument of the United States according to which the Panel cannot review the 1916 Act as such under Article VI and the Anti-Dumping Agreement. We will also consider the defence of the United States based on the alleged "mandatory/non-mandatory" nature of the 1916 Act. If we proceed with the analysis of Article VI of the GATT 1994 and the Anti-Dumping Agreement, we shall consider the scope of our jurisdiction under those provisions. We shall also address the relationship between Article VI and the Anti-Dumping Agreement and how this relationship should affect the findings we shall make.

6.22 Once this is done, we may also consider the claims of Japan under Article XI of the GATT 1994, and Articles XVI:4 of the Agreement Establishing the WTO and 18.4 of the Anti-Dumping Agreement.

---

[435] We note that Japan referred to the negative trade impact of the 1916 Act, in particular the "chilling effect" it has on exports from Japan. However, Japan did not link its statement to the violation of any particular provision, nor to a non-violation claim. We therefore did not entertain it.

[436] Since the term "legislative history" is used throughout this report in relation to the preparation of US pieces of legislation, it will be given the meaning it has under US practice, i.e. "The background and events, including committee reports, hearings, and floor debates, leading up to the enactment of a law." *Black's Law Dictionary*, 6th Ed. (1990), p. 900.

[437] Hereinafter also referred to as the "DSB".

6.23 However, before reviewing the substantive issues of the case, we will address the procedural issues raised by the parties in the course of the proceedings.

(c) Burden of Proof

6.24 We recall the Appellate Body Report on *United States - Measure Affecting Imports of Woven Wool Shirts and Blouses from India*,[438] which stated that:

> "the burden of proof rests upon the party, whether complaining or defending, who asserts the affirmative of a particular claim or defence. If that party adduces evidence sufficient to raise a presumption that what is claimed is true, the burden then shifts to the other party, who will fail unless it adduces sufficient evidence to rebut the presumption."

6.25 Applying this rule to the factual evidence submitted in the present case, Japan, as the complainant, should adduce sufficient evidence to raise a *prima facie* case that each of its claims has merit. If it were to do so, it would then be for the United States to adduce sufficient evidence to rebut that *prima facie* case. If the United States were to assert the affirmative of a particular defence, it would bear the burden of proving it. This rule however is only applicable to determine whether and when a party bears the burden of proof. Once both parties have submitted evidence meeting those requirements, it is up to the Panel to weigh the evidence as a whole. In cases where the evidence as a whole regarding a particular claim or defence remains in equipoise, the issue must be decided against the party bearing the burden of proof on that claim or defence.

6.26 With respect to the interpretation of the covered agreements, the Panel will be aided by the arguments of the parties but will not be bound by them. Pursuant to Article 3.2 of the DSU, our decision on such matters must be in accord with the rules of treaty interpretation applicable to the WTO.

3. *Relationship of this Case with the EC Complaint*

6.27 The subject matter of the present case is basically the same as that of the case on *United States - Anti-Dumping Act of 1916*, complaint by the EC (WT/DS136), and some of the issues that have to be addressed by the Panel are largely similar. However, the claims and arguments made by Japan and the arguments developed by the United States in reply in the present case are sometimes quite different from the claims and arguments of the European Communities and the arguments submitted by the United States in WT/DS136. We also recall that, even though this Panel is composed of the same members as the panel which addressed the EC complaint, the two panels are procedurally distinct. As a matter of fact, the proceedings initiated by Japan started several months after the beginning of the case initiated by the EC and none of the parties requested that the panels harmonise their timetables or hold concurrent deliberations in the two procedures (WT/DS136 and WT/DS162). The United States objected to concurrent deliberations by the two panels and the European Communities was not in favour of delaying the proceedings in WT/DS136, which

[438] Appellate Body Report, *United States - Measure Affecting Imports of Woven Wool Shirts and Blouses from India, supra*, footnote 27, at 335.

concurrent deliberations would have resulted in. In such a context, the panel in the EC complaint considered that it had to conduct its review independently from the present case initiated by Japan, both in terms of procedure and of analysis of the substantive issues before it.

6.28 The same reasoning should apply to this case. Consequently, each case has to be decided on the basis of the claims and arguments submitted by the parties in that specific case. This also implies that our reasoning on a similar issue may sometimes be different, depending on the arguments developed by the parties. We note, *inter alia*, that since the defence of the United States has, in our opinion, evolved between the two cases, this Panel had to consider aspects that the panel in WT/DS136 did not have to consider and it would not be consistent with the obligation of the two panels to separately conduct their examination of the 1916 Act to review the findings of the panel in WT/DS136 on the basis of the arguments raised in this case, and *vice-versa*. However, whenever the claims and arguments of the parties raise issues identical to those addressed by the panel in WT/DS136, we will apply the same reasoning as has been applied by the panel in WT/DS136.

B. Preliminary Issues

1. Request for Enhanced Third Party Rights by the European Communities

6.29 The European Communities reserved its third party rights in this case and made both a written submission and an oral presentation to this Panel at our first substantive meeting. On 25 August 1999, the EC also requested enhanced third party rights so as to allow it to fully participate in the proceedings, that is to be present throughout both substantive meetings of the Panel and to be able to make a submission on each occasion. The EC recalled that a similar decision had been taken in the case on *European Communities - Measures Concerning Meat and Meat Products ("Hormones").*[439] In that case, the Appellate Body found that "Although Article 12.1 and Appendix 3 of the DSU do not specifically require the Panel to grant this opportunity [...] we believe that this discussion falls within the sound discretion and authority of the Panel, particularly if the Panel considers it necessary for ensuring to all parties due process of law."

6.30 Japan informed the Panel that it shared the concern of the European Communities and accepted its request for enhanced third party rights. In turn, Japan requested access to the documents exchanged by the parties in WT/DS136 and the right to attend the second substantive meeting of the panel in that case. The United States strongly objected to the request of the EC. In the opinion of the United States, enhanced third party rights were not necessary in order to obtain access to the submissions of the parties. In the *EC - Hormones* case, the panels had granted enhanced

[439] Panel Report, *EC Measures Concerning Meat and Meat Products (Hormones) - Complaint by the United States*, WT/DS26/R/USA, adopted 13 February 1998, DSR 1998:III, 699; Panel Report, *EC Measures Concerning Meat and Meat Products (Hormones) - Complaint by Canada*, WT/DS48/R/CAN, adopted 13 February 1998, DSR 1998:II, 235, hereinafter the "*EC - Hormones*" case.

third party rights essentially because they intended to conduct concurrent deliberations in the case initiated by the United States and in the case initiated by Canada. The United States mentioned that it would not support concurrent deliberations in this case and that it could not agree to a request of which the apparent purpose was to provide the third party with an opportunity to make an additional submission in relation to its own panel process.

6.31 On 13 September 1999, the Panel, through its Chairman, informed the parties and the European Communities that it could not accede to the request of the EC. The Panel reserved its right to reconsider the issue in light of subsequent events and informed the parties and the European Communities that it would address the matter in detail in its findings.

6.32 The Panel carefully considered the arguments raised by the parties. While the DSU does not provide for enhanced third party rights, neither Article 10 of the DSU nor any other provision of the DSU prohibits panels from granting third party rights beyond those expressly mentioned in Article 10. We also note that Article 9.3 of the DSU, which deals with situations where more than one panel is established to examine complaints related to the same matter, does not address the question of enhanced participation of third parties. Finally, we recall that the Appellate Body in the *EC - Hormones* case confirmed that granting enhanced third party rights was part of the discretion of panels under Article 12.1 of the DSU.[440]

6.33 However, we note that the DSU differentiates in terms of rights between main parties and third parties and that this principle should be respected in order to keep within the spirit of the DSU in that respect. Enhanced third party rights have so far been granted for specific reasons only. In the *EC - Hormones* case, like in this case and the case initiated by the European Communities (WT/DS136), the two panels were composed of the same panelists and dealt with the same matter. While these elements appeared to play a significant role in the decisions taken by the panels and in their confirmation by the Appellate Body, we consider that they are not decisive. Otherwise, enhanced third party rights would have to be granted in almost all cases where the same matter is subject to two or more complaints with the same panel composition.[441] We note that particular circumstances existed in the *EC - Hormones* case which certainly contributed to the decisions of the panels to review the two cases concurrently, such as their highly technical and factually intensive nature, as well as the fact that the panels had decided to hold one single meeting with the parties and the experts consulted pursuant to Article 11.2 of the Agreement on Sanitary and Phytosanitary Measures. These decisions were largely based on practical reasons and due process had to be preserved. We conclude from the reports in the *EC - Hormones* case that enhanced third party rights were granted primarily because of the specific circumstances.

6.34 We find that no similar circumstances exist in the present matter, which does not involve the consideration of complex technical facts or scientific evidence. Moreover, none of the parties requested that the panels harmonise their timetables or

[440] *Op. Cit.*, para. 154.

[441] Our remark is based on our understanding of the current state of the WTO practice. It is without prejudice to the question whether enhanced third party rights would be advisable or not in general.

hold concurrent deliberations in the two procedures (WT/DS136 and WT/DS162). In fact, the United States objected to concurrent deliberations.

6.35 We therefore find that there was no reason to grant enhanced third party rights to the European Communities in these proceedings.

2. *Context in which the 1916 Act Should Be Examined by the Panel*

(a) Issue before the Panel

6.36 We note that Japan contests the compatibility of the 1916 Act as such - not of particular instances of application - with certain provisions of the WTO Agreement. While it is clear from the terms of Article 3.2 of the DSU that it falls within the competence of the Panel to "clarify the existing provisions of [the covered agreements] in accordance with customary rules of interpretation of public international law", the DSU does not expressly provide how panels should address domestic legislation. Article 11 of the DSU only specifies that panels "should make [...] an objective assessment of the facts of the case". However, both Article 3.2 of the DSU and the practice of the Appellate Body make it clear that we should, whenever appropriate, take into consideration the practice of international tribunals in this respect.

6.37 This case has an additional dimension. Although panels often have to address domestic laws, in the present case we are called upon to review the consistency of a law which was drafted more than eighty years ago, and the historical, cultural, legal and economic context of the time undoubtedly influenced its terms. We also note that the parties seem to have diverging views regarding the weight which the Panel should give to the court decisions relating to that law.

6.38 Furthermore, the 1916 Act was seldom applied since its enactment. It is the understanding of the Panel, based on the information provided by the parties, that no criminal case was ever prosecuted under the 1916 Act and that, until the early 1970's, there was only one reported court decision based on the civil procedure provided for in the 1916 Act.[442] Since 1975, there has been only a limited number of judicial interpretations of the provisions of the 1916 Act. All these interpretations come from US circuit courts of appeals or US district courts.[443] No claim under the 1916 Act was ever expressly reviewed by the Supreme Court of the United States.[444]

6.39 Therefore, we find it appropriate to clarify from the outset how we shall take into consideration the text of the 1916 Act itself, the historical context of its enactment (including the legislative history) and its subsequent interpretation as it results from the US case-law and any other relevant element of information.

---

[442] *H. Wagner and Adler Co. v. Mali*, F.2d 666 (2d Cir. 1935).

[443] Federal courts (district courts and circuit courts of appeals) are competent to review cases brought under the 1916 Act, under the supervision of the Supreme Court of the United States (hereinafter also the "Supreme Court").

[444] In *United States v. Cooper Corporation* (312 U.S. 600, 1941), hereinafter the "*Cooper*" case, p. 745, the Supreme Court made a reference to the 1916 Act as "supplemental" to the Sherman Act. This decision is discussed further in section VI.C.2(d)(ii) below.

(b) How Should the Panel Consider the Text of the 1916 Act, the Context of its Enactment, the Case-Law Relating to it and other Relevant Pieces of Information?

(i) Arguments of the Parties and Approach of the Panel

6.40 Japan claims that the text of the 1916 Act is unambiguous. Thus, the Panel's analysis should begin and end with the text. The Panel should not defer to the characterisation of the 1916 Act by the United States as an "anti-trust" remedy. The existence and characteristics of the 1916 Act are questions of fact that are "left to the discretion of a panel as a trier of facts". The term "examination", as used by the Appellate Body in its report on *India - Patent Protection for Pharmaceutical and Agricultural Chemical Products*[445] encompasses all the aspects of the "objective assessment of the matter" provided for in Article 11 of the DSU. Thus, the Panel should not accept the US judicial interpretation of the 1916 Act as binding.

6.41 Japan also considers that the historical context and the legislative history confirm the textual interpretation of the 1916 Act.

6.42 Moreover, Japan claims that official statements by members of the executive branch of the US government contradict the position taken by the United States in the present case. Japan refers to letters of US officials to congressmen or statements before the US Congress that the 1916 Act was "grandfathered" under GATT 1947 as "existing legislation" within the meaning of the Protocol of Provisional Application. For Japan these statements demonstrate that, for years, the United States has viewed the 1916 Act as GATT-inconsistent and requiring grandfathering.

6.43 Finally, Japan refers to a 1995 document of the US Department of Justice and the US Federal Trade Commission, called *Antitrust Enforcement Guidelines for International Operations*,[446] which states that "the 1916 Act is not an antitrust statute, it is a trade statute that creates a private claim against importers". This document shows that the two US government agencies that enforce US anti-trust law agree that the 1916 Act is not an anti-trust law, but an anti-dumping law. Japan also refers to a compilation prepared for the Committee on Ways and Means of the US House of Representatives, which includes the 1916 Act as a trade statute.

6.44 The United States argues that it is an accepted principle of international law that municipal law is a fact to be proven before an international tribunal. In *India - Patent (US)*, the Appellate Body affirmed the panel's review of India's domestic law as a question of fact. It was proper for the panel to conduct an extensive review of the Indian law at issue to determine whether India had met its obligations under the TRIPS Agreement. The Appellate Body had also approved the fact that the panel had not interpreted Indian law as such but, rather, had reviewed that law to determine whether it was WTO-consistent. This Panel must determine the fact of the 1916 Act

[445] Appellate Body Report, *India - Patent Protection for Pharmaceutical and Agricultural Products*, WT/DS50/AB/R, adopted 16 January 1998, DSR 1998:I, 9, paras. 66-67, hereinafter "*India - Patent (US)*".

[446] April 1995, available on http://www.usdoj.gov/atr/public/guidelines/internat.txt.

under US law, which includes US judicial decisions interpreting the 1916 Act. If the Panel were to interpret the 1916 Act, it would run the risk of adopting an interpretation that does not match the true application of the law in the United States. The Panel should deem the case-law interpreting the 1916 Act as dispositive for purposes of determining the fact of US law. The role of the Panel is to assess the facts and then determine their conformity with the relevant WTO agreements, which generally entails interpreting the scope and applicability of those agreements to the facts. The proper interpretation of the 1916 Act is a question of fact to be established, as it is an accepted principle of international law that municipal law is a fact to be proven before international tribunals. The Panel must review the current weight of judicial authority and decide for itself whether the 1916 Act is inconsistent with any WTO obligations. However, it is not the role of the Panel to agree or disagree with any US judicial decision relevant to the interpretation of the 1916 Act.

6.45 The United States also considers that statements of officials of the executive branch of government of the United States cited by Japan deserve no weight in the Panel's consideration for two reasons. First, statements as to the GATT consistency of an amendment to the 1916 Act are not relevant in this case because the amendments were never enacted. Second, the United States considers that the notifications to the GATT of its "grandfathered" laws (document L/2375/Add.1), which does not include the 1916 Act, is evidence that the official view of the United States that the 1916 Act was not incompatible with Part II of the GATT 1947. Thus, the statements referred to by Japan are mistaken as a matter of fact.

6.46 Finally, the United States mentions that the *Antitrust Enforcement Guidelines for International Operations* are not regulations with the force of law, but rather are intended to provide anti-trust guidance to businesses engaged in international operations on questions that relate specifically to the relevant agencies' international enforcement policy. The United States also points at its codification system, which classifies the 1916 Act as a text dealing with unfair competition, and at a compilation prepared for the Committee on the Judiciary, which lists the 1916 Act as one of the US anti-trust laws.

6.47 The Panel is of the view that the understanding of a law, the WTO-compatibility of which has to be assessed, begins with an analysis of the terms of that law. However, we consider that we should not limit ourselves to an analysis of the text of the 1916 Act in isolation from its interpretation by US courts or other US authorities, even if we were to find that text to be clear on its face. If we were to do so, we might develop an understanding of that law different from the way it is actually understood and applied by the US authorities. This would be contrary to our obligation to make an objective assessment of the facts of the case, pursuant to Article 11 of the DSU. Therefore, we must look at all the aspects of the domestic law of the United States that are relevant for our understanding of the 1916 Act. However, looking at all the relevant aspects of the domestic law of a Member may raise some methodological difficulties, such as how much deference must be paid to that Member's characterisation of its legislation. In that context, we will determine first how to deal with that aspect of the examination of a domestic law and how we should consider the case-law related to it, since courts are, *inter alia*, responsible for interpreting the law. Moreover, in light of the fact that the law at issue was enacted more than eighty years ago and not regularly invoked, and since the parties have referred to other elements such as the historical context, the legislative history and subsequent declarations of US authorities made in relation to the 1916 Act, we shall also explain how we will consider them.

(ii) Consideration by Panels of Domestic Law in General

6.48 We note that in *India - Patent(US)*, the Appellate Body addressed in some detail the issue of how panels should consider municipal law. The Appellate Body stated that:

> "In public international law, an international tribunal may treat municipal law in several ways. Municipal law may serve as evidence of fact and may provide evidence of State practice."[447]
>
> "It is clear that the examination of the relevant aspects of Indian municipal law [...] is essential to determining whether India has complied with its obligations under Article 70.8(a) [of the TRIPS Agreement]. [...] To say that the Panel should have done otherwise would be to say that only India can assess whether Indian law is consistent with India's obligations under the *WTO Agreement*. This, clearly, cannot be so."[448]

6.49 The extent to which panels may examine the laws of Members was illustrated by the Appellate Body in the same report. Having to determine whether India provided for legal protection commensurate with the requirements of Article 70.8 of the TRIPS Agreement, the Appellate Body asked itself the question of "what constitutes [...] a sound legal basis in Indian law".[449] Moreover, it agreed with the conclusion of the panel that "the current administrative practice [of India, based on so-called "administrative instructions" from the government] creates a certain degree of legal insecurity in that it requires Indian officials to ignore certain mandatory provisions of the Patent Act."[450] The Appellate Body also agreed that "it was necessary for the Panel in this case to seek a detailed understanding of the *operation* of the Patent Act as it relates to the 'administrative instructions' in order to assess whether India had complied with Article 70.8(a) [of the TRIPS Agreement]."[451]

6.50 Thus, our understanding of the term "examination" as used by the Appellate Body is that panels need not accept at face value the characterisation that the respondent attaches to its law. A panel may analyse the operation of the domestic legislation and determine whether the description of the functioning of the law, as made by the respondent, is consistent with the legal structure of that Member. This way, it will be able to determine whether or not the law as applied is in conformity with the obligations of the Member concerned under the WTO Agreement.[452]

---

447 *Op. Cit.*, para. 65. See also M.N. Shaw, *International Law* (1995), at p. 106, mentioning that domestic law "can be utilised as evidence of compliance or non-compliance with international obligations".

448 *Ibid.*, para. 66.

449 *Ibid.*, para. 59.

450 *Ibid.*, para. 63, Panel Report, para. 7.35.

451 *Ibid.*, para. 68 (emphasis added).

452 This is evidenced by the examples used by the Appellate Body (*Ibid.*, para. 67):

(iii) Consideration of the Case-Law Relating to the 1916 Act

6.51 In the present case, unlike India in the *India - Patent (US)* case, the United States does not claim that some administrative interpretation determines the meaning of the 1916 Act. The situation is different to the extent that both parties rely, in order to support their claims, on a number of judgements by US courts which have applied and interpreted the 1916 Act since the 1970's.[453] In many Members, final judicial decisions regarding the interpretation of a given law may not be contested any further, whereas administrative interpretations of a law may generally be overruled by a domestic judge called upon to apply that law. However, an administrative interpretation will normally provide one single interpretation. In contrast, depending on the judicial structure of a Member, judicial interpretations may emanate from several courts positioned at different levels in the judicial order. The diversity of the sources of the case-law may make it more difficult to assess the respective value of the judgements of which that case-law is composed.

6.52 We recall that the International Court of Justice, in the *Elettronica Sicula S.p.A (ELSI)* case, referred to the judgement of the Permanent Court of International

---

> "Previous GATT/WTO panels also have conducted a detailed examination of the domestic law of a Member in assessing the conformity of that domestic law with the relevant GATT/WTO obligations. For example, in *United States - Section 337 of the Tariff Act of 1930* [footnote omitted], the panel conducted a detailed examination of the relevant United States' legislation and practice, including the remedies available under Section 337 as well as the difference between patent-based Section 337 proceedings and federal district court proceedings, in order to determine whether Section 337 was inconsistent with Article III:4 of the GATT 1947."

[453] The following - final or interlocutory - court decisions relate to claims made under the 1916 Act: *H. Wagner and Adler Co. v. Mali, Op. Cit.*; *In re Japanese Electronic Products Antitrust Litigation*, 388 F.Supp. 565 (Judicial Panel on Multidistrict Litigation, 1975) (hereinafter "*In re Japanese Electronic Products I*"); *Zenith Radio Corp. v. Matsushita Electric Industrial Co., Ltd.*, 402 F.Supp. 244 (E.D. Pa. 1975) (hereinafter "*Zenith I*"); *Zenith Radio Corp. v. Matsushita Electric Industrial Co., Ltd.*, 402 F.Supp. 251 (E.D. Pa. 1975) (hereinafter "*Zenith II*"); *Outboard Marine Corp. v. Pezetel*, 461 F. Supp. 384 (D. Del. 1978); *Schwimmer v. Sony Corp. of America*, 471 F. Supp. 793 (E.D.N.Y. 1979); *Schwimmer v. Sony Corp. of America*, 637 F.2d 41 (2nd Cir. 1980); *Jewel Foliage Co. v. Uniflora Overseas Florida*, 497 F. Supp. 513 (M.D. Fla. 1980); *Zenith Radio Corp. v. Matsushita Electric Industrial Co., Ltd.*, 494 F.Supp. 1190 (E.D. Pa. 1980) (hereinafter "*Zenith III*"); *In re Japanese Electronic Products Antitrust Litigation (Zenith Radio Corp. v. Matsushita Electric Industrial Co., Ltd.)*, 723 F.2d 319 (3d Cir. 1983) (hereinafter "*In re Japanese Electronic Products II*"); *Western Concrete Structures Co. v. Mitsui & Co.*, 760 F.2d 1013 (9th Cir. 1985); *Isra Fruit Ltd. v. Agrexco Agr. Export Co.*, 631 F. Supp. 984 (S.D.N.Y. 1986); *In re Japanese Electronic Products Antitrust Litigation (Zenith Radio Corp. v. Matsushita Electric Industrial Co., Ltd.)*, 807 F.2d 44 (3d Cir. 1986) (hereinafter "*In re Japanese Electronic Products III*") *Helmac Products Corp. v. Roth (Plastics) Corp.*, 814 F. Supp. 560 (E.D. Mich. 1992) (hereinafter "*Helmac I*"); *Helmac Products Corp. v. Roth (Plastics) Corp.*, 814 F.Supp. 581 (E.D. Mich. 1993) (hereinafter "*Helmac II*"); *Geneva Steel Company v. Ranger Steel Supply Corp.*, 980 F.Supp. 1209 (D. Utah 1997) (hereinafter "*Geneva Steel*"); *Wheeling-Pittsburgh Steel Corporation v. Mitsui Co.*, 35 F.Supp.2d. 597 (S.D. Ohio 1999) (hereinafter "*Wheeling-Pittsburgh*").

Justice[454] in the *Brazilian Loans* case - to which the United States also refers in its submissions - and noted that:

> "Where the determination of a question of municipal law is essential to the Court's decision in a case, the Court will have to weigh the jurisprudence of the municipal courts, and 'If this is uncertain or divided, it will rest with the Court to select the interpretation which it considers most in conformity with the law' (*Brazilian Loans*, PCIJ, Series A, Nos. 20/21, p. 124)." [455]

We are fully aware that our role is to clarify the existing provisions of the covered agreements so as to determine the compatibility of a domestic law with those agreements. We are also aware that, in the *Brazilian Loans* case, the PCIJ was asked to apply domestic legislation to a given case. We are nevertheless of the view that there is nothing in the text of the DSU, nor in the practice of the Appellate Body, that prevents us from "weigh[ing] the jurisprudence of municipal [US] courts" if it is "uncertain or divided". This would not require us to develop our own independent interpretation of US law, but simply to select among the relevant judgements the interpretation most in conformity with the US law, as necessary in order to resolve the matter before us.[456]

6.53 We note that the 1916 Act is applied by US federal courts. Interpretations by the Supreme Court of the United States prevail over interpretations made by the courts of appeals of the various circuits. Interpretations by courts of appeals, in turn, prevail over interpretations by district courts, but only within the same circuit.[457]

6.54 We understand from the submissions of the parties that the Supreme Court has yet to address the interpretation of specific provisions of the 1916 Act. It mentioned the 1916 Act in only one of its judgements.[458] Thus, the case-law submitted by the parties that would allow us to understand the actual meaning of the 1916 Act today essentially comes from district courts and courts of appeals of various circuits of the US federal judicial system. We also note that the parties in their submissions have relied on different judgments, which they claim support their interpretations of the 1916 Act.

6.55 We will respect the formal hierarchy of court decisions in the US federal system to the extent that it is applicable. In that context, we should allow a circuit

---

454 Hereinafter "PCIJ".

455 *Case Concerning Elettronica Sicula S.p.A. (ELSI)* (United States of America v. Italy), ICJ Reports 1989, p. 15, at p.47, para. 62.

456 We do not consider that this would be engaging into *interpreting* US law, with the risks highlighted by the United States in its submissions. Our approach is consistent with the reasoning of the PCIJ in the *Brazilian Loans* case, where it stated that:

> "It follows that the Court must pay the utmost regard to the decisions of the municipal courts of a country, for it is with the aid of their jurisprudence that it will be enabled to decide what are the rules which, in actual fact, are applied in the country the law of which is recognized as applicable in a given case." (PCIJ, Series A, Nos. 20/21, p. 124)

457 A description of the organization of the US federal judicial system is found in para. 2.14 and footnote 20 above.

458 *Cooper, Op. Cit.*

court of appeals decision to prevail over a district court decision. However, applying such a formal approach may prove insufficient in some instances, for example when the decisions to be compared come from different circuits.[459] Therefore, in all instances, we shall first ascertain whether the judgements subject to our comparison address (i) the same issue, and (ii) at the same level of detail. In other words, we should always make sure that a comparison can reasonably be made, both in terms of fact and in terms of the legal issues addressed, before giving preference to the interpretation contained in one judgement compared with the interpretation contained in another judgement of a court belonging to another circuit.

6.56 Moreover, we should normally, with respect to a given issue, allocate more weight to a final judgement than to an interim or "interlocutory" decision, since the latter does not definitively determine a cause of action, but only "decides some intervening matter pertaining to the cause."[460] However, we should also determine which argumentation is more convincing. Again, we will not substitute our judgement for that of US courts. Our analysis should be based not only on the quality of the reasoning, but also on what we would perceive to be in line with the dominant interpretation, "paying utmost regard to the decision of the municipal courts". This is consistent with the US court practice that if a precedent is not binding, the weight afforded to it will depend on the persuasive value of the reasoning in the decision.

6.57 If, after having applied the above methodology, we could not reach certainty as to the most appropriate court interpretation, i.e. if the evidence remains in equipoise, we shall follow the interpretation that favours the party against which the claim has been made, considering that the claimant did not convincingly support its claim.

6.58 Finally, we also consider that we should not accept at face value the use of certain terms such as "dumping", "anti-dumping", "anti-trust", "protectionism" or "predatory pricing" in court decisions, in other administrative documents or in academic works, when those terms are not further substantiated. We recall that the mere description or categorisation of a measure by a Member, be it internally or before a panel, should not be considered as a decisive factor for the application of the WTO Agreement to that measure.[461] In the present case, such descriptions or categorisations may be valid under US law but not necessarily in the WTO context. Likewise, having regard to the importance of the legislative history in the interpretation of statutes by the US judiciary branch, terms used in 1916 will have to be interpreted within

---

[459] From the replies of the United States to our questions, we understand that the *stare decisis* effect which can be attached to precedents in common law does not apply between court decisions handed down in different circuits.

[460] See *Black's Law Dictionary* (1990), p. 815.

[461] See, Panel Report on *EEC - Regulation on Imports of Parts and Components*, adopted on 16 May 1990, BISD 37S/132 (hereinafter "*EC - Parts and Components*"), paras. 5.6 and 5.7. In para. 5.7, the panel stated that:

> "if the description or categorization of a charge under the domestic law of a contracting party were to provide the required "connection with importation", contracting parties could determine themselves which of these provisions would apply to their charges."

the meaning they had at the time, not in light of the meaning they have today, unless we have evidence that US courts have done so.

(iv) Consideration of the Historical Context and other Evidence of the Meaning of the 1916 Act

6.59 The historical context of the 1916 Act encompasses several elements. The first one, to which US courts also extensively refer in order to determine "the intent of Congress", is the legislative history as it appears, *inter alia*, from the Congressional Records. Since we have to examine the 1916 Act and understand its actual scope and operation, we should, as US courts do, pay attention to the legislative history of that statute, as appropriate. The political and economic context as it emerges from public declarations of the time or studies of the period may also be relevant. When considering this evidence, we should not lose sight of the degree of development of anti-trust and trade law concepts at the time of the enactment of the 1916 Act.

6.60 Regarding the statements of US officials referred to by Japan,[462] we note that Japan considers them as showing that for many US executive branch officials, including officials of the current Administration, the 1916 Act could be maintained under GATT 1947 only because it was "grandfathered." We also note that the United States considers that these statements do not represent the official position of the United States and are mistaken as a matter of fact. The 1916 Act was not included in the survey of existing mandatory legislation not in conformity with part II of the GATT 1947[463] because the 1916 Act was GATT-legal and therefore did not require "grandfathering".

6.61 The main question is whether these statements should be treated as admissions of facts or of the legal nature of the 1916 Act under the WTO. We note that the factual accuracy of the statements mentioned in this case has been put in doubt by the United States before the Panel. While this is not sufficient to reject those statements out of hand, we are reluctant to consider them as "admissions" of the United States without prior verification of the context in which they were made.

6.62 For these reasons, we consider that these statements should be used only to the extent that they confirm other established evidence.

6.63 Japan and the United States have also referred to compilations prepared for committees of the US Congress. Japan refers to the *Overview and Compilation of US Trade Statutes*, prepared for the House Committee on Ways and Means. The United States considers this document to be an unofficial compilation which has not been officially approved by that committee and may not reflect the views of its members. As a result, it should be given less weight than a compilation made for the use of the Committee on the Judiciary of the US House of Representatives, which is the committee also responsible for the revision and codification of the statutes of the United States under Rule 10 of the Rules of the US House of Representatives. This compilation confirms that the 1916 Act is an anti-trust statute. We consider these docu-

462 The arguments of the parties on this issue are reported in section III:D.2.(c) above.

463 See GATT Doc. L/2375/Add.1 of 19 March 1965.

ments to be informative regarding the opinions of the authorities of the United States as to the classification of the 1916 Act as an anti-trust or as an anti-dumping statute. However, as such, the codification of the 1916 Act or its inclusion in a compilation for a committee of the US Congress cannot, in our view, affect our determination of the compatibility of the 1916 Act with the WTO provisions.[464]

6.64 With regard to the 1995 *Antitrust Enforcement Guidelines for International Operations* of the US Department of Justice and the US Federal Trade Commission referred to by Japan, we note their role as "antitrust guidance to business engaged in international operations". We therefore consider that they are indicative of the position of a particular department of the executive branch of the US government. Moreover, to the extent that these guidelines do not substantiate the reasons why the 1916 Act should be considered as a trade statute and, in fact, mention that "its subject-matter is closely related to the anti-trust rules regarding predation", we consider that we should refer to them only as a confirmation of other established evidence, if necessary.

6.65 Having clarified how we shall consider the materials before us in assessing the WTO-compatibility of the 1916 Act, we now proceed to discuss the preliminary issue of the applicability of Articles III:4 of the GATT 1994, and of Article VI of the GATT 1994 and the Anti-Dumping Agreement.

3. *Relationship between, on the One Hand, Article III of the GATT 1994 and, on the Other Hand, Article VI of the GATT 1994 and the Anti-Dumping Agreement*

(a) Issue before the Panel

6.66 Japan claims that the 1916 Act violates Article VI of the GATT 1994 and certain provisions of the Anti-Dumping Agreement. It also claims that the 1916 Act violates Article III:4 of the GATT 1994.[465] The United States claims that the 1916 Act is not subject to the disciplines of Article VI essentially because it is not aimed at counteracting injurious dumping and because it does not impose border measures in the form of anti-dumping duties.

6.67 Article III:4, first sentence, of the GATT 1994 provides in relevant parts as follows:

> "The products of the territory of any contracting party imported into the territory of another contracting party shall be accorded treatment no less favourable than that accorded to like products of national ori-

[464] See Panel Report on *EC - Parts and Components, Op. Cit.*, para. 5.7. That panel addressed the description or categorisation of a charge under domestic law and concluded that if the description or categorisation of a charge under the domestic law of a contracting party were to provide the required "connection with importation", contracting parties could determine themselves which of these provisions would apply to their charges. With such an interpretation the basic objective underlying Articles II and III could not be achieved. We consider that the same reasoning applies with respect to the application of Article VI.

[465] Japan also claims a violation of Article XI of the GATT 1994. However, we find it appropriate to address the relationship of Article XI with Article VI and Article III:4 once we have dealt with the relationship between Article III:4 and Article VI.

gin in respect of laws, regulations and requirements affecting their internal sale, offering for sale, purchase, transportation, distribution or use."

6.68 Article VI provides in relevant parts as follows:

"1. The contracting parties recognize that dumping, by which products of one country are introduced into the commerce of another country at less that the normal value of the product, is to be condemned if it causes or threatens material injury to an established industry in the territory of a contracting party or materially retards the establishment of a domestic industry. [...]

2. In order to offset or prevent dumping, a contracting party may levy on any dumped product an anti-dumping duty no greater in amount than the margin of dumping in respect of such product. [...]"

6.69 The arguments of the parties raise the question whether the 1916 Act could, by its nature, fall within the scope of Article VI only, of Article III:4 only, or partly or wholly within the scope of both. This question is prompted by the positions taken by the parties on this issue. According to Japan, a measure found inconsistent with Article VI can also violate Article III:4 by regulating imported products under a separate, less favourable regime than applicable to domestic products. For the United States, a law falls within the scope of Article III:4 when it can be characterised as an "internal" law. Since the 1916 Act does not provide for border adjustment measures, such as the imposition of duties on an imported product, it is an "internal" law subject to Article III:4 of the GATT 1994.

6.70 It seems to us that Articles III and VI are based on different premises: Article III (entitled "National Treatment") operates on the basis of a comparison between the treatment granted to domestic and imported products respectively, once the latter have been cleared through customs. Thus, Article III:4 applies to measures imposed by Members internally, irrespective of the objective of the measures. In contrast, Article VI does not compare the treatment of domestic and imported products, since it applies only to imported goods. The basis for the applicability of Article VI to the law of a Member does not seem to be the type of *measures* which is imposed by that Member, since other reasons than dumping may lead to the imposition of duties, but the type of trade practice *at the origin* of the measure.

6.71 The Panel thus is of the opinion that the *nature* of the 1916 Act might be such as to affect the relevance of the claims made by Japan under Article III:4 or Article VI. Irrespective of the question of judicial economy, the Panel considers that it has the "competence of its competence", i.e. that it may determine whether a given claim can be addressed, irrespective of the positions expressed by the parties on the issue.[466] Japan, in its submissions to the Panel, addressed first its claims based on Article VI. However, the Panel should not be obliged to address those claims if it were to

[466] This is different from exercising judicial economy, which is based on the necessity to address a claim in light of findings made on another claim. It is also different from determining whether a claim is properly before the Panel on the basis of the request for establishment of a panel. It is a question of knowing whether the Panel can rule on two claims which, on the basis of a first consideration of the facts and arguments before it, might be mutually exclusive.

find that Article VI is not applicable because the *qualification juridique* made by Japan is not correct.[467] On the other hand, the Panel may not have to address Japan's claims under Article III:4 if it were to find that the 1916 Act falls exclusively within the scope of Article VI.

6.72 Therefore, it would be relevant to consider whether Article III:4 or Article VI of GATT 1994 - or both - are *applicable* to the 1916 Act, irrespective of whether the 1916 Act is *compatible* with those provisions or not.

(b) Approach to be Followed by the Panel

6.73 The issue whether the 1916 Act should be addressed under Article III:4 only, Article VI only, or both, is not obvious from the outset. In our opinion, reaching conclusions on this matter requires that we address the substance of the case, since one of the issues before us is whether the 1916 Act can be subject to the disciplines of Article VI and the Anti-Dumping Agreement. It is therefore appropriate to address this question as part of the substantive issues of this case, but separately from the actual WTO-compatibility of the 1916 Act. Based on our findings regarding the applicability of Articles III:4 and VI to the 1916 Act, we shall proceed to review the compatibility of that law with either provision or both.

6.74 However, even though we do not reach yet any conclusion on the applicability of either provision, we need to decide at this stage whether to begin our analysis with Article VI or Article III:4.

6.75 It is a general principle of international law recalled by the Appellate Body that, when applying a body of norms to a given factual situation, one should consider that factual situation under the norm which most specifically addresses it.[468] As a result, one way to reply to the question above is to determine which article more specifically addresses the 1916 Act. We agree that this will require us to touch upon the substance of the case, but we recall that this test is used here for purely procedural reasons, that is to determine the order of our review. Such a *prima facie* analysis is, of course, without prejudice to the final findings on the issue of the applicability of Articles III:4 and VI, to be reached after a more detailed review of the scope of each provision, as necessary.

6.76 We note that the parties agree that the 1916 Act deals with transnational price discrimination. We also note that dumping is a form of transnational price discrimination. However, the United States argues that other requirements under the 1916 Act, such as the fact that it does not lead to the imposition of border measures, make

---

[467] For instance, if a complainant were to claim a violation of Article XI of GATT 1994 in relation to a small tariff increase, the panel called upon to address the issue may be entitled to reject the claim on the ground that the measure at issue is not a quantitative restriction within the meaning of Article XI, without addressing any further the claim and the related arguments.

[468] See Appellate Body Report on *European Communities - Regime for the Importation, Sale and Distribution of Bananas*, WT/DS27/AB/R, adopted on 25 September 1997 (hereinafter "*European Communities - Bananas*"), DSR 1997:II, 591, para. 204, and PCIJ decision in the *Serbian Loans* case (1929), where the PCIJ stated that "the special words, according to elementary principles of interpretation, control the general expression" (PCIJ, Series A, No. 20/21, at p. 30). See also György Haraszti, *Some Fundamental Problems of the Law of Treaties* (1973), at p. 191.

that law fall outside the scope of Article VI and into the realm of Article III:4. We recall that Article III:4 states that imported products:

> "shall be accorded treatment no less favourable than that accorded to like products of national origin in respect of laws, regulations and requirements affecting their internal sale, offering for sale, purchase, transportation, distribution or use."

It is not *a priori* impossible to determine that damages, fines or imprisonment, which are imposed on persons, may accord less favourable treatment to imported products with respect to their internal sale, offering for sale, purchase, transportation, distribution or use. This was done by previous panels.[469] However, a preliminary examination of the scope of application of Article III:4 (i.e. internal sale, offering for sale, purchase, transportation, distribution or use) would tend to show that the terms of Article III:4 are less specific than those of Article VI when it comes to the notion of transnational price discrimination. Indeed, the 1916 Act refers to internal sales, but such sales relate to imported products and the application of the 1916 Act is based on an international price difference, like Article VI. We also consider that the main object of the 1916 Act is to counteract a certain form of price discrimination, and that the sanctions imposed are, in that respect, the instruments of that object, not the object itself.

6.77 In application of the principle recalled by the Appellate Body in *European Communities - Bananas* and by the Permanent Court of International Justice in the *Serbian Loans* case,[470] there seems to be reasons to reach the preliminary conclusion that we should review the applicability of Article VI to the 1916 Act first, as that article apparently applies to the facts at issue more specifically. This preliminary conclusion is based on our understanding of the arguments of the parties and on a preliminary review of the terms of Articles III:4 and VI.

6.78 Our preliminary conclusion does not address the question whether the 1916 Act could fall within the scope of both provisions. Should we determine that the 1916 Act actually falls within the scope of Article VI, we would continue with Japan's claims of violation of Article VI and the Anti-Dumping Agreement, as necessary to enable the DSB to make sufficiently precise recommendations and rulings. Once this part of our terms of reference has been addressed, we shall also decide whether pursuing our review with an analysis of the applicability of Article III:4 would be necessary to enable the DSB to make sufficiently precise recommendations and rulings so as to allow for prompt compliance "in order to ensure effective reso-

---

[469] See, e.g., Panel Report on *United States - Section 337 of the Tariff Act of 1930*, adopted on 7 November 1989, BISD 36/345, para. 5.10. See also Panel Report on *Italian Discrimination Against Imported Agricultural Machinery*, adopted on 23 October 1958, BISD 7S/60, which mentioned at para. 12 that:

> "The selection of the word "affecting" [in Article III:4] would imply, in the opinion of the Panel, that the drafters of the Article intended to cover in para. 4 not only the laws and regulations which directly governed the conditions of sale or purchase but also any laws or regulations which might adversely modify the conditions of competition between the domestic and imported products on the internal market."

[470] See footnote 464 above.

lution of disputes to the benefit of all Members."[471] If we do not find that the 1916 Act falls within the scope of Article VI of the GATT 1994, we will proceed to consider the applicability of Article III:4 to the 1916 Act and, if applicable, the compatibility of the 1916 Act with that provision.

6.79 Consequently, we proceed with a review of the applicability of Article VI to the 1916 Act. However, before doing that, we need to address the question of the relationship between Article VI and the Anti-Dumping Agreement. Indeed, Japan makes claims based concurrently on Article VI and the Anti-Dumping Agreement. The United States argues that the jurisdiction of the Panel under the Anti-Dumping Agreement is limited to situations where specific measures have been adopted; the Panel cannot review the conformity of a law as such under the Anti-Dumping Agreement. Moreover, the United States argues that the Panel cannot entertain claims based on Article VI independently from the Anti-Dumping Agreement. In other words, the United States argues that the Panel has no jurisdiction to review Japan's claims under either Article VI of the GATT 1994 or the Anti-Dumping Agreement.

4. *Relationship between Article VI of the GATT 1994 and the Anti-Dumping Agreement*

(a) Issues before the Panel

6.80 We note that Japan, in its request for establishment of a panel, states that the 1916 Act

> "is neither consistent with nor justified by the following relevant provisions:
>
> [...]
>
> (2) Article VI of GATT 1994 and the Anti-Dumping Agreement, and in particular:
>
> - Article VI:2 of GATT 1994 and Article 18:1 of the Anti-Dumping Agreement which permit imposition of anti-dumping duties as the only possible remedies for dumping;
> - Articles 1, 2, 3, 4, 5, 9 and 11 of the Anti-Dumping Agreement which stipulates necessary requirements for an anti-dumping duty to be applied only under the circumstances provided for in Article VI of GATT 1994."[472]

6.81 In its first submission, Japan has concurrently invoked the violation of Article VI of the GATT 1994 and of Articles 1, 2, 3, 4, 5, 9, 11 and 18.1 of the Anti-Dumping Agreement.

6.82 The United States has argued that, as demonstrated by the Appellate Body in *Guatemala - Cement*, the only matter that may be challenged under the Anti-

---

[471] See Appellate Body Report on *Australia - Measures Affecting Importation of Salmon*, ("*Australia - Salmon*"), WT/DS18/AB/R, adopted on 6 November 1998, DSR 1998:VIII, 3327, para. 223.

[472] WT/DS162/3.

Dumping Agreement are the three types of anti-dumping measures set forth in the Anti-Dumping Agreement (i.e. a definitive anti-dumping duty, acceptance of a price undertaking, or a provisional measure). Similarly, in light of the reasoning of the panel in *Brazil - Measures Affecting Desiccated Coconut*, which was affirmed by the Appellate Body, the Panel has no jurisdiction to decide a claim under Article VI because that article is not independently applicable to a dispute to which the Anti-Dumping Agreement is not applicable.

6.83 In our opinion, the fact that Japan has claimed a violation of Article VI in relation to a violation of certain provisions of the Anti-Dumping Agreement would seem to imply that the Panel is expected to make findings under both Article VI of the GATT 1994 and the Anti-Dumping Agreement. In that context, the arguments of the parties require the Panel to address the following issues:

(i) what is the actual scope of the "jurisdiction" of the Panel under the Anti-Dumping Agreement and to what extent does that scope influence the Panel's "jurisdiction" under Article VI? And

(ii) what is the relationship between Article VI of the GATT 1994 and the Anti-Dumping Agreement in terms of the respective application of those provisions and of the findings to be made (including judicial economy)?

We will address these questions successively.

(b) Jurisdiction of the Panel under Article VI of the GATT 1994 and the Anti-Dumping Agreement

6.84 We first consider the provisions of the Anti-Dumping Agreement relating to consultation and dispute settlement. Paragraphs 1 to 4 of Article 17 provide as follows:

> "17.1 Except as otherwise provided herein, the Dispute Settlement Understanding is applicable to consultations and the settlement of disputes under this Agreement.
>
> 17.2 Each Member shall afford sympathetic consideration to, and shall afford adequate opportunity for consultation regarding, representations made by another Member with respect to any matter affecting the operation of this Agreement.
>
> 17.3 If any Member considers that any benefit accruing to it, directly or indirectly, under this Agreement is being nullified or impaired, or that the achievement of any objective is being impeded, by another Member or Members, it may, with a view to reaching a mutually satisfactory resolution of the matter, request in writing consultations with the Member or Members in question. Each Member shall afford sympathetic consideration to any request from another Member for consultation.
>
> 17.4 If the Member that requested consultations considers that the consultations pursuant to paragraph 3 have failed to achieve a mutually agreed solution, and if final action has been taken by the administering authorities of the importing Member to levy definitive anti-dumping duties or to accept price undertakings, it may refer the matter to the Dispute Settlement Body ("DSB"). When a provisional meas-

> ure has a significant impact and the Member that requested consultations considers that the measure was taken contrary to the provisions of paragraph 1 of Article 7, that Member may also refer such matter to the DSB."

6.85 We first note that Article 17 of the Anti-Dumping Agreement does not replace the DSU as a coherent system of dispute settlement for that Agreement.[473] In this respect, the Appellate Body in *Guatemala - Cement* explained that "the rules and procedures of the DSU [...] apply to disputes brought pursuant to the consultation and dispute settlement provisions contained in Article 17".[474]

6.86 We also note that nothing in the terms of either Article 17.2 or Article 17.3 limits the scope of possible consultations under the Anti-Dumping Agreement. The Appellate Body in *Guatemala - Cement* explained that Article 17.3 was not listed in as a special or additional provision in Appendix 2 of the DSU because "it provides legal basis for consultations to be requested by a complaining member under the *Anti-Dumping Agreement*. Indeed, it is the equivalent provision in the Anti-Dumping Agreement to Articles XXII and XXIII of the GATT 1994, which serves as the basis for consultation and dispute settlement under the GATT 1994 [and] under most of the other agreements in Annex 1A of the *Marrakesh Agreement Establishing the World Trade Organization*". Thus, nothing in Articles 17.2 and 17.3 of the Anti-Dumping Agreement supports the view that consultations are limited to circumstances where certain measures have been adopted by the Member investigating dumping.

6.87 In our opinion, Article 17.4 deals with a particular situation under the Anti-Dumping Agreement, hence its status of a special or additional provision under the DSU. As stated by the Appellate Body in *Guatemala - Cement*:

> "We see the special or additional rules and procedures of a particular covered agreement as fitting together with the generally applicable rules and procedures of the DSU to form a comprehensive, integrated dispute settlement system for the *WTO Agreement*. The special or additional provisions listed in Appendix 2 of the DSU are designed to deal with the particularities of dispute settlement relating to obligations arising under a specific covered agreement, while Article 1 of the DSU seeks to establish an integrated and comprehensive dispute settlement system for all of the covered agreements of the *WTO Agreement* as a whole. It is, therefore, only in the specific circumstance where a provision of the DSU and a special or additional provision of another covered agreement are mutually inconsistent that the special or additional provision may be read to *prevail* over the provision of the DSU."[475]

6.88 This paragraph illustrates the function of Article 17.4. Article 17.4 deals with the particular question of challenging actions taken by anti-dumping authorities. However, there is nothing in that provision expressly limiting the scope of applica-

[473] *Op. Cit.*, para. 67.
[474] *Ibid.*, para. 64.
[475] *Ibid.*, para. 66.

tion of the DSU except in relation to the specific issue of Members' anti-dumping actions.

6.89 Our reading of Article 17.4 is not only confirmed by the immediate context of that provision, i.e. Article 17.1, 17.2 and 17.3, but also by other provisions of the Anti-Dumping Agreement. Article 18.4 provides that:

> "Each Member shall take all necessary steps, of a general or particular character, to ensure, no later than the date of entry into force of the WTO Agreement for it, the conformity of its laws, regulations and administrative procedures with the provisions of this Agreement as they may apply for the Member in question."

We understand the term "to ensure, no later than the date of entry into force of the WTO Agreement" in Article 18.4 of the Anti-Dumping Agreement as requiring the conformity of Members' anti-dumping laws as of the date of entry into force of the WTO Agreement for those Members. Moreover, a Member's anti-dumping legislation must be compatible with the WTO Agreement continuously, whether that legislation is applied or not. If dispute settlement could be initiated in relation to some specific anti-dumping *action* only, i.e. if the conformity of a domestic anti-dumping law could only be reviewed when that law is applied, the provisions of Article 18.4 would be deprived of their meaning and useful effect. A Member could maintain a WTO-incompatible law in total impunity as long as none of the measures referred to in Article 17.4 is adopted. Even if, on the occasion of a review of a particular action, the law on which the action was based could be found to be WTO-incompatible, the interpretation advocated by the United States would still fail to give meaning and legal effect to the terms of Article 18.4 and would be contrary to the principle of effectiveness.[476] Moreover, Article 18.4 requires that *all necessary steps*, of a general or particular nature, be taken by Members to ensure the conformity of their laws. These terms would be redundant if the anti-dumping laws of Members only had to be WTO-consistent in specific instances of application.

6.90 As could already be noticed from the previous paragraphs, the interpretation of Article 17 of the Anti-Dumping Agreement by the Appellate Body confirms our view. The argument of the United States is essentially based on an interpretation of paragraph 79 of the Appellate Body Report in *Guatemala - Cement* taken out of its context.[477] The facts at issue in the *Guatemala - Cement* case were different from

---

[476] See, e.g., Appellate Body Report on *Argentina - Safeguard Measures on Imporst of Footwear*, WT/DS121/AB/R, adopted 12 January 2000, DSR 2000:I, 515, para. 88 and Appellate Body Report on *United States - Standards for Reformulated and Conventional Gasoline*, WT/DS2/AB/R, adopted 20 May 1996, DSR 1996:I, 3 at 15.

[477] The Appellate Body Report in the *Guatemala - Cement* case, *supra*, footnote 433 referred to by the United States reads as follows:

> "79. Furthermore, Article 17.4 of the *Anti-Dumping Agreement* specifies the types of "measure" which may be referred as part of a "matter" to the DSB. Three types of anti-dumping measure are specified in Article 17.4: definitive anti-dumping duties, the acceptance of price undertakings, and provisional measures. According to Article 17.4, a "matter" may be referred to the DSB *only if* one of the relevant three anti-dumping measures is in place. This provision, when read together with Article 6.2 of the DSU, requires a panel request in a dispute brought

those before us. In that case, Mexico contested a specific investigation carried out by Guatemala against imports of Portland cement from Mexico. If one reads the reasoning of the Appellate Body in the factual context to which it pertains, it is not possible to draw the extensive conclusion suggested by the United States. The specific scope of the findings in that case is confirmed by the Appellate Body itself in the paragraph following the one quoted by the United States:

> "80. For all of these reasons, we conclude that the Panel erred in finding that Mexico did not need to identify "specific measures at issue" in this dispute. We find that in disputes under the *Anti-Dumping Agreement* relating to the initiation and conduct of anti-dumping investigations, a definitive anti-dumping duty, the acceptance of a price undertaking or a provisional measure must be identified as part of the matter referred to the DSB pursuant to the provisions of Article 17.4 of the *Anti-Dumping Agreement* and Article 6.2 of the DSU." (emphasis added)

Thus, the findings of the Appellate Body in *Guatemala-Cement* were limited to the taking of action in situations contemplated in Article 17.4. They could not be - and actually were not - intended to exclude the review of anti-dumping laws as such.

6.91 We therefore conclude that Article 17 of the Anti-Dumping Agreement does not prevent us from reviewing the conformity of laws as such under the Anti-Dumping Agreement, irrespective of whether the measures referred to in Article 17.4 have been adopted or not. The same applies, *a fortiori*, with respect to Article VI of the GATT 1994. In that respect, we consider that the findings of the panel and the Appellate Body in *Brazil - Desiccated Coconut* referred to by the United States are not applicable to this case, since those findings dealt with the question of the non-applicability of the Agreement on Subsidies and Countervailing Measures to existing measures or investigations initiated pursuant to applications made before the entry into force of that Agreement.[478]

(c) Relationship between Article VI of the GATT 1994 and the Anti-Dumping Agreement

6.92 Regarding the relationship between Article VI and the Anti-Dumping Agreement and, in particular, the question whether we could make findings regarding Arti-

---

under the *Anti-Dumping Agreement* to identify, as the specific measure at issue, either a definitive anti-dumping duty, the acceptance of a price undertaking, or a provisional measure. This requirement to identify a specific anti-dumping measure at issue in a panel request in no way limits the nature of the *claims* that may be brought concerning alleged nullification or impairment of benefits or the impeding of the achievement of any objective in a dispute under the *Anti-Dumping Agreement*. As we have observed earlier, there is a difference between the specific measures at issue - in the case of the *Anti-Dumping Agreement*, one of the three types of anti-dumping measure described in Article 17.4 - and the claims or the legal basis of the complaint referred to the DSB relating to those specific measures. In coming to this conclusion, we note that the language of Article 17.4 of the *Anti-Dumping Agreement* is unique to that Agreement."

[478] See Article 32.3 of the Agreement on Subsidies and Countervailing Measures.

cle VI independently from the Anti-Dumping Agreement, we note that the issue addressed by the panel and the Appellate Body in *Brazil - Desiccated Coconut*, to which the United States refers, must be differentiated from the one before us. In *Brazil - Desiccated Coconut*, the question was one of application of Article VI of the GATT when the WTO Agreement on Subsidies and Countervailing Measures did not apply. In the present case, the issue is whether the Panel can make findings in relation to Article VI only or whether the link between Article VI and the Anti-Dumping Agreement is such as to make impossible a finding under Article VI only.

6.93 We note that the panel in the *India - Quantitative Restrictions on Imports of Agricultural, Textile and Industrial Products*[479] case did not make findings under Article XVIII:11 of the GATT 1994 in isolation from the Understanding on Balance-of-Payments Provisions of the GATT 1994. Likewise, we have no intention to address Article VI in isolation from the Anti-Dumping Agreement. In the present case, the complainant has made claims based on the violation of provisions of Article VI and the Anti-Dumping Agreement. In our opinion, if the panel in *Brazil - Desiccated Coconut* confirmed that Article VI and the Agreement on Subsidies and Countervailing Measures were an "inseparable package of rights and obligations", this is because the solution proposed by the complainant would have led to apply Article VI in total disregard of the Agreement on Subsidies and Countervailing Measures. Such a solution cannot even be considered in our case. Article VI and the Anti-Dumping Agreement are part of the same treaty: the WTO Agreement. In application of the customary rules of interpretation of international law, we are bound to interpret Article VI of the GATT 1994 as part of the WTO Agreement and, pursuant to Article 31 of the Vienna Convention,[480] the Anti-Dumping Agreement forms part of the context of Article VI. This implies that we must look at Article VI and the Anti-Dumping Agreement as part of an "inseparable package of rights and obligations" and that Article VI should not be interpreted in a way that would deprive either Article VI or the Anti-Dumping Agreement of meaning.[481] However, this obligation does not prevent us from making findings in relation to Article VI only, as the panel did in its report on *India - Quantitative Restrictions*.

6.94 We conclude that we can make findings under Article VI without, at the same time, having to make findings under the provisions of the Anti-Dumping Agreement,

[479] Panel Report, *India – Quantitative Restrictions on Imports of Agricultural, Textile and Industrial Products*, ("*India - Quantitative Restrictions*"), WT/DS90/R, adopted 22 September 1999, DSR 1999:V, 1799, paras. 5.18-5.19. These findings were not modified by the Appellate Body.

[480] We recall that the official title of the Anti-Dumping Agreement is "Agreement on Implementation of Article VI of the General Agreement on Tariffs and Trade 1994". This agreement is essential for the interpretation of Article VI. Articles 1 and 18.1 of the Anti-Dumping Agreement confirm the close link between Article VI and the Anti-Dumping Agreement. Moreover, as was recalled by the Appellate Body in the case on *Brazil - Desiccated Coconut, supra*, footnote 434, the WTO Agreement is a single treaty instrument which was accepted by the WTO Members as a single undertaking. As a result, the Anti-Dumping Agreement is part of the context of Article VI since Article 31.2 of the Vienna Convention provides that "the context for the purpose of the interpretation of a treaty shall comprise, [...] the text, including its preamble and annexes...". We are therefore not only entitled to consider the Anti-Dumping Agreement, but we are also *required* to do so under the general principles of interpretation of public international law.

[481] See, also, *Argentina - Safeguards, supra*, footnote 476, paras. 74 and 81-83.

and *vice-versa*. However, the fact that Article VI and the Anti-Dumping Agreement represent an inseparable package of rights and disciplines requires that we interpret each of the provisions invoked by Japan in its claims in conjunction with the other relevant provisions of this "inseparable package", so as to give meaning to all of them.

C. Applicability of Article VI of the GATT 1994 and of the Anti-Dumping Agreement to the 1916 Act

1. Preliminary Remarks on the Possibility of Interpreting the 1916 Act in a WTO-Compatible Manner and on its "Mandatory/Non-Mandatory" Nature

(a) Issue before the Panel

6.95 The United States argues that if the complaining party is challenging a law as such, the first question for the Panel is whether that law is mandatory or discretionary. The United States contends that the 1916 Act is non-mandatory legislation within the meaning of the GATT1947/WTO practice essentially because (i) with respect to both civil and criminal proceedings, there is a possibility for US courts to interpret the provisions of the 1916 Act in a manner consistent with the WTO obligations of the United States - as evidenced by court decisions so far - and (ii) the US Department of Justice has discretion to initiate or not criminal proceedings under the 1916 Act.[482] Japan considers that the 1916 Act is mandatory legislation because it is not susceptible of a range of meanings but rather mandates the imposition of sanctions. Japan adds that panels have consistently ruled that laws that mandate GATT/WTO-inconsistent actions can be challenged as such. Japan also considers that the obligation set out in Article XVI:4 of the Agreement Establishing the WTO "to ensure the [WTO] conformity of [...] laws, regulations and administrative procedures" should apply in the present dispute, rather than the mandatory/non-mandatory dichotomy.

6.96 For the reasons presented below, we shall address these arguments as part of our review of the claims raised by Japan under Article VI of the GATT 1994 and the Anti-Dumping Agreement and, if necessary, Article III:4 of the GATT 1994, rather than as a question of admissibility of the claims of Japan.[483]

---

[482] The United States does not seem to allege that a similar discretion exists in relation to the civil proceedings which would make the 1916 Act non-mandatory.

[483] Such an approach is also consistent with the practice of other panels, which addressed this issue in the course of their review of the conformity of measures with provisions of the GATT 1947. See *United States - Measures Affecting the Importation, Internal Sale and Use of Tobacco*, adopted on 4 October 1994, BISD 41S/131, para. 118. That report refers to the Report of the Panel on *United States - Taxes on Petroleum and certain Imported Substances*, adopted on 17 June 1987, BISD 34S/136, p. 160; the Report of the Panel on *EEC - Regulation on Imports of Parts and Components, Op. Cit.*, pp. 198-199; the Report of the Panel on *Thailand, Restrictions on Importation of and Internal Taxes on Cigarettes*, adopted on 7 November 1990, BISD 37S/200 pp. 227-228; the Report of the Panel *on United States - Measures Affecting Alcoholic and Malt Beverages*, adopted on 19 June 1992, BISD 39S/206, pp. 281-282, 289-290; and the Report of the Panel on *United States - Denial of MFN Treatment as to Non-Rubber Footwear from Brazil*, adopted on 19

6.97 As a preliminary remark, it should be noted that, even though the parties have used the terms "mandatory/non-mandatory" or "discretionary" legislation in their arguments with respect to different aspects of the 1916 Act, we consider that we should differentiate the issues before us. We consider that the question whether the US Department of Justice has discretion to initiate or not criminal proceedings under the 1916 Act is indeed a question of application of the doctrine on mandatory/non-mandatory legislation within the meaning usually given to it in the GATT and in public international law. The question whether the 1916 Act could be, or has been, interpreted in a way that would make it fall outside the scope of Article VI is, however, simply a question of assessing the current meaning of the law.

(b) The Possibility of Interpreting the 1916 Act in a WTO-Compatible Manner

6.98 Concerning the argument according to which US courts have interpreted in the past and/or could in the future interpret the 1916 Act in a manner consistent with the WTO obligations of the United States, the United States refers to the panel report on *United States - Measures Affecting the Importation, Internal Sale and Use of Tobacco*[484] as being the case whose facts most closely resemble the present case. For the United States also, there is a presumption that if a law is susceptible to an interpretation that is WTO consistent, domestic authorities will interpret that law so as to avoid a conflict with WTO obligations. This presumption may be seen as underlying the finding of the Panel in *United States - Tobacco* that a domestic law susceptible of multiple interpretations would not violate a party's international obligations so long as one possible interpretation permits action consistent with those obligations.

6.99 In our opinion, the United States refers to *United States - Tobacco* for essentially two reasons. First, the United States argues that a law which can be interpreted in a WTO-consistent manner is a law that does not mandate a WTO-illegal action. Second, the United States claims that, for Japan's challenge to succeed, Japan must demonstrate not only that the 1916 Act authorises WTO-inconsistent action, but that it mandates such action. In other words, it must show that this legislation is not susceptible to an interpretation that would permit the US government to comply with its obligations.

6.100 The issue in this case is primarily, like in the *United States - Tobacco* case, a question whether the text of a law contains ambiguities or not. However, in our opinion, similarities are limited to that aspect. In the *United States - Tobacco* case, the panel had to deal with the question whether the ambiguous term at issue mandated a violation of Article VIII of GATT 1947. In the present case, what is at issue is whether the terms of the 1916 Act are such as to make Article VI *applicable* to that law. We are consequently at an earlier stage of our analysis than the panel in the *United States - Tobacco* case. Moreover, in the *United States - Tobacco* case, the United States had as yet neither changed the fee structure nor promulgated rules implementing the law at issue. In the present case, the 1916 Act did not require any

June 1992, BISD 39S/128, p. 152. See also, under the WTO Agreement, the report of the panel on *Canada Aircraft*, *supra*, footnote 32, para. 9.124.

[484] *Op. Cit.*, hereinafter "*United States - Tobacco*".

implementing measures from the US government and, contrary to the law at issue in the *United States - Tobacco* case, it has been applied in a number of instances by US courts. Consequently, the situations faced by this Panel and the panel in the *United States - Tobacco* case are factually different.

6.101 These differences have implications for the burden of proof. In the *United States - Tobacco* case, the extensive burden of proof imposed on the complainants was obviously related to the absence of any application of the ambiguous term by the executive branch of the US government at the time of the findings. The United States had until then applied its law in conformity with Article VIII of the GATT 1947 and there was no evidence that the United States intended to apply the law in a GATT-incompatible manner. Therefore, imposing on the complainants the burden to prove that the US law at issue could not be applied in a GATT-consistent manner was consistent with the presumption that the United States would continue to apply the GATT in good faith.

6.102 In contrast, several courts have interpreted and applied the 1916 Act. In fact, reaching a decision on the US argument requires the Panel to determine whether the interpretation of the 1916 Act by US courts has been such as to actually make the 1916 Act WTO-compatible by making it fall outside the scope of Article VI of the GATT 1994 and the Anti-Dumping Agreement. In such a context, Japan only needs to prove that the 1916 Act, as it has been interpreted and applied so far by US courts, meets the conditions to fall within the scope of Article VI and the Anti-Dumping Agreement. If Japan succeeds in proving this, we will proceed with a review of the compatibility of the 1916 Act with Article VI and the Anti-Dumping Agreement.

6.103 The question whether there could be a possibility to interpret the 1916 Act in the future so that it would fall outside the scope of Article VI would be relevant, according to the *United States - Tobacco* case, only if the 1916 Act had not yet been applied. Since the 1916 Act has actually been applied and has been subject to interpretation by US courts, the issue before us is (i) whether Article VI and the Anti-Dumping Agreement are found to be applicable to the 1916 Act on the basis of the current court interpretation of the terms of the 1916 Act and (ii) whether a violation of Article VI and/or the Anti-Dumping Agreement by the 1916 Act as currently applied, is identified.

6.104 Even if the factual circumstances in the present case and in the *United States - Tobacco* case were considered to be comparable, we recall that, in *United States - Tobacco*, a crucial element in the finding of the panel had been the presence of an *ambiguity* in the text of the law under review. In that case, the term "comparable" could be interpreted in GATT-compatible as well as in GATT-incompatible ways. Assuming that the reasoning of the panel in the *United States - Tobacco* case could be extended to the present situation in spite of the differences highlighted above, if we find that no such ambiguity exists regarding the applicability of Article VI to the text of the 1916 Act itself or as interpreted by the US courts, (i) the burden of proof which the United States alleges was applied in the *US - Tobacco* case will not apply in this case and (ii) we will conclude that the 1916 Act falls within the scope of Article VI of the GATT 1994 and the Anti-Dumping Agreement and will address its compatibility with these provisions as we would for any other legislation.[485]

(c) Mandatory/Non-Mandatory Nature of the 1916 Act

6.105 The United States argues that, in relation to the criminal proceedings provided for in the 1916 Act, the US Department of Justice has the discretion to decide whether or not to bring a criminal prosecution. In other words, while the 1916 Act authorises the Department of Justice to bring a criminal prosecution, it does not mandate it. Japan is of the view that the obligation set out in Article XVI:4 of the Agreement Establishing the WTO and Article 18.4 of the Anti-Dumping Agreement should apply in the present dispute, rather than the mandatory/non-mandatory dichotomy drawn from GATT 1947 practice.

6.106 We note that the terms of Article 18.4 of the Anti-Dumping Agreement require that Members bring their laws into conformity with the Anti-Dumping Agreement at the time of the entry into force of that agreement for them. This requirement seems to contradict the concept of mandatory/non-mandatory legislation, which does not require laws as such to be compatible, but only instances of application.[486] We recall that Article 16.6(a) of the Tokyo Round Agreement on Implementation of Article VI of GATT[487] contained provisions almost identical to Article 18.4 of the Anti-Dumping Agreement. We also note that, in relation to Article 16.6(a) or its equivalent under the Tokyo Round Agreement on Interpretation and Application of Articles VI, XVI and XXIII of GATT,[488] past panels found that a countervailing duty law a such could be reviewed by a panel and that the discretion to initiate an investigation was insufficient to consider as "non-mandatory" a law reviewed under those agreements.[489]

---

485 If we conclude that the 1916 Act falls within the scope of Article VI, we will not need to take position on the issue whether, in light of Article XVI:4 of the Agreement Establishing the WTO, the reasoning in the *United States - Tobacco* report, which was adopted under the GATT 1947, would still be valid after the entry into force of the WTO Agreement.

486 We recall that the panel on *United States - Section 301-310 of the Trade Act of 1974*, adopted on 20 January 2000, WT/DS152/R, claimed that its findings did not require the wholesale reversing of earlier GATT and WTO jurisprudence on mandatory and discretionary legislation (see para. 7.54 and footnote 675). We nevertheless understand that the reasoning of the panel in that case was apparently based on the fact that Article 23 of the DSU may prohibit legislation with certain discretionary elements and therefore the very fact of having in the legislation such discretion could, in effect, preclude WTO consistency. We note that Article 18.4 of the Anti-Dumping Agreement may have a similar effect.

487 Hereinafter the "Tokyo Round Anti-Dumping Agreement".

488 Hereinafter the "Tokyo Round Subsidies Agreement".

489 See *Panel on United States Definition of Industry Concerning Wine And Grape Products*, adopted on 28 April 1992, BISD 39S/436 (hereinafter "*United States - Definition of Wine Industry*") and the report of the panel on *EC - Anti-Dumping Duties on Audio Tapes in Cassettes Originating in Japan*, ADP 136, 28 April 1995 (hereinafter "*EC - Audio Cassettes*"). The latter was not adopted. However, we recall that in its report on *Japan - Taxes on Alcoholic Beverages, supra*, footnote 78, at 108, the Appellate Body confirmed that "a panel could nevertheless find useful guidance in the reasoning of an unadopted panel report that it considered to be relevant." Therefore, we will refer to the reasoning of the panel in *EC - Audio-Cassettes* as guidance to our own reasoning.

6.107 From the above, it would seem to us that the issue of the "mandatory/non-mandatory" nature of a law has apparently been addressed differently under Article VI of the GATT 1947 and the Tokyo Round anti-dumping and subsidies agreements than under Article III of the GATT 1947 and the other GATT 1947 provisions referred to by the United States. In order to avoid making unnecessary findings, we consider it appropriate to address this issue once we have determined whether the 1916 Act falls within the scope of Article VI and the Anti-Dumping Agreement or not, a determination to be made in any event for the reasons mentioned in the previous paragraphs.

2. *Does the 1916 Act Fall within the Scope of Article VI of the GATT 1994 and the Anti-Dumping Agreement?*

(a) Preliminary Remarks

(i) Scope of Article VI of the GATT 1994 and Scope of the Anti-Dumping Agreement

6.108 A first methodological question to be clarified from the outset is how we should approach the compatibility of the 1916 Act with Article VI and with the Anti-Dumping Agreement, respectively. In this respect, we note that Article 1.1 of the Anti-Dumping Agreement establishes a link between Article VI and the Anti-Dumping Agreement:

> "An anti-dumping measure shall be applied only under the circumstances provided for in Article VI of GATT 1994 and pursuant to investigations initiated [footnote 1 omitted] and conducted in accordance with the provisions of this Agreement."

Article 18.1 of the Anti-Dumping Agreement also confirms this link:

> "No specific action against dumping of exports from another Member can be taken except in accordance with the provisions of GATT 1994, as interpreted by this Agreement.[footnote 24]"[490]

We also recall our consideration of the relationship between Article VI and the Anti-Dumping Agreement in section VI.B.4.(c) above. We concluded that Article VI and the Anti-Dumping Agreement are one "single package of rights and obligations". We are of the view that if we find that the 1916 Act falls within the scope of the provisions of Article VI of the GATT 1994 dealing with dumping, it also must fall within the scope of the Anti-Dumping Agreement. As a result, we will consider primarily whether the 1916 Act falls within the scope of the provisions on anti-dumping of Article VI, bearing in mind the terms of the Anti-Dumping Agreement and the extent to which they may influence the interpretation of Article VI.

---

[490] Footnote 24 to Article 18.1 reads as follows:

> "This is not intended to preclude action under other relevant provisions of GATT 1994, as appropriate."

(ii) Approach of the Panel to the Question of the Definition of the Scope of Article VI of GATT 1994 in Relation to the 1916 Act

6.109 According to Japan, Article VI of GATT 1994 and the Anti-Dumping Agreement address international price discrimination where prices in the importing market are lower than prices in the exporting market. When these conditions giving rise to this type of price discrimination are met, a law, whatever it may be called, is an anti-dumping measure and must conform to Article VI of GATT 1994 and the Anti-Dumping Agreement. Japan considers that the terms of the 1916 Act are unambiguous. The conduct targeted by the 1916 Act is the same as "dumping" as defined in Article VI and the Anti-Dumping Agreement and the addition of qualifying elements on the core features of the law does not alter the fundamental nature of the 1916 Act as an anti-dumping law.

6.110 The United States considers that Article VI only addresses actions taken for the purpose of offsetting or preventing injurious dumping, not actions that are not designed to offset or prevent injurious dumping, as is the case with the 1916 Act. Nowhere does the text of Article VI or the Anti-Dumping Agreement state that its disciplines govern any law based upon the concept of international price discrimination regardless of any other elements required to be proven under the law. The 1916 Act addresses a specific form of price discrimination with predatory intent. Moreover, the 1916 Act imposes damages on importers, not a border adjustment in the form of a duty on imported products. The nature of the measure imposed in application of the law removes any doubt that the 1916 Act is an "internal law" subject only to Article III of GATT 1994.

6.111 We note that the views of the parties are diametrically opposed as to the criteria that should be used to determine the applicability of Article VI of the GATT 1994 to the 1916 Act. Japan favours a broad interpretation of Article VI based on the definition of dumping found in Article VI:1. The United States favours a narrow interpretation: Article VI applies only when a Member wishes to address dumping practices through anti-dumping duties.

6.112 First, the Panel considers that its role, pursuant to Article 3.2 of the DSU, is to clarify the meaning of Article VI in order to determine whether it applies, as claimed by Japan, to the type of measures addressed by the 1916 Act. For the sake of clarity, we consider that we should first address the applicability of Article VI to the *terms* of the 1916 Act as such, in isolation from subsequent interpretation(s). We will then review the circumstances of the enactment of the 1916 Act (including the legislative history) as well as the relevant US court case-law and determine to what extent they may affect the conclusions that we will have reached on the basis of the text only.[491]

---

[491] As recalled in para. 6.58 above, the mere description or categorization of a measure under the domestic law as well as the policy purpose behind the measure cannot be a decisive factor in the categorization of that measure under the WTO Agreement. We therefore do not consider as decisive the classification of the 1916 Act under the US Code or the fact that it is generally called the "Anti-dumping Act of 1916". We consider that we should exclusively rely at this stage on what the text of the law expressly says. This does not mean that we should disregard the objective of the 1916 Act.

6.113 Second, we note that we are called upon to consider the compatibility of a specific law with Article VI of GATT 1994, not to make an interpretation of the scope of that Article in absolute terms. Thus, any assessment we may make regarding the scope of Article VI will be limited to the specific issues raised by the terms of the 1916 Act.

6.114 Third, in the light of the arguments of the parties and of the above-mentioned comment, we note that the determination of the scope of Article VI *vis-à-vis* the 1916 Act requires that we reply to the following questions:

(i) Does the 1916 Act address the same type of price differentiation as Article VI?

(ii) If this is the case, is the type of "effects" targeted by the 1916 Act (i.e. "intent of destroying or injuring an industry in the United States, or of preventing the establishment of an industry in the United States, or of restraining or monopolizing any part of trade and commerce in such articles in the United States") relevant to determining whether the 1916 Act falls within the scope of Article VI? And;

(iii) is the type of measures imposed under the 1916 Act relevant to determining whether the 1916 Act falls within the scope of Article VI?[492]

(b) Analysis of the text of the 1916 Act in light of Article VI:1 of the GATT 1994

(i) Does the 1916 Act Address the Same Type of Price Discrimination as Article VI of the GATT 1994?

6.115 Article VI:1 provides, in relevant parts, as follows:

> "The contracting parties recognize that dumping, by which products of one country are introduced into the commerce of another country at less than the normal value of the products, is to be condemned if it causes or threatens material injury to an established industry in the territory of a contracting party or materially retards the establishment of a domestic industry. For the purpose of this article, a product is to be considered as being introduced into the commerce of an importing country at less than its normal value, if the price of the product exported from one country to another
>
> (a) is less than the comparable price, in the ordinary course of trade, for the like product when destined for consumption in the exporting country, or,

However, for now we will consider it only to the extent that it results from the terms of the law only, to the exclusion of the legislative history or the subsequent court practice, which we will address later. This also seems to be consistent with US court practice. In *Zenith I* (1975), *Op. Cit.*, at p. 246, Judge Higginbotham stated that "as always, when a court is called to construe a statute, it is wise to begin by reading the statute itself."

[492] This question is different from the issue whether anti-dumping duties are the only remedy allowed under Article VI. This issue is addressed in the section concerning the violation of Article VI:2.

(b) in the absence of such domestic price, is less than either

(i) the highest comparable price for the like product for export to any third country in the ordinary course of trade, or

(ii) the cost of production of the product in the country of origin plus a reasonable addition for selling cost and profit.

Due allowance shall be made in each case for differences in conditions and terms of sale, for differences in taxation, and for other differences affecting price comparability." [notes *Ad Article VI:1* omitted]

6.116 We note that, for measures to be applied under Article VI, three conditions have to be met: there must be (a) "dumping", i.e. the pricing practice at the origin of the application of Article VI; (b) material injury or threat of material injury to an established domestic industry or material retardation of the establishment of a domestic industry, i.e. the effect of the dumping; and (c) a causal link between the two. Article VI and the Anti-Dumping Agreement clearly separate these conditions.

6.117 Article VI:1 defines "dumping" as the introduction of products of one country into the commerce of another country at less than their normal value.[493] Apart from an additional explanation of how to determine normal value,[494] this definition of "dumping" is not qualified anywhere in Article VI.[495] The conditions for "dumping" to exist are the following:

(i) there must be products imported and cleared through customs ("introduction into the commerce"); and

(ii) those imported products must be priced at a price lower than their normal value, i.e. their price in a foreign country, be it the country of production or another country of export, or a constructed value based on a calculation of cost and profits.

In other words, dumping within the meaning of Article VI exists when there is a price difference between like products sold in two markets, one of which is not within the jurisdiction of the same Member. In addition, the price of the products in the country of exportation must be lower than the price of the like products in the country of production or in a third country to which they are exported.[496]

---

[493] We note that this definition is close to the definition of dumping given by Jacob Viner in *Dumping, A Problem in International Trade* (1923), p. 3, i.e. "price-discrimination between national markets." The court in *Zenith III, Op. Cit.*, p. 1213, refers to the 1966 edition which includes, at p. 4, a slightly revised definition: "price discrimination between purchasers in different national markets."

[494] We do not read the language "For the purpose of this article, a product is to be considered as being introduced into the commerce of an importing country at less than its normal value, if the price of the product exported from one country to another..." as qualifying anything but the term "normal value".

[495] See Article VI:2, second sentence, which provides that "For the purposes of this Article, the margin of dumping is the price difference determined in accordance with the provisions of para. 1." Additional conditions have been introduced in the Anti-Dumping Agreement, such as the *de minimis* requirement for the margin of dumping (Article 5.8 of the Anti-Dumping Agreement) but they do not affect the original definition to such an extent that they would change our conclusions.

[496] The existence of a price difference between two markets *located in two different Members*, together with a lower price in the importing country that in the country of export, are essential fea-

6.118 Neither the context of the first paragraph of Article VI, nor the object and purpose of the GATT 1994 or the WTO Agreement contradicts this assessment. On the contrary, Article VI:1(a) and (b) confirm that no qualification applies to the definition of the price difference requirement. There is no requirement that the export price be above or below fixed or variable costs or that price undercutting, price suppression or price depression be identified for "dumping" to exist, even though they may be considered for injury purposes. In other words, dumping exist as soon as there is a price difference, as small as it may be, subject to the *de minimis* provisions of the Anti-Dumping Agreement.

6.119 When considering the terms of the 1916 Act, we note that it also contains a price discrimination test:

> "It shall be unlawful for any person *importing or assisting in importing* any articles from any foreign country into the United States, commonly and systematically to import, sell or cause to be imported or sold such articles within the United States *at a price substantially less than the actual market value or wholesale price of such articles, at the time of exportation to the United States, in the principal markets of the country of their production, or of other foreign countries* to which they are commonly exported after adding to such market value or wholesale price, freight, duty, and other charges and expenses necessarily incident to the importation and sale thereof in the United States..." (emphasis added)

This test includes requirements similar to the requirement of Article VI (i.e., the introduction of the dumped product into the commerce of one Member) since it refers to "import or sell or cause to be imported or sold [...] within the United States". We further note that the 1916 Act is premised on a comparison between two prices, one in the United States, the other in the country of production of the product or in a third country where the product is also sold. There is consequently a very close similarity between the definition of dumping in Article VI and the transnational price discrimination test found in the 1916 Act.

6.120 The United States argues that the 1916 Act has additional requirements compared with Article VI. In the first place, the 1916 Act requires the price difference to be "substantial" and the importation and sales to be done "commonly and systematically". Secondly, the 1916 Act includes additional requirements that are not found in Article VI, which make it an instrument addressing specific forms of price discrimination in an anti-trust context.

6.121 We do not consider that conditions which make the establishment of dumping more difficult, such as the requirement of substantial price difference and of common and systematic dumping are such as to make the price discrimination test of the 1916 Act fall outside the scope of the definition of Article VI:1. The fact that additional requirements make a finding of dumping more difficult does not affect the applicability of Article VI as long as the test of the 1916 Act requires a price difference between two markets, each located in the territory of a different Member. Members

tures to differentiate dumping from other forms of price discrimination and pricing practices. See, e.g., Viner, *Op. Cit.*, pp. 2-3.

remain free to apply requirements which make the imposition of measures more difficult, but they may not exempt themselves from the rules and disciplines of the WTO Agreement when counteracting dumping as such.

6.122 This said, would there be other elements in the text of the 1916 Act that would lead us to conclude that the transnational price discrimination test in the 1916 Act nevertheless does not meet the definition of dumping in Article VI? We note that the 1916 Act relies not only on the actual market value but also on wholesale price. We consider that the meaning of the terms "comparable price, in the ordinary course of trade, for the like product when destined for consumption in the exporting country" found in Article VI:1(a) is broad enough to include the phrase "principal markets of the country of [...] production [of the imported merchandise]" or of "other foreign countries to which they are commonly exported". The 1916 Act also refers to sales on the "principal markets" of "other foreign countries to which they are commonly exported". This may not be the "highest comparable price for the like product for export to any third country in the ordinary course of trade" found in Article VI:1(b) but, once again, the criteria of Article VI:1 are sufficiently broad to encompass such sales. Moreover, the criteria used in the 1916 Act do not refer to other concepts that could be differentiated from those found in Article VI:1. Finally, we note that the 1916 Act does not refer to the possibility to use a "constructed" normal value, within the meaning of Article VI:1(b)(ii). However, this only makes the transnational price discrimination test in the 1916 Act "narrower" than the definition of "dumping" in Article VI:1. It does not make it fall outside the scope of that article. We also note that the 1916 Act provides for adjustments. Even though these adjustments are not those found in the last sub-paragraph of Article VI:1, they do not affect the scope of the price discrimination test in the 1916 Act in relation to Article VI. On the contrary, they confirm the similarity of the two texts as far as the identification of the pricing practice at issue is concerned.

6.123 This does not mean that the criteria for establishing price discrimination under the 1916 Act would always be compatible with the requirements of Article VI of the GATT 1994. This means only that we do not find in these criteria anything that would make us consider that the 1916 Act transnational price discrimination test would partly or totally fall outside the definition of dumping found in Article VI:1.

6.124 The United States argues that the Panel's description of the 1916 Act price discrimination test (i.e. "commonly and systematically to import, sell or cause to be imported or sold such articles within the United States at a price substantially less than the actual market value or wholesale price of such articles") is incomplete. The 1916 Act addresses a particular type of price discrimination, namely, predatory pricing. For this reason, the price discrimination test in the 1916 Act includes not just the language quoted by the Panel, but also the additional language describing the predatory intent that is required to be shown.[497]

6.125 We understand the US argument as meaning that price discrimination for anti-dumping purposes is of a different nature than price discrimination for anti-trust purposes. We noted above that Article VI differentiates between the pricing practice

[497] We note that this additional language corresponds to what the Panel has described as the "intent" test under the 1916 Act.

("dumping") and its effects (material injury). We note that the Anti-Dumping Agreement confirms this differentiation by addressing dumping and injury in two separate provisions (Articles 2 and 3). We also look at the 1916 Act as requiring two separate inquiries, the second one qualifying the results of the first. The first one deals with the identification of a transnational price difference in the form of a lower price on the US market than in the exporting country or a third country of export. The second one deals with the identification of an intent to affect in some ways a US industry or US commerce. However, even if this "intent" were to imply the finding of a certain type of pricing practice on the US market, it would not affect the basic requirement of a price difference between two markets, one located in the United States and one in the exporting country or a third country of export. As noted, this basic requirement is identical to that of Article VI:1.

6.126 Similarly, the United States considers that the prices to be considered under the 1916 Act are not the same as those considered under Article VI and the Anti-Dumping Agreement. The 1916 Act provides that the US import price is the price at which the product at issue is imported or sold *within* the United States. In contrast, the US import price found in the Article VI definition of dumping, as further described in Article 2 of the Anti-Dumping Agreement, is normally the price in the United States that is "made at the same level of trade, normally at the ex-factory level, and in respect of sales made at as nearly as possible the same time" as the price in the exporting country or third country used to establish the *normal value*, with due allowances made for price comparability purposes. The foreign price under the 1916 Act is similar to, but nevertheless different from, the foreign price found in the Article VI definition of dumping, as further described in Article 2 of the Anti-Dumping Agreement.

6.127 We note that the terms of Article VI are sufficiently broad to include the types of prices used in the 1916 Act. We also recall our reasoning in paragraph 6.125 above. There is nothing in the types of prices referred to in the 1916 Act that would be of such a nature that they would be specific to anti-trust, to the exclusion of anti-dumping. On the contrary, the type of prices on which the 1916 Act is based meets the criteria of "normal value" and "export price" within the meaning of Article VI and the Anti-Dumping Agreement. The differences, far from making the 1916 Act fall outside the scope of Article VI, should rather be seen as violations of the requirements of the Anti-Dumping Agreement.

6.128 We therefore conclude that the 1916 Act addresses the same type of price discrimination as Article VI of the GATT 1994.

(ii) Is the Type of "Effects" Targeted by the 1916 Act Relevant to Determining whether the 1916 Act Falls within the Scope of Article VI of the GATT 1994?

6.129 We note that Article VI:1, first sentence, provides that dumping is to be condemned "if it causes or threatens" material injury. Taken in accordance with their ordinary meaning, the terms of the first sentence of Article VI:1 mean that, even though the condition for action against dumping by a Member is the existence of some injury, the prerequisite for such action is the presence of "dumping" as defined in that sentence.

6.130 We recall that the price discrimination addressed by the 1916 Act must be done with the intent of (a) "destroying" or (b) "injuring an industry in the United States", or of (c) "preventing the establishment of an industry in the United States", or of (d) "restraining" or (e) "monopolizing any part of trade and commerce [in the goods concerned] in the United States." We note that the first three tests are very similar to the material injury and retardation tests of Article VI:1, while the two last ones are more of the type used in an anti-trust context[498] and thus clearly different from the requirement of material injury of Article VI:1. However, we found above that the existence of "dumping" within the meaning of Article VI:1 is a condition *sine qua non* for a Member to take action under Article VI. Likewise, it is our understanding from the US case-law that, before identifying any intent under the 1916 Act, US judges would also have to establish that there has been importation or that there has been sales at discriminatory prices of the type required by that law.[499] Moreover, we have been presented with no evidence that transnational price discrimination under the 1916 Act could be presumed when the court had only established the existence of an intent to destroy, injure or prevent the establishment of an industry in the United States, or to restrain or monopolise any part of the trade in the product concerned within the United States. Therefore, we conclude that the existence in the 1916 Act of the additional requirements referred to by the United States, which are not found in Article VI, does not *per se* suffice to make the 1916 Act fall outside the scope of Article VI.

6.131 Moreover, we recall that dumping "is to be condemned if it causes or threatens" to cause certain effects listed in Article VI:1. We consider that Article VI:1 should be interpreted as limiting the use of measures against dumping as such to the situations expressly foreseen in Article VI.[500] The implicit meaning of Article VI:1, first sentence, is that if dumping has none of the injurious effects contemplated by that Article, it is not to be "condemned". We note in this respect that the terms of Article VI:1, first sentence, are quite broad. If, as the United States argues, Article VI:1 had been designed merely as a carve-out to the obligations of Article II of the

---

[498] See the Robinson-Patman Act, which provides that the "effect of such discrimination may be substantially to lessen competition or tend to create a monopoly in any line of commerce, or to injure, destroy, or prevent competition with any person who either grants or knowingly receives the benefit of such discrimination or with customers of either of them."

[499] See the statement of the court in *In Re Japanese Electronic Products II* (1983), at p. 324, that:

> "The first element necessary to a finding of dumping under the 1916 Act is proof that a price differential exists between two comparable products, one of which is imported or sold in the United States and the other of which is sold in the exporting country."

See also *Helmac II* (1993), p. 591,which recognised that "dumping: the pricing of goods on the American market at a price lower than on the home market" was "the key to liability under the [1916] Act".

[500] That such a limitation was clearly envisaged by the drafters of Article VI is confirmed by the Report of the Sub-Committee at the Havana Conference. The Sub-Committee considered the provision which was to replace the original Article VI in the GATT 1947 and noted that "The Article as agreed to by the Sub-Committee condemns *injurious 'price dumping'* as defined therein and does not relate to other types of dumping." (emphasis added) (Havana Reports, p. 74, para. 23, as reported in *GATT, Analytical Index: Guide to GATT Law and Practice, Updated 6th Edition* (1995), p. 222)

GATT 1994, applicable only when a Member wishes to impose anti-dumping duties, the term "is to be condemned" would not have been used. Rather, the term "is to be subject to anti-dumping duties" would have been used. Since we have to regard the text of the treaty as the most achieved expression of the intent of the parties to that treaty,[501] we cannot assume that the terms of the treaty were not carefully selected to meet the intent of the parties. Therefore, we do not read the terms of Article VI:1 in their ordinary meaning and in their context as supporting the view of the United States.

6.132 In our opinion, accepting the allegation of the United States that the disciplines of Article VI are only applicable to the extent a Member wants to address situations of material injury, threat thereof or material retardation of the establishment of a domestic industry would defeat the purpose of Article VI and the Anti-Dumping Agreement. From the terms of Article VI, we deduce that the purpose of that provision is to define the conditions under which the imposition of anti-dumping measures is allowed. This purpose is confirmed by the context of Article VI. Article 1, first sentence, of the Anti-Dumping Agreement provides that:

> "An anti-dumping measure shall be applied *only under the circumstances provided for in Article VI of GATT 1994* and pursuant to investigations initiated [footnote 1 omitted] and conducted in accordance with the provisions of this Agreement." (emphasis added)

Article 18.1 of the Anti-Dumping Agreement also confirms this understanding:

> "No specific action against dumping of exports from another Member can be taken *except in accordance with the provisions of GATT 1994*, as interpreted by this Agreement. [footnote 24 omitted]"[502] (emphasis added)

This implies that, by adopting Article VI of the GATT 1994 and the Anti-Dumping Agreement, Members have agreed to use only one permissible approach against "dumping" as such. The interpretation suggested by the United States would undermine the useful effect of the provisions of Article VI and of the Anti-Dumping Agreement. In this respect, we do not read footnote 24 to Article 18.1 as undermining our position. Article VI is the only provision of the GATT 1994 addressing specifically the conditions for imposing measures against dumping. Reading footnote 24

[501] See Mustafa Kamil Yasseen: *L'Interprétation des Traités d'après la Convention de Vienne sur le Droit des Traités*, Recueil des Cours de l'Académie de La Haye (1974) p. 1:

> "[...] le texte est surtout l'expression authentique de l'intérêt des parties, il est supposé incarner ce que les parties ont voulu".

See also the report of the International Law Commission to the UN General Assembly, Yearbook of the International Law Commission (1966), Vol. II, A/CN.4/SER.A/1966/Add.1, p. 221:

> "The second principle [contained in para. 1 of Article 31 of the Vienna Convention] is the very essence of the textual approach: the parties are to be presumed to have that intention which appears from the ordinary meaning of the terms used by them."

[502] We did not overlook the terms of footnote 24. Footnote 24, as we understand it, does not affect our conclusion that, when dealing with dumping as such, Members must comply with Article VI of the GATT and the Anti-Dumping Agreement. See our discussion of footnote 24 in section VI:D.2(c) below.

as permitting actions other than anti-dumping actions allowed under other provisions, as long as the measure does not address dumping as such, is fully consistent with the principle of useful interpretation.

6.133 For these reasons, we do not consider that the existence of other "effect" tests than those provided for under Article VI would be sufficient to exclude the 1916 Act from the scope of Article VI. The 1916 Act may be targeting particular effects of cross-border price discrimination. However, to the extent that such price discrimination meets the definition of "dumping" contained in Article VI:1, it is, in our view, subject to the disciplines of Article VI and the Anti-Dumping Agreement.[503]

6.134 Finally, the United States argues that the existence of an anti-trust objective in a law regulating cross-border price discrimination removes it from the scope of Article VI of the GATT 1994. While we agree that Article VI applies when Members have recourse to a given trade policy instrument, i.e. anti-dumping action, we do not agree that the application of Article VI is dependent on the objective pursued by the Member concerned. As we have demonstrated in the previous paragraphs, Article VI is based on an objective premise. If a Member's legislation is based on a test that meets the definition of Article VI:1, Article VI applies. The stated purpose of the law cannot affect this conclusion.[504]

6.135 We therefore conclude that the fact that the 1916 Act may have an anti-trust objective or be categorized in US law as an anti-trust law does not *per se* make it fall outside the scope of Article VI, unless it is demonstrated that this objective and this categorisation have an impact on the operation of the 1916 Act. In light of our findings, this would require that the terms of the transnational price discrimination test of the 1916 Act be understood in such a way that it would not meet the definition of "dumping" of Article VI:1 of the GATT 1994. We further address this question in section VI.C.2.(c) and (d) below.

(iii) Is the Type of Measures Imposed under the 1916 Act Relevant to Determining whether the 1916 Act Falls within the Scope of Article VI of GATT 1994?

6.136 The United States argues that the 1916 Act does not fall within the scope of Article VI because it does not impose anti-dumping duties. Rather, the 1916 Act sanctions the importer, not imports, through clearly "internal" measures. Article VI, as a carve-out to Article I and Article II of the GATT 1994, only deals with the impo-

---

[503] We understand that the United States did not argue that the tests at issue were less stringent than the material injury/material retardation tests of Article VI. Therefore, we do not address this point.

[504] We note that a similar approach was taken in the report of the panel on *EC - Parts and Components, Op. Cit.*, para. 5.6, where the panel examined whether the policy purpose of a charge was relevant to determining whether the charge at issue was imposed "in connection with importation", within the meaning of Article II:1(b) of GATT 1947. The panel noted that:

> "the policy purpose of charges is frequently difficult to determine objectively. Many charges could be regarded as serving both internal purposes and purposes related to the importation of goods. Only at the expense of creating substantial legal uncertainty could the policy purpose of a charge be considered to be relevant in determining whether the charge falls under Article II:1(b) or Article III:2."

sition of duties. Japan claims that the type of measures imposed does not change the nature of the law as an anti-dumping law.

6.137 We noted above that the premise on which Article VI is based is the existence of dumping. We recall that the US argument is based on the premise that the circumstances provided for in Article VI are not the only circumstances in which dumping as such can be counteracted. We concluded above that Article VI provided for the only circumstances in which dumping as such could be targeted by Members. We therefore conclude that the type of measures imposed under the 1916 Act is not relevant to determining whether the 1916 Act falls within the scope of Article VI.[505]

(iv) Conclusion

6.138 We find that the 1916 Act, based on an analysis of its terms, objectively addresses a type of transnational price discrimination that meets the definition of "dumping" contained in Article VI:1 of the GATT 1994 and, thus, should be subject to the disciplines of Article VI.

6.139 However, our findings are based on the definition of dumping as in Article VI:1 of the GATT 1994 and on the terms of the 1916 Act in their current meaning. As we recalled above,[506] we must pay due regard to the fact that we are dealing with a text drafted more that eighty years ago. If, by the time it was enacted, the 1916 Act was not designed to address "dumping", in other words if the terms found in the 1916 Act had a different meaning in 1916 than they appear to have today, this should be apparent from the legislative history and the context of its enactment. We therefore proceed with the legislative history of the 1916 Act and the context of its adoption.

6.140 The United States also claims that the true nature of the 1916 Act as an antitrust statute may be more difficult to discern simply from the text of the 1916 Act, but the case law interpreting the 1916 Act removes any doubt on this point. Having regard to our conclusions in paragraph 6.135 above that this would require that the price discrimination test of the 1916 Act be interpreted in such a way that it would no longer meet the definition of Article VI:1, we must also address this argument, as well as the contention of Japan that, in fact, US courts have applied the 1916 Act as an anti-dumping instrument.

(c) Impact of the Historical Context and of the Legislative History of the 1916 Act

(i) Approach of the Panel

6.141 Both parties have referred the Panel to the historical context of the 1916 Act and to its legislative history as it results, *inter alia*, from the Congressional Records. Japan considers that the historical context and legislative history of the 1916 Act show that the US Congress sought to enact an anti-dumping law to address the com-

[505] This does not mean however that Article VI is indifferent to the type of measures applied against dumping. This issue will be addressed in the section dealing with remedies allowed under Article VI:2.

[506] See section B.2. above.

mercial problem of dumping, i.e. international price discrimination. The United States considers that Japan's description of the 1916 Act's legislative history is incomplete and misleading. The 1916 Act was part of the policy of the second Wilson Administration to reinforce the US anti-trust legislation. The bill proposed by Representative Kitchin, which was to become the 1916 Act, was intended to supplement the existing anti-trust laws. Moreover, the United States is of the view that the Panel's role is not to weigh the legislative history of the 1916 Act itself. The legislative history is cited only as confirmation or to help explain the courts' holdings.

6.142 Our understanding is that the legislative history of an act of the US Congress is an important tool for US courts to identify the "intent of Congress".[507] The legislative history allows US courts to interpret a law in accordance with what they perceive to be the original intent of the US Congress when the text of that law is not clear. US courts may also use legislative history, when necessary, to confirm the clear meaning of a law.[508] Since, as mentioned above,[509] we have to identify how the 1916 Act is understood within the US legal system, we need to address the arguments of the parties based on the historical context and the legislative history of the 1916 Act. In doing this, we shall take due account of the use that US courts made of those tools of interpretation in practice.

6.143 We have found that the key to the applicability of Article VI:1 of the GATT 1994 to the 1916 Act is whether that law objectively addresses "dumping" within the meaning of that article. We have also found that the terms of the 1916 Act, on their face, showed that the transnational price discrimination test in that law met the definition of "dumping" in Article VI:1 of the GATT 1994. We consider that we now have to determine whether there is evidence in the legislative history or the historical context of the enactment of the 1916 Act that we should understand the price discrimination test of the 1916 Act differently than we have on the basis of the text of the law.

(ii) Review of the Historical Context and Legislative History

6.144 In light of the arguments of the parties regarding the scope of the 1916 Act, we consider it useful to determine whether the historical context and the legislative history confirm the following elements: (i) how the term "dumping" was understood at the time of the adoption of the 1916 Act and (ii) whether the fact that the 1916 Act may have been considered at the time as addressing "unfair competition" from foreign producers should have in practice an influence on how we must understand the transnational price discrimination test contained in the 1916 Act. Having reviewed

---

[507] In the *Zenith III* case, p. 1213, the court mentioned that the Supreme Court had "recently observed that 'courts, in construing a statute, may with propriety recur to the history of the times when it was passed; and this is frequently necessary in order to ascertain the reason as well as the meaning of particular provisions in it.' Leo Sheep Co. v. United States, 440 U.S. 668, 669, 99 S.Ct. 1403, 1405, 59 L.Ed.2d 677 (1979)".

[508] US courts had recourse to the legislative history of the 1916 Act in a number of cases. See, e.g., the *Zenith I* (1975) and *Zenith III* (1980) judgements.

[509] See section B.2. above.

the materials submitted by the parties, we have found no indication that the terms of the price discrimination test found in the 1916 Act were understood differently at the time of its enactment than we understand them today. In its 1919 *Information Concerning Dumping and Unfair Foreign Competition in the United States and Canada's Anti-Dumping Law*, at p. 9, the United States Tariff Commission included a definition of "dumping" identical in substance to the concept addressed by Article VI:

> "Dumping may be comprehensively described as the sale of imported merchandise at less than its prevailing market or wholesale price in the country of production. The definition derives particular importance from a not infrequent tendency to confuse with dumping [...] certain other trade practices which are generally considered unfairly competitive."

This statement of the Tariff Commission shows that dumping was probably not the only price practice which could be considered as "unfairly competitive". However, the Tariff Commission added that:

> "The anti-dumping act of Congress of September 8, 1916, [footnote omitted] somewhat modifies the above definition by condemning importation as well as sale, if commonly and systematically resorted to with the purpose specified in the law."

While not part of the legislative history of the 1916 Act as such, this document of the Tariff Commission indicates that the practice addressed by the 1916 Act was already clearly understood to be "dumping" as we define it today. The Tariff Commission definition of "dumping" is, with some exceptions which we found not to affect the applicability of Article VI:1 of the GATT 1994,[510] similar to the definition of transnational price discrimination in the 1916 Act. Therefore, it seems reasonable to conclude that the US Congress, when it passed the 1916 Act, was fully aware of the fact that that law addressed "dumping" and not another form of price discrimination. This fact was acknowledged in the *Zenith II* case, where the court stated that "The practice [of dumping] itself long outdated the passage of the Antidumping Act of 1916 [...], which clearly implies that Congress knew whereof it wrote when it enacted the statute."[511]

6.145 Moreover, even though the 1916 Act might pursue anti-trust objectives, we found no *express* indication in the legislative history that, in the 1916 Act, price discrimination as such should be understood in any particular anti-trust context.

6.146 The United States argues that the historical context and the legislative history show that the 1916 Act was intended to *supplement* or *complement* the rules applicable to US products in an anti-trust context. The United States deduces from this that the 1916 Act is an anti-trust law not subject to the disciplines of Article VI of the GATT 1994. The United States refers, *inter alia*, to the statement of Representative Claude Kitchin:

---

[510] See para. 6.122 above.

[511] See *Zenith II, Op. Cit.*, p. 258. See also the comments of Senator Penrose, criticizing the effectiveness of the 1916 Act in comparison with the Canadian anti-dumping legislation, 53 Cong. Rec. S13080 (1916), quoted by Japan at para. 3.173 above.

> "We believe that the same unfair competition law which now applies to the domestic trader should apply to the foreign import trader."[512]

6.147 We also note that the US Secretary of Commerce William Redfield explained in 1915 that

> "Unfair competition is forbidden by law in domestic trade, and the Federal Trade Commission exists to determine the facts and abate the evil wherever found. The door, however, is still open to "unfair competition" from abroad which may seriously affect American industry for the worse."[513]

The two statements refer to the extension of "unfair competition" rules applicable to US domestic commerce to imports. We have noted above that the US Congress had used in the 1916 Act a definition of transnational price discrimination which was already at that time understood as "dumping". We have also concluded in paragraph 6.135 above that the fact that the 1916 Act had an anti-trust objective was not relevant and did not make the 1916 Act fall outside the scope of Article VI of the GATT 1994. Likewise, we are not convinced that the fact that the 1916 Act was presented at the time of its enactment as "supplementing" or "complementing" the existing anti-trust laws necessarily requires that the 1916 Act be interpreted as an anti-trust law. In our opinion, the argument of the United States is only valid if the United States can prove that the historical context and the legislative history of the 1916 Act gave indications that anti-trust and anti-dumping were already separate legal concepts. If the two were not clearly identified but, rather, were still part of one single notion of "unfair competition", the US argument should be rejected.

6.148 We note that, at the time of the enactment of the 1916 Act, the current distinction between anti-trust and anti-dumping did not apply in the United States. We reviewed the materials submitted by the parties and the extensive analysis of the legislative history of the 1916 Act in the *Zenith III* case. While it appears, *inter alia* from the quotations above, that the US Administration and US lawmakers of that time considered that the 1916 Act "complemented" or "supplemented" the unfair competition rules applied to domestic products essentially under the Sherman Act and the Clayton Act,[514] it also seems that no clear legal distinction had yet been made in the United States between unfair competition resulting from dumping and unfair competition resulting from other practices, as it is made today.[515] Dumping as de-

---

[512] 53 Cong. Rec. App. 1938 (1916), as quoted in *Zenith III*, p. 1222.

[513] *Annual Report of the Secretary of Commerce* 43 (1915), as quoted in *Zenith III*, p. 1219.

[514] See J. Viner, *Dumping: A Problem in International Trade* (1923), *Op. Cit.*; pp. 242-243:

> "[The Wilson Administration] therefore recommended that any measure adopted to meet the problem should be divorced from customs legislation [in the sense of imposition of higher tariffs] and should take the form of a further extension to those engaged in the import trade of the restraints against unfair competition which had been imposed on domestic commerce."

> See also the excerpt from the letter of Samuel J. Graham, Assistant Attorney General, to the New York Times, 4 July 1916, included in a footnote to the above quotation.

[515] Even though dumping is now subject to specific international disciplines and may have acquired other purposes, the origins of anti-trust and that of anti-dumping were essentially the same, as high-

fined in Article VI:1 of the GATT 1994 was just one specific cause of action under anti-trust law,[516] as noted in 1923 by Jacob Viner:

> "This antidumping provision, beyond the fact that it makes the participation of the importer both as to act and intent in predatory dumping *specifically unlawful and not merely unlawful by construction as a practice by which competition can be restrained or monopoly established*, adds nothing to the Sherman Act. Beyond the fact that it makes unnecessary the proof of conspiracy between the importer and others, it adds nothing to the Wilson Act of 1894" (emphasis added).[517]

6.149 Even if we were to agree with the United States that the objective of the law is decisive, the historical context and legislative history do not confirm that the 1916 Act had a purely "anti-trust" purpose, within the meaning of that concept today. Rather, it appears that anti-dumping, as it is known today in international trade law, and anti-trust laws dealing with predatory pricing were part of the same notion of "unfair competition."

(iii) Conclusion

6.150 We note that evidence from the historical context of the 1916 Act supports our finding that the 1916 Act transnational price discrimination test corresponds to "dumping" within the meaning of Article VI. We also note that, at the time of the enactment of the 1916 Act, there would have been no need to give any different meaning to that test in order to make it fall within the scope of US anti-trust law because, at that time, "dumping" had not yet been conceptually isolated from the body of US anti-trust laws. In any event, the United States has not submitted evidence from the historical context or the legislative history of the 1916 Act that the terms of the transnational price discrimination test of the 1916 Act were understood differently because of the anti-trust objective of the law or that that objective was such as to make the 1916 Act fall outside the scope of Article VI.

---

lighted by the 1974 report of the *Ad Hoc* Committee on Antitrust and Antidumping of the American Bar Association Section on Antitrust Law, which stated as follows:

> "Both U.S. antidumping and antitrust law and policy have historic roots, and both were intended to protect and engender the fundamental U.S. economic policy of free and fair competition.
>
> [...] antidumping policy seeks to accommodate the legitimate need for legislation which protects American competition from unfair price discrimination by foreign concerns."

43 Antitrust L J 653, 691-93 (1974), as reproduced in J. H. Jackson & W. Davey, *Legal Problems of International Economic Relations*, 2d Ed. (1986). This is an additional reason for not deciding on the applicability of Article VI of the GATT 1994 to the 1916 Act on the basis of the general objective of the law.

[516] In that context, the statement of the court in the *Zenith III* case, at p. 1220, that "the political and legal history of the era supports our conclusion from the statutory text that the 1916 Act was an antitrust based unfair competition law, not a protectionist one" does not support the US position. From the paras. preceding that conclusion, we understand it as meaning that the court opposed the use of selective "unfair competition" instruments to the application of higher tariffs as part of a protectionist policy.

[517] J. Viner, *Dumping: A Problem in International Trade* (1923), *Op. Cit.*; p. 244.

6.151 We therefore conclude that the historical context and the legislative history of the 1916 Act, while showing that there was an intent to parallel the rules applicable to US and foreign companies, do not lead us to conclude any differently than we have on the basis of the terms of the 1916 Act as such. Therefore, we proceed to review the impact of the US case-law relating to the 1916 Act.

(d) Impact of the US Case-Law Relating to the 1916 Act

(i) Approach of the Panel

6.152 We recall our determinations under section VI.B.2 above on how we should consider the various court decisions regarding the 1916 Act and their interrelationship. We note that the United States claims that the case-law is evidence that the 1916 Act was applied as an anti-trust statute. We would like to make two preliminary remarks in relation to what is essentially a defence of the United States.

(a) First, as already mentioned, the categorisation of the 1916 Act as an anti-trust law or an anti-dumping law by the US courts should not be decisive in determining the WTO-compatibility of that law.[518] Since the point of our review of the US case-law is to ascertain the actual meaning of the 1916 Act in order to assess its conformity with the WTO Agreement, the classification of this law by US courts can only be of limited impact for the purpose of the present case. For the Panel, it is the reasoning, if any, behind the classification that matters.

(b) Second, we found that the 1916 Act price discrimination test met, on its face, the definition of Article VI:1 of GATT 1994, and that the other tests of the 1916 Act based on the "intent" of the exporter engaged in "dumping" do not have any bearing on that conclusion. As a result, we are of the view that we need not consider any court interpretation of the 1916 Act relating to any other test than the transnational price discrimination test.

We must therefore identify the instances, if any, where courts, in applying the 1916 Act, have addressed the "dumping" test contained in that law and determine whether US courts have applied/interpreted that test in such a way that it would no longer meet the definition of Article VI:1 of the GATT 1994.

6.153 Since we have already found that the text of the 1916 Act, on its own, supports the conclusion that Article VI is applicable to that law, we consider that, in order for that conclusion to be confirmed, it is not necessary for Japan to demonstrate that there was no court decision that applied the 1916 Act in such a way that it would not fall within the scope of Article VI. If we find that the US court practice is not sufficiently well established, or that there is no prevailing interpretation, or no sufficiently clear reasoning regarding the way the transnational price discrimination test of the 1916 Act should be applied, we shall rely on the text of the law itself. However, for the United States to prevail, it would be sufficient in our view to show that

---

[518] See *EC - Parts and Components, Op. Cit.*, para. 5.19. In that context, the statement of the court in *Zenith III* (1980) that "the 1916 Act is an antitrust, not a protectionist statute" is for us of limited assistance if this statement is not followed by specific conclusions in terms of interpreting the price discrimination test of the 1916 Act.

there is one definitive interpretation supporting its position. As a result, we first determine whether there is any relevant Supreme Court decision which would provide us with a definitive authority at the highest level of jurisdiction. If not, we will review the circuit court decisions.

(ii) The Supreme Court and the 1916 Act

6.154 We first note that the Supreme Court has not yet been called upon to interpret the text of the 1916 Act. However, as highlighted by the United States, in the *Cooper* case,[519] the Supreme Court described the 1916 Act as "supplemental" to the Sherman Act, as part of an illustration that "Congress had in mind the distinction between public and private remedies". The United States concludes from this that the 1916 Act is an anti-trust instrument. However, the Supreme Court also referred to the 1916 Act as "the antidumping provisions of the Revenue Act of 1916". Even if the Supreme Court regarded the 1916 Act as an anti-trust law, the fact that it refers to "antidumping provisions" leaves the issue of the interpretation of the price discrimination test of the 1916 Act open, since US courts may well apply the 1916 Act as an anti-trust law when it comes to the "intent" test, while applying the price discrimination test without any additional requirements than those contained in the text of the 1916 Act.

6.155 What the Supreme Court meant by "supplemental" is not clear in the absence of an agreed technical definition under US law. The 1916 Act could be "supplemental" to anti-trust statutes in a number of other ways than that suggested by the United States. For instance, an anti-dumping law could "supplement" a domestic predatory pricing law. The context of the statement in the decision is of limited use.[520]

6.156 Therefore, we are not in a position to draw any definitive conclusion from the US Supreme Court statements in the *Cooper* case. Even if the Supreme Court had expressly stated that the 1916 Act was an anti-trust or an anti-dumping law, this statement would have no relevance for this Panel as long as it was not supported by an explanation of the reasons why the Supreme Court thought that way, or of the implications of that statement on the interpretation of the transnational price discrimination test of the 1916 Act.

6.157 As a result, any conclusion on the basis of the US case-law becomes delicate because there is no unambiguous authority at the highest level of US jurisdiction. This does not mean that we will not find an unanimous interpretation, or even a prevailing interpretation that would be convincing. Indeed, many decisions are final as a practical matter at the level of the circuit court of appeals, *inter alia,* because the possibility to appeal before the US Supreme Court is not automatically granted.

---

[519] *Op. Cit.*, p. 308.

[520] The term "supplemental" was also used by US Secretary of Commerce Redfield in his legislative proposal of 1915 (*Annual Report of the Secretary of Commerce* (1915), *Op Cit.*) when he said "I also recommend that legislation supplemental to the Clayton Antitrust Act be enacted..." However, we already expressed the view when we addressed the historical context and the legislative history of the 1916 Act that the borderline between anti-dumping and anti-trust was not so clear at that time, if only because anti-dumping was at an early stage of development and because it was probably not yet perceived in the United States as a trade instrument separate from anti-trust.

(iii) The Interpretation of the Transnational Price Discrimination Test of the 1916 Act at the Circuit Court Level

"Dumping" as an international trade concept applied in an anti-trust context

6.158 Considering the other cases mentioned by the parties and decided either at the district court level or at the court of appeals level, the Panel notes that the parties discussed at length the decision of the court in *Zenith III* (1980). We first note that the court in *Zenith III* stated that the 1916 Act

> "should be interpreted whenever possible to parallel the "unfair competition" law applicable to domestic commerce. Since the 1916 Act is a price discrimination law, it should be read in tandem with the price discrimination law, section 2 of the Clayton Act, which was amended by the Robinson-Patman Act of 1936 in 1936."

6.159 The United States relies heavily on this and other similar statements[521] to argue that the 1916 Act addresses anti-competitive pricing practices and should be interpreted similarly to the Robinson-Patman Act. However, as outlined in section VI.C.2(c) above, the fact that the 1916 Act was adopted for anti-trust purposes and the fact that it combines a "dumping" test with other tests which are typical of US anti-trust legislation are, in our view, of no relevance in this case. [522] What matters for us is the way transnational price discrimination has been addressed by US courts.

6.160 The United States considers that the *Zenith III* judgement is the leading lower court case addressing how specific provisions of the 1916 Act should be interpreted. We note, with respect to price discrimination *stricto sensu*, that the court, after having recalled Viner's definition of dumping, stated that "to restate the obvious, the Antidumping Act of 1916 is a prohibition of international price discrimination." This would tend to confirm that the court applied the transnational price discrimination test of the 1916 Act without reading into it additional anti-trust-like requirements which would modify its meaning. The Court also recalled that "as a price discrimination statute, the Antidumping Act of 1916 is functionally similar to the price discrimination statutes which are applicable to domestic business." However, this was before the introduction - implicitly in the *In Re Japanese Electronic Products III* case or explicitly in the *Brooke Group* case - of the predatory pricing/recoupment test. We have no clear evidence that, before those judgements, the price discrimination test of the 1916 Act was applied in a manner different from that suggested by the wording of this Act. More particularly, we have no convincing evidence that any criteria exclusively found in anti-trust practice to establish price discrimination were used by the US courts in that context.[523] On the contrary, we recall that the courts in *Zenith III* and in *In Re Japanese Electronic Products II* confirmed that the phrase "actual mar-

---

[521] See *Zenith III*, p. 1223. See also paras. 3.225 and 3.331 above, where the United States refers to statements of the courts in the *Zenith II* (1975) and *In Re Japanese Electronic Products II* (1983).

[522] We note in this respect that the *Zenith III* decision shows that even the judgement on which the United States relies to qualify the 1916 Act as an anti-trust law seems to acknowledge that the 1916 Act was a combination of anti-dumping and anti-trust.

[523] See *Zenith III*, *Op. Cit.*, pp. 1197 and 1229-1230.

ket value or wholesale price of such articles" in the 1916 Act was a term of art borrowed from the Tariff Act of 1913 - a customs law - and defined in that Act. The court in *Zenith III* also specified that it would hold that there is no violation of the 1916 Act unless the standards of similarity of the customs appraisement law were met.[524]

6.161 We have not found in the decisions referred to by the United States other elements which would demonstrate that the price discrimination test of the 1916 Act, as such, was affected by attempts to parallel the Robinson-Patman Act. In fact, the court in *Zenith II* (1975) largely used "standard dictionary definitions" to interpret the terms of the 1916 Act that had been challenged by the defendants on grounds of vagueness. This was the case for the terms "commonly and systematically", and "other charges and expenses necessarily incident to the importation and sale". Regarding the term "substantially", the court only referred to the case-law regarding the Clayton Act to conclude that if the term "substantially" in "substantially to lessen competition" in the Clayton Act was not found unconstitutionally vague the term " substantially less" in the 1916 Act cannot be either. Finally, the court also referred to the 1913 Tariff Act to interpret the phrase "actual market value or wholesale price."

6.162 The United States also mentions that the court's analysis in the seminal *Zenith III* case has been supported by other US courts which have considered the nature of the 1916 Act. We note however that a number of these cases were concerned with the issue of *locus standi* in a 1916 civil action[525] or more generally with the problem of establishing a cause of action.[526] If they confirm *Zenith III*, it seems to be essentially by reason of not objecting to its conclusions, which we have found not to affect our initial findings based on the terms of the 1916 Act alone. In fact, it seems that courts have concentrated their efforts on other aspects of the 1916 Act, such as the standing and damages provisions, which were found "essentially the same as those applicable to the antitrust laws under section 4 of the Clayton Act" and the criminal penalty clause which is "virtually identical to, and specifies the same penalties as, the corresponding clauses of the Sherman Antitrust Act as then in force."[527]

6.163 Other elements tend to show that courts approached the transnational price discrimination test found in the 1916 Act as "dumping" within the meaning of Article VI of the GATT 1994. For instance, a number of those decisions, including the cases cited by the United States in support of its position, refer to the definition of dumping by Jacob Viner, i.e. "price discrimination between purchasers in different national markets"[528] and generally address the price discrimination test found in the 1916 Act as "dumping", without any further qualification. In this respect, the court in

---

[524] *Ibid.*, see also *In Re Japanese Electronic Products II*, p. 324.

[525] See *Schwimmer v. Sony Corp. of America* (1979), *Op. Cit.*; *Schwimmer v. Sony Corp. of America* (1980), *Op. Cit.*; *Western Concrete Structures Co. v. Mitsui & Co.* (1985), to which Japan refers expressly in its submissions.

[526] *Jewel Foliage Co. v. Uniflora Overseas Florida* (1980), *Op. Cit.*; *Outboard Marine Corporation v. Pezetel* (1978), *Op. Cit.*

[527] *Zenith III*, p. 1214.

[528] J. Viner, *Dumping: A Problem in International Trade*, 1966 edition, p. 4. See, e.g., *Zenith II* (1975), *Outboard Marine Corporation v. Pezetel* (1978), p. 408; *Zenith III* (1980); *In re Japanese Electronic Products II* (1983), p. 321

Zenith II did not find it necessary to look any further than that definition and the popular title of the 1916 Act to conclude that:

> "An economic regulatory statute could scarcely acquire the designation of an 'antidumping Act' unless the business community to which the statute was addressed knew what 'dumping' was."[529]

6.164 The United States argues that the court used a colloquial definition of "dumping", not one based on examination of "fair value" and "material injury" concepts. Moreover, the district court went on to stress that the 1916 Act contains the additional element of "specific, predatory, anti-competitive intent". We do not contest the assessment of the 1916 Act made by the court. In our opinion however, the "intent" aspect of the 1916 Act is not a determining factor to conclude on the applicability of Article VI and the Anti-Dumping Agreement to the 1916 Act. As demonstrated in our analysis of Article VI:1, the key to the application of those provisions is the existence of a transnational price discrimination. Once a Member plans to address this type of price discrimination as such, not its causes such as subsidisation or monopolization in the exporting country, or its effects, such as increased sales at the expense of domestic competitors, it can only do it if "injury" within the meaning of Article VI and the Anti-Dumping Agreement is found.

6.165 We are therefore of the view that these examples are evidence that a number of US courts, irrespective of their interpretation of the other parts of the 1916 Act, considered that the transnational price discrimination test had to be interpreted as "dumping", as it is also understood in international trade, and on the basis of US trade law standards.

The *Brooke Group* recoupment test

6.166 The United States notes that the 1916 Act is not directed at the simple price difference that constitutes dumping under the anti-dumping rules. Pricing practices under the 1916 Act must be "predatory pricing". In that context, the United States argues that, since the 1986 Third Circuit Court of Appeals decision *In Re Japanese Electronic Products III* and the 1993 Supreme Court decision in *Brooke Group Ltd.*

---

529 *Zenith II*, p. 258. See also the statement of the court in *Zenith III*, p. 1196:

> "We also have occasion to compare the 1916 Act, which creates a private right of action for treble damages and provides criminal penalties for dumping, with the Antidumping Act of 1921"

The terms used by the court and the subsequent developments in the judgement show that "dumping" in the 1916 Act and in the 1921 Act, which was the US anti-dumping law based on administrative investigations applied until the entry into force of the Tokyo Round Anti-Dumping Agreement, were not understood differently. The fact that the understanding of the meaning of "dumping" by US courts corresponds to the definition of that concept in Article VI:1 of the GATT 1994 is confirmed by the following statement of the court in *In Re Japanese Electronic Products II*, at p. 324:

> "The first element necessary to a finding of dumping under the 1916 Act is proof that a price differential exists between two comparable products, one of which is imported or sold in the United States and the other of which is sold in the exporting country."

See also *Helmac II* (1993), p. 591, which recognised that the key to liability under the 1916 Act was "dumping: the pricing of goods on the American market at a price lower than on the home market".

v. Brown & Williamson Tobacco Corporation,[530] courts have applied the anti-trust predatory pricing/recoupment test developed in those cases.[531]

6.167 We understand the predatory pricing/recoupment test in the *Brooke Group* case to require that (i) the complainant establish that the prices complained of are below an appropriate measure of its rival's costs and that (ii) the complainant demonstrate that the competitor had a reasonable prospect of recouping its investment in below-cost prices.[532] The Supreme Court further held that evidence of below-cost pricing is not on its own sufficient to permit an inference of probable recoupment and injury to competition. Determining whether recoupment of predatory losses is likely requires an estimate of the cost of the alleged predation and a close analysis of both the scheme challenged by the plaintiff and the structure and conditions of the relevant market.[533]

6.168 It is not clear whether the recoupment test should be analysed as part of the transnational price discrimination test or as part of the "intent" test of the 1916 Act. As a result, in order to consider the applicability of the *Brooke Group* test to the price discrimination test of the 1916 Act, we have to assume that price recoupment is more related to the type/amount of price discrimination that can be achieved by the importer than to its intent to affect the US market. If the Brooke Group test relates to the "intent" test of the 1916 Act, it cannot affect the transnational price discrimination test of the 1916 Act, as the Panel has already repeatedly argued.

6.169 This said, regarding the first criterion of the *Brooke Group* test, i.e. below cost prices, we do not consider that the introduction of a below-cost price test would make Article VI of the GATT 1994 no longer applicable to the 1916 Act, essentially because the definition of dumping in Article VI:1 does not incorporate a notion of magnitude of price difference. We are aware that Article 5.8 of the Anti-Dumping Agreement provides that there "shall be immediate termination in cases where the authorities determine that the margin of dumping is *de minimis*", i.e. that it is less than 2 per cent, expressed as a percentage of the export price. We have no evidence that this *de minimis* dumping margin bears any link with any kind of below-cost test as applied in the anti-trust context. The application of a below-cost price test in the 1916 Act may make the establishment of a transnational price difference more difficult, but it does not affect the basic requirement that a price difference has to be established under the 1916 Act, which is also the basic requirement of Article VI:1 of the GATT 1994.

6.170 As far as the cost recoupment criterion is concerned, we do not believe either that the introduction of a recoupment requirement under the 1916 Act would make Article VI of the GATT 1994 no longer applicable to the 1916 Act for essentially two reasons. First, the definition of dumping set out in Article VI:1 would still apply.

---

[530] 509 U.S. 209, 118 S.Ct. 2578, hereinafter the "*Brooke Group* case".

[531] Even though the parties have discussed the implication of the court decision *In Re Japanese Electronic Products III*, we do not find it necessary to determine whether the court actually applied in that case the predatory pricing/recoupment test later established by the Supreme Court in the *Brooke Group* case. For the sake of our analysis, we will assume that the court in *In Re Japanese Electronic Products III* actually applied a standard similar to the *Brooke Group* test.

[532] *Brooke Group, Op. Cit.*, pp. 2587-2588.

[533] *Ibid.* p. 2589.

Even if a cost recoupment were to be required in addition to a price difference, a price difference must always be found in the first place. The second reason is more of an economic nature. Since, in transnational price discrimination, an exporter may benefit from an isolated domestic market where it may maximise its profits, recoupment on the *export* market may not always occur in a situation of international predatory pricing. The recoupment requirement, which may be justified in cases of price discrimination within the United States, may be an economically questionable requirement in cases of transnational price discrimination, at least whenever the exporter does not need to recoup its costs on the US market. Indeed, the company exporting at dumped prices may benefit from a simultaneous recoupment of its "dumping" costs through more profitable sales on its domestic market.

6.171 However, this Panel is called on to clarify WTO provisions, not to discuss specific anti-trust issues. Therefore, having expressed the above-mentioned reservations, we proceed to consider if, effectively, the *Brooke Group* test has been actually and consistently applied by US courts in their interpretation of the 1916 Act.

6.172 If the Supreme Court decision in *Brooke Group* is applicable to the 1916 Act, one would expect the other courts which had to consider complaints under the 1916 Act to apply that test as well. We have no clear evidence that this has been the case, even if one assumes that the test was already applicable since *In Re Japanese Electronic Products III* (1986), as it would appear from the reaction of the courts in the *Geneva Steel* [534]and *Wheeling-Pittsburgh* cases.[535]

6.173 In that context, the parties have discussed the content of the *Helmac I* case (1992). We understand that the court in the *Helmac I* case concluded that the complainant did not have to establish recoupment. On the contrary, the court noted the importance of the difference in terminology between the 1916 Act and the US antitrust statutes. According to the court, the 1916 Act:

> "focuses upon intent while the antitrust statutes focus upon effect. Beside injury to competition, the Antidumping Act also provides a cause of action when the defendant attempts to, among other things, injure an industry in the United States."[536]

The court only stated as a possibility that the adoption of the recoupment theory would be appropriate if Helmac, the complainant in that case, had claimed that the defendant's conduct injured *competition*. Since Helmac alleged an attempt to injure an *industry* in the United States, the court concluded that proving ability to recoup losses was not necessary.[537] In the *Helmac II* decision (1993) the court differentiated between liability, of which a finding of dumping was the key, and the calculation of the harm caused to the domestic industry.[538]

6.174 Therefore, we consider that we do not have sufficient evidence of the actual application of the *Brooke Group* test to 1916 Act cases in relation to the establishment of the price discrimination required by that law.

---

[534] *Op. Cit.* See para. 6.177 below.

[535] *Op. Cit.* See para. 6.179 below.

[536] *Helmac I, Op. Cit.*, pp. 575-576.

[537] *Ibid.*, p. 575.

[538] *Helmac II, Op. Cit.*, at p. 591.

The interlocutory decisions relied upon by Japan

6.175 Japan alleges that two interlocutory judgements in the *Geneva Steel* and *Wheeling Pittsburgh* cases support its claims that the 1916 Act addresses dumping within the meaning of Article VI of the GATT 1994. Japan also considers that these decisions show the lack of relevance of the *Zenith III* decision, because it ignored the text of the 1916 Act. The United States argues that these two decisions are neither final nor conclusive under US law. Therefore, they cannot, at the present time, be considered by the Panel as authoritative interpretations of US law.

6.176 We are fully aware of the fact that these decisions are only interlocutory judgements issued in different circuits than the *Zenith* decisions. We consider that our review of the other - final - judgements referred to by the parties already shows that US courts did not interpret the transnational price discrimination test of the 1916 Act in such a way that it would fall outside the scope of Article VI of the GATT 1994. However, we recall that we are required to make an objective assessment of the facts of the case. Since these two interlocutory judgements have, like the *Zenith* cases, actually discussed in detail the origin, objectives and practical operation of the 1916 Act, we found it relevant to consider also those cases. We also note that these two cases are subsequent to the *Zenith* cases and the Supreme Court decision in the *Brooke Group* case. Considering them is appropriate in light of the arguments of the United States based on those decisions. Finally, as mentioned in paragraph 6.152(a) above, we are interested in the *reasoning* followed by the US courts as a clarification of how the transnational price discrimination test of the 1916 Act operates. If this reasoning is convincing, we feel justified in taking it into account in our examination.[539]

6.177 In *Geneva Steel*, the district court addressed the question whether the 1916 Act always requires evidence of antitrust-like predatory pricing. Since the intent of predatory pricing in our opinion does not affect the transnational price discrimination test of the 1916 Act, we do not consider that judgement to be directly relevant to our case. However, we note that the court considered that "By the words it chose, Congress protected United States industry from unfair dumping."[540] Having regard to our conclusions regarding the use of the word "dumping" in other judgements, we assume that the court consciously used the word "dumping" in the same meaning as this word is given in Article VI:1 of the GATT 1994.

6.178 Other reasonings of the court are relevant in so far as they seem to confirm our understanding of the case-law. For instance, the court in *Geneva Steel* considered the conclusion in *Zenith III* that the 1916 Act was "an antitrust, not a protectionist statute". It stated that such conclusion did not appear to be necessary to support the

---

[539] Since the Panel's second substantive meeting with the parties there have apparently been further developments in the *Wheeling-Pittsburgh* case. According to the United States, the plaintiff in that case, Wheeling-Pittsburgh Steel Corporation, has voluntarily dismissed its claims against the remaining defendants at the trial court level so that all that remains is an appeal of an interlocutory opinion regarding injunctive relief currently pending before the US Court of Appeals for the Sixth Circuit. We do not consider that these recent developments affect our approach to the *Wheeling-Pittsburgh* case.

[540] *Geneva Steel*, p. 1217.

finding of the court in the *Zenith III* case that the term "such articles" in the 1916 Act included also "similar" articles.[541] The reason for this conclusion was, as we understand it, that the relevant text in the 1916 Act had been imported from the 1913 Tariff Act, a customs statute which provided for a "similarity" standard. We also note that the court in *Geneva Steel* found the terms of the 1916 Act unambiguous,[542] as we did - at least with respect to the transnational price discrimination test - when we considered the text of the 1916 Act in isolation from the subsequent case-law.

6.179 The court in the *Wheeling-Pittsburgh* case did not address the price discrimination test of the 1916 Act as such, but the question whether predatory intent had to be demonstrated. Its reasoning is therefore less relevant for this case, except for its discussion of the inclusion of the predatory pricing/price recoupment test in the 1916 Act.[543] In that respect, like in the *Geneva Steel* case, the court in *Wheeling-Pittsburgh* rejected the application of this test with respect to certain circumstances of application of the 1916 Act because it created a double burden of proof for the complainants. Indeed, the court considered that the *Zenith III* decision had added "an antitrust type of predatory pricing, including the reasonable prospect of resultant market control and price recoupment", to the "intent" to injure or destroy or prevent the establishment of a domestic industry contained in the text of the 1916 Act.[544]

6.180 The *Geneva Steel* and *Wheeling-Pittsburgh* cases shed additional light on the interpretation of the pricing/recoupment test because they have addressed quite specifically the question of its application. They also represent additional evidence that some district courts do not find themselves compelled, at least at an early stage of consideration of an issue, to apply the *Brooke Group* predatory pricing/price recoupment test to claims under the 1916 Act.

(iv) Conclusion

6.181 We find that that the assessment made by courts of the price discrimination test of the 1916 Act was based essentially on the text of the 1916 Act itself, without any significant additions. We also find that, at best, we have no clear evidence of a consistent application of the cost recoupment test - or any other "anti-trust" standards, such as below-cost prices - in the implementation of the transnational price discrimination test of the 1916 Act. In accordance with our approach,[545] we conclude that the US case-law supports our original conclusion that the 1916 Act addresses "dumping" within the meaning of Article VI:1 of the GATT 1994.

---

[541] *Geneva Steel*, p. 1218.

[542] *Ibid.*, p. 1222-1223.

[543] The Court in *Wheeling-Pittsburgh* (1999) gave its views as to why the "predatory pricing" part of the *Brooke Group* test could not apply to cases under the 1916 Act. The court stated that "by requiring a plaintiff to prove 'intent to injure a domestic industry' by below-cost-pricing, the Anti-dumping Act of 1916 does require proof of predatory intent, albeit of a different kind" (p. 601). However, since its reasoning was based only on the "intent" requirement of the 1916 Act, we do not find it necessary to address it.

[544] *Wheeling-Pittsburgh, Op. Cit.*, p. 605.

[545] See paras. 6.152-6.153 above.

3. *Conclusions on the Applicability of Article VI of the GATT 1994 and of the Anti-Dumping Agreement to the 1916 Act*

(a) The 1916 Act Falls within the Scope of Article VI of the GATT 1994 and of the Anti-Dumping Agreement

6.182 Having interpreted Article VI of the GATT 1994 in accordance with the Vienna Convention, we have reached the conclusion that the rules and disciplines of that article apply to laws that address "dumping" as defined in Article VI:1. Having examined the text of the 1916 Act, we have found that the transnational price discrimination test incorporated in that law falls within the definition of "dumping" of Article VI:1 of GATT 1994. On the basis of our interpretation of Article VI, we have also found that none of the additional conditions or requirements contained in the text of the 1916 Act is such as to make the transnational price discrimination test of the 1916 Act fall outside the scope of the definition of "dumping" in Article VI:1 or otherwise modify our conclusions. We found no convincing evidence in the legislative history that should lead us to understand the terms of the price discrimination test of the 1916 Act differently than we have. Finally, our review of the US court decisions submitted by the parties did not show that courts had interpreted the transnational price discrimination test of the 1916 Act in such a way that it would no longer meet the definition of Article VI:1 of the GATT 1994.

6.183 This conclusion also disposes of the argument of the United States that the 1916 Act has been interpreted in such a manner that it would fall outside the scope of Article VI of the GATT 1994.

6.184 Having found that Article VI of the GATT 1994 applies to the 1916 Act, and having regard to the relationship between that Article and the Anti-Dumping Agreement, as highlighted in paragraphs 6.92-6.94 above, we find that the applicability of Article VI to the 1916 Act also implies the applicability of the Anti-Dumping Agreement to the 1916 Act.

(b) The 1916 Act is a Mandatory Law within the Meaning of GATT 1947/WTO Practice

6.185 With respect to the discretion enjoyed by the US Department of Justice which would, according to the United States, make the 1916 Act non-mandatory, we recall our reasoning in paragraphs 6.106-6.107 above.

6.186 We note that anti-dumping laws may involve a large degree of discretion for the investigating authorities in terms of deciding on the initiation of an investigation. If one were to apply the "mandatory/discretionary" doctrine suggested by the United States, such a degree of discretion might well be sufficient for a panel to declare that, as far as criminal proceedings are concerned, the 1916 Act does not *mandate* WTO-inconsistent actions. However, we note that Article 18.4 of the Anti-Dumping Agreement, to which Japan referred in the proceedings, reads as follows:

> "Each Member shall take all necessary steps, of a general or particular character, to ensure, no later than the date of entry into force of the WTO Agreement for it, the conformity of its laws, regulations and administrative practices with the provisions of this Agreement, as they may apply to the Member in question."

6.187 Japan also argues that Article 18.4 applies in this case instead of the mandatory/non-mandatory dichotomy suggested by the United States. The United States argues that there is nothing inherent in the anti-dumping context that renders the generally applicable distinction between mandatory and non-mandatory legislation inapplicable.

6.188 We note that Article 18.4 requires that Members ensure that their anti-dumping laws are in conformity with the provisions of the Anti-Dumping Agreement as of the time of the entry into force of that Agreement for the Member concerned. Since we have found that the 1916 Act is subject to Article VI and the Anti-Dumping Agreement, the obligations of Article 18.4 apply to it and the United States should have taken all necessary steps, of a general or particular character, to bring the 1916 Act into conformity with the Anti-Dumping Agreement. We also note that Article 18.4 creates an obligation of conformity of the *laws* of a Member *no later* than the date of entry into force of the Anti-Dumping Agreement for that Member. In other words, Article 18.4 requires (i) the conformity of the law as such, regardless of whether it is applied or not and (ii) this conformity must be achieved as of the entry into force of the WTO Agreement for the Member concerned and *permanently* thereafter. In contrast, the mandatory/non-mandatory doctrine is based on the conformity of the law only in *instances* of application.

6.189 The notion of "mandatory/non-mandatory legislation" is a generally recognised concept of international law, whereas Article 18.4 is a treaty provision. Even if one were to assume that this concept is actually a norm of customary international law, it is well established under general international law that treaty provisions normally prevail over norms of customary international law.[546] We therefore conclude that, to the extent that Article 18.4 requires the conformity of the 1916 Act with the Anti-Dumping Agreement as of the date of entry into force of the WTO Agreement for the United States, the notion of mandatory/non-mandatory legislation is no longer relevant in determining whether the Panel can or cannot review the conformity of the 1916 Act with the Anti-Dumping Agreement. We note in this respect the approach followed by the panel in the report on *EC - Audio Cassettes*. This report, which was not adopted,[547] considered why the mere fact that the initiation of anti-dumping investigations was discretionary would not make the EC legislation at issue non-mandatory. The panel stated that:

> "[it] did not consider in any event that its task in this case was to determine whether the EC's Basic Regulation was non-mandatory in the sense that the initiation of investigations and impositions of duties were not mandatory functions. Should panels accept this approach,

[546] See, e.g., ICJ judgement *Military and Paramilitary Activities in and against Nicaragua* (Nicaragua v. United States of America), ICJ Reports 1986, p. 137, which stated at para. 274 that:

> "In general, treaty rules being *lex specialis*, it would not be appropriate that a State should bring a claim based on a customary-law rule if it has by treaty already provided means for settlement of such a claim".

[547] *Op. Cit.* On the legal value of unadopted panel reports, see footnote 489 above and its reference to the Appellate Body report on *Japan - Taxes on Alcoholic Beverages.*

> they would be precluded from ever reviewing the content of a party's anti-dumping legislation."[548]

The *EC - Audio Cassettes* panel expressly based its reasoning on the fact that this approach would undermine the obligation contained in Article 16.6 of the Tokyo Round Anti-Dumping Agreement. That provision, which contained terms almost identical with Article 18.4 of the WTO Anti-Dumping Agreement, provided that parties had to bring their laws, regulations and administrative procedures into conformity with the provisions of the Tokyo Round Anti-Dumping Agreement.[549]

6.190 Like the panel on *EC - Audio-Cassettes* with respect to Article 16.6(a) of the Tokyo Round Anti-Dumping Agreement, we consider that interpreting the provisions of Article 18.4 differently would undermine the obligations contained in that article and would be contrary to the general principle of effectiveness[550] by making many disciplines of the Anti-Dumping Agreement non-enforceable as soon as a Member would claim that the investigating authority has discretion to initiate or not an anti-dumping investigation.[551]

6.191 We therefore conclude that the discretion enjoyed by the US Department of Justice to initiate a case under the 1916 Act should not be interpreted as exempting the 1916 Act from scrutiny under Article VI of the GATT 1994 and the Anti-Dumping Agreement.

6.192 As a result, we consider that the United States, as the party having raised this defence, failed to supply convincing evidence that the 1916 Act should be considered as "non-mandatory legislation" within the meaning of GATT 1947/WTO practice.[552] We therefore find that the 1916 Act cannot be considered to be a "non-mandatory" law.[553]

(c) Concluding Remarks on the Applicability of Article VI of the GATT 1994 and the Anti-Dumping

---

548 *Op. Cit.*, para. 362.

549 Article 16.6(a) ("National Legislation") of the Tokyo Round Anti-Dumping Agreement provided as follows:

> "Each government accepting or acceding to this Agreement shall take all necessary steps, of a general or particular character, to ensure , not later than the date of entry into force of this Agreement for it, the conformity of its laws, regulations and administrative procedures with the provisions of this Agreement as they may apply to the Party in question."

550 See *United States - Gasoline* and *Argentina - Safeguards, supra*, footnote 476.

551 We also find support for our reasoning in the report of the panel *on United States - Section 301-310 of the Trade Act of 1974*, WT/DS152/R, adopted 27 January 2000, DSR 2000:II, 815, para. 7.54 and footnote 675.

552 We recall that we found in paras. 6.101-6.102 above that the burden of proof established by the *US - Tobacco* panel was not applicable in the present case. In application of the rules on burden of proof recalled in paras. 6.24-6.26 above, we consider that it was up to the United States to provide sufficient evidence to establish a *prima facie* case for its defence.

553 Having found that the 1916 Act cannot be considered as "non-mandatory" legislation within the meaning of that concept under GATT1947/WTO practice, we do not find it necessary to address the arguments of the parties on the impact of Article XVI:4 of the Agreement Establishing the WTO on the application of that concept.

Agreement to the Price Discrimination Test of the 1916 Act

6.193 First, we would like to recall that our findings are based on an objective interpretation of the terms of Article VI and the Anti-Dumping Agreement. Our findings do not contest the fact that the US authorities and US courts may, in good faith, consider that the 1916 Act addresses anti-trust issues. With respect to the interpretations made by the US courts, our findings do not affect certain aspects of the 1916 Act which could be claimed to be of an anti-trust nature, since the interpretations made by US courts did not affect the price discrimination test which we found was similar to the definition of "dumping" in Article VI.

6.194 The United States warned the Panel of the implications of an interpretation of the price discrimination test of Article VI that would be so broad that it could make Article VI of the GATT 1994 applicable to all anti-trust laws, including those of Japan, when such laws address situations of transnational price discrimination.

6.195 We recall that we were requested to review the conformity of the 1916 Act with the provisions of the WTO Agreement, not to address the general issue of the relationship between trade law and anti-trust law. In order to assess the WTO-compatibility of the 1916 Act, we interpreted the provisions of Article VI:1 of the GATT 1994 in conformity with the general principles of interpretation of public international law, as embodied in the Vienna Convention. This exercise led us to conclude that the terms of Article VI, interpreted in their context and in the light of the object and purpose of GATT 1994 and the WTO Agreement, applied to the form of transnational price discrimination addressed by the 1916 Act. The United States did not provide us with any evidence or argument that would demonstrate that we should have read in Article VI:1 a limitation addressing the risk highlighted by the United States in the previous paragraph.[554] As recalled by the Appellate Body, we are not to import into the text of the WTO Agreement conditions that do not appear from its terms interpreted in accordance with the Vienna Convention.[555] Our conclusion is, therefore, fully consistent with our mandate.

---

[554] We note that, in any event, the scope of the WTO Agreement does not exclude *a priori* restrictive business practices. Thus, the fact that the 1916 Act would be an anti-trust law would not *per se* be sufficient to exclude the application of WTO rules to that law. We note that panels under GATT 1947 and the WTO have addressed various aspects of restrictive business practices initiated by governments when such practices had the effect of impeding market access of foreign products or entry of foreign enterprises (see e.g., *Japan - Trade in Semiconductors,* adopted on 4 May 1988, BISD 35S/116; *Panel Report on Japan – Measures Affecting Consumer Photographic Film and Paper ("Japan – Films"),* WT/DS44R, adopted 22 April 1998, DSR 1998:IV, 1179 and M. Matsushita: *Restrictive Business Practices and the WTO/GATT Dispute Settlement Process in International Trade Law and the GATT/WTO Dispute Settlement System* E.-U. Petersmann Ed. (1997), p. 359. Consequently, we do not consider the dichotomy trade law/anti-trust law, to the extent that it would be based on the assumption that WTO disciplines are not intended to apply to business restrictive practices, to be a limitation to the application of WTO rules and disciplines.

[555] See, e.g., Appellate Body Report in *India - Patent (US), supra,* footnote 55, para. 45, where the Appellate Body stated that the principles of interpretation contained in Article 31 of the Vienna Convention "neither require nor condone the imputation into a treaty of words that are not there or the importation into a treaty of concepts that were not intended."

6.196 In any event, we are not convinced that our conclusion, if applied outside the context of this dispute, would generate the effect referred to by the United States.

6.197 First, we note that transnational price discrimination of the type covered by the definition of "dumping" in Article VI:1 of GATT 1994 is only one narrowly defined type of price discrimination. Other types of price discrimination, beginning with primary-line price discrimination under the Robinson-Patman Act, do not fall within the scope of the definition of "dumping" in Article VI:1.[556] In particular, the definition of Article VI:1 does not address price discrimination within the territory of a given jurisdiction.

6.198 Second, under Article VI:1 of the GATT 1994, the identification of "dumping" is the starting-point for any determination of injurious dumping. It is the only possible basis for the initiation of an anti-dumping investigation by a Member and for the imposition of measures. Injury not causally linked to the dumping cannot be addressed through anti-dumping action.[557] Comparatively, under anti-trust law, the causes of a given market disruption can be several. When determining what could be at the origin of certain prices, anti-trust investigators will try to identify specific practices such as price conspiracy or abuse of dominant position. It is the understanding of the Panel that, under anti-trust law, transnational price discrimination of the type covered by the definition of "dumping" in Article VI:1 of GATT 1994 is not sufficient *as such* to form the basis for a claim of violation of anti-trust law, even in the presence of a disruption on the export market based on the prices found on that market. It is necessary to demonstrate other specific practices, such as monopoly, abuse of dominant position, price agreement or concerted practices, of which transnational price discrimination may constitute, at most, only supporting evidence.

6.199 We therefore conclude that the possibility that our findings with respect to Article VI:1 of the GATT 1994 could affect the application of anti-trust laws of Members is very limited, since transnational price discrimination as defined in Article VI :1 of GATT 1994 is only one limited form of price discrimination that may be considered under anti-trust law. Moreover, transnational price discrimination is unlikely to constitute *by itself* a practice which anti-trust law would consider to be a cause for imposition of sanctions.

6.200 Having found that Article VI of the GATT 1994 is applicable to the 1916 Act because the latter addresses "dumping" and Article VI and the Anti-Dumping Agreement are applicable as soon as a Member's measure objectively addresses "dumping" within the meaning of Article VI, we proceed to address the claims of violation of Article VI:2 and the Anti-Dumping Agreement. On the basis of our findings, we will consider whether it is necessary to address the issue of the applicability and violation of Article III:4 of the GATT 1994.

---

[556] At our request, the United States confirmed that in order for the Robinson-Patman primary-line price discrimination to apply, both commodities involved in the alleged price discrimination must be sold for use, consumption or resale in the United States (see also *Zenith I, Op. Cit.*, p. 246).

[557] See Article 3.5 of the Anti-Dumping Agreement, which provides that injuries caused by certain factors must not be attributed to the dumped imports and includes among those factors "trade restrictive practices of and competition between the foreign and domestic producers". This provision would seem to imply that transnational price discrimination of the kind defined in Article VI:1 is not considered to be part of the "competition" practices between the foreign and domestic producers.

D. *Violation of Article VI:2 of the GATT 1994 and of Article 18.1 of the Anti-Dumping Agreement*

1. *Approach of the Panel*

6.201 Japan claims that the 1916 Act violates Article VI:2 of the GATT 1994 and Article 18.1 of the Anti-Dumping Agreement because it provides for other sanctions than anti-dumping duties, such as damages, fines or imprisonment. In support of its claim, Japan argues that Article VI:2 of the GATT 1994 authorises only one type of measure in response to dumping: the imposition of anti-dumping duties. Article 18.1 of the Anti-Dumping Agreement reaffirms the understanding that Article VI of the GATT 1994 is the sole GATT-authorised remedy for dumping.

6.202 The United States replies that Article VI and the Anti-Dumping Agreement do not govern all measures directed at dumping, but only laws and measures that attempt to counteract injurious dumping through the imposition of duties. Other measures are allowed as long as they are not inconsistent with other provisions of the GATT 1994.

6.203 In support of their respective positions, the parties refer to the ordinary meaning of the terms of Article VI:2 and of Article 18.1. They also refer to the context of those provisions, such as footnote 24 to Article 18:1 of the Anti-Dumping Agreement and Articles I:1 and II:2(b) of the GATT 1994. They also consider the object and purpose of the GATT 1994 and the Anti-Dumping Agreement and they address the negotiating history of GATT 1947 and the Anti-Dumping Agreement, as well as the Tokyo Round Anti-Dumping Agreement. In application of Article 31 of the Vienna Convention, we find it relevant to consider Article 18.1 as part of the context of Article VI:2

6.204 We note that Japan based its claim on both Article VI:2 of the GATT 1994 and Article 18.1 of the Anti-Dumping Agreement. We recall that, in section VI.B.4.(c) above, we considered the relationship between Article VI of the GATT 1994 and the Anti-Dumping Agreement to be similar to the relationship between Article VI of the GATT 1994 and the Agreement on Subsidies and Countervailing Measures and that between Article XIX of the GATT 1994 and the Agreement on Safeguards, as established by the Panel Report on *Argentina - Safeguards* and confirmed by the Appellate Body in the same case.[558] As a result, we shall ensure that our findings are made "in a way that gives meaning to [both] of them, harmoniously." In this respect, we recall that Article 18.1 provides that "No specific action against dumping of exports from another Member can be taken *except in accordance with the provisions of GATT 1994*, as interpreted by this Agreement" (emphasis added). On the basis of these terms, we are of the view that if we find a violation of Article VI:2 considered in its context (in particular the Anti-Dumping Agreement, including if it adds to the content of Article VI:2),[559] a violation of Article 18.1 will be automatically established.[560] If we do not find that the terms of Article VI:2, inter-

---

[558] See Appellate Body Report, *Argentina – Safeguards, supra*, footnote 476, para. 81.

[559] See Panel Report in *Brazil - Desiccated Coconut*, supra, footnote 269, para. 246 and Appellate Body Report in the same case, supra, footnote 434, at 182.

[560] We are aware of the content of footnote 24 to Article 18.1. However, this footnote, like the rest of Article 18.1, are part of the context in which Article VI:2 must be interpreted. If we reach the

preted in their context and in the light of the object and purpose of the GATT 1994 and the WTO Agreement, support Japan's claim, we will proceed to review Article 18.1 as we will have done with Article VI:2.

6.205 Therefore, having regard to the arguments raised by the parties, we shall clarify the meaning of Article VI:2 of the GATT 1994 by applying the general principles of interpretation of public international law as embodied in the Vienna Convention,[561] as we are instructed by Article 3.2 of the DSU and the Appellate Body practice.

6.206 We are aware of the fact that Article 31 of the Vienna Convention provides for one "General Rule of Interpretation", as its title states. For the sake of clarity, we will address one after the other the factors to be reviewed pursuant to that Article. However, each of these steps should be seen as part of one single process. If necessary to confirm the meaning resulting from the application of Article 31, or to determine the meaning if the interpretation under Article 31 leaves the meaning ambiguous or obscure or leads to results manifestly absurd or unreasonable, we may have recourse to the supplementary means of interpretation under Article 32 of the Vienna Convention. On that basis, we will determine whether the 1916 Act, because it pro-

---

conclusion that Article VI:2 has been violated by the 1916 Act in spite of the terms of footnote 24, there will be no reason for not finding a violation of Article 18.1.

[561] Article 31 (*General Rule of Interpretation*) of the Vienna Convention reads as follows:

> "1. A treaty shall be interpreted in good faith in accordance with the ordinary meaning to be given to the terms of the treaty in their context and in the light of its object and purpose.
>
> 2. The context for the purpose of the interpretation of a treaty shall comprise, in addition to the text, including its preamble and annexes:
>
> (a) any agreement relating to the treaty which was made between all the parties in connexion with the conclusion of the treaty;
>
> (b) any instrument which was made by one or more parties in connexion with the conclusion of the treaty and accepted by the other parties as an instrument related to the treaty.
>
> 3. There shall be taken into account together with the context:
>
> (a) any subsequent agreement between the parties regarding the interpretation of the treaty or the application of its provisions;
>
> (b) any subsequent practice in the application of the treaty which establishes the agreement of the parties regarding its interpretation;
>
> (c) any relevant rules of international law applicable in the relations between the parties.
>
> 4. A special meaning shall be given to a term if it is established that the parties so intended."

Article 32 of the Vienna Convention (*Supplementary Means of Interpretation*) reads as follows:

> "Recourse may be had to supplementary means of interpretation, including the preparatory work of the treaty and the circumstances of its conclusion, in order to confirm the meaning resulting from the application of article 31, or to determine the meaning when the interpretation according to article 31:
>
> (a) leaves the meaning ambiguous or obscure; or
>
> (b) leads to a result which is manifestly absurd or unreasonable."

The Panel is mindful that other provisions of the Vienna Convention, such as Article 33 (*Interpretation of Treaties Authenticated in Two or More Languages*) are also relevant for the interpretation of international agreements.

vides for other forms of sanctions than anti-dumping duties, violates Article VI:2 and Article 18.1 of the Anti-Dumping Agreement.

2. *Analysis of the Terms of Article VI:2 of the GATT 1994*

(a) Arguments of the Parties

6.207 Japan argues that Article VI of the GATT 1994 authorises only one measure in response to dumping: the imposition of an anti-dumping duty. Under Article VI:2, a Member may levy an anti-dumping duty equal to the margin of dumping or less than the margin of dumping, or it may decide to take no action. Any other action would violate Article VI. The text of Article 18.1 and footnote 24 of the Anti-Dumping Agreement reaffirm the understanding that Article VI of the GATT 1994 is the sole GATT-authorised remedy for dumping. A Member may affect imports through actions authorised by other provisions of the GATT 1994. For example, in a situation involving dumping, a Member could impose a safeguard measure after complying with the provisions of Article XIX of the GATT 1994 and the Agreement on Safeguards. However, the objective of the action itself would not be to address the dumping, but rather its effect. Footnote 24 simply avoids the possible conflict between other actions against imports under the WTO and the obligation under Article 18.1 not to take other action against dumping. No provision of the GATT 1994 justifies the procedures and penalties provided by the 1916 Act. The reference of the United States to Article III is irrelevant since this article does not enable a Member to take specific measures against dumping.

6.208 The United States argues that Japan's interpretation that Article VI:2 of the GATT 1994 and Article 18.1 of the Anti-Dumping Agreement establish that anti-dumping duties are the exclusive remedy for injurious dumping is contradicted by the ordinary meaning of the terms used by the two articles in question. As made clear by footnote 24 to Article 18.1, a Member may take a measure against injurious dumping even when such measures are not explicitly set forth in Article VI of the GATT 1994 or the Anti-Dumping Agreement, as long as the measure is not inconsistent with the other provisions of the GATT 1994. Nothing in Article VI:2 addresses whether anti-dumping duties are the exclusive remedy for dumping. It simply states that a Member "may" levy an anti-dumping duty to offset or prevent dumping, it does not state that a Member "may only" levy anti-dumping duties. If the word "only" had been intended, the text could and would have said so.

6.209 Moreover, according to the United States, Article VI only governs laws and measures that attempt to counteract injurious dumping through the imposition of duties, based on findings of "dumping" and "injury". When Article VI is read in the context of Articles I:1 and II:1 of the GATT 1994, it can be seen that the coverage of Article VI is limited to laws or measures that attempt to counteract injurious dumping through the imposition of anti-dumping duties. Article VI establishes a right to impose duties, it does not prohibit the imposition of other measures. Moreover, Article VI does not address the issue. It is Article 18.1 of the Anti-Dumping Agreement that addresses that issue, and it makes clear that a Member may take whatever other action is consistent with other GATT 1994 provisions. If a law imposes damages on importers, it does not fall within the scope of Article VI, since it does not impose duties, but it would be an internal law subject to Article III:4 of the GATT 1994.

(b) Ordinary Meaning of Article VI:2, First Sentence, of the GATT 1994

6.210 We note that with respect to Article VI:2 of the GATT 1994, the parties have exclusively referred to the first sentence, which provides as follows:

> "In order to offset or prevent dumping, a contracting party may levy on any dumped product an anti-dumping duty not greater in amount than the margin of dumping in respect of such product."

6.211 In that article, the only term the meaning of which is actually debated by the parties is the verb "may". The ordinary meanings of the verb "may" as an auxiliary verb include "have ability or power to, can"[562] Taken on its own, this verb could mean that Members have the possibility only to impose duties or that they have a choice between duties and other types of measures. If the word "may" was used in the first meaning, it could be argued that the term "only" should have been added right after it so as to limit its meaning. However, such an argument disregards the immediate context of the word "may". The terms "in order to offset or prevent dumping" set up the framework in which the term "may" must be understood. By specifying that the purpose of anti-dumping is to "offset" dumping, not to impose punitive measures, Article VI:2, first sentence, limits the meaning of the word "may" to giving the choice between a duty equal to the dumping margin or a lower duty, not between anti-dumping duties and other measures.

6.212 In other words, the thrust of the first sentence of Article VI:2 is to make the *imposition* of duties facultative and to limit in any event that amount to the dumping margin. If, as suggested by the United States, that sentence, and in particular the word "may" had been meant to allow other measures than anti-dumping duties, it is reasonable to expect that this would have been specified. We recall that Article VI was meant to regulate the use of anti-dumping by WTO Members. It would have been logical to list the other possible sanctions, especially if those sanctions could be more severe than the imposition of offsetting duties.[563] We therefore conclude that the ordinary meaning of the terms of the first sentence of Article VI:2 support the view that anti-dumping duties are the only type of remedies allowed under Article VI of the GATT 1994.

(c) Context of Article VI:2 of the GATT 1994

6.213 We note that the immediate context of Article VI:2 within Article VI confirms our understanding of the word "may". The United States stresses the fact that the words "may" was used in Article VI:2, rather than "shall", as in other paragraphs of Article VI. In our opinion, the term "shall", as used in paragraphs 3 to 6 was not

[562] See *The New Shorter Oxford English Dictionary* (1993), p. 1721. It is evident that while we review the ordinary meaning, our reading of the dictionary is already made selective by the broad context of the term. For instance, we left aside the definition of "may" as "have the possibility, opportunity or suitable conditions to..." or the definition of "may" which, in the interpretation of some statutes means "shall, must".

[563] We note in that respect that Article 7.2 of the Anti-Dumping Agreement, which provides for the types of provisional measures that may be imposed, lists the measures that may be taken, i.e. "provisional duty or, preferably, a security".

necessary in paragraph 2 of Article VI if it was meant to be permissive, not mandatory to *impose* duties, and "shall" was not necessary either to express the idea that only anti-dumping duties could be imposed.

6.214 As noted above, we see Article VI and Article 18.1 as part of the same "package" of rights and obligations, if only because the Anti-Dumping Agreement interprets Article VI of the GATT 1994 (see the terms of Article 18.1, below). As a result, Article 18.1 is particularly relevant as context of Article VI, but we shall also review the other provisions referred to by the parties: Article I and II of the GATT 1994 and Article 1 of the Anti-Dumping Agreement.

6.215 Article 18.1 provides as follows:

> "No specific action against dumping of exports from another Member can be taken except in accordance with the provisions of GATT 1994, as interpreted by this Agreement. [footnote 24]"

Footnote 24 to Article 18.1 reads as follows:

> "24 This is not intended to preclude action under other relevant provisions of GATT 1994, as appropriate."

6.216 We consider that the provisions of Article 18.1 as such limit the *anti-dumping instruments* that may be used by Members to those expressly contained in Article VI and the Anti-Dumping Agreement. Except for provisional measures and price undertakings, the only type of remedies foreseen by the Anti-Dumping Agreement is the imposition of duties. We also note that Article 9.1 of the Anti-Dumping Agreement[564] establishes a clear connection between the calculation of a dumping margin provided for in Article 2 of that agreement and the final measures that may be imposed. We therefore conclude that the context of Article VI confirms the provisional conclusion we had reached on the basis of the ordinary meaning.

6.217 The United States argues that the terms of footnote 24 to Article 18.1 of the Anti-Dumping Agreement, like footnote 16 to Article 16.1 of the Tokyo Round Anti-Dumping Agreement, does not "lock" a Member into levying anti-dumping duties when faced with a factual situation constituting injurious dumping. Footnote 24 leaves the option open for applying other measures that are in accordance with the GATT 1994. According to the United States, if the measure is of a nature that is simply not regulated by the GATT 1994, as is the case for the 1916 Act, the measure is *a fortiori* consistent with GATT 1994.

6.218 We consider that footnote 24 does not prevent Members from addressing the causes or effects of dumping through other trade policy instruments allowed under the WTO Agreement. Nor does it prevent Members from adopting other types of measures which are compatible with the WTO Agreement. Such a possibility does

[564] Article 9.1 provides as follows:

> "The decision whether or not to impose an anti-dumping duty in cases where all requirements for the imposition have been fulfilled, and the decision whether the amount of the anti-dumping duty to be imposed shall be the full margin of dumping or less, are decisions to be made by the authorities of the importing Member. It is desirable that the imposition be permissive in the territory of all Members, and that the duty be less than the margin if such lesser duty would be adequate to remove the injury to the domestic industry."

not affect our conclusion that, when a law of a Member addresses the type of price discrimination covered by Article VI and makes it the cause for the imposition of anti-dumping measures, that Member has to abide by the requirements of Article VI and the Anti-Dumping Agreement. Whether or not Article VI applies does not depend on whether a Member addresses dumping through the imposition of duties or through the imposition of other remedies, with the implication that Article VI applies only if a Member addresses dumping through the imposition of duties, as opposed to, e.g., fines on importers. In our opinion, the application of Article VI depends on whether the practice that triggers the imposition of the measures is "dumping" within the meaning of Article VI:1 of the GATT 1994. If the interpretation suggested by the United States were to be followed, Members could address "dumping" without having to respect the provisions of Article VI of the GATT 1994 and the Anti-Dumping Agreement. Such an interpretation would deprive Article VI of the GATT 1994 and the Anti-Dumping Agreement of their useful effect within the framework of rules and disciplines imposed by the WTO Agreement.

6.219 The United States argues that the coverage of Article VI, read in the context of Articles I:1 and II:1 of the GATT 1994, is limited to laws or measures that attempt to counteract injurious dumping through the imposition of anti-dumping duties. Article VI is a carve-out to those articles, and merely allows Members to impose anti-dumping duties above the relevant bound rate and on a non most-favoured-nation basis. It does not follow that Article VI (or Article 18.1 of the Anti-Dumping Agreement) would itself act as a prohibition against actions that Members may take. Rather, according to the United States, Article VI is properly viewed as establishing a right that a Member has, that is the right to impose duties to counteract injurious dumping.

6.220 We do not regard the US argument as compelling. The fact that Article VI provides for a carve-out to Articles I and II or, as the panel report on *United States - Countervailing Duties on Fresh, Chilled and Frozen Pork from Canada* puts it, "an exception to basic principles of the General Agreement",[565] does not support the argument that Article VI only applies to laws that purport to address injurious dumping through anti-dumping duties. It merely confirms that duties may be imposed under Article VI without violating Articles I and II of the GATT 1994. This conclusion does not affect our interpretation of Article VI:2 based on the ordinary meaning of that provision.

6.221 As part of the context of Article VI:2, we find the terms of Article 1 of the Anti-Dumping Agreement more relevant. Article 1 provides as follows:

> "An anti-dumping measure shall be applied only under the circumstances provided for in Article VI of GATT 1994 and pursuant to investigations initiated [footnote 1] and conducted in accordance with the provisions of this Agreement. The following provisions govern the application of Article VI of GATT 1994 in so far as action is taken under anti-dumping legislation or regulations."

Footnote 1 to Article 1 reads as follows:

[565] Adopted on 11 July 1991, BISD 38S/30, para. 4.4. We note that the reasoning of the panel in that case related to Article VI:3 of the GATT 1947.

"1 The term "initiated" as used in this Agreement means the procedural action by which a Member formally commences an investigation as provided in Article 5."

6.222 In this respect, we requested the parties to provide us with their understanding of the meaning of the term "measure" in Article 1, so as to have a clearer view of the impact of the context of Article VI:2. Both parties referred to the three types of measures allowed under the Anti-Dumping Agreement. In addition, the United States argued that the word "measure" is qualified by the term "anti-dumping", stating that this term limits the scope of Article 1. In our opinion, an anti-dumping measure is a measure aimed at counteracting dumping as such, as defined in Article VI:1 of the GATT 1994. Members may decide to address under other WTO provisions the causes or the effects of dumping. By doing so, they would not adopt "anti-dumping measures" within the meaning of Article VI and the Anti-Dumping Agreement. However, if they objectively address a form of price discrimination that meets the definition of Article VI, this must be in accordance with Article VI and the Anti-Dumping Agreement, which themselves do not refer to any other remedy than duties. We therefore conclude that the context of Article VI:2 of the GATT 1994 confirms our understanding of the meaning of that provision based on its ordinary meaning.

(d) Object and Purpose

6.223 We note that the parties have not, in their arguments regarding the meaning of Article VI:2 addressed the object and purpose of the GATT 1994, of the Anti-Dumping Agreement or of the WTO Agreement in general. We recall that the preamble of a treaty may assist in identifying the object and purpose of that treaty. However, as far as dumping is concerned, the preambles of the WTO Agreement and the GATT do not provide precise directives. We note however that both preambles refer to the "substantial reduction of tariffs and other barriers to trade and to the elimination of discriminatory treatment in international trade relations". We also note that the WTO preamble refers to the development of a "more viable and durable multilateral trading system". We consider that the approach of the United States which would allow Members to take any type of measure against dumping as such outside the framework of Article VI, as long as they are not incompatible with other provisions of the WTO Agreement, does not seem to be commensurate with the objectives highlighted above.

6.224 Moreover, the fact that dumping may only be subject to countermeasures if it causes injury and then only through anti-dumping duties promotes, in our opinion, the durability and viability of the trading system. As a matter of fact, the WTO Agreement does not regulate dumping, but anti-dumping, even though by doing so it also recognises the negative effect of dumping. One should also recall that the developments that took place through the various agreements on anti-dumping have imposed clearer conditions on recourse by Members to anti-dumping instruments. The effect of these efforts would be significantly limited if a Member could be exempted of their obligations by simply choosing to impose any other measure than anti-dumping duties to counteract dumping as such.

6.225 We therefore consider that the object and purpose of the WTO Agreement and the GATT 1994 confirm our interpretation of the terms of Article VI:2 taken in their context.

(e) Preparatory Work

6.226 We could conclude our interpretation of Article VI:2 of the GATT 1994 on the basis of the rule of Article 31 of the Vienna Convention. However, since the parties have discussed the meaning of the negotiating history at length, we consider it in order to determine if it confirms the meaning of Article VI:2 we have identified under Article 31.

6.227 The parties have referred to a number of documents relating to the negotiation of the Havana Charter and the GATT.[566] We do not consider it necessary to review all these materials since our analysis under Article 31 of the Vienna Convention does not leave the meaning of Article VI ambiguous or obscure and does not lead to a manifestly absurd or unreasonable result. We recall, however, that the parties have, in particular, discussed the Report of the Working Party on Modifications to the General Agreement, which was adopted by the CONTRACTING PARTIES on 1-2 September 1948 in the context of the revision of Article VI of GATT 1947.[567] This report mentions that:

> "endorsing the views expressed by Sub-Committee C of the Third Committee of the Havana Conference, [footnote omitted] [it] agreed that measures other than compensatory anti-dumping and countervailing duties may not be applied to counteract dumping or subsidization except in so far as such other measures are permitted under other provisions of the General Agreement."[568]

6.228 We consider that the first part of the sentence ("measures other than compensatory anti-dumping and countervailing duties may not be applied to counteract dumping or subsidization") confirms our understanding of Article VI. The second part of the sentence ("except in so far as such other measures are permitted under other provisions of the General Agreement"), may be understood as allowing Members to counter dumping through other measures than anti-dumping duties.[569] The United States argues that a number of measures could be legally applied against dumping, such as raising unbound tariffs, tariff renegotiation, safeguard measures or countervailing measures. We note, however, that even though those measures may be legally applied to address dumping, the basis for their imposition would not objectively be "dumping", but its causes or effects. Safeguard measures or the increase of unbound tariffs would apply on a most-favoured-nation basis. So would the results of a tariff renegotiation. Unless all Members were dumping, dumping could not be

---

566 See section III.E.3. above.

567 See the discussion in section III.F above.

568 BISD Vol. II, p. 41 (1952), para. 12.

569 We note in this respect that the United States refers to John H. Jackson, *World Trade and the Law of GATT* (1968), p. 411, where it is mentioned that:

> "Although Article VI carves out an exception to GATT obligations for anti-dumping or countervailing duties, nevertheless, measures that do not violate other GATT provisions can also be used to counteract dumping or subsidies. Thus, insofar as tariffs on a particular product are not bound in a GATT schedule, a country that found that the product was being dumped could raise its tariffs without limit to counteract the dumping, and go even further and punish the dumper."

considered as the objective reason for the imposition of the measures or of the renegotiated tariff *vis-à-vis* each Member. Countervailing measures can only be imposed in relation to subsidies. The fact that those subsidies may allow their beneficiaries to dump is not directly relevant to the imposition of the countervailing measures. Therefore, the sentence quoted above can only be understood as having the same meaning as footnote 24 to Article 18.1 of the Anti-Dumping Agreement.[570]

6.229 We conclude that the supplementary means of interpretation of Article 32 of the Vienna Convention confirm our interpretation of Article VI:2 of the GATT 1994 based on the ordinary meaning of its terms taken in their context and in the light of the object and purpose of the WTO Agreement.

3. *Conclusion*

(a) Conclusion on the Violation of Article VI:2 of the GATT 1994 and Article 18.1 of the Anti-Dumping Agreement

6.230 We therefore find that Article VI:2 of the GATT 1994 provides that only measures in the form of anti-dumping duties may be applied to counteract dumping as such[571] and that, by providing for the imposition of fines or imprisonment or for the recovery of treble damages, the 1916 Act violates Article VI:2 of the GATT 1994.

---

[570] See para. 6.218 above. We also recall the reasons stated in the report of the Working Party established by Sub-Committee C of the Third Committee of the Havana Conference (E/CONF.2/C.3/C/18, 22 January 1948) for the deletion of para. 6 of Article 34 of the Geneva Draft Charter of the International Trade Organisation. Para. 6 was similar to para. 7 of the original Article VI of the GATT 1947 and read as follows:

> "No measures other than anti-dumping or countervailing duties shall be applied by any contracting party in respect of any product of the territory of any other contracting party for the purpose of offsetting dumping or subsidization."

The question had been prompted by the issue whether para. 6 should be deleted or amended in the event that it could be interpreted so as to limit action permitted under Articles 13 and 14 of the Geneva Draft. The report stated that:

> "The Working Party was evenly divided as to whether the terms of para. (6) could be construed as limiting the rights of Members under Articles 13 and 14. It was in agreement, however, that para. (6) was unnecessary and that its deletion would not effect any change in substance."

These statements confirm the intent to restrict the measures allowed to counteract dumping *as such* to offsetting duties. The fact that Article VI allows only for duties to counteract dumping practices as such is also confirmed by the Report of the Review Working Party on "Other Barriers to Trade", which mentions that:

> "With respect to para. 3 of Article VI, the Working Party considered a proposal submitted by New Zealand which would have permitted under certain circumstances the use of quantitative restrictions to offset subsidization or dumping. This proposal did not receive the support of the Working Party, and has not been recommended." (BISD 3S/223, as quoted in *GATT, Analytical Index: Guide to GATT Law and Practice*, Updated 6th Edition (1995), p. 238)

[571] This is of course without prejudice to the acceptance of price undertakings, as provided for in the Anti-Dumping Agreement.

6.231 Having regard to our comments in paragraph 6.204 above and for the reasons mentioned therein, we conclude that the 1916 Act, because it violates Article VI:2 of the GATT 1994 by providing for other remedies than anti-dumping duties, is not "in accordance with the provisions of GATT 1994 as interpreted by [the Anti-Dumping Agreement]", within the meaning of Article 18.1. As a result, the 1916 Act also violates Article 18.1 of the Anti-Dumping Agreement.

6.232 We also recall our conclusion in paragraph 6.183 above. Since we found a violation of Article VI:2 of the GATT 1994 and of Article 18.1 of the Anti-Dumping Agreement, we do not find it necessary to determine what would be the legal consequences of a consistent WTO-compatible interpretation of the 1916 Act by US courts *in the future*.

(a) Remarks on the Burden of Proof with Respect to the Violation of Article VI:2 of the GATT 1994 and of Article 18.1 of the Anti-Dumping Agreement

6.233 The Panel divided its own analysis along lines that did not always correspond to the argumentation followed by each party, since each adopted a different approach to the problem before us.[572] However, we consider that Japan has established a *prima facie* case for each point addressed by the Panel in relation to the applicability of Article VI and the Anti-Dumping Agreement and regarding the violation of Article VI:2 of the GATT 1994 and Article 18.1 of the Anti-Dumping Agreement.[573] The United States did not sufficiently rebut them. Moreover, we consider that the United States did not establish such a *prima facie* case with respect to the defences it raised, especially regarding the jurisdiction of the Panel under Article VI and the Anti-Dumping Agreement and the non-mandatory nature of the 1916 Act.

E. Violation of Article VI of the GATT 1994 and of Articles 1, 2, 3, 4, 5, 9, 11, and 18.1 of the Anti-Dumping Agreement

1. Preliminary Remarks

6.234 We recall that Japan makes several additional claims under Article VI of the GATT 1994 and the Anti-Dumping Agreement. We already found that the 1916 Act violates Article VI:2 of the GATT 1994 and Article 18.1 of the Anti-Dumping Agreement by providing for damages, fines or imprisonment, which are not allowed under those provisions. We are of the view that "adapting" the 1916 Act, by amendment or otherwise, to the requirement of Article VI:2 and Article 18.1 may not be sufficient to make the 1916 Act fully WTO-compatible.[574] We also recall that, as

[572] See para. 6.111 above.

[573] Since Article 18.1 of the Anti-Dumping Agreement specifies that actions must be taken "in accordance with the provisions of GATT 1994 as interpreted by this Agreement" and since we found a violation of Article VI of the GATT 1994 , we consider that such a violation automatically leads to a violation of Article 18.1.

[574] While this statement is not made under Article 19.1 of the DSU, we note that, pursuant to that provision, we are entitled to suggest ways in which the Member concerned could implement the Panel's recommendations.

mentioned by the Appellate Body in its report on *Australia - Measures Affecting Importation of Salmon,*[575]

> "A panel has to address those claims on which a finding is necessary in order to enable the DSB to make sufficiently precise recommendations and rulings so as to allow for prompt compliance by a Member with those recommendations and rulings 'in order to ensure effective resolution of the dispute to the benefit of all Members.'"

We are of the view that additional findings with respect to the other claims of Japan under Article VI and the Anti-Dumping Agreement would assist the DSB in making sufficiently precise recommendations and rulings so as to allow for prompt compliance by the United States with those recommendations and rulings. We therefore proceed to address those claims to the extent necessary, reserving our right to exercise judicial economy if we consider that certain additional findings are not necessary, within the meaning of the quote from the Appellate Body Report above.

6.235 We also note that Japan, in its request for the establishment of a Panel (WT/DS162/3), did not specify the paragraphs of the provisions of the Anti-Dumping Agreement which it cited in support of its claims. Furthermore, in its claims based on both Article VI and the Anti-Dumping Agreement, Japan did not specify either which paragraph of Article VI it considered to be breached. We note that, in *Korea - Definitive Safeguard Measures on Imports of Certain Dairy Products*, the Appellate Body considered that the complainant in that case should have been more specific in presenting its claims in its request for the establishment of a panel, mostly since the provisions to which it referred had several paragraphs, each containing distinct obligations.[576] In this respect, the situation in the present case is quite similar. However, unlike Korea in the above-mentioned case, the United States did not claim that it had been prejudiced by the lack of precision of Japan's claims under the Anti-Dumping Agreement and Article VI of the GATT 1994. We read the requirements of Article 6.2 of the DSU in the light of the above-mentioned Appellate Body report and in the light of the Appellate Body Report in *European Communities - Bananas* as primarily designed to protect the respondent. We therefore consider that if the respondent does not argue that it has been prejudiced by the lack of specificity of the claims and the Panel is satisfied that it can make an objective assessment of the matter before it, including an objective assessment of the applicability of and conformity of the measure at issue with the relevant covered agreements, there is no reason for the Panel to reject the claims concerned *propio motu*.

6.236 We note however that the United States does not specifically reply to each of the claims of Japan. It states that the claims raised by Japan under various provisions of the Anti-Dumping Agreement and Article VI rest on the assumption that the Panel has already found the 1916 Act to be in violation of Article VI:2 of the GATT 1994 and Article 18.1 of the Anti-Dumping Agreement. Thus, according to the United States, each of these claims has the same faulty premises.

---

[575] See Appellate Body Report on *Australia - Measures Affecting Importation of Salmon, supra*, footnote 471, para. 223.

[576] Appellate Body Report on *Korea - Definitive Safeguard Measures on Imports of Certain Dairy Products*, WT/DS98/AB/R, adopted 12 January 2000, DSR 2000:I, 3, paras. 129 and 131.

6.237 Having regard to our findings under Article VI:2 of the GATT 1994 and Article 18.1 of the Anti-Dumping Agreement, we also take note of the arguments of the United States and do not assimilate its absence of reply to an acknowledgement that Japan's claims are justified.

2. *Review of the Additional Claims of Japan under Article VI of the GATT 1994 and the Anti-Dumping Agreement*

(a) Violation of Article VI:1 of the GATT 1994 and Article 1 of the Anti-Dumping Agreement

6.238 Japan claims that the 1916 Act provides for the application of sanctions outside the circumstances specified in Article VI:1 of the GATT 1994 and Article 1 of the Anti-Dumping Agreement. Specifically, the 1916 Act provides for the imposition of measures in the absence of an investigation initiated and conducted in accordance with the provisions of the Anti-Dumping Agreement, and without establishing facts required by Article 1 thereof.

6.239 We recall that Article 1 of the Anti-Dumping Agreement reads as follows:

> "An anti-dumping measure shall be applied only under the circumstances provided for in Article VI of GATT 1994 and pursuant to investigations initiated and conducted in accordance with the provisions of this Agreement. The following provisions govern the application of Article VI of GATT 1994 in so far as action is taken under anti-dumping legislation or regulations."

6.240 We note a violation of Article 1 may result, *inter alia*, from the fact that the 1916 Act does not provide for investigations consistent with the Anti-Dumping Agreement. Japan has made other claims under other provisions of the Anti-Dumping Agreement. If we find that any of these claims is justified, we will conclude that Article 1 is violated.

6.241 Likewise, since Japan makes other, more specific claims with regard to Article VI:1, we will suspend our decision regarding a potential violation of that provision until we have addressed them. Indeed, we note that Article VI:1, *inter alia*, mentions circumstances under which an anti-dumping measure may be applied. If we find another cause of violation of Article VI:1, it will not be necessary for us to make a finding of violation of Article VI:1 in relation to a violation of Article 1 of the Anti-Dumping Agreement.

(b) Violation of Article VI:1(a) of the GATT 1994 and Article 2.1 and 2.2 of the Anti-Dumping Agreement

6.242 Japan argues that the 1916 Act prohibits the importation of products at a price "substantially less" than the "actual value or wholesale price of [the products] [...] in the principal markets of the country of their production, or of other foreign countries to which they are commonly exported [...]." In contrast, Article VI:1(a) of the GATT 1994 and Article 2.1 and 2.2 of the Anti-Dumping Agreement require that the first benchmark against which the price of the imported product is compared be the actual price of the product for sale in the exporting country. Under Article VI:1(a) and Article 2.1, the primary and preferred benchmark for comparison is "the comparable price, in the ordinary course of trade, for the like product when destined for consumption in the exporting country".

6.243 We note that the terms of Article VI:1(a) of the GATT 1994 and Article 2 of the Anti-Dumping Agreement are different from those used in the 1916 Act. In order to determine whether this textual difference results in a violation, we need to consider whether those terms have been, or, in the absence of any past interpretation, could be interpreted consistently with the provisions of Article VI:1(a) and Article 2.

6.244 We first note that, contrary to Article VI:1 of the GATT 1994 and Article 2 of the Anti-Dumping Agreement, the 1916 Act does not make the comparable *price when destined for consumption in the exporting country* the preferred basis for the establishment of the normal value. In the 1916 Act, actual value or wholesale price of the products "in the principal markets [...] of other foreign countries to which they are commonly exported" seems to be equally applicable, even if an appropriate comparable price for consumption in the domestic market of the exporting country exists. However, we note that nothing in the terms of the 1916 Act would prevent the introduction in practice of an order of precedence between the "actual value or wholesale price of [the products] [...] in the principal markets of the country of their production" and the actual value or wholesale price of [the products] [...] in the principal markets of other foreign countries to which they are commonly exported" compatible with the requirement of Article VI:1 of the GATT 1994 and Article 2 of the Anti-Dumping Agreement.

6.245 Japan also argues that Article 2.4.1 of the Anti-Dumping Agreement provides that those against whom dumping is alleged can have protection against currency fluctuations. The 1916 Act provides no such protection.

6.246 Article 2.4.1 provides as follows:

> "When the comparison under paragraph 4 requires a conversion of currencies, such conversion should be made using the rate of exchange of the date of sale [footnote 8], provided that when a sale of foreign currency on forward markets is directly linked to the export sale involved, the rate of exchange in the forward sale shall be used. Fluctuation in exchange rates shall be ignored and in an investigation the authorities shall allow exporters at least 60 days to have adjusted their export prices to reflect sustained movements in exchange rates during the period of investigation."

Footnote 8 reads as follows:

> "Normally, the date of sale would be the date of contract, purchase order, order confirmation, or invoice, whichever establishes the material terms of sale."

6.247 We note that the mechanism provided for in Article 2.4.1 of the Anti-Dumping Agreement is not mentioned in the 1916 Act. We also note that nothing in the terms of the 1916 Act would prevent the use of that mechanism in the actual application of the 1916 Act.

6.248 Japan's arguments raise the question whether the mere fact that the 1916 Act does not expressly incorporate a WTO requirement, while at the same time not preventing the implementing authority from reading that requirement into the 1916 Act, can be considered as a violation of Article VI:1 and Article 2 of the Anti-Dumping Agreement.

6.249 We recall that, at our request, the United States explained that, pursuant to the doctrine established by the US Supreme Court in *Murray v. Schooner Charming Betsy*,[577] in the absence of conflict, US judges should, whenever possible, interpret US laws in conformity with the international obligations of the United States. Applied to the present case, this doctrine would imply that any judge before whom claims similar to those of Japan would be raised, would be expected to interpret the 1916 Act in conformity with the US obligations under Article 2 of the Anti-Dumping Agreement, provided there is no conflict between the relevant US legislation and international law. In other words, the fact that the 1916 Act is silent regarding some WTO requirements does not mean *a priori* that, when it comes to applying the 1916 Act to a particular case, those requirements would be disregarded.

6.250 We note that Japan did not give us grounds for believing that we should consider that the 1916 Act violates Article VI and the Anti-Dumping Agreement by the mere fact that it is silent with respect to certain requirements contained in those provisions. We also note that the terms of the 1916 Act are, as such, not incompatible with the above-mentioned requirements. Those requirements could be read into the 1916 Act through interpretation. Japan did not refer the Panel to any court decisions relating to the 1916 Act which would have specifically discussed the issue covered by Article 2.4.1 of the Anti-Dumping Agreement and applied an inconsistent decision. Japan did not point either at any other US law which would apply in relation to the 1916 Act (e.g., procedural rules) and would be in conflict with international law, thus preventing the application of the *Charming Betsy* doctrine in the first place. In our opinion, it is not for the Panel to "make the case" of the complainant.[578] As a result, we conclude that Japan did not establish a *prima facie* case that the 1916 Act violates Article VI:1(a) and Article 2.1 and 2.2 of the Anti-Dumping Agreement.

(c) Violation of Article VI.1 and VI:6(a) of the GATT 1994 and Article 3 of the Anti-Dumping Agreement

6.251 Japan claims that Articles VI:1 and VI:6(a) of the GATT 1994, and Article 3 of the Anti-Dumping Agreement, require a Member to find that a given dumping practice causes or threatens to cause material injury to its domestic industry (or retards the establishment of a domestic industry) before applying an anti-dumping measure. These articles also set forth criteria which define and govern the determina-

[577] 6 U.S. (2 cranch) 64, 118 (1804). The United States also refers to *Footwear Distributors and Retailers of America v. United States*, 852 F. Supp. 1078, 1088 (CIT), appeal dismissed, 43 F.3d 1486 (Table) (Fed. Cir. 1994), citing *DeBartelo Corp. v. Florida Gulf Coast Building and Trade Council*, 485 U.S. 568 (1988).

[578] We are of the view that we face a situation resembling that addressed in the case on *Japan - Measures Affecting Agricultural Products,* Panel and Appellate Body Reports, adopted 19 March 1999, WT/DS76/R, DSR 1999:I, 315 and WT/DS76/AB/R, DSR 1999:I, 277, (see Appellate Body Report., paras. 125-131). In that case, the complainant had not made a particular argument. The panel then deduced that argument from the experts' answers to its questions. The Appellate Body considered that, even though Article 13 of the DSU and Article 11.2 of the Agreement on Sanitary and Phytosanitary Measures suggested that panels had significant investigative authority, this authority could not be used by a Panel to rule in favour of a complaining party which had not established a *prima facie* case of inconsistency based on specific legal claims asserted by it.

tion of injury. In contrast, the 1916 Act only requires a showing of intent. Moreover, the intent requirement in the 1916 Act is defined as an intent to destroy or injure a United States industry or to prevent its establishment. Thus, the 1916 Act contains no requirement similar to "material injury" within the meaning of Article VI of the GATT 1994 and the Anti-Dumping Agreement.

6.252 We note that Article VI:1 of the GATT 1994 requires the existence of material injury or a threat thereof to an established industry or material retardation of the establishment of a domestic industry. The 1916 Act does not refer to material injury or threat of material injury or material retardation of the establishment of a domestic industry but to the *intent* of, *inter alia*, "destroying or injuring an industry in the United States, or of preventing the establishment of an industry in the United States". In certain circumstances, the existence of an intent to injure may be more difficult to prove than the existence of actual injury. The United States executive branch early considered that the requirement of an "intent" made the imposition of remedies under the 1916 Act almost impossible.[579] The Panel also recalls that the Supreme Court in the *Brooke Group* case considered, with respect to a company's planning documents speaking of a desire to slow the growth of a given segment of industry, that "even an act of pure malice by one business competitor against another does not, without more, state a claim under the federal anti-trust law". Thus, assuming that the *Brooke Group* test applies to the 1916 Act, and assuming further that it relates to the "intent" aspect of the law,[580] evidence of predatory pricing and prospects of recoupment are necessary. A statement of aggressive policy in an internal company document does not seem to be sufficient. However, we are not convinced that such requirements could be interpreted as having substituted an "actual effect" test to the "intent" test found in the text of the 1916 Act. Even in the circumstances mentioned above, the existence of an "intent" may not always imply the existence of actual injury, actual threat of injury or actual retardation. Interpreting the term "injuring an industry or [...] preventing the establishment of an industry in the United States" in the 1916 Act as meaning "causing material injury or materially retarding the establishment of a domestic industry" as in Article VI of the GATT 1994 might be possible under US law. However, reading the "intent" requirement out of the 1916 Act would, in our view, amount to a *contra legem* interpretation of which we have seen no instance yet in relation to this case.

6.253 For these reasons, we find that the 1916 Act, to the extent that it provides for the identification of an "intent" on the part of the defendant rather than for the actual injury requirements of Article VI, is not compatible with Article VI:1 of the GATT 1994. We note that Article VI:6(a) does not, in substance, contain additional obligations with respect to the existence of material injury, threat of injury or material retardation of the establishment of a domestic industry.[581] However, from the terms of

---

[579] See *Geneva Steel, Op. Cit.*, at p. 1220, quoting a statement recorded in 56 Cong. Rec. 346 (Dec. 9, 1919):

> "The Tariff Commission declares that [the 1916 Act] is not workable, for the reason that it is almost impossible to show the intent on the part of the importer to injure or destroy business in the United States by such importation or sale".

[580] See our opinion in this respect in paras. 6.168-170 above.

[581] Article VI:6(a) provides as follows:

Article VI:6(a), it seems to us that the objective of that paragraph is to require a *determination* by the authorities of the importing Member that dumping is such as to cause material injury, threat thereof or material retardation.[582] Having regard to the evidence before us, we do not consider that Japan has established a *prima facie* case of violation of Article VI:6(a) based on the fact that the 1916 Act would not provide for a *determination* by the US authorities.

6.254 Since we have found above that the 1916 Act violates Article VI:1 by not providing for an injury test compatible with the terms of that Article and since Article 3 of the Anti-Dumping Agreement simply addresses in more detail the requirement of "material injury" contained in Article VI:1, we do not find it necessary to make specific findings under Article 3. We therefore exercise judicial economy with respect to the claim made by Japan under Article 3 of the Anti-Dumping Agreement, as we are entitled to do pursuant to GATT 1947 panel practice and WTO panel and Appellate Body practice.[583]

(d) Violation of Articles 4 and 5 of the Anti-Dumping Agreement

6.255 Japan claims that Articles 4 and 5 of the Anti-Dumping Agreement set forth requirements limiting the party or parties that may properly pursue an anti-dumping claim. Article 5.1 requires that a request for initiation of an anti-dumping investigation be made by or on behalf of the domestic industry. Article 4.1 defines "domestic industry" for the purpose of the Anti-Dumping Agreement. Article 5.4 requires the investigating authorities to determine that an application is supported by "those producers which collective output constitutes more than 50 per cent of the total production of the like product" of those producers supporting or opposing the application. Moreover, under no circumstances can an investigation be initiated if those supporting the application account for less than 25 per cent of total domestic production of the like product. In contrast, as evidenced by the most recent cases initiated under the 1916 Act, a complaint under the 1916 Act can be initiated by a single United States producer. Article 5 also requires that applications contain evidence of the three elements of dumping, injury and causation, and sets a *de minimis* threshold applicable to the dumping element. The 1916 Act contains none of these elements. On the contrary, Japan argues that, under the US Federal Rules of Civil Procedure 8(a)(2), a complainant under the 1916 Act needs only to present a short and plain statement of its claims. Finally, Article 5.10 of the Anti-Dumping Agreement requires Members to

---

> "No contracting party shall levy any anti-dumping or countervailing duty on the importation of any product of the territory of another contracting party unless it determines that the effect of the dumping or subsidization, as the case may be, is such as to cause or threaten material injury to an established domestic industry, or is such as to retard materially the establishment of a domestic industry."

[582] See, e.g., Panel Report on *New Zealand - Imports of Electrical Transformers from Finland*, adopted on 18 July 1985, 32S/55, para. 4.4.

[583] See, e.g. Panel Report on *Canada - Administration of the Foreign Investment Review Act*, adopted on 7 February 1984, BISD 30S/140, para. 5.16; Panel Report on *Brazil - Desiccated Coconut*, *supra*, footnote 269, para. 293; Appellate Body Report on *United States - Measures Affecting Imports of Woven Wool Shirts and Blouses from India*, *supra*, footnote 27, at 339.

complete their investigations and decide whether or not to impose duties within 18 months. The 1916 Act contains no such deadline.

6.256 We note that Japan's claims under Article 4 and 5 of the Anti-Dumping Agreement are closely linked because one of the conditions for the initiation of an investigation under Article 5.1 is that the application be made on behalf of the domestic industry, which is defined in Article 4.1.

6.257 We recall that civil proceedings under the 1916 Act are available to "any person injured in his business or property" by reason of a violation of the 1916 Act. This term is nowhere qualified by a statement that this person should be sufficiently representative of an industry of the United States, within the meaning of Article 4 of the Anti-Dumping Agreement. We note that the 1916 Act refers to the intent of destroying or injuring an *industry* in the United States, or of preventing the establishment of an *industry* in the United States. However, we have no evidence that a minimum representation level for a given industry must be established by the complainant before filing a case before a federal court. On the contrary, we note that all cases so far have, in fact, been initiated by individual companies under their own responsibility. The fact that, in certain cases, these companies may have represented a very large portion of the US industry in the economic sector concerned does not seem to be linked to any legal requirement of representation under the 1916 Act and is most probably fortuitous. We have not been referred to any provisions of the US Federal Rules of Civil Procedure which would qualify the terms of the 1916 Act in line with the terms of Article 4 and 5 of the Anti-Dumping Agreement. In light of the terms of the 1916 Act, especially the term "*any person* injured in his business or property"[584] which is clear, we have no reason to believe that US federal courts will be in a position to interpret that provision - which conflicts with the terms of the Anti-Dumping Agreement - to meet the requirements of Articles 4 and 5 of the Anti-Dumping Agreement in terms of representation of the complainants.

6.258 Regarding the requirement of Article 5.2 that applications contain evidence of the three elements of dumping, injury and causation, we note that Japan referred to the provisions of the US Federal Rules of Civil Procedure to support its argument that no such requirement applies to complainants under the 1916 Act. We note that the United States did not contest, as a matter of fact, the applicability to the 1916 Act of the provisions of the US Federal Rules of Civil Procedure cited by Japan. We also recall that the 1916 Act does not require the establishment of injury within the meaning of Article VI of the GATT 1994. We therefore conclude that there is no obligation for a complainant under the 1916 Act to respect the obligations of Article 5.2 of the Anti-Dumping Agreement in terms of the type of evidence to be included in an application.

6.259 Finally, Japan argues that Article 5.10 of the Anti-Dumping Agreement requires Members to complete their investigations and decide whether or not to impose duties within 18 months. Japan claims that the 1916 Act contains no such deadline.

6.260 As we noted in a similar situation for certain claims of Japan under Article 2 of the Anti-Dumping Agreement, the fact that the 1916 Act does not include a deadline for the completion of proceedings is not as such sufficient to establish a viola-

[584] Emphasis added.

tion. We do not consider it *a priori* impossible that US courts, in the absence of a conflict, read that deadline into the text of the 1916 Act in application of the *Charming Betsy* doctrine.[585] Japan did not submit evidence that the absence in the 1916 Act of an express deadline compatible with the provisions of Article 5.10 of the Anti-Dumping Agreement was a violation of the WTO Agreement. Even though we are not sure that the 18-month deadline could always be imposed by the judge on the parties to a 1916 Act case, we consider that Japan, as a complainant, did not establish a *prima facie* case in that respect and we refrain from making a finding under Article 5.10 on the 1916 Act.

6.261 We therefore find that the 1916 Act, because it does not require a minimum representation of a US industry in applications for the initiation of proceedings under the 1916 Act, violates Article 4.1 and Article 5.1, 5.2 and 5.4 of the Anti-Dumping Agreement.

(e) Violation of Article VI of the GATT 1994 and Articles 9 and 11 of the Anti-Dumping Agreement

6.262 Japan argues that the 1916 Act ignores the regime provided for in Article 9 of the Anti-Dumping Agreement[586] with respect to the imposition and collection of anti-

---

[585] See para. 6.249 above.

[586] Article 9 of the Anti-Dumping Agreement provides as follows:

> "9.1 The decision whether or not to impose an anti-dumping duty in cases where all requirements for the imposition have been fulfilled, and the decision whether the amount of the anti-dumping duty to be imposed shall be the full margin of dumping or less, are decisions to be made by the authorities of the importing Member. It is desirable that the imposition be permissive in the territory of all Members, and that the duty be less than the margin if such lesser duty would be adequate to remove the injury to the domestic industry.
>
> 9.2 When an anti-dumping duty is imposed in respect of any product, such anti-dumping duty shall be collected in the appropriate amounts in each case, on a non-discriminatory basis on imports of such product from all sources found to be dumped and causing injury, except as to imports from those sources from which price undertakings under the terms of this Agreement have been accepted. The authorities shall name the supplier or suppliers of the product concerned. If, however, several suppliers from the same country are involved, and it is impracticable to name all these suppliers, the authorities may name the supplying country concerned. If several suppliers from more than one country are involved, the authorities may name either all the suppliers involved, or, if this is impracticable, all the supplying countries involved.
>
> 9.3 The amount of the anti-dumping duty shall not exceed the margin of dumping as established under Article 2.
>
>> 9.3.1 When the amount of the anti-dumping duty is assessed on a retrospective basis, the determination of the final liability for payment of anti-dumping duties shall take place as soon as possible, normally within 12 months, and in no case more than 18 months, after the date on which a request for a final assessment of the amount of the anti-dumping duty has been made. [footnote 20] Any refund shall be made promptly and normally in not more than 90 days following the determination of final liability made pursuant to this sub-para.. In any case, where a refund is not

dumping duties by imposing measures incompatible with that Article. Japan also

---

made within 90 days, the authorities shall provide an explanation if so requested.

9.3.2 When the amount of the anti-dumping duty is assessed on a prospective basis, provision shall be made for a prompt refund, upon request, of any duty paid in excess of the margin of dumping. A refund of any such duty paid in excess of the actual margin of dumping shall normally take place within 12 months, and in no case more than 18 months, after the date on which a request for a refund, duly supported by evidence, has been made by an importer of the product subject to the anti-dumping duty. The refund authorized should normally be made within 90 days of the above-noted decision.

9.3.3 In determining whether and to what extent a reimbursement should be made when the export price is constructed in accordance with para. 3 of Article 2, authorities should take account of any change in normal value, any change in costs incurred between importation and resale, and any movement in the resale price which is duly reflected in subsequent selling prices, and should calculate the export price with no deduction for the amount of anti-dumping duties paid when conclusive evidence of the above is provided.

9.4 When the authorities have limited their examination in accordance with the second sentence of para. 10 of Article 6, any anti-dumping duty applied to imports from exporters or producers not included in the examination shall not exceed:

(i) the weighted average margin of dumping established with respect to the selected exporters or producers or,

(ii) where the liability for payment of anti-dumping duties is calculated on the basis of a prospective normal value, the difference between the weighted average normal value of the selected exporters or producers and the export prices of exporters or producers not individually examined,

provided that the authorities shall disregard for the purpose of this para. any zero and *de minimis* margins and margins established under the circumstances referred to in para. 8 of Article 6. The authorities shall apply individual duties or normal values to imports from any exporter or producer not included in the examination who has provided the necessary information during the course of the investigation, as provided for in subparagraph 10.2 of Article 6.

9.5 If a product is subject to anti-dumping duties in an importing Member, the authorities shall promptly carry out a review for the purpose of determining individual margins of dumping for any exporters or producers in the exporting country in question who have not exported the product to the importing Member during the period of investigation, provided that these exporters or producers can show that they are not related to any of the exporters or producers in the exporting country who are subject to the anti-dumping duties on the product. Such a review shall be initiated and carried out on an accelerated basis, compared to normal duty assessment and review proceedings in the importing Member. No anti-dumping duties shall be levied on imports from such exporters or producers while the review is being carried out. The authorities may, however, withhold appraisement and/or request guarantees to ensure that, should such a review result in a determination of dumping in respect of such producers or exporters, anti-dumping duties can be levied retroactively to the date of the initiation of the review."

Footnote 20 reads as follows:

"It is understood that the observance of the time-limits mentioned in this subparagraph and in subparagraph 3.2 may not be possible where the product in question is subject to judicial review proceedings."

argues that Article 11 of the Anti-Dumping Agreement[587] limits the duration of anti-dumping measures and requires periodic reviews of the need for continued imposition of anti-dumping duties. The 1916 Act contains no provisions regarding duration of measures or review.

6.263 We found above that, by not imposing anti-dumping duties within the meaning of Article VI and the Anti-Dumping Agreement, but other types of measures such as fines, imprisonment or damages, the 1916 Act violates Article VI:2 of the GATT 1994 and Article 18.1 of the Anti-Dumping Agreement. Since we found that the *type* of measures imposed under the 1916 Act is not compatible with the WTO Agreement, we do not find it necessary to determine whether the way those measures *operate* is compatible with Article VI of the GATT 1994 and the Anti-Dumping Agreement. We therefore exercise judicial economy in respect of these claims.

---

587 Article 11 provides as follows:

> "11.1 An anti-dumping duty shall remain in force only as long as and to the extent necessary to counteract dumping which is causing injury.
>
> 11.2 The authorities shall review the need for the continued imposition of the duty, where warranted, on their own initiative or, provided that a reasonable period of time has elapsed since the imposition of the definitive anti-dumping duty, upon request by any interested party which submits positive information substantiating the need for a review.[footnote 21] Interested parties shall have the right to request the authorities to examine whether the continued imposition of the duty is necessary to offset dumping, whether the injury would be likely to continue or recur if the duty were removed or varied, or both. If, as a result of the review under this para., the authorities determine that the anti-dumping duty is no longer warranted, it shall be terminated immediately.
>
> 11.3 Notwithstanding the provisions of paras. 1 and 2, any definitive anti-dumping duty shall be terminated on a date not later than five years from its imposition (or from the date of the most recent review under para. 2 if that review has covered both dumping and injury, or under this para.), unless the authorities determine, in a review initiated before that date on their own initiative or upon a duly substantiated request made by or on behalf of the domestic industry within a reasonable period of time prior to that date, that the expiry of the duty would be likely to lead to continuation or recurrence of dumping and injury.[footnote 22] The duty may remain in force pending the outcome of such a review.
>
> 11.4 The provisions of Article 6 regarding evidence and procedure shall apply to any review carried out under this Article. Any such review shall be carried out expeditiously and shall normally be concluded within 12 months of the date of initiation of the review.
>
> 11.5 The provisions of this Article shall apply *mutatis mutandis* to price undertakings accepted under Article 8."

Footnote 21 reads as follows:

> "A determination of final liability for payment of anti-dumping duties, as provided for in para. 3 of Article 9, does not by itself constitute a review within the meaning of this Article."

Footnote 22 reads as follows:

> "When the amount of the anti-dumping duty is assessed on a retrospective basis, a finding in the most recent assessment proceeding under subparagraph 3.1 of Article 9 that no duty is to be levied shall not by itself require the authorities to terminate the definitive duty."

3. *Conclusion*

6.264 For the reasons mentioned above, we find that the 1916 Act violates Article VI:1 of the GATT 1994 and Articles 4.1, 5.1, 5.2 and 5.4 of the Anti-Dumping Agreement. In light of our findings and for the reasons mentioned in paragraphs 6.239-6.241 above, we also find that the 1916 Act violates Article 1 of the Anti-Dumping Agreement. We also recall that Japan made a claim under Articles 1 and 18.1 based on the violation of other provisions of the Anti-Dumping Agreement. Article 18.1 provides that specific actions against dumping must be taken "in accordance with the provisions of GATT 1994, as interpreted by [the Anti-Dumping Agreement]". Since we found that the 1916 Act violates Article VI of the GATT 1994 and a number of provisions of the Anti-Dumping Agreement, we reach the same conclusion regarding the violation of Article 18.1 as we did regarding Article 1.

F. *Violation of Article III:4 of the GATT 1994*

6.265 We recall that Japan does not request the Panel to make a finding of violation of Article III:4 of the GATT 1994 in the alternative. Rather, Japan considers that, in the present case, the 1916 Act violates Article VI as an anti-dumping law not in conformity therewith; it also violates Article III:4 by regulating imported products under a separate, less favourable regime than is applicable to domestic products.

6.266 Article III:4 provides as follows:

> "The products of the territory of any contracting party imported into the territory of any other contracting party shall be accorded treatment no less favourable than that accorded to like products of national origin in respect of all laws, regulations and requirements affecting their internal sale, offering for sale, purchase, transportation, distribution or use. The provisions of this paragraph shall not prevent the application of different internal transportation charges which are based exclusively on the economic operation of the means of transport and not on the nationality of the product."

6.267 In section VI.C above, we have found that Article VI of the GATT 1994 and the Anti-Dumping Agreement were applicable to the 1916 Act. We have also found in sections VI.D and E above that the 1916 Act violates certain provisions of Article VI and of the Anti-Dumping Agreement. We also recall that it is a well established practice of panels under the GATT 1947 and the GATT 1994 to exercise judicial economy when applicable and that this practice has been confirmed by the Appellate Body.[588]

6.268 When we considered the relationship between Article VI and Article III:4 of the GATT 1994, we noted that Article VI seemed to address the basic feature of the 1916 Act (i.e. transnational price discrimination) more directly than Article III:4. In our findings, we concluded that Article VI applies to a measure whenever that measure objectively addresses a situation of transnational price discrimination, as defined in Article VI:1. Thus, we found that the 1916 Act was *fully* subject to the provisions of Article VI of the GATT 1994 and the Anti-Dumping Agreement and could not

[588] See footnote 583 above.

escape the disciplines of Article VI by the mere fact that it had anti-trust objectives, did not address *injurious dumping* as such, included additional requirements of an anti-trust nature or led to the imposition of measures other than anti-dumping duties that were not border adjustment measures.

6.269 However, even though we considered that Article VI deals specifically with the type of price discrimination at issue, we did not address the question whether Article VI applied to the 1916 Act *to the exclusion* of Article III:4. In this regard, we recall that, in its report on *European Communities - Bananas*, the Appellate Body noted that:

> "Although Article X:3(a) of the GATT 1994 and Article 1.3 of the *Licensing Agreement* both apply, the Panel, in our view, should have applied the *Licensing Agreement* first, since this agreement deals specifically, and in detail, with the administration of import licensing procedures. If the Panel had done so, then there would have been no need for it to address the alleged inconsistency with Article X:3(a) of the GATT 1994."[589]

We are mindful of the fact that Article X:3(a) of the GATT 1994 deals with the way domestic trade laws in general should be applied, whereas Article 1.3 of the Agreement on Import Licensing Procedures deals with the way rules should be applied in the specific sector of import licensing. In contrast, it may be said that Articles III:4 and VI do not share the same purpose. However, we view the Appellate Body statement as applying the general principle of international law *lex specialis derogat legi generali.* This is particularly clear from its remark that the *Agreement* on Import Licensing Procedures "deals specifically, and in detail, with the administration of import licensing procedures". In our opinion, Article VI and the Anti-Dumping Agreement "deals specifically, and in detail, with the administration of" anti-dumping. In the present case, the question of the applicability of Article III:4 was essentially raised by the type of measures imposed under the 1916 Act. On the basis of the reasoning of the Appellate Body, we conclude that, even assuming that Article III:4 is applicable, in light of our findings under Article VI and the Anti-Dumping Agreement, we do not need to make findings under Article III:4 of the GATT 1994.

6.270 We nevertheless recall that, as stated by the Appellate Body in its report on *Australia - Measures Affecting Importation of Salmon*,[590] our findings must be complete enough to enable the DSB to make sufficiently precise recommendations and rulings so as to allow for prompt compliance "in order to ensure effective resolution of disputes to the benefit of all Members."

6.271 Having regard to our findings under Article VI and the Anti-Dumping Agreement, and keeping in mind that, in our view, Article VI and the Anti-Dumping Agreement deal specifically and in detail with laws addressing dumping as such, we do not consider that making *additional* findings under Article III:4 is necessary in order to enable the DSB to make sufficiently precise recommendations and rulings so as to allow prompt compliance by the United States in order to ensure an effective resolution of this dispute.

---

[589] *Supra*, footnote 468, para. 204.

[590] *Supra, footnote 471,* para. 223.

6.272 Therefore, we find that we are entitled to exercise judicial economy and decide not to review the claims of Japan under Article III:4 of the GATT 1994.

G. *Violation of Article XI of the GATT 1994*

6.273 Japan claims that the 1916 Act violates the obligations of the United States under Article XI:1 of the GATT 1994 because it establishes impermissible import "prohibitions or restrictions other than duties, taxes or other charges", within the meaning of that article. Japan argues that the 1916 Act, being a statute of the United States with binding effects, is unquestionably a "measure". Also, the 1916 Act imposes "restrictions other than duties, taxes or other charges" in the form of treble damages and imprisonment. Finally, the 1916 Act applies to the importation of products into the United States. Japan adds that, in essence, the 1916 Act establishes product-specific minimum price levels to protect US industries similar to the minimum import price system declared inconsistent with Article XI by the panel on *EEC - Programme of Minimum Import Prices, Licenses and Surety Deposits for Certain Processed Fruits and Vegetables.*[591] The fact that it applies to persons rather than products is in this respect immaterial.[592]

6.274 The United States argues that, in general, Article XI prohibits, with certain exceptions, quantitative restrictions on imports or exports. The 1916 Act contains no provision which would enable a court to impose any sort of prohibition or restriction upon the importation of products. Courts may impose on the defendant in a law suit, and not on any other persons not involved in the case, a monetary sanction or a criminal sentence, which obviously does not apply to any particular product. In the opinion of the United States, there is no basis for Japan's assertion that the 1916 Act establishes product-specific minimum price levels. The reports referred to by Japan can be differentiated from the present situation: in *EEC - Processed Fruits and Vegetables*, there was a prohibition to import below a certain price which fell within the ambit of Article XI. The reliance of Japan on the report of the panel on *United States - Section 337* is also misplaced. There is no language in Article XI concerning whether a measure affects the conditions of competition between domestic and imported products.

6.275 Article XI:1 of the GATT 1994 provides as follows:

> "No prohibitions or restrictions other than duties, taxes or other charges, whether made effective through quotas, import or export licences or other measures, shall be instituted or maintained by any contracting party on the importation of any product of the territory of another contracting party or on the exportation or sale for export of any product destined for the territory of any other contracting party."

6.276 In section VI.C above, we have found that Article VI of the GATT 1994 and the Anti-Dumping Agreement were applicable to the 1916 Act. We have also found

---

[591] Adopted on 18 October 1978, BISD 25S/68, para. 4.9, hereinafter "*EEC - Processed Fruits and Vegetables*".

[592] Japan refers to the Panel Report on *United States - Section 337, Op. Cit.*, para. 5.10, whereby, under Article III:4 of the GATT, a measure applied to importers by imposing penalties on them also affects imported products.

in sections VI.D and E above that the 1916 Act violates certain provisions of Article VI and of the Anti-Dumping Agreement. We recall that it is a well established practice of panels, confirmed by the Appellate Body, to exercise judicial economy where applicable.

6.277 With respect to the necessity to make findings under Article XI of GATT 1994, we are of the view that the same reasoning as with Article III:4 applies. In our opinion, Article VI addresses the basic feature of the 1916 Act (i.e. transnational price discrimination) more directly than Article XI:1. In our findings, we concluded that Article VI applies to a measure whenever that measure objectively targets a situation of transnational price discrimination, as defined in Article VI:1. Thus, we found that the 1916 Act was *fully* subject to the provisions of Article VI of the GATT 1994 and the Anti-Dumping Agreement and could not escape the disciplines of Article VI by the mere fact that it had anti-trust objectives, did not address *injurious dumping* as such, included additional requirements of an anti-trust nature or led to the imposition of measures other than anti-dumping duties.

6.278 However, the fact that Article VI deals specifically with the type of price discrimination at issue does not mean that it applies to the 1916 Act *to the exclusion* of Article XI. However, we recall that, in its report on *European Communities - Bananas*, the Appellate Body noted that although both Article X:3(a) of the GATT 1994 and Article 1.3 of the Agreement on Import Licensing Procedures applied, the panel should have applied the Agreement on Import Licensing Procedures first, since this agreement dealt specifically, and in detail, with the administration of import licensing procedures. The Appellate Body concluded that, if the panel had done so, there would have been no need for it to address the alleged inconsistency with Article X:3(a) of the GATT 1994."[593] We conclude that, even assuming that Article XI:1 is applicable, Article VI deals specifically and in detail with the administration of anti-dumping actions. In light of our findings under Article VI and the Anti-Dumping Agreement, we do not need to make findings under Article XI:1 of the GATT 1994.

6.279 We also recall that, as stated by the Appellate Body in its report on *Australia - Measures Affecting Importation of Salmon*,[594] our findings must be complete enough to enable the DSB to make sufficiently precise recommendations and rulings so as to allow for prompt compliance "in order to ensure effective resolution of disputes to the benefit of all Members."

6.280 Having regard to our findings under Article VI and the Anti-Dumping Agreement, and keeping in mind that, in our view, Article VI and the Anti-Dumping Agreement deal specifically and in detail with laws addressing dumping, we do not consider that making *additional* findings under Article XI is necessary in order to enable the DSB to make sufficiently precise recommendations and rulings so as to allow prompt compliance by the United States in order to ensure an effective resolution of this dispute.

6.281 Therefore, we find that we are entitled to exercise judicial economy and decide not to review the claims of Japan under Article XI.

---

[593] *Supra*,footnote 468, para. 204.

[594] *supra*, footnote 471, para. 223.

H. *Violation of Article XVI:4 of the Agreement Establishing the WTO and of Article 18.4 of the Anti-Dumping Agreement*

6.282 Japan claims that the United States is in breach of its obligations under Article XVI:4 of the Agreement Establishing the WTO and Article 18.4 of the Anti-Dumping Agreement because it has failed to conform to its obligations under the WTO Agreement. Article XVI:4 applies to all WTO agreements, including the GATT 1994 and the Anti-Dumping Agreement. Article 18.4 of the Anti-Dumping Agreement is reflective of the general obligation set out in Article XVI:4 as it applies to anti-dumping. Article 18.4 imposes an additional obligation to take all necessary steps, of a general or particular character, to ensure the conformity of laws, regulations and administrative procedures. Under Article 18.4, it is sufficient for a law to provide for WTO-inconsistent actions in order for that law to violate Article 18.4. The fact that there is a possibility of a WTO-consistent action is irrelevant.

6.283 The United States contends that, since the 1916 Act is susceptible to an interpretation that is fully consistent with all US obligations and, in fact, has been so interpreted to date, there is no requirement under Article XVI:4 of the Agreement Establishing the WTO that the United States take action to change that law, just as there is nothing inherent in the anti-dumping context that renders the generally applicable distinction between mandatory and non-mandatory legislation inapplicable. This distinction is consistent with the presumption against conflicts between national and international law. Regarding Article 18.4 of the Anti-Dumping Agreement, the United States considers that, although the language is not identical to Article XVI:4, there were similar provisions in the Tokyo Round agreements on anti-dumping and subsidies which have been generally interpreted as requiring the parties to those agreements to adopt laws, regulations and procedures that permits them to act in conformity with their obligations under those agreements. Article 18.4 of the Anti-Dumping Agreement should be interpreted in the same way.

6.284 Article XVI:4 of the Agreement Establishing the WTO reads as follows:

> "Each Member shall ensure the conformity of its laws, regulations and administrative procedures with its obligations as provided in the annexed Agreements."

6.285 Article 18.4 of the Anti-Dumping Agreement provides that:

> "Each Member shall take all necessary steps, of a general or particular character, to ensure, no later than the date of entry into force of the WTO Agreement for it, the conformity of its laws, regulations and administrative procedures with the provisions of this Agreement as they may apply to the Member in question."

6.286 Since Article 18.4 specifically applies to the Anti-Dumping Agreement, we shall first determine whether the 1916 Act violates Article 18.4. The meaning of Article 18.4 which immediately comes to mind when reading that article is that when a law, regulation or administrative procedure of a Member has been found incompatible with the provisions of the Anti-Dumping Agreement, that Member is also in breach of its obligations under Article 18.4.[595] We found that the 1916 Act violates Articles 1, 4.1, 5.1, 5.2, 5.4 and 18.1 of the Anti-Dumping Agreement. We conclude that, by violating those provisions, the United States also violates Article 18.4 of the Anti-Dumping Agreement.

6.287 With respect to Article XVI:4 of the Agreement Establishing the WTO, we note that, if some of the terms of Article XVI:4 differ from those of Article 18.4, they are identical and unqualified as far as the basic obligation of ensuring the conformity of laws, regulations and administrative procedures found in both articles is concerned. The same reasoning as for Article 18.4 applies to Article XVI:4 regarding the terms found in both provisions. In other words, if a provision of an "annexed Agreement" is breached, a violation of Article XVI:4 immediately occurs. GATT 1994 is one of the "annexed Agreements" within the meaning of Article XVI:4. Since we found that provisions of Article VI of the GATT 1994 has been breached, we conclude that, by violating this provision, the United States violates Article XVI:4 of the WTO Agreement.

6.288 We therefore find that, by violating Articles 1, 4.1, 5.1, 5.2, 5.4 and 18.1 of the Anti-Dumping Agreement, the United States violates Article 18.4 of the same Agreement. We also find that by violating provisions of Article VI of the GATT 1994, the United States violates Article XVI:4 of the WTO Agreement.[596]

I. Summary of Findings

6.289 Our findings may be summarized as follows:[597]

(a) in order to review the conformity of the 1916 Act with the provisions of the WTO Agreement, we were entitled, consistently with the practice of the Appellate Body and of other international tribunals, to carry out an examination of the US domestic law, including a review of the relevant legislative history and an analysis of the relevant case-law;

(b) Article VI:1 of the GATT 1994 and the Anti-Dumping Agreement, interpreted in accordance with the Vienna Convention, must be understood as applying to the type of transnational price discrimination defined therein, irrespective of whether it is combined with additional requirements or leads to other measures than anti-dumping duties;

---

[595] We did not exercise judicial economy with respect to Article 18.4 because, in that context, a violation of Article 18.4 automatically results from the breach of another provision of the Anti-Dumping Agreement.

[596] In that context, we do not find it necessary to determine whether the violation of provisions of the Anti-Dumping Agreement lead to a breach of Article XVI:4 of the Agreement Establishing the WTO. Since we did not identify any conflict within the meaning of Article XVI:3 of the Agreement Establishing the WTO between Article XVI:4 of the Agreement Establishing the WTO and Article 18.4 of the Agreement on Anti-Dumping, we do not need to address further the relationship between the two provisions.

[597] Having regard to the fact that the articles of the WTO agreements referred to by Japan in its claims have multiple paras., most of which contain at least one distinct obligation, the Panel strictly circumscribed its findings to the paras. effectively found to be violated on the basis of the evidence and arguments submitted by the parties.

(c) on the basis of the terms of the 1916 Act, the transnational price discrimination test found in that law meets the definition of Article VI:1 of GATT 1994. The legislative history of the 1916 Act and the subsequent interpretation by US courts do not lead to a different conclusion;

(d) by providing for the imposition of treble damages, fines or imprisonment, instead of anti-dumping duties, the 1916 Act violates Article VI:2 of GATT 1994 and Article 18.1 of the Anti-Dumping Agreement;

(e) by not providing for a number of procedural requirements found in Article VI of the GATT 1994 and the Anti-Dumping Agreement, the 1916 Act also violates Article VI:1 of the GATT 1994 and Articles 1, 4.1, 5.1, 5.2, 5.4 and 18.1 of the Anti-Dumping Agreement;

(f) by violating Article VI:1and VI:2 of GATT 1994, and Articles 1, 4.1, 5.1, 5.2, 5.4 and 18.1 of the Anti-Dumping Agreement, the 1916 Act violates Article XVI:4 of the Agreement Establishing the WTO and Article 18.4 of the Anti-Dumping Agreement;

(g) in accordance with Article 3.8 of the DSU, since violations have been established that have not been rebutted by the United States, the United States nullifies or impairs benefits accruing to Japan under the WTO Agreement.

J. Request of Japan for a Specific Recommendation of the Panel

6.290 We recall that Japan requests that we recommend that the United States repeal the 1916 Act in order to bring the 1916 Act into conformity with US obligations under the WTO. We note that Article 19.1 of the DSU provides that:

> "When a panel or the Appellate Body concludes that a measure is inconsistent with a covered agreement, it shall recommend that the Member concerned [footnote omitted] bring the measure into conformity with that agreement [footnote omitted]. In addition to its recommendations, the panel or the Appellate Body may suggest ways in which the Member concerned could implement the recommendations."

6.291 From the first sentence of Article 19.1, we conclude that the type of recommendations we are entitled to make are limited to recommend that the Member concerned bring the measure at issue into conformity with the relevant WTO agreements. As a result, we cannot make the recommendation requested by Japan.

6.292 We nevertheless note that, pursuant to Article 19.1 of the DSU, we may suggest ways in which the Member concerned could implement our recommendations. We also recall that we reviewed all the claims on which, in our opinion "a finding [was] necessary in order to enable the DSB to make sufficiently precise recommendations and rulings so as to allow for prompt compliance by a Member with those recommendations and rulings 'in order to ensure effective resolution of the dispute to the benefit of all Members.'"[598] In light of our findings, we are of the view that, in

[598] See Appellate Body Report on *Australia - Measures Affecting Importation of Salmon, supra*, footnote 471, para. 223.

order to bring the 1916 Act as such into conformity with its WTO obligations, the United States would probably have to amend that law to such an extent that it may no longer have a number of its current main features. We also note that the 1916 Act has been seldom applied compared with other anti-dumping or anti-trust instruments of the United States and that, when applied, it is has never led to the imposition of any remedies by courts.[599] Finally, we recall that Article 3.7, fourth sentence, of the DSU provides that:

> "In the absence of a mutually agreed solution, the first objective of the dispute settlement mechanism is usually to secure the withdrawal of the measures concerned if these are found to be inconsistent with the provisions of any of the covered agreements."

As a result, we suggest that one way for the United States to bring the 1916 Act into conformity with its WTO obligations would be to repeal the 1916 Act.

VII. CONCLUSIONS AND RECOMMENDATIONS

7.1 We *conclude* that

(i) the 1916 Act violates Article VI:1 and VI:2 of GATT 1994;

(ii) the 1916 Act violates Articles 1, 4.1, 5.1, 5.2, 5.4, 18.1 and 18.4 of the Anti-Dumping Agreement;

(iii) the 1916 Act violates XVI:4 of the Agreement Establishing the WTO; and

(iv) as a result, benefits accruing to Japan under the WTO Agreement have been nullified or impaired.

7.2 We therefore *recommend* that the DSB request the United States to bring the 1916 Act into conformity with its obligations under the WTO Agreement.

[599] Our remark only applies to the remedies provided for in the 1916 Act as such. We nevertheless recall that settlements have been reached between the parties in the *Wheeling-Pittsburgh* case. We have no evidence of the extent of the involvement of the US authorities, in particular the US court concerned, in sanctioning the settlements reached between the parties in that case. Moreover, no claim was made by Japan in this respect. We therefore do not have to take position on the WTO-conformity of these settlements.

CANADA - CERTAIN MEASURES AFFECTING THE AUTOMOTIVE INDUSTRY

Arbitration under Article 21.3(c) of the Understanding on Rules and Procedures Governing the Settlement of Disputes

WT/DS139/12, WT/DS142/12

Circulated to Members on 4 October 2000

I. INTRODUCTION

1. On 19 June 2000, the Dispute Settlement Body (the "DSB") adopted the Appellate Body Report[1], and the Panel Report[2] as modified by the Appellate Body Report, in *Canada - Certain Measures Affecting the Automotive Industry* ("*Canada - Automotive Industry*"). On 19 July 2000, Canada informed the DSB, pursuant to Article 21.3 of the *Understanding on Rules and Procedures Governing the Settlement of Disputes* (the "DSU"), that it would implement the recommendations and rulings of the DSB in this dispute.[3] At the DSB meeting of 27 July 2000, Canada said that it would require a "reasonable period of time" to do so, under the terms of Article 21.3 of the DSU, with regard to certain aspects of the measures at issue in the dispute, in particular, the DSB's recommendations pursuant to Article I:1 and Article III:4 of the General Agreement on Tariffs and Trade 1994 ("GATT 1994") and Article XVII of the General Agreement on Trade in Services ("GATS").[4]

2. In view of the impossibility to reach an agreement with Canada on the period of time required for the implementation of those recommendations and rulings, the European Communities and Japan requested that such period be determined by binding arbitration pursuant to Article 21.3(c) of the DSU.[5]

3. By joint letter of 23 August 2000, Canada, the European Communities and Japan notified the DSB that they had agreed that the duration of the "reasonable period of time" for implementation should be determined through binding arbitration, under the terms of Article 21.3(c) of the DSU, and that I should act as Arbitrator. The parties also indicated in that letter that they had agreed to extend the time period for the arbitration, fixed at 90 days by Article 21.3(c) of the DSU, until 6 October 2000.

---

[1] Appellate Body Report, *Canada - Certain Measures Affecting the Automotive Industry* ("*Canada - Automotive Industry*"), WT/DS139/AB/R, WT/DS142/AB/R, adopted 19 June 2000, DSR 2000:VI, 2995.

[2] Panel Report, *Canada - Certain Measures Affecting the Automotive Industry* ("*Canada - Automotive Industry*"), WT/DS139/R, WT/DS142/R, adopted 19 June 2000, as modified by the Appellate Body Report.

[3] Communication from Canada, WT/DS139/9, WT/DS142/9, 19 July 2000.

[4] DSB Meeting of 27 July 2000, WT/DSB/M/86, para. 40. With respect to the findings under Article 3.1(a) of the *Agreement on Subsidies and Countervailing Measures*, the DSB recommended that Canada withdraw the export subsidy within 90 days. Accordingly, these findings are not at issue in this arbitration under Article 21.3(c) of the DSU.

[5] WT/DS139/10, WT/DS142/10, 8 August 2000.

Notwithstanding this extension of the time period, the parties stated that the arbitration award would be deemed to be an award made under Article 21.3(c) of the DSU. My acceptance of this designation as Arbitrator was conveyed to the parties by letter of 24 August 2000.

4. Written submissions were received from Canada, the European Communities and Japan on 31 August 2000, and an oral hearing was held on 14 September 2000.

II. ARGUMENTS OF THE PARTIES

A. *Canada*

5. Canada submits that the "reasonable period of time" needed for full compliance with the recommendations and rulings of the DSB relating to the Canadian value-added requirements (the "CVA requirements") and the duty exemption is "11 months, 12 days", that is, until 1 May 2001. In its written submission, Canada proposes to implement these recommendations and rulings through the repeal or amendment of the Motor Vehicles Tariff Order, 1998 (the "MVTO 1998")[6] and the Special Remission Orders (the "SROs")[7] promulgated by the Government of Canada.

6. Canada noted that it was on schedule to withdraw the export subsidy component of the measures, namely the production-to-sales ratio requirements, by 17 September 2000, as recommended by the DSB. However, to do so, Canada "drastically foreshortened" its normal law-making process. Canada's ability to withdraw the export subsidy component so quickly has no bearing on the "reasonable period of time" for implementing recommendations and rulings of the DSB relating to the CVA requirements and the duty exemption.

7. Canada argues that for these aspects of the measures at issue, the normal rules for determining a "reasonable period of time" under Article 21.3(c) arbitrations apply. According to Canada, past Arbitrators have recognized the sovereign prerogative of Members to determine the most appropriate and effective method of implementing the recommendations and rulings of the DSB, including the choice and timing of the steps necessary to do so. Canada states that the "reasonable period of time" which it has proposed is based on this rule.

8. Canada notes that it will implement the recommendations and rulings through administrative measures, and explains the regulation-making process in Canada as follows.

9. In Canada's legal system, the basic process to be followed for the making of regulations is prescribed by the Statutory Instruments Act and the Government of Canada Regulatory Policy (the "Regulatory Policy"). The Regulatory Policy imposes a succession of steps on authorities sponsoring regulations, as well as obligations of

---

[6] The MVTO 1998 is a regulation promulgated by the Governor-General-in-Council, on the recommendation of the Minister of Finance, under the authority of the Customs Tariff, S.C. 1997, c. 36, subsections 14(2) and 16. See Panel Report, *Canada - Automotive Industry*, *supra*, footnote 2, footnote 24.

[7] The SROs are regulations promulgated by the Governor-General-in-Council, on the recommendation of the Minister of Finance and the Minister of Industry, under the authority of the Financial Administration Act, R.S.C. 1985, c. F-11, s. 23. *Ibid.*, footnote 25.

transparency and consultation. Canada explains that the length of time required for each of the steps in the regulatory process depends on both the nature and the consequences of the proposed regulation. The Federal Regulatory Process Guide (the "Process Guide") elaborates the process for obtaining approval for Governor-in-Council regulations.

10. Once the Canadian government has identified a problem, it is required to consult with all concerned stakeholders in order to determine the key elements of the issue, identify the best course of action for remedying the situation, and allow Canadians an opportunity to participate in developing or modifying regulations and regulatory programs. Consultation occurs prior to the drafting of the regulations and following "pre-publication" of the draft regulations.

11. In the normal course of events, the department with responsibility for the area in which the problem has arisen (in this case, Canada's Department of Finance) will include information about the problem in its Report on Plans and Priorities, a document which is tabled in Parliament. Where this is not possible, in order to ensure that the public is involved in isolating and defining the problem and selecting a solution, the department may use other forms of early notice. For example, the department may publish a "Notice of Intent" seeking public advice and comment.

12. The responsible department is then required to draft a proposed regulation. It must also prepare a Regulatory Impact Analysis Statement ("RIAS"), which describes the purpose of the draft regulation, the alternatives considered, a benefit-cost analysis, the results of consultations with interested parties, the department's response to the concerns raised, and how the regulation will be enforced. The RIAS is to be drafted both to provide concise information for decision-makers, and to give the public the information it needs to evaluate and comment upon a regulatory proposal.

13. Once the proposed regulation and supporting documentation, including the RIAS, have been prepared in both of Canada's official languages and approved by the responsible department's legal services and senior management, they must be sent to three central agencies. The Department of Justice must examine the regulation to ensure that it has a proper legal basis and is not inconsistent with the *Canadian Charter of Rights and Freedoms* or the *Canadian Bill of Rights*. The Clerk of the Privy Council Office ("PCO") must ensure that the proposal is consistent with the government's overall program, and that the responsible department has adequately considered the communications aspects of the proposed regulatory action. The Regulatory Affairs and Orders-in-Council Secretariat of the PCO must review the proposal in order to ensure that it is consistent with the Regulatory Policy and, in particular, that: the responsible department has considered alternatives; the benefits of the regulation or amendments clearly outweigh the costs; adequate consultation with the public has taken place; and the responsible department has cooperated with Canada's provincial governments.

14. Once the foregoing reviews have been completed, the Minister of the responsible department approves the regulation and supporting documentation and submits them to the PCO for consideration by the Cabinet's Special Committee of Council ("SCC"). The SCC is the Cabinet committee that gives Governor-in-Council approval for the pre-publication of a draft regulation and its accompanying RIAS.

15. The Regulatory Policy requires pre-publication of a regulation in order to provide the Canadian public at large with an opportunity to comment. Upon approval by the SCC ministers, the regulation and its RIAS are pre-published in the *Canada*

Gazette, Part I, and are open for public comment for a minimum period of 30 days. This period will vary from case-to-case depending on the impact of the proposed regulatory changes and the extent of the consultation that occurred prior to drafting. Comments received from the public must be weighed on their merits and changes to the proposed regulation must be considered. If the proposed regulation is changed, the Department of Justice must again examine and approve the revised version before it is sent to the SCC for final approval by the ministers. If the proposed regulation is amended, its RIAS must also be changed to reflect the amendment.

16. If the ministers approve the regulation, it is registered under a statutory orders and regulations number within seven days. The regulation will come into force on a date specified or, where not so specified, on the day of registration.

17. The approved regulation and its RIAS are then forwarded for publication in the *Canada Gazette*, Part II. Pursuant to subsection 11(1) of the Statutory Instruments Act, publication must take place no later than 23 days after registration. Once published, the regulation becomes enforceable as law, since the public is deemed to have notice of the change in the regulatory regime.

18. Canada presents a chart in which it estimates the time needed for each stage of the implementation process. Canada submits the following estimated periods. First, Canada estimates 150 days for the "Pre-Drafting" process, including identification and assessment of the problem and publication of a Notice of Intent in the *Canada Gazette*. Then, Canada estimates 178 days for the "Drafting/Approval Process", which includes the following time periods: 60 days for drafting the proposed regulation and completing the RIAS, submission to central agencies, submission to PCO for SCC approval, and SCC decision, followed by pre-publication in the *Canada Gazette*; 30 days for receipt of questions and comments from the public; 30 days for a response to the public questions and comments; 30 days for the amendment of the regulation and the RIAS as required; 14 days for submission to PCO for SCC final approval; 7 days for SCC final approval and signature of the Governor General; and 7 days for registration of the regulations.

19. In addition, Canada submits that two other factors are relevant in determining the "reasonable period of time" in this dispute. First, the elimination of the customs duty exemption for motor vehicles has significant implications for the administration of Canada's customs regime. The Government of Canada is currently undertaking a major re-engineering of customs operations to develop enhanced processes available to all importers. A new customs system, known as "Customs Self-Assessment", or "CSA", will streamline the import process. Because qualifying manufacturers under the Agreement Concerning Automotive Products Between the Government of Canada and the Government of the United States of America (the "Auto Pact")[8], are the largest users of Canada's customs system, Canada's measures to comply with the recommendations and rulings of the DSB in this dispute must fully address the planned CSA system. In making the changes necessary to comply with the recommendations of the DSB, the Government of Canada has a responsibility to find ways to avoid administrative delays and other trade disruptions resulting from a change in tariff regimes and to ensure the earliest transition to the new CSA system. At the oral

[8] See 4 International Legal Materials 302.

hearing, Canada cited previous arbitration awards as establishing a preference for full and effective implementation[9], and as allowing a period for transition to replacement measures as part of the "reasonable period of time".[10]

20. Second, Canada argues that its treaty obligations under the Auto Pact must be taken into account in determining the "reasonable period of time". Under the Auto Pact, Canada is required to accord duty-free treatment to motor vehicles from the United States, if they are imported by manufacturers that meet certain conditions. Since Canada will have to eliminate this duty-free treatment in order to comply with the recommendations of the DSB, Canada will have to strike a balance between its co-existing international obligations. To achieve this balance, Canada considers that it will need to consult with the United States. During the oral hearing, Canada clarified that it is not seeking to extend the "reasonable period of time" because of such consultations, as it believes that such consultations can be carried out simultaneously with the regulatory reform needed for implementation.

B. European Communities

21. The European Communities notes that the DSB's recommendations gave Canada 90 days to withdraw the export subsidy component of the measures found to be inconsistent with Canada's WTO obligations. With regard to the aspects of the measures that were found to be inconsistent with Article I:1 and Article III:4 of the GATT 1994 and Article XVII of the GATS, Canada's obligation was to brings its measures into conformity with its obligations under these provisions. The European Communities notes that Canada indicated that it would require a "reasonable period of time" for implementation of these aspects of the measures under Article 21.3(c), as Canada considered that it would be "impracticable" to comply with the recommendation "immediately".

22. The European Communities submits that the 15 month period mentioned in Article 21.3(c) for the "reasonable period of time" is a "guideline" for the arbitrator, not an "average" or "usual" period. The European Communities argues that past arbitrations make clear that the "reasonable period of time" should be the shortest period of time possible within the legal system of the Member to implement the recommendations and rulings of the DSB. Article 21.3(c) refers to the notion of "particular circumstances" that can influence the "reasonable period of time". The "particular circumstances" of each case determine the length of this period.

23. Examining the "particular circumstances" of this dispute, the European Communities considers that a period of three months from the adoption of the Panel and Appellate Body reports, that is, until 17 September 2000, is a "reasonable period

---

[9] Canada's Oral Statement, para. 23 (citing Award of the Arbitrator, *Chile - Taxes on Alcoholic Beverages – Arbitration under Article 21.3(c) of the DSU* ("*Chile - Alcoholic Beverages*"), WT/DS87/15, WT/DS110/14, 23 May 2000, DSR 2000:V, 2589.

[10] Canada's Oral Statement, para. 26 (citing Award of the Arbitrator, *European Communities - Regime for the Importation, Sale and Distribution of Bananas - Arbitration under Article 21.3(c) of the DSU*, ("*EC – Bananas III*"), WT/DS27/15, 7 January 1998, DSR 1998:I, 3; Award of the Arbitrator, *Australia - Measures Affecting Importation of Salmon - Arbitration under Article 21.3(c) of the DSU* ("*Australia - Salmon*"), WT/DS18/9, 23 February 1999, DSR 1999:I, 267.

of time" for implementation. The European Communities' assessment is based on the following "particular circumstances".

24. The European Communities first notes that the MVTO 1998 and the SROs are not legislative acts, but regulations in the form of Orders in Council, which can, therefore, be amended or repealed by means of another Order in Council. The European Communities further argues that most of the steps in Canada's regulation making process are not subject to any deadlines, either mandatory or indicative. As a result, there is a large measure of discretion for the Canadian administrative authorities to act promptly if they wish to do so.

25. Next, the European Communities submits that the "problem" requiring the adoption of a regulation has already been clearly identified by the DSB's recommendations, and the Government of Canada has stated that it has consulted with "stakeholders" throughout the WTO dispute process, so their views are well-known. The European Communities also states that the implementing options are limited since Canada has no choice but to repeal the MVTO 1998 and the SROs, and the drafting of such a regulatory change is a simple task. Moreover, given that repeal is the only option, comments from the public cannot result in much alteration of the proposed regulatory text.

26. The European Communities raises two examples of regulatory amendments that were accomplished in only three months, as evidence that Canada could bring the measures at issue into conformity within this time-period. First, Canada will withdraw the export subsidy component of the measures at issue within three months. Second, in another WTO dispute, Canada accomplished a regulatory change within three months as well.

27. At the oral hearing, the European Communities challenged Canada's reliance on the reform of its customs regime, as well as its reliance upon the need to consult with the United States regarding the Auto Pact, as factors relevant to the determination of a "reasonable period of time" for implementation. In the view of the European Communities, Canada has provided no evidence in support of its assertions that massive and costly changes to its system will be necessary, that no alternative solutions can be put in place until the new customs system has begun operation, or that neither the "Big Three"[11] nor the Canada customs regime can quickly shift to the procedures used for importation under the NAFTA. As regards the alleged need for consultations with the United States regarding the Auto Pact, the European Communities notes that Canada does not argue that it needs to amend or terminate the Auto Pact in order to implement the DSB's recommendations and rulings. Furthermore, since the *Marrakesh Agreement Establishing the World Trade Organization* ("*WTO Agreement*") is a subsequent treaty to the Auto Pact, the rule set out in Article 30.3 of the *Vienna Convention on the Law of Treaties*[12] means that the Auto Pact continues to apply between the United States and Canada only to the extent that it is still "compatible" with the provisions of the *WTO Agreement*.

---

[11] DaimlerChrysler Canada Inc., Ford Motor Company of Canada Limited and General Motors of Canada Limited.

[12] Done at Vienna, 23 May 1969, 1155 U.N.T.S. 33; 8 International Legal Materials 679.

C. Japan

28. Japan believes that Canada should take all necessary steps to implement all of the recommendations of the DSB within 90 days of the date of the adoption of the Panel and Appellate Body reports.

29. Japan notes that Canada has accepted that the measures found to be inconsistent with the *Agreement on Subsidies and Countervailing Measures* ("*SCM Agreement*") will be brought into conformity within such a 90-day period, and emphasizes that all measures addressed by the Panel and the Appellate Body are administrative rather than legislative measures. For these reasons, Japan considers that all DSB recommendations and rulings should be implemented "immediately" by Canada, unless Canada can demonstrate that immediate implementation is impracticable. In Japan's view, the reference to "prompt compliance" in Article 21.1 of the DSU and previous arbitration awards establish that an implementing Member bears the burden of proving that immediate compliance is impracticable, and that the "reasonable period of time" it proposes for implementation is appropriate.

30. Japan recalls that a "reasonable period of time" is the shortest period of time required to amend the relevant laws and provisions in order to implement DSB recommendations and rulings. In determining a "reasonable period of time" relevant factors include whether implementation will occur by administrative or legislative means, the "complexity" of the measures required for implementation, and the extent to which specific procedures, such as opportunity for public comments, are legally required as part of the process for introducing implementing measures. In contrast, Japan argues that other factors, such as the domestic, social and economic impact of implementing measures, and any necessary structural adjustment, are irrelevant to the determination of a "reasonable period of time".

31. In this case, Japan stresses the "inseparable nature" of the measures at issue. The import duty exemption is granted only when qualifying manufacturers satisfy both the CVA requirements and the ratio requirements. The two requirements and the duty exemption are properly regarded as inseparable elements of one system, all of which should be simultaneously brought into conformity with the *WTO Agreement* in order to comply with the DSB's recommendations and rulings. Japan considers that the two-stage implementation proposed by Canada would effectively remove a quantitative limit on the number of motor vehicles imported duty-free, thereby allowing qualifying companies to benefit from the tariff exemption as long as they satisfy the CVA requirements, and effectively leading to an "aggravation" of Canada's violation of the *WTO Agreement* for as long as the remaining measures remain in force. Japan concludes that, in order for Canada to comply with the recommendations and rulings of the DSB, Canada must repeal both the ratio requirements and the CVA requirements simultaneously, within 90 days of the adoption of the Panel and Appellate Body reports.

32. At the oral hearing, Japan expressed "strong reservations" concerning the need for consultations prior to the various steps of regulatory reform proposed by Canada, as well as the length of time that Canada allocates to each step in the process. Canada has consulted with interested parties throughout these dispute settlement proceedings, and further consultations should not be necessary. Japan does not accept other Canadian estimates of the time needed for each step of the regulatory process, in particular since most of these steps have no legally binding duration, and the

fact that Canada will simply repeal the MVTO 1998 and the SROs means that the drafting of regulations and impact analysis statements should be easy.

33. Japan rejects Canada's reliance on the proposed reform of its customs procedures and on the need for consultations with corporations, such as the "Big Three", that may be affected by implementation. For Japan, neither the administrative burden nor the effect of implementation on concerned private corporations are relevant to the determination of a "reasonable period of time".

III. REASONABLE PERIOD OF TIME

34. Canada has stated that it will comply with the recommendations and rulings of the DSB in *Canada - Automotive Industry*.[13] There are two aspects to these recommendations and rulings. First, the DSB recommended that Canada bring its measures found to be inconsistent with Canada's obligations under Article I:1 and Article III:4 of the GATT 1994 and Article XVII of the GATS into conformity with its obligations under those agreements. Second, with respect to the findings under Article 3.1(a) of the *SCM Agreement*, the DSB recommended that Canada withdraw the export subsidy within 90 days.

35. Canada has taken steps to comply with the latter aspect of the DSB's recommendations, that is, that Canada withdraw the export subsidy within 90 days.[14] Canada's actions relating to compliance with this recommendation of the DSB are not at issue in this arbitration under Article 21.3(c) of the DSU.

36. With respect to the DSB's recommendations relating to Article I:1 and Article III:4 of the GATT 1994 and Article XVII of the GATS, Canada has asserted that it is "impracticable to comply immediately with the recommendations and rulings" and, therefore, Canada requests a "reasonable period of time" in which to implement the DSB's recommendations under Article 21.3 of the DSU.

37. As the duration of the "reasonable period of time" in this case has not been agreed by the parties, they have requested that I determine this period of time through binding arbitration under Article 21.3(c) of the DSU. Thus, the issue to be resolved in this arbitration is the following: what is the "reasonable period of time" for implementation of the recommendations and rulings of the DSB in *Canada - Automotive Industry* relating to Article I:1 and Article III:4 of the GATT 1994 and Article XVII of the GATS?

38. My mandate in this arbitration is governed by Article 21.3(c) of the DSU. Article 21.3(c) provides that when the "reasonable period of time" is determined through arbitration:

> ... a guideline for the arbitrator should be that the reasonable period of time to implement panel or Appellate Body recommendations should not exceed 15 months from the date of adoption of a panel or Appellate Body report. However, that

[13] Communication from Canada, WT/DS139/9, WT/DS142/9, 19 July 2000. Canada's submission, para. 5.

[14] Canada's submission, para. 5.

> time may be shorter or longer, depending upon the particular circumstances.

39. Thus, when the "reasonable period of time" is determined through arbitration, the guideline for the arbitrator is that this period should not exceed 15 months from the date of adoption of the panel report and/or the Appellate Body report. This does not mean, however, that the arbitrator is obliged to grant 15 months in all cases. Article 21.3(c) makes clear that the "reasonable period of time" may be shorter or longer, depending upon the "particular circumstances". The "particular circumstances" of a dispute may influence the determination of what is a "reasonable period of time" for implementation, as has been stated by previous Arbitrators.[15]

40. The meaning of Article 21.3(c) is elucidated by its context. Paragraph 1 of Article 21 provides:

> *Prompt* compliance with recommendations or rulings of the DSB is essential in order to ensure effective resolution of disputes to the benefit of all Members. (emphasis added)

41. Thus, the DSU explicitly recognizes the importance of "prompt" compliance. In recognition of this principle, previous Arbitrators have established that the most important factor in establishing the length of the "reasonable period of time" is the following:

> ... it is clear that the reasonable period of time, as determined under Article 21.3(c), should be the *shortest period possible within the legal system of the Member* to implement the recommendations and rulings of the DSB.[16] (emphasis added)

42. I now turn to an examination of the arguments made by Canada, the European Communities and Japan in order to determine what would be a "reasonable period of time" in the "particular circumstances" of this dispute.

43. In its written submission, Canada requested "11 months, 12 days" from the adoption of the Panel and Appellate Body Reports on 19 June 2000 for implementation, which, according to Canada, is until 1 May 2001.[17] I note that the period from 19 June 2000 to 1 May 2001 is actually 10 months and 12 days. However, since Canada has made reference to the date 1 May 2001 four times in its written submission and twice in its oral statement at the hearing, I consider that Canada's request is that the "reasonable period of time" expire on 1 May 2001.[18]

---

[15] See, e.g., Award of the Arbitrator, *Chile - Alcoholic Beverages, supra*, footnote 9, paras. 39, 41-45; Award of the Arbitrator, *Canada - Patent Protection of Pharmaceutical Products - Arbitration under Article 21.3(c) of the DSU* ("*Canada - Pharmaceutical Patents*"), WT/DS114/13, 18 August 2000, para. 48.

[16] Award of the Arbitrator, *EC Measures Concerning Meat and Meat Products (Hormones, - Arbitration under Article 21.3(c) of the DSU* ("*EC - Hormones*"),WT/DS26/15, WT/DS48/13, 29 May 1998, DSR 1998:V, 1833, para. 26; quoted with approval in Award of the Arbitrator, *Korea - Taxes on Alcoholic Beverages - Arbitration under Article 21.3(c) of the DSU* ("*Korea - Alcoholic Beverages*"), WT/DS/75/16, WT/DS84/14, 4 June 1999, DSR1999:II, 937, para. 37; and Award of the Arbitrator, *Australia - Salmon, supra*, footnote 10, para. 38.

[17] Canada's submission, para. 9.

[18] *Ibid.*, paras. 7, 9, 45 and 70; Canada's oral statement, paras. 36 and 38.

44. Canada has made arguments in its written submission and at the oral hearing in justification of the period it has proposed for the "reasonable period of time". First, Canada estimates 150 days for the "Pre-Drafting" process, including identification and assessment of the problem and publication of a Notice of Intent in the *Canada Gazette*. Then, Canada estimates 178 days for the "Drafting/Approval Process", which includes the following time periods: 60 days for drafting the proposed regulation and completing the Regulatory Impact Analysis Statement ("RIAS"), submission to central agencies, submission to the Privy Council Office ("PCO") for Special Committee of Council ("SCC") approval, and the SCC decision, followed by pre-publication in the *Canada Gazette*; 30 days for receipt of questions and comments from the public; 30 days for a response to the public questions and comments; 30 days for the amendment of the regulation and the RIAS as required; 14 days for submission to PCO for SCC final approval; 7 days for SCC final approval and signature of the Governor General; and 7 days for registration of the regulations.[19] Canada notes that these estimates will result in implementation by mid-May 2001, but Canada expects to be able to accomplish some of these steps in less time, and, therefore, Canada considers that it can achieve implementation by 1 May 2001.[20]

45. In response, the European Communities and Japan argue that Canada needs only 90 days to implement the DSB's recommendations, that is, until 17 September 2000. Both the European Communities and Japan argue that Canada was able to implement the other recommendation of the DSB, that it withdraw the export subsidy, within 90 days, and that Canada has provided insufficient justification as to why it cannot also implement the DSB's recommendations at issue here within 90 days.

46. In the present case, the parties agree that the measures at issue are certain regulations of the Government of Canada, namely the MVTO 1998 and the SROs. In the oral hearing, Canada stated that "in all likelihood" it would implement the DSB's recommendations through the repeal of these regulations, and would also make consequential amendments to other regulations.[21] I note that the specific implementation steps proposed by Canada are required under the Statutory Instruments Act[22] and/or prescribed in the Government of Canada Regulatory Policy (the "Regulatory Policy")[23] and the Federal Regulatory Process Guide (the "Process Guide").[24] I have taken both the steps required under the Statutory Instruments Act and the steps (and any durations specified) under the Regulatory Policy and the Process Guide into account in evaluating and calculating a "reasonable period of time".[25]

---

19 Canada's submission, Annex.

20 *Ibid.*, para. 45.

21 Canada's response to questioning at the oral hearing.

22 Statutory Instruments Act, R.S.C. 1985, c. S-22 (Exhibit 2 of Canada's submission).

23 Government of Canada Regulatory Policy, November 1999 (Exhibit 3 of Canada's submission). The Regulatory Policy was approved by Cabinet in November 1999.

24 Federal Regulatory Process Guide (Exhibit 4 of Canada's submission). The Process Guide sets out the steps required to develop, process and obtain approval of regulations.

25 These same instruments were at issue before the Arbitrator in Award of the Arbitrator, *Canada - Pharmaceutical Patents, supra,* footnote 15. Like the Arbitrator in that dispute, I accept, for purposes of this arbitration, that the steps mandated under the Regulatory Policy, though not legally binding in the sense of a law or regulation, can nevertheless constitute part of the "reasonable period of time" for implementation. *supra*, footnote 15, para. 54.

47. After examining Canada's arguments concerning the "reasonable period of time", it is clear that certain of the steps proposed by Canada for implementation of the DSB's recommendations and rulings in this dispute are not fixed either by law or by regulation. Rather, they are estimates made by the Government of Canada. The actual time taken to implement the DSB's recommendations and rulings in this case is subject to the discretion of the Government of Canada, and Canada has considerable flexibility in this regard. I recall the guidance provided by Article 21.1 of the DSU, which states that "[*p*]*rompt* compliance with recommendations or rulings of the DSB is essential in order to ensure effective resolution of disputes to the benefit of all Members." (emphasis added) Thus, it is incumbent upon the Government of Canada to use its discretion to ensure that compliance with the DSB's recommendations at issue is "prompt".

48. I am not persuaded that the implementation schedule proposed by Canada properly reflects the objective of "prompt" compliance. In particular, it appears that the Government of Canada could use the discretion inherent in its Regulatory Policy to implement the recommendations of the DSB in this case in a shorter period of time while still following the normal procedures for modifying regulations. Two of the steps proposed by Canada illustrate the generous nature of the estimates provided by Canada.

49. First, Canada has proposed that it be given 150 days for what it terms "Pre-Drafting". Canada identifies two aspects of the "Pre-Drafting" process. The first aspect is "Identification and assessment of problem". The second aspect is "Publication of Notice of Intent in *Canada Gazette*, Part I." Canada notes that the explanation of this stage can be found in the Process Guide, at pages 3-4 and 38-39. However, nowhere in the Process Guide is a time period specified. In response to questioning at the oral hearing, Canada was not able to provide me with a sufficient justification for its request of 150 days for this stage of the implementation process. Canada's primary explanation appears to be the need for consultations between certain Canadian government departments, as well as consultations between the Canadian government and various "stakeholders". While I agree that such consultations are important, 150 days appears to be more than is reasonably necessary when "prompt compliance" is the objective. In my view, Canada did not provide a satisfactory explanation as to why these consultations should take 150 days. I note further that Canada, in its RIAS relating to its efforts to withdraw the export subsidy published in the *Canada Gazette* on 5 August 2000, indicates that it will "*continue consultations* with stakeholders and the provinces to determine how and when Canada will implement those findings."[26] (emphasis added) Moreover, in this same RIAS, Canada acknowledges that various Canadian government departments have been consulting with "stakeholders" throughout the WTO dispute settlement process.[27] Under these circumstances, Canada's request for 150 days for consultations in the "Pre-Drafting" stage appears excessive.

50. Second, in the "Drafting/Approval" stage, upon receipt of public questions and comments after pre-publication of draft regulations in the *Canada Gazette*, Can-

---

26 See Exhibit 1 of Canada's submission.

27 *Ibid.*

ada has asked for 30 days so that it might prepare a "response to public comments" and another 30 days for "amendment of regulation and RIAS as required" in response to the public comments. However, I note that the regulations in question are likely to be very straightforward. In response to questioning at the oral hearing, Canada stated that "in all likelihood" it would simply repeal the MVTO 1998 and the SROs. Thus, 30 days to prepare a "response to public comments" and another 30 days for "amendment of regulation and RIAS as required" are unlikely to be necessary.

51. In my view, Canada's proposal does not make sufficient use of the discretion built into the Regulatory Policy to achieve the "prompt" compliance required by Article 21.1 of the DSU.

52. The European Communities and Japan have both argued that Canada should be able to implement the DSB's recommendations here at issue within 90 days. The European Communities and Japan argue that since Canada was able to implement the DSB's recommendations under Article 3.1(a) of the *SCM Agreement* within 90 days, it should be able to implement the DSB's recommendations relating to Article I:1 and Article III:4 of the GATT 1994 and Article XVII of the GATS within 90 days as well.

53. I agree with Canada, taking account of the normal process for adopting regulations in Canada, that 90 days does not constitute a "reasonable period of time" for implementation of the DSB's recommendations relating to Article I:1 and Article III:4 of the GATT 1994 and Article XVII of the GATS.[28] In its written submission, Canada confirmed that it intends to withdraw the export subsidy within 90 days.[29] However, Canada took this action in accordance with the DSB's recommendations and rulings relating to Article 3.1(a) of the *SCM Agreement*, made pursuant to the special dispute settlement procedures in Article 4 of that Agreement. Article 4.7 of the *SCM Agreement* requires that if a measure is found to be a prohibited subsidy, the panel *shall* recommend that the subsidizing Member "withdraw the subsidy without delay". To this end, the DSB recommended that Canada withdraw the export subsidy within 90 days. Canada has stated that it will comply with this recommendation, and in order to do so, will take, in its words, "extraordinary action".[30] In my view, Canada's ability to take "extraordinary action" to withdraw the export subsidy "without delay", in accordance with the provisions of Article 4.7 of the *SCM Agreement* and pursuant to the recommendation of the DSB, is not relevant for determining the "reasonable period of time" under Article 21.3(c) of the DSU for implementation of the recommendations of the DSB relating to Article I:1 and Article III:4 of the GATT 1994 and Article XVII of the GATS.

54. Canada has placed great emphasis on the "significant implications" that implementation of the DSB's recommendations in this case will have for the "administration of Canada's customs regime"[31] Canada has explained, in detail, how implementation will cause difficulties for the ongoing "major re-engineering" of its cus-

---

[28] For example, I note that Canada has highlighted the risk that regulations may be subject to judicial challenge by affected parties if there has not been sufficient opportunity for public consultation. Canada's submission, para. 25.

[29] *Ibid.*, para. 5.

[30] *Ibid.*

[31] *Ibid.*, paras. 46-66.

toms operations, under which it is establishing a new system known as "Customs Self-Assessment"[32] This reform process was begun at the end of 1999, and the legislation necessary to effect it is scheduled to be introduced into Parliament this fall. This reform is a continuing process, with the final phase of implementation to begin in late April 2001, and the testing of the system with clients to continue through 2004.[33] The relevance of the implementation of this new customs administration system to Canada's argument on the "reasonable period of time" for implementation is not clear. In its written submission, Canada appears to be arguing that the establishment of the new customs system would require a *delay* in implementation of the DSB's recommendations in this case.[34] However, in response to questioning at the oral hearing, Canada stated that implementation of the DSB's recommendations would occur *sooner* as a result of the adoption of the new customs administration system, if I accept the "reasonable period of time" proposed by Canada.

55. Regardless of Canada's specific argument on this issue, I wish to emphasize that factors unrelated to an assessment of the shortest period of time possible for a Member to implement, within its legal system, the recommendations and rulings of the DSB in a particular case are irrelevant to determining the "reasonable period of time" under Article 21.3(c) of the DSU.[35] While it might be more convenient for Canada to implement the DSB's recommendations in this case on the same timeline as it has planned for the reform of its customs administration regime, this factor is not relevant in determining the "shortest period possible" within Canada's legal system for implementation of the DSB's recommendations.[36] As noted by the Arbitrator in *Canada - Pharmaceutical Patents*, the determination of the "reasonable period of time" for implementation must be a legal judgment based on an examination of relevant legal requirements.[37]

IV. THE AWARD

56. I determine that the "reasonable period of time" for Canada to implement the recommendations and rulings of the DSB relating to Article I:1 and Article III:4 of the GATT 1994 and Article XVII of the GATS in this case is *8 months* from the date

---

32 Canada's submission, paras. 53, 55.

33 See Exhibit 6 of Canada's submission.

34 Canada's submission, paras. 56-58.

35 See Award of the Arbitrator, *Canada - Pharmaceutical Patents, supra,* footnote 15, para. 52. See also, Award of the Arbitrator, *Indonesia - Certain Measures Affecting the Automobile Industry - Arbitration under Article 21.3(c) of the DSU* (*"Indonesia Autos"*), WT/DS54/15, WT/DS55/14, WT/DS59/13, WT/DS64/12, 7 December 1998, DSR1998:IX, 4029, para. 23; Award of the Arbitrator, *Japan - Taxes on Alcoholic Beverages – Arbitration under Article 21.3(c) of the DSU ("Japan – Alcoholic Beverages II"*), WT/DS8/15, WT/DS10/15, WT/DS11/13, 14 February 1997, DSR 1997:I, 3, paras. 19 and 27.

36 I note further that, according to Canada, legislation relating to the proposed reform of Canada's customs regime is scheduled to be introduced into Parliament this fall. As with any legislative process, there is always an element of uncertainty in the specific timing for enactment of legislation. Therefore, it seems to me that Canada has placed undue reliance on its customs reform process as a factor in determining the "reasonable period of time" for implementation.

37 *Supra*, footnote 15, para. 52.

of adoption of the Appellate Body Report and the Panel Report, as modified by the Appellate Body Report, by the DSB on 19 June 2000. The "reasonable period of time" will thus expire on *19 February 2001*.

CANADA - TERM OF PATENT PROTECTION

Report of the Appellate Body
WT/DS170/AB/R

Adopted by the Dispute Settlement Body on
12 October 2000

Canada, *Appellant*
United States, *Appellee*

Present:
Lacarte-Muró, Presiding Member
Bacchus, Member
Ganesan, Member

TABLE OF CONTENT

I. INTRODUCTION

1. Canada appeals from certain issues of law and legal interpretations developed in the Panel Report in *Canada - Term of Patent Protection* (the "Panel Report").[1] The Panel was established to consider claims made by the United States that the term of patent protection provided in Canada's *Patent Act*[2] is inconsistent with Canada's obligations under Articles 33 and 70 of the *Agreement on Trade-Related Aspects of Intellectual Property Rights* (the "*TRIPS Agreement*").

---

[1] Panel Report, *Canada - Term of Patent Protection,* WT/DS170/R, adopted 12 October 2000.

[2] Canadian *Patent Act*, R.S.C., 1985, c.P-4, s.45. For more detailed discussion of the measure, see paras. 2.1-2.11 of the Panel Report.

2. The measure at issue in this dispute is Section 45 of Canada's *Patent Act*. Before 1 October 1989, Canada provided patent protection for a term of seventeen years from the date of grant of a patent. Canada changed the law, with effect from 1 October 1989, to provide patent protection for a term of twenty years from the date of filing of the application for a patent. However, no mechanism was provided in the legislation to allow for conversion from one system to the other.[3] Consequently, Section 44 of the *Patent Act* establishes the new rule for applications filed after 1 October 1989, while Section 45 maintains the seventeen year from grant rule for patent applications filed before 1 October 1989.[4]

3. Sections 44 and 45 of Canada's *Patent Act* read as follows:

> 44. Subject to Section 46[5], where an application for a patent is filed under this Act on or after October 1, 1989, the term limited for the duration of the patent is twenty years from the filing date.
>
> 45. Subject to Section 46, the term limited for the duration of every patent issued under this Act on the basis of an application filed before October 1, 1989, is seventeen years from the date on which the patent is issued.

4. Thus, Section 44 provides for a term of twenty years from the date of *application* for a patent for patent applications filed on or after 1 October 1989, while Section 45 provides for a term of seventeen years from the date of *grant* of a patent for patent applications filed before that date. Patents which are subject to Section 44 are commonly described in Canada as "New Act patents", while those subject to Article 45 are described as "Old Act patents". The Old Act patents are the subject of this dispute.

5. In accordance with Article 65.1 of the *TRIPS Agreement*, on 1 January 1996, the *TRIPS Agreement* became applicable for Canada. According to statistics provided by Canada, and uncontested by the United States, on 1 October 1996, 93,937 or just under 40 per cent of Old Act patents then in existence had terms that would, subject to the continued payment of the requisite maintenance fees, expire in less than twenty years measured from their respective application dates.[6] Furthermore, 66,936 or just under 40 per cent of these Old Act patents that were still in force on 1 January 2000 will, subject to the payment of annual maintenance fees, expire in less than twenty years measured from their respective application dates.[7]

6. In the Panel Report, circulated to WTO Members on 5 May 2000, the Panel concluded that:

---

[3] Panel Report, *supra*, footnote 1, para. 2.4.

[4] By virtue of Section 27 of *An Act to Amend the Patent Act and to Provide for Certain Matters in Relation Thereto*, 17 November 1987, see paras. 2.2-2.5 of the Panel Report.

[5] Section 46 provides for the payment of maintenance fees to maintain the rights accorded by a patent once it has been issued. It further provides for the deemed expiry of the patent where those fees are in default. See Canada's appellant's submission, para. 11, footnote 9. See also Panel Report, para. 2.1, footnote 5.

[6] Panel Report, *supra*, footnote 1, para. 2.7.

[7] *Ibid.*, para. 2.9.

(i) the reference to "subject matter...which is protected" on the date of application of the *TRIPS Agreement* in Article 70.2 includes inventions that are currently protected by patents in accordance with Section 45 and that were protected by patents on 1 January 1996, and this is not affected by Article 70.1; and

(ii) Section 45 of Canada's *Patent Act* does not make available a term of protection that does not end before 20 years from the date of filing as mandated by Article 33.[8]

7. The Panel, therefore, recommended that the Dispute Settlement Body (the "DSB") request Canada to bring its measures into conformity with its obligations under the *Marrakesh Agreement Establishing the World Trade Organization* (the "*WTO Agreement*").[9]

8. On 19 June 2000, Canada notified the DSB of its decision to appeal certain issues of law covered in the Panel Report and certain legal interpretations developed by the Panel, pursuant to Article 16.4 of the *Understanding on Rules and Procedures Governing the Settlement of Disputes* (the "DSU"), and filed a Notice of Appeal with the Appellate Body pursuant to Rule 20 of the *Working Procedures for Appellate Review* (the "*Working Procedures*").[10] On 29 June 2000, Canada filed an appellant's submission.[11] The United States filed an appellee's submission on 14 July 2000.[12] On 25 July 2000, at the request of the Appellate Body Division hearing the appeal, the participants submitted additional memoranda on certain issues of legal interpretation arising under Articles 70.1 and 70.2 of the *TRIPS Agreement*.[13] The Division afforded each participant an opportunity to respond to the additional memoranda submitted by the other participant.[14]

9. The oral hearing in the appeal was held on 1 August 2000.[15] The participants presented oral arguments and responded to questions put to them by Members of the Division hearing the appeal.

II. ARGUMENTS OF THE PARTICIPANTS

A. *Claims of Error by Canada - Appellant*

1. *Articles 70.1 and 70.2 of the TRIPS Agreement*

10. Canada appeals the finding of the Panel that the "non-retroactive application rule"[16] contained in Article 70.1 of the *TRIPS Agreement*, with respect to "acts"

---

8 Panel Report, *supra*, footnote 1, para. 7.1.

9 *Ibid.*, para. 7.2.

10 WT/DS170/4, 19 June 2000.

11 Pursuant to Rule 21 (1) of the *Working Procedures*.

12 Pursuant to Rule 22 (1) and Rule 23(3) of the *Working Procedures*.

13 Pursuant to Rule 28.1 of the *Working Procedures*.

14 Pursuant to Rule 28.2 of the *Working Procedures*.

15 Pursuant to Rule 27 of the *Working Procedures*.

16 Canada's appellant's submission, para. 2.

which occurred prior to the date of application of the *TRIPS Agreement* for a Member, does not override the rule in Article 70.2 of the *TRIPS Agreement*, with respect to existing "subject matter" which was protected on the date of application of the Agreement for the Member in question. Canada appeals the Panel's conclusion that Canada is required to apply the obligation under Article 33 to inventions which, on 1 January 1996, the date of application of the *TRIPS Agreement* for Canada, were protected by patents, even though these patents were the result of acts of grant that occurred prior to 1 January 1996.

11. Canada relies on Article 28 of the *Vienna Convention on the Law of Treaties* (the "*Vienna Convention*")[17] which provides that a treaty's provisions do not operate to bind a party in relation to any act, fact or situation which pre-dates the treaty's entry into force for that party. In the view of Canada, Article 70.1 of the *TRIPS Agreement* confirms the non-retroactivity rule of Article 28 of the *Vienna Convention*, while the remaining paragraphs of Article 70 "variously amplify or modify the general rule" set out in Article 70.1, in order to address the special circumstances that negotiators of the *TRIPS Agreement* anticipated would be encountered in bringing the Agreement into effect.[18]

12. Canada recalls that in its submissions before the Panel, Canada argued that the obligation in Article 33 of the *TRIPS Agreement* is activated by both the *act* of filing a patent application and the *act* of granting the patent itself. The obligation in Article 33 is an obligation to provide a term of patent protection measured from the date of filing the patent application. The term of protection is activated by the act of filing and is created by the act of grant of the patent. The term of protection is, thus, an integral part of these two acts. Canada submits that the *TRIPS Agreement* does not give rise to obligations that flow from the acts of filing an application for, or of granting, a patent, where those acts occurred prior to 1 January 1996.

13. Canada further submits that the Panel erred in its interpretation by failing to consider the contextual relationship between Articles 70.1 and 70.2 of the *TRIPS Agreement*. According to Canada, a contextual interpretation of Articles 70.1 and 70.2 would reveal that both Articles address obligations to which the *TRIPS Agreement* either does or does not give rise. When the two Articles are read together, it is clear from their ordinary meaning and the "excepting language" of Article 70.2 that the obligations to which the *TRIPS Agreement* gives rise preclude any obligations described in Article 70.1.[19]

14. Canada also submits that in presenting its argument to the Panel, Canada addressed the distinction between Articles 33 and 28 of the *TRIPS Agreement*, in order to explain the manner in which Article 70.1 operates to exclude the obligations imposed by the latter provision but not the former. Canada contends that Article 70.1 has no application to Article 28 because, unlike Article 33, which addresses the "term" of protection, and is, therefore, attached to the "acts" of filing and grant, the rights conferred by Article 28 flow merely from the fact that the patent exists. Canada considers that in rejecting these arguments on the ground that Canada had ad-

---

17 Done at Vienna, 23 May 1969, 1155 U.N.T.S. 331; 8 International Legal Materials 679.

18 Canada's appellant's submission, para. 220.

19 Canada's appellant's submission, para. 231.

vanced no evidence in support of them, the Panel erred by treating the arguments, which relate solely to a question of law, as propositions of fact.

15. Canada considers that the Panel erred further in its finding that Canada's argument, if correct, would nullify Articles 70.6 and 70.7 of the *TRIPS Agreement*. According to Canada, the error stems from the Panel's misconception that Canada was arguing that patents granted prior to 1 January 1996 were not subject to any of the obligations of the *TRIPS Agreement*. Canada states that Article 70.6 applies to authorizations granted by a government for the use of patent rights without the owner's authorization. Article 70.6 specifically provides that Articles 31 and 27.1 do not apply to such authorizations granted before the *TRIPS Agreement* became known, a date which, in Canada's view, is "generally accepted to be 20 December 1991, when the Dunkel Draft of the *TRIPS Agreement* was released by the GATT Secretariat".[20] Article 70.6 is, thus, a provision clearly intended to be applied retroactively to the general application date of the *TRIPS Agreement*.

16. Canada argues further that the Panel erred by failing to apply the interpretative maxim *lex specialis derogat legi generali*, which stipulates that a general rule such as that in Article 70.1 must yield to one such as that in Article 70.6, which is more specific.

17. Canada submits that the Panel made the same error with respect to Article 70.7 of the *TRIPS Agreement*. Article 70.7 applies to patent applications which were pending at the date of application of the *TRIPS Agreement* and provides that such applications may be amended to claim any enhanced protection provided under that Agreement. The same interpretative maxim that applies to Article 70.6 applies to Article 70.7 as well. While the act of filing an application is generally exempt from the *TRIPS Agreement* under Article 70.1, Article 70.7 provides a specific exception that where an application is pending on the date of application of the *TRIPS Agreement*, such an application can be amended to claim enhanced protection. Canada submits that by failing to apply the relevant interpretative principle, the Panel erred in law.

18. Accordingly, Canada requests the Appellate Body to reverse the findings and conclusions of the Panel and find that "the excepting phrase which introduces Article 70.2 subordinates the rule in that Article to the rule in Article 70.1 in those circumstances where the two rules ostensibly give rise to obligations in respect of the same act", and, that, as a consequence, the complaint of the United States is unfounded.[21]

2. *Article 33 of the TRIPS Agreement*

19. Canada appeals the finding of the Panel that the term of protection provided under Section 45 of the Canadian *Patent Act* is inconsistent with the minimum standard prescribed in Article 33 of the *TRIPS Agreement*. Canada also appeals the Panel's finding that a term of protection that does not end before twenty years from the filing date of a patent application is not "available" under Section 45 of the Canadian *Patent Act*, and that Section 45 is, therefore, inconsistent with Article 33 of the *TRIPS Agreement*.

---

20 *Ibid.*, para. 249.

21 Canada's appellant's submission, para. 261.

20. Canada argues that it acknowledged, before the Panel, that the term of protection provided by Section 45 of its *Patent Act* is different in language, and thus in form, from that prescribed in Article 33 of the *TRIPS Agreement*. However, Canada considers that the "substantive" or "*effective*" term of protection contemplated by both Section 45 and Article 33 are equivalent, and, therefore, consistent in substance.

21. According to Canada, both the text and context of the *TRIPS Agreement* contradict the Panel's finding that there is no textual or contextual support for interpreting Article 33 of the *TRIPS Agreement* as requiring Members to provide a term of "*effective*" protection. Read together, Articles 31.1 and 31.2 of the *Vienna Convention* clearly require that treaty provisions be interpreted in their context, having particular regard to the treaty's object and purpose.

22. Canada notes that the preamble to the *TRIPS Agreement* declares the purpose of the Agreement as, *inter alia*, to promote and provide "*effective* and adequate protection" of intellectual property rights. Canada submits that further contextual contradictions of the Panel's finding appear in Article 62.2 of the *TRIPS Agreement*, which allows Members to complete their pre-grant procedures "within a reasonable period of time" so long as this does not lead to an "unwarranted curtailment of the period of protection". Canada argues that, in drafting the *TRIPS Agreement*, the negotiators understood the effect of the "pendency period" on a term of protection counted from the filing date and therefore undertook to ensure an effective period or term of protection. Canada maintains further that the terms of protection elsewhere referred to in the *TRIPS Agreement* as being the minimum available period are "*nominal*" terms that are subject to the curtailment which Article 62.2 "expressly recognizes and condones".[22]

23. Canada observes that, having conceded that Article 62.2 of the *TRIPS Agreement* provides the context for interpreting the term of protection referred to in Article 33, the Panel nevertheless rejected Canada's contextual interpretation on the ground that Articles 33 and 62.2 create separate obligations: an obligation to provide a term of patent protection and an obligation not to curtail unreasonably that term, respectively. The Panel reasoned that Canada's interpretation requires the creation of a third and distinct obligation, the obligation to provide an effective term of protection. According to Canada, such a characterization misconstrues the Canadian argument, which is that the two Articles, whatever their form, must be read contextually, and if they are thus read together, they produce a substantive result, namely, an "*effective*" term of protection. As Section 45 of Canada's *Patent Act* produces substantively the same result as the *TRIPS Agreement*, Section 45 is consistent with the obligations imposed by the *TRIPS Agreement*.

24. Canada contends that the related operation of Articles 33, 62.2 and 28 together with Articles 44, 45.1 and 45.2 of the *TRIPS Agreement* provides further support for Canada's contextual interpretation. These latter Articles define the various legal remedies which serve to enforce the exclusive rights conferred by a patent. Whereas, under Article 33, the term of protection is counted from the date of filing, in reality it is not until the patent is actually granted that the exclusive rights and the attendant enforcement remedies come into play. Without these rights and remedies,

[22] Canada's appellant's submission, para. 90.

there is no real protection and, consequently, no term of protection. Canada argues that, in failing to take account of the contextual import of the relationship between these various Articles, "the Panel could not discover the substantive meaning of what is prescribed" in Article 33 of the *TRIPS Agreement*.[23]

25. Canada argues further that the Panel failed to appreciate the nature and import of the figures advanced in support of Canada's "*equivalence*" argument. In presenting evidence establishing that the majority of Old Act patents benefited from terms of protection of twenty years or more counted from the filing date, Canada merely demonstrated that as a matter of form, these patents came within the standard required under Article 33 of the *TRIPS Agreement*. Further, in presenting "pendency period" statistics in respect of New Act patents, Canada sought to demonstrate, as a matter of substance, the curtailment of the effective term and its downward variance from the nominal term referred to in Article 33. Canada did not argue that averages produce consistency in and of themselves, but simply that when viewed against the fixed term available under Section 45, there is consistency between Section 45 and the variable term of substantive protection available under Article 33 of the *TRIPS Agreement*.

26. Canada submits that Article 33 of the *TRIPS Agreement* makes clear that the critical element of the obligation it imposes on Members is that the specified term of protection be made *available*. In Canada's view, the ordinary meaning of "available" is "able to be used or obtained".[24] Applying this meaning to both the language of Section 45 and to the associated practices and procedures relating to Section 45 applications plainly demonstrates the *availability* of a term of protection of twenty years counted from the filing date.

27. Canada recalls that Section 45 of the Canadian *Patent Act* confers a term of protection of seventeen years from the date a patent is granted. Canada submits that the actual period between the date of an originating application and patent expiry depends on the length of time that the "pendency period" adds to the fixed seventeen-year term. The "pendency period" is taken up by administrative requirements to which a patent applicant must respond, and the search and examination of the substance of the application conducted by the Patent Office. Under the Canadian law, a term of protection "equal to or greater than" the twenty year period mentioned in Article 33 of the *TRIPS Agreement* was invariably "available" to every Old Act applicant because "the system permitted the applicant to control the pace of the process so as either to retard or to accelerate the examination of its application".[25]

28. Canada contends that the evidence shows that an applicant could postpone the processing of its application by simply asking the Patent Office, which did not refuse such requests, to "retard or backup its position in the pendency queue".[26] The evidence also shows that an applicant could further retard the prosecution of its application by simply making full use of the limitation periods prescribed for the completion of the various statutory steps. In such a case, the applicant alone could control and obtain twenty eight months of "pendency", which was in addition to the "one-to-two year normal period required by the Patent Office to complete both the search and

[23] Executive Summary of Canada's appellant's submission, p. 6.
[24] Executive Summary of Canada's appellant's submission, p. 7.
[25] Canada's appellant's submission, para. 124.
[26] *Ibid.*, para. 125.

examination of the application".[27] In the extraordinary event that the Patent Office discharged its duties in six months, an applicant wishing to postpone its application by another six months could default on its issuance fees and then, "as a matter of right, make good on the default at the end of the six month statutory limit in which to do so".[28] Canada argues, therefore, that an applicant who desired such a term could "prosecute its application" in a manner that made available a term of protection equivalent to that in Article 33.[29]

29. In conclusion, Canada requests that the Appellate Body reverse the findings and conclusions of the Panel and find that the term of patent protection available under Section 45 of the *Patent Act* is equivalent to and consistent with the term of protection envisaged by Articles 33 and 62.2 of the *TRIPS Agreement*. Canada also requests the Appellate Body to find that the term of protection referred to in Article 33 is, and has been, available under the Canadian law and practice relating to Section 45 of the *Patent Act*.

B. Arguments by the United States - Appellee

1. Articles 70.1 and 70.2 of the TRIPS Agreement

30. The United States requests that the Appellate Body reject Canada's appeal and uphold the finding of the Panel that Section 45 of Canada's *Patent Act* is inconsistent with Article 33 of the *TRIPS Agreement*, as made applicable by Article 70.2, to inventions existing and protected by patents in Canada on 1 January 1996.

31. The United States notes that, according to the Panel, the threshold issue raised by Articles 70.1 and 70.2 of the *TRIPS Agreement* must first be resolved before any determination regarding the possible violation of Article 33 of the *TRIPS Agreement* can be made.

32. The United States submits that the Panel correctly found that, contrary to Canada's assertion, the obligations arising with respect to existing protected "subject matter" under Article 70.2 are not eliminated by Article 70.1, which establishes that the obligations of the *TRIPS Agreement* do not apply to "acts" that occurred prior to 1 January 1996. The requirement under Article 70.1 with respect to "acts" that occurred prior to the date of application for a Member is not an exception to the obligations that arise under Article 70.2 with respect to "subject matter existing at the date of application which is protected". In the view of the United States, these two provisions are separate and distinct.

33. The United States argues that Canada's emphasis of the "interrelationship" between Articles 70.1 and 70.2, due to their common use of the phrase "give rise to obligations", does not detract from the distinction between the two provisions: that is, one exclusively addresses "acts", while the other exclusively addresses "subject matter". When Articles 70.1 and 70.2 are interpreted based on their ordinary meaning, in their context and in light of the object and purpose of the *TRIPS Agreement*, it is clear that the obligations of the *TRIPS Agreement* apply, for Canada, to protected

27 Executive Summary of Canada's appellant's submission, p. 7.

28 Executive Summary of Canada's appellant's submission, p. 7.

29 Canada's appellant's submission, para. 215.

"subject matter" in existence on 1 January 1996, but not to "acts" commenced and concluded before 1 January 1996. The United States thus considers that the only relevant question is whether this dispute involves "existing subject matter" or "acts".

34. In response to this question, the United States concludes that this dispute involves "existing subject matter" the protection of which will expire before the period provided for in Article 33, and that, for this reason, Article 70.2, and not Article 70.1, applies. The United States recalls that the Panel came to this same conclusion when it found that the "reference to 'subject matter . . . which is protected' on the date of application" of the *TRIPS Agreement* in Article 70.2 includes inventions that were under patent protection in Canada on 1 January 1996.

35. The United States notes Canada's argument that "the rights enumerated by Article 28 flow from the fact that the patent exists and not from the act of grant" but argues that, as is the case with the obligation under Article 33, the patent from which the rights in Article 28 flow also came into existence *because* of the act of filing a patent application and the Canadian government's act of granting a patent. The United States submits that it could just as easily be argued, following the logic of Canada's argument, that the rights of Article 28 are an "integral part" of the acts of filing an application and granting a patent. It could even be argued that every obligation under the *TRIPS Agreement* can be linked to an act or a series of acts.[30] The United States, therefore, considers that the distinction Canada attempts to draw among the obligations of the *TRIPS Agreement* to support its claim that Article 33 *alone* is subject to the exception provided by Article 70.1 is arbitrary, and must be dismissed.

36. The United States challenges Canada's argument that the Panel erred in finding that Canada's arguments would reduce Articles 70.6 and 70.7 of the *TRIPS Agreement* to inutility. According to the United States, Article 70.6 is an exception to Article 70.2: Article 70.6 enumerates two obligations of the *TRIPS Agreement* that do not apply to a protected subject matter existing on the date of application for a Member if the unauthorized use was granted by the government before the "date this Agreement became known". For the interpretative maxim *lex specialis derogat legi generali* to be applicable, however, there must first be a conflict between the two Articles at issue. When interpreted correctly, there is no conflict between Articles 70.1 and 70.6. In the view of the United States, the Panel adopted the proper interpretation of the Articles in paragraph 6.48 of the Panel Report. The United States submits further that there is a strong presumption against conflict in interpreting treaties.

37. The United States argues that, when interpreted correctly, there is also no conflict between Article 70.1 and Article 70.7, which permits patent applicants with pending applications on the "date of application of this Agreement" to amend them so as to "claim any enhanced protection provided under the provisions of this Agreement".

30 United States' appellee's submission, para. 12.

2. *Article 33 of the TRIPS Agreement*

38. The United States also requests that the Appellate Body reject Canada's appeal and uphold the finding of the Panel that Section 45 of Canada's *Patent Act* is not consistent with Article 33 of the *TRIPS Agreement*.

39. The United States notes Canada's "equivalence" argument, namely, that the average term of protection available to its Old Act patents is equivalent to the obligation created through Articles 33 and 62.2 of the *TRIPS Agreement* conjunctively, which, if accepted, would only then require Canada to provide a patent protection term of fifteen years from the date of grant, regardless of whether this fifteen-year term expired prior to twenty years counted from the filing date. The United States argues that Article 33 states that the term of protection available shall not expire before twenty years counted from the filing date, while Article 62.2 separately requires that the term of protection shall not be unreasonably curtailed by procedures for grant or registration that affect the term's commencement. In the view of the United States, the obligations in Articles 33 and 62.2 are two independent obligations that cannot be interpreted conjunctively to create an additional obligation that overrides the obligations concerning the dates of commencement or expiry of the term of protection.

40. The United States submits that Canada's argument requires that the Appellate Body ignore the ordinary meaning of Article 33, which states unequivocally that the term of protection available for a patent "shall not end before the expiration of a period of twenty years counted from the filing date." The United States notes Canada's argument that an "equivalence" analysis is necessary and appropriate because "pendency periods" typically and routinely erode the twenty-year period of protection referred to in Article 33 and, consequently, the negotiators of the *TRIPS Agreement* must have intended that an effective period or term of protection be established by looking beyond the nominal term of protection in Article 33. The United States submits, however, that nothing in the text or context of Article 33 supports Canada's argument that a specific minimum term of protection for patents is somehow established in the *TRIPS Agreement*. Instead, the twenty-year period mandated by Article 33 serves expressly and unambiguously as "a measuring unit" to determine the earliest date on which a term of protection of a patent may end without violating the *TRIPS Agreement*.

41. The United States argues that Canada's application of Article 31 of the *Vienna Convention* is inappropriate. Although Canada correctly states that provisions of the *TRIPS Agreement* must be interpreted in good faith in accordance with the ordinary meaning to be given to the terms of the treaty in their context and in light of its object and purpose, Canada misuses Article 62.2 to construe and calculate a patent term of protection that the clear language of Article 33 of the *TRIPS Agreement* does not permit. The United States acknowledges that Article 62.2 is part of the context of Article 33 because it is part of the text of the *TRIPS Agreement*. However, the United States insists that one Article of the *TRIPS Agreement* "cannot be used to distort the ordinary meaning of another as Canada proposes".[31]

42. The United States maintains that the Panel correctly rejected Canada's argument that a term of protection that does not end before twenty years from the date of

[31] United States' appellee's submission, para. 19.

filing was "available" under Section 45 of Canada's Patent Act. The Panel correctly found that the ordinary meaning of the word "available" as used in Article 33 of the *TRIPS Agreement*, in light of the object and purpose, suggests that patent right holders are entitled, as a matter of right, to a term of protection that, in the words of Article 33, does not end "before the expiration of a period of twenty years counted from the filing date".

43. The United States submits further that, contrary to Rule 22 of the *Working Procedures*, elements of Canada's "availability" defence are not directed toward "errors in the issues of law", nor do they involve the Panel's "legal interpretations". Rather, they arise seemingly from Canada's disagreement with the Panel's factual findings. Such arguments are not within the mandate of Article 17.6 of the DSU, which makes it clear that "[a]n appeal shall be limited to issues of law covered in the panel report and legal interpretations developed by the panel." The United States recalls that this limited scope has been further confirmed by the Appellate Body.[32]

44. The United States notes Canada's argument that the Panel completely disregarded the factual evidence before it. The United States submits that, in making this argument, Canada is merely questioning the weight the Panel gave to certain factual evidence. According to the United States, the Panel discussed the evidence submitted by Canada, but was ultimately not persuaded by Canada's evidence that postponement requests by Old Act patent applicants were never refused. The United States submits that the Panel correctly found that the relevant issue was not whether an Old Act applicant knew ten years after the last Old Act patent was filed that postponement requests were granted, but whether such applicant knew with certainty at the time he was requesting a postponement that such a request would be honoured. Given the Panel's focus on the real issue of whether an applicant had a legal right to a postponement, the Panel was justified in giving less weight to Canada's evidence regarding the history of postponement requests.

45. The United States asserts that Canada is, in effect, claiming that the Panel erred when it relied on the plain meaning of the text of Canada's law to find that the procedural delays described by Canada to extend "pendency periods" for Old Act patent applicants might not always be granted as a matter of right, but would instead be subject to the discretion of the Canadian Patent Commissioner. Canada essentially argues that this plain meaning of the text of the Canadian law should be ignored. In presenting this defence, however, Canada fails to establish a justification for its assertion.

46. The United States submits that Canada was obligated, as from 1 January 1996, to make available a patent term that will not expire until at least twenty years from the filing date. It is uncontested that this requirement was not made available for all Old Act patents as from that date. Therefore, according to the United States, it does not matter whether a patent applicant might have been able to manipulate the patent system to obtain a term of twenty years counted from the filing date. What matters is that, when Canada had the obligation to make available a term of protec-

[32] Appellate Body Report, *EC Measures Concerning Meat and Meat Products (Hormones)* ("*EC - Hormones*"), WT/DS/26/AB/R, WT/DS48/AB/R, adopted 13 February 1997, DSR 1997:I, 135, para. 132.

tion that does not end until at least twenty years counted from the filing date for all its Old Act patents, it did not do so, and it still does not do so. Thus, the United States submits that the Article 33 benefit is not "available" for purposes of the *TRIPS Agreement* because Old Act patent holders cannot take advantage of the benefit any time after the *TRIPS Agreement* entered into force for Canada. In the view of the United States, for this reason alone, Canada's "availability" argument must fail.

47. Accordingly, the United States requests that the Appellate Body reject Canada's appeal and uphold the findings of the Panel that Section 45 of the Canadian *Patent Act* is not consistent with Canada's obligation under Article 33 of the *TRIPS Agreement*, as made applicable by Article 70.2 to inventions existing and protected by patents in Canada on 1 January 1996.

III. ISSUES RAISED IN THIS APPEAL

48. This appeal raises the following issues:

(a) whether the Panel erred in concluding that Article 70.2, and not Article 70.1, of the *TRIPS Agreement* is applicable to inventions protected by Old Act patents on the date of application of the *TRIPS Agreement* for Canada, and that, therefore, the obligation in Article 33 to provide a term of protection of not less than twenty years from the date of filing is applicable to Old Act patents; and

(b) whether the Panel erred in interpreting and applying Article 33 of the *TRIPS Agreement* and, in particular, in concluding that Section 45 of Canada's *Patent Act*, which provides a term of seventeen years from the date of grant for Old Act patents, is inconsistent with Article 33.

IV. ORDER OF ANALYSIS

49. The measure before us in this appeal is Section 45 of Canada's *Patent Act*. As applied by Canada, and as both parties agree, this measure relates to patents for which the applications were filed before 1 October 1989, and which were in force on 1 January 1996, the date on which the *TRIPS Agreement* became applicable for Canada ("Old Act patents"). As in every appeal, a threshold question is whether the measure before us falls within the scope of one of the covered agreements, in this case the *TRIPS Agreement*. For this reason, we begin our analysis of the legal issues raised in this appeal by considering Article 70, because this Article determines the overall applicability of the obligations of the *TRIPS Agreement*, including the obligation found in Article 33, to the measure in dispute. Only if we conclude from addressing Article 70 that the measure before us does fall within the scope of the *TRIPS Agreement* will it become necessary for us to examine the consistency of Section 45 of Canada's *Patent Act* with Article 33 of that Agreement.

V. ARTICLES 70.1 AND 70.2 OF THE *TRIPS AGREEMENT*

50. Canada appeals the Panel's conclusion that Article 70.2, which addresses "subject matter existing ... and which is protected" on the date of application of the *TRIPS Agreement* for a Member applies, in the case of Canada, to Old Act patents;

and that Article 70.1, which addresses "acts which occurred" before that date, does not. Canada argues that the patent term obligation in Article 33 is, to use Canada's phrase, an "integral part"[33] of the "act" of filing a patent application and also the "act" of granting a patent. Canada argues that, with respect to Old Act patents, Article 33 thus becomes an obligation in respect of "acts which occurred" before the date of application of the *TRIPS Agreement* for Canada, and that, because of Article 70.1, the obligation in Article 33 does not apply. According to Canada, Articles 70.1 and 70.2 are not mutually exclusive, as shown by the "excepting language" at the beginning of Article 70.2 - "[e]xcept as otherwise provided for in this Agreement ... ."[34]

51. The Panel rejected Canada's arguments. Looking first at Article 70.2, the Panel found that "subject matter existing ... and which is protected" at the date of application of the *TRIPS Agreement* for Canada includes *inventions* protected by Old Act patents. Turning to Article 70.1, the Panel found that, as the protection accorded under Old Act patents in respect of inventions is a "situation which has not ceased to exist" at the date of application of the *TRIPS Agreement* for Canada, this situation cannot be related to "acts which occurred" before that date and thereby brought within the scope of Article 70.1 of the *TRIPS Agreement*.[35] The Panel found that Articles 70.1 and 70.2 are mutually exclusive, and that the clause "[e]xcept as otherwise provided in this Agreement ..." in Article 70.2 does not refer to Article 70.1.[36] In the view of the Panel, any other interpretation would reduce Articles 70.6 and 70.7 to redundancy or inutility.[37] Finally, the Panel rejected Canada's argument that, while the other patent rights under the *TRIPS Agreement* may apply to inventions protected by Old Act patents, the patent term right alone under Article 33 does not. The Panel saw no textual or contextual legal basis for such a distinction in the *TRIPS Agreement*.[38]

52. In addressing this issue, we will proceed as follows. First, we will examine whether Article 70.1 provides that the obligations of the *TRIPS Agreement* do *not* apply to Old Act patents. Next, we will examine whether Article 70.2 provides that the obligations of the *TRIPS Agreement do* apply to Old Act patents. And, finally, we will examine whether, for the purposes of Article 70, the patent term obligation in Article 33 should be treated differently from other obligations under the *TRIPS Agreement*.

53. Canada claims that the Panel erred in finding that Article 70.1 does not prevent the obligations of the *TRIPS Agreement* from applying to Old Act patents. In addressing this issue, we look first, as always, at the text of the treaty provision, in accordance with the general rule of interpretation in Article 31 of the *Vienna Convention on the Law of Treaties* (the "*Vienna Convention*").[39] Article 70.1 states:

---

33 Oral statement of Canada at the Second Panel Meeting, Panel Report, *Canada - Term of Patent Protection, supra*, footnote 1, para 66. See also response of Canada to question 37 from the Panel, Panel Report, *supra*, footnote 1, at 161.

34 Canada's appellant's submission, para. 238.

35 Panel Report, *supra*, footnote 1, para. 6.41.

36 *Ibid.*, para. 6.44.

37 *Ibid.*, para. 6.48-6.49.

38 *Ibid.*, para. 6.52-6.54.

39 Done at Vienna, 23 May 1969, 1155 U.N.T.S. 331; 8 International Legal Materials 679. We have previously confirmed this approach in Appellate Body Report, *United States - Standards for*

Article 70

Protection of Existing Subject Matter

> 1. This Agreement does not give rise to obligations *in respect of acts which occurred* before the date of application of the Agreement for the Member in question. (emphasis added)

54. Our main task is to give meaning to the phrase "acts which occurred before the date of application" and to interpret Article 70.1 harmoniously with the rest of the provisions of Article 70. We are of the view that the term "acts" has been used in Article 70.1 in its normal or ordinary sense of "things done", "deeds", "actions" or "operations". In the context of "acts" falling within the domain of intellectual property rights, the term "acts" in Article 70.1 may, therefore, encompass the "acts" of public authorities (that is, governments as well as their regulatory and administrative authorities) as well as the "acts" of private or third parties. Examples of the "acts" of public authorities may include, in the field of patents, the examination of patent applications, the grant or rejection of a patent, the revocation or forfeiture of a patent, the grant of a compulsory licence, the impounding by customs authorities of goods alleged to infringe the intellectual property rights of a holder, and the like.[40] Examples of "acts" of private or third parties may include "acts" such as the filing of a patent application, infringement or other unauthorized use of a patent, unfair competition, or abuse of patent rights.[41]

55. Article 70.1 provides that, where such "acts" "occurred" before the date of application of the *TRIPS Agreement* for a Member, that is to say, where such "acts" were done, carried out or completed before that date, no obligation of the *TRIPS Agreement* is to be imposed on a Member in respect of those "acts". Those "acts" themselves cannot be called in question after the date of application of the *TRIPS*

Conventional and Reformulated Gasoline ("*US - Gasoline*"), WT/DS2/AB/R, adopted 20 May 1996, DSR 1996:I, 3, at 15; Appellate Body Report, *Japan - Taxes on Alcoholic Beverages* ("*Japan – Alcoholic Beverages II*"), WT/DS8/AB/R, WT/DS10/AB/R, WT/DS11/AB/R, adopted 1 November 1996, DSR 1996:I, 97, at 104; and, most recently, in Appellate Body Report, *Argentina - Safeguard Measures on Imports of Footwear*, WT/DS121/AB/R, adopted 12 January 2000, DSR 2000:I, 515, para. 81.

[40] Article 2 of the *TRIPS Agreement* provides, in pertinent part, that, with respect to Part II of the Agreement, which includes Section 5 relating to "Patents", "Members shall comply with Articles 1 through 12, and Article 19, of the *Paris Convention* (1967)", which is defined in footnote 2 of the *TRIPS Agreement* as the Stockholm Act of 14 July 1967 of the *Paris Convention for the Protection of Industrial Property*, done at Paris on 20 March 1883. Reference to various Articles of the *Paris Convention* that relate to patents will also show that patents are granted for protection of "inventions", and that inventions are the "*subject matter*" of patents. The word "acts" is mentioned in Article 4B of the *Paris Convention*, notably in the context of certain "acts" of third parties. This indicates to us that part of the wider context for such terms, as used in the *TRIPS Agreement*, is the way in which the same terms are used in the *Paris Convention* (1967). We note in the World Intellectual Property Organization (WIPO) treatise, Introduction to Intellectual Property, Theory and Practice (Kluwer Law International Ltd., 1997), a description of: "actions" by public authorities in relation to the grant and publication of patents (p. 134, paras. 7.78-7.85); and "invention" (p. 123, paras. 7.1). Similarly, we note also the descriptions in this WIPO treatise of "subject matter" as that term relates to patents (p. 124, para. 7.8). These descriptions are consistent with the interpretations we give to these terms in this Report.

[41] For examples discussed by the Panel, see Panel Report, *supra*, footnote 1, para. 6.40.

Agreement for a Member. In this regard, we note that, in this dispute, the United States has repeatedly emphasized that it is not challenging or complaining against any "act" of any Canadian public authority or private party that took place before 1 January 1996, the date of application of the *TRIPS Agreement* for Canada.[42]

56. However, in the realm of intellectual property rights, it is of fundamental importance to distinguish between "acts" and the "rights" created by those "acts". In the field of patents, for example, the grant of a patent (which is clearly an "act") confers at least the following substantive rights on the grantee, according to the provisions of the *TRIPS Agreement*: national treatment (Article 3); most-favoured-nation treatment (Article 4); product and process patents being available in all fields of technology; non-discrimination between imported and domestic products (Article 27.1); the term of protection (Article 33); and "reversal of burden of proof" in the case of process patents (Article 34).

57. With respect to Article 70.1, the crucial question for consideration before us is, therefore: if patents created by "acts" of public authorities under the Old Act continue to be in force on the date of application of the *TRIPS Agreement* for Canada (that is, on 1 January 1996), can Article 70.1 operate to exclude those patents from the scope of the *TRIPS Agreement*, on the ground that they were created by "acts which occurred" before that date?

58. The ordinary meaning of the term "acts" suggests that the answer to this question must be no. An "act" is something that is "done", and the use of the phrase "acts which occurred" suggests that what was done is now complete or ended. This excludes situations, including existing rights and obligations, that have *not* ended. Indeed, the title of Article 70, "Protection of Existing Subject Matter", confirms contextually that the focus of Article 70 is on bringing within the scope of the *TRIPS Agreement* "subject matter" which, on the date of the application of the Agreement for a Member, is existing and which meets the relevant criteria for protection under the Agreement.

59. A contrary interpretation would seriously erode the scope of the other provisions of Article 70, especially the explicit provisions of Article 70.2. Almost any existing situation or right can be said to have arisen from one or more past "acts". For example, virtually all contractual and property rights could be said to arise from "acts which occurred" in the past. If the phrase "acts which occurred" were interpreted to cover all *continuing* situations involving patents which were granted before the date of application of the *TRIPS Agreement* for a Member, including such rights as those under Old Act patents, then Article 70.1 would preclude the application of virtually the whole of the *TRIPS Agreement* to rights conferred by the patents arising from such "acts". This is not consistent with the object and purpose of the *TRIPS Agreement*, as reflected in the preamble of the Agreement.

60. We conclude, therefore, that Article 70.1 of the *TRIPS Agreement* cannot be interpreted to exclude existing rights, such as patent rights, even if such rights arose through acts which occurred before the date of application of the *TRIPS Agreement*

[42] Rebuttal submission of the United States, para. 30, Panel Report, *Canada - Term of Patent Protection*, *supra*, footnote 1, at 56. Oral statement of the United States at the Second Panel Meeting, para. 21, Panel Report, *supra*, footnote 1, at 61.

for a Member. We, therefore, confirm the finding of the Panel that Article 70.1 does *not* exclude from the scope of the *TRIPS Agreement* Old Act patents that existed on the date of application of the *TRIPS Agreement* for Canada.

61. Canada also appeals the Panel's determination that Article 70.2 and, therefore, Article 33, applies to Old Act patents. We recall that the Panel first found that the "subject matter ... which is protected" on the date of application of the *TRIPS Agreement* for Canada includes "inventions" protected by Old Act patents.[43] The Panel then found that, under Article 70.2, the *TRIPS Agreement* gives rise to obligations in respect of those patented inventions.[44] Canada does not contest that the "subject matter ... which is protected" in this case is the patented inventions existing at the time the *TRIPS Agreement* became applicable for Canada. However, Canada does not accept that the obligation in Article 33 applies to Old Act patents.

62. We begin our examination of Article 70.2 with the text of the provision, which states:

> Article 70
>
> *Protection of Existing Subject Matter*
>
> ....
>
> 2. Except as otherwise provided for in this Agreement, this Agreement gives rise to obligations *in respect of all subject matter existing* at the date of application of this Agreement for the Member in question, and which is *protected* in that Member on the said date, or which meets or comes subsequently to meet the criteria for protection under the terms of this Agreement ... (emphasis added)

63. In examining the text of this treaty provision, the first interpretative issue is whether Old Act patents are "subject matter existing ... which is protected" on the date of application of the *TRIPS Agreement* for Canada. The second is to determine whether the clause "[e]xcept as otherwise provided", which qualifies Article 70.2, applies to the issue raised in this appeal. We deal with each of these issues in turn.

64. We first examine the meaning of the term "subject matter". On this issue, the Panel said:

> ... the term "subject matter" refers to particular "material", including literary and artistic works, signs, geographical indications, industrial designs, inventions, layout-designs of integrated circuits and undisclosed information, which, if they meet the relevant requirements set out in Part II of the Agreement, will attract protection in the form of the corresponding intellectual property rights which are set out in Sections 1 to 7 of Part II of the *TRIPS Agreement*.

---

43 Panel Report, *supra*, footnote 1, para. 6.36.

44 *Ibid.*

The Panel concluded:

> We therefore find that the reference to "subject matter...which is protected" on the date of application of the *TRIPS Agreement* in Article 70.2 includes "inventions" that were under patent protection in Canada on 1 January 1996.[45]

65. We agree with the Panel's reasoning that "subject matter" in Article 70.2 refers, in the case of patents, to *inventions*. The ordinary meaning of the term "subject matter" is a "topic dealt with or the subject represented in a debate, exposition, or work of art".[46] Useful context is provided by the qualification of the term "subject matter", in the same sentence of Article 70.2, by the word "protected", as well as by the phrase "meet the criteria for protection under the terms of this Agreement" appearing later in the same sentence. As noted earlier, the title to Article 70 also uses the words "Protection of Existing Subject Matter". We can deduce, therefore, that the "subject matter", for purposes of Article 70.2, is that which is "protected", or "meets the criteria for protection", under the terms of the *TRIPS Agreement.* As, in the present case, patents are the means of protection, then whatever patents protect must be the "subject matter" to which Article 70.2 refers.

66. Articles 27, 28, 31 and 34 of the *TRIPS Agreement* also use the words "subject matter" with respect to patents and provide an equally useful context for interpretation. Article 27, entitled "Patentable Subject Matter", states: "patents shall be available for any *inventions*" ... .[47] This Article identifies the criteria that an invention must fulfill in order to be eligible to receive a patent, and it also identifies the types of inventions that may be excluded from patentability even if they meet those criteria. On the other hand, in Articles 28, 31 and 34, the words "subject matter" relate to patents that are granted pursuant to the criteria in Article 27; that is to say, these Articles relate to inventions that are protected by patents granted, as distinguished from the "patentable" inventions to which Article 27 refers. These Articles confirm the conclusion that *inventions* are the relevant "subject matter" in the case of patents, and that the "subject matter" in Article 70.2 means, in the case of patents, patentable or patented inventions. Article 70.2 thus gives rise to obligations in respect of all such inventions existing on the date of application of the *TRIPS Agreement* for a Member. In the appeal before us, where the measure in dispute is Section 45 of Canada's *Patent Act*, which applies to Old Act patents, the word "subject matter" means the inventions that were protected by those patents. We, therefore, confirm the conclusion of the Panel in this regard.

67. We now consider whether the qualifying provision at the beginning of Article 70.2 applies in this case. Article 70.2 begins with the words "Except as otherwise provided for in this Agreement". Canada argues that Article 70.1 constitutes an exception for "subject matter existing ... and which is protected" on the date of application of the *TRIPS Agreement* for Canada; that Article 70.1 is, therefore, "otherwise provided", within the meaning of this qualifying provision; and that, accordingly,

[45] Panel Report, *supra*, footnote 1, para. 6.36.

[46] *The New Shorter Oxford English Dictionary*, Lesley Brown (ed.), (Clarendon Press, 1993), Vol. I, p. 1849.

[47] Emphasis added.

Article 70.1 overrides Article 70.2. Canada concludes, as a consequence, that the obligation in Article 33 does not apply to Old Act patents.

68. In addressing this issue, the Panel stated:

> Because we consider that the word "acts" and the term "subject matter" are different concepts with disparate meanings and the term "acts" as used in Article 70.1 refers only to discrete acts which predate the date of application of the *TRIPS Agreement* and not to subsequent acts to apply the Agreement, including to situations that have not ceased to exist on that date, there is no inconsistency between paragraphs 1 and 2 of Article 70. Article 70.1 therefore does not fall within the exception and does not set aside Article 70.2.[48]

69. Like the Panel, we see Articles 70.1 and 70.2 as dealing with two distinct and separate matters. The former deals with past "acts", while the latter deals with "subject matter" existing on the applicable date of the *TRIPS Agreement.* Article 70.1 of the *TRIPS Agreement* operates only to exclude obligations in respect of "acts which occurred" before the date of application of the *TRIPS Agreement*, but does *not* exclude rights and obligations in respect of *continuing situations.* On the contrary, "subject matter existing ... which is protected" is clearly a continuing situation, whether viewed as protected inventions, or as the patent rights attached to them. "Subject matter existing ... which is protected" is not within the scope of Article 70.1, and, therefore, the "[e]xcept as otherwise provided for" clause in Article 70.2 can have no application to it. Thus, for the sake of argument, even if there is a relationship between Article 70.1 and the opening proviso in Article 70.2, Canada's argument with respect to Old Act patents fails nonetheless, as we have concluded that the continuing rights relating to Old Act patents do not fall within the scope of Article 70.1.

70. We wish to point out that our interpretation of Article 70 does not lead to a "retroactive" application of the *TRIPS Agreement.* Article 70.1 alone addresses "retroactive" circumstances, and it excludes them generally from the scope of the Agreement. The application of Article 33 to inventions protected under Old Act patents is justified under Article 70.2, not Article 70.1. A treaty applies to existing rights, even when those rights result from "acts which occurred" before the treaty entered into force.

71. This conclusion is supported by the general principle of international law found in the *Vienna Convention*, which establishes a presumption against the retroactive effect of treaties in the following terms:

> Article 28
>
> *Non-retroactivity of treaties*
>
> Unless a different intention appears from the treaty or is otherwise established, its provisions do not bind a party in relation to any act or fact which took place or any *situation which*

[48] Panel Report, *supra*, footnote 1, para. 6.44.

> *ceased to exist* before the date of the entry into force of the treaty with respect to that party. (emphasis added)[49]

72. Article 28 of the *Vienna Convention* covers not only any "act", but also any "fact" or "situation which ceased to exist". Article 28 establishes that, in the absence of a contrary intention, treaty provisions do *not* apply to "any situation which ceased to exist" before the treaty's entry into force for a party to the treaty. Logically, it seems to us that Article 28 also necessarily implies that, absent a contrary intention, treaty obligations *do* apply to any "situation" which has *not* ceased to exist - that is, to any situation that arose in the past, but continues to exist under the new treaty. Indeed, the very use of the word "situation" suggests something that subsists and continues over time; it would, therefore, include "subject matter existing ... and which is protected", such as Old Act patents at issue in this dispute, even though those patents, and the rights conferred by those patents, arose from "acts which occurred" before the date of application of the *TRIPS Agreement* for Canada.

73. This interpretation is confirmed by the Commentary on Article 28, which forms part of the preparatory work of the *Vienna Convention*:

> If, however, an act or fact or situation which took place or arose prior to the entry into force of a treaty continues to occur or exist after the treaty has come into force, it will be caught by the provisions of the treaty. The non-retroactivity principle cannot be infringed by applying a treaty to matters that occur or exist when the treaty is in force, even if they first began at an earlier date.[50]

This point is further explained by the Special Rapporteur:

> The main point ... was that "the non-retroactivity principle cannot be infringed by applying a treaty to matters that occur or exist when the treaty is in force, even if they first began at an earlier date". In these cases, the treaty does not, strictly speaking, apply to a fact, act or situation falling partly within and partly outside the period during which it is in force; it applies only to the fact, act or situation which occurs or exists after the treaty is in force. *This may have the result that prior facts, acts or situations are brought under consideration for the purpose of the application of the treaty; but this is only because of their causal connexion with the subsequent facts, acts or situations to which alone in law the treaty applies.*[51] (emphasis added)

---

[49] We have endorsed this general principle of international law in Appellate Body Report, *Brazil - Measures Affecting Desiccated Coconut* ("*Brazil – Desiccated Coconut*"), WT/DS22/AB/R, adopted 20 March 1997, DSR 1997:I, 167, at 179, and in Appellate Body Report, *European Communities - Regime for the Importation, Sale and Distribution of Bananas*, ("*EC – Bananas III*"), WT/DS27/AB/R, adopted 25 September 1997, DSR 1997:II, 591, para. 235.

[50] See D. Raushning, ed., *Vienna Convention on the Law of Treaties, Travaux Préparatoires*, (Alfred Metzner Verlag, 1978), observation 3 on Article 28 of the International Law Commission Final Draft, p. 220.

[51] *Ibid.*, observation 3 on the Waldock Report VI, p. 218.

74. We note that Article 28 of the *Vienna Convention* is not applicable if "a different intention appears from the treaty or is otherwise established". We see no such "different intention" in Article 70. Despite some differences in wording and structure from Article 28, we do not see Article 70.1 as in any way establishing "a different intention" within the meaning of Article 28 of the *Vienna Convention.*

75. The Panel found that Article 70.2 makes the obligations of the *TRIPS Agreement* applicable to inventions protected by Old Act patents. Canada does not argue in this appeal that *none* of the obligations in the *TRIPS Agreement* relating to patent rights applies to Old Act patents. Canada argues, instead, that, although Article 70.2 may make *some* obligations under the *TRIPS Agreement* applicable to Old Act patents, Article 70.2 does not make the obligation in Article 33 relating to the *patent term* applicable to such patents. Thus, Canada seeks to distinguish the obligation to provide a particular patent term from the other obligations relating to patents in Section 5 of the *TRIPS Agreement,* notably those relating to exclusive rights in Article 28, by showing that the obligation to provide a patent term of not less than twenty years from the filing date, unlike the other obligations in Section 5, is an "integral part"[52] of the "acts" of granting and filing.

76. The Panel's description of Canada's argument, a description which Canada specifically endorses in its appellant's submission[53], is as follows:

> [U]nlike Article 33 which is temporal in nature because of its linkage of both the commencement and the expiry dates of the term of protection with the acts of filing and granting, the obligation in Article 28 does not depend upon the occurrence of any act. According to Canada, the operation of Article 28 depends solely upon a patent being in existence.[54]

Responding to this argument, the Panel said:

> Neither the textual nor the contextual reading of Section 5 of Part II supports the notion that one obligation can be detached from the patent issued to the right holder or that Members need not comply with all relevant *TRIPS* obligations in relation to them.[55]

77. We agree. Article 70.2 applies the obligations of the *TRIPS Agreement* to "all subject matter existing ... and which is protected" on the date of application of the *TRIPS Agreement* for a Member. A Member is required, as from that date, to implement *all* obligations under the *TRIPS Agreement* in respect of such existing subject matter. This includes the obligation in Article 33. We see no basis in the text for isolating or insulating the obligation in Article 33 relating to the duration of a patent term from the other obligations relating to patents that are also found in Section 5 of the *TRIPS Agreement.* There is nothing whatsoever in Section 5 to indicate that the

---

[52] Oral statement of Canada at the Second Panel Meeting, Panel Report, *Canada - Term of Patent Protection supra*, footnote 1, para. 66. See also response of Canada to question 37 from the Panel, Panel Report, *Canada - Term of Patent Protection, supra*, footnote 1, at 161.

[53] Canada's appellant's submission, para. 222.

[54] Panel Report, *supra*, footnote 1, para. 6.28.

[55] *Ibid.*, para. 6.53.

obligation relating to patent term in Article 33 differs in application in any respect from the other obligations in Section 5. An obligation that relates to duration must necessarily have a beginning and an end date. On that ground alone, it cannot be argued that the obligation is attached to, and arises uniquely from, certain "acts". Although Canada has not done so, it could just as easily be argued that the exclusive rights under Article 28 are also an "integral part" of the "act" of granting a patent, as those rights also can arise only from the grant and consequent existence of a patent.

78. We note, furthermore, that, despite the presence of several other paragraphs in Article 70 that provide clarifications or exceptions to the general rules set out in paragraphs 1 and 2, none of these other paragraphs states that the obligation in Article 33 has a different status from the other obligations in the *TRIPS Agreement*. Sometimes the absence of something means simply that it is not there. And, in our view, the distinction that Canada sees between the obligation in Article 33 and the other obligations in Section 5 is not contemplated by the *TRIPS Agreement*: it is not there.

79. For all these reasons, we conclude that Article 70.2, and not Article 70.1, of the *TRIPS Agreement* applies to inventions protected by Old Act patents and to the rights conferred by those patents, because they are "subject matter existing ... and which is protected" on the date of application of the *TRIPS Agreement* for Canada. We, therefore, conclude that Canada is required to apply the obligation contained in Article 33 of the *TRIPS Agreement* to Old Act patents.

VI. ARTICLE 33 OF THE *TRIPS AGREEMENT*

80. Having concluded from our examination of Article 70 that the measure at issue in this appeal does fall within the scope of coverage of the *TRIPS Agreement*, and having concluded that Canada is, therefore, required to apply the obligation in Article 33 of the *TRIPS Agreement* from the date of application of the Agreement for Canada, we must next ask whether Canada has done so.

81. Canada appeals the Panel's finding that Section 45 of Canada's *Patent Act* is inconsistent with Article 33. Canada argues that the Panel misinterpreted Article 33 in two principal ways: first, in finding that there is no textual or contextual support for the view that Article 33 requires Members to provide patent holders with a term of "effective" protection[56]; and, second, in adopting a "specialized, extra-ordinary and obsolete meaning"[57] of the word "available" that excludes consideration of the various administrative steps in Canada's patent-granting procedure from being used to calculate the earliest date on which the term of protection of a patent may expire.

82. The application of Article 33 to Section 45 of Canada's *Patent Act* raises a preliminary issue with respect to Canada's interpretation of the term "available" in Article 33. In the context of Section 45 of Canada's *Patent Act*, we are persuaded that the Panel was correct in finding that whether a patent term ending not earlier than twenty years after filing was "available" *at the time of filing and grant of the patent under the Old Act* is irrelevant in examining the consistency of Section 45 with Arti-

---

[56] Panel Report, *supra*, footnote 1, para. 6.92.

[57] Canada's appellant's submission, paras. 4, 117, 136, 150 and 151.

cle 33 of the *TRIPS Agreement.*[58] The procedures regarding the "availability" of a patent term before the date of application of the *TRIPS Agreement* for Canada relate to "acts which occurred" *before* the date of application of the Agreement and are, therefore, under Article 70.1, not subject to the obligations of the Agreement.

83. That said, we will nonetheless examine the arguments of Canada relating to the notion of "availability". We will look first at the meaning of Article 33. Then we will examine whether Section 45 of Canada's *Patent Act* is consistent with Article 33.

84. We begin with the text of Article 33 of the *TRIPS Agreement*, which states:

> The term of protection available shall not end before the expiration of a period of *twenty years counted from the filing date.* (emphasis added)

85. In our view, the words used in Article 33 present very little interpretative difficulty. The "filing date" is the date of filing of the patent application. The term of protection "shall not end" before twenty years counted from the date of filing of the patent application. The calculation of the period of "twenty years" is clear and specific. In simple terms, Article 33 defines the earliest date on which the term of protection of a patent may end. This earliest date is determined by a straightforward calculation: it results from taking the date of filing of the patent application and adding twenty years. As the filing date of the patent application and the twenty-year figure are both unambiguous, so too is the resultant earliest end date of the term of patent protection.

86. Section 45 of Canada's *Patent Act* provides that:

> ... the term limited for the duration of every patent issued under this Act on the basis of an application filed before October 1, 1989, is *seventeen years from the date on which the patent is issued.* (emphasis added).

87. The meaning of Section 45 is straightforward. Section 45 defines the term of patent protection in terms of the starting date (the date of "issue" of the patent) and of a duration (seventeen years). These terms are unambiguous. As a result, so too is the end date of patent protection. It is derived through simple calculation: the date of issue of the patent plus seventeen years.

88. Article 33 requires a Member to make a term of protection "available". Canada argues that Section 45 of its *Patent Act* makes "available", on a sound legal basis, a twenty-year term to every patent applicant because, under the Canadian regulatory practices and procedures, every patent applicant has statutory and other means to control and delay the patent-granting process. The Panel rejected this argument, and interpreted the word "available" in the following terms:

> *Black's Law Dictionary* defines the word "available" as "having sufficient force or efficacy; effectual; valid" and the word

---

[58] The Panel stated:

> According to Article 65.1, Canada became obligated to apply Article 33 on 1 January 1996. In our view, no Member can implement an obligation by reference to a state of affairs which ceased to exist in respect of Old Act patents at the time the obligation to make available a term of protection that does not end before 20 years from the date of filing became applicable.

See Panel Report, *supra*, footnote 1, para. 6.120.

> "valid" in turn means "having legal strength or force...incapable of being rightfully overthrown or set aside." The dictionary meaning of the word "available" would suggest that patent right holders are entitled, as a matter of *right*, to a term of protection that does not end before twenty years from the date of filing.[59]

89. The Panel concluded that:

> ... the discretionary nature of both a patent examiner's authority to grant informal delays as well as the Commissioner's power to grant statutory delays so as to allow patent applicants to obtain a term of protection that does not end before 20 years from the date of filing does not make available, as a matter of right, to patent applicants a term of protection required by Article 33.[60]

90. We agree with the Panel that, in Article 33 of the *TRIPS Agreement*, the word "available" means "available, as a matter of right", that is to say, available as a matter of legal right and certainty.

91. The key question for consideration with respect to the "availability" argument is, therefore, whether Section 45 of Canada's *Patent Act*, together with Canada's related regulatory procedures and practices, make available, as a matter of legal right and certainty, a term of protection of twenty years from the filing date for each and every patent. The answer is clearly in the negative, even without disputing the assertions made by Canada with respect to the many statutory and other informal means available to an applicant to control the patent process. The fact that the patent term required under Article 33 can be a by-product of possible delays in the patent-granting process does not imply that this term is available, as a matter of legal right and certainty, to each and every Old Act patent applicant in Canada.

92. To demonstrate that the patent term in Article 33 is "available", it is not sufficient to point, as Canada does, to a combination of procedures that, when used in a particular sequence or in a particular way, *may* add up to twenty years. The opportunity to obtain a twenty-year patent term must not be "available" only to those who are somehow able to meander successfully through a maze of administrative procedures. The opportunity to obtain a twenty-year term must be a readily discernible and specific right, and it must be clearly seen as such by the patent applicant when a patent application is filed. The grant of the patent must be sufficient *in itself* to obtain the minimum term mandated by Article 33. The use of the word "available" in Article 33 does not undermine but, rather, underscores this obligation.

93. Canada also appeals the Panel's rejection of the view that Article 33 embodies a notion of "effective" protection. This notion, advanced by Canada, would allow a different end date from that specified in Article 33, so long as the result was equivalent "effective" protection measured from the date of grant of the patent to its expiry.

94. Taking note of the clear wording of Article 33, the Panel concluded that:

---

59 Panel Report, *supra*, footnote 1, para. 6.102.

60 *Ibid.*, para. 6.109.

> In relation to the equivalence argument, we find that the term of protection under Section 45 is inconsistent with the minimum standard of Article 33 of the *TRIPS Agreement* because, within the calculation of the average period of effective protection, there are Old Act patents with a term of protection that ends before 20 years from the date of filing.[61]

95. The text of Article 33 gives no support to the notion of an "effective" term of protection as distinguished from a "nominal" term of protection. On the contrary, the obligation in Article 33 is straightforward and mandatory: to provide, as a specific right, a term of protection that does not end before the expiry of a period of twenty years counted from the filing date.

96. In support of this notion of "effective" protection, Canada argues that Article 33 must be read conjunctively with Article 62.2, which recognizes the fact that the length of the patent-granting process invariably involves some curtailment of the period of protection. According to Canada, so long as patents are granted "within a reasonable period of time" and there is no "unwarranted curtailment of the period of protection", Article 33, when read with Article 62.2, permits a Member to provide a term of "effective" protection that is equivalent to the nominal term of twenty years from filing prescribed in Article 33.[62] As the American, European and Canadian patent offices take, on an average, from four to five years to grant a patent[63], this period must, in Canada's view, be regarded as "a reasonable period of time", and, therefore, the term of seventeen years from the grant of the patent that is provided under Section 45 of Canada's *Patent Act* must be regarded as "equivalent" to the term of twenty years from the filing of the patent application that is prescribed by Article 33.[64]

97. We see no merit in this argument of Canada. Article 62.2 deals with procedures relating to the acquisition of intellectual property rights. Article 62.2 does not deal with the duration of those rights once they are acquired. Article 62.2 is of no relevance to this case. This purely procedural Article cannot be used to modify the clear and substantive standard set out in Article 33 so as to conjecture a new standard of "effective" protection. Each Member of the WTO may well have its own subjective judgement about what constitutes a "reasonable period of time" not only for granting patents in general, but also for granting patents in specific sectors or fields of complexity. If Canada's arguments were accepted, each and every Member of the WTO would be free to adopt a term of "effective" protection for patents that, in its judgement, meets the criteria of "reasonable period of time" and "unwarranted curtailment of the period of protection", and to claim that its term of protection is substantively "equivalent" to the term of protection envisaged by Article 33. Obviously, this cannot be what the Members of the WTO envisaged in concluding the *TRIPS Agreement*. Our task is to interpret the covered agreements harmoniously.[65] A har-

---

[61] Panel Report, *supra*, footnote 1, para. 6.100.

[62] Canada's appellant's submission, paras. 90-91 and 94.

[63] Canada's appellant's submission, para. 71.

[64] *Ibid.*, paras. 51 and 59.

[65] Appellate Body Report, *Korea - Definitive Safeguard Measure on Imports of Certain Dairy Products* ("*Korea – Dairy*"), WT/DS98/AB/R, adopted 12 January 2000, DSR 2000:1, 3, para. 81; Appellate Body Report, *Argentina - Footwear Safeguards*, *supra*, footnote 39, para. 81.

monious interpretation of Article 33 and Article 62.2 must regard these two treaty provisions as distinct and separate Articles containing obligations that must be fulfilled distinctly and separately.

98. In assessing the consistency of Section 45 with Article 33, we observe that the term of patent protection set out in Section 45 is seventeen years from the date on which the patent is granted, while the term of patent protection required by Article 33 is a minimum of twenty years from the date of filing. Thus, Section 45 will meet the minimum standard prescribed in Article 33 only if the period between the filing and the issue of the patent (the "pendency period", during which a patent application is examined) is equal to or greater than three years. This may not always be the case, since the "pendency period" may be *less* than three years in many cases. In fact, in this case, Canada has provided uncontested evidence that 66,936 patents existing on 1 January 2000, about 40 per cent of the Old Act patents then in force, end earlier than required under Article 33, by virtue of Section 45.[66]

99. We find, therefore, that the Panel correctly interpreted Article 33 of the *TRIPS Agreement*, and correctly found that Section 45 of Canada's *Patent Act* is inconsistent with Canada's obligations under Article 33 of the *TRIPS Agreement*. Consequently, we uphold the Panel's finding that a term of protection that does not end before twenty years counted from the date of filing is not available under Section 45 of Canada's *Patent Act*, and that, accordingly, Section 45 is inconsistent with Article 33 of the *TRIPS Agreement*.

100. In conclusion, we wish to point out that our findings in this appeal have no effect whatsoever on the transitional arrangements found in Part VI of the *TRIPS Agreement*. The provisions in Part VI establish *when* obligations of the *TRIPS Agreement* are to be applied by a WTO Member and not what those obligations *are*. The issues raised in this appeal relate to what the obligations are, not to when they apply.

101. Also, we note that our findings in this appeal do not in any way prejudge the applicability of Article 7 or Article 8 of the *TRIPS Agreement* in possible future cases with respect to measures to promote the policy objectives of the WTO Members that are set out in those Articles. Those Articles still await appropriate interpretation.

VII. FINDINGS AND CONCLUSIONS

102. For the reasons set out in this Report, the Appellate Body:

(a) upholds the conclusion of the Panel that Article 70.2, and not Article 70.1, of the *TRIPS Agreement* applies to inventions protected by Old Act patents because such inventions are "subject matter existing ... and which is protected" on the date of application of the *TRIPS Agreement* for Canada and, consequently, Canada is required to apply the obligation contained in Article 33 of the *TRIPS Agreement* to Old Act patents; and

[66] Panel Report, *supra*, footnote 1, para. 2.9.

(b) upholds the finding of the Panel that a term of protection that does not end before twenty years counted from the date of filing is not available under Section 45 of Canada's *Patent Act*, and that, accordingly, Section 45 is inconsistent with Article 33 of the *TRIPS Agreement*.

103. The Appellate Body recommends that the DSB request Canada to bring Section 45 of its *Patent Act* into conformity with Canada's obligations under the *TRIPS Agreement*.

9 780521 828567